GLOBAL WOMEN'S WORK

This volume considers how women are shaping the global economic landscape through their labor, activism, and multiple discourses about work. Bringing together an interdisciplinary group of international scholars, the book offers a gendered examination of work in the global economy and analyses the effects of the 2008 downturn on women's labor force participation and workplace activism.

The book addresses three key themes: exploitation versus opportunity; women's agency within the context of changing economic options; and women's negotiations and renegotiations of unpaid social reproductive labor. This uniquely interdisciplinary and comparative analysis will be crucial reading for anyone with an interest in gender and the post-crisis world.

Beth English is Director of the Project on Gender in the Global Community at the Liechtenstein Institute on Self-Determination at Princeton University's Woodrow Wilson School of Public and International Affairs.

Mary E. Frederickson is a Visiting Professor at Emory University in the Rollins School of Public Health, and Professor of History Emerita at Miami University, Oxford, Ohio, where she taught from 1988 to 2015.

Olga Sanmiguel-Valderrama is an Associate Professor in the Department of Women's, Gender and Sexuality Studies and the Director of the Latin American, Caribbean and Latinx Studies Program and the Social Justice Certificate at the University of Cincinnati.

Routledge IAFFE Advances in Feminist Economics

IAFFE aims to increase the visibility and range of economic research on gender; facilitate communication among scholars, policy makers, and activists concerned with women's wellbeing and empowerment; promote discussions among policy makers about interventions which serve women's needs; educate economists, policy makers, and the general public about feminist perspectives on economic issues; foster feminist evaluations of economics as a discipline; expose the gender blindness characteristic of much social science and the ways in which this impoverishes all research – even research that does not explicitly concern women's issues; help expand opportunities for women, especially women from underrepresented groups, within economics; and, encourage the inclusion of feminist perspectives in the teaching of economics. The IAFFE book series pursues the aims of the organization by providing a forum in which scholars have space to develop their ideas at length and in detail. The series exemplifies the value of feminist research and the high standard of IAFFE sponsored scholarship.

12 New Frontiers in Feminist Political Economy
Edited by Shirin M. Rai and Georgina Waylen

13 Gender and Climate Change Financing
Coming Out of the Margin
Mariama Williams

14 Feminist Economics and Public Policy
Edited by Jim Campbell and Morag Gillespie

15 Economics and Austerity in Europe
Gendered Impacts and Sustainable Alternatives
Edited by Hannah Bargawi, Giovanni Cozzi and Sue Himmelweit

16 Women, Work and Gender Justice in the Global Economy
Ruth Pearson

17 Gender and Risk-Taking
Economics, Evidence and Why the Answer Matters
Julie A. Nelson

18 Global Women's Work
Perspectives on Gender and Work in the Global Economy
Edited by Beth English, Mary E. Frederickson and Olga Sanmiguel-Valderrama

For more information about this series, please visit www.routledge.com/Routledge-IAFFE-Advances-in-Feminist-Economics/book-series/IAFFE

GLOBAL WOMEN'S WORK

Perspectives on Gender and Work in the Global Economy

Edited by Beth English, Mary E. Frederickson and Olga Sanmiguel-Valderrama

LONDON AND NEW YORK

First published 2019
by Routledge
2 Park Square, Milton Park, Abingdon, Oxon OX14 4RN

and by Routledge
711 Third Avenue, New York, NY 10017

Routledge is an imprint of the Taylor & Francis Group, an informa business

© 2019 selection and editorial matter, Beth English, Mary E. Frederickson and Olga Sanmiguel-Valderrama; individual chapters, the contributors

The right of Beth English, Mary E. Frederickson and Olga Sanmiguel-Valderrama to be identified as the authors of the editorial material, and of the authors for their individual chapters, has been asserted in accordance with sections 77 and 78 of the Copyright, Designs and Patents Act 1988.

All rights reserved. No part of this book may be reprinted or reproduced or utilised in any form or by any electronic, mechanical, or other means, now known or hereafter invented, including photocopying and recording, or in any information storage or retrieval system, without permission in writing from the publishers.

Trademark notice: Product or corporate names may be trademarks or registered trademarks, and are used only for identification and explanation without intent to infringe.

British Library Cataloguing-in-Publication Data
A catalogue record for this book is available from the British Library

Library of Congress Cataloging-in-Publication Data
A catalog record has been requested for this book

ISBN: 978-1-138-03658-1 (hbk)
ISBN: 978-1-138-03659-8 (pbk)
ISBN: 978-1-315-17847-9 (ebk)

Typeset in Bembo
by Integra Software Services Pvt. Ltd.

Printed and bound in Great Britain by
TJ International Ltd, Padstow, Cornwall

CONTENTS

List of figures   *viii*
List of tables   *x*
List of contributors   *xi*
Acknowledgements   *xviii*

Introduction: perspectives on gender and work in the global economy   1
Beth English, Mary E. Frederickson, and Olga Sanmiguel-Valderrama

PART I
Women's agency   **13**

1 Recognizing the home workplace: making workers through global labor standards   17
   Eileen Boris

2 Empowerment revisited: capitalist development and women workers in China's reform era   36
   Xiaodan Zhang

3 Peasant women's agency in Bolivia during the global recession: the movement of the Confederación Nacional de Mujeres Campesinas Indígenas Originarias y Afrodescendentes de Bolivia–Bartolina Sisa   56
   Anne Marie Ejdesgaard Jeppesen

4 Global women's work in transition: the case of entrepreneurial Bolivian women in apparel production in São Paulo, 2013–2014 71
Katiuscia Moreno Galhera and João Paulo Candia Veiga

5 Gender equality in the European employment strategy 91
Gabriella Berloffa, Eleonora Matteazzi, and Paola Villa

6 From sister to co-worker: new patterns of feminization of labor in Turkey 109
Esra Sarıoğlu

7 Gender, work, and recession: two views from the United States 125
Brigid O'Farrell

PART II
Exploitation vs. opportunity 155

8 Women in the Russian workforce: a retreat from equality? 161
Carol Nechemias

9 Working poor women in Mexico facing another crisis: domestic workers, struggling with structural disadvantages, and the 2008 recession 190
Georgina Rojas-García and Mónica Patricia Toledo González

10 Women's work in Kenya's Athi River Export Processing Zone: opportunity or exploitation? 215
Kelly Pike

11 Women and trade liberalization in Egypt 234
Heba Nassar

12 Women's university attainment and labor force participation in Gulf Cooperation Council countries 250
Alessandra L. González

13 The politics of women and work in Iran 263
Valentine M. Moghadam

PART III
Negotiations of social and reproductive labor 283

14 Change and the status quo in home-based industry in south
Tamil Nadu, India: women beedi workers confront shifts
in the organization of labor and capital 287
Meena Gopal

15 Mexican and Puerto Rican women in Chicago: a gendered
analysis of the 2008 recession 299
Ivis García and Maura I. Toro-Morn

16 The economic crisis and women's part-time work in Hungary 319
Erika Kispeter

17 Gendered austerity policies: inequality on the rise in the
European Union including Ireland 336
Ursula Barry

18 From kick-start to U-turn? Gender equality in Sweden 353
Anita Nyberg

Index *387*

FIGURES

4.1	Reproductive work distribution, by marital status and children	78
4.2	Distribution of tasks according to origins (urban or rural)	82
5.1	Gender equality in the labor market: a comparison between the feminist approach (social justice) and the EES approach (efficiency)	97
7.1	Labor force changes for women over the past fifty years	127
7.2	Recession and recovery	132
10.1	A Woman's Work in the Athi River EPZ	219
12.1	GCC ratio of percentage of female to male tertiary enrollment, 1995–2013, based on World Bank data	253
12.2	GCC Women Labor Force Participation Rates (%, Total Labor Force), based on World Bank data	255
12.3	GCC Energy Production (kt of oil equivalent) (1995–2011), based on World Bank data	256
12.4	GCC GDP/Capita (1995–2013), based on World Bank data	259
14.1	The headquarters of the Seyadu Beedi Company, referred to as the House of Seyad	290
18.1	Percent of children aged 1–5 years in publicly financed childcare, Sweden, 1990–2016	361
18.2	Percent of fathers among total number of recipients of parental allowance and of total number of parental allowance days, Sweden, 1974–2016	364
18.3	Percent of employed women and men 16–64 years and of mothers and fathers with children 0–6 years of age, Sweden, 1963–2016	369
18.4	Number of employees, in thousands, women and men in different sectors, Sweden, 1964–2016	370

18.5 Percent absent of the employees, women and men, Sweden, 1963–2015 373
18.6 Percent part-time employed of the employed, mothers and fathers with children 0–6 years old and working age women and men, Sweden, 1965–2016 374
18.7 Percent underemployed of the employed, women and men, Sweden, 1965–2015 375

TABLES

5.1	The changing position of gender equality in the European Employment Strategy	94
5.2	Predicted probabilities of employment statuses and gender marginal effects among young Europeans (aged 16–24) by country group in 2005 and 2011	101
5.3	Predicted probabilities of employment statuses and gender marginal effects among young Europeans (aged 25–34) by country group in 2005 and 2011	102
7.1	Domestic work and skilled trades in the United States, 2012	133
9.1	Lack of Social Security among Mexican Workforce, 2007–2012	194
9.2	Weekly working hours among Mexican Workforce, 2007–2012	195
9.3	Monthly income among Mexican Workforce, 2007–2012	196
9.4	Percentage of women's average monthly wage relative to men's in Mexico, 2014	197
9.5	Sociodemographic characteristics and working conditions of domestic workers' Mexico by percentages, 2007 and 2014	201
10.1	Average wages of Kenyans in EPZ employment	220
10.2	U.S. apparel imports from Kenya	222
10.3	Key indicators of Kenya's apparel export sector	222
12.1	GCC women's education and labor force statistics	252
15.1	Key demographics in Chicago (1970–2010)	308
15.2	Socioeconomic changes for women workers from 2005 to 2012	313
17.1	Contraction in EU employment rates	339

CONTRIBUTORS

Ursula Barry is a Senior Lecturer and Deputy Head of the School of Social Justice and Women's Studies at the University College Dublin in Ireland. She specializes in social economics with a particular focus on gender, equality, and public policy in Ireland and the European Union. She is the author of a wide range of research reports, articles, and books. She is editor and contributor to the volume *Where Are We Now? New Feminist Perspectives on Women in Contemporary Ireland* (2009).

Gabriella Berloffa is a Professor in Economics and Management at the University of Trento in Italy. Her main field of research is political economy. Her research interests are mainly on economic choices of households (consumption, savings and labor supply) and their consequences in terms of welfare, both theoretically and empirically, particularly in Italy, Britain and the USA. Her most recent publication, co-authored together with F. Modena, and Paola Villa, is *Changing Labour Market Opportunities for Young People in Italy and the Role of the Family of Origin*.

Eileen Boris is the Hull Professor and Chair of the Department of Feminist Studies at the University of California, Santa Barbara, where she directs the Center for Research on Women and Social Justice. An interdisciplinary historian, she specializes in women's labors in the home and other workplaces and on gender, race, work, and the welfare state. She has authored numerous books, articles, and policy reports on the feminization of poverty, the wages of care, and welfare reform. Her non-academic writings have appeared in *The Nation*, *LA Times*, *New Labor Forum*, *Labor Notes*, *Salon*, *Dissent*, *Women's Review of Books*, and the *Washington Post*.

João Paulo Candia Veiga is a researcher at the Center of International Negotiations Studies (CAENI) and is a full-time Professor at the School of Philosophy,

Literature and Human Sciences, in the Department of Political Science (DCP) and the Institute of International Relations (IRI) at the University of São Paulo in Brazil. His research focuses on political economics and institutions. He has published multiple articles and book chapters, and is currently conducting research on the impact of environmental certification on Brazilian foreign trade.

Beth English is Director of the Project on Gender in the Global Community at the Liechtenstein Institute on Self-Determination at Princeton University's Woodrow Wilson School of Public and International Affairs. Her research and teaching focus on historical and contemporary labor and working class issues, gender, deindustrialization, and the U.S. and global South. She is the author of *A Common Thread: Labor Politics and Capital Mobility in the Textile Industry*, and her recent articles include, "Global Women's Work: Historical Perspectives on the Textile and Garment Industries" (*Journal of International Affairs*). Her research has been funded by the National Endowment for the Humanities.

Mary E. Frederickson is a Visiting Professor at Emory University in the Rollins School of Public Health and Professor of History Emerita at Miami University, Oxford, Ohio, where she taught from 1988–2015. Her research and teaching focus on gender, race, labor studies, and the social impact of disease. She is the author of *Looking South: Race, Gender, and the Transformation of Labor* and co-editor of *Sisterhood and Solidarity: Workers' Education for Women, 1914–1984* and *Gendered Resistance: Women, Slavery, and the Legacy of Margaret Garner*. Her published articles include works on labor and cultural history, new trajectories in women's history, and the relationship between historical consciousness and activism. Her research has been funded by the National Council for Research on Women, Fulbright-Hays, the American Association for State and Local History, and the National Endowment for the Humanities.

Ivis García is an Associate Professor at the University of Utah in the Department of City and Metropolitan Planning. Her research focuses on grassroots stakeholders of urban planning, community development, housing, and identity politics. Prior to her appointment at the University of Utah, she was a researcher at the Nathalie P. Voorhees Center for Community Improvement, a research center within the University of Illinois at Chicago. She has led several large-scale housing projects, such as the BRAC Homeless Assistance Submission for the Concord Community Reuse Project and a program evaluation for the Chicago Low-Income Housing Trust Fund.

Alessandra L. González is a Lecturer in Public Policy Studies at the University of Chicago. She is the principal investigator of the Islamic Social Attitudes Survey Project (ISAS), a study in conjunction with Baylor ISR on Islamic Religiosity and Social Attitudes, including Women's Rights Attitudes in the Arab Gulf

Region. She has forthcoming book chapters in *Women's Encounter with Globalization* (Frontpage Publications) and *Islam and International Relations: Mutual Perceptions* (Cambridge Scholars Publishing).

Meena Gopal is an Associate Professor at the Tata Institute of Social Science and the Center for the Study of Social Difference of Columbia University in the United States. Her research interests focus on of feminist theories, feminist research methodologies, violence against women, socialization, and sexuality and sexual violence. Her recent publications include the article, "Sexuality and Social Reproduction, Reflections from an Indian Feminist Debate" (*Indian Journal of Gender Studies*).

Anne Marie Ejdesgaard Jeppesen is an Associate Professor in the Department of English, German and Romance Languages and the Founder and Coordinator of the Centre for Latin American Studies at the University of Copenhagen in Denmark. Her research interests focus on labor movements and peasant organization in Bolivia. She is the author of numerous books, book chapters, and articles, including "Memories of Repression and the Creation of a Political Instrument for Social Change in Bolivia," (*Latin American Perspectives*).

Erika Kispeter is a Research Fellow at the Warwick Institute for Employment Research at the University of Warwick, UK. Her research focuses on women's working lives as they are shaped by the welfare state and work organizations, focusing especially on Eastern Europe. Her latest publication co-authored with E. Fodor is, "Making the 'Reserve Army' Invisible: Lengthy Parental Leave and Women's Economic Marginalisation in Hungary," (*European Journal of Women's Studies*).

Eleonora Matteazzi is a Research Assistant in economics at the University of Trento in Italy, and an affiliate researcher at OFCE-Presage (Sciences Po Economic Research Centre, France) program on gender thinking. Her main research fields are household behavior and family economics, time allocation and labor supply, gender discrimination, and working conditions on the labor market. Her latest publication, coauthored with Eleonora Matteazzi, Ariane Pailhé, and Anne Solaz, is, "Part-Time Wage Penalties for Women in Prime Age: A Matter of Selection or Segregation? Evidence from Four European Countries" (*Industrial & Labor Relations Review*).

Valentine M. Moghadam is Director of the International Affairs Program and a Professor of Sociology at Northeastern University. She has studied and worked internationally in Canada, Finland, France, the Middle East, and North Africa. Her areas of research are globalization, transnational feminist networks, civil society and citizenship, and gender and development in the Middle East and North Africa. Among her recent publications are *Modernizing Women: Gender and*

Social Change in the Middle East, *Globalizing Women: Transnational Feminist Networks*, and *Globalization and Social Movements: Islamism, Feminism, and the Global Justice Movement*.

Katiuscia Moreno Galhera is a Katiuscia M. Galhera holds a PhD in Political Science (2018) from the Universidade Estadual de Campinas (UNICAMP) in Brazil. During 2016–2017, she was Visiting Scholar in the School of Labor and Employment Relations at Pennsylvania State University (PSU), which is affiliated with the Global Labour University (GLU). She has worked as a consultant and researcher in Brazil for international trade unions such as SASK (Finland), KU Leuven (Belgium), and the Trade Union Confederation of the Americas (TUCA), as well as the Solidarity Center (USA) and, most recently, the International Labor Organization (ILO). She is the author of refereed journals articles and published book chapters in English and Portuguese on labor politics, gender, and labor transnationalism. The most recent is (with João Paulo Cândia Veiga and Scott B. Martin) "Walmart in Brazil: From Global Diffusion to National Institutional Embeddedness"; in Carolina Bank Muñoz, et al., eds., *Walmart in the Global South: Workplace Culture, Labor Politics, and Supply Chains* (University of Texas, May 2018). She is currently Adjunct Lecturer at the Universidade Federal de Grande Dourados, where she taeaches undergraduate courses on international relations, feminist theory, NGO/third sector studies, and Latin American social and political thought and advised undergraduate theses.

Heba Nassar is a Professor of Economics and Political Science at Cairo University and was previously the Vice President of the University. Her research interests include labor markets, international economics, and macroeconomics. She has authored or contributed to numerous policy publications and reports, including for the United Nations Development Programme, World Bank, and the ILO and is Director of Review of Economics and Political Review Journal-Egypt.

Carol Nechemias is an Associate Professor emerita of Public Policy and Political Science at Penn State Harrisburg. Her areas of specialization include Russian domestic politics and women in politics. Her work on Russian living standards has appeared in *Slavic Review, Soviet Studies, Urban Studies, Studies in Comparative Communism*, and *Social Science Quarterly*. Her essays on women's status in post-Soviet Russia have been published in *Women and Politics* and *Demokratizatsiya* and in book chapters focusing on such topics as women's access to legislative seats, the development of a women's movement, women's political participation, and women's health issues. Nechemias is co-editor of two books, *The Encyclopedia of Russia Women's Movements*, and *Post-Soviet Women Encountering Transition: Nation Building, Economic Survival, and Civic Activism*. In 2004–05 she was a Fulbright Scholar at Volgograd State University in Russia, teaching and conducting research.

Anita Nyberg is a Professor emerita at the University of Stockholm in Sweden. Her research focuses on gender, work and the economy. She is the former General Secretary of Sweden's government committee on the distribution of economic power and economic resources between women and men. In 2015, she contributed to the official reports about gender equality where she wrote about economic gender equality and economic independence. She is a co-editor of *Kön och makt i Norden (Gender and Power in the Nordic Countries)*, and author of "Women and Poverty," "Education and Training for Women," and "Women and the Economy" in Beijing + 15:The Platform for Action and the European Union", a Report from the Swedish Presidency of the Council of the European Union.

Brigid O'Farrell is an independent scholar whose research and writing has focused on employment equity, especially for women in non-traditional jobs. A sociologist by training, she delves into labor history to better understand the issues and barriers confronting today's workers. Her latest book is *She Was One of Us: Eleanor Roosevelt and the American Worker*, and is the co-author of, *Rocking the Boat: Union Women's Voices 1915–1975*, with Joyce Kornbluh. O'Farrell is currently director of the project "Using History Today" at Mills College in Oakland, CA. She is also affiliated with the Eleanor Roosevelt Papers Project, George Washington University. Previous positions include affiliated scholar at Stanford University's Institute for Research on Women and Gender and study director at the National Research Council/National Academy of Sciences. She has written or edited seven books, including *Beyond Gender: The New Politics of Work and Family*, with Betty Friedan.

Kelly Pike is an Assistant Professor in the Work and Labour Studies program at York University in Canada. She specializes in the role of worker's voice and participation in the regulation of international labor standards, with a particular focus on the global garment industry in sub-Saharan Africa. She has published peer-reviewed journal articles, book chapters, and reports and discussion papers for the ILO. Before her appointment at York, she worked as a consultant for the World Bank, reporting on working conditions in the garment industry in Lesotho and Kenya. During this time, she also taught courses in negotiations and labor relations at the Centre for Industrial Relations and Human Resources at the University of Toronto.

Georgina Rojas-García is a Professor at the Centro de Investigaciones y Estudios Superiores en Antropología Social (CIESAS) in Mexico City. Her research focuses on economic restructuring and the labor market in Mexico, household economics and migrations. She is author of various peer reviwed publications including most recently, "Reproducción social estratificada: El trabajo doméstico remunerado en México y la interacción entre mujeres de estratos medios y populares," in *Población y trabajo en América Latina: Abordajes teórico-conceptuales y tendencias empíricas recientes* (UNFPA).

Olga Sanmiguel-Valderrama is an Associate Professor in the Department of Women's, Gender and Sexuality Studies at the University of Cincinnati. She is the Director of the Latin America, Caribbean, and Latinx Studies Program and Social Justice Certificate. Her teaching and research are multidisciplinary, including Law and Society, Labor Studies, Latin American Studies, Women's and Feminist Studies, and Globalization. Her research and publications are sociolegal examinations of the contradictions between on the one hand, neoliberal economic policies and military aid and, on the other hand, respect for individual and collective human rights—in particular labor, environmental, and equality rights for women and racial minorities. She has published numerous peer-reviewed articles and book chapters in the areas of trade and labor, women's, and human rights in Colombia, South America, and Latino/a immigrants in the USA. Her research has been supported by competitive grants from the Social Sciences and Humanities Research Council of Canada, the Charles Phelps Taft Research Center, and the University of Cincinnati Research Council.

Esra Sarıoğlu is an Assistant Professor in the Department of Sociology at Yeditepe University, Istanbul, Turkey. Her research and teaching interests include gender, self, subjectivity, labor, and globalization. She is currently researching She is the author of the article, "Slowly but Surely? The Rise of Women Participating in the Labour Force in Turkey."

Mónica Patricia Toledo González is the Coordinator of the Licenciatura de Ciencias de la Familia en la Facultad de Ciencias para el Desarrollo Humano de la Universidad Autónoma de Tlaxcala in Mexico. Her research focuses on paid domestic work, quality of work, family, care, and reproductive work. She is author of various publications, including co-author of "Reproducción social estratificada: El trabajo doméstico remunerado en México y la interacción entre mujeres de estratos medios y populares," in *Población y trabajo en América Latina: Abordajes teórico-conceptuales y tendencias empíricas recientes*, Fondo de Población de las Naciones Unidas (UNFPA).

Maura I. Toro-Morn is a Professor of Sociology at Illinois State University. She is a scholar in the fields of immigration and sociology, focusing on global migration and on the questions of why people move, how, and what are the consequences of their movements. She is the author or editor of numerous publications, including most recently the co-edited volume, *Immigrant Women Workers in the Neoliberal Age*.

Paola Villa is a Professor in Economics and Management at the University of Trento in Italy. Her main field of research is labor economics. She is the author of numerous studies with specific reference to the dynamics of employment and unemployment. In recent years her research has focused on identifying barriers for women's integration in the labor market, the interrelationships between family dynamics and the labor market, and female labor participation and fertility trends. Her most recent publication, co-authored with F. Modena and Gabriella Berloffa, is *Changing Labour Market Opportunities for Young People in Italy and the Role of the Family of Origin*.

Xiaodan Zhang is an Associate Professor in Sociology and Gender Studies at the City University of New York's York College. She was previously a research scholar with the Weatherhead East Asian Institute of Columbia University. Her research focuses on changing labor relations resulting from economic reform in China, how women's social movements in China adopt, apply and redefine feminist theories from the West, and more broadly, on the construction and reproduction of power relations in society. She centers her theoretical questions on the relations between institution, human action, and social change. She also examines cultural factors, particularly how and why certain cultural elements survive different social systems.

ACKNOWLEDGEMENTS

The editors would like to thank the Liechtenstein Institute on Self-Determination at Princeton University (LISD) and the Institute's Project on Gender in the Global Community for generously sponsoring the Symposium on Global Women's Work in September 2014, where our network of contributing scholars first met and began the collaborative conversation that resulted in *Global Women's Work*.

Beth English is particularly grateful to Wolfgang Danspeckgruber, Founding Director of LISD, for his support not only of this book project but the broader work undertaken by the Project on Gender in the Global Community. Likewise, thanks is due to Princeton colleagues Doyle Hodges, Uriel Abulof, Rana Ibrahem, Jacqueline Gufford, Jordi Graupera, Angella Matheney, and Trisha Barney who have offered their support, in large and small ways. In its critical early phases, Julia Tréhu assisted in compiling and copyediting submissions to the volume. Thanks as well to Barbara Buckinx who has most recently become a valued collaborator and colleague.

Mary Frederickson would like to thank the Graduate Institute for the Liberal Arts at Emory University, which provided support for the project in its earliest stages. Kevin Corrigan, Allen Tullos, Elizabeth Goodstein, Michael Moon, Peter Wakefield, Ari Eisen, and Kim Loudermilk offered encouragement at crucial points along the way. Over the past three years the Rollins School of Public Health and the Department of Behavioral Sciences and Health Education housed the project at Emory and provided a stimulating environment for research and writing. Special thanks go to Colleen McBride, Nancy Thompson, and Colin Talley, and also to Ashley Mastin, Yenawa Robinson, and Brittani Magee who were always willing to help.

Olga Sanmiguel-Valderrama is especially grateful to the TAFT Research Center at the University of Cincinnati, for granting financial support and providing an intellectually stimulating venue that fostered engagement with the project and facilitated the presentation of this research at domestic and international conferences. Thanks also goes to the faculty and students at the Women's Gender and Sexuality Studies department at UC for their unconditional encouragement of writing and research for this book.

We benefitted tremendously from the careful editing work of Jeanne Barker-Nunn. Her skill, good humor, and support made an enormous difference in how the volume came together. At Routledge, we thank Jill Rubery for initially inviting us to submit the manuscript to the press, and then for including it in the IAFFE Advances in Feminist Economics Series. We appreciated the assistance of Emily Kindleysides and Anna Cuthbert. Lisa Lavelle did a wonderful job of propelling the manuscript once it arrived at Routledge and we are most grateful for her skill, efficiency, and most importantly, her interest in the book.

We each thank our families and friends: for Beth, Steven Barnes for his constant love and support, Simon and Graham Barnes for their love, laughter and silliness, and David English, who died before the publication of the volume, for his lifetime of hard work, sacrifice, support and love; for Mary, love and support from Clinton Joiner and Evan, Megan, Anthony, and Arden, provided inspiration and perspective. Sarah Knox offered crucial encouragement, Nancy Schick never failed to ask how the book was progressing, and Katie Colville kept things moving; and for Olga, with loving gratitude to her daughter Ana Patricia Sanmiguel-Valderrama for running along with her on trips and to endless meetings that allowed her to be part of the project, her father, Eduardo Sanmiguel-Arciniegas (R.I.P.) and mother, Emma Valderrama de Sanmiguel, for their endless sacrifices and loving support. Also thank you to Eileen Ryan, who generously fulfilled mothering duties when Olga had to be away.

Finally, we thank the wonderful group of scholars who contributed essays to *Global Women's Work*. You came from a dozen different countries to participate in this unique collaboration on women's work across the globe. We appreciate your knowledge, insights, and hard work, and your willingness to join us in what has become an ongoing conversation about gender, agency, opportunity, and oppression in the twenty-first century.

INTRODUCTION

Perspectives on gender and work in the global economy

Beth English, Mary E. Frederickson, and Olga Sanmiguel-Valderrama

At 4:30 a.m. EST on January 20, 2017, demonstrators began marching in the streets of Tokyo. They launched what became one of the largest protests in world history and the largest demonstration ever organized in the United States. As Inauguration Day progressed in Washington, D.C., marchers lined up and took to the streets in Osaka, Japan, on the Antarctic Peninsula, and in Brussels, Miraflores, Peru, and Madrid. Tens of thousands of locals and American expats lined up to march in Australia, "because we don't want to stand by and let the bigotry rhetoric of Donald Trump prevail," as Ayebatonye Abrakasa, co-founder of the Women's March in Sydney told *Al Jazeera*. "We're standing up for our country, for the rights of the indigenous people ... for the rights of women who deserve to be able to own their own bodies. We're fighting for everyone, this is an all-inclusive event."[1]

An estimated five million people, of diverse backgrounds, marched in these protests. More than 60 countries on seven continents were represented, including Thailand, South Korea, New Zealand and Australia, as well as nations from across Central, Eastern and Western Europe, the Middle East, Africa, and in Central, South and North America. The morning after Inauguration Day, across the United States, in cities large and small, marchers from all 50 states rallied against Donald Trump's presidency and his political positions on women's rights, healthcare, immigration, environmental issues, religious freedom, violence against women and more.

The worldwide nature of the Women's Marches underscored the determination of women across the globe to protect the strides made and rights gained in the previous decades. The united front exhibited by women and men who came together in opposition to a right-wing political and social agenda and social policies articulated a global vision of indivisibility of rights for women that cut across national and cultural boundaries. Right-wing strength in the United States mirrored gains made by reactionary government leaders in France, Britain, India, Egypt, and Russia. This rightward shift accompanied individual rights and expanding opportunities for women, immigrants and workers, that gave way to downward pressures on wages, restrictions on public protest, and severe cutbacks in spending for healthcare, education, and infrastructure across the globe.

The undeniable power of the activism underpinning the Women's March is part of a long history of women's agency in both the public and private spheres. Building on this history, collective actions among women workers have taken on new meanings in the decade since the 2007–2008 global economic recession. Women workers in particular have embraced innovative approaches to organizing, and momentum has continued to build, with movements by women workers under a globalized economy showing resilience and courage in the face of growing obstacles. Wildcat-strikes and other workers' protests have taken place around the world, from Brazil (where the rate of unionization has increased in the twenty-first century) and Argentina, South Africa, Germany, and France, to the outstanding workers' mobilizations taking place in industrialized China, where spontaneous and organized strikes have been increasing rapidly in the last 20 years. As Chris Tilly and Marie Kennedy report regarding China, "So-called 'mass incidents,' of which experts estimate about a third to be strikes, numbered 85,000 in 2005, and were unofficially pegged at 120,000 in 2008."[2] This growth in strike activity has correlated with a major demographic shift as millions of young workers, predominantly women, have moved from rural communities to manufacturing centers. In China and throughout the Global South—thanks to the broad economic slowdown started by the 2007–2008 global recession, a combination of lower rates of profit for businesses, and workers who are more aware of their worth and less willing to stoically endure hardships and lower wages—women workers are demanding their rights and labor unrest is increasingly present.

These vigorous worldwide mobilizations have opened a new conversation about the endurance of women's rights in the workplace and broader society, and of individual freedoms fought for and achieved over the course of the twentieth century. As part of this tidal wave of activism spreading across the United States, the European Union, the Middle East, Central and South America, Australia, Africa, and Asia, women have drawn on long-standing practices of protest and dissent, from public protest to private opposition and marching in the streets, to organizing demonstrations. As Annelise Orleck writes in *"We Are All Fast-Food Workers Now:" The Global Uprising Against Poverty Wages*, "In Bangladesh, Cambodia, Myanmar, India, Vietnam, and Ethiopia, garment workers have taken to the streets. They are sick from breathing toxic fumes and tired of factory owners who flee to other countries owing workers months of back pay. Hundreds of thousands have joined these protests."[3]

As such protests have spread, established forms of networking have given way to the creative use of social media that supports organization on a global scale. Women across the world have long influenced and shaped the nature of their own lives, even when faced with the most difficult economic and cultural circumstances. The present moment however represents a major turning point as women from around the globe work to sustain past gains and to staunch the tide of abrogated rights going forward.

Within this context and that of the global economic recession and rapidly shifting macroeconomic trends, this particular period in the modern age of globalization offers an unusual opportunity for reflection and analysis on issues of gender, class, and the nature of work. *Global Women's Work* does this by addressing the central question, "How are women currently shaping the global economic landscape through their labor, activism, and multiple discourses about work?" and by bringing together the scholarship of an interdisciplinary group of international scholars to engage in a gendered examination of work in the wake of the global financial crisis that began in 2007–2008.

The broad scope of *Global Women's Work* reflects the interests of the editors—two historians of U.S. women's labor and an international feminist legal scholar who specializes in Latin America and immigrant rights—and our desire to compare and contrast the experiences of women workers across the globe during the financial crisis following 2007. To this end, we assembled a group of scholars with wide-ranging expertise, from economics to sociology, women's studies to international affairs, history to political science. Throughout this process, we worked to engage researchers from across the globe and to decenter the role of the United States. In October 2014 we brought together 20 scholars from more than a dozen countries for a two-day symposium on Global Women's Work at Princeton University's Woodrow Wilson School of Public and International Affairs. Sponsored by the Liechtenstein Institution on Self-Determination's Project on Gender in the Global Community, symposium participants debated how to broaden the scope of individual research through comparative analysis and collective scholarship. Each participant spoke about their research from a national perspective and then worked with others to compare and contrast the experiences of women across the globe, with an emphasis on the dynamic years following the 2007 economic downturn. Gradually, as the group shared ideas and areas of expertise, national specificities gave way to global commonalities and *Global Women's Work* is the collaborative product of this group of international scholars.

A collective work from beginning to end, *Global Women's Work* analyzes the effects of the global economic downturn on women's labor force participation and workplace activism through microstudies and analyzes the impact of geopolitical economic transformation on the gendering of work in industrialized, industrializing, and deindustrialized regions of the world. Somewhat ironically, in some countries and regions, the contraction of the economy provided new opportunities for women workers; in other regions, the opposite was true, and women workers lost ground. The broad spectrum of economic systems and work experiences analyzed here provides new evidence about the range and scope of women's participation in the global economy.

Broad themes

Global Women's Work addresses three broad themes: 1) women's agency within the context of changing economic options; 2) exploitation versus opportunity for women within the context of global capitalism; and 3) women's negotiations and renegotiations of unpaid social reproductive labor. There is a significant and growing body of scholarship offering important theoretical and practical perspectives on women's work in the global economy. However, interdisciplinary and comparative work—in terms of both place and time—on women's economic participation in various regions of the world, especially in the post-crisis period, remains limited. The threatened collapse of the global economy in 2008 imparted new urgency to processes long underway: movements of labor, capital, and technology from the Global North to the Global South, the decline of western—especially U.S.—economic hegemony, the tensions between neoliberal free trade and economic nationalism, and the race to the bottom in wages and working conditions.

Historically, women have been the "canaries in the coal mine" for the global workforce, and the expansion or unwinding of labor standards for women are often the first indicators of what will eventually become normative for all workers. The "Great Recession" therefore, is a pivot point to probe how women workers have already, and will in the future, fit into local, national, regional, and transnational economies, while considering the challenges posed especially to women workers by racist and patriarchal structures of global capitalism and the international division of labor.[4]

The essays that follow address the first broad theme of women's agency by focusing on where women have choices and what they are doing with them. Part of this involves analyzing how women are negotiating the future for themselves and their families through economic options and how those choices have changed in the face of global recession. Exploitation versus opportunity for women within the context of global capitalism is the focus of the second theme of the volume. In many ways, women are victims of some of the worst forms of economic exploitation—human trafficking, the proliferation of sweatshops, and notions of women's second-class social and economic status. However in the current economic landscape, women also have unique opportunities for advancement, whether it be through attaining waged work in a local manufactory, securing a microfinance loan and taking a step toward entrepreneurship, joining a union, or migrating to undertake service work. The third and final broad theme explores women's negotiations and renegotiations of unpaid social reproductive labor. The feminization of the paid economy in post-industrial, developing, and emerging economies has transformed social relations and affected the unpaid physical, emotional, and mental work traditionally undertaken within families and communities. The intricate challenges of balancing paid labor with the unpaid work of reproduction fall primarily to women and this gender gap in unpaid care work influences not only women's ability to participate in the labor market, but define paid labor occupational segregation, and women's bargaining power within the household and in the labor market. Time is a limited resource and the division of labor between paid and unpaid labor, stretches women thin. Moreover, the devaluation of reproductive work, considered at once a private matter and a woman's responsibility, reduces women's power vis-à-vis men's in confronting the patriarchy, capital, and the state.

Specific concerns

Each chapter in *Global Women's Work* examines women's work in a particular state from multiple perspectives that include the scope of industrial and technological development, the level of proto-colonization and zones of dependency, the existing political system, gendered dynamics of citizenship, and the efficacy of democratic institutions. We encouraged our contributors to pay careful attention to women's economic roles and to incorporate detailed information about wage and salary structures in specific economic sectors and divisions in the workforce by gender, race, ethnicity, and age. Attention is paid to divisions between the formal and informal economies in each nation, with a particular emphasis on measuring the economic impact of female workers. Working conditions for women and girls are documented across time and place, with a detailed analysis that relies on data collected through fieldwork undertaken by the authors, and by reliable NGOs and/or international agencies. Workplace data available in each nation varies, however, and our contributors have worked to focus on issues including working time, sexual harassment, job security, unfree labor, workplace violence, and occupational safety and health. The authors incorporate data on independent national, regional, and local trade unions whenever possible and pay attention to state-sponsored worker organizations and company unions. Microfinance opportunities for women have been examined in detail in those nations where such sponsorship is available. Throughout the volume, the global recession forms a powerful backdrop against which scholars analyze the intricacies of women's paid and unpaid labor in national and global contexts.

Global recession

The 2007 economic downturn that began in the United States when the housing bubble burst and financial chaos followed spread worldwide through 2008. This represented the deepest global economic downturn since the 1930s, with the world economy slowing and ultimately contracting in 2009. From the world's most highly developed economies the recession rippled out, spreading rapidly from the epicenter, and resulting in negative global GDP growth for the first time since World War II. Globally, wages sank, unemployment increased, economic insecurity skyrocketed, and importantly, the slow but steady and promising progress that had been made in the decade before in closing gender gaps in the global labor force reversed.

Between 1997 and 2007 the global gender gap in employment remained high at nearly 25 percent but was on a downward trajectory. In the immediate pre-crisis years, women realized higher employment growth rates than men across all regions, with 1.8 percent growth for women compared to 1.6 percent for men. As the global economic downturn deepened through 2009, employment growth rates for women fell below that of men, with women's employment growth rates dropping below those of men by 0.1 percent.[5] Globally, the gender gaps in unemployment that had likewise been trending toward convergence before 2008, began to grow again, exacerbating the gender gap between employed and unemployed. Overall unemployment increased to a record number of 210 million worldwide by the end of 2009, with millions more who simply stopped looking for work and effectively dropped out of the labor force. Globally, 2017 unemployment rates for women stood at 6.2 percent compared to 5.5 percent for men, with some significant regional variations. While the unemployment gap in both developing and developed countries has narrowed, in the Arab States and North Africa for example, the unemployment gap between men and women remains stubbornly high—a combination of both recession and other sociocultural factors—with women's unemployment rates topping 20 percent, more than twice the rate of men.[6]

By 2017 gender gaps in the labor market remained one of the most persistent and pressing issues in the global economy, with women, according to the ILO, "substantially less likely than men to participate," as the female labor force participation rate hovered at 49 percent, nearly 27 percentage points lower than the rate for men. The largest gender gap in participation rates remained in emerging economies at 30.6 percent, with the smallest participation gap—due in large part to the economic necessity for women to work for wages—in developing countries at 12.3 percent.[7] The recession, too, stressed existing systems and in the case of women workers in most nations across the globe, inequalities in wages and quality of work, caregiving, and vulnerable labor became more deeply entrenched and, in some cases, have been exacerbated. Sectoral and occupational segregation remained highly segregated by gender, with women's share in the service sector—wherein jobs are often low-skill, low-wage, and high-turnover—by 2012 representing nearly half of all women workers globally. In advanced economies 85 percent of the female workforce worked in the service sector. Further, crisis-response policies undertaken by governments, both stimulus and austerity measures, frequently hit women workers especially hard. Stimulus packages focusing on manufacturing, construction, and trade-oriented industries were, because of sectoral segregation, most beneficial to male workers. Austerity measures targeting the public sector impacted social safety-net provisions and fell most hard on women, contributing to both a rise in part-time work among women and increased hours spent on non-waged family care. As late as 2016, while on average 81 percent of working-age men participated through work in the formal economy, only 54 percent of women did, and persistent gaps remain in waged work with women's average earnings almost half those of men.[8]

Comparative histories

Three specific examples, of women workers in China, Russia, and the United States, illustrate the broad spectrum of similarities and differences experienced by workers who have experienced dramatic economic transformation and dislocation in the decade since the economic crisis began. In China, as scholar Xiaodan Zhang puts it, the "very visible, brawny hand of the state," reacted quickly with a RMB4 trillion (US$700 billion) rescue package to reenergize the Chinese economy in the wake of repercussions from the sudden and deep U.S. recession. In Russia, another nation emerging from the painful transition from a socialist economy to a new capitalist order, the lives of women have been dramatically affected by back-to-back recessions, the first in the 1990s, the second in 2008. As political scientist Carol Nechemias argues, in Russia the political ramifications of the 2008 crisis actually outweigh the economic because of Russia's pursuit of political decisions that bode ill for women's status. And in the United States itself, emerging from the Great Recession women have regained job losses, but have not moved toward greater equality in the workplace. As scholar Brigid O'Farrell asserts, the expanding global economic landscape, coupled with declining union membership, has added increased challenges that have kept wages stagnant. The Great Recession she argues, escalated a development that began in 1979 when the nation's productivity began a sharp ascent and workers' median compensation remained flat. By 2016, global trade and investment were recovering, but full-time employment and wages were not.

In China, Russia, and the United States, the global financial crisis generated vigorous debates about gender roles and women's identity. When Chinese employment levels dropped after 2007, the state urged women to "return home." Changing ideologies about women's roles, declining opportunities for women in the workplace, and increasing wages for male workers, have turned women's empowerment on its head in China and pushed women back toward a more traditional gendered division of labor. Likewise, when the 2008 global recession hit Russia hard, the state responded by fending off the encroachment of "immoral western values." The West came to be seen as standing for a "genderless and infertile" morality, leaving Russia as the defender of traditional family values. Protecting Russian society from the pull of western neoliberal thinking includes not only hostility to gay rights but also to western-style feminism. Authoritarian crackdowns, a priority on boosting birth rates, and a resurgent Russian Orthodox Church together have shaped an ideology regarding women's special role as "guardian of the home, loving and careful wife and mother" that has impacted women's workplace status in Russia.

In the United States, the Great Recession of 2007–2008 brought conflicting strategies and tactics center stage in American culture and politics. On the one hand, conservative politicians renewed their efforts to make abortion illegal and birth control difficult to obtain. Many school districts, especially those in states with conservative legislatures, instituted abstinence-only sex education. Evangelical politicians and church leaders in the United States articulate ideas laced with the same anti-feminist rhetoric heard in Putin's Russia and Xi's China. But on the other hand, throughout the United States, a major post-recession effort has focused on improving workers' lives through demonstrations, legislation, education, and training. As Brigid O'Farrell discusses, the National Domestic Workers Alliance, organized in 2007, has 42 affiliate organizations with over 10,000 nannies, housekeepers, and caregivers for the elderly in 26 cities and 18 states. In 2013 the Department of Labor announced a new rule extending minimum wage and overtime protections to nearly two million home care workers. Across the board, the recession strengthened the resolve of domestic workers, individually and collectively, to push the government for protective legislation, to organize against exploitation, and to fight against economic insecurity. As in China and Russia, however, these gains remain vulnerable in the face of right-wing leaders determined to dismantle legislation that protects the rights of women workers to equal pay for equal work and protection from sex discrimination in the workplace.

Past, present, and future

Everything has a history and global women's work is no exception. The chapters in this book expand the narrative arc of women's experiences, across time and place, to use the resources at their disposal to shape the world in which they live and work. Women's agency in economies from Asia to Africa, the Americas to Europe and the Middle East, takes myriad forms, including entrepreneurship, organizing, mobilization, protest and legislation, to name a few. While the essays in *Global Women's Work* focus on the years surrounding the global economic crisis that began in 2007, the long history of women and work undergirds each chapter. Each generation adopts new forms of entrepreneurship, political strategies, defensive actions, and ways to negotiate social and reproductive labor. But at the same time, certain opportunities and forms of exploitation remain consistent over time. Economies across the world undervalue women's labor, paid and unpaid, in the workplace and at home. Women's associations have the potential to wield economic clout, to shape legislation, to influence those in power. Collective actions multiply the influence of those working for social, political, and economic change. The importance of this cannot be underestimated, especially in the face of sexual harassment, discrimination, and assault, in the workplace and beyond.

We live in a present that is influenced by strongmen. As journalist Thomas Friedman argued in early 2018, passé titles like "president" and "prime minister" no longer suffice. China's Xi wants to be emperor, Russia's Putin wants to be czar, Turkey's Erdogan wants to be Caliph, Egypt's el-Sisi wants to be pharaoh, Hungary's Orban wants to be king, Iran's Khamenei "already has the most coveted title du jour, supreme leader, and he's bent on keeping it," and the U.S.'s Trump has said of Xi Jinping's new "president for life" status, "I think it's great. Maybe we'll want to give that a shot someday."[9] Globalization, rapid changes in the workplace, perpetual armed conflicts, and global financial crises have exacerbated the insecurities of people around the globe, making them long for leaders who "can stop the winds of change."

But "winds of change" that bring strongmen to power, also fan the flames of resistance. The resistance launched during the Women's Marches of 2017 was replicated on International Women's Day—March 8, 2018—when women in more than 60 nations around the world marched again for their rights, with some 5.3 million women in Spain alone joining a 24-hour strike to protest working conditions in their wage-paying jobs and the unpaid work of social reproduction they undertake in their homes.[10] In Turkey, Afghanistan, South Korea, the Philippines, China, England, France, Italy, and elsewhere around the world, the 2018 International Women's Day events focused on gender parity, sexual dynamics, and the treatment of women in the workplace. In the age of #MeToo and Time's Up, a new sense of urgency imbued the marches and strikes that marked this annual celebration first observed in the United States in 1909, made a national holiday in Soviet Russia in 1917, and adopted by the United Nations in 1975. Past, present, and future coalesced in the actions of women on March 8, 2018, who protested "with pots and pans, raised fists and howls of rage," and in the words of Cintia González, a social activist in Argentina, who spoke before a march that drew hundreds of thousands to downtown Buenos Aires, "This isn't a day to celebrate … we're taking to the streets to demand equality and justice."[11]

Strategies for addressing the gaps for women in the global labor force continue to be created every day in all corners of the world. Workers take action on the shop floor, in the streets, in state houses, and within their own homes, using tactics honed for generations—collective bargaining, agitation, education, and organization. At certain junctures, optimism runs high and a new future seems close at hand; at other times, women ask, are we taking "one step forward, two steps back?"[12]

Nothing illustrates this paradox more powerfully than the collapse of the Rana Plaza building in the Dhaka District, Bangladesh, on April 24, 2013. One thousand, one hundred and thirty workers plunged to their deaths and over 2,500 were seriously injured, many losing an arm or a leg, or facing lifelong paralysis. In the years that have followed, Bangladeshi workers have continuously organized and protested to obtain safer working conditions and better wages. There has been some progress, but much remains to be done. At the 2015 White House Summit on Workers Voice, President Barack Obama cautioned the attendees, including women workers from across the globe, "You can't just keep on doing the same things, thinking you're going to get a different outcome." He challenged the gathering to develop innovative new strategies and models for making a difference that included unions, as well as alternative organizing efforts and organizations. When Nobel Laureate Muhammad Yunus, the Bangladeshi pioneer of both social business and microcredit, wrote about the Rana Plaza collapse, he asked the same question:

> [Rana] has created a huge wound and deep pain in the minds of the people of this country. I pray that this deep pain compels us towards resolving the core of the problems in our national life. [Rana] is the creation of our dysfunctional politics. When we watched more than [1,100] helpless deaths, the loss of limbs of hundreds on our TV screen throughout the country it made us aware at every moment, what our dysfunctional politics has led us to. After all this, will we just keep on watching as it keeps happening again and again? When will we come to our senses?[13]

On April 24, 2016, the three-year anniversary of the collapse of the Rana Plaza building in Dhaka, Bangladesh, hundreds of workers and family members again gathered at the site to mourn the workers killed on that day in 2013 and to push for health and safety reforms in garment factories.

The Rana Plaza collapse, the deadliest garment-factory accident and the deadliest accidental structural failure on record in the world, has become the latest powerful symbol of industrial exploitation. But before it collapsed, the Rana Plaza building had represented something very different—employment opportunities for 5,000 workers, the majority of whom were young women. Bangladeshi journalist Zafar Sobhan, in writing about an earlier catastrophic fire at the Tazeen Fashions garment factory outside Dhaka that killed 112 workers in 2012, captured the stark contrast between exploitation and opportunity in the global workplace this way:

> [I]t is this dehumanizing, exploitative trade that has provided employment to over 3 million impoverished Bangladeshi citizens, the vast majority of them women, and utterly transformed the economic and social landscape of the country. In the 40 years since independence, the poverty rate has plummeted from 80 percent down to less than 30 percent today, GDP growth has averaged around 5-6 percent for over 20 years, and the garment industry has had a lot to do with it.[14]

Significantly, the Rana Plaza collapse happened in the wake of the Great Recession and the subsequent global economic contraction that severely reduced the number of jobs in export-led sectors—especially in the garment industry—as demand in the West decreased. To cope with the financial crisis, companies laid off workers, kept many jobs part time or implemented a stretch out, making employees work longer hours without an increase in pay. Cutting corners in enforcement of everything from building codes to safety regulations, from wage rates to work hours, lowered the price of doing business to unprecedented global levels. Western corporations flocked to Bangladesh where an invisible system of subcontracting protected brand names and made the price of doing business dirt-cheap. The results can be seen in the history of Rana Plaza, a tragedy that symbolizes the failure of globalization to protect workers, the failure of state systems to control corruption, and the failure of reforms that too frequently get lost in the debris of the most recent industrial disaster.

This powerful symbol of failure, a structure that once promised such hope, challenges us to remember the past, even as we plan for a more inclusive, safer, and egalitarian future. As Eleanor Roosevelt wrote in her last book, *Tomorrow is Now*, we must "think and plan on a broader scale than ever before, on a scale that goes beyond our own borders, a scale that encompasses the world."[15] In this time of globalization we can afford to do no less. The chapters presented here, written by scholars from across the globe, trace the narratives of women workers who have done just that, and have used the resources they had at hand to create a better future for themselves, their families, and the communities in which they live and work.

Notes

1 "Women's March on Washington Kicks off Down Under," *Al Jazeera*, 21 January 2018. "Women's March: All the US Protests Taking Place in One Map," *The Independent*, 20 January 2017.
2 Chris Tilly and Marie Kennedy, "On Strike in China: A Chinese New Deal in the Making?" in Armagan Gezici et al., eds., *Real World Globalization: A Reader in Economics, Politics, and Social Policy* (15th ed., Boston: Dollars and Sense, 2016), 147; Eli Friedman, *Insurgency Trap: Labor Politics in Post-Socialist China* (Ithaca, NY: Cornell University Press, 2014).
3 Annelise Orleck, *"We Are All Fast-Food Workers Now": The Global Uprising Against Poverty Wages* (Boston: Beacon Press, 2018), 2.
4 The current volume contributes to a growing body transnational studies of women's work in the modern global economy, which most recently includes Annelise Orleck's *"We Are All Fast-Food Workers Now"*; Maria Karamessini and Jill Rubery, eds., *Women and Austerity: The Economic Crisis and the Future for Gender Equality* (London: Routledge, IAFFE Advances in Feminist Economics Series, 2014); Sharon Harley, ed., *Women's Labor in the Global Economy: Speaking in Multiple Voices* (New Brunswick: Rutgers University Press, 2007); and Barbara Ehrenreich and Arlie Russell Hochschild, eds., *Global Woman: Nannies, Maids, and Sex Workers in the New Economy* (New York: Henry Holt Publishers, 2002). This scholarship provides new transnational perspectives on women's economic negotiations in a world increasingly dependent on corporate expansion, international labor pools, and global markets. The current volume likewise expands upon the pre-recession focus of Ellen Mutari and Deborah M. Figart, eds., *Women and the Economy* (New York: Routledge, 2003); Joyce P. Jacobsen, *The Economics of Gender* (3rd ed., New York: Wiley-Blackwell, 2007); and Dorothy Sue Cobble, ed., *The Sex of Class: Women Transforming American Labor* (Ithaca, NY: ILR Press, 2007). More recent books that address issues analyzed in *Global Women's Work* include Valentine Moghadam et al., eds., *Making Globalization Work for Women: The Role of Social Rights and Trade Union Leadership* (Albany, NY: SUNY Press, 2011), Erica G. Polakoff and Ligaya Lindio-McGovern, eds., *Gender and Globalization: Patterns of Women's Resistance* (Whitby, ON: de Sitter Publications, 2011); and Heidi Gottfried, *Gender, Work, and Economy: Unpacking the Global Economy* (Cambridge, UK: Polity, 2012). The Moghadam et al., and Polakoff and Lindio-McGovern volumes explore resistance in the global economy from a gendered perspective. Through a

feminist lens and case studies of specific global cities that have been affected by globalization, Gottfried explores the hidden worlds of gender and work where structural inequalities persist and the power relations that shaped old forms of work endure.

5 International Labour Organization, *Global Employment Trends for Women* (Geneva: International Labour Office, 2012), vi. See also, United Nations, Department of Economic and Social Affairs, *The World's Women 2015: Trends and Statistics* (New York: United Nations, 2015), 87–95.
6 ILO, *World Employment Social Outlook* (2017), 1–2.
7 International Labour Organization, *Global Wage Report 2010/11: Wage Policies in Times of Crisis* (Geneva: International Labour Office, 2010), v; International Labour Organization, *World Employment Social Outlook: Trends for Women 2017* (Geneva: International Labour Office, 2017), 5–8; ILO, *Global Employment Trends for Women* (2012), 4.
8 Measured in average global earned income for women and men. World Economic Forum, *The Global Gender Gap Report 2016* (Geneva: World Economic Forum, 2016), 30; ILO, *Global Employment Trends for Women* (2012), especially 22–29. See also, ILO, *World Employment Social Outlook: Trends for Women* (2017). On the gendered nature of austerity policies see also, Karamessini and Rubery, eds., *Women and Austerity*.
9 Thomas L. Friedman, "When the Cat's Away …," *New York Times*, 27 February 2018, A23; "'President for Life'? Trump's Remarks about Xi Find Fans in China," *New York Times*, 4 March 2018. http://www.nytimes.com/2018/03/04/world/asia/donald-trump-xi-jinping-term-limits.html.
10 BBC, "International Women's Day: 'Millions' Join Spain Strike," 8 March 2018. http://www.bbc.com/news/world-europe-43324406.
11 Elisabetta Povoledo, Raphael Minder, and Yonette Joseph, "Beyond #MeToo: Pride, Protests and Pressure," *New York Times*, 9 March, 2016, A4.
12 Nadine Sika and Yasmin Khodary, "'One Step Forward, Two Steps Back?' Egyptian Women with the Confines of Authoritarianism," *Journal of International Women's Studies* (13:5) October 2012, 91.
13 Muhammad Yunus, "After the Savar tragedy, time for an international minimum wage," *The Guardian*, 12 May, 2013.
14 Marc Bain and Jenni Avins, "The Thing That Makes Bangladesh's Garment Industry Such a Huge Success Also Makes It Deadly," *Quartz*, 24 April 2015; Zafar Sobhan, "Progress and Globalization in Bangladesh: The Tazreen Fashions Garment Factory Fire," *Vice*, 2 December 2012.
15 Eleanor Roosevelt, *Tomorrow is Now* (1963; reprint NY: Penguin, 2012), 71.

PART I
Women's agency

The chapters in Part I look at women's agency from multiple vantage points and geographic positions. Women's agency, by which we mean the capacity of an individual or group to make choices and act on them, together with activism and organization, provide key lenses through which to examine and analyze women's experiences in, and interaction with, a social and economic world that stretches beyond home and family. Part of this involves analyzing how women are negotiating the future for themselves and their families through economic options, and how those choices changed in the face of the 2007–2008 global recession when protections against gender discrimination established in the late twentieth century, were bypassed, ignored, or rescinded with the onset of the economic crisis.

The set of essays that follows looks at women's agency from a global perspective, a macroregional standpoint, and from the viewpoint of the nation-state. From a global perspective, Eileen Boris engages grassroots feminist campaigns that became international efforts to combat capitalist restructuring of home labor during the last third of the twentieth century and into the 2000s. She evaluates a series of home work campaigns in which women challenged the usual definitions of employee and worker, and developed new tactics to redress the traditional categories of labor long used by the International Labour Organization (ILO). Subsequent essays focus on China, Bolivia, Brazil, Turkey, and the United States, nation-states that vary widely in their interpretations and policies regarding women's agency. From a macroregional perspective, Gabriella Berloffa, Eleonora Matteazzi, and Paola Villa analyze women's employment in the European Union (EU) in the two decades following the inception of the European Employment Strategy (EES) in 1997. They ask whether the strength and visibility of gender equality in the EU in the 1990s was the result of women's agency and a shared concern about gender equality as a goal in itself, or whether it was seen as a necessary tool for the achievement of the overall employment targets agreed upon within the EU. As the global recession deepened, gender disparities increased, especially for young mothers who experienced a much lower employment probability than young fathers. By 2016, they find large gender disparities in all European countries and call for a reconsideration of the gender equality issue within the EU.

In sharp contrast to the regionally centralized policies regarding gender equality in the EU, national strategies in China, Bolivia, Brazil, Turkey, and the United States vary widely in terms of the consequences of potential intersections between women's agency, activism and organization, and the state. In China, as Xiaodan Zhang documents, capitalist development run by the Chinese Communist State had a deep impact on women workers' empowerment and disempowerment in the reform era between 1978 and 2010 when an increasingly market-driven economy and patriarchal state contributed to a movement of "returning home" for women workers whose wage-earning capacity had once empowered them. Like Berloffa, Matteazzi, and Villa, Zhang calls for a review of women's agency in the context of an increasingly gendered Chinese society, a growing class gap, and a neocapitalist ideology that legitimizes the disempowerment of women. As we witness the widespread growth of strike activity in China in the past 15 years, the patriarchal state–led movement calling women to return home, documented by Zhang, highlights the historical complicity between capital and patriarchy using socially and culturally ascribed gender roles to maintain continuing economic growth.

Ongoing research in Bolivia, Brazil, and Turkey also reveals complex patterns of women's agency reflected in rapidly increasing labor force participation and attendant new forms of relationships, activism, and organization. In Bolivia, women's agency has been strikingly evident in the organizing capacity of poor peasant women and their struggle for political recognition and better living conditions. Among the poorest in Bolivia, these women incorporated the activist and organizing traditions of both labor and peasant movements into their own independent women's organization, while belonging to the "National Confederation of Peasant Workers in Bolivia." Documented in the work of Anne Marie Jeppesen, these women have gained political influence despite barriers that include poverty, illiteracy, family responsibilities, male chauvinism, racism, and harassment. Jeppesen argues that in the interconnected and globalized world of post–2008, national government policies and female agency make a vital difference in overcoming the effects of social inequality. Bolivian women migrants to Brazil, interviewed by Katiuscia Moreno Galhera and João Paulo Candia Veiga, demonstrated the same capacity to gain greater agency and turn oppressive situations into opportunities for emancipation by carving out places for themselves in the garment clothing chain in the city of São Paulo. Moreover, whenever possible, these women become entrepreneurs who, while a minority among female Bolivian migrants to Brazil, own their own sewing machines and workshops. Seeking new horizons in another country instead of engaging in collective action at home. "Neoliberalism and poverty *create* agency," one of Galhera and Viega's interviewees, a Bolivian anarchist, argued. The entrepreneurial *mulieres advenus*—"adventurous" Bolivian women—who are part of the Bolivian diaspora and the subject of Galhera and Viega's research, demonstrate the complexity of women's agency filtered through the variables of class, race/ethnicity, nationality, age, gender, religion, generation, and personal aspirations.

Like the entrepreneurial *mulieres advenus* migrating out of Bolivia to new lives in Brazil, in Turkey, women have entered a new era of waged labor. The rise of an urban economy dominated by services rather than industrial production has prompted a shift in the feminization of labor, as well as the development of a gendered work culture in urban Turkey. In response, women workers have cultivated new bodily and interactional forms of agency, adopted new norms of sexualized behavior, and developed new language patterns. Traditional concepts of sexual modesty and propriety have been challenged, or given way entirely, as women have expanded their roles in the public sphere and shaped new forms of agency.

Many of the changes women are experiencing as they move into the urban workforce in Turkey in the twenty-first century, were faced by late nineteenth-century women in the United States. Nevertheless, despite a century of workforce participation by U.S. women, equality in the workplace remains an elusive goal. Brigid O'Farrell's chapter on "Gender, Work, and Recession," examines the effects of the Great Recession on women workers in two distinct occupational categories: low-wage domestic caregiving and higher-wage jobs in the construction trades. As she highlights ongoing job segregation within these occupations in the context of a global economic framework, O'Farrell argues that legislation and enforcement provide a critical framework for achieving gender equity in the global economy. She also contends that legal strategies are not enough. Examples of activism, organization, and agency by domestic workers and tradeswomen provide insights into strategies for achieving gender equality despite economic setbacks, increasing class inequality, and political resistance from conservative governments in the United States and around the world.

Each of the essays in Part I of *Global Women's Work*, underscore the critical nature of women's agency and its reflection in deliberate and independent gendered actions within the family, the workplace, and the community. At the same time, this work emphasizes the relative fragility of women's agency, as in the compelling case of the EU and its governmental retraction of women's rights in the face of the global economic slowdown and EU-wide economic crisis; the long history of women workers fighting for gender equality in the workplace in the United States; and the massive retrenchment of women's empowerment in China since 1978. This unevenness of women's agency across time and place underscores the importance of examining the connections between nation-states, regional economies, and global economic platforms.

1
RECOGNIZING THE HOME WORKPLACE

Making workers through global labor standards

Eileen Boris

Apologizing for her absence from a union meeting, Ahmedabad resident Shanta, a twenty-eight-year-old mother of six with a tubercular husband, explained, "I didn't go because I thought if the *seth* [subcontractor] finds out, he won't give me any work. That meant no food for my children, or going back to domestic help." Still, she told the canvasser from the Self-Employed Women's Association (SEWA), "I prayed for the meeting's success." Although the work rolling *agarbatti* (incense sticks) as part of India's expanding informal sector in the 1980s was demanding, it paid better than working as domestic help and could be combined with watching one's own children.[1] Nearly a quarter of a century later, other Asian women workers returned to household work when garment manufacturing left for cheaper locations, an organizer from HomeNet Thailand reported in 2013.[2] In places such as the Philippines, some paid women workers labored in the homes of nearby women, joining the ranks of transnational mothers cooking, cleaning, and caring for yet another group of women—those who entered the labor market as part of the managerial professional class in Los Angeles, New York, Rome, and elsewhere (Parreñas 2001; Huang, Yeoh, and Abdul Rahman 2005; Ray and Qayun 2009; Lutz 2011).

Outworker, household worker, working mother, employer of other women, and consumer of their goods: these often distinct positions in the global economy converged at the end of the twentieth century and were sometimes held by the same woman. This chapter examines grassroots feminist campaigns that moved to the international scale to combat capitalist restructuring that uses living dwellings as places of employment. It considers two sides of home labor: putting-out systems, known as outsourcing, for the making of goods; and bringing-in systems, known as insourcing, for the making or maintenance of people exemplified through paid domestic and care work. Over the last half-century, home workplaces, rather than disappearing as relics of an earlier state of economic development, have expanded in the wake of profound transformations in the gendered international political economy.

From a theoretical perspective, this analysis distinguishes between processes often conflated under the term *outwork*: manufacturing work and housework or care work, which are often dichotomized as productive and reproductive labor (Estévez-Abe and Hobson 2015). It is true that for employers, paying for household work is outwork insofar as a woman or family provides its reproductive labor to another. But from the standpoint of the home as a place of employment, it is more accurate to speak of the employment of domestic workers as insourcing because the worker comes into the home. Paid domestic work is commodified labor, but its outputs are a mixture of intangibles and material products that forge or produce the home and its people. The labor involved dissipates through the very quotidian nature of cooking and cleaning or becomes manifested in the bodies that incorporate such offerings, including caring. In contrast, outwork moves production from factories, offices, and other sites into living spaces; commodities made in dwellings subsequently circulate from their place of fabrication to be sold like any other good. Each form of home labor suffers from what Maria Mies labels "housewiferization," the mystification that the worker is just a housewife or that she labors for love, not money. Homeworkers often claim to be undertaking piecework for pin money, or as a leisure activity, and thus do not appear as real workers in their own minds nor in the minds of others (Mies 1982). Observers often have interpolated the household worker with the housewife. But most cleaners and caregivers understand that they are workers even if they develop attachments to homes and families that can complicate these relations (Glenn 2010).

The rich academic literature on gender and globalization considers transnational motherwork and migrant domestic work as one category and microenterprises and industrial outwork as another (Anderson 2000; Mehrotra and Biggeri 2005; Lutz 2008; Cox 2013; English 2013).[3] In discussing their interconnection through the broader category of the home as a workplace, I build upon my previous scholarship on each form to consider developments during the last third of the twentieth century and first years of the twenty-first, arguing that the new outwork and the newly prominent household work posed similar challenges to a labor standards regime forged with the industrial worker (marked as male and white) in mind (Boris 1994a, 1994b; Boris and Prügl 1996; Boris and Parreñas 2010; Boris and Klein 2012; Boris and Fish 2014a). My concern is less with documenting the global order than with campaigns that occurred to make home labor legible as a type of employment and thus covered by minimum wage rules and occupational safety and other labor standards. But standard-making has come with a price, as it squeezed home labor into categories based on the male industrial and formal sector worker as the norm (Vosko 2010). SEWA and other feminist organizations thus have had to balance creating new entities to meet the circumstances of their members by insisting on being treated just like any other kind of worker, maintaining demands for special treatment to compensate for a gendered-derived precarity as part of the quest for social justice.

On a global scale, campaigns for acceptance of home labor as work occurred through the convention-making process of the International Labour Organization (ILO). Unique among international organizations, the ILO has three components: the International Labour Office (the Office), the International Labour Conference (ILC), and the Governing Body (GB). Its tripartite organization—all national delegations have government, employer, and worker representatives, as do most committees—distinguishes the organization from other institutions of global governance. The Office and regional branches provide technical assistance and research, ranging from advising on labor bureaus and statistical collection to consulting with grassroots NGOs. The Office itself has many departments, only some of which address women's work. Though aspirational in nature, ILO conventions become legally binding upon ratifying nations, offering organizers an additional tool to press for legislative and legal changes at home (Riegelman Lubin and Winslow 1990; Rodgers et al. 2009). Beginning in the 1980s, homeworker advocates, and later organized household workers, went to the ILO to push for social protections and standards for labor hidden in homes. Through archival research and feminist theory, I extend previous ethnographic, social science, and legal studies on convention making at the yearly ILC in Geneva that have tended to reinforce the singularity of those events, whereas I am interested in the connections among them (Prügel 1999; Blackett 2011; Tomei 2011; Schwenken and Prügel 2011; Schwenken 2012; Becker 2013, 32–55; Kawar 2014; McCann 2014).[4]

Both home-based piece-rate and household workers parlayed transnational networks and funding to push for national laws, form worker cooperatives (for cleaning and care services as well as goods production), and redefine the significance of home labor for the global economy. After a decade of mobilization, SEWA achieved international protection for the home-based workers in 1996 when the ILO passed Convention 177, "Home Work." This successful placement of home outworkers under an international treaty set the stage for a similar victory for household workers fifteen years later. In the mid-2000s, national and regional associations and unions of domestic or household workers[5] joined forces as the International Domestic Worker Network (IDWN) and, within a half decade, won ILO Convention 198, "Decent Work for Domestic Workers" in 2011. In October 2013, this coalition established the first woman-run international labor federation dominated by women members, the International Domestic Workers Federation (IDWF). Feminist NGOs (especially for domestic workers), international trade union federations, and ILO staff facilitated the ILO convention process. Such organizing by home laborers themselves has promised redress, but not necessarily elimination, of exploitation (Prügl 1999; Boris and Fish 2014b).

This chapter proceeds chronologically. After considering the global context of home labor during the last third of the twentieth century, I discuss the home work campaign in which the social relations of outwork challenged the usual definitions of employee and worker. SEWA was not the only group in India or elsewhere pushing for an ILO convention, but by the mid-1980s it had become, for women staff at the ILO and feminists within other international circles, the exemplar organization mobilizing home-based workers and offering a model for relieving "third world" poverty (Riegelman Lubin and Winslow 1990; Rodgers, Lee, Sweptson, and Van Daele 2009). I then assess the efforts of household and domestic workers in the 2000s, during which household "in-workers" built upon the prior legitimizing of the home as a workplace forged by the outworkers but developed new tactics in response to the obstacles posed by the tripartite operations of the ILO. With coalition partners and allies, these activists are in the process of institutionalizing their movement in ways that have eluded home-based outworkers.

Contexts

Following WWII, sociologists and policy makers alike predicted the demise of domestic service and home-based manufacturing as consequences of modernization. Neither totally disappeared. Beginning in the 1970s, with the reorganizing of the global economy through market fundamentalism, business flexibility, financialization, and structural adjustment, inequality between and within nations grew—and so did home labor (Coser 1973, 197; Mitter 1985; Boris 1994a; Lindio-McGovern 2012). Other factors fed into the reappearance of household work and industrial home work as social and economic problems: the dispossession of people from land, the shift in garment manufacturing from the global North to the global South (and the "third world" within), the computerization of offices, and the privatized response to the crisis in domestic and care work generated by the increased labor force participation of women in the global North and elsewhere (Gornick and Meyers 2005; Heymann 2007).

With export processing zones as a development strategy, some people's homes became extensions of factories and offices, what Marx (commenting on the first Industrial Revolution) referred to as the "invisible threads" that tied the home to the mill, or what we might rephrase as the linking of reproduction to production (Marx 1967, 461). Rationalized as allowing flexibility to combine wage earning with caregiving and household chores, such arrangements gained employer approval by facilitating a different form of flexibility: the ability to slough off obligations when competition required fewer personnel or lower wages. Capital additionally could reduce costs by transferring responsibility for equipment and infrastructure, like electricity and the workspace itself, to the woman worker herself, who then would enlist children and other family members to finish the task in the allotted time, a double form of sweating, to use the old term for such practices. Investigators found that homeworkers "rarely enjoy legal status nor adequate protection" compared to formal sector counterparts. Uncounted as workers by censuses, they were "invisible." Their inability to participate in collective bargaining, advocates argued, had negative "long-term implications for the labour movement, development, status of women and welfare of families."

These laborers remained predominantly women with children, most of who were married.[6]

Offshore production and home work were also spreading beyond their historical presence in the garment and textile industries to include the making of other consumer goods, electronics, and plastics. These processes of production thrived on what trade union leader and Indian Parliamentarian Ela R. Bhatt, the founder of SEWA, described as "increasing landlessness and poverty."[7] Where independent artisan and handicraft production persisted, such skilled workers became dependent on middlemen for materials and marketing. Following the computer revolution, telework and home assembly of components updated the practice of clerical homework in Australia, Canada, and other "developed" nations, but also served as additional forms of offshoring from North to South and from expensive to cheaper labor markets (Freeman 2000).[8]

By the twenty-first century, poor women in the global South, but also immigrants and ethnic and racial minorities in the global North, engaged in a variety of home labors, circulating between outwork, domestic service, and unpaid family household and care work. Some also performed domestic labors in institutional settings such as hospitals and schools (Boris and Klein 2012). They had become the vanguard of an exploding informal economy in which the characteristics once thought of as adhering to feminized labor—part-time and irregular hours, low wages, lack of benefits, and temporary assignments outside of regulation or unionization—have become components of all kinds of work, for men as well as women, throughout the world (Peterson 2010). In the early 2000s, the estimated worldwide home-based workforce reached a hundred million, 80 percent of them women, including 10 percent of non-agricultural workers in "developing countries," with between 25 and 60 percent of those in the garment and textile industries (Spooner and Mather 2012, 7).

Simultaneously with this commodification of family or domestic labor, more people's homes were functioning as waged workplaces for women from subordinate groups hired to perform chores associated with wives and mothers. Despite its naturalized status as a private sphere for women and family life, the home continued as a place of production, procreation, and social reproduction, the latter two also shaping possibilities for income generation from increased numbers of workers and, in the case of welfare states, from additional cash supports. Some women turned to surrogacy, transforming their bodies into biocapital (Vora 2015). To balance "work" and "family" labor, the better-off hired nannies and housecleaners; poorer women, especially in places without formal sector jobs, turned to outwork. Under neoliberal globalization, opportunities for some women intensified the exploitation of other women in a manner made visible through faster communication across space and over time (Heyzer et al. 1994; Chang 2000; Parreñas 2001; Harvey 2005).

In this context, women at the low end of the labor market have organized to combat the precarity resulting from the home as a workplace under capitalist social relations on a worldwide scale. Fighting for dignity and recognition, they have taken multiple approaches, combining institution building, grassroots mobilization, and campaigns for international labor conventions. They have not only called for coverage under labor standards and social security schemes, but have demanded "access to basic amenities of housing, water, sanitation or subsidized rations"; redress from "harassed social conditions (lack of male contribution, desertion, alcoholism by males and abuse, high indebtedness, child labor)"; alleviation of health problems from "continuous reproduction, physical stress due to intensive labour in low skilled occupations"; and enhanced visibility. They strove to counter other social impediments, such as "low self-perceptions, caste networks, reproductive roles, and [limited] mobility." In short, seeking the means to maintain daily life, they politicized reproductive labor, seeing it as facilitating production but also central to their capacity to act and to the very survival of families and communities.[9] When they could not find relief within the wage relationship, they produced and marketed their own wares as own-account workers, yet remained dependent on middlemen or contractors.[10] The persistent presence of the contractor led them to question the standard classifications of an employee under the law and labor policy and hence to demand a broader definition under ILO conventions to include all home laborers.

A new kind of union

Registered as an Indian trade union in 1972, SEWA emerged as an independent women's organization in the early 1980s, when its membership stood at nearly two thousand. By the time of ILO deliberations on the home work convention in 1995, its membership had jumped to about 145,000. Women from various informal sector occupations joined, about twenty-three thousand of them home-based. Many members were own-account workers, defined as self-employed despite actually being dependent on distributors or suppliers.[11] In 2014, membership reached 1.8 million (Jhabvala, personal communication, January 2015). SEWA used its membership strength for advocacy joined with direct protest, as in a struggle by garment outworkers in Gujarat for inclusion in the state's minimum wage, where it pushed for coverage under social security and welfare provisions, such as health insurance, housing, and childcare, demonstrating the link between reproductive and productive labor. It also generated alternative forms of production that at times improved the going rate of employers by offering competition (Rose 1992; Jhabvala 1995, 17–18, 20–22, 25–26; Boris 2017, 79–98).[12]

By combining self-help and self-organizing, lobbying and microenterprise, research and dissemination, SEWA appealed to a wide range of political actors. Its leadership consisted of college graduates and local women without education. It gained technical and financial assistance from international organizations, including both NGOs like OXFAM and global labor federations like the International Confederation of Free Trade Unions (ICFTU), now the International Trade Union Confederation (ITUC). Such support provided the material basis for its operations. So did monies from the governments of the Netherlands, Norway, and Sweden and the ILO. The latter funded some of its operations by having SEWA run the "Participatory Action Research Project on the Development of Effective Monitoring Systems and the Application of Legislation for Home-Based Producers" in 1986. Donors facilitated the purchase of transport vehicles, materials for income-generation projects and cooperatives (such as embroidery, spinning, weaving, and dairying), the construction of the SEWA Reception Centre in the heart of Ahmedabad, and the holding of training sessions and clinics.[13] During the United Nations Decade for Women, SEWA became a local organization that participated in a transnational women's movement.

SEWA offered a form of organizing that, quoting the title of one of its documents, would lead to "Generating Awareness in Workers."[14] ILO feminists in the Geneva-based Programme on Rural Women and the India regional office recognized that SEWA understood that organizing did "not simply mean joining SEWA."[15] Organizing required empowering often illiterate and always "spread out" or isolated workers. One tactic that it relied upon was formal gatherings called camps that allowed such women "to move out of their home, visit SEWA, meet other workers and learn about their rights."[16] Eager to support projects that combined standard setting with technical cooperation, the ILO financed such camps to create a bridge between legal training and organizing. The camps provided a space for participants to share their thoughts, discover similarities, and develop demands for economic improvement and safer and fairer work.[17]

Through a participatory action methodology, SEWA gathered data on working conditions, compensating for the neglect of this population in official statistics—a lacunae that India shared with nations worldwide. From the women's own knowledge, it established ergonomic standards and redesigned tools. Part of "awareness" was gaining the courage and know-how to transform embodied knowledge into public actions. At the camps, SEWA instructed the women in techniques in lobbying, sharing information on who to contact and how.[18]

But SEWA found its parliamentary initiatives blocked. In 1988, Parliamentarian Bhatt introduced a "Bill for the Protection of Home-Based Workers" as a private member's measure, but the government failed to put it on the docket for consideration.[19] To gain leverage, SEWA moved to the international arena to push for an ILO convention to win labor and social protections on the national level in India. It hoped to use the ratification process to push for the implementation of local regulations and as the basis for legal action against those who broke them. So its interests and those of key players at the ILO Office and its Indian bureau dovetailed. Though SEWA was not the only group, or India the only country, in which technical cooperation (or assistance) projects operated (there others were in Pakistan, Philippines, Indonesia, and Thailand), it was the go-to grassroots organization within ILO circles.[20]

Convention 177

SEWA's quest for a convention began after discussions with an ILO official during the 1985 Nairobi Conference on Women, where it presented a panel

(Jhabvala and Tate 1996, 14), but the Programme on Rural Women already was promoting its activities as a model for the self-organization of rural women. Already in late 1983, Martha Loutifi from the Rural Employment Policies Branch/Programme on Rural Women had been arguing for "a need for some kind of instrument focused on domestic outworkers" in recommending the topic to the Governing Body; her colleagues found this suggestion premature but met to discuss information gathering. When the usual survey of governments and legislation proved inadequate, SEWA offered a new approach, collaborating with committed ILO feminists like Loutifi and Gisela Schneider de Villegas in Geneva, and Andrea M. Singh and Anita Kelles-Viitanen in New Delhi, on a series of "action-oriented projects" financed predominantly by Nordic countries and the Netherlands.[21] International unions also funded a series of seminars and workshops that proved crucial for documenting the home work problem. Like resolutions passed by ILO committees, trade unions, and feminist NGOs, such meetings served as venues for convincing the annual ILC in Geneva to place labor standards for home work on its agenda.[22] In 1994 and 1995, SEWA would mobilize to influence national responses to the ILO questionnaire that preceded drafting a convention. It also marshaled support at the 1995 UN Women's Conference at Beijing.[23]

To advance international action, Indian, British, and Dutch activists organized HomeNet International (Delaney 2009, 78–97). This international network extended from Asia and Europe to South Africa, Canada, and Australia, building upon earlier regional connections. Local and national groups in Asia (including Thailand and India) and Europe (United Kingdom, Netherlands, and Portugal) had exchanged information and offered support throughout the 1980s. Field visits served as a tool for "cross-fertilization," "to learn and draw inspiration from each other," as SEWA's secretary and chief trade union organizer Renana Jhabvala and West Yorkshire activist Jane Tate explained. A series of international meetings—in the Netherlands in 1990, Washington, DC, in 1991, and Belgium in 1994—formalized the network, which initially Tate ran from England (Jhabvala and Tate 1996, 13–14).

But SEWA and its HomeNet collaborators could not define the agenda at the ILO. SEWA gained access to ILO deliberations because of its relationship with the International Union of Food, Agricultural, Hotel, Restaurant, Catering, Tobacco and Allied Workers' Associations (IUF), which had admitted it to membership in 1983, giving it entry to the ICFTU and thus at the ILO. Still, its reach was limited. Along with other kinds of NGOs, the trade union federations held observer status at the ILO, which meant they could participate in committees, but only nation-appointed delegates could speak during the ILC except during limited designated times. As a representative of a recognized observer group, Ela Bhatt from SEWA attended worker committee meetings. Additionally, the ILO appointed her to the Committee on Experts deliberating on home-based labor because of her knowledge. But no homeworkers or their organizers had full standing to speak at the ILC during the 1995 or 1996 deliberations.

The Workers' Group was behind placing home work on the ILO agenda. In 1988, the International Textile, Garment, and Leather Workers' Union (ITGLWF) and the ICFTU supported an international instrument covering homeworkers (Jhabvala and Tate 1996, 15; Spooner and Mather 2012, 28–29). The unions agreed with SEWA that broad definitions were in order. SEWA recommended inclusion of the self-employed during various ILO deliberations on the informal sector. Offering an expansive experiential conception of the worker, they called for social protection beyond pensions to include housing, healthcare, childcare, and education.[24]

Action on home-based labor would come as the ILO considered the informal sector and sought to promote self-employment in the face of unemployment, yet own-account workers fell out of the scope of concerns. In 1990, the same year that the ILC passed a resolution on self-employment, the GB convened a Committee of Experts on Home Work (ILC 1991, 7, 15). But, in an attempt to placate governments, the resulting instruments considered homeworkers as employees, asking the many nations that failed to count homeworkers as such to revise their practices. Employers, for their part, attempted to obscure deliberations by conflating the home-based piece-rate worker with the professional who worked from home. They equated industrial homeworkers with teleworkers, even though it was generally understood that the convention was to address conditions in developing nations and the informal sector, meaning that computer home work might require its own instrument. They claimed that the convention confused "a commercial contract and an employment contract" and presented such examples to argue for the vagueness of the terms and thus the impossibility of capturing the nature of home work through a convention. The final definitions responded to this critique even while rejecting its conclusions and thus excluded those defined as self-employed.[25]

Initial discussion in various committee meetings recuperated discourses of invisibility, marginalization, vulnerability, and isolation that had long haunted home work. Fearing "a return to the conditions of the nineteenth century" through "modern slavery, camouflaged" as independent contracting, Worker Group speakers argued for adopting a convention that would "bring ... a smile to the unfortunate faces of those who have never been given any hope ..." What workers viewed as a generator of exploitation, employers portrayed as "the cradle or kindergarten of enterprise" and engine of economic growth,[26] arguing that home work offered opportunities to women who otherwise would not be able to leave their families, thereby ending their marginalization. In contrast, workers saw it as taking unfair advantage of customary and employer discrimination. The ITGLWF, which had refined its position on home work from prohibition to regulation, pictured Ahmedabad women under the weight of piles of garments, their children denied a childhood as "family life is tethered to the ever-present work." Employers also connected home and work as they too drew upon hegemonic understandings of the family, but to defend "the genius and culture of domestic establishment, particularly involving women workers," from interference by regulatory bureaucracy or to charge that "'equality of treatment'" would destabilize "domestic life" and "the family system."[27] Employer experts "stressed the positive potential for job creation, reduced costs, flexibility," while their worker counterparts "saw the advantages as going mainly to the employers ... often the only advantage for the homeworker was to have work and some income instead of having no work and no income at all." Rather than alleviate poverty, according to this reasoning, home work damaged the fiscal health of the state, as much of it was underground, illegal, and invisible. Employers claimed the convention would simply push such work further underground.[28]

During these deliberations, the homeworker appeared to be like the woman worker, covered by other conventions and equal to the hegemonic worker of the standard employment contract, but in need of special treatment because of the unique circumstance of her place of labor.[29] She too would have "freedom of association, protection against discrimination in employment, occupational safety and health, remuneration and maternity protection," but obtaining these standards required additional recordkeeping by employers, workers, and government agencies as well as inspections, despite the lingering belief in the privacy of home spaces.[30]

The inability of the experts to agree on the scope of the problem, on the definitions of homeworker, intermediary (subcontractor), and employer, or on much else led to a request to the GB to decide whether the ILO should engage in standard setting at all. In 1993, the GB agreed to place the question on the ILC agenda in 1995 and 1996. The rancor over the appropriateness of action foreshadowed the breakdown of tripartism during the 1996 passage of what emerged from the conference standard setting committee as a very general convention and a non-binding detailed recommendation on implementation. The employer delegates, refusing to participate in deliberations over the convention, abstained en masse during the ILC vote. Their attempt to undermine the needed quorum failed, however.[31] Convention 177 brought to a head a long-simmering disjunction between the organization of the ILO and the Employer Group's negation of its procedures. In that moment of ascendent neoliberal thought, employers wanted less, not more, oversight.

Despite all the talk, the homeworker herself was mute. Employers blocked a proposal to have Bhatt address the plenary session during the final deliberation on the convention. Given how the ILO works, all tripartite partners had to approve an observer speaking at the assembly. The employers certainly feared Bhatt's power to move delegates—what political theorist Elisabeth Prügl, who witnessed the proceedings, described as "her symbolic power evoking the image of home-based assembly workers" that would cut through employers' constructs of "the new flexible labor force" as consisting of white-collar workers choosing their space of labor. The ILC could only view, not hear, an exhibit hung outside of the meeting. This display, probably put together by the Office from materials provided by SEWA and its allied campaigners, underscored homeworker diversity. Passersby saw the beedi workers in India, the garment workers in Bangkok and all over the rest of the world, the British woman assembling Christmas crackers, the tele-homeworkers in Canada and Australia, and the women in Madeira, Portugal, who do the most beautiful hand embroidery.

(ILC 1996, pp. 213–214)

These representations spoke to homeworkers' standing as part of "those workers who are in need of protection" whose plight remained the ILO's mission to relieve through standard setting—that is, as victims of global capitalism rather than active campaigners in their own right against its abuses.[32]

Decent work for domestics

The Employer Group correctly predicted that few nations would ratify Convention 177, which came into force in 2000 and today has ten signatories. They lobbied vigorously against ratification.[33] Only three years after passage, more countries had accepted the domestic worker convention, Convention 189, than have signed the earlier one on home-based labor.[34] But the home work campaign set the stage for the domestic worker victory in numerous ways. With Convention 177, the ILO for the first time recognized work in the home as worthy of a labor standard of its own. It ended the distinction between public and private on the basis of the location or the characteristics of the worker rather than the nature of the labor process itself. Technical assistance and standard setting on home work solidified institutional support for the informal sector, helping to redirect ILO efforts to the reproductive labor that occurs in that realm. Finally, home work activism revealed the kind of transnational networking and coordinated strategy necessary for success within the ILO system and highlighted the necessity of obtaining trade union support for admittance into the ILO deliberative process (Keck and Sikkink 1998; Franzway and Fonow 2011).

As McGill law professor Adelle Blackett, who served on the ILO Secretariat during the "Decent Work for Domestics" process in 2010 and 2011, has argued,

> the negotiation and adoption of the new convention and recommendation reflected the ILO's effort to address and respond to a social movement ... [that] left an indelible imprint both on the process and the substance of the new convention and recommendation.
>
> *(Blackett 2012, p. 791)*

The movement of domestic workers for human rights, under which inclusion in labor standards belongs, challenged the workings of the ILO, opening up the process to NGOs in creative ways and enabling the organization to address the contours of work under twenty-first-century precarity and informality.

Household workers challenged both trade unions and employer organizations. The global union federations, however, had learned to support workers not organized in traditional forms. Aided by the NGOs, which lobbied governments, they pushed the GB to include "decent work for domestic workers," which became an agenda item at the 2010 and 2011 ILC (IRENE and IUF 2008, 10). Even the Employers Group overcame their initial skepticism to accept a human rights framework, though they continued to insist that the particularities of domestic work distinguished it from other occupations and thus undercut the appropriateness of a convention. As with outwork, they wrangled over definitions, seeking to exclude those employed by "commercial" enterprises and those who worked under contractors. They questioned standardizing labor that defied standards as well as the inspection of homes and the capability of employers of domestics to keep records, which were old shibboleths brought up whenever standards for household workers came to the fore in many nations. But they were shamed into permitting the convention.[35]

As I have discussed more fully elsewhere, a changing political economy, which encouraged organizing among household and domestic workers on local, national, and regional levels, laid the basis for transnational networks and international action (Boris and Fish 2014a). By 2010, the ILO estimated the number of domestic and household workers had reached nearly fifty-three million women and men, nineteen million more than fifteen years before, accounting for some 7.5 percent of women's labor across the globe, with larger percentages in specific regions (ILO 2013, 2). Domestic work became recognized as an issue of migrant as well as child labor. As such, it fit into the ILO's focus on both "fair globalization" and "decent work."

The transnational forces that encouraged migrant domestic work also facilitated transnational networks among women and enhanced activities by global labor federations. From the 1980s, household workers throughout Latin America and the Caribbean, in Hong Kong and South Africa, and among migrants in Asia, Europe, and the United States created associations and unions, some of which were part of larger labor federations or left-leaning political parties. Activists and unionists in the Netherlands proved, as with HomeNet, central to bringing these groups together, convening an action conference in Amsterdam in November 2006. They built upon a prior 2005 meeting, aptly titled "Out of the Shadows" in keeping with dominant reform discourse, that focused on what trade unions could do to organize and "protect" domestic workers in Europe. These sponsors included migrant rights, feminist, and human rights NGOs as well as unions, especially the ITUC and IUF, some of these groups the ILO would approve as participants in the Committee on Domestic Work during its deliberations. Particularly important was the Latin American and Caribbean Confederation of Household Workers, or CONLACTRAHO.[36]

Despite the years between the home work and domestic work battles, what is striking is the overlapping of approaches taken by their supporters. The IUF, which remained a progressive organization of low-waged food and service sectors, became the first global union to include domestic work as part of its agenda, just as it had earlier embraced SEWA. It then helped to incubate the international movement.[37] Similarities also can be attributed to the influence of Women in Informal Employment: Globalizing and Organizing (WIEGO), described as "an NGO development and advocacy group" that relies on "research, policy assessment and promotion, and information provision" to aid women in the informal sector. In 1997, SEWA's Jhabvala was one of the three founders of WIEGO, which subsequently provided technical advice and coordination for IDWN (Delaney 2009).[38] The domestic workers who would form the International Domestic Worker Federation (IDWF) mobilized by providing their own knowledge of the labor compiled through participatory research methods like those deployed by SEWA. They too held preparatory meetings where activists and NGOs mapped strategy and endorsed a convention. They also relied on the politics of affect, representational displays, observer status, and the knowledge and skill of interested feminists in the ILO Office, including Manuela Tomei, then heading the Conditions of Work and Employment Programme.

But two aspects of the later campaign stand in contrast to the one mobilized for home-based workers. The first is that the domestic workers demanded their right to be heard as well as recognition as workers and respect for their skill. As Marcolina de los Milagros Infante Ramirez of Peru explained, "We are tired of hearing others speak in our name." As they frequently noted, such workers "often care for the most vulnerable of society, the children, sick and elderly, increasing the well-being of all," but received "contempt and abuse" rather than respect. They asked, "How Can I Be Proud of Myself When You See Me As a Victim?" (IRENE and IUF 2008, 14, 13, 18). To this end, domestic workers, unlike the outworkers, maneuvered around ILO procedures to seize a voice at the main assembly of the ILC. They did so by winning representation on official national delegations, but they also engaged in a politics of messaging by wearing t-shirts printed with their demands and bending the rules by breaking into song and unfurling banners. Their palpable presence stood witness to the living bodies subjected to conventions and recommendations, making it difficult for delegates to vote "no" (Fish 2017).

Second, while the campaign traveled from the local to the regional and then to the international level of struggle, it had stronger local organizations ready to press for ratifications (Schwenken and Prügl 2011; Blodfield 2012; Becker 2013, 32–55; Boris and Fish 2014a). All of this took intense labor to teach low-waged women of various levels of education and knowledge about their rights and how to access them, what we might classify as a form of reproductive labor. As South African Hester Stephens reflected on the transformed consciousness that struggle engendered, "I feel proud as a domestic worker, and I also believe in our union" (Schwenken and Prügl 2011, 445–446).

Domestic worker advocates brought that kind of energy into their formal remarks at the ILC. As substitute delegates or observer representatives, a handful of activists received speaker rights, including Shirley Pryce, a household worker from Jamaica.[39] The old tropes of vulnerability, victimization, slavery, and exploitation certainly persisted. As a Worker delegate from Chile described the ethical imperative for action, "Domestic workers in private homes find that their hours are endless, that their days of rest are not respected, and the treatment which they experience cannot be considered decent work." Worker delegates from India and Kuwait spoke of relieving "suffering." Countering the notion that they were just one of the family were assertions that "We too are workers," as Bolivian Quenta Jucumari, an alternate Worker representative, declared during the final debate in 2011. Household workers asked for coverage under health and safety, non-discrimination, and social security laws as well as wage and hour regulations. Earlier IUF representative Vicky Kanyoka, a Tanzanian leader in IDWN, offered a different vision to the general one that dismissed the worth of such labor:

> As domestic workers themselves say, we are the oil in the wheels. It is our work in households that enables others to go out and be economically active.... Yet it is us who take care of your precious children and your sick and elderly; we cook your food to keep you healthy and we look after your property when you are away[40]
> (Record of Proceedings, *99th Session 2010*, 8/41)

The observation of a Singapore Government delegate exposed the usual understanding about this labor: "Employers did not hire domestic workers to increase their business profits, but rather to help in the household."[41] That is, he viewed domestic work as not really like other work. The representative of the Holy See echoed the feminist analysis of the global care chain as "structurally built on the disruption of basic family relationships for all women involved," but with the goal of maintaining the heterosexual family, the site of "human and economic development."[42] Therein were the bonds of care that advocates deployed to effect change through affect, an approach not available to outworkers. In short, as a Sri Lanka Worker delegate explained, domestic workers had earned coverage because "they visibly and invisibly contribute their blood and sweat to keep afloat the living standards of society as a whole, particularly in the sending countries."[43]

Gender mattered, but so did "the human element." While a Canadian Government delegate stressed gender-neutral language, his Australian counterpart compared the proposed convention with existing ones for seafarers. Not only would standards for domestics cover around a hundred million workers, compared to 1.2 million under maritime regulations, but she also reiterated a concern for dignity and the "end to scandalous situations" expressed at a recent Maritime committee.[44] Domestic workers deserved no less; this was a women's issue, she argued, the resolution of which could advance gender equality.

Conclusion

Considering the campaign for Convention 189 in light of the earlier struggle for Convention 177 illuminates key aspects of women's organizing under globalization that are applicable in the current moment. First, it takes transnational networks to push policy through international institutions. Second, feminist NGOs and women worker groups have "mastered" a multiscalar approach, generating a synergy between the local, national, regional, and global. In doing so, they have engaged in advocacy learning, transferring strategies, knowledge, and techniques (Keck and Sikkink 1998). Domestic in-workers could build upon the legacy of the home outworkers in part because some key players applied lessons learned from the latter to the former.

Like SEWA, domestic worker associations and unions continue to work on many fronts: creating cleaning cooperatives, shifting legal responsibility for wages and other conditions from labor boards to rights commissions, and building their own capacity for leadership and campaigning. Through organizing the whole woman and paying attention to relationships between family and paid labor, they are waging a prolonged battle in which the changing of attitudes toward home labor is the first step.

Only the most committed Gandhian would offer love to putting-out manufacturers and their contractors. But domestic worker associations stress cooperation and love in appeals to the women and households that employ them. For the threads of connections are visible even when the employment relation is denied. These bonds are dual: linking worker and employer in ways that obscure economic bondage. The ties of outwork harbor the illusion that the worker is just a housewife rather than like a housewife, laboring without standard protections. Whether the labor standards regime developed for industrial work is flexible enough to address home labors in all their commodified forms is an unfolding story.

Notes

1 "The Home-Based are Workers Too," typescript draft, p. 4, in WEP 10–4–04–158, Jacket 2, ILO Archives, Geneva. Unless noted otherwise, all archival folders are from this repository.
2 Author's field notes, Founding Congress, International Domestic Worker Federation, Montevideo, Uruguay, 25 October 2013; http://wiego.org/wiego/homenet-thailand.
3 Outwork, especially industrial homework, has become part of the literature on global supply chains, but scholars usually study specific local examples.
4 Tomei was the key staff person at ILO for the domestic worker convention.
5 There is debate within the movement whether to call themselves domestic or household workers, and thus I alternate. Latin Americans reject the term "domestic," while others find it in keeping with their national laws and usages.
6 To Mrs. Ahmad, Mr. Chai, Mr. Martin from Martha F. Loutfi, Memo, "Items for First Discussion at 72nd (1986) I.L.C., 19.12.83, WEP 10–4–04–018, Jacket 1.
7 "Speech Given by SMT. Ela R. Bhatt at the 14th World Congress, 14–18 March 1989, Melbourne," WEP 10–4–04–21–1–33–02, Jacket 6.
8 ILO, Documents of the Meeting of Experts on the Social Protection of Homeworkers, "Social Protection of Homeworkers," Geneva, 1990, MEHW/1990/7, 7–9, and passim.
9 Azad, Nandini. n.d. "Overview of Women Workers in the Unorganised Sector," WEP 10–4–04–21–1–33–02 Jacket 2. She was a consultant with NIPCCD, an agency connected to the Indian government's Women's Ministry.
10 For example, Letter to Anita Berar Amed from Reena Nanavaty, 5 July 1993; SEWA, "An invitation to International Applique Exhibition '99 France," both in EMP 63-4-1–2, Jacket 1.

11 "Project Description: Follow Up Activities Toward An ILO Discussion on Homework," EMP 63–4-1, Jacket 1; accessed 17 August 2014, http://www.sewa.org/About_Us_Structure.asp,
12 See also, Memo, S. Selliah to C.F. Poloni, "SEWA Rural Study," 21.04.1988, 38, WED 31–0-33–3, Jacket 1.
13 Memo, S. Selliah to C.F. Poloni, "SEWA Rural Study," 35–38; Jhabvala (1995, 18).
14 "Generating Awareness in Workers," SEWA document, n.d., WEP 10–4-04–21-1–33-02, jacket 6.
15 Memo, Anita Kelles-Viitanen to Philippe Egger, 17 October 1986, "Legal Camp for Women Beedi Workers in Indore," WEP-10–4-04–21-1–33-02, Jacket 2.
16 "Generating Awareness in Workers." See, Boris (2017, 88–91).
17 "Report of Mission to Indore, Madya Pradesh, 2–7 September 1986," 5–7.
18 Kelles-Viitanen, Anita "Minutes of a Meeting held on 22 July 1986," WEP-10–4-04–21-1–33-02, Jacket 1.
19 Letter to Ms. Crow from Andrea Singh; Email from Renana Jhabvala to author, 25 January 2015, in author's possession.
20 "Project Document: Employment Promotion and Social Protection of Home-Based Workers in Asia."
21 Letter to Ms. Crow from Andrea Singh, 13 April 1993, CWL 7–1-11–3 Jacket 1; To Mrs. Ahmad, Mr. Chai, Mr. Martin From Martha F. Loutfi, Memo, "Items for First Discussion." Singh and Kelles-Viitanen were prominent in India; Loutifi, Zubeida Ahmad, Rounaq Jahan, and then others in Geneva.
22 "Project Description: Follow Up Activities Toward an ILO Discussion on Homework;" "Project Document: Employment Promotion and Social Protection of Home-Based Workers in Asia" (1992), 4, WEP 10–4-04–028-158, Jacket 3.
23 Letter to Madhubala Nath from Ela Bhatt, 3/6/1994 in EMP 63–4-1, Jacket 1.
24 "Resolutions for UN Social Summit 1995 Proposed at SEWA General Body Meeting, 15–17 April 1994," 5–6; "Asian Regional Workshop on the ILO Convention," both in EMP 63–4-1–2, Jacket 1.
25 "Report of the Committee on Home Work: Submission, discussion and adoption," *Record of Proceedings*, 82nd Session, 27\/24; GB, "Report of the Meeting of Experts on the Social Protection of Homeworkers," Meeting of the Governing Body, 248th Session, Geneva 12–16 November 1990, III/1–2, GB 248–1–5 GB Sess. 248.
26 "Report of the Committee on Home Work: Submission, discussion and adoption," 27/32, 44, 37.
27 *Record of Proceedings*, 77th Session, 19/37–39; "Report of the Committee on Home Work: Submission, discussion and adoption," 27/38; "Report of the Committee on Home Work: Submission and Discussion,", 219.
28 ILO, "Meeting of Experts on the Social Protection of Homeworkers," 5–9, passim.
29 "Report of the Committee on Home Work: Submission, discussion and adoption," 27\/21.
30 "Report of the Committee on Home Work: Submission, discussion and adoption," 27\/32, 34.
31 ILC, *Record of Proceedings*, 82nd Session, 1995 (Geneva: ILO, 1996), 252, 27/19ff; "Record of Votes," *Proceedings*, 83rd Session, 1996, 7–10.
32 "Report of the Committee on Home Work: Submission and Discussion," 213–14; e-mail E. Prügl to E. Boris, 21 August 2014.
33 Jhabvala to Boris; Ratifications at http://www.ilo.org/dyn/normlex/en/f?p=1000:11300:0::NO:11300:P11300_INSTRUMENT_ID:312322, accessed 20 August 2014.
34 This number stands at 25 and is growing. http://www.ilo.org/dyn/normlex/en/f?p=1000:11300:0::NO:11300:P11300_INSTRUMENT_ID:2551460, last accessed 16 August 2018.

35 International Labor Conference, *Record of Proceedings*, 99th Session, 2010 (Geneva: ILO, 2010): 12/4.
36 They were: IRENE, International Restructuring Education Network Europe; FNV Mondiaal, a Netherlands trade union; Committee for Asian Women; Asian Domestic Workers' Network; Asia Monitor Resource Centre; WIEGO, Women in the Informal Economy Globalizing and Organizing; BLINN, Bonded Labour in the Netherlands Humanitas/Oxfam; GLI, Global Labour Institute; and PICUM. Platform for International Cooperation on Undocumented Migrants, and IUF.
37 *Decent Work for Domestic Workers*, Report IV(1) (Geneva: ILO, 2010), 78–83.
38 "Organizing Homeworkers," accessed 20 August 2014 http://wiego.org/, 97–98; field notes, Montevideo, October 24–309, 2013.
39 International Labor Conference, *Record of Proceedings*, 100th Session, 2011 (Geneva: ILO, 2011): 10/42. Other activists who spoke at the ILC assembly were Fish Ip from Hong Kong and IUF and Ida Le Blanc of Trinidad.
40 *Record of Proceedings*, 99th Session: 8/10, 8/15, 8/20, 8/37–38, 8/41. For Jucumari, International Labor Conference, *Record of Proceedings*, 100th Session, 2011 (Geneva: ILO, 2011): 9/35.
41 *Record of Proceedings*, 99th Session: 12/6.
42 *Record of Proceedings*, 100th Session: 9/9.
43 *Record of Proceedings*, 100th Session: 9/34.
44 *Record of Proceedings*, 100th Session: 15/9.

References

Anderson, Bridget. 2000. *Doing the Dirty Work: The Global Politics of Domestic Labor*. London: Zed Books.

Becker, Jo. 2013. *Campaigning for Justice: Human Rights and Advocacy in Practice*. Stanford, CA: Stanford University Press.

Blackett, Adelle. 2011. "Introduction: Regulating Decent Work for Domestic Workers," *Canadian Journal of Women and the Law*, 23(1): 1–46.

Blackett, Adelle. 2012. "Current Development: The Decent Work for Domestic Workers Convention and Recommendation, 2011," *American Journal of International Law*, 106 (October): 778–794.

Blodfield, Merike. 2012. *Care Work and Class: Domestic Workers' Struggle for Equal Rights in Latin America*. University College, PA: The Pennsylvania University State Press.

Boris, Eileen. 1994a. *Home to Work: Motherhood and the Politics of Industrial Homework in the United States*. New York, NY: Cambridge University Press.

Boris, Eileen. 1994b. "The Home as a Workplace: Deconstructing Dichotomy," *International Review of Social History*, 39(December): 415–428.

Boris, Eileen. 2017. "SEWA's Feminism," in *Women's Activism and "Second Wave" Feminism: Transnational Histories*, Barbara, Molony and Nelson, Jennifer, eds. New York, NY: Bloomsbury Academic, 79-98.

Boris, Eileen and Fish, Jennifer. 2014a. "'Slaves No More': Making Global Labor Standards for Domestic Workers," *Feminist Studies*, 40(2): 411–443.

Boris, Eileen and Fish, Jennifer. 2014b. "Domestic Workers Go Global: The Birth of the International Domestic Workers Federation," *New Labor Forum*, 23(3): 76–81.

Boris, Eileen and Klein, Jennifer. 2012. *Caring for America: Home Health Workers in the Shadow of the Welfare State*. New York, NY: Oxford University Press.

Boris, Eileen and Parreñas, Rhacel, eds. 2010. *Intimate Labors: Cultures, Technologies, and the Politics of Care*. Stanford, CA: Stanford University Press.

Boris, Eileen and Prügl, Elisabeth, eds. 1996. *Homeworkers in Global Perspective: Invisible No More*. New York, NY: Routledge.
Chang, Grace. 2000. *Disposable Domestics: Immigrant Women Workers in the Global Economy*. Boston, MA: South End Press.
Coser, Lewis. 1973. "Servants: The Obsolescence of an Occupational Role," *Social Forces*, 52(1): 31–40.
Cox, Rosie. 2013. "House/Work: Home as a Space of Work and Consumption," *Geography Compass*, 7(12): 821–831.
Delaney, Annie. 2009. *Organising Homeworkers: Women's Collective Strategies to Improve Participation and Social Change*. PhD dissertation, La Trobe University, School of Management, in author's possession.
English, Beth. 2013. "Global Women's Work: Historical Perspectives on the Textile and Garment Industries," *Journal of International Affairs*, 67(1): 67–82.
Estévez-Abe, Margarita and Hobson, Barbara. eds. 2015. "Social Politics: International Studies in Gender, State, and Society," Special issue *The Politics, Policies and Political Economy of Outsourcing Domestic Work*, 22(2): 133–241.
Fish, Jennifer N. 2017. *Domestic Workers of the World Unite! A Global Movement for Dignity and Human Rights*. New York, NY: New York University Press.
Franzway, Suzanne and Fonow, Mary Margaret. 2011. *Making Feminist Politics: Transnational Alliances between Women and Labor*. Urbana, IL: University of Illinois Press.
Freeman, Carla. 2000. *High Tech and High Heels in the Global Economy: Women, Work, and Pink-Collar Identities in the Caribbean*. Durham, NC: Duke University Press.
Glenn, Evelyn Nakano. 2010. *Forced to Care: Coercion and Caregiving in America*. Cambridge, MA: Harvard University Press.
Gornick, Janet and Meyers, Marcia. 2005. *Families That Work: Policies for Reconciling Parenthood and Employment*. New York, NY: Russell Sage.
Harvey, David. 2005. *A Brief History of Neoliberalism*. New York, NY: Oxford University Press.
Heymann, Jody. 2007. *Forgotten Families: Ending the Growing Crisis Confronting Parents and Children in the Global Economy*. New York, NY: Oxford University Press.
Heyzer, Noeleen, Lycklama à Nijeholt, Geertje, and Weerakoon, Nedra, eds. 1994. *The Trade in Domestic Workers: Causes, Mechanisms and Consequences of International Migration*. London: Zed Books.
Huang, Shirlena, Yeoh, Brenda, and Noor Abdul, Rahman, eds. 2005. *Asian Women as Transnational Domestic Workers*. Singapore: Marshall Cavendish Academic.
ILC. 1991. "Resolution Concerning Self-Employment Promotion," *Record of Proceedings*, 77th Session, 1990, Geneva: ILO.
ILO. 2013. *Domestic Workers Across the World: Global and Regional Statistics and the Extent of Legal Protection*. Geneva: ILO.
IRENE and IUF. 2008. *Respect and Rights: Protection for Domestic/Household Workers*. Tilburg and Geneva: IRENE and IUF.
Jhabvala, Renana. 1995. "SEWA's Programmes for the Organization of Home-Based Workers—India," in *Action Programmes for the Protection of Homeworkers: Ten Case Studies from Around the World*, Huws, Ursula, ed. (Geneva: ILO), 15-26.
Jhabvala, Renana and Tate, Jane. 1996. "Out of the Shadows: Home-Based Workers Organize for International Recognition." SEED Working Paper #18, Series on Homeworkers in the Global Economy. Geneva: ILO.
Kawar, Leila. 2014. "Making the Machine Work: Technocratic Engineering of Rights for Domestic Workers at the International Labour Organization," *Indiana Journal of Global Legal Studies*, 21(2): 483–511.

Keck, Margaret and Sikkink, Kathryn. 1998. *Activists Beyond Borders: Advocacy Networks in International Politics*. Ithaca, NY: Cornell University Press.

Lindio-McGovern, Ligaya. 2012. *Globalization, Labor Export and Resistance: A Study of Filipino Migrant Domestic Workers in Global Cities*. New York, NY: Routledge.

Lutz, Helma, ed. 2008. *Migration and Domestic Work: A European Perspective on a Global Theme*. Aldershot: Ashgate Publishing.

Lutz, Helma. 2011. *The New Maids: Transnational Women and the Care Economy*. London: Zed Books.

Marx, Karl. 1967. *Capital*, Vol. I. New York, NY: International Publishers.

McCann, Deidre. 2014. "Equality through Precarious Work Regulation: Lessons from the Domestic Work Debates in Defense of the Standard Employment Relationship," *International Journal of Law in Context*, 10(4): 507–521.

Mehrotra, Santosh and Biggeri, Mario. 2005. "Can Industrial Outwork Enhance Homeworkers' Capabilities? Evidence from Clusters in South Asia," *World Development*, 33(10): 1735–1757.

Mies, Maria. 1982. *The Lace Makers of Narsapur*. London: Zed Books.

Mitter, Swatsi. 1985. "Industrial Restructuring and Manufacturing Homework: Immigrant Women in the UK Clothing Industry," *Capital and Class*, 9(3): 37–80.

Parreñas, Rhacel. 2001. *Servants of Globalization: Women, Migration and Domestic Work*. Stanford, CA: Stanford University Press.

Peterson, V. Spike. 2010. "Informalization, Inequalities and Global Insecurities," *International Studies Review*, 12(2): 244–270.

Prügl, Elisabeth. 1999. *The Global Construction of Gender*. New York, NY: Columbia University Press.

Ray, Raka and Seemin Qayum. 2009. *Cultures of Servitude: Modernity, Domesticity, and Class in India*. Stanford, CA: Stanford University Press.

Riegelman Lubin, Carol and Winslow, Anne. 1990. *Social Justice for Women: The International Labor Organization and Women*. Durham, NC: Duke University Press.

Rodgers, Gerry, Lee, Eddy, Sweptson, Lee, and Van Daele, Jasmien, eds. 2009. *The ILO and the Quest for Social Justice, 1919–2009*. Ithaca, NY: Cornell University Press.

Rose, Kalima. 1992. *Where Women Are Leaders: The SEWA Movement in India*. London: Zed Books.

Schwenken, Helen. 2012. "From Maid to Worker," *Queries*, 7(1): 14–21.

Schwenken, Helen and Prügl, Elisabeth. 2011. "An ILO Convention for Domestic Workers: Contextualizing the Debate," *International Feminist Journal of Politics*, 13(3): 437–461.

Spooner, Dave and Mather, Celia. March 2012. "Promoting the ILO Home Work Convention (C177) and the Rights of Homeworkers: A Manual for Workers' Educators and Facilitators," accessed July 22, 2015 at http://wiego.org/sites/wiego.org/files/resources/files/HNSA_GLI_Promoting_ILO_Convention_C177.pdf.

Tomei, Manuela. 2011. "Decent Work for Domestic Workers: Reflections on Recent Approaches to Tackle Informality," *Canadian Journal of Women and the Law*, 23(1): 185–212.

Vora, Kalindi. 2015. *Life Support: Biocapital and the New History of Outsourced Labor*. Minneapolis: University of Minnesota Press.

Vosko, Leah F. 2010. *Managing the Margins: Gender, Citizenship, and the International Regulation of Precarious Employment*. New York, NY: Oxford University Press.

2
EMPOWERMENT REVISITED

Capitalist development and women workers in China's reform era

Xiaodan Zhang

The 2008 economic crisis caused economic reverberations in nations across the globe, and China was no exception. As a market economy with strong state control, however, China responded differently than many other countries. Concerned with possible repercussions from the United States' sudden and deep recession, the Chinese state reacted quickly with a four trillion *renminbi* (RMB) (US$700 billion) rescue package to reenergize the economy.[1] This package consisted of increases in three parts: fixed asset investment, consumption, and net exports. Although this package saved China from an immediate crisis, the economy became unbalanced as the majority of the rescue package went into fixed asset investments, followed by consumption and net exports (Huang and Wang 2010). These imbalances had actually occurred even before 2008, as China's economic reforms had been ramping up to the full-speed capitalist development since the beginning of the twenty-first century. In 2008, however, 670,000 labor-intensive small- and medium-sized firms reportedly closed down in the major industrial cities in Guangdong Province and 6.7 million jobs disappeared. In the spring of 2009, an additional 20 million migrant workers were laid off and forced to return to their rural hometowns.[2] Politically, the state and the market became further integrated and exerted more control over people's daily activities. Scholars have explored the direct impact of the 2008 economic crisis on Chinese women workers in terms of job loss and reductions in public welfare (Chow and Zou 2011). This chapter moves beyond that analysis to focus on how capitalist development has subjected women workers to the power of the state and the market and what consequences this has had on gender inequality.

While existing studies have condemned the exploitation of Chinese women workers, they also tend to celebrate human agency in the process of laboring. They especially point out the similar features that Chinese women workers share with their sisters elsewhere, such as opportunities to work outside the family and the empowerment that results from financial independence. They highlight women workers' resistance to the social system, including shop floor slowdowns, defiance toward the state's family planning policy, and especially their manipulation of some gender discrimination to turn this disadvantage to their advantage while interacting with the state and the market (Lee 1998; Gaetano and Jacka 2004; Zheng 2004; Pun 2005; Yan 2008; Otis 2012). This chapter acknowledges all these findings; but also devotes particular attention to the specific social conditions under which women's resistance has taken place. Drawing on a series of forty interviews with female and male migrant workers, this study analyzes the ideas and the social arenas that fostered women's empowerment. In other words, this chapter evaluates women's agency within the context of an increasingly market-driven economy run by the state and argues that the integration of the state and the market have further consolidated, rather than changed, a society divided by gender. In this gendered world, women's resistance takes place not only individually in informal, transitory, and fragmented forms, but also collectively confined within an ideological framework promoted by Chinese authorities.

Based on both first- and second-hand ethnographic stories collected from migrant workers and retirees during 2012–2014,[3] this chapter unfolds in four separate sections. The first section covers women's pursuit of liberation and gender equality during the socialist revolution that took place from the 1950s to the 1970s. It provides a historical perspective on current gender issues and compares what has changed and what remained the same after these economic reforms were put into place. The second and third sections examine women workers' interactions with both the market and the state since the economic reforms began at the end of the 1970s. They focus on how this dual force impacted women workers' minds and bodies through work, consumption, institutional arrangements, and ideological indoctrination. The fourth section evaluates changes in women workers' relationships to their families as a result of their new positions outside of the domestic domain and analyzes how the current trend of "home returning" illustrates the dilemma women workers encounter in their search for gender equality in twenty-first-century China. Discussing the influence of market economic principles, a state-promoted discourse of middle-class values, and lingering traditional views of women's social roles, the chapter demonstrates that globalized market and state regulations take place in a gendered world, and that the development of a capitalist system has deepened gender inequality through creating a huge class gap, an ideology that legitimizes it, and ultimately a predicament that women workers must shake free of or be buried by.

Gender equality: the Maoist approach and its impacts (1950s–1970s)

In the 1950s, at the dawn of socialism, the newly formed state led by the Chinese Communist Party (CCP) made several institutional and organizational arrangements to champion women's liberation. Among these, Yang (1999) rightly highlights the Chinese Constitution (1954), which stipulates that women have equal rights in the political, economic, cultural, educational, social, and familial realms; the Marriage Law (1950), which abolishes polygamy, arranged marriages, child-bride marriages, prostitution, the buying and selling of women, and other overt abuses against women; and the All China Women's Federation (ACWF), which was created as part of the state apparatus to represent women at the state's request. The state did act as a protector of women's interests and an advocate of gender equality at a time when women were a weaker social group and perceived as such.

The state also promoted women's full participation in the labor force. Women's participation in wage labor in China had begun in the early twentieth century, long before the establishment of the socialist regime, but this was the first time that the principle of "equal work, equal pay" was formulated as a state policy and that women's work was given important political significance. Women were encouraged to "venture out of home into society" (走出家庭；走进社会) against the traditional division of labor that viewed society as an "outside" or public sphere and home as an "inside" or private domain, two separate spaces reserved for men and women, respectively. This social movement infused the concept of "work" (工作) with a sense of pride and made it a symbol of social advancement, while the economic independence that women gained from earning wages was considered one of the preconditions for women's liberation. As a result, a large number of women were brought into both the industrial and the agricultural labor forces. My conversations with factory women workers show that the practice has had a profound impact on women's views of formal employment in factories.

For example, Ms. Li, a sixty-five-year-old retiree in Shanghai, said that she remembered how happy she was when she was assigned a job in a state-owned textile factory upon her graduation from middle school. "We looked down upon those who didn't work but relied on their husbands," she recalled. "At that time, everyone worked. If you didn't work, people would despise you. You yourself would feel ashamed if you did not have a job." Another retiree, Ms. Chen, said that she never even thought of not working. To her, working was always a "must." Ms. Zhou, a retired worker who came with Ms. Chen to meet me, said, "What would you do if you did not work?" During the 1980s and 1990s, when many women workers were either laid off or asked to take early retirement due to the bankruptcy or downsizing of their companies, especially in the textile and electronics industries, most of them found other paid jobs in the service sector. When asked why they continued their employment at the time of being laid off or forced to take early retirement, everyone I interviewed said that it was unthinkable for them to stop working at such a young age—they were in their late thirties or early to mid-40s then.

At work, women workers were given the same opportunities as men to move to the managerial level. Ms. Li, a former textile worker, told me that her ambition was to become a cadre in her workshop's production office, which was called 工转干 (to be promoted to a managerial position from the rank and file). Women were also encouraged to seek honor from winning skill competitions. Among the seven retired women workers I interviewed two had been honored as municipal model workers in the 1960s and 1970s, one in a textile factory and the other in a wool sweater factory. Both of them said they had won the title due to their work ethic and skills and that they felt honored, even though the prize they won was usually just a piece of paper certifying the title.[4]

These institutional measures along with the ideological advocacy significantly improved women's social status in general, although in the beginning, they created conflicting ideas and practices regarding gender. The first of such conflicts lay in the confusion about whether men and women are the same. Chairman Mao Zedong's famous aphorisms, such as "Women hold up half the sky" and "Women can do whatever men can" were banners women used to march into public spheres in which men had previously been either the sole occupants or total dominators. Thus, initially, when talking about men and women being the same, people seemed to understand that biological differences did not prevent women from doing things that men could do. As this so-called "sameness" was not really clearly defined however, women were under the impression that they should challenge their biological limitations, such as physical strength. The "iron girl" model the party-state promoted pushed to an extreme the idea that if women were willing, they could do as well as men in physically demanding jobs.[5] This model was never accepted completely or widely (Honig 2000) in reality because biological differences between men and women could not be wiped out simply by belief; on the contrary, in agriculture, the labor done by women sometimes did not have the same pay rate as labor engaged in by men (e.g., moving heavy loads), while in industry, more women were assigned to textile industries, whereas more men were assigned to steel mills. There was apparently a gap between the ideals embedded in the "iron girl" model under Mao's "highest teaching" (最高指示) and reality in which men and women experienced and perceived biological differences. It thus made people wonder if women's liberation and gender equality would ever be possible if they were to be based on the denial of gender differences.

Second, the state's protection of women had its own limits. Women's full participation in the labor force gave women, especially those in cities, much more economic independence than their mothers' generations had had. But as a group, women were still perceived as being "weak" and remained so because their own voices were not always directly heard or made any impact on policymaking. A group under protective policies necessarily subordinates itself to the state. It was the state that promoted gender equality, and it was the state that established women's organizations as part of the state's controlling devices. The Chinese party-state's efforts to eliminate gender discrimination in public resource distribution fell under the term "state feminism" (Yang 1999), but this concept was not always applicable in the Chinese context. The Chinese paternalistic state had total control over society, and therefore Chinese women were protected if the state handed down protections; however, they were unable to fight for protections they believed in if the state did not allow them. Women lacked power as a group and were still very much dependent on the state to achieve any form of progress in society. Thus, despite the institutional arrangements in women's favor, the ideology on which those institutions were based was unable to effectively eradicate the traditional bias against women. Consequently, families, especially those living in the countryside, often preferred to spend their limited resources on their sons, not on their daughters (for schooling, for example). Paternalistic control gave rise to the phenomenon that changes came only from the top, which created a gap between state regulations and local implementation due to limited resources and slowly changing belief systems.

Third, women experienced discrepancies between the dominant discourse and reality regarding family responsibilities. As pointed out earlier, the socialist state encouraged women to leave the home and seek success outside the family. The workplace and the home became dichotomized, and the former was valued more highly than the latter. Women were made to believe that devotion to "society" was more important and that one should "not allow one's family to be a burden at work" (别让家庭拖后腿). In the eight "model dramas" that became a major form of entertainment during the Cultural Revolution in the 1970s, most of the female protagonists were single without personal relationships as they focused only on their work in "socialist construction." In reality, however, the state's attempt to socialize such services as childcare and community canteens was cut short and could not meet all demands; despite some men's starting to share housekeeping chores, women were still considered the main family caregivers in people's minds.

My retired women interviewees admitted that earning money and contributing to the family income had made them feel much more respected by others and gave them decision-making power at home. The husbands and male colleagues I interviewed did some cooking, dishwashing, and laundry, but wives did much more housework, especially in terms of childcare. Ms. Zhou, the model worker, said that she had four children in her care while working full-time. Her mother usually helped care for the older children, but the younger ones were always her responsibility. She used to breastfeed her baby and eat lunch at the same time during her half-hour lunch break. Ms. Zhang, a retiree from an electronics company, shared similar experiences that occurred when her baby was in her factory's nursery. Ms. Li, who was finally promoted to a foreman position, said that she found women workers difficult to control at work because they constantly asked for leave to deal with their family affairs. Due to the severe housing shortage in the 1970s in Shanghai, many families had a multigenerational living arrangement in one apartment (Davis 2000). While grandmothers often helped with cooking and babysitting, conflicts between mothers and daughters-in-law often occurred as part of the daily routine. Ms. Li remembered that a lot of women workers were distracted by this kind of conflict at home, which affected their morale at work. They were often criticized for being selfish and passive (落后) and lacking the desire to improve their skills by their superiors. This formed a common impression that women workers did not take their job wholeheartedly among employers and people in general, and as a result, women workers were often among the first to be laid off when state-owned enterprises underwent structural reforms in the 1980s.

In summary, the paternalistic state did improve women's social status through a series of institutional arrangements and ideological promotions. The revolution to enact gender equality based on women's participation in the labor force on a large scale, however, is far from complete; it is also a revolution led by a state that is patriarchal in nature, under which women are asked to meet physical and mental standards set for men. Women are often seen as passive and are sometimes confused about their own liberation, especially when juggling the double burden of work and family.

Women workers and the market: gender inequality in a money economy

In 1978, the state initiated economic reforms to save the faltering economy and its own political legitimacy after the death of Mao, the chairman of the Communist Party of China from its founding in 1949 to his death in 1976. One of the main aims of these reforms was to introduce market elements into the existing planned economy in order to create a so-called socialist market economy. Starting in the early 1980s, an export-oriented economy began to take shape, bringing more than two hundred million peasants from the countryside to seek jobs in the industrial and service sectors, mostly in coastal cities. Of these new industrial workers, according to the 2000 Chinese census, more than half were rural women.

In the beginning of these market reforms, rural women sought job opportunities in cities not just to make money but also to see the world. As discussed earlier, gender equality in the countryside had always lagged behind that in the cities, but the political meaning of formal employment shaped their concept of work. In Yang's research, men were more likely to migrate for economic reasons than women, although the difference was small (Yang 2000, 203). The poverty and boredom of their rural lives were indeed the driving forces for both men and women migrant workers at that time, but among these early women migrant workers, many claimed that going to the city meant seeing the outside world and being free from their parents' control. Some thought of going to the city as what they "should" do. From Shanxi Province, Ms. Zhou was a thirty-five-year-old security guard in an elevator company in Jiangsu Province. She left home at age sixteen because, as she claimed, girls were not valued (重男轻女) in her hometown. "I was so happy when I got my first monthly payment," she said. "It was 100 *yuan*. Now I know it is really a small amount. But I was happy then. I sent 80 *yuan* back home. I wanted to show my parents I am useful, too."

Twenty or thirty years later, after decades of working in the city, these same migrant women claimed that money was now their primary reason for working. This is even more true for the younger generations of migrant women workers in recent years. Apparently, their own experience with the market economy, especially through the process of working, has changed their view on work. These changes are vividly reflected in a couple of studies on female service workers in today's China (Zheng 2004; Otis 2012).

Tiantian Zheng's research on bar hostesses in Dalian illuminates a "dark corner" in which women provide sexual services to men.[6] The resurgence of prostitution beginning in the late 1970s resulted from a relaxation of the strict social controls enforced by the CCP, which was deemed necessary to developing a market economy. Zheng describes how these young rural women tried every trick at their disposal to solicit high tips from their male clients and willingly relinquished their bodies to their desire for money. From Zheng's accounts of their own words, however, we can also see how these young women changed their views on work. One girl admitted her regret for not exchanging her virginity for 10,000 *yuan* offered by a client when she had just started working as a hostess. She called herself a fool and now believes "that's the most important thing—to have money in your own pocket" (Zheng 2004, 95). Certainly, choosing to be a bar hostess provided much higher wages and required less strenuous labor than performing manual labor on a factory shop floor or a menial position scraping hotel floors, but in the beginning, most of these women were not yet accustomed to a market system in which women's bodies are commodities, sellable by individual parts: breasts, hymens, vaginas, etc. Experiencing a deepened market economy and an enhanced patriarchal order that was never completely eliminated under the socialist promotion of gender equality, they gradually changed their views of their own bodies, which drove them to manipulate their clients for high tips, access to their clients' high-powered social networks, and hopes of becoming a long-term hostess or an even more highly paid mistress. It goes without saying that these women were not completely passive, even in asymmetric power relations, but there was something more at play here: if the strategies these women utilized were to play the roles of "unruly whore," "demure virgin," or sympathetic "Cinderella" (Zheng 2004), using those images to cater to male clients' sexual tastes or fantasies actually reinforced patriarchal domination. Especially when these strategies succeeded in winning the respect of their *Mami* (madam) and their peers, they regenerated and reconsolidated the association between money and power again and again in the minds of these bar hostesses. Making money by any means necessary took priority over any other concerns to such an extent that they no longer needed a moral justification for prostitution because making money had become a moral justification in itself.

Although Zheng's research offers extreme examples of the submission of women workers' bodies and minds to a cash economy, Eileen Otis's research on service workers in hotels and other informal service sectors came to similar conclusions (Otis 2012, 6). Otis claims that women workers' bodies are market-conditioned now, as their floor labor practice is organized along, not only gender, but also class lines. Although those women were recruited based on their perceived gender characteristics, their work also reinforced class differences between workers and customers, between workers and managers, and even among customers. As Otis points out, femininity was programmed into marketable traits, such as caregiving, sexual modesty, and putting others before oneself (77). In other words, even though the women workers Otis studied neither provided sexual services nor received tips, their perceived feminine qualities, in terms of both body and mind, were measured in monetary terms; thus inevitably, as Otis states, their bodies were subjected to a hierarchy based on class and gender and the body experience in turn affected their view of work.

In the beginning of the economic reform era, people were already using different words to distinguish employment in formal workplaces, either state-owned or collectively owned, from jobs in private companies or outside of official payrolls and benefit systems. The former was "工作" (work) and the latter "打工" (labor). The rural migrant workers were thus called 打工仔 (blue collar boys) or 打工妹 (blue collar girls) (Entwisle and Henderson 2000). This distinction indicates the different emphases placed on work under two different systems of production. In people's minds, the two words carried different values. Labor (打工) connoted lower social status than work (工作), the former referring only to making a living and the latter meaning inclusion in the socialist system and thus reflecting greater respect. However, during the development of the market economy, this distinction slowly blurred. For more and more people, work meant making money, which surpassed other concerns. On the industrial shop floor, managers often closely watched how workers spent every minute and workers' performance was measured in monetary terms (financial rewards or penalties). For example, in both state and private enterprises, tardiness incurred fines that would be deducted from a worker's wages depending on how many minutes the worker was late. Consequently, the purpose of labor (打工) became simple: everything was about money and everything was for money. In my fieldwork, I often heard workers, both male and female, say with resignation that enduring hardships at work was necessary for the sake of money (看在钱的份上).

Prioritizing earning money over other concerns to justify one's acceptance of hardships, including unfair treatment, was an act of "free will" that was not completely free. Even when the bar hostesses in Zheng's study attached a "price tag" to each of their body parts, their sense of degradation was reflected in their sarcastic comments that they should cut and weigh their body parts to determine whose body parts should fetch higher prices (Zheng 2004, 94–95). Several interviewees in another study expressed their unhappiness about being called "blue collar girls" (打工妹) or "blue collar boys" (打工仔) because they viewed the terms as intended to put them down (Lin and Zhang 2008). However, the newly developed consumer culture became another strong gravitating force in women workers' moral struggles. Two aspects of women workers as consumers are worth noting. First of all, as product makers or service providers, they saw in person the close connection between consumption and power or social status. They had firsthand experience, often negative, of the power that their managers and customers had over them (Pun 2005; Otis 2012). Second, the newly developed consumer culture during the reform era inevitably targeted women workers despite their limited purchasing power. Quite a few researchers in the field have explored the impact of consumer culture on women workers in China, particularly its association with the dominant discourse of modernity (Zheng 2004; Pun 2005; Yan 2008; Otis 2012). Migrant women workers from rural areas were often looked down upon for lacking cultural sophistication (土气) and made to believe that through consuming material goods, they could shed their sense of inferiority to city dwellers and become accepted urban inhabitants in this modern world. Pun and others have found that many women workers possess a great passion for consumption (Pun 2005, 158),[7] and that spending their hard-earned money allows them to momentarily change their role from serving to being served, although they know their wallets are very light compared to those of the people they serve. Nevertheless, consumer culture creates a false hope of equality that informs the worldview of these women.

Women workers and the state: a continuation of paternalistic power

The Chinese socialist state, defying predictions of its decline as a result of the market economy, remains as powerful as ever in both the political and economic arenas. Chinese women workers in the reform era thus encountered two controlling masculine forces: the market and the state. Both forces entailed individual aggression, competitiveness, and hierarchical power. The economic reforms seem to have wiped out, almost overnight, the progress the state made for women under socialism. Evidence of this can be found in the reemergence of prostitution, in female infanticide, and in other practices that degrade women. In twenty-first-century China, the treatment of women workers in the workplace has often been brutal: urban women workers were particularly vulnerable when the state- and collectively owned enterprises went bankrupt, and rural migrant women workers were usually hired in labor-intensive sweatshops.

The state, though the initiator, designer, and enforcer of the economic reforms, tried to maintain some socialist traditions by continuing gender policies in favor of equal treatment for women, at least on paper. For example, the state policy of equal pay for equal work remained in place. In 1988 the state issued "Regulations Concerning Labor Protection of Female Employees,"[8] which continued the development of policies regarding female employees in the "Regulations on Labor Insurance," stipulated in January 1953. In this 1988 document, policies about pregnancy, childbirth, the post-partum period, and breastfeeding are much more specific. In 2012, these regulations were further revised into "Special Rules on Labor Protection of Female Employees."[9] In this new legal document, eight additional days with full pay were added to the original ninety-day maternity leave. Employers were also banned from hiring women in mining and other positions requiring heavy lifting. Female employees were not allowed to lift anything more than 20 kg six times within an hour, or more than 25 kg intermittently. These newly added regulations indicate that the state recognizes biological differences in strength between men and women, a clear refutation of the "iron girl" model.

Because of the state's attempts to ensure gender equality through policy-making, women continue to rely on the state to protect them and to grant them rights and equal treatment. In return, their complete loyalty to the state is expected. The nature of the All China Women's Federation (ACWF) reflects the relationship between the state and women in China. The ACWF was established by the CCP as a government-sponsored mass organization for women. The organization is set up to represent women on behalf of the state. Like the other two mass organizations of the same nature, the All China Federation of Trade Unions and the All China Youth Federation, ACWF is a centralized organization that has branches at every administrative level and in every state-owned enterprise, all under the control of the party branch within the same organization.

These institutional and organizational arrangements for women have not been able to protect them at all times, let alone raise women's status. This is not because the state has been weakened by the implementation and development of the market economy; on the contrary, the discrepancy between what is written in law and regulations and what actually happens in reality is a clear reflection of the state's paradoxical attitude toward women and its behavior on gender issues. The ways in which the state promotes the market economy render its protective policies less effective in realizing gender equality than in the pre-reform era. Taking a pro-business stand, the state usually lends no support to the idea that workers, male and female, should be able to directly negotiate with management; all it does is to continue emphasizing workers' legal rights in the media. No organization of workers is allowed, but both trade union and ACWF branches in companies are utilized to assist management in improving productivity. One retired woman worker recalled that the branch of ACWF in her work unit in the 1970s and 1980s organized production campaigns on management's behalf and selected women as model workers, literally titled the "March-Eighth Flag Holder" (三八红旗手). Before the reforms, ACWF branches in the workplace were also responsible for helping solve family conflicts between employees and their spouses or in-laws, whereas in the post-reform era, they shifted to the role of a referee if there were conflicts between management and workers. ACWF branches are rarely present in private companies.

ACWF branches at each government level organize training programs for female migrant workers, especially for those working as domestics. Besides teaching specific skills, these workshops often target rural women's "backwardness" and emphasize the necessity for women to improve their so-called human qualities (素质) through their own efforts (Gaetano 2004; Yan 2008). Young women from the countryside learn to perceive themselves as uneducated, unskilled, and inadequate as workers in the "modern era." Even domestic chores, which women are supposed to be good at, must be relearned step by step to their employers' satisfaction. As reported on the ACWF's website, the fifth Household Service Competition for "home support workers" was organized by Chongqing's Municipal Women's Federation and other organizations on November 28, 2014.[10] Forty household service firms took this opportunity to publicize their own agendas. As Yan (2008) points out, these training programs basically shape women workers' bodies and minds by teaching them the best strategy for keeping their jobs, namely, to be obedient and loyal to their employers. Whether emphasizing women's rights for fair treatment or helping them acquire skills, the state and its ACWF convey the message that women lag behind in social development and thus need to be both protected and taught how to behave.

While these programs and other ACWF activities transmit the beliefs that the state wants women to acquire, ACWF-sponsored newspapers and magazines directly communicate ideological propaganda to women. The notion of "modernity" again subjects women, especially rural migrant women workers, to a "controlling gaze" (Sun 2004). Sun's study of ACWF publications discovered two "ideal" models of women that were being promoted: one a woman who took her own life in order to escape forced prostitution, the other a worker-turned-entrepreneur. Through these two models, the state in the form of ACWF propagates the ideas that women should be independent, strong, confident, and proud (Sun 2004, 112). These publications also suggest that most Chinese women have not yet met these criteria.

Several problems are manifested in these publications. First, as Sun points out, the state does not address structural inequality since it firmly supports the market reforms, and second, the value-loaded discourse in the two ideal models (an entrepreneur and a "virtuous woman" who would rather die than have her virtue compromised) is inherently paradoxical (Sun 2004, 110). In both these models, being independent, strong, confident, and proud is connected to becoming wealthy. Although a legitimate way of making money is encouraged through the promotion of entrepreneurship and denouncement of prostitution, in reality, it is very difficult for migrant women workers to become rich through entrepreneurship. The ACWF did provide funds for women to start small businesses, but the government funds were so limited that most women had to rely on themselves to accumulate capital. Very few women managed to do so on the low wages they were paid, especially if they had families to support. These women also lacked the social connections needed to borrow money. Thus, the level of success the state defined for women workers to pursue was actually impossible for the vast majority of migrant women workers. Furthermore, the state could not change the fact that sex sells for higher prices than menial labor in the post-reform Chinese marketplace. Under the state-promoted creed that "getting rich is glorious," selling one's body offers a faster route to accruing wealth, and the condemnation of it as illegitimate carries less and less weight in people's mind. Ironically, the high profitability of the hostess business has enabled some women to fulfill their entrepreneurial dreams (Zheng 2004).

Another kind of paradoxical discourse found in ACWF publications is embedded in their endorsement of conflicting values. A review of ACWF magazines that are published by the head office and provincial branches—*Chinese Women*, by the ACWF; *Women's Life*, by the Henan provincial branch; *Modern Family*, by the Shanghai municipal branch; *Women's Friend*, by the Heilongjiang provincial branch; and *Soul Mate*, by the Hubei provincial government and women's federation—reveals two common themes: the importance of maintaining a marriage and of family life for women. These periodicals printed stories about movie stars' successful marriages, romantic love stories, and model stepmothers and good daughters-in-law and advice on how to solve conflicts between husbands and wives, to rear children, and to find a suitable marriage partner. *Women's Life*, for example, focuses on how to rear, communicate with, and teach children, emphasizing that the purpose of a woman's life is mainly to become a "modern mother." One article in *Soul Mate* is entitled "A Successful Marriage is the Only Measure of Women's Happiness" (July 2014). Another report in *Chinese Women* cites an old saying, "Don't ruin a marriage, as it is far worse than abolishing ten monasteries," to emphasize the importance of protecting a marriage (August 2014). Only one article in all of the magazines I read was about a successful German female politician. Its title, however, was "A Super Mother's Political Skills" (*Women's Friend*, July 2014). Another article in *Women's Life* (August 2014) introduced ten famous cities, but the title of the article reads, "The Great Ten Cities Where You Can Most Easily Run into A Wealthy Man." When the significance of women's social roles is tied mostly to their roles in the family and the opportunity to meet a wealthy man is highlighted to attract readers, the promotion of women's independence in the same publications sounds discordant and disingenuous.

Furthermore, these magazines are run like commercial publications, not as the publishing arm of a non-profit advocacy organization. The cover of every issue of *Chinese Women* in 2014 featured a female movie star. On the ACWF's website, a movie star's wedding was one of the top news stories. Shopping guides are also featured in these magazines. In *Chinese Women* (August 2014), one article guides women on the purchase of green jade jewelry. *Modern Family* features fashions, lifestyles, and entertainment that target upper- and middle-class female readers and transmit middle-class tastes and values.

The state-run ACWF, integrated with market forces, exerts its influence in a paternalistic and authoritarian way that teaches women how to conduct themselves, body and mind. Under socialism, women's liberation was thought of as part of the proletarian mission to eliminate class inequality. Since market reform, although the CCP still claims socialism as its ideology, class inequality is now considered not only a harsh reality but also an accepted social norm, endorsed by the government-controlled media. Since the CCP opened its membership to business owners as representatives of China's advanced production force, advocating for class equality is no longer relevant. The party's mission has obviously and dramatically changed. The rhetoric of gender equality is mixed with hidden support for class stratification, a prerequisite for the success of a burgeoning capitalist market economy. At the same time, the state's open emphasis on women's social roles as wives and mothers pushes women to "return home."

Women workers' roles in family: back to the home

As discussed earlier, in the 1950s, the socialist state encouraged women to leave their families to seek success in the wider world. Consequently, the space outside the home was generally termed "society" (社会), and family (家庭) and society (社会) were given different values as the former became subordinate to the latter. In this context, the shift to an emphasis on women's roles within the family in the official media can be viewed as a subversion of the women's liberation norm that socialist China had previously advocated.

Rural migrant workers, unlike their urban sisters, experienced more gender discrimination before they became wage earners in cities in the 1980s. If family resources allowed for the education of only one or two children, the parents' priority was always on their sons. Even if the resource was not an issue, in many people's mind, there was no need for girls to have formal school education. Ms. Wang, from Anhui province, now a housekeeper in Shanghai, told me that her father did not allow her to go to school. Even after her teacher came to her home to persuade him that it was tuition-free, her father responded, "What's the point for a girl to go to school?" But her five younger brothers all went to school. She said that her mother understood her persistence, but her father beat her when she repeatedly begged him. Later, when her aged father, unable to find the care he needed in his sons' homes, came to live with her, she said to him with a bit of vengeance, "Didn't you say sons were better than daughters?"

Recent research, including my own, indicates that many female migrant workers left home at least in part to escape this kind of discrimination. Some interviewees told me that in their hometowns, older daughters, before their marriage, had a responsibility to help with family expenses, especially their brothers' education. They were responsible for their brothers' wedding expenses, as well as their own dowries. It is still a common practice for young women workers to send a large portion of their earnings back home. These women agreed that they earned some respect from their families for doing so. The convention is that a daughter's obligation to her parents must be fulfilled before she marries because her responsibility after marriage will be mainly to her husband's family. Most twenty-first-century women workers stop their monthly financial contributions to their parents after they marry, though they do help out when "big things" happen, such as the death of a parent. These women shared a general belief that after they married, their brothers should assume the majority of the responsibility for their parents. Nevertheless, whether still in their parents' homes or later with their own families, being able to contribute financially elevated their status in the eyes of their parents and siblings.

In the first wave of rural-to-urban migration in the 1990s, regardless of a woman's age, two general patterns occurred: unmarried women moved to cities mostly with friends, and married women usually moved with their spouses. Ms. Song, one of my interviewees, came to Shanghai with her husband in 1992 from Liuan County in Anhui province. Her husband, Mr. Wei, first sold coal balls, while she found a cleaning job in a hospital. They left their land to Wei's brother and their two children (an eight-year-old daughter and a six-year-old son) to Wei's parents. After more than twenty years working in Shanghai, he became a truck driver and she held four cleaning jobs—full-time for the hospital and part-time for three households, twice a week each. I asked her why she still worked so hard after their two children had grown up and they had purchased a three-bedroom apartment in their hometown of Liuan. She said that they had yet to pay all the debts from their children's wedding expenses, which included RMB 150,000 (roughly US$25,000) for a new house for their son and a similar amount of cash for their daughter's dowry. As they had to continuously work in Shanghai, they rented a small room in Minhang and leased their apartment in Liuan to another family. Her daughter, now a migrant worker herself in a garment factory in one of the satellite cities of Shanghai, visited her parents every Saturday or Sunday with her husband. When I went to Ms. Song's home one Saturday, I met her husband and her daughter. Her husband prepared an eight-course meal for us that day. As we talked about big decisions, I asked who was usually the decision maker in the family. Although he claimed that a man is still the master of a family (一家之主), Ms. Song gently yet firmly disagreed, saying, "Even so, all decisions are made after a discussion between the two [of us]." Her daughter nodded and said that she and her husband first discuss and then make decisions together.

Ms. Wang was among the few married migrant women who had left their husbands at home. She came to Shanghai in her late fifties after a relative recommended her for a live-in position caring for an elderly person. She first said that her purpose in migrating was to earn money to pay the big debt her family owed after her two sons married, each with a new house as a wedding gift from their parents (roughly US$7,000 and US$17,000, respectively). Gradually she revealed that her husband, who often beat her was, in her eyes, an incompetent carpenter. She wanted to divorce him but did not because she feared "losing face." After a few years working in Shanghai, she cleared the debt but did not want to go back home. She said that since she started making money for the family, her husband no longer beat her and she had become the main decision maker. She sent half of her earnings back to her husband each month, as he had some health problems, but she remained in Shanghai.

Most of the other male and female interviewees said that in their homes, husbands and wives made decisions together, except Mr. Li, a young male worker from Heilongjiang. In front of his four male colleagues, Mr. Li said, "In my hometown, men are the decision makers. Women must follow men's demands. Yes, they seem to discuss things with their women; but it is not really a negotiation but an announcement from men." He probably expected that his colleagues would nod to his macho posture, but the other four male workers laughed and called him "a male chauvinist." Taking into consideration that I, the interviewer, am a woman, I cannot exclude the possibility that they said this because they thought I would approve of it, nor can I verify what these male interviewees actually did at home. Yet what they said at least shows they believed that husbands and wives should make decisions together. The discrepancy in the ideas among the five interviewees apparently reflects regional differences and individual experiences.

The rising status of migrant women workers within the family can propel women to focus more on the families they have built for themselves, especially if they have children. But two other factors are equally, if not more important, in pushing them in this direction. One is the state's promotion of family values for women, as discussed in the previous section, and the other is that the nature of work for most women is such that it lacks meaning and fulfillment beyond making a living. Compared with their counterparts in the pre-reform period, women workers today have fewer opportunities to be promoted to managerial positions and less chance of gaining any power in the process of production. Their experiences of hardship, exploitation, and powerlessness in the workplace lead them to seek a meaningful life domestically.

Among my interviewees were three young women workers from the same factory in Kunshan: Ms. Zhou, Ms. Li, and Ms. Xiong, who migrated from their native villages (in Shanxi, Henan, and Jiangxi Provinces, respectively) between the mid- and late 1990s. Ms. Zhou had three daughters, Ms. Li had one daughter, and Ms. Xiong had a son. Although they all said they did not care whether they had a son or not, they claimed that their parents-in-law did care. Since Ms. Xiong had a son, she seemed firm about not needing to have a second child and about concentrating all her limited resources on bringing up her only child. Ms. Li was not sure, although she did say that families in the Zhejiang, Jiangsu, and Shanghai areas followed the family planning policy more closely than those in her hometown in Henan Province. It seemed to me that satisfying the desire of their husbands' families for a male heir or their own desire to have a son was more of a concern than abiding by the state's family planning regulation. Ms. Zhou finally had a tubal ligation operation due to health issues after giving birth to her three daughters, but she did not admit that she wanted a son and kept emphasizing to me that daughters are as valuable as sons. She missed her daughters because she and her husband worked in Jiangsu and her daughters were with their paternal grandparents in Guizhou. Ms. Xiong's time on weekend was devoted to her son, as he was taking extra-curricular classes in karate and calligraphy, which she said were expensive. All of the women told me that since having children, they rarely purchased clothes and cosmetics for themselves as they had when single. Some of them also stopped their educational pursuits after marriage.[11] Ms. Xiong said that she acutely felt her own deficits when working in the IT office in the factory with two other college graduates, which made her feel ashamed, but she was too busy to take any classes to improve her own computer skills. All she hoped was that her son would have a better future. The fourth interviewee, Ms. Wei (Ms. Song's daughter from Anhui Province), expressed to me that she wanted her daughter to have everything the other children had. Her determination was shared by many young mothers. This stemmed not only from competition but a genuine hope that their children could move up the social ladder through a good education.[12] Their total devotion included being willing to quit their jobs at any time if their children need them. When asked who would stay home if necessary, both men and women said that it would be whoever made less money. In reality, however, if children are not in their grandparents' care, mothers are more likely to stay home.

Most of the younger women workers I spoke to had met their husbands at work. Both Ms. Li and Ms. Xiong said that the best part of their migration experience was having met their husbands. In the past, they would not have had as many chances to meet men from outside their hometowns, and marriages were largely made through matchmakers with their parents' approval. Before meeting her husband, Ms. Li moved between cities and changed jobs several times. She met her husband in Beijing. During the interview, she kept mentioning that she was not very pretty but had luckily met her husband, who was a lawyer and six years her senior. She then settled in the Suzhou region, her husband's hometown. Ms. Zhou, from Shanxi, met her husband in Shenzhen, where they both worked as migrant workers. She moved to Guizhou with him after they married. She said she was shocked at how poor her husband's hometown was even though she herself came from a poor region in Shanxi. Still, she said she felt fortunate to have met her husband, a gentle and caring man. As mentioned earlier, Ms. Li, Ms. Xiong, Ms. Zhou, and others shifted their attention from their birth families to their own husbands and children once they married.

However, the older women among those I interviewed, such as Ms. Song and Ms. Wang, did not put their children's interests above their own, as their daughter's generation would do, and resisted the expectation that they would stop working and take care of their grandchildren, especially their sons' children, based on a long-established practice. Because Ms. Song wanted to continue her employment in Shanghai, she instead bought her son a new house in her daughter-in-law's hometown, as the tacit agreement was that the child's maternal grandmother would bear the responsibility of taking care of the child. Ms. Wang said that her younger daughter-in-law was mad at her for staying in Shanghai and stopped talking to her because she did not return home to take care of her grandson as she had for her older daughter-in-law before she became a caregiver in Shanghai. She believes that when she gets old and cannot work anymore, her children will provide her with care only in exchange for her doing their household chores. I asked her why she did not go back if she knew her children would take care of her only if she helped them first. She, as well as Ms. Song, told me she intended instead to save money for retirement. My understanding was that they could not look forward to state protection, as the government's social safety net included very little or no pension for elder migrant workers. Nevertheless, they did not seem to entertain any expectation about their children's financial support. "There is no free lunch," Ms. Wang said to me with a cynical tone in her voice.

Yet there was no doubt that migrant women workers, regardless of their age, were devoted to their families, especially in terms of caring for their children, but the development of a market economy has shaken the traditional multigenerational family structure in China. The change is reflected in the different behaviors of women workers in different age groups. Women approaching their retirement, despite their love for their children and an expectation of their children's reciprocation, tended to rely more on their own wage labor than on their family network for financial support. The sense of responsibility for caring for grandchildren was still there but significantly diminished.

These empirical cases suggest that the financial contributions of today's migrant women workers earned them decision-making power and respect from their spouses within a family structure without their in-laws. This path is very similar to the one that women workers took to their empowerment at home under socialism. Compared with those retired women workers from state-owned enterprises (SOEs) discussed in the first section, however, migrant women workers have different attitudes and practices in the face of possible conflicts between work and family in a market economy. For younger women workers, once the initial empowerment of earning wages had made their life seem more meaningful and tied them more closely to their own families, they were often willing to give up their jobs, either because of their husbands' earning power or because their children needed their full-time care. In the view of both husbands and wives, there should be equality at home. That said, men are still the main breadwinners in most families. This has to do with economic concerns, institutional arrangements (men still earn more than women), media promotion of traditional gender roles, disempowering situations at work, and women's own experiences with their children, for whom they have hopes for a better life. The dilemma of their lives is that the working role that empowers them eventually leads to their willing retreat to a gender role that limits their future prospects.

Many older migrant women workers chose to continue working rather than going back home to care for their grandchildren. They were also tied closely to families in which they felt empowered and worthy, but since they had to be concerned with retirement, they did not give up their work as easily as their daughters had. They have directly experienced the impact of the market on their traditional family structures and belief systems, even though they may not be conscious of the forces that have brought about these changes.

Both generations, however, appeared to be quite determined when facing choices between work and family. As the meaning of work for women in twenty-first-century China is mostly limited to economic gain, women are seeking meaning elsewhere so that they may endure the soulless hardships they face at work. There is also a new balance between a self-aware hardship from work experience and selfless devotion as mother, wife, and daughter, even though in the new era women's family devotion takes place mostly between parents and children in a nuclear family. For women approaching retirement age, however, financial self-reliance can take precedence over caring for grandchildren.

Conclusion

In socialist China, women's liberation was an integral part of a proletarian revolutionary movement. Those committed to the CCP believed that the issue of gender inequality would be automatically resolved. This understanding guided women's search for gender equality, and some successes were achieved. At the same time, Maoist China sowed the seeds of future problems. One of these problems is that under market reform, gender issues have been eclipsed by class inequality, becoming a lesser concern or even no concern at all. Women's power and social status are closely linked to how much money they earn or obtain through means other than work such as a marriage or a mistress position. The state's ambivalent attitude about gender equality further reinforces a class-oriented patriarchal order in which women's roles are restricted and gender inequality is perpetuated. Women share more common interests with their male counterparts in the same class than with women from different classes. Under the market economy in China, rural migrant women workers in the lowest classes of society have far fewer chances to overcome class barriers than their middle-class female counterparts. Of course, that does not mean that power based on money is gender neutral. Structured class inequality shapes people's cognition and judgments about power and powerlessness across the divisions between men and women and the barriers between urban and rural. These kinds of divisions allow certain groups of people to harbor a sense of superiority or inferiority in relationship to others.

This brings us full circle, back to our earlier discussion of women's empowerment gained from economic earning power. We saw that in China, under both socialism and the market economy, after women joined the labor force, they gained a certain degree of respect and freedom to make choices, including whom to marry. While this kind of empowerment indeed contributes to gender equality, an overly optimistic celebration of this progress prevents us from understanding just how fragile this equality really is. Other social forces—changing ideologies about women's roles, declining promotion opportunities for women in the workplace, increasing wages for male workers—have turned women's empowerment on its head and pushed women back toward a more traditional gendered division of labor. With the advent of the market economy in China over the past two decades, women have been disempowered and are experiencing a new round of subjugation in the process. Although women have been able to strategically maneuver within the political, economic, and social constraints imposed upon them, under the state's watchful eye and with the return to traditional ideas about women's social roles in China, individualized resistance is not powerful enough to topple a new patriarchal order buoyed by a deepened and globalized capitalism that deems class inequality and gender discrimination natural.

Notes

1. The exchange rate between the U.S. dollar and the Chinese RMB was approximately 1 dollar to 6 *yuan* in 2014.
2. http://factsanddetails.com/china/cat9/sub59/item1106.html
3. I conducted face-to-face interviews with about forty migrant workers (both men and women) in 2012, 2013, and 2014, and with eight retired workers (six of whom were women) in 2014.
4. They were sometimes given towels or thermos as the tokens of the awards.
5. The Iron Girls were a group of young rural women who broke gender barriers by doing physically strenuous farming work usually reserved only for their male colleagues.
6. According Zheng, bar hostesses did not always engage in sexual intercourse as prostitutes do; but their male clients often treated them as potential hookers without much respect (2004, 94).
7. My research shows that this behavior may change after marriage, as discussed in more detail in the fourth section.
8. See www.lawinfochina.com
9. See http://en.acftu.org/28616/201408/26/140826131330762.shtml
10. http://www.womenofchina.cn/womenofchina/html1/news/action/1411/3091-1.htm
11. The data in Lin and Zhang (2008) indicate that women workers were more active and willing to pay for training programs than men in hopes of changing their jobs through acquiring education.
12. Although rare, there are stories about successful children of first-generation migrant workers. One of my interviewees, for example, was proud that her son is a college graduate and her daughter received a master's degree in law.

References

Chow, Esther Ngan-ling and Yuchun, Zou. "Globalization and Locality: Gendered Impact of the Economic Crisis on Intersectionality, Migration, and Work in China." In *Analyzing Gender, Intersectionality, and Multiple Inequalities: Global, Transnational and Local Contexts*, 95–120. Edited by Esther Ngan-ling Chow, Marcia Texler Segal, and Lin Tan Bingley, UK: Emerald Books, 2011.

Constitution of the People's Republic of China. Peking: Foreign Languages Press, 1954.

Croll, Elisabeth. *Feminism and Socialism in China*. London: Routledge and Kegan Paul, 1978.

Davis, Deborah S. "Reconfiguring Shanghai Households." In *Re-Drawing Boundaries: Work, Households, and Gender in China*, 245–260. Edited by Barbara Entwisle and Gail Henderson. Berkeley: University of California Press, 2000.

Entwisle, Barbara and Henderson, Gail E. (eds.). *Re-Drawing Boundaries: Work, Households, and Gender in China*. Berkeley: University of California Press, 2000.

Gaetano, Arianne M. "Filial Daughters, Modern Women: Migrant Domestic Workers in Post-Mao Beijing." In *On the Move: Women and Rural-to-Urban Migration in Contemporary China*, 41–79. Edited by Arianne M. Gaetano and Tamara Jacka. New York: Columbia University Press, 2004.

Gaetano, Arianne M. and Jacka, Tamara (eds.). *On the Move: Women and Rural-to-Urban Migration in Contemporary China.* New York: Columbia University Press, 2004.

Honig, Emily. "Iron Girls Revisited: Gender and the Politics of Work in the Cultural Revolution, 1966-76." In *Re-Drawing Boundaries: Work, Households, and Gender in China*, 97–110. Edited by Barbara Entwisle and Gail Henderson. Berkeley: University of California Press, 2000.

Huang, Yiping and Bijun, Wang. "Rebalancing China's Economic Structure." In *China: The Next Twenty Years of Reform and Development*, 293–317. Edited by Ross Garnaut, Jane Golley, and Ligang Song. Canberra, Australia: Australian National University Press, 2010.

The Marriage Law of the People's Republic of China. Peking: Foreign Languages Press, 1950.

Lee, Ching Kwan. *Gender and the South China Miracle: Two Worlds of Factory Women.* Berkeley: University of California Press, 1998.

Lin, Zhibin and Lixin, Zhang. *Migrant Workers: Participatory Action Research.* Beijing: Social Sciences Academic Press, 2008. (In Chinese).

Otis, Eileen M. *Markets and Bodies: Women, Service Work, and the Making of Inequality in China.* Stanford: Stanford University Press, 2012.

Pun, Ngai. *Made in China: Women Factory Workers in a Global Workplace.* Durham: Duke University Press, 2005.

Sun, Wanning. "Indoctrination, Fetishization, and Compassion: Media Constructions of Migrant Woman." In *On the Move: Women and Rural-to-Urban Migration in Contemporary China*, 109–130. Edited by Arianne M. Gaetano and Tamara Jacka. New York: Columbia University Press, 2004.

Yan, Hairong. *New Masters, New Servants: Migration, Development, and Women Workers in China.* Durham: Duke University Press, 2008.

Yang, Mayfair Mei-hui. *Spaces of Their Own: Women's Public Sphere in Transnational China.* Minneapolis: University of Minnesota Press, 1999.

Yang, Xiushi. "Interconnection among Gender, Work and Migration: Evidence from Zhejiang Province." In *Re-Drawing Boundaries: Work, Households, and Gender in China*, 197–213. Edited by Barbara Entwisle and Gail Henderson. Berkeley: University of California Press, 2000.

Zheng, Tiantian. "From Peasant Women to Bar Hostesses: Gender and Modernity in Post Mao Dalian." In *On the Move: Women and Rural-to-Urban Migration in Contemporary China*, 80–108. Edited by Arianne M. Gaetano and Tamara Jacka. New York: Columbia University Press, 2004.

3

PEASANT WOMEN'S AGENCY IN BOLIVIA DURING THE GLOBAL RECESSION

The movement of the Confederación Nacional de Mujeres Campesinas Indígenas Originarias y Afrodescendentes de Bolivia–Bartolina Sisa

Anne Marie Ejdesgaard Jeppesen

In January 2009, when the world economic and financial crisis was just beginning to show its devastating consequences in many countries, 61 percent of Bolivian voters approved a new political constitution. Under the leadership of Silvia Lazarte, the Constituent Assembly wrote a truly revolutionary new Carta Magna. Silvia Lazarte is an indigenous peasant woman who dresses in traditional indigenous clothing. She has no formal training and only a few years of schooling at the primary level, but she is also a leader of the peasant women's organization, the National Confederation of Original, Indigenous, and Afro-descendant peasant Women of Bolivia—Bartolina Sisa, whose members are also known as Bartolinas.[1]

This study focuses on the organizing capacity of these poor peasant women and their struggle for political recognition and better living conditions. These women, among the poorest in Bolivia, have incorporated the activist and organizing traditions of both labor and peasant movements into their own independent women's organization, while ascribed to the "National Confederation of Peasant Workers in Bolivia." Through this effort, they have gained political influence against barriers such as poverty, illiteracy, family responsibilities, male chauvinism, racism, and harassment.

My main point is that, even in an interconnected and globalized world, national government policies and female intellectual emancipation and agency can make a difference in overcoming the effects of economic and social inequality and the international crisis. This chapter thus shows that historical situations of discrimination, marginalization, exclusion, and poverty can be changed—in spite of not-so-favorable international circumstances—if women are able to grasp opportunities and fight for their rights. It is a testament of how women can use existing traditions for organizing for their own purposes, while focusing on women's problems, strengthen their leaders, preserve independence from other organizations dominated by men and at the same time collaborate with them.

The analysis is based on documents and previous literature as well as life stories and interviews with the leaders of the Bartolinas in the department of Santa Cruz, including Silvia Lazarte, which I conducted between 2011 and 2014.[2] Analytically, this study examines how gender intersects with social class and ethnicity to shape the identity construction of the organization and how this multilayered identity is related to its strong affinity with the government of Morales. After providing a brief explanation of the effects of the 2008 financial crisis on the Bolivian economy and the socioeconomic position of peasant women in Bolivia, the chapter examines peasant women's agency, the history of the Bartolinas, and the organization's identity and claims.

Bolivia and the results of the 2008 economic crisis

According to a 2012 study, the financial crisis did not have a severe impact on the Bolivian economy because of its low degree of integration with world markets and the low level of direct foreign investment in the country outside of the mining and the hydrocarbon sectors. This means that, what at another time in the economic history of the country could have appeared as a weakness, was actually a benefit at this particular historical moment (Fundación Unir 2012). It also means that we must go further back in time to gain an in-depth understanding of low-income peasant women's agency and their subsequent political participation, situation, and challenges after 2008 and to recognize that although the international crisis was indeed international, its effects on local economies varied.

This does not mean that the crisis had no effect in Bolivia. The rate of growth in gross domestic product (GDP) fell from 6.1 percent in 2008 to 3.4 percent in 2009, but according to numbers from the Economic Commission for Latin American and the Caribbean (ECLAC 2016), it began to rise immediately after 2009 and had gone up to 6.8 percent in 2013, but then slowly decreased to 4.3 in 2016. Although foreign direct investments fell to 19 percent in 2009, most significantly in the mining sector, Chinese foreign direct investments (FDI) increased substantially in the same period, mostly in land and food production in Santa Cruz (Farthing and Kohl 2014, 80; Fundación Unir 2012, 170). Although general unemployment in Bolivia rose from 7 percent in 2007 to 8 percent in 2009, this was not as high as it had been in 1987, when it was 12 percent (ECLAC 2016)). By 2010, the unemployment rate was back to 6.5 percent, lower than before the global economic recession started.

What most affected the daily lives of the majority of Bolivians was probably the rising prices of food crops due to a series of climate conditions that impacted local food production. Bolivia imports important basic food staples such as wheat, further adding to the cost of living (Fundación Unir 2012, 45). Peasant women are both producers and consumers of foodstuffs, and their production is dependent on such factors as climate change, market prices of agricultural raw materials and technology, access to loans, and opportunities for earning an income in the labor market, since their husbands, and sometimes they themselves, may have to migrate to supplement their earnings. Peasant families generally must diversify their activities to avoid risks and dependency on a single source of income, a strategy that can make them less economically vulnerable in times of crisis.

Another impact of the crisis on the lives of a large group of Bolivians was that remittances from Bolivian migrants in Europe diminished. Remittances fell by 8.5 percent during the final months of 2008 and 11.9 percent during the first months of 2009, which affected both domestic consumption and microinvestments (Fundación Unir 2012, 45).

For low-income peasant women in Bolivia, however, the effects of the crisis were not perceived as a breakdown of the economy or as a completely new situation, but rather as a continuation of a long line of difficulties they had been forced to deal with throughout their lives. Poverty had risen ever since neoliberal policies were introduced into the country in 1985, and only recently have low-income Bolivians been able to see changes for the better. The new government of Evo Morales and its handling of the country's economy and of the economic and social exclusion of the majority of the population that it had inherited from previous governments were much more important to these women than the international crisis in 2008. Equally important to peasant women was the recognition of their organizations in national public life after decades of neglect and struggle. New opportunities that enabled these women's participation in society and politics were important forms of progress, even amid the global economic crisis.

Women, work, and poverty in Bolivia

This section provides a brief overview of the living conditions of peasant women in Bolivia. The women who represent 42 percent of the economically active population in Bolivia are primarily self-employed in services, sales, or agriculture. In the agricultural sector, women made up 26.6 percent of the workforce in 2012 (Censo 2012, 15).

It is normal for a peasant woman to get up at four o'clock in the morning to prepare food for her family, complete several other household chores, join her husband in the fields, and then return home to complete housework and prepare supper. Women also typically take care of the domestic animals and sell the family's products at the local markets.[3]

According to the 2012 census, 67.5 percent of the Bolivian population lived in cities and 32.5 percent in rural areas. These numbers, however, do not account for the people who live "double lives," that is, who work in the cities but return to their communities to cultivate their land for periods of time.[4] During times of crisis, migration to the cities, the lowlands, Argentina, or even Spain is a common strategy.

The most extreme poverty in Bolivia is geographically concentrated in rural areas and closely related to ethnicity and gender. The general poverty rate is 32.7 percent, but 54.1 percent in rural areas (ECLAC 2016 The highest levels of poverty persist where indigenous people compose the majority of the population and where women tend to suffer such hardships that the phrase "indigenous woman" is synonymous with being poor (Baudoin 2009). There are, however, significant differences between rural areas, and extreme poverty is predominantly concentrated in the Andean departments of Potosí and Oruro.

Government initiatives during the government of Evo Morales have made some improvements in the living conditions of the poor and have had some success in ameliorating poverty and enhancing production in rural areas. From 2005 to 2012, the number of persons living in poverty fell from 60 percent in 2005 to 50 percent in 2012, and the infant mortality rate fell from 80 per 1,000 live births in 2005 to 30 in 2015. The GDP per capita also grew from US$1,044 in 2005 to US$2,232 in 2012 and to US$3,100 in 2016 (ECLAC 2016 Farthing and Kohl 2014, 33; Fundación Unir 2012, 78).[5] Life expectancy increased from sixty-three years in 2000 to seventy years in 2016, although regional differences are again notable: in Potosí, it was sixty-one years, whereas in the most prosperous department of Santa Cruz, it was sixty-nine in 2012 (Fundación Unir 2012, 70).

Poverty manifests in ways beyond economic hardship. Illiteracy is higher among the female population than in the male population, but again, regional differences exist. In a poor department such as Potosí, the level of illiteracy among females older than fifteen was 11 percent in 2012 compared to just 2.6 percent In Santa Cruz, although this is an enormous improvement compared to 1976, when 54 percent of females over fifteen in Potosí were illiterate (Censo Nacional de Población y Vivienda 2012, 11).

About half of Bolivia's peasant families live in the highland departments on plots of land so small that they can barely provide basic subsistence. Permanent or periodical migration from these areas is frequent. Another 20 percent of peasants now live in lowland departments, where their plots are larger. Communal land and collective ownership exist in highland departments, lowland departments, and the valleys. Large estates exist primarily in two lowland departments, Santa Cruz and Beni.

Since 2001, the landownership situation for women has improved. The Agrarian Reform Law, which was passed in 1953, distributed land among peasants in the highland departments, but very few women received land. If they did, it was because they were widows or single mothers. In all other cases, the landowner was a man (Deere, Lastarria-Cornheil, and Ranaboldo 2011, 29). In 2001, the law required registering the name of the wife together with the name of the husband on the land title document, but in 2006, during the first Morales administration, a new law required the name of the wife to be mentioned first on the document. Finally, the New Political Constitution of 2009 eliminated discrimination against women in the access to land, ownership, and heritage. Two years later 37.2 percent of the land held by individuals was listed in the name of men and 24.1 percent in the name of women (Deere, Lastarria-Cornheil, and Ranaboldo 2011, 59). This improved situation for women is very important because, as Farah and Salazar note, land is key to economic opportunities in rural areas (Farah and Salazar 2009, 113).

To be a peasant in Bolivia almost always means to be indigenous. According to the 2001 census, 68 percent of the population considered themselves indigenous. In the 2012 census, this number had changed, however, and only 41 percent answered that they belonged to an indigenous people (Censo Nacional 2012). Of thirty-six different indigenous nations and peoples, the Quechua-speaking people is the largest, and the Aymara speaking people the second. But at the same time, peasants in Bolivia, both male and female, consider themselves to be workers, as evidenced by the name of the largest and most important peasant organization, the Unified Confederation of Peasant Workers of Bolivia, the CSUTCB, which organizes millions of peasant families in branch unions at the community level. The following analysis considers the construction of peasant women and touches upon the complex intersections of social class, ethnicity, and gender.

Women's participation and the Bartolinas

Peasant women have organized at the national level under the Bartolinas organization, which is affiliated directly with the national leadership of the CSUTCB as an independent, parallel organization. The Bartolinas strongly support Evo Morales' government and the Movement for Socialism-Political Instrument for the Sovereignty of the Peoples (MAS-IPSP) which has put more women on its lists than any other political party (Ardaya 2012), and since the 2014 elections, women make up 48 percent of the Plurinational Legislative Assembly. Women have participated alongside their male partners in the peasant movement since the beginning, including on some occasions where they acted as a human shield against police abuse. During interviews, both Silvia Lazarte and Felipa Merino described how women would march at the front of the marches because the police and the army would be less violent toward the females and thus it would take them more time to get to the men.[6] This additional time would dilute the intensity of the force used against the men, who would be beaten up less badly.

The Bartolinas have gained influence through their support for solutions to the nation's problems as well as their fight for women's rights. Silvia Lazarte's being named president of the Constituent Assembly clearly shows respect for and acknowledgment of the Bartolinas' efforts on the part of the government. Yet important problems and difficulties must still be overcome to achieve full recognition of women's place and equality in Bolivian society. This chapter next discusses some of these challenges before examining them in the local context of Santa Cruz.

The Bartolinas' affiliation with the the Unified Confederation of Peasant Workers of Bolivia, the CSUTCB creates both tensions and strengths for the organization. To comprehend the unusual situation this creates for a women's organization, we must understand the character of community organization among Bolivian peasants. Bolivian peasants started organizing themselves into community-based unions (*sindicatos de base*) in the department of Cochabamba in the 1930s (Dandler 1969). After the 1952 revolution, this form of organization spread to most rural areas in Bolivia, in some places as a voluntary effort carried out by the peasants themselves, in other areas due to pressure from the government and the El Movimiento Revolucionario Nacional (MNR), the political party that led the revolution of 1952.[7]

The Bolivian revolution of 1952 was organized by the MNR with the support of the miner's unions and some sectors of the peasantry. It was a violent uprising against the mining and agrarian elites that controlled the country. Its most important results were the nationalization of the tin mines, universal suffrage that included the indigenous majority and women for the first time, agrarian reforms that distributed land to the indigenous peasantry of the Andean highlands, and the introduction of universal and obligatory education in rural areas (Farthing and Kohl 2014; Fundación Unir 2012; Klein 1992; Zegada et al. 2011).

The lowest level of the peasant organization is the *sindicato de base,* or the local peasant community, which organizes the whole life of the community as a kind of autonomous self-government. The community elects its leaders in a system of rotation, and being a leader at some point in one's life is seen as an obligation to the community. This form of organization has its roots in the ancient system of *ayllus*, indigenous communities and extended family organizations that existed in the Andean region prior to Spanish colonization. The community unions constitute the lowest level of the nationwide CSUTCB or, in the case of the areas dominated by migration, the Confederation of Intercultural Communities of Bolivia (*Confederación Sindical de Comunidades Interculturales de Bolivia*, CSIB).[8] Both peasant organizations are affiliated with the Bolivian Workers' Central, a nationwide organization of workers' unions from industries, public services, street vendors, transport sectors, and others. The CSUTCB is the largest of all the organizations affiliated with the Workers' Central in collaboration with the largest women's organization, the Bartolinas.

The first concrete steps toward an independent women's organization were taken on January 10, 1980 when a Federation of Peasant Women was founded in La Paz (García Linera, Chávez León, Costas Monje 2004, 504), although the first initiative took place in 1978 when peasant women from the La Paz region assembled a local meeting for women only (Alanes Bravo 1997; Ejdesgard Jeppesen 2015). It is important to note that the initiative did not come from the local community level, as had been the case with the mixed peasants' organization in the 1930s in Cochabamba. The women's way of organizing is nevertheless built on a similar structure, which means that the community union is the basis of the entire organization, although we do not find Bartolinas in all communities. It is noteworthy that, compared to the CSUTCB, the leadership of the Bartolinas can make decisions without consulting the base unions first. This would be unthinkable in the CSUTCB organization, but probably reflects a lack of time and resources in the case of the Bartolinas, as the communities are dispersed and a lack of public transport makes communication difficult. Another difference is that the Bartolinas at the community level cannot claim to represent the whole community as the *sindicato* can. It can only represent the women, and sometimes not even all of the women.

One of the first documents of the Bartolinas stated as one of their objectives that they wanted to develop actions in collaboration with the CSUTCB and the COB (García Linera et al. 2004, 505).[9] From the very beginning, the organization has experienced a tension between a desire for independence and a need for integration and participation in the struggles of the mixed *sindicato* dominated by men. This aspiration reflects that peasant women are also producers and form part of the family unit that constitutes the basis of both the community and the organization of peasants.[10] This is a dilemma that the women have to deal with on a daily basis, on an individual as well as an organizational level.

Bolivia has a long history of both active and courageous women and of male chauvinism and discrimination against women and their participation in social organizations. Silvia Lazarte told me in an interview that the independent women's organization was necessary because in a meeting where both sexes are present, the women will prefer keeping quiet.[11] This silence is based on structural and cultural rules that grant men privileges in the public sphere at the expense of women. These rules are partly due to the traditional division of labor in the countryside, in which the private home is the sphere of women and the public space is reserved for men (García Forés 2011, 16; Farah and Salazar 2009, 106).

When decisions made among family members in their homes are presented in the public space of community meetings, they are therefore presented by men (León and Monje 2004/2005, 506). But unfortunately one of the consequences of this division of space is a lack of experience and political schooling among women. The peasant movement provides schooling for participants and leaders through a learning process that means that a newly elected leader begins with less responsibility and later rises in the hierarchy. As a result of this learning system, leaders gradually acquire a political language and the proficiency to undertake a political analysis of both local and international problems (Ejdesgaard Jeppesen 2002, 2012). A leader will also gradually learn how to write political documents, how to take minutes and direct a meeting, how to organize the economy of the organization and manage accounts, and so on. This informal learning system is efficient in various ways and for many peasants is the only education they will receive throughout their lives. In this sense, democracy in Bolivia owes much to this informal education of its citizens. President Evo Morales, who was also educated through the structures of the *Sindicato Agrario*, is probably the first president in the history of the country who knows the system from within and who can fully acknowledge this contribution to democracy.

For women who wish to participate in the organization, however, the internal schooling system can create a vicious circle. Very often women have not learned to read and write sufficiently, and their Spanish might be poor because they stay in their home communities and only speak their native language. Because they keep mostly silent during the meetings of the community, traditionally all seated together at the back of the room, they do not get to practice speaking in public and therefore do not get elected as leaders. Breaking this vicious circle requires considerable courage and strength. Nevertheless, some manage to do so.[12] Several women have told me that their fathers had been active in the peasant organizations and that they have learned the importance of organizing through them, so even if this has not been the intention, experiences have been passed on from father to daughter.

An additional issue regarding women's participation is that childcare is almost exclusively a female responsibility. This means that if a woman wants to participate in the political work of the organization, she must leave her children with another woman or simply abandon her home for a period, which creates strong feelings of guilt.[13] In combination with strong opposition or a negative attitude from her partner, this can interfere with her wishes to participate (Farah and Salazar 2009, 109; García Forés 2011, 74). Nevertheless, some women leaders talk about how their husbands resisted their participation initially but later grew accustomed to it enough to support them.[14]

There are nonetheless regional differences in the political participation of women. According to Gloria Ardaya, there are higher levels of women's political participation in the lowland departments, such as Beni, Pando, Tarija, and Santa Cruz, which are also the departments with the lowest degree of violence against women (Ardaya 2012, 278). The highland departments of La Paz, Potosí, Oruro, Chuquisaca, and partly Cochabamba are where the traditional Andean community organizations are found and where the peasants' organizations have most members from the small-scale subsistence peasantry. The lowland departments, in contrast, are characterized by a relatively late colonization and a high degree of immigration. The following section will focus on the lowland department of Santa Cruz, one of the departments with the strongest representation of Bartolinas.

Bartolinas in a local context: Santa Cruz de la Sierra

The Bartolinas in Santa Cruz, as in other areas, have built their organizations inside the mixed peasant unions, but the creation of the organization has required a tremendous effort as they face all the difficulties mentioned above. Hilda Villalba de Pérez, a member of the executive committee of the Bartolinas, told me that she must walk for kilometers to go to a meeting and that it can be very difficult for her to meet with other women, who do not have money for public transport and do not own vehicles. She has also felt racism and discrimination. Commenting on the general political climate in the region and the situation of peasant women, she claimed that "here in Santa Cruz they do not value us." She nevertheless feels it is very important that women assemble, organize, and work together, and she emphasizes the fact that the Bartolinas, in general, see themselves as part of a much broader social and political process.[15]

This priority is also clearly stated in the regulations of the organization in Santa Cruz, which set forth this goal: "To fight for the spaces for decision making of the original, indigenous, peasant women in the department of Santa Cruz, on the basis of unity, reciprocity, and solidarity with the country's social movements." Not only do the Bartolinas see themselves as part of this broad process in which all social movements play a role, their regulations also state a more specific political goal: "To fight for a participatory, communitarian, true, solidary, and freeing democracy with social justice which rejects all forms of exploitation, oppression, and discrimination and gives equal opportunities for all women and men" (Federación Departamental 2010). This is a clear example of intertextually with the New Political Constitution, in which participatory and communitarian democracy is the basis of all the political principles of the Bolivian State.

When asked why they support the government of Evo Morales, Silvia Lazarte and other Bartolinas immediately mentioned government social support programs like the Bono Juancito Pinto for school children;[16] the Bono Juana Azurduy, a subsidy to help pregnant women get medical checks and offer support for their children;[17] the Renta Dignidad, pensions for the elderly; programs fighting illiteracy; and the very important credit schemes for small-scale peasants.[18] These programs, which were introduced by the Morales government as general means to ease the situation of poverty for the majority of poor Bolivians, also probably diminished the effects of the crisis of 2008. As Silvia Lazarte stated with reference to the president and the MAS-IPSP, "Before, they made us believe that Bolivia was a poor country, but now we have someone on the inside [i.e., in the government, AMEJ] that makes demands for us."[19] This statement clearly outlines the contrast to those periods when social demands were rejected by former governments as well as a feeling of relief because the situation has changed. The women I interviewed identified with the president because of both ethnicity and class and the common experiences they share in spite of gender differences.

Among the women I interviewed, a very important motivation for organizing was the future of their children. "We want them to study," they told me; "If, we, the women, do not organize, our children will become 'pongos' like before."[20] The women specifically mentioned wanting their children to study agriculture or become veterinarians or doctors, which incidentally are professions to which they do not have access to in their daily work and lives.

The Bartolinas also wish to fight illiteracy and to make education public and free of charge for themselves and their families on the basis of "intraculturality, interculturality, and plurinationality." These concepts are symbols of the new Bolivia and are expressed in the New Political Constitution. Their importance hinges upon experiences of exclusion based on ethnicity and poverty, but they also express the tremendous challenge the new Bolivian state is facing in a country with 36 different languages.

Male chauvinism is another important topic addressed in the Bartolinas' regulations, which state that the Bartolinas want to fight against "all kinds of physical or psychological violence against original, indigenous peasant women" (Federación Departamental de Mujeres Campesinas Indígenas Originarias de Santa Cruz "Bartolina Sisa" 2010). This point is much more important than is suggested by the simple and undramatic phrasing. According to Bolivian newspapers a woman is murdered every other day in Bolivia simply because she is a woman (El Diário 2013; La Razón Digital 2013). The government passed a new law in February 2013 consisting of 169 articles that define abuse against women as crimes against the public that will be punished with thirty years in prison, with no right to release on parole in the case of femicide.

Ardaya's work shows that political participation of women in the lowlands is more frequent than in the Andean areas, where there is the most poverty and less participation by women in the public space in general and higher levels of harassment and political violence against women (Ardaya 2012). It was, for example, in the highland department of Chuquisaca that Silvia Lazarte was physically assaulted when she was doing her work as the president of the Constituent Assembly. The lower level of political harassment against women in general in Santa Cruz may be one reason why we find a stronger organization of the Bartolinas in Santa Cruz, despite the general climate of harassment there against indigenous migrants from the highlands that often has been directed against women who dress traditionally and who are therefore more visibly different.

But another factor, which is not taken into consideration in Ardaya's study, is that women in Santa Cruz are very often migrants who stay permanently in their new environments. Perhaps their participation in politics in Santa Cruz suggests that at least some of these women have left their traditions of passivity behind. We know from other studies that migrant women often become more independent and that traditional relationships between men and women can change due to the distinct experiences of the migrants, whereas the paternalistic traditions of the indigenous communities in the highlands can be difficult to alter.

The goals of the Bartolinas are both political and social. They address the exclusion of the indigenous majority of the Bolivian population as well as the situation of peasant women, but the specific gender demands mainly concern space for decision making and the fight against violence against women. Both demands are clearly based on problems that peasant women confront on a daily basis and are responses to a high level of male chauvinism within the peasant movement and in the Bolivian society in general. The results that the Bartolinas have obtained confirm that it has been important for them to organize in their own organization. One important goal has been to become part of the base of the Morales government, which is built on the social movements in Bolivia. Their voice is now being taken into account in a way that no other government has previously done. Most of the social funding that has been granted by the government has been directed toward women and children. Other important results are that women's ownership of land is now recognized and violence against women is penalized as a severe crime. Seeing one of their leaders as the president of the Constituent Assembly has showed them that things have changed dramatically. However, there are still many problems to be addressed, primarily the difficulties presented by a multifaceted identification as peasants, indigenous, women, and producers, as discussed next.

Identity and agency

The regulations of the Federation of Bartolinas in Santa Cruz express their priority of including women as an integral part of the process of change in Bolivia. They also express the members' identity as producers, peasants, women, and indigenous people. One of their important goals is "to fight for equality in the social, economic, political and cultural rights of the original, indigenous peasant women of the Department of Santa Cruz" (Federación Departamental de Mujeres Campesinas Indígenas Originarias de Santa Cruz "Bartolina Sisa" 2010). The phrase "original, indigenous, peasant," which also appears in the New Political Constitution of the State, reflects the strong influence of the social movements in the text of the constitution the intertextually between it and the regulations of the CSUTCB.

After the revolution in 1952, Bolivian society sought to change the oppression of the indigenous majority of the population after centuries of racism and exclusion. Indigenous people (or Indians, as they were known in Bolivia) were to be integrated as citizens and given the right to vote and participate in society. Although using the term "peasant" instead of "Indian" seemed appropriate to most people the Bolivian peasant movement has been fighting for decades for recognition of the people's dual identity as both peasants and indigenous people. One leader expressed the relationship as walking with both feet on the ground, referring to both social class and ethnicity. The intersection of the two identities is present in the documents of the CSUTCB from the start (*Documentos y Resoluciones*, V, VI & VII) and has finally found acceptance with the government of Evo Morales and the New Political Constitution. The Bartolinas have been participating actively in the fight for the recognition of this dual identity, as can be seen from the regulations, but the importance of ethnic identity for the Bolivian peasantry, and for peasant women in particular, has not always been widely understood within Bolivian society.

As Susan Paulson and Pamela Calla point out, institutions of the Bolivian State historically have separated gender and ethnicity, creating one *subsecretaría* for gender and another for ethnicity, each with their own areas of responsibility: family, reproductive health, and domestic violence in the case of the gender office, and territoriality in the case of the office for ethnicity (2000). Although the authors claim that academic researchers have sought to combine rather than separate these terms or see them as polarized or antagonistic, such has not always been the case. For instance, the analysis of Álvaro García Linera, Marxa Chávez León, and Patricia Costas Monje (2004) identifies two components in the identity of the Bartolinas, one that the authors claim is very strong—the peasant condition, i.e., social class—and another that is weaker—gender. This analysis is based on an interview with the executive secretary of the Bartolinas, Nemesia Achacollo, who clearly expresses her ideas about the organization and their identity as based on gender as well as on ethnicity and social class. But by maintaining a complete silence on the ethnic component of their interview with the leader, they deny a very important part of the self-identification of this individual and her organization, as if they doubt what Nemesia Achollo is telling them. The intersections between these various elements, however, are harder to overlook today.

If we analyze the phrase "original indigenous peasant women," we can see how an identity and a self-identification are constructed on the basis of categories that the academic literature has traditionally treated as belonging to different social groups. As Esther del Campo states, it is important to ask how different kinds of inequalities operate together because they are more than just the sum of the categories (del Campo 2012). Studies of intersectionality intend to prevent this separation.

According to Stéphanie Rousseau, the term *intersectionality* is based on a critique of studies about identity and social categories (e.g., "women," "workers") that are essentialist and marginalize the experiences of many groups or individuals with multiple identities (e.g., "women workers"). According to Rousseau, quoting Denis (2008), intersectionality is "the concurrent analysis of multiple, intersecting sources of subordination/oppression, and is based on the premise that the impact of a particular source of subordination may vary, depending on its combination with other potential sources of subordination (or relative privilege)" (Rousseau 2011, 7). The aim of this perspective is to recognize that the concepts of gender, ethnicity, and class do not exist independently from one another but in every specific historical context will produce social identities, mechanisms of exclusion, positions, and possibilities that may vary and be difficult to predict. This is clearly the case in Bolivia at present, where we see that ethnicity is being used as a new powerful political weapon.

The Bartolinas insist on maintaining an identity of being both peasants and indigenous people. This complex identity combines gender, social class, and ethnicity that appears to historically have been only recognized and understood by their male partners in the CSUTCB and in the MAS-IPSP. This complex identity also allows them to include and integrate women with very different experiences in the areas of migration like Santa Cruz, where women come from different places, speak different languages, and represent different cultures. This is probably why the Bartolinas have managed to become a strong social movement in this part of Bolivia. They are now represented in local governments, including all municipalities in the department of Santa Cruz, as well as at the national level as important representatives of the MAS-IPSP.

Conclusion

The Bolivian economy's relatively low level of integration with the world market has been an advantage during and after the 2008 economic crisis. More important for indigenous peasant women's lives, however, were government programs intended to eradicate poverty and social exclusion as well as legal reforms protecting women. Political participation of Bolivian women in general has grown during the administrations of Evo Morales, and more women have been elected members of parliament and local governments. We find more women in all institutions exerting a much more direct influence on the government via the social movements that represent the majority of Bolivians as well as peasant women's organizations like the Bartolinas. Whereas this denotes that peasant women are much more visible in politics than ever before, it does not mean that all problems of inequality between men and women have been resolved or that poverty has been alleviated. It continues to be true that the great majority of the poor and most vulnerable in times of crisis are women and children from indigenous and peasant backgrounds. We still find high levels of male chauvinism that women must confront on a daily basis. This is what led Silvia Lazarte to continue to ask, "How long must we women be marginalized?" Yet she herself is part of an impressive effort and organizing capacity of poor peasant women in Bolivia who are now agents of change in their own society. The changes they initiate will lead to a different society for all, men and women, in spite of international financial crises and economic hardships.

Notes

1. Bartolina Sisa is the name of the wife of Túpac Catari, an Aymara leader who rebelled against the Spaniards in El Alto Perú (now Bolivia) in 1780. Bartolina Sisa and her husband were both tortured and killed by the Spanish authorities after the defeat of the uprising.
2. I have interviewed Silvia Lazarte on several occasions in 2011, 2012, and 2014, and the general secretary, Felipa Merino, as well as Hilda Villalba and other members of the executive committee of the Bartolinas, in 2012 and again in 2014 in group and individual interviews. My fieldwork in Bolivia was funded by the University of Copenhagen.
3. Author interview with Hilda Villalba, 15 May 2014, Santa Cruz.
4. Bolivia, situated in the heart of South America, has a population of ten million people according to the latest census in 2012. Geographically, it is divided between the highland, Andean areas, with a high plateau and summits up to 6,000 meters above sea level, the valleys, and the lowlands with tropical rainforests. It has one of the highest bio-diversities in the world. The 2009 political constitution defines the country as a plurinational, decentralized state with nine departments.
5. Bolivia is the poorest country in South America. In 2010, the gross national income (GNI) per capita was US$1.993 compared to US$11.888 per capita in Chile (Fundación Unir 2012, 77, based on numbers from the WB and ECLAC).
6. Interviews in Santa Cruz in 2012.
7. MNR, Movimiento Nacional Revolucionaria, National Revolutionary Movement.
8. The organization was originally named Confederación Sindical de Colonizadores but it changed its name during the Morales administration.

9   COB, Central Obrera Boliviana, the Bolivian Workers' Central, represents workers, peasants, and indigenous peoples.
10 Interview with Hilda Villalba, Santa Cruz, May, 2014.
11 Interview with Silvia Lazarte, Santa Cruz, May 2014.
12 In 1983, Lidia Flores was elected executive secretary for the Federation of Peasant Workers in Santa Cruz, the first time a woman was elected the leader of a peasant organization. In 1992, the young Elsa Guevara, the representative from the Regional Central from the Province of the Sur Cinti in Chuquisaca, was elected president of the fifth Congress of the CSUTCB (Alanes Bravo 1997, 45).
13 This was mentioned in several individual interviews as well as in group interviews in Santa Cruz, 2012 and 2014.
14 My interview with Silvia Lazarte, October, 2011; (García Forés, 2011).
15 Interview with Hilda Villalba, October, 2012.
16 The Bono Juancito Pinto is an annual payment of 200 Bolivianos (about US$29) given to every child up to the fifth grade when finishing the school year. The idea is to reduce dropouts, and it seems that it has been successful.
17 The subsidy is about US$250, and it has proven to bring down the high maternal mortality rate by more than half in just four years.
18 Interviews, Santa Cruz, May 2014.
19 Interview, Silvia Lazarte, Santa Cruz, May, 2014.
20 Interview with Bartolinas, Santa Cruz, 1012. The "pongo" was a slave-like bonded laborer or servant who worked for the estate owner. It was an obligation for the indigenous peasant population to serve in the landowner's house. The term is used for the most denigrating of all the obligations and situations of the indigenous population.

References

Alanes Bravo, Zulema (1997): *La mujer en los sindicatos: Bajo el Signo de la Discriminación*. La Paz: CEDOIN.

Ardaya, Gloria (2012): "Mujeres y representación política de las mujeres en la Bolivia en tiempos del socialismo comunitario." In de Esther del Campo (ed.): *Mujeres Indígenas en América Latina: Política y políticas públicas*. Madrid: Editorial Fundamentos. Colección Ciencia.

Baudoin, Luis F (2009): "Crisis y Pobreza Rural en América Latina: el caso de Bolivia." In *Documento de Trabajo No. 40, Programa Dinámicas Territorialidades Rurales*. Santiago: Rimisp. 2–45.

Censo Nacional de Población y Vivienda (2012): *Un Pincelazo a las Estadísticas con base a Datos de Censos*. La Paz: Estado Plurinacional de Bolivia.

Dandler, Jorge (1969): *El Sindicalismo Campesino en Bolivia. Los Cambios Estructurales en Ucureña*. La Paz: Centro de Estudios de la Realidad Económica y Social.

Deere, Carmen Diana, Susana Lastarria-Cornhiel & Claudia Ranaboldo (2011): *Tierra de Mujeres. Reflexiones sobre el Acceso de las Mujeres Rurales a la Tierra en América Latina*. La Paz: Fundación Tierra. Coalición Internacional para el Acceso a la Tierra.

del Campo, Esther del, ed. (2012): *Mujeres Indígenas en América Latina: Política y políticas públicas*. Madrid: Editorial Fundamentos. Colección Ciencia.

Denis, Ann (2008): "Intersectional Analysis: A contribution of Feminism to Sociology." *International Sociology* 23 (5): 677-694.

ECLAC, Economic Commission for Latin America and the Caribbean. (2016): http://interwp.cepal.org/cepalstat/WEB_cepalstat/Perfil_nacional_economico.asp?Pais=BOL&idioma=i; http://estadisticas.cepal.org/cepalstat/Perfil_Nacional_Economico.html?pais=BOL&idioma=english

Ejdesgaard Jeppesen, Anne Marie (2002). "Reading the Bolivian Landscape of Exclusion and Inclusion: The Law of Popular Participation," In *In the Name of the Poor. Contesting Political Space for Poverty Reduction*. Neil Webster and Lars Engberg-Pedersen, eds. Zed Books: London.

Ejdesgaard Jeppesen, Anne Marie (2006): "Discursos de otredad, conflictos políticos y movimientos sociales en Bolivia." In En Nicolas A. Robins (ed.): *Conflictos sociales y movimientos sociales en Bolivia*. La Paz: Plural.

Ejdesgaard Jeppesen, Anne Marie (2012): "Global Discourses, Local Meanings: Indigenous and Nationalistic Responses to Neoliberal Globalization in Bolivia." In Manuela Nilsson & Jan Gustafsson (eds.): *Latin American Responses to Globalization in the 21st Century*. London, New York: Palgrave. Macmillan.

Ejdesgaard Jeppesen, Anne Marie (2015): "Identidades entrecruzadas. Las Bartolinas de Santa Cruz." In Mario Velázquez, Helene Balslev & A. M. Ejdesgaard Jepesen (eds.): *Los nuevos Caminos de los Movimientos Sociales en América Latina*. México: Editorial Tilde.

El Diário, March 10, 2013.

García Forés, Estefanía (2011): *El Proceso de Cambio en Bolivia. Una Mirada desde las "Bartolinas"*. La Paz: Veterinarios Sin Fronteras.

Farah, Ivonne & Cecilia Salazar (2009): "Neoliberalismo y desigualdad entre mujeres: Elementos para replantar el debate en Bolivia." Biblioteca CLACSO. Edu. Arg. Género y Globalización.

Farthing, Linda C. & Benjamin H. Kohl (2014): *Evo's Bolivia. Continuity and Change*. Austin: University of Texas Press.

Federación Departamental de Mujeres Campesinas Indígenas Originarias de Santa Cruz "Bartolina Sisa". (2010): *Estatuto Orgánico y Reglamento Interno*. Aprobado los días 2 y 3 de octubre del 2010.

Fundación Unir (2012): *Perfiles de la Conflictividad Social en Bolivia (2009-2011). Análisis multifactorial y perspectivas*. La Paz: Santa Cruz, Cochabamba.

García Linera, Álvaro (coordinador) Marxa Chávez León & Patricia Costas Monje (2004/2005): *Sociología de los Movimientos Sociales en Bolivia. Estructuras de movilización, repertorios culturales y acción política*. La Paz: Diakonia; Oxfam. Plural Editores.

Klein, Herbert S. (1992): *Bolivia. The Evolution of a Multi-Ethnic Society*. Second Edition, Oxford, UK: Oxford University Press.

La Razón Digital, May 6, 2013. http://www.la-razon.com

Paulson, Susan & Pamela Calla (2000): "Gender and Ethnicity in Bolivian Politics: Transformation or Paternalism?" *The Journal of Latin American Anthropology* 5 (2): 112–149.

Rousseau, Stéphanie (2011): "Indigenous and Feminist Movements at the Constituent Assembly in Bolivia. Locating the Representation of Indigenous Women." *Latin American Research Review* 46 (2): 6–28.

Zegada, María Teresa, Claudia Arce, Gabriela Canedo & Alber Quispe (2011): *La Democracia desde los Márgenes. Transformaciones en el campo político boliviano*. La Paz: CLACSO. Muela del Diablo Editores.

4

GLOBAL WOMEN'S WORK IN TRANSITION

The case of entrepreneurial Bolivian women in apparel production in São Paulo, 2013–2014

Katiuscia Moreno Galhera and João Paulo Candia Veiga

> We are not born, but rather become, women.
>
> *Simone de Beauvoir*

> We are not born, but rather become, women and migrants. It's a contingency. [Nosotras no nacemos mujeres, no nacemos inmigrantes. Es una contingencia.]
>
> *Christiane Vieira Nogueira, Coordinator for the Eradication of Slave Labor in São Paulo Folha de S. Paulo (2014)*

The changes in economic, social, cultural, and political contexts driven by global economic conditions impact the lives of millions of people around the globe as a result of macroeconomic imbalances in the economies of developed countries that increase unemployment on a global scale (International Labor Organization 2009). The so-called side effects of global economic crises directly affect the daily lives of international organizations, governments, and institutions. In Brazil, examples of such side effects have been new waves of international immigration from Haiti (due to earthquakes and other adverse economic conditions), Colombia (due to institutional political instability with the guerrillas), Bolivia (due to poor living conditions) other nations (such as Syria, for instance), and Venezuela (due to humanitarian crisis). These new waves of immigration are often a matter of concern to nation states, as reflected in xenophobic policies. Co-constitutions of multiple and varied institutional arrangements and local realities might have no hierarchy between them (Sassen 2010) and are, thus, the institutionality of a contemporary globalized economy. For instance, the 2008 international crisis triggered by banks has affected the lives of thousands of immigrants who, in turn, have rearranged family spaces, friendships, and work relationships.

This is not to suggest that individuals are passive agents of globalization and its impacts. A person's agency is complex, and any apparent fixed relation of cause and effect between macro- and microstructures is premeditated. Nobody likes to passively watch their own poverty. In fact, neoliberalism and poverty *create* agency, as one of our interlocutors, a Bolivian anarchist, argued. From an individual and emancipatory perspective, immigrants often seek new horizons in other countries instead of engaging in collective action or other organized efforts at home.

If individual immigration is due mainly to factors of repulsion from the country of origin linked to economic, political, and social factors, then a myriad of variables make that diaspora complex: an immigrant is not a *homo economicus*, although he or she usually behaves like one upon arrival in the receiving country. Based on our research, we can point to several variables that make this social subject more complex, such as class, race/ethnicity, nationality, age, gender, religion, generation, personal aspirations, and dreams. This entrepreneurial *mulieres advenus*, adventurous woman, and the constellation of issues that she brings with her are the focus of this chapter.

Women in this chapter – entrepreneurial Bolivians – are an exception among Bolivian immigrants in São Paulo, most of whom are working class and employed in small sweatshops dispersed throughout the city. After a long and torturous process of social and professional integration, these women have managed to become owners of sewing machines and workshops, although they have very few resources and tend to assist the heads of these small businesses, who are usually men, rather than occupy the main role in the public sphere. Opting for a non-essentialist perspective, this chapter examines approaches to the logic of opportunity that drives these women, who are motivated by an entrepreneurial spirit (linked to migration) and a search for greater autonomy and personal fulfillment. What, this study asks, distinguishes entrepreneurial women from other immigrants? What are the common characteristics of these women that lead them to embrace entrepreneurship in an oppressive environment? Why have they become entrepreneurs? How can they embody Beauvoir's quote that opens this chapter without ever having read it?

The picture of the Bolivian migrant women painted here is that of poor women, often from a rural area and physically marked by the typical traits of indigenous peoples. This study examines whether market mechanisms can provide opportunities for women's empowerment in an environment where few other opportunities for social emancipation exist. Therefore, this analysis examines entrepreneurship in the broader sense of demonstrating personal initiative and a certain fearlessness in taking action to gain greater financial independence and physical and emotional autonomy within the social conditions in which the migrant woman operates. Entrepreneurship, therefore, is here understood in the strict sense as owning a business, but investigated in terms of the variable of gender and the specific situations faced by poor Bolivian women. For instance, it asks how, given emotional factors related to Bolivian notions of the family and Catholic ethics, do Bolivian women deal with the ambivalence that affects most women who are active outside the home, especially in the xenophobic environment migrant women face?

In this chapter, we wish to dismantle the perspective that treats women as passive agents of local and global events or unfavorable historical consequences. By developing this perspective, we do not wish to ignore structuralist perspectives that highlight the subordination of women but to demonstrate that these perspectives do not necessarily preclude individual entrepreneurship. Such entrepreneurial projects may not escape, for example, the gendered division of labor or the socially undervalued tasks that these women perform, but surprisingly turn those into niches of opportunity and fuel the trajectory of these entrepreneurial women.

In their contact with the city, as we shall see, these women experience both oppressive factors (i.e., xenophobia) and empowering cultural influences (i.e., acculturation, sisterhood, other cultures of the city); the workplace includes both female subordination (gendered division of labor) and opportunities for social mobility (capital accumulation); their responsibility for their children both burdens the women and provides incentives for daily work. Moments of oppression and agency are largely contingent and depend on both the individual women's actions and the effect of the macroeconomic scenario within which they operate on both their broader social relations and personal trajectories. As we shall see, however, some factors increase the chances that a woman will become entrepreneurial, including formal education, acculturation, urban or rural origin, and contact with other cultures.

This chapter first addresses the 2008 crisis and the main countries of destination for Bolivians. Next, it provides a profile of Bolivian immigrant women and the chauvinist context they come from and that is reproduced in their destination country (Brazil), as well as other market and institutional challenges to their social and economic rise. The third part aims to identify elements common to Bolivian entrepreneurial women within the apparel sector of São Paulo. Finally, it offers some concluding thoughts.

The 2008 crisis and international immigration

Currently, Brazil is the eighteenth-largest economy in the world measured in gross domestic product (GDP). Although it is currently facing political and economic crises, in the decade between 2003 and 2013, the country experienced economic growth and social progress in which more than 25 million people rose out of poverty and inequality was reduced, although such reductions have been showing signs of stagnation: GDP growth has recently slowed and inflation has increased (World Bank 2015).

The apparel industry in Brazil is not export-led and is highly outsourced. Subcontracted factories employ workers (both immigrants and nationals) who are economically and socially vulnerable. A restructuring of the industry began in the mid-1980s but accelerated in the 1990s due to trade liberalization. Central features of this restructuring process include the introduction of new production technologies, organization of companies, trade and product differentiation, and the incorporation of new styles and designs that are sensitive to new fashion and seasonal trends and new market dynamics (Freitas 2013a, 81). In the 2000s, the sector's production level remained generally stable despite the 2008 international financial crisis.

The Bolivian diaspora can be better understood by looking at both the socioeconomic and political issues of the country of origin and the needs of the country of destination (Baeninger 2013). Thus, we point out some repulsion factors of Bolivia, some of which were derived from the 2008 crisis and other long-term issues in the region. For example, Bolivia ranks as one of the poorest countries in Latin America and as one of the countries with the lowest levels of Human Development Index (HDI) worldwide (the 108th position in 2013). We also point out aspects of attraction of foreigners to Brazil, explained mainly by the economic growth in the country in the last decade.

The 2008 crisis

The subprime crisis affected the growth of both Bolivia's and Brazil's GDP, although not to the same extent when compared with Europe and the United States. It would be more correct in this regional situation to use the term *economic slowdown*. Additionally, this impact differed depending on the country. The Bolivian GDP per capita at constant prices fell from 4.4% in 2008 to 1.7% the following year, and in Brazil from 4.2% to 1.2%. What distinguishes the Bolivian from the Brazilian case is the degree of economic recovery. In 2010, the year with the highest recovery in both countries, Bolivia increased its GDP by 2.5%, while Brazil increased its by 6.6%. This fast Brazilian recovery was reflected in then-President Luiz Inacio "Lula" da Silva's polemic statement that the Brazilian crisis would not be a "tsunami" as seen in the Global North, but rather a "small wave."

Unfortunately, due to the illegal nature of part of the international migration, it is impossible to infer with certainty whether Bolivian immigration increased in intensity in some countries over others. In 2012, according to the Census of Population and Housing of Bolivia (*Censo de Población y Vivienda*), the main destinations of Bolivian migrants were Argentina (38.25% of the Bolivian diaspora), followed by Spain (23.84%), Brazil (13.21%), Chile (5.94%), and the United States (4.21%). In 2006, around 20% of the Bolivian population lived outside the country (De La Torre 2006, quoted in Freitas 2013a).

Another interesting indicator related to the crisis that may have influenced Bolivians' decision to immigrate is the annual average consumer price index, which erupted in late 2007 and early 2008 due to the sharp increase in inflation, the highest in twelve years. Due to the danger of hyperinflation, Evo Morales' government imported tariff-free food before the crisis (Uol Economia 2007).

However, the deceleration of GDP that derived from the international crisis and the increase in consumer prices were not themselves adequate to explain the historical immigration flows from Bolivia: rather, the crisis should be seen as a cyclical event and combined with historical events linked mainly to poverty in the country. Moreover, women's decision to migrate is linked more to social ties than to strict economic need, as we shall see below.

Structural repulsion factors

Economic activity is not vigorous in Bolivia, although this has been changing recently. Historically, the formal sector has been small, but the informal sector is not a source of wealth, either. It is common to see children working alongside adults and older people in informal functions. The main economic activities contributing to the country's recent GDP are, in order of participation, personal and communal services, minerals, manufacturing, agriculture, trade, financial intermediation, construction and electricity, gas, and water (CEPAL 2014a). Remunerations are, in general, low: in the private sector, according to the Ministry of Labor, Employment, and Social Security of Bolivia (*Ministerio de Trabajo, Empleo y Prevision Social*), mining offered the best incomes, which in December 2008 were clearly not very high, just BS 168.24 (US$24) per month (Instituto Nacional de Estadística 2014a).

In summary, low economic activity coupled with low wages and little purchasing power has perpetuated poverty in the country. Although this situation may become even worse with international crises and inflation, indicators show that poverty is likely to be a long-term situation in Bolivia.

Thus, the level of migration and the remittances derived from it run along a continuum, from high to low, that can be deepened by national or international crises. Private unilateral remittances show great sensitivity to events in the global economy. Migrant workers, because of their vulnerability (related to the absence of formal employment contracts), have sent fewer remittances to Bolivia in the post-crisis years, from 2008–2015. As the crisis continued, more people migrated, but remittances decreased. We deduce that this has occurred, at least in part, because approximately 40% of these migrants were in Spain, one of the countries most affected by the crisis.

Attraction factors: the Brazilian case

Alongside the repulsion factors, pull factors (Tilly 1990) have attracted migration to Brazil, such as the stabilization of politics, currency, and economic growth following democratization in Brazil and a higher per capita income than in

Bolivia. In these flows within the Global South, Brazil has received immigrants from Bolivia, Haiti, Paraguay, Peru, and other countries.

In comparison to the Brazilian annual GDP per capita, Bolivian low general wages become evident. Although Brazil is an emerging country, it is not considered developed. However, Brazil is rich compared to Bolivia. Income differences between the countries are quite significant.

According to our fieldwork, in which we administered a survey to seventy-two Bolivian workers in São Paulo in 2013–2014, Bolivian immigration was due to Brazil's high economic performance plus previous ties to someone in the workplace (familial or personal). In the case of immigrant women, the ties of kinship and friendship were reportedly the most important factors in their decision to immigrate. The main answers to the question "Why Brazil and not another country as a destination?" were previous ties (60%), economic aspects (17%), and other types of recommendations (6%). São Paulo, as a global city, is a magnet for global migrant workers. The metropolis is the site of economic concentration and restructuring processes (Sassen 1990) and has been a "traditional destination of Bolivian migrants for several decades" (Gordonava 2010, 4, our translation).

The profile of migrants according to the Brazilian census

According to the last Brazilian census (2010), the typical Bolivian migrant then economically active in the state of São Paulo (group I) was male and single (59% and 60% of the sample, respectively), young (thirty-two years on average), worked forty-two hours per week, received a wage of BRL 1,400.00 (US$440.65) per month, and had completed high school or some college (36% of sample).

Within this general profile, the undisputed majority, 68.35%, worked in the manufacturing sector (group II). In this profile, most were still single men (56.1% male and 60% single), although younger (twenty-nine years on average), worked approximately forty-three hours per week, and received a wage of BRL 1.776 (US$559). There was greater participation of women in this group (43.9% versus 41.16% generally); the average age was twenty-nine years old; it included child labor (we found three incidences of children from ten to thirteen years old); and the compensation was much lower (BRL 837.04 or US$263.46, even with the inclusion of divergent/high salaries). The education level of this group was lower, they worked more hours per week (43.37 hours), and included more unmarried people and more precarious workers, such as those engaged in self-employment (60.98% rather than 52.23% more generally), and unregistered immigrants (28.11% rather than 27.19%); fewer had steady jobs, such as those with formal contract (9.66% rather than 15.35%) or were employers (0.88% compared to 1.54%).

Data from the Census of Population and Housing of Bolivia for 2012 show that most Bolivian migrants exit the country at the age they usually start working. The same census also demonstrates that most migration is from urban areas. If we define the profile of the working migrant by the variable "female" (group III) and compare it to the group of male workers in group II, the numbers change a little more. There is no major difference in age (females are on average 28.5 years old), numbers of hours worked in the productive space, or marital status. However, Bolivian women and migrant workers in the apparel production have, compared to their male counterparts and under the same context, a lower educational level (37% have some or no instruction) and lower compensation (the average salary is GBP 704.11), which supports the thesis of the "feminization of poverty" (True 2012). The category of stable jobs disappears and unstable jobs increase even further; self-employed women represent 69.01%, informal workers 29.58% of these workers, and employers 1.44% of these female workers (Instituto Brasileiro de Geografia e Estatística 2010).

Macroeconomic and macro social data

What explains these differences between men and women? Data available from the Economic Commission for Latin America and the Caribbean (CEPAL) for 2010 demonstrate that in Bolivia, there were clear challenges for gender equity: the rate of women without their own incomes (37.8%) was much higher than the rate for men (11.1%), and, on average, women earned US$79.70 for every US$100 earned by men (CEPAL/Objetivos do Milênio 2013). Additionally, in 2013 more women than men were working in informal jobs (66% and 52.8%, respectively), and women did not participate equally in Parliament (25.4%) (CEPAL Objetivos do Milênio 2013). Once these women moved to Brazil, many of the same gender inequalities found in Bolivia were reproduced there.

According to True (2012), sex, domestic service, and employment in sweatshops are the main professional occupations of migrant women. Sewing is a skill usually learned informally, usually passed from mother to daughter, which is not paid and has no formal qualifications and therefore is socially undervalued (Kergoat 1987). Additionally, although sewing is historically done by women (although in São Paulo most Bolivian workers in the sector are men), this income is typically seen as complementing the husband's. While Bolivians are devalued in a way that makes them vulnerable, Bolivian women are devalued in a way that makes them even more vulnerable.

Woman in the (re)productive space

Although the Brazilian Census offers a big-picture view of Bolivian workers, only through a special survey could we glean a closer idea of gendered relations within the productive and reproductive spheres.

According to our data, men led the diaspora. When women were married or dating, they came according to the availability of jobs in the sweatshops, which means that jobs for women are more dependent on the fluctuation and demand of the market than those of their partners. Married women or those in stable relationships (46%) made up the largest group of female migrants. The majority of these women had children (58.33%). Single women followed, making up 37% of women migrants. Divorced women comprised 14% of the group. Among these women, married women dedicated more time to reproductive work, whereas single and divorced women were practically equivalent to one another in reproductive work (see Figure 4.1). Common comments by the women that reflected this expectation are "women do everything while the men just sew" and "it is the woman who generally goes to the kitchen."

Due to the dynamics of sewing work, couples that work together have higher incomes and productivity levels. As an effect, married women have higher incomes (BRL 812.50 or US$255.74), followed by women in stable relationships (BRL 866.67 or US$272.79), divorced women (BRL 615 or US$193.57), and single women (BRL 614.29 or US$193.35). We also verified that the workshop owners, whose monthly incomes varied from BRL 2,000 (US$629.50) to BRL 4,000 (US$1,259.01), were married or in stable relationships. Therefore, married women, and mainly those with children, dedicated themselves more to work, both in the productive or reproductive sphere. Despite these earnings, about half of the women (51%) surveyed reported that they felt prejudice against them or the Bolivian community, and that they wanted to return to Bolivia within two years.

Other challenges: legal and market

Thus, as we have shown, Bolivian women face economic and social challenges, in the macro and micro levels, that have real consequences for their material lives.

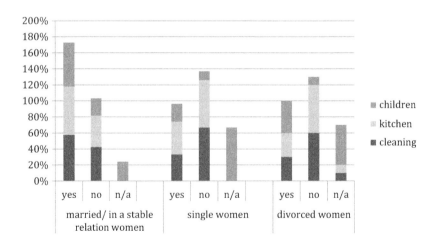

FIGURE 4.1 Reproductive work distribution, by marital status and children

Our findings indicated that other aspects and challenges related to their legal status and the market also affect their working and living conditions.

With regard to legal aspects, currently the easiest and cheapest way to obtain legal status in Brazil is through the MERCOSUL Agreement about Residence for National from the States Parties, Chile and Bolivia (*Acordo sobre Residência para Nacionais dos Estados Partes do MERCOSUL, Chile e Bolívia*), decree No. 6975/09 (Brazil 2009). However, the registration lasts only two years, and the fees are too high for most apparel workers; just the first step in the process costs BRL 188.81 (US$80.85).

With regard to market aspects, it is worth mentioning that the actual frame of apparel production in São Paulo is the result of a restructuring process that has occurred globally since the 1970s that affected this sector especially: factories that previously hired employees with more stable regimes, full-time schedules, and guaranteed rights gradually gave way to sweatshops in greenfields—small sweatshops within cities or areas of a country that offer cheap and hand-labor, low tax collection, and low labor union participation, such as in Bangladesh and Vietnam.

Although this reconfiguration has brought high profit margins for brand-named clothing corporations, the same is not true for sweatshop owners. In today's segmented system in which large companies buy products from small producers around the globe, market competitiveness reaches unimaginable levels. This new structure not only reduces the ability of workers to fight for better wages, but also decreases the profit margins and management maneuvering for small producers (Anner 2011):

> These structural constraints faced by small suppliers became apparent during a visit to an apparel export factory in El Salvador for the first time. The owner was a Cuban-American woman living in El Salvador, Rosa Hernandez. Rosa made girls' dresses for Kmart, which supplied her not only with the patterns for the design of the dresses but also with all the material needed to make them. For sewing the dresses and packaging them for export, Rosa was paid one dollar per dress.
>
> Her cost structure was tight, but Rosa was able to cover her expenses and still have something left over for her income. Because all the material was provided, and she did not need to cover transportation costs or advertising expenses, her biggest expense was her workers, whom she paid the minimum wage.
>
> Then the Salvadoran government raised the minimum wage by approximately 10%. Suddenly Rosas's finances were in the red. She could not pay the workers the higher wages mandated by law and still produce the dresses for one dollar a piece. She decided to call Kmart and explain her predicament. Kmart's response was quick and clear: it would not alter its one-dollar-per-item price. If Rosa could not produce the girl's dresses for that price, then Kmart knew of many other factories in the region that would accept the contract.
>
> *(Anner 2011, 40)*

During the fieldwork carried out among Bolivian entrepreneurs in São Paulo, it was clear that there were no external signs of wealth in this population. While there were few advantages to being an entrepreneur in the apparel sector in São Paulo, certainly being an employee was worse, not necessarily due to economic aspects, but because of subjective aspects, such as greater freedom, as discussed next.

Bolivian entrepreneurial women in the apparel sector in São Paulo

To discuss the Bolivian women's case in São Paulo, it's worth touching on the concept of intersectionality (Brah 2006; McClintock 1995). There are intersections among gender, class, and ethnicity, and these "social markers of difference" explain the Bolivians' working conditions, especially the women's. The intersectionality concept was chosen by us—as well as the concept of sexual (gendered) division of labor (Kergoat 2010)—because this constructionist approach presumes some agency, although it is highly limited by structural factors. The migration is itself the action of the social agent, even though structurally limited.

This analysis has shown that the immigrants analyzed face many challenges and that, because of these challenges, the percentage of entrepreneurial women is low. Considering that there are entrepreneurial women despite all these difficulties, we wish to answer the following questions: what motivates these women to engage in a business, and what characteristics do these women share?

We intended to uncover the characteristics shared by these women to develop an ideal type (Weber 1999) using the methodology of life stories (Kofes 1994), in which women report their histories and the researcher compiles the main variables, concepts, and categories consistent with the literature and other forms of fieldwork. This section discusses the commonalities derived from the personal narratives collected by the study.

Formal education

As demonstrated by Freitas (2013b), people with higher levels of education tend to get better-remunerated jobs. In our fieldwork, women from urban areas with some level of technical education (for example, in accounting and typing) were those who became sweatshop owners.

According to Fertala (2006), self-employment (a fairly common form of entrepreneurship among women) can be a refuge for migrants formally educated within the destination country. Indeed, our interviewed entrepreneurs, who used to be employees but were now self-employed, had taken but not completed technical courses of study connected to the management of a company. Although these women had left their studies to work in Brazil due to lack of opportunities in Bolivia, they brought with them some knowledge of management and accounting. This technical knowledge brought these women some facility for dealing with aspects of small workshops that went beyond the sewing work itself, such as issuing invoices and calculating costs of production.

Origins and acculturation

In addition, these women came mainly from urban areas. Experience living in cities meant that these women brought with them not only the technical knowledge they had acquired, worldviews linked to city life, but werealso more communicative. The dynamics of cities, their complexity, and the demands of relationships within the public sphere created a competitive advantage for these women because being a business woman requires specific knowledge and more cosmopolitan forms of behavior.

Although women from rural areas had knowledge about land and agriculture, they had little expertise immediately applicable in the apparel chain in São Paulo. Moreover, women from rural areas were more geared to the private sphere in which habits and customs did not require a great degree of social relations based on the capitalist exchanges that happen in the public sphere. Women from rural areas performed remunerated activities linked to the reproductive space (the home) (Kergoat 2010), such as cleaning activities within an apparel workshop.

Thus, women from rural areas were less entrepreneurial due to their lack of knowledge related to the life in the city; their more vulnerable insertion into the sweatshops, compared to that of men and women from the city; and their lower wages, which diminished their capacity to save the money needed to open an enterprise. According to one interviewee,

> If [a woman] is from a rural area, she will always be shy and feel submissive. If she is from the city, she will always be self-overcoming and know how things work [in the city]. [For women from rural áreas, there is a] lack of knowledge of the process, the things of the city.
>
> *(Field Interview)*

Our interviews revealed that women from rural areas spent more time engaged in reproductive tasks—cleaning, cooking, taking care of children—than their counterparts from urban areas, (see Figure 4.2). We found, on the other hand, that urban women, from Cochabamba, followed by women from La Paz, Oruro, and Potosí, reproduced gender inequalities less often. According to one of the women, "The woman from Cochabamba is always more rational, less sentimental, assumes responsibility, and assumes man tasks, such as to install a lamp."

Moreover, children were frequently the main motivation for these women's daily efforts, as revealed in one woman's answer to the question "And how did you stop being an employee and became an owner?"

> I saved money and, moreover, my daughter was suffering a lot. The daughter of the owner used to lock my daughter out. It hurt me and I felt pain. And I said that I would do something. I told my daughter that I would do something, then I opened my business. I thought I would have

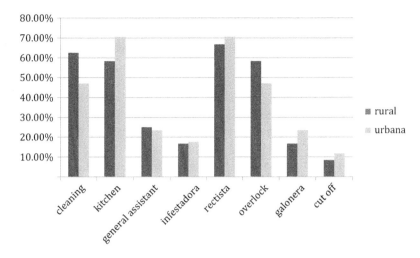

FIGURE 4.2 Distribution of tasks according to origins (urban or rural)

more time for my daughter, but I didn't. I work more now; I have to pay the bills.... But no one hurts her anymore; she walks in the workshop, so I'm satisfied with this. I didn't win a lot of money, but now my daughter can walk, go to the backyard, she even has a dog.

(Field Interview)

When the interviewer asked a follow-up question, "I've noted that a great motivation of you is your daughter, isn't she?" she responded, "My daughter, yes! I have dreams for her, that she could have a profession. And I also have dreams. I want to study."

Finally, the women reported that their family helped them in times of greatest need. As one woman explained, her ex-husband "went away with everything and I started from the ground again. My mother lent me US$120 to buy a machine and I started from the zero again. I started working with caps and used to employ twenty-five people."

Oppression and the possibility of emancipation

Some authors have highlighted the potential for emancipation, autonomy, and freedom that entrepreneurship brings to migrant women (Castells and Portes1989; Malheiros and Padilla 2010). Others, however, also note the ways in which it can reproduce gender inequalities (Phizacklea and Wolkowitz 1995). We argue, in this analysis, that migrants experience subordination and social mobility simultaneously (Salazar 2001). In this sense, we argue, poverty can create agency, gender inequities can create niches for empowerment, and oppression can create spaces of emancipation.

By making these statements, we do not wish to deny the negative aspects of poverty, gender inequities, and oppression. We should consider that there are few institutions that work in favor of these women. Thus, poverty, gender inequities, and oppression are constants in their lives. These women are, under clear structural boundaries, imaginatively managing possibilities for emancipation. In this sense, "survival strategies" (for getting by) are close to "mobility strategies" (for getting away) (Jurik 1998), and both are often interspersed, depending on market fluctuations, marital status, the birth of a child, etc. As Bailey points out,

> The daily life of migrant women is basically negotiated by the convergence of diverse cultural influences and limited by different power structures. Their experiences are lived in and out of a "displaced space." This space is constructed by interests of differentiation and inequality.
>
> *(2013, 16; our translation)*

The experiences of the women we interviewed, who began their "careers" sewing and then became owners of small workshops, were similar to those of the entrepreneurs in Portugal studied by Malheiros and Padilla (2010), whose income allowed them to negotiate traditional roles performed at home.

The collected narratives also showed that when these entrepreneurs worked with their marital companions (the property of a small workshop was often shared by a couple), a gendered division of labor within the management took place, but their "feminine expertise" helped women better motivate their employees to be more careful with the clothing and so on. According to one, "It's about the human relationship, the way the woman speaks."

If entrepreneurship is characterized by self-employment (with no social security), at the same time it is often the only alternative for women with children and for those responsible for the housework. Domestic violence is another factor that led women to seek to gain financial and personal autonomy from their marital partners. As one woman reported, "He hurt me a lot, so I left him." Again, while self-employment does not break down the gendered division of labor, but it is sometimes the only alternative under a specific social context:

> It was he [the former husband] who was the head [of the workshop]. I helped him. I had to see the quality of the service, to see if the clothes were matching the invoice. And I had my tasks at home, right? With my children, as wife… [When the separation came], I had no Brazilian documents. He wanted me to leave and I wanted to stay with the house, with the children, with the machines, with everything. [Under this context] I worked alone and had two children to take care of. When I got divorced, I talked with my children and said, "Look, I need to work."
>
> *(Field Interview)*

Conclusion

This study researched the experiences of poor, female Bolivian immigrant workers in São Paulo, from 2013 to 2014, with a special focus on entrepreneurial women, who were an exception in this context. Two themes, structure and agency, were used to analyze these women's experiences. The studied women's decision to migrate was not linked to strictly economic issues, but also to social ties linked to family, friends, and other close relations. Once in Brazil, power imbalances between workers were reflected in such intersecting variables as gender, immigration status, race, children, and age. Variables that helped women in their projects of gaining greater agency were formal education, origins, acculturation, and viewing oppressions as opportunities for emancipation.

Some conclusions may be drawn. The first is that the Bolivian migrant entrepreneurial women we interviewed in São Paulo, especially after the restructuring of the apparel sector, negotiated and renegotiated their own working conditions. These women perform multiple tasks and face the numerous rational and emotional contingencies that come their way, from destabilizing personal and work experiences to physical displacement, from the birth of a child to currency devaluation, from a divorce to a new production demand.

Our interviewees had no intention of returning to Bolivia, although all complained of the current conditions of the Brazilian market. Given that their families had been reconstituted in the country and that the economic conditions were worse in Bolivia, they saw remaining in Brazil as more advantageous than returning. It was evident that their decision to stay was based on a blend of reason and emotion. Bolivian women in Brazil found that oppressive and emancipatory elements existed concomitantly. At the same time the subaltern insertion in Brazil offers oppressive elements, such as discrimination, it also includes the possibility of emancipation. Difference, diversity, and differentiation can offer a constellation of such possibilities within a diaspora (Brah 2006).

Appendix

Questionnaire provided to Bolivian women workers in the apparel chain

EL TRABAJO DE LA MUJER IMIGRANTE EN SÃO PAULO

Entrevistadora: _____

Edad _____ Nombre _____

Estado civil ( ) casada ( ) soltera ( ) divorciada ( ) concubinada

Hijos? ( ) Si ( ) No. Cuántos? _____ Cuántos años tienen ellos?
_____

Departamento: _____

Provincia: _____ ( ) ciudad/áreaurbana ( ) campo/área rural

1. En que trabajas? _____

1.1 Como trabajas?
( ) soy autónoma/vendo mis pezas ( ) tengo un jefe/soy (sub)contratada
Vivesen el mismolugar de trabajo? ( ) si ( ) no
El alquiler de la casa donde vives es descontado de susueldo? ( ) si ( ) no

1.2 De que trabajas? Especifique (marque más que una si necesario):
Trabajo – Esta función es remunerada? Pagan a tipor la función?
( ) limpieza ( ) si ( ) no

( ) cocina ( ) si ( ) no

( ) ropas ( ) si ( ) no

( ) cuidado con los niños ( ) si ( ) no

( ) ayudante ( ) si ( ) no

( ) infestadora ( ) si ( ) no

( ) rectista ( ) si ( ) no

( ) overlockista ( ) si ( ) no

( ) galonera ( ) si ( ) no

( ) corte ( ) si ( ) no

( ) pago (sueldos, tejido, alquiler etc) ( ) si ( ) no

( ) transporte ( ) si ( ) no

( ) negociación con las compañías ( ) si ( ) no

( ) otros ( ) si ( ) no – Especificar otros:_____

1.3 Como es el trabajoen el taller? Cuales son las etapas del trabajo?

_____

_____

1.4 Hay trabajoshechospor hombres y otrospormujeres?

_____

_____

1.5 En que trabajabasen Bolivia?

_____

A ti le gustaba su trabajo en Bolivia?

_____

El trabajo en Brasil es mejor? Por qué decidiste venir a Brasil?

_____

_____

Y porqué Brasil (no Argentina, Estados Unidos, España e etc.)?

_____

_____

Usted o su familia pagó los custos del viaje? ( ) si ( ) no.
Quién lo hize?

_____

1.6 Fue lo que esperabas al venir a Brasil? ( ) si o ( ) no. Por que?

_____

Sabías que ibatrabajaren la costura? ( ) si o ( ) no

1.7 Su documento se quedó con su jefe? ( ) si ( ) no

1.8 Lo que debes o debióenBrasil? ( ) comida ( ) aluguel ( ) pasaje ( ) nada

1.9 Tienes una cartera de empleo en Brasil (es formalizada)? ( ) si ( ) no

Sabes que enBrasil los trabajadores y trabajadoras tienen derechos como sueldo mínimo, ferias, jornada de 8 horas? ( ) si ( ) no
Usted tiene acceso a los mismos derechos de los brasileños? ( ) si ( ) no.
Porque?

_____

1.10 Como son las condiciones en su empleo? ( ) buenas ( ) malas

El trabajo es exhaustivo? ( ) si ( ) no

Hay niños en el mismo local de empleo? ( ) si ( ) no

Los niños ayudan sus madres o papas en el trabajo? ( ) si ( ) no

Hay muchas personas en el sitio de trabajo? ( ) si ( ) no

Sientes calor o frio en el ambiente de trabajo? ( ) si ( ) no

Como es la iluminación? ( ) Buena ( ) Mala

Las máquinas ofrecen un peligro para la salud (cables o partessueltas, etc.)? ( ) si ( ) no

Usted o alguna de los suyos compañeros de trabajo tienen o tuvieron algún accidente de trabajo o enfermedad debido al trabajo? ( )si ( ) no.

___

Cuánto usted recibe por pieza?

___

Y por mes?

___

¿Qué se puede hacer para mejorar su condiciónen el trabajo? Y para ganar más?

___

1.11 Tú trabajas de que horas hasta que horas?

___

2. Tú pareja vive contigo en Brasil?

Si vives contigo en Brasil: te ayuda con limpieza, cocina, ropas o cuidado con los niños dónde viven ustedes hoy? ( ) Si ( ) No En que?

___

3. Cuales son la dificultades que enfrentas aquí? ___

Creche (guardería) ( ) Si ( ) No En que?

___

Salud ( ) Si ( ) No En que?

___

Por qué no reclamas? _____

_____

4. Quieresvolver a Bolivia? ( ) si ( ) no. En cuánto tiempo? _____

Es feliz en Brasil? _____

Percibes

prejuicio? _____

Deseas decir alguna cosa más?

_____

Informaciones adicionales:

_____

_____

References

Anner, M. (2011) *Solidarity Transformed: Labor Responses to Globalization and Crisis in Latin America*, kindle version (Ithaca: Cornell University Press).

Baeninger, R. (2013) 'Notas acerca das migrações internacionais no século 21' in R. Baeninger (eds.). *Migração internacional* (Campinas: Núcleo de Estudos de População), 9–23.

Bailey, O.G. (2013) 'Mulheres Africanas Migrantes: Histórias de Agência e Pertencimento', *Perspectivas*, 43, 159–182.

Brah, A. (2006) 'Diferença, diversidade, diferenciação', *Cadernos Pagu*, 26, 329–365.

Brazil. 2009. Acordo sobre Residência para Nacionais dos Estados Partes do Mercado Comum do Cone Sul (Mercosul), Chile e Bolívia: Decreto no. 6.975, de 7 de outubro pde 2009, http://www.planalto.gov.br/ccivil_03/_Ato2007-2010/2009/Decreto/D6975.htm, date accessed 1 December 2013.

Castels, M., and A. Portes (1989) 'World Underneath: The Origins, Dynamics and Effects of the Informal Economy' in A. Portes and M. Castells (eds.). *The Informal Economy: Studies in Advanced and Less Developed Countries* (Baltimore: Johns Hopkins University Press), 11–37.

CEPAL (2014a) Perfiles Nacionales, http://interwp.cepal.org/cepalstat/WEB_cepalstat/Per fil_nacional_economico.asp?Pais=BOL&idioma=e, date accessed 10 September 2014.

CEPAL Objetivos do Milênio (2013) Perfiles Nacionales, http://estadisticas.cepal.org/cepal stat/WEB_CEPALSTAT/perfilesNacionales.asp?idioma=e, date accessed 29 November 2013.

Fertala, N. (2006) Determinants of successful entrepeneurship in the Federal Repúblic of Germany, https://publikationen.uni-tuebingen.de/xmlui/bitstream/handle/10900/47470/pdf/Fertala_Dissertation.pdf?sequence=1, date accessed 15 September 2014.

Field work Interviews. João Paulo Candia Veiga and Katiuscia Moreno Galhera.

Folha de S. Paulo (2014). Mujeres inmigrantes de América Latina son las protagonistas de un seminario en São Paulo, http://www1.folha.uol.com.br/internacional/es/loshermanos/2014/08/1503271-mujeres-inmigrantes-de-america-latina-son-las-protagonistas-de-un-seminario-en-sao-paulo.shtml, date accessed 4 June 2015.

Freitas, P. T. (2013a) "Bolivianos(as) por entre oficinas de costura na cidade de São Paulo: Novos aspectos da dinâmica migratória no século 21" in R. Baeninger (ed.). *Processos Migratórios no Estado de São Paulo* (Campinas: Núcleo de Estudos de População).

Freitas, P. T. (2013b) 'Trajetórias laborais/residenciais dos locais de origem e projeto migratório – A migração boliviana para o setor de confecção da cidade de São Paulo' in R. Baeninger; C. Deddeca (ed.). *Processos Migratórios no Estado de São Paulo* (Campinas: Núcleo de Estudos de População).

Gordonava, A. H. (2010) Procesos migratorios transnacionales en Bolivia y Cochabamba, http://www.cesu.umss.edu.bo/webmigra/images/migracion/pdf/flaco.pdf, date accessed 15 September 2014.

Instituto Nacional de Estadística (2014a) Índice de Salario Medio Real, según Actividad (Ministerio de Trabajo, Empleo y Prevision Social), http://www.ine.gob.bo/indice/indice.aspx?d1=0201&d2=6, date accessed 9 September 2014.

International Labor Organization (2009) OIT diz que emprego está aumento devido à crise econômica, http://www.oit.org.br/content/oit-diz-que-o-desemprego-est%C3%A1-aumentando-devido-%C3%A0-crise-econ%C3%B4mica, date accessed 15 September 2014.

Jurik, N. (1998) 'Getting Away and Getting By. The experience of self-employed homeworkers', *Work and Occupations*, 25, 7–35.

Kergoat, D. (1987) 'Em defesa de uma sociologia das relações sociais. Da análise crítica das categorias dominantes à elaboração de uma nova conceituação' in A.Kartchevsky-Bulport (org.). *O sexo do trabalho* (Rio de Janeiro: Paz e Terra).

Kergoat, D. (2010) 'Dinâmica e consubstancialidade das relações sociais', *Novos estudos CEBRAP*, 86, 93–103.

Kofes, S. (1994) 'Experiências sociais, interpretações individuais: Histórias de vida, suas possibilidades e limites,' *Cadernos Pagu*, 3, 117–141.

McClintock, A. (1995) *Imperial leather: Race, gender and sexuality in the colonial contest* (New York: Routledge).

Padilla, B. and J.Malheiros (2010) *Mulheres imigrantes empreendedoras*, 1st edn (Lisboa: Comissão para a Cidadania e Igualdade de Gênero).

Phizacklea, A. and C. Wolkowitz (1995) *Homeworking women: Gender, racism, and class at work* (Thousand Oaks: Sage).

Salazar, R. P. (2001) *Servants of globalisation: Women, migration and domestic work* (California: Standford University Press).

Sassen, S. (2002) 'Global Cities and Survival Circuits' in *Global Woman: Nannies, Maids, and Sex Workers in the New Economy*, 254–274.

Sassen, S. (2010) *Sociologia da Globalização* (Porto Alegre: Artmed).

Tilly, C. (1990) 'Transplanted Networks' in V. YANS-Mclaughlin (ed.). *Immigration Reconsidered* (Oxford: Oxford University Press, 1990).

True, J. (2012) *The political economy of violence against women* (New York: Oxford University Press).

Uol Economia (2007) Bolívia vai importar alimentos sem tarifa para reduzir inflação, http://economia.uol.com.br/ultnot/efe/2007/11/07/ult1767u107084.jhtm, date accessed 5 September 2014.

Weber, M. (1999) *Economia e sociedade: Fundamentos da Sociologia Compreensiva* (Brasília: Editora da UNB).

World Bank (2015) Brazil Overview, http://www.worldbank.org/en/country/brazil/overview, date accessed 4 June 2015.

5
GENDER EQUALITY IN THE EUROPEAN EMPLOYMENT STRATEGY

Gabriella Berloffa, Eleonora Matteazzi, and Paola Villa

Employment policy coordination at the European Union (EU) level has been in place since 1997, when the European Employment Strategy (EES) was launched, and it has been influential in shaping policy thinking and inducing governments to implement policy reforms in labor market policies. The promotion of female employment, gender equality, and equal opportunities was a key component of the EES, certainly in its initial phase. The EU commitment to promoting gender equality was strengthened when member states agreed to coordinate their employment policy via the Open Method of Coordination (OMC).

Gender equality and equal opportunities between women and men are fundamental values of the EU, acknowledged in the EU Treaty, reaffirmed in several documents, and pursued through different policy tools (from directives to soft law instruments). The visibility of the EU's commitment to gender equality in employment was high in its early years. The evolution in the formulation of the EES has resulted, however, in a progressive loss of visibility of gender equality and equal opportunities, culminating in the disappearance of gender mainstreaming from the latest reformulation in 2010.

This chapter presents a critical analysis of the EES and considers the evolution of its formulation since its launch in 1997 to verify whether the pursuit of the quantitative target in terms of an increase in the female employment rate has been matched by the pursuit of gender equality. It investigates whether the emphasis on gender equality and equal opportunities between women and men in the labor market that was quite visible in the early formulation of the EES reflects a concern with the pursuit of gender equality as a goal in itself, or if gender equality in the labor market is conceived of as a tool necessary for the achievement of the overall employment targets agreed upon at the EU level.

The EES and gender equality

The promotion of gender equality was high in the EU agenda when the EES was launched through an innovative mode of governance. However, the evolution of the strategy, documented in the EU official documents, shows how gender equality progressively lost visibility. This declining attention to gender equality is mirrored into the individual policy recommendations to member states for corrective actions, i.e. the Country Specific Recommendations (CSRs) proposed every year by the European Commission (EC).

The emergence of the EES and its mode of governance

The post-Second World War period, which has been characterized as the golden age of the European economy, was interrupted by the oil shocks of the 1970s. During the 1980s, high and rising unemployment was accompanied by weak economic growth, a high incidence of long-term unemployment, low employment rates (especially among young people, older workers, and women), an aging population, and increasing difficulties in the sustainability of welfare systems.

At the European Community level, the debate over policies to improve employment performance began in 1993 with the publication of the white paper "Growth, Competitiveness and Employment" by Jacques Delors, then the president of the European Commission. The white paper marked a turning point in the debate, shifting the focus from high unemployment (measuring the disequilibrium in the labor market) to low employment rates (measuring the low share of working age people integrated into paid employment, because either unemployed or inactive) and seeking to combine labor market policies with other macroeconomic policies of a Keynesian type. The debate was animated, with a crescendo of documents, declarations, and resolutions on the subject of employment. This process led the Council of Amsterdam (in June 1997) to include in the revised EU treaty an entire chapter on employment and the Council of Luxembourg (in November 1997) to formally launch the EES, a system of governance based on the coordination of national employment policies aimed at achieving objectives agreed to at the EU level.

When the process of European economic integration began in 1957, social policies were left to the national states. The primacy of economic and monetary integration at the community level was reinforced in the 1990s with the enactment of the Maastricht Treaty in 1992.[1] Though reforms of the national employment and welfare regimes could be carried out only by member states, concerns about high unemployment, low employment rates, and the sustainability of the so-called European social model (i.e., national welfare systems) started to rise dramatically in the 1990s at the EU level.[2] Various attempts to develop the social dimension of economic integration had been made in previous decades, but with very limited success. In the 1990s, the various actors involved in the framing of policy orientation at the EU level identified the ultimate goal of those attempts:

an increase in overall employment. This goal had to be pursued through a coordinated employment strategy that was formally included in the Amsterdam Treaty, approved in 1997.

The EES, as designed by the treaty, is formulated in terms of non-mandatory employment guidelines (GLs) for national governments in the field of labor market policies. These employment GLs identify what are perceived to be problematic areas of the European labor markets and suggest changes to be adopted by national policy makers. The process requires the council, following the commission's proposal, to adopt common employment GLs. These must be translated into national employment policies on which the individual member states report on a yearly basis in their annual national documents, which are then analyzed by the commission, which makes specific policy recommendations to member states.

This new mode of governance, called the Open Method of Coordination (OMC), relies on "soft law" mechanisms, such as policy recommendations, benchmarking and peer review, monitoring, and the sharing of best practices.[3] In the sector of European employment policy, the OMC has a legal basis, but failure to follow the employment GLs (i.e., if a member state does not implement policies according to the agreed priorities) is not subject to sanctions. Since 1999, the annual review by the council can suggest that developments in some policy areas are less than satisfactory or that some member states should take action in certain policy areas. These country-specific recommendations (CSRs) allow for a differentiation of policy guidance among member states according to their respective situations and progress in implementation, including gender equality issues and gender mainstreaming.

The evolution of the EES and the visibility of gender equality

The EES pursues employment objectives through regulatory policies of the labor market, not through macroeconomic action. In fact, the initial diagnosis made by the EES was that the high structural unemployment was symptomatic of the insufficient capacity of the labor market (i.e., workers and jobs) to adapt to change. The strategy proposed assumed that low employment rates were related to the economic characteristics of the working age population and to the obstacles to an active work life. Hence the policy prescriptions were based on a supply-side approach, assigning a key role to activation policies aimed at stimulating the entry into the labor market of the highest possible number of people, especially women.

Indeed, the largest potential labor supply was made of inactive women (and this was, and still is, the case in southern countries). Thus, the idea was to make a move from a male breadwinner family model toward a dual-earner household. But how can women be encouraged to work outside the home? This can be done by reducing gender inequalities in the labor market, by promoting affordable child-care services and organizational solutions that allow for a combination of paid work with family responsibilities, and by encouraging sharing responsibilities between partners. Thus, despite the shortcomings of the approach adopted in EU official documents, the reorientation from lowering unemployment among previously employed workers (and the traditional passive policy approach to address it) to increasing the rate of employment among the population as a whole as the main target of the employment policy was welcomed from a gender perspective. It encouraged job creation, integration into paid work, and gender equality in employment (Rubery et al. 1999). However, subsequent reformulations of the EES have resulted in significant changes in the way in which the gender equality goal has been designed.

The EES has been reformulated several times since its launch in 1997. It is possible to identify four distinct phases of the EES (summarized in Table 5.1), each of which is characterized by significant changes in the relative position of gender equality (Villa and Smith 2012, 5).

TABLE 5.1 The changing position of gender equality in the European Employment Strategy

	The evolving structure of EES	*Visibility of equal opportunities and gender equality*	*EU enlargement*
Phase 1 1998–2002	4 Pillars; around 18–22 employment GLs	1 Pillar (out of 4) on Equal Opportunities; 3 GLs on gender issues; 1 horizontal GL on Gender Mainstreaming was added in 1999	15 Member States
Phase 2 2003–2005	3 overarching objectives: full employment; quality and productivity at work; social cohesion and an inclusive labor market 10 employment GLs	1 GL on equal opportunities, including the systematic Gender Mainstreaming of new policies	25 Member States in 2004
Phase 3 2006–2009	The employment GLs and the BEPGs are presented jointly in a single annual set of "integrated guidelines" 24 integrated GLs, of which 8 are employment GLs	No GL (out of the 8 employment GLs) on equal opportunities; there is a simple mention in the preamble: "*Equal opportunities and combating discrimination are essential for progress. Gender mainstreaming and the promotion of gender equality should be ensured in all action taken*" (CEC 2005, 29)	27 Member States in 2007
Phase 4 2010–2020	10 integrated GLs, of which 4 are employment GLs	No GL (out of the 4 employment GLs) on equal opportunities;there is a simple sentence in the preamble stating "*... visible gender equality perspective, integrated into all relevant policy areas*" (EC 2010f)	28 Member States in 2013

Notes: GL = Guideline; BEPG = Broad economic policy guideline.
Source: Villa (2013, 141).

In the first phase, 1997 to 2002, equal opportunity was one of the so-called four pillars of the EES (i.e. the four main issues around which the strategy was organized in the early years), which included three guidelines regarding gender issues (out of a total of eighteen to twenty-two guidelines). This was also the phase that introduced gender mainstreaming to the EES processes (in 1999). The principle of gender mainstreaming requires all policies to be tested for their gender impacts on design, development, implementation, and evaluation. The agreement on a ten-year plan and quantitative targets at the 2000 Lisbon Council further focused attention on the contribution that gender equality could make to the aim of a high employment rate, with a target of 60 percent for women and 70 percent overall by 2010. The headline status of equal opportunities, accompanied by specific gender-related targets, marked the high point of the visibility of gender issues (Rubery 2002; Fagan et al. 2006; Smith and Villa 2010).

The second phase, 2003 to 2005, saw a streamlining of the EES: the pillar structure was abolished and replaced by three new overarching objectives (full employment, quality and productivity at work, social cohesion and an inclusive labor market) and only ten guidelines, with gender equality turned from a higher-order principle into one of the guidelines (Rubery et al. 2003; Devetzi 2008, 5).

Phase three, 2006 to 2009, integrated previously separate reporting mechanisms on employment and economic policies into National Reform Programs (NRPs). This major reformulation led to gender falling out as a separate guideline and reliance being placed on gender mainstreaming of the employment chapters of NRPs as the key monitor of gender equality. Combined with the greater focus on creating more jobs, the loss of a specific guideline on gender equality was a significant blow to the status of gender equality (Pfister 2008).

The fourth phase was marked by the end of the Lisbon Process of 2010 and the formulation of a new strategy to take the EU into 2020. The Europe 2020 strategy further marginalized gender equality with none of the ten integrated guidelines related specifically to equal opportunities and only four related to employment. Gender mainstreaming was not mentioned. Furthermore, this reformulation occurred in the middle of the economic crisis, when policy makers' attention was focused on its immediate impact on male employment (Bettio and Verashchagina 2013), a context in which the gains made in raising female employment during the Lisbon Process were quickly overlooked (Villa and Smith 2013; Smith and Villa 2014).

The evolution of the EES shows that, from its high profile in phase one, gender equality progressively lost its centrality to the employment strategy and became sidelined into parallel initiatives. In fact, gender equality goals were increasingly focused on initiatives parallel to the EES, such as the *Road Map* and the *Pact for Gender Equality* in 2006, the *Women's Charter* in 2010, the *Gender Equality Strategy for 2010–2015* adopted by the commission in 2010, the new *Pact for Gender Equality 2011–2020* adopted by the council in March 2011, and specific campaigns on pay gaps and work-life balance (Villa 2013, 148). These political declarations state important principles and areas of action for the commission and member states. These parallel initiatives (i.e. new soft law instruments), however, are not backed by any kind of monitoring and reporting mechanisms, as those developed within the EES. It follows that their impact on member states' policymaking processes is likely to be extremely weak, if not insignificant. Although gender equality is still on the EU agenda, it is now outside the disciplining mechanisms of European-wide targets, as well as the processes of monitoring, learning, and diffusion between member states. Moreover, gender mainstreaming has been put aside in phase four.

Country specific recommendations and their view on gender equality

Since 1999, within the EES, the commission has issued individual policy recommendations to the member states for corrective actions. These Country Specific Recommendations (CSRs) are supposed to suggest the most important issues to be addressed by national governments in order to move in the direction of the guidelines agreed upon at the EU level. The CSRs must be endorsed by the council so that some room exists for bargaining between the commission and council representatives. Because the OMC does not rely on legal mechanisms and sanctions, the toughest kind of sanction amounts to the "naming and shaming" of the poorest performers; however, council representatives have always been resistant to use this approach. Thus, CSRs tend to be rather mild and to tone down any criticism. Performances are assessed and individual recommendations are adopted, but without any ranking of member states. Notwithstanding the drawbacks of this type of tool, examining the evolution in the sets of CSRs can shed light on the role attributed to gender equality issues over time. Although it is not easy to provide a synthetic overview of the changing role of gender equality issues in the EES by means of the CSRs because of several changes that occurred after 1997,[4] here below we provide some insights based on the empirical evidence presented in Villa (2013, 152–153).

First, in quantitative terms, the number of member states that received a recommendation on gender issues drastically declined over time; whereas in phase one (2000, 2001, and 2002), nearly three-quarters of countries received an individual recommendation to reduce gender inequality, in phase four (2011, 2012, and 2013), only around a third of countries received an individual recommendation that included concerns related to gender inequality in employment.

Second, in qualitative terms, the concern for gender inequality appears to be relatively narrow, if not disappointing. The content of the CSRs has been identified on the basis of key words used in the specification of recommendations: gender segregation and gender imbalances in occupations and/or sectors, gender pay gap, childcare and/or reconciliation, female participation, raising hours worked and/or part-time/full-time, and second earners and/or lone parents (Villa 2013, 160–161).

Childcare and/or reconciliation emerged as the most critical areas, especially in phase four. Overall, for phase four (2011, 2012, and 2013), twelve countries received at least one recommendation on "increasing the availability of child care" and/or "ensuring better reconciliation of work and private life."[5] The second issue in terms of frequency of mention was female participation in employment, which was identified as critical at least once for eight countries.[6] This issue is implicitly linked to the relatively low number of women in employment in the southern countries and the very high share of part-timers in the Netherlands and Austria. Gender segregation and gender imbalances in the labor market were identified as areas of concern in only two countries in 2007 (Austria and Slovakia), with the addition of Cyprus in 2008; the wide gender pay gap emerged as a problem in very few countries.[7] Finally, the term "second earners" was used in the 2011, 2012, and 2013 CSRs to implicitly describe women's employment position. This wording is problematic because it reinforces the notion of women as a secondary priority in the labor market and their reliance on male breadwinner wages. Moreover, it makes explicit that the only real concern is the low participation of women, not gender inequalities in the family and in the labor market.

The analysis of CRSs over time, though partial and provisional, is quite revealing. It shows, first of all, a declining attention to gender equality and no real evidence of a gender mainstreaming approach to the issues raised, and second, that gender equality issues have been incorporated into the EES with a very narrow perspective. More precisely, gender equality is pursued almost exclusively by recommending to policy makers the removal of obstacles for working mothers of small children—that is, more affordable child-care services and the option to work part-time.

To show the limits of the approach followed in promoting gender equality within the EU employment strategy, Figure 5.1 illustrates two opposite views: the efficiency approach (implicitly assumed by the EES), in which gender equality in the labor market is conceived of as a tool necessary for the achievement of the overall employment target, and the social justice approach (the feminist view), in which gender equality is conceived of as a goal in itself.

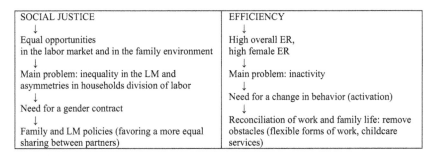

FIGURE 5.1 Gender equality in the labor market: a comparison between the feminist approach (social justice) and the EES approach (efficiency)

According to the EES approach to gender equality, the ultimate goal of policy action is to improve the efficiency of the economic system. Europe needs higher overall employment rates, including higher female employment rates. The main problem to be tackled is labor force inactivity (not so much gender inequality); thus, labor market policies must be reformed in order to change workers' behavior, specifically the behavior of inactive women, which should be accomplished by removing obstacles to that participation. The solutions proposed can be summarized in two main policy thrusts: reconciliation of paid work and family life (through increasing the availability of affordable child-care facilities) and more flexible work (by allowing a high share of women to be employed part-time or in atypical jobs). Within this approach, gender equality is a policy tool for reaching efficiency; thus, reconciliation of paid work (in the labor market) and unpaid work (in the family) is conceived of from a narrow perspective that does not include family policies and the interaction between inequalities in the labor market (i.e., in paid work) and inequalities in the households (i.e., in unpaid work).

If one takes a feminist approach, the causal relationship changes radically, as shown in Figure 5.1. From this perspective, gender equality is conceived of as an ultimate goal for social justice; therefore, family policies are included in the analysis. It holds that every human being deserves a good life, which might include things such as having a family, a desired number of children, time for both personal life and paid work, and a high-quality job. But men and women do not have equal opportunities in the labor market (due to segregation, the gender pay gap, atypical contracts, etc.), which is a main obstacle for social justice. Labor market policies can play a role, but they will not be sufficient. True gender equality calls for a gender contract that promotes gender equality in the relationship between women and men in the family and in society and for family policies that should favor a more equal sharing between partners inside the family. Only by changing gender roles inside the family, hence in society, will it be possible to tackle gender inequalities in the labor market. This complex issue cannot be left solely up to individuals to resolve in their private lives.

Gender equality and the Great Recession

In 2009, the European Union recorded the sharpest contraction in real gross domestic product (GDP) in its history: −4 percent. The EU's response to the downturn was the launch, in December 2008, of the *European Economic Recovery Plan*, a massive and coordinated policy initiative comprising financial rescue policies, fiscal stimulus measures, and structural reforms implemented at the national level. The resulting financial rescue of banks, the fall in tax revenues, the rise in expenditures on unemployment benefits, and the implementation of fiscal stimulus plans resulted in substantial overall support of the economy in 2009–2010, but with significant differences across countries. By 2010, the public finances of many member states were destabilized and the policy responses quickly changed course; austerity measures were adopted to reduce debt and deficits. Thus, a double dip recession (a second recessionary period) was experienced by the majority of EU countries.

For women, the Great Recession exhibited a pattern somewhat different from that observed in previous downturns. Female employment was hit earlier and more severely than in previous recessions. Moreover, in the EU the crisis had been preceded by strong growth in female employment and a decade during which women had been called upon to play a key role in the success of the EES (Karamessini and Rubery 2013). Thus, the period furnishes an important research opportunity for the analysis of national policies from a gender perspective.

The anti-crisis measures were by and large concerned with the direct impact of the economic crisis on employment. Because the fall in employment and the increase in unemployment were initially larger for men than for women, most of the adopted measures focused on support for either male employment or income. Much of the policy effort to promote consumer demand and protect jobs in 2009–2010 was focused on a narrow range of sectors supporting male employment, particularly construction and automobiles. Also, the promotion of short-time working arrangements, a key part of the European strategy to limit rises in unemployment and maintain contact between workers and jobs, supported male income. As a result of the segregation of employment, men tended to benefit more than women from short-time working schemes (by virtue of their employers applying for these schemes). Such schemes created two groups of involuntary part-timers: compensated involuntary part-timers in sectors affected by the crisis (mostly men) and uncompensated involuntary part-timers who could not find full-time work (mostly women).

The subsequent fiscal consolidation (i.e. austerity measures enacted to reduce excessive public deficits) also involved cuts in public spending that were not gender neutral (Rubery 2015). The radical changes in public-sector spending negatively impacted women for several reasons. First, the majority of public-sector workers are women and thus subject to pay freezes, job cuts, and reduced pension entitlements. Second, women use public services more intensely than men to meet their own needs and to help manage their caregiving responsibilities. Third, women are more likely than men to pick up extra unpaid work resulting from cuts in public services. Finally, women have a higher dependency on benefits due to their higher participation in unpaid care work and their lower earnings. To sum up, cuts in public spending may have not only direct negative results on the quantity and quality of jobs in female-dominated public sector jobs, but also indirect effects on gender inequality in the household; austerity measures reduce the availability and affordability of services and have inevitable repercussions on unpaid work.

Despite European guidance on gender mainstreaming policies, anti-crisis measures as well as fiscal consolidation were planned and implemented without an integrated gender dimension. It is worth noting that the European Commission had spent much of the pre-crisis decade promoting gender mainstreaming in employment policy machinery. Gender mainstreaming implies assessing how policies impact the lives and positions of both women and men—and taking responsibility to readdress them if necessary. The way to make gender equality a concrete reality in the lives of women and men is by creating space for everyone within organizations and communities to contribute to the process of articulating a shared vision of sustainable human development and translating it into reality.

Unfortunately, the commitment to, and the implementation of gender mainstreaming waned over time—a point clearly revealed in policies developed and implemented in response to the recession. One feature shared by the EU initiatives during the first wave of the crisis was the low visibility of gender in the analysis of, and policy proposals for, labor markets. In the second wave of the crisis, the European Commission and the Council focused on devising a reinforced system of economic governance that ensured that Eurozone members honored their debt and deficit commitments. In this scenario, gender mainstreaming was set aside at both the EU and the national levels.

The increased policy activity at the member state level during both the first and the second wave of the crisis produced policies that were even less likely to be gender mainstreamed than policies that had been developed in the preceding years of the EES. This conclusion is supported by a series of detailed analyses of the national reporting mechanisms conducted by a European Expert Group on Gender and Employment (EGGE) and its gender-sensitive analyses of member states' labor market policies during 2008–2011 (Smith and Villa 2014). These national-level analyses, based on a common methodology for analyzing employment policies in terms of their gender impact and the extent of gender mainstreaming, show that very few anti-crisis policies, and even fewer fiscal consolidation measures, were regarded by national experts on gender equality (producing reports for EGGE) as being adequately gender mainstreamed. In short, a gender-blind approach in policy responses was adopted, with direct and indirect implications for gender inequality.

Some empirical evidence for young Europeans

Gender disparities are still large in all European countries. This can be understood by looking at the labor outcomes of young Europeans before, during, and after the recent economic crisis. Berloffa et al. (2015, 2016) estimated the likelihood of being employed, unemployed, in education, or inactive for two age groups (sixteen to twenty-four and twenty-five to thirty-four), four country groups (Nordic, Anglo-Saxon, Continental, and Mediterranean countries), and two years (2005 and 2011). Selected results from their estimation are reported in Tables 5.2 (ages sixteen to twenty-four) and 5.3 (ages twenty-five to thirty-four).[8]

As regards young Europeans aged sixteen to twenty-four, all other things being equal, females generally have a higher probability of being in education and a lower probability of being employed and inactive. More precisely, the probability of being in education is about 10–13 percentage points higher for females

TABLE 5.2 Predicted probabilities of employment statuses and gender marginal effects among young Europeans (aged 16–24) by country group in 2005 and 2011

	2005								2011							
	Employed		Unemployed		In education		Inactive		Employed		Unemployed		In education		Inactive	
	Coeff	Std. Err.	Coeff	Std. Err.	Coeff	Std. Err.	Coeff	Std. Err.	Coeff	Std. Err.	Coeff	Std. Err.	Coeff	Std. Err.	Coeff	Std. Err.
Nordic Countries																
Pred. prob.	**0.161**	0.006	**0.042**	0.003	**0.750**	0.007	**0.047**	0.003	**0.151**	0.006	**0.077**	0.004	**0.734**	0.007	**0.038**	0.003
Female	−0.048	0.010	−0.008	0.005	**0.100**	0.012	−0.044	0.005	−0.045	0.010	−0.009	0.007	**0.095**	0.013	−0.041	0.005
Anglo-Saxon Countries																
Pred. prob.	**0.461**	0.012	**0.064**	0.006	**0.429**	0.012	**0.047**	0.005	**0.327**	0.014	**0.135**	0.009	**0.496**	0.014	**0.042**	0.006
Female	−0.051	0.022	−0.013	0.010	**0.052**	0.022	0.012	0.008	0.014	0.024	−0.045	0.017	0.035	0.027	−0.004	0.009
Continental Countries																
Pred. prob.	**0.254**	0.005	**0.059**	0.003	**0.639**	0.006	**0.049**	0.003	**0.279**	0.121	**0.044**	0.003	**0.631**	0.274	**0.046**	0.002
Female	−0.102	0.010	−0.005	0.005	**0.131**	0.012	−0.023	0.005	−0.089	0.010	−0.015	0.004	**0.124**	0.011	−0.020	0.004
Mediterranean Countries																
Pred. prob.	**0.248**	0.005	**0.102**	0.003	**0.563**	0.006	**0.089**	0.003	**0.156**	0.004	**0.146**	0.004	**0.613**	0.005	**0.085**	0.003
Female	−0.109	0.009	**0.023**	0.006	**0.112**	0.011	−0.026	0.006	−0.055	0.007	−0.018	0.007	**0.108**	0.010	−0.035	0.006

Notes: Age, education, citizenship, parents' education and working conditions, country, and quarter of interview are controlled for. Predicted outcome probabilities and marginal effects are computed at the sample mean of the variables. Bold values are statistically significant at 10 percent level of significance or lower.

TABLE 5.3 Predicted probabilities of employment statuses and gender marginal effects among young Europeans (aged 25–34) by country group in 2005 and 2011

<table>
<tr><th rowspan="3"></th><th colspan="8">2005</th><th colspan="8">2011</th></tr>
<tr><th colspan="2">Employed</th><th colspan="2">Unemployed</th><th colspan="2">In education</th><th colspan="2">Inactive</th><th colspan="2">Employed</th><th colspan="2">Unemployed</th><th colspan="2">In education</th><th colspan="2">Inactive</th></tr>
<tr><th>Coeff</th><th>Std. Err.</th><th>Coeff</th><th>Std. Err.</th><th>Coeff</th><th>Std. Err.</th><th>Coeff</th><th>Std. Err.</th><th>Coeff</th><th>Std. Err.</th><th>Coeff</th><th>Std. Err.</th><th>Coeff</th><th>Std. Err.</th><th>Coeff</th><th>Std. Err.</th></tr>
<tr><td colspan="17">Nordic Countries</td></tr>
<tr><td>Pred. prob.</td><td>0.842</td><td>0.006</td><td>0.039</td><td>0.003</td><td>0.062</td><td>0.004</td><td>0.058</td><td>0.004</td><td>0.861</td><td>0.007</td><td>0.043</td><td>0.004</td><td>0.052</td><td>0.005</td><td>0.043</td><td>0.005</td></tr>
<tr><td>Female</td><td>−0.011</td><td>0.016</td><td>−0.008</td><td>0.008</td><td>0.010</td><td>0.009</td><td>0.009</td><td>0.011</td><td>−0.035</td><td>0.016</td><td>0.004</td><td>0.009</td><td>0.013</td><td>0.008</td><td>0.018</td><td>0.010</td></tr>
<tr><td>Parenthood: father</td><td>0.115</td><td>0.021</td><td>−0.035</td><td>0.011</td><td>−0.052</td><td>0.014</td><td>−0.028</td><td>0.014</td><td>0.105</td><td>0.023</td><td>−0.020</td><td>0.011</td><td>−0.062</td><td>0.016</td><td>−0.023</td><td>0.014</td></tr>
<tr><td>Parenthood: mother</td><td>−0.091</td><td>0.016</td><td>0.013</td><td>0.008</td><td>−0.006</td><td>0.010</td><td>0.085</td><td>0.010</td><td>−0.050</td><td>0.017</td><td>−0.015</td><td>0.011</td><td>−0.008</td><td>0.010</td><td>0.073</td><td>0.010</td></tr>
<tr><td colspan="17">Anglo–Saxon Countries</td></tr>
<tr><td>Pred. prob.</td><td>0.855</td><td>0.008</td><td>0.024</td><td>0.003</td><td>0.016</td><td>0.003</td><td>0.105</td><td>0.007</td><td>0.804</td><td>0.026</td><td>0.076</td><td>0.007</td><td>0.017</td><td>0.029</td><td>0.102</td><td>0.009</td></tr>
<tr><td>Female</td><td>−0.014</td><td>0.022</td><td>−0.013</td><td>0.008</td><td>0.004</td><td>0.005</td><td>0.023</td><td>0.021</td><td>0.019</td><td>0.034</td><td>−0.037</td><td>0.018</td><td>−0.011</td><td>0.020</td><td>0.030</td><td>0.027</td></tr>
<tr><td>Parenthood: father</td><td>−0.001</td><td>0.025</td><td>0.007</td><td>0.008</td><td>−0.005</td><td>0.007</td><td>0.000</td><td>0.024</td><td>0.020</td><td>0.051</td><td>0.037</td><td>0.017</td><td>−0.029</td><td>0.048</td><td>−0.029</td><td>0.031</td></tr>
<tr><td>Parenthood: mother</td><td>−0.243</td><td>0.020</td><td>0.022</td><td>0.008</td><td>−0.006</td><td>0.005</td><td>0.227</td><td>0.018</td><td>−0.219</td><td>0.027</td><td>0.041</td><td>0.018</td><td>0.005</td><td>0.010</td><td>0.173</td><td>0.022</td></tr>
</table>

Continental Countries

Pred. prob.	**0.845**	0.005	**0.061**	0.003	**0.018**	0.002	**0.076**	0.004	**0.874**	0.024	**0.044**	0.025	**0.017**	0.010	**0.064**	0.003
Female	−0.030	0.013	−0.004	0.007	−0.002	0.002	**0.036**	0.011	−0.007	0.010	−0.006	0.006	0.000	0.002	**0.014**	0.008
Parenthood: father	**0.099**	0.016	**−0.036**	0.009	**−0.025**	0.005	**−0.038**	0.014	**0.096**	0.021	−0.019	0.012	**−0.030**	0.017	**−0.048**	0.012
Parenthood: mother	**−0.172**	0.012	**0.022**	0.008	**−0.010**	0.003	**0.160**	0.009	**−0.132**	0.012	0.013	0.009	−0.013	0.008	**0.131**	0.008

Mediterranean Countries

Pred. prob.	**0.802**	0.004	**0.084**	0.002	**0.015**	0.001	**0.098**	0.003	**0.762**	0.004	**0.144**	0.003	**0.012**	0.001	**0.083**	0.003
Female	**−0.108**	0.008	**0.033**	0.005	**0.002**	0.001	**0.073**	0.006	**−0.059**	0.009	0.007	0.007	**0.004**	0.001	**0.049**	0.006
Parenthood: father	**0.125**	0.016	−0.003	0.010	**−0.024**	0.006	**−0.099**	0.014	**0.076**	0.017	0.007	0.012	**−0.024**	0.007	**−0.059**	0.013
Parenthood: mother	**−0.146**	0.010	**0.035**	0.007	**−0.011**	0.003	**0.123**	0.007	**−0.139**	0.012	**0.040**	0.010	−0.013	0.003	**0.111**	0.007

Notes: Age, education, citizenship, parenthood, living arrangements, parents' education and working conditions, country and quarter of interview are controlled for. Predicted outcome probabilities and marginal effects are computed at the sample mean of the variables. Bold values are statistically significant at 10 percent level of significance or lower.
Source: Berloffa et al. (2015, Tables A.1–A.4).

than for males in both 2005 and 2011 in all country groups, except in Anglo-Saxon countries (where it was 5 percentage points higher in 2005, but the coefficient was not significant in 2011). This is reflected in a lower probability of being employed (between 5 and 11 percentage points) and of being inactive (between 2 and 5 percentage points) everywhere. This suggests that females invest more in education and for this reason less likely to be inactive in this age group, but they also enter the labor market later than males.

The picture changes completely when we focus on the subsequent age group (twenty-five to thirty-four). Gender effects in this case are mainly, but not exclusively, related to parenthood. Non-mothers present a lower probability of being employed and a higher probability of being inactive compared to non-fathers in all country groups, except in Anglo-Saxon countries (about 3–4 percentage points in Nordic and Continental countries, 6–11 percentage points in Mediterranean countries). However, the largest differences emerge when we compare fathers and mothers. In all country groups, with the exception of Anglo Saxon countries, being a father is associated with a higher probability of being employed (about 10 percentage points) and a lower probability of being unemployed, in education, or inactive (about 2 to 5 percentage points in each category) compared to non-fathers. On the contrary, being a mother is associated with a lower probability of being employed (from 5 to 24 percentage points) and in education (1 to 5 percentage points), and a higher probability of being inactive (from 7 to 23 percentage points) compared to non-mothers. These marginal effects imply a gender gap of about 20–25 percentage points in employment rates of males and females with children in all country groups. This gap appears to be somewhat smaller in 2011, but the reduction is only about 2–4 percentage points.

Taken together, these results imply that gender disparities in labor market opportunities for young people are still large in all European countries, especially those related to parenthood. This suggests that the decision to have children still creates huge problems for females in the labor market, even where females' participation rates are higher, and calls for a reconsideration of the gender equality issue within European policies.

Conclusion

Within the EES, the pursuit of gender equality in employment certainly occupied a central place, especially in the initial formulation. Since its launch, however, repeated reformulations of the EES have led to a progressive loss of visibility of gender equality and equal opportunities, culminating in the final disappearance of gender mainstreaming in the latest reformulation, the Europe 2020 strategy.

As pointed out by several feminist researchers, the EES is based on a rather narrow understanding of the way in which gender equality is conceptualized and policy goals are determined (Rubery 2002; Stratigaki 2004; Lewis 2006a; Villa 2013). The pursuit of gender equality in employment has tended to be connected to dominant economic goals of increasing competitiveness and growth and the sustainability of public finance. In short, gender equality has been translated into the higher female employment rates required to improve the economic performance of EU countries and to allow the sustainability of welfare systems. As a consequence, the economic goal of increasing female participation rates has resulted in a rather instrumental vision of gender equality. Gender equality and equal opportunities between women and men are acknowledged explicitly as fundamental values of the European Union in the EU Treaty and reaffirmed in several documents; however, the pursuit of these important goals at the EU level has been historically linked as much to the pursuit of economic efficiency as to social justice (Lewis 2006b, 149).

Albeit with some limits, the EES's commitment to promoting gender equality has significantly influenced member states' policies on equal opportunity issues (Rubery 2002; Rubery et al. 2003; Fagan et al. 2006). Employment was the first policy area to use the soft law approach based on agreed upon common guidelines that also included recommendations to reduce gender inequalities. From the field of employment, the soft law approach was extended to social inclusion and other social policy areas. By far, however, the most important EU influence on equal opportunity policies at the level of member states has been exerted by the EES. Although the EES may be considered insufficiently powerful to bring about job creation or any major reorientation on member states' labor market policies or gender equality, the need for member states to report regularly on specific guidelines, actions taken, and progress with respect to certain policy targets and to be accountable for these to the commission and the council does provide some influence on their policy agendas. Therefore, the progressive loss of visibility and the watering down of the EU's commitment to gender equality within the employment guidelines enables national governments, especially those half-hearted toward gender equality issues, to ignore the gender dimension in policymaking.

Some researchers had argued that the fallout from the crisis offered an opportunity to create a fairer distribution of resources between rich and poor (Jolly 2010; Vos 2010) and a potentially transformative moment for creating more gender-equal societies (Seguino 2009). In the European context, a major transformation would have required an explicit strategy to integrate gender equality into responses to the crisis, fiscal consolidation measures, and the exit strategy from the Great Recession, with the goal of pushing forward to a more gender-equal labor market. By and large, the reality turned out that the crisis was more of a threat to gender equality priorities. The threat came from policy makers "reverting to type" and paying little attention to gender in the urgency of their responses to the crisis. Implicit and explicit priority given to male breadwinners may induce moves toward policies that do not reflect the realities of dual earning for many European households. A gender-blind approach in policy responses that ignores their impact on the household misses the opportunity to adopt a "win-win" strategy: supporting male employment in the short run but also readdressing some structural weaknesses in the longer run. In particular, investing in social infrastructure would help to address the longer-term challenges of aging, caregiving deficits, and raising employment rates. This is particularly important given that young people in Europe still face large gender disparities in the labor market, especially those related to parenthood, with young mothers generally experiencing a much lower employment probability than young fathers. This calls for a reconsideration of the gender equality issue within European policies.

Notes

1 The Maastricht Treaty (1992), with the establishment of the European Monetary Union (EMU) and the Stability and Growth Pact (SGP), made the primacy of economic (i.e. market-making) interests very explicit, setting stronger constraints on national governments' capacities to realize self-defined sociopolitical goals.
2 The European Union (EU) system of governance is based on a division of labor between the European and the national levels, with certain policies decided at the EU level (market integration, competition law, monetary policy) and others decided at the national level (employment, social policy, pensions, education, etc.).
3 This mode of governance was first introduced in the European Employment Strategy (EES) and then spread rapidly through a wide range of social policy sectors (social inclusion, education, pension reform, etc.).
4 First, there were several reformulations of the European Employment Strategy (EES), modifying the number of employment Guidelines (GLs) and their specification; second, the EU enlargement brought ten new member states in 2004 and another two in 2007; third, since 2005, the employment GLs have been merged with the Broad Economic Policy Guidelines (BEPGs), so that member states are asked to report all their economic and employment policies in a single document (National Reform Programme) on the basis of the so-called integrated guidelines. Consequently, Country Specific Recommendations (CSRs) span all the integrated guidelines. Finally, the style used to formulate the CSRs has changed over time (e.g., in terms of the total number of CSRs, length of each recommendation, etc.).
5 AT, CZ, DE, ES, HU, IE, IT, LT, LV, MT, PL, UK.
6 AT, EL, HU, IT, MT, NL, PL, SK.
7 CZ, SK in 2007, also CY in 2008, only AT in 2011 and 2012.
8 Countries included in the estimations are: DK, FI, NO, and SE for Nordic countries; AT, BE, FR, DE, CH, and NL for Continental countries; IE and UK for Anglo-Saxon countries; and CY, EL, IT, MT, ES, and PT for Mediterranean countries. The four groups of countries are representative of the great heterogeneity of European labor market institutions and welfare regimes. A multinomial logit model is estimated separately for each year, age group and country group. Variables included in the estimation are an individual's age, education, citizenship, living arrangements, parents' education and working conditions, and country dummies.

References

Berloffa, Gabriella, Eleonora Matteazzi, and Paola Villa. 2015. "Households and youth employment." In *Work-Poor and Work-Rich Families: Influence on Youth Labour Market Outcomes*, edited by Gabriella Berloffa, Marianna Filandri, Eleonora Matteazzi, Tiziana Nazio, Nicola Negri, Jacqueline O'Reilly, Paola Villa, and Carolina Zuccotti.STYLE Working Papers 8.1. http://www.style-research.eu/wordpress/wp-content/uploads/ftp/STYLE-Working-Paper-WP8_1.pdf.

Berloffa, Gabriella, Eleonora Matteazzi, and Paola Villa. 2016. "Family background and youth labour market outcomes across Europe." ECINEQ, WP 2016 396. http://www.ecineq.org/milano/WP/ECINEQ2016-393.pdf.

Bettio, Francesca, and Alina Verashchagina. 2013. "Women and men in the 'Great European Recession'." In *Women and Austerity*, edited by Maria Karamessini and Jill Rubery. 57–81. New York: Routledge.

CEC (Commission of the European Communities). 2005. Integrated guidelines for growth and jobs (2005–08). COM(2005) 141 final. http://ec.europa.eu/economy_finance/publications/pages/publication6410_en.pdf

Fagan, Colette, Damian Grimshaw, and Jill Rubery. 2006. "The subordination of the gender equality objective: the national reform programmes and 'Making Work Pay' Policies." *Industrial Relations Journal*, 37(6), 571–592.

Jolly, Richard. 2010. "Employment, basic needs and human development: elements for a new international paradigm in response to crisis." *Journal of Human Development and Capabilities*, 11(1), 11–36.

Karamessini, Maria, and Jill Rubery, eds. 2013. *Women and Austerity: The Economic Crisis and the Future for Gender Equality*. New York: Routledge.

Lewis, Jane. 2006a. "Work/family reconciliation, equal opportunities, and social policies: the interpretation of policy trajectories at the EU level and the meaning of gender equality." *Journal of European Public Policy*, 13(3), 420–437.

Lewis, Jane. 2006b. "What instruments to foster what kind of gender equality?" *Revue française des affaires sociales*, 5, 147–166.

Pfister, Thomas. 2008. "Mainstreamed away? Assessing the gender equality dimension of the European Employment Strategy." *Policy and Politics*, 36(4), 521–538.

Rubery, Jill. 2002. "Gender mainstreaming and gender equality in the EU: the impact of the EU employment strategy." *Industrial Relations Journal*, 33(5), 500–522.

Rubery, Jill. 2015. "Austerity and the future for gender equality in Europe." *ILR Review*, 68(4), 715–741.

Rubery, Jill, Damian Grimshaw, and Colette Fagan. 2003. "Gender equality still on the European agenda. But for how long?" *Industrial Relations Journal*, 34(5), 477–497.

Rubery, Jill, Mark Smith, and Colette Fagan. 1999. *Women's Employment in Europe. Trends and Prospects*. London and New York: Routledge.

Seguino, Stephanie. 2009. "The global economic crisis, its gender implications and policy responses." Paper prepared for the 'Gender Perspective on the Financial Crisis' Panel, 53rd Session of the Commission on the Status of Women, United Nations. March 7, 2009. https://www.uvm.edu/~sseguino/pdf/global_crisis.pdf.

Smith, Mark, and Paola Villa. 2010. "The ever-declining role of gender equality in the European Employment Strategy." *Industrial Relations Journal*, 41(6), 526–543.

Smith, Mark, and Paola Villa. 2014. "The long tail of the great recession: Foregone employment and foregone policies." *Revue de l'OFCE*, 133, 85–119.

Stratigaki, Maria. 2004. "The cooptation of gender concepts in EU policies: the case of 'reconciliation of work and family'." *Social Politics*, 11(1), 30–56.

Villa, Paola. 2013. "The role of the EES in the promotion of gender equality in the labour market." In *Gender and the European Labour Market*, edited by Francesca Bettio, Janneke Plantenga, and Mark Smith. 135–167. London: Routledge.

Villa, Paola, and Mark Smith. 2012. "Gender equality and the evolution of the Europe 2020 strategy." In *Labour Markets, Industrial Relations and Human Resources Management: From Recession to Recovery*, edited by Roger Blanpain. 3–23. Alphen aan den Rijn: Kluwer Law International.

Villa, Paola, and Mark Smith. 2013. "Policy in the time of Crisis: Employment policy and gender equality in Europe." In *Women and Austerity. The Economic Crisis and the Future for Gender Equality*, edited by Maria Karamessini and Jill Rubery. 273–294. New York: Routledge.

Vos, Rob. 2010. "The crisis of globalization as an opportunity to create a fairer world." *Journal of Human Development and Capabilities*, 11(1), 143–160.

6
FROM SISTER TO CO-WORKER

New patterns of feminization of labor in Turkey

Esra Sarıoğlu

A remarkable feature of the labor market in Turkey is that female labor force participation rates are low by international standards. As of 2016, female labor force participation in Turkey was only 30 percent, while women's labor force participation rates on a world scale averaged 49.5 percent (World Bank 2017). Turkey is characterized by a prevalent gender discourse on women's work comprising patriarchal norms, Islamic principles, and cultural constructions of modernity that controls female labor, setting norms and determining whether women can join the workforce, and, if so, when and under what conditions. The discourse has functioned largely as an obstacle to women's employment outside the home, although it differs across class lines. For instance, working outside the home is considered not only appropriate but also desirable for educated middle- and upper-middle-class women in Turkey. Underlying this view is the cultural construction of modernity, originating from Turkey's westernization project, which began with the foundation of the country as a secular republic in 1923. In the initial decades of the Republic, the modernity of the new regime was signaled through the refashioning and display of new gender identities. Of particular importance here was the display of the image of the modern Turkish woman via regulating women's appearance and clothing in the public sphere. For the Turkish Republican elite, the emancipation of women from religious constraints and traditional ties was a necessary precondition for modernization; the image of a modern, westernized, liberated woman in the public sphere was attained by women's removal of the veil.

Although the modern Turkish woman was a working woman, she was not supposed to work as a factory worker or as a cleaning lady. Women's work outside the home was sanctioned only if it was a profession rather than a low-skilled job, and working women succeeded in reaching the standards of modernity only if they were educated. Lower-class women, however, were stigmatized because of the type of economic activity they engaged in, and laboring in textile workshops or cleaning houses was seen as traditional and backward rather than modern. If women in urban Turkey did leave their houses to work at factories or do domestic work in strangers' homes, it besmirched their reputations as honorable women, and their husbands were perceived as failed breadwinners.

Religiosity also compounded the constraining effects of discourse on women's work by reinforcing women's reliance on the family rather than the market. In addition, in Turkey, where the majority of the population is Muslim, Islamic principles have long shaped women's lives through community norms and behavioral codes. For instance, the principle of piety, which addresses the notions about personal modesty and governs women's clothing choices, places restrictions on women's movement outside the domestic sphere and on interactions with non-kin men. These norms and codes associated with piety have long functioned as a cultural barrier that kept women from working outside the domestic sphere.

Since the introduction of export-oriented manufacturing in the 1980s, women began to move into the workforce and largely occupied jobs in the labor-intensive branches of the manufacturing sector. At those workplaces, family and kinship shaped the gender dynamics and the general organization of industrial waged work, with the workplace relations being modeled on patriarchal hierarchies within the family. As a result, a woman's subordinate status in the family extended into the workplace so that she was treated as a subordinate sister, daughter, or wife at work.

Whereas export-oriented production failed to create a feminized workforce in Turkey during the 1980s, the urban shift from industrial to service economies, beginning in the early 1990s, transformed both women's employment trends and the cultural politics of gender relations at work. Having increasingly developed over the last decade, the service sector has become the largest employer of women in urban Turkey. With this has come the expansion of spaces for consumer consumption as well as new employment opportunities for women. Gendered implications of this transformation for working class women in urban Turkey are the subject of this chapter.

New workers in the global era

On a hot July day in 2011, I met Dilara, a twenty-three-year-old married saleswoman. The hypermarket (combined supermarket and department store) at which she worked is located in an open-air shopping complex outside of Istanbul's city center. In addition to housing more than fifty stores, the shopping complex includes an amusement park, an open-air concert square, movie theaters, and an ice-skating rink. I picked her up at lunchtime, and we went to a coffeehouse within the complex. Before the interview, she said, "This is my spot. We often come here after work and talk about the day's events, like how customers and our supervisors treat us at the store." After a week or so, I met Nihal, a twenty-six-year-old single saleswoman. Her description of her first day at the retail store illustrates the promise that working at these new consumption spaces offers:

> I can't forget my first day at MajorMarket. The workers inside the store were at ease with each other, joking with one another and making plans to go out after work. I mean, they looked so free to me. Back then, it never occurred to me that I would hang out after work and drink beer. Now it is something I take for granted.
> *(Saleswoman, Nihal, 2010, Istanbul Interviews)*

Throughout my research, I spent a lot of time with many saleswomen I met at these new consumption sites, which emerged as a result of Turkey's rapid integration into global networks. As my research progressed, it became clear that these workers spent most of their time in these consumption spaces to work, to shop, and to meet with their friends at the coffee shops, restaurants, and nearby stores For service workers, these spaces have multiple functions in their everyday lives. New consumption spaces not only expand employment opportunities for working-class women, but also provide them with spaces of sociability, where they can spend their leisure time without risking their respectability.

This chapter examines how the rise of an urban economy dominated by services rather than industrial production has prompted a transformation in women's employment patterns as well as the gendered work culture in Turkey during the global era. More particularly, it investigates how the working-class construction of femininity in Turkey is shaped by the new service work culture as well as the commercialization of leisure that global capitalism promotes by drawing on historical studies exploring the creation of working-class women's culture in the United States in the late nineteenth and early twentieth centuries (Benson 1986; Peiss 1986). This study first demonstrates that Turkey's transformation into a heavily urbanized and service-based economy created a new pattern in the feminization of labor in the global era, which, at the same time, sustains modern working class femininities. Second, based on fifteen months' field research in Istanbul, through both ethnography and in-depth interviews, it investigates female retail workers' work experiences on the sales floor and their leisurely practices in the new consumption spaces to show that these spaces reinforce the formation of a heterosocial public culture, fostering a particular form of sociability based on non-familial personal interactions, peer-group culture, and gender-mixing.

New patterns of feminization of labor in the global era

Over the last three decades, the feminization of labor has attracted wide attention from scholars who have investigated women's incorporation into waged work in so-called developing countries during the recent global economic restructuring (Standing 1989; Tiano 1994). Earlier studies documenting the employment of women, especially of young women, in multinational factories located in Export Processing Zones have drawn attention to the feminization of textile, garment, and electronics industries in the sense that these industries have become characterized by a predominance of women workers, low wages, employment insecurity, and exploitation of women's labor (Fernandez-Kelly 1983; Ong 1987). The Marxist paradigm of the reserve army of labor has provided the theoretical foundations on which studies into the feminization of labor have been built. According to this model, women form an ideal reservoir of labor that can be tapped in times of boom or labor shortage and easily discarded when no longer needed. Studies in this vein have illustrated the ways in which such global processes as outsourcing, subcontracting, and structural adjustment programs have drawn women into precarious forms of employment as homeworkers, cleaning ladies, or factory workers in different non-core countries, such as Turkey (White 1994), Mexico (Salzinger 2003), and China (Lee 1998). Since then, scholars have focused on precarious forms of work but paid little attention to novel types of work, such as the interactive service occupations emerging in the metropolises of so-called developing countries.

By investigating the characteristics of the female workforce employed in the corporate retail sector in Turkey, this study explores uncharted dynamics of the feminization of labor in a so-called developing country. In particular, it shows that the case of the feminization of labor presented in this study does not fit into the Marxist reserve army of labor paradigm. As global networks penetrate Turkey, supermarkets, shopping malls, restaurants, hotels, and bars thrive in the urban landscape. These globalized spaces of commerce and leisure are now the principal source of jobs for women in urban centers. In these new settings, both the skill requirements and the labor process facilitate the emergence of new work forms as well as new workers. The traits of docility, subordination, and dexterity that assisted women's earlier incorporation into manufacturing industries are no longer demanded in the new service industries. Rather, traits of sociability, extraversion, and open-mindedness constitute working-class women's value in the labor market. Underlying these skill requirements are corporate retailers' strategies for making a profit from a consumer market niche. One such strategy is to cater to the shared values, tastes, and aspirations of particular consumer segments. Thus, corporate service employers hire workers on the basis of physical appearance and interpersonal skills, unlike manufacturing employers, who look for "nimble fingers." Interactive service occupations, unlike manufacturing jobs, are not necessarily fraught with insecurity and flexibility. Instead, these jobs are regular, stable, and unionized, offering both full-time and part-time employment with no significant wage gap between male and female workers. Yet women's career advancement efforts apparently confront a glass ceiling. Women account for a large proportion of entry-level workers, a small proportion of managers, and a very small proportion of top-ranked retail employees.

Given these differences in skill requirements, the work experiences of interactive service workers differ noticeably from those of their counterparts still working in factories. Instead of working to produce tangible goods, service workers cultivate and express certain styles of social intercourse, accommodating consumers' desires, habits, and preferences. By definition, interactive service work involves customers as part of the work process and entails considerable interaction with customers and clients. The interactive requirements of service jobs, at least in Turkey, translate into a gendered work culture, where gender-mixing is a rule. This makes service settings look quite different from their counterparts in the industrial sector. While, for instance, female workers in factories are stigmatized for displays of personal interaction with male coworkers at work, the new service work requires and promotes face-to-face interactions between genders.

The feminization of labor in service industries in Turkey, therefore, forces us to reconsider the dynamics of feminization of labor in so-called developing countries during global restructuring. This chapter looks at the gendered organization of service work embedded with particular meanings and norms of sexualized behavior, gendered interactions, as well as sociability, and commodification of leisure to highlight a new pattern in the feminization of labor in Turkey. It draws on the concept of aesthetic labor inspired by Pierre Bourdieu's (1984) notion of habitus as well as the historical literature on the women's working-class cultures in the United States in the late nineteenth and early twentieth centuries. Such an account, which highlights previously ignored dimensions of the gendered work culture and working class femininities, also offers an alternative way to analyze both the opportunities offered to working-class women and the power relations they undergo in the context of globalization.

Research setting and method

A third-world metropolis in the 1980s, Istanbul has quickly ascended into the higher echelons of global networks in just two decades and now aspires to be a global city. Successive waves of economic liberalization have replaced industrial production within business and commercial services, while the service sector has become the city's key source of employment. Data show that more than 60 percent of the labor force in Istanbul is employed in service occupations, and half of this service labor force is employed in consumer services, such as retailing, hotels, and restaurants (Turkish Statistical Institute, TUIK 2014).

The field research for this study focused on a particular segment within the broader category of low-wage interactive service workers, namely female retail workers. The reason for the selection is twofold. First, the rapid rise of heavily capitalized and corporate retailers in the last two decades makes retailing an ideal site to examine new types of low-wage service occupations in Turkey. For instance, the number of hypermarkets and supermarkets in Turkey increased from 2,979 to 11,588 between 2000 and 2011 (Confederation of Turkish

Tradesmen and Craftsmen, TESK 2012). Second, the retail workforce is becoming increasingly feminized in Turkey, with employment in this subsector representing one-third of women's service employment in Turkey, apart from being one of the fastest growing subsectors, alongside wholesale, restaurants, and hotels (Toksöz 2012).

The demographic characteristics of female retail workers exhibit striking similarities with respect to their age, educational credentials, and family background.[1] While no large-scale survey of the female retail workforce in Istanbul has been attempted, the following can be said of its demographic makeup within this study. The age of informants varied from twenty to forty-two with a median age of twenty-nine. Almost all of the women were at least high school graduates, although there were some retail workers with university diplomas or post-graduate degrees. The informants came from both working-class and lower-middle-class families. These women were among the first generation of women in their families to attain a high school education and the first to be employed outside the home. As of 2011, women's starting wages in the retail sector ranged from US$400 a month to US$440. Although the wages are above the poverty line, a sole head of a household would not be able to live over the poverty line with this income. None of the women workers were sole heads of households. More than half of my informants (around 65 percent) were married with children. The married and single women differed regarding household responsibilities and motherhood. Their differences also tended to be reflected in their work schedules, patterns of sociability, and cliques of friends who regularly met for lunch or dinner or got together after work hours. The majority of married women lived in nuclear family households, and almost half also stated that they lived in close proximity to members of their extended family, making it easier for them to share child-rearing with them. All the married women in this study relied on female kin, particularly grandmothers, for childcare, which was essential for making married women's waged work possible. The residential patterns of single women workers confirmed the norm of single women living with their parents until they were married.

Turkey, like many countries, was not able to escape the impact of the global recession. Indeed, the Turkish economy suffered severely. The export-oriented manufacturing sector was hit particularly hard due to the contraction of demand in the so-called developed world. In 2009, unemployment rose to 16 percent. To minimize the effects of the recession, the government reduced taxes, offered vocational training for the unemployed, and regulated the use of credit cards. Following this, the Turkish economy achieved relatively high growth rates beginning in 2010, and unemployment rates fell to 11 percent. The retail sector was among the least impacted industries thanks to the strong consumer spending and rapid economic recovery (Kearney 2012). In the aftermath of the global recession, the retail sector continued to be one of the leading sectors in employing women in urban Turkey. For instance, in 2013, the retail sector ranked second in increasing women's formal employment in Turkey (The Economic Policy Research Foundation of Turkey, TEPAV 2014).

A new feminization of labor: modern and sociable women workers in Turkey

In Turkey, corporate retailers like MajorMarket, which target the urban, secular, educated, middle- and upper-middle classes with western lifestyles, have developed brand images informed by the core values and norms of modernity. As a part of this strategy, corporate retail employers recruit and prepare their workforce in ways that appeal to the cultural tastes of their target consumers. To ensure their appeal to those customers with secular orientations and westernized lifestyles, retail employers hire workers on the basis of their personal style, manner, comportment, and physical appearance, creating a modern female workforce that reflects their brand image. In other words, service employers select workers with the required aesthetic characteristics.

Based on the notion of habitus elaborated by Pierre Bourdieu to explain class-coded patterns of acquired habits, preferences, and dispositions, the concept of aesthetic labor refers to the role that personality, manner, and appearance requirements play in employment in service-sector occupations (Warhurst and Nickson 2007; Williams and Connell 2010). Service workers perform aesthetic labor when they express these patterns as part of their work. In line with MajorMarket's aesthetic labor requirements, female retail workers are expected to maintain an urban individual identity embodied in modern styles of physical appearance, speaking, and interacting with both customers and coworkers. Thus, employers hire women who have already acquired the desired habitus, a particular urban habitus including traits of sociability, extroversion, openness, and friendliness. In short, the hiring of modernized women is a basic strategy utilized by corporate retailers to guarantee customers a modern shopping experience.

In Turkey, western and secularist notions of modernity have been historically irreconcilable with women's veiling. Therefore, the image of a headscarf-wearing female worker is incompatible with the modern image that MajorMarket wants to project. Indeed, there is a tacit agreement among those corporate retailers that target the urban and secularized middle and upper-middle classes in Turkey that women wearing headscarves are not eligible to work on the sales floor.[2] All human resources employees that I interviewed stated that there was no written rule about wearing headscarves but admitted that those retail companies do not hire women with headscarves for cashier and sales positions. From the corporate retailers' point of view, women wearing headscarves, whose religious lifestyle and appearance tend to be perceived by secular Turks as a threat to secular lifestyles, do not portray the desired modern image for corporate retailers targeting affluent urban customers who have adopted secular lifestyles.

In addition to looking modern, ideal women workers on the sales floor are expected to act modern. On the sales floor, interactions between men and women constitute an integral part of service encounters. In Turkey, public interaction between men and women is accepted in urban life, and the social mixing of genders has been constructed as modern in line with early Turkish modernity. On the other hand, Islamic norms regarding female seclusion, which restrict interactions between men and women to a certain extent, prevail both in urban and rural areas. For retail employers who seek the ideal workers on the sales floor, modern woman workers are those whose interactional capacity is not restricted by Islamic norms of seclusion.

Of all the preferred dispositions, sociability is, therefore, the most desirable skill requirement in the corporate retail sector. As the human resource manager of a major corporate retail company explained, "We want our workers to be presentable and sociable. We cannot work with shy people. Our customers are coming from very different cultural backgrounds; tourists and people from different religions are also shopping here." High school graduate urban women, management believes, are more likely to possess such skills as sociability and open-mindedness, so they are considered well-suited for work in retail stores. Ela, a 33 year-old MajorMarket worker, explained why high school graduates were better suited to the work environment in corporate retail stores:

> Generally, people who are tolerant and open-minded about interactions with the opposite sex get hired. And high school graduates are more suitable for working here because at school, girls and boys sit next to each other in the classroom. If a girl is a high school graduate, she thinks it normal that girls and boys are close friends because interacting with boys is a part of her upbringing and education. She probably has had a couple of romantic relationships, too. But if a girl has only a primary school diploma, it means that, later in her life, she lives in seclusion. She would find it strange that girls and boys are close friends, working all day and sometimes at night together. Just as the guys [her coworkers] here feel uneasy when they talk with a gay person, the girl with a primary school diploma would feel uneasy interacting with men, customers, and coworkers alike.
>
> (Saleswoman, Ela, 2010, Istanbul Interviews)

The practice of aesthetic labor, on the one hand, explains why a particular group of women is hired in the corporate retail sector in Turkey while, on the other hand, obscures the power relations and discrimination affecting women's opportunities in the labor market. For instance, if an employer does not hire an applicant wearing a headscarf for one of the service jobs, it is not due to illegal employment discrimination; the employer is legitimately looking for someone whose appearance, manner, and habitus matches the brand. Depending on the company's image, which is highly subjective, some other employer might not want to hire a woman without a headscarf or a woman with a Kurdish accent. As a result, service workers are increasingly hired on the basis of their ethnicity, gender, and habitus as indicators of their skills because they have this additional task of reflecting the company image. In this sense, aesthetic labor, a widespread practice in the service sector, offers a justification for employer discrimination, masking it under the guise of skill requirements.

Inside the non-familial and sociable space of work

At MajorMarket, sociability is not only a skill requirement, but also a principle guiding interactions between supervisors and staff, customers and workers, and among the workers themselves. Corporate organizations typically install programs of workplace and organizational restructuring with the aims of disciplining employees, enhancing customer satisfaction and thereby increasing profitability, and reinforcing a particular form of sociability at the workplace. The pivotal organizational cultural practices of tropes about the family and the team have been extensively discussed in the literature on globalization and labor control (Freeman 2000; Otis 2008; Pettinger 2005). Studies show the ways in which corporate culture, in the guise of a team or family, shapes the work environment, functioning as a guiding principle of workplace interactions.

In Turkey, scholarly research on the feminization of labor in the manufacturing sector in the global era indicates that the family model is heavily endorsed among industrial workers (Sarioglu 2013; White 1994). As Jenny B. White observed in her study *Money Makes Us Relatives* (1994), small-scale production in Istanbul is regulated by kinship logic. In the production process, a woman's labor is conflated with her gender identity, reflecting her subordinate position within the family. In these workplaces, traditional gender hierarchies are imposed on the work setting in such a way that managers, who employ the family metaphors, are able to cast female workers as daughters or wives and, by doing so, are able to discipline them according to family rules. The organization of relations between workers and management in terms of kin, at the same time, obscures the exploitation and subordination of female workers.

My research shows that the work culture inside corporate retail stores in Istanbul did not seem to be imbued with this family rhetoric. Rather, the organizational culture that pervaded the workplace through language forms and codes of behavior, shaping interpersonal interactions in the workplace was defined by the absence of familial codes. These non-familial aspects of the organizational culture of the retail stores in Istanbul are manifested primarily in the process of the assignment of workers to stores. MajorMarket, like other retail corporations, has a strictly enforced company policy that bans spouses and siblings from working at the same store. While the company hires married couples, fathers and children, and brothers and sisters, such family members are not allowed to work in the same store. If two employees working in the same store get married, which is a widespread phenomenon, one of them must be transferred to another store. The company's rationale for this is the prevention of nepotism. This policy is widely supported by female workers, although for different reasons. Women believe that the policy helps them avoid family surveillance at work. For example, Banu, who married one of her coworkers, described the sense of ease and freedom she felt after her husband was transferred to another store:

> I feel very comfortable now. I smoke a lot, but my husband doesn't. If he was here, he would be nagging me about smoking all the time. Plus, he would kind of control me. Without him being around, I feel free at the store. I hang out with my coworkers without thinking about whether my husband is bothered by my behavior. If he was around me, I would have to watch myself constantly. You know, he is a typical Turkish man.[3] He would probably be jealous seeing me spending a lot of time with the guys working here.
>
> (Saleswoman, Banu, 2010, Istanbul Interviews)

The retail setting also encourages workers to cast relationships with their coworkers and managers in non-familial terms, as clearly reflected in the terms that the workers use to refer to each other. They call each other by their names and address each other as "Mr." and "Mrs." or "Ms." in the presence of customers. For female retail workers, the way employees address each other at MajorMarket signals that the salesfloor has been freed from paternalistic norms and behaviors. In industrial production sites, in contrast, workers' interpersonal interactions are often framed in kinship terms through the use of gendered familial terms that evoke a paternalistic disposition towards women. For example, female factory workers are regularly called "sister" [*bacı*], denoting a low-status kin position, whereas the absence of gendered familial language in the retail stores flattens familial hierarchies among workers. The modern forms of addressing and absence of family evocative on the shopping floor allow female workers to cast themselves as sociably equal to their male coworkers. Many of the female retail workers cited this non-familial language as a positive aspect of their work environment. As Esma put it, "I like working here because there is no *bacı* talk here. We call each other by our names; it is not like the factory."

Sociability, which is associated with such personal traits as being extraverted, friendly, and courteous, also rearranges the normative context of personal interactions between the sexes on the sales floor. In a work setting where sociability is the dominant form of personal interaction, female workers are no longer considered morally questionable because of their interactions with unfamiliar men in public. On the contrary, the requirement of sociability sanctions close personal interactions between the sexes in public, a behavior that was formerly prohibited and which is still deemed immoral in some industrial production sites in Turkey. This shift allows female workers to work in gender-integrated environments and closely interact with men without subsuming their gender identities under a familial identity. Sociability requirement at the interactive service settings, in this sense, reframes the moral context of interactions between the sexes, removing women's interactional behavior from the clutches of sexual modesty and propriety.

The social mores embedded in the notion of sociability enhance the work experience of female workers. Many of them believe that relaxed norms about social interactions between the sexes turn the shopping floor into a freer, less inhibited, and radically different workplace from the factories. For single female workers, sociability is particularly important, and the workplace is a setting to meet new people and make friends. "I could have worked at a small office, but I didn't want to because I knew I could make a lot of friends here at the store," said Canan, a twenty-six-year-old MajorMarket worker. For young workers, the opportunity to socialize was the biggest perk of the service floor, apart from the wages. When asked about friendship ties on the shopping floor, Zehra said in excitement,

> The staff canteen is like a university canteen. Young people like me come together and talk about different things, like fun places to go, books, movies, and even inter-rail. I have come to meet a lot of college students here. We work together and have fun together.
> (Saleswoman, Zehra, 2010, Istanbul Interviews)

Sociability, however, is a double-edged sword. On the one hand, it enhances workers' employment experiences; on the other hand, it functions as an instrument of supervisory control by removing the need for direct control over workers. By fostering sociability and ensuring the formation of a work team resembling a wide circle of friends, management is better able to guarantee workers' commitment to their employers. In this way, management coaxes workers into long hours of work and manages their intense stress. Creating a friendly environment allows the supervisors to expect greater cooperation from the workers in response to requests for overtime and to generally demand high-quality work as well as small favors like making tea and picking up take-out lunch for a supervisor during a break.

Women in spaces of leisure

New types of leisure activities flourishing at the new consumption sites also extend the sociability emerging in the workplace outside of work. Using their hard-won cash, female workers enthusiastically pursue leisure activities at these new consumption sites. Leisure, like work, reinforces their autonomy by removing them from parental and community control. As Nihal put it, "I am usually outside the home. I spend a lot of time with my friends after work and on my off days. When I was a kid, my parents used to keep me at home most of the time." Women's leisure patterns and time spent in leisure, however, varies with marital status. While unmarried women workers have a large amount of leisure time at their disposal and spend much of their free time apart from their families, married women workers' leisure time is limited, and they spend much of it with their families.

For female workers, leisurely sociability functions as an arena for the articulation of certain values and behaviors, offering them an opportunity to articulate less conventional gender identities for themselves. Of particular importance here is the increasing prominence of friendship within mixed-gender groups. Female workers go to movies and concerts with male coworkers, get together with them after work at fast-food outlets and other restaurants, and hang out with them on their days off, playing backgammon games in cafés. On these occasions, women work through and define the ways in which they relate to and interact with men. Framing their interpersonal interactions with men within the context of friendship enables women to move beyond the customary attachments embodied in gender roles, such as wife, fiancée, or romantic partner. In this context, women are neither the repository of male honor nor morally flawed. Leisure occasions mark a sphere where women workers can negotiate the tropes about being a woman in Turkish society. Ela's description of her leisurely pursuits illustrates how a lively peer culture cultivates a new sense of identity among working women in this study:

> When I started working at MajorMarket in 1994, I liked the friendship ties best. I grew up within a conservative family. Things like going to a bar were unthinkable for my parents. The first time I went to a bar was when I started working at MajorMarket. Back then, I, just like my parents, was thinking that bars are morally dubious places. I thought that women and men who go to bars are either promiscuous or are the type of people who do drugs. But that night we went there with my male coworkers, and they treated me like a friend. That night I noticed that going out to [a] bar is something that one can do with her friends just to have fun and let it all hang out.
>
> (Saleswoman, Ela, 2010, Istanbul Interviews)

These gatherings in which female workers participate represent a new leisure pattern for women in urban Turkey. Previously, women's involvement in leisure activities in public spaces was, to a certain extent, deemed immoral. For instance, the presence of women in public spaces, particularly behaviors such as being on the streets just for the sake of socializing and entertainment, was considered a sign of sexual availability that provoked harassment. Additionally, there were very few mixed gender leisure spaces like cafés, restaurants, and cinemas available to women in Turkey. However, the new consumption spaces that have flourished with the expansion of the service economy in the context of globalization take on a new meaning as women utilize these venues so as to affirm their personal and financial autonomy. Especially unmarried women embrace the friendship ties forged in these gatherings, which offer freedom and companionship as an alternative to domestic lifestyles.

Furthermore, female workers utilize leisurely pursuits to articulate their own ideas about work and life. When they leave the familiar context of family and community for a new world of work and leisure marked by novel norms, rules, demands, and experiences, these women are increasingly confronted with new situations for which the conventional repertoire of rules and forms of behavior are no longer sufficient. As they strive and grope for a new repertoire of norms and patterns of behavior, they rely, to a significant extent, on friendship ties. Of all the leisurely pursuits that attract unmarried women workers, "getting together with the girls" in a café is their greatest passion. After a long day of working in the store, they change their clothes and hurry out to a fast-food outlet or café to meet up with their female coworkers. In these gatherings, conversations often help women discover their own informal rules of interaction. For example, they discuss how to respond to a male coworker who shows a lack of respect for women, how to negotiate with a supervisor whose patronizing behavior intimidates female workers, how to guard themselves against "nosy" female workers, and how to draw boundaries with male coworkers. At one of these gatherings that I attended, the women extensively discussed the issue of friendship between male and female workers. Pelin, for instance, specified the conditions under which she becomes friends with male coworkers:

> For a woman to be friends with a man, the guy should have already experienced certain things. Then, he won't misinterpret the woman's behavior. I can only be a friend with a guy who has already had a romantic relationship with a woman. Other guys mistake your friendliness for sexual interest. Take this guy, Mehmet. I added him on Facebook and now he thinks that I have a crush on him.
>
> *(Saleswoman, Pelin, 2011, Istanbul Interviews)*

In these gatherings, women also frequently discuss their careers, assessing new job opportunities on the basis of working hours, wages, social security, future prospects, and workplace relationships. They also talk about ways to enhance their social mobility, such as affordable language courses, college programs, and computer learning courses. Closely tied to the topic of careers are women's aspirations. Many female workers have left behind the expectations and experiences typical of their families as a result of their education and employment. Now, their life plans are different from their mothers', and some of them have started to question things that their mothers took for granted regarding romantic relationships, divorce, education, and age of marriage. In one of these gatherings, Nesrin expressed her own aspirations resolutely by saying,

> I am not the type of person who dedicates herself to her husband, takes care of the kids, and cooks all day. I want to go to college and in ten years be a woman who can stand on her own feet.
>
> *(Saleswoman, Nesrin, 2010, Istanbul Interviews)*

Conclusion

With Turkey integrating itself into European and world markets undergoing global restructuring, the growth of new types of service industries has changed the employment landscape and a dramatic shift has taken place in employment opportunities: from manufacturing to services, from male to female, and from muscle power to cultural capital. This chapter has examined how an urban service economy has reshaped the patterns of the feminization of labor in Turkey, addressing the opportunities as well as the limitations for women that are emerging with globalization. This analysis has located the feminization of labor in relation to recent scholarship on aesthetic labor and the literature on gendered cultural shifts that occur within the context of workplace and economic restructuring.

As it has shown, the new patterns of the feminization of labor, here identified, relate to the skill requirements in the interactive service sector. Given that a worker's self-presentation and interactive competency constitute a major part of the service product, service employers carefully screen women's habitus in the hiring process. In the case of MajorMarket, a particular group of women discursively constructed as modern and sociable make ideal workers on the sales floor, and another group of women, constructed as traditional, are not eligible for working in corporate retail stores. Practices of aesthetic labor, which at times allow employers to legitimize discrimination at the hiring stage, create a new stratum of female workers within the working class in Turkey. This study demonstrates that female high school graduates who are not constrained by Islamic principles of seclusion have expanded employment opportunities and it is important for future research to empirically evaluate whether the less educated, migrant, and female workers with headscarves are more likely to be marginalized in the interactive service sector.

By focusing on new consumption spaces, this chapter has also investigated the transformation of gendered interactions in public spaces, another novel dimension of the recent feminization of labor. Through an analysis of sales floor culture and new types of leisure activities, this chapter has shown that new consumption spaces, as venues of both leisure and work, reinforce the formation of a heterosocial public culture, fostering a particular form of sociability based on non-familial personal interactions, peer-group culture, and gender-mixing that undermines the prevailing industrial workplace culture characterized by protectionist paternalism. On the sales floor as well as in the new consumption spaces, familial hierarchies that define industrial workplaces are flattened. Women's status is not that of a submissive sister, but of a coworker and friend, making women feel that they are at least sociably equal to men on the sales floor. Contractual rather than protectionist relationships characterize these new consumption spaces, which in turn represents a cultural shift towards liberal relationships in the working-class work environment in Turkey.

Notes

1 The research I conducted in Istanbul included two interconnected methodologies: in-depth, semi-structured interviews and participant observation. I conducted sixty in-depth interviews with the research participants, who consisted of thirty-five female retail workers, four human resources employees of individual retail companies, one Turkish retail council representative, and one union leader. Participant observation was another source of field data. Between May 2011 and August 2011, I worked as a cashier at MajorMarket (a pseudonym for a large supermarket in Istanbul), a joint venture owned by European and Turkish holding companies that was located in an upscale urban neighborhood on the European side of the city and targeted the market segment between those of the mass discounters and the luxury markets.
2 This unwritten rule has been strictly enforced by joint venture retailers owned by TNCs (an acronym for Transnational Corporation) and Turkish holding companies, such as IKEA, Migros, and CarrefourSA. In contrast, both national retailers such as BIM and local supermarkets owned by Islamic-oriented individuals that target the lower-middle classes and the pious middle classes employ headscarf-wearing women for cashier and sales positions.
3 By "typical Turkish man," Banu was referring to the traits of masculinity regarded as normal in Turkey, in which a man would be threatened by his female partner's close interactions with other men, experience a feeling of loss of patriarchal control, and, in response, feel entitled to display aggressive behavior toward her.

References

Benson, Susan Porter. *Counter Cultures: Saleswomen, Managers, and Customers in American Department Stores 1890–1940*. Urbana: University of Illinois Press, 1986.
Bourdieu, Pierre. *Distinction*. Cambridge, MA: Harvard University Press, 1984.
Fernández-Kelly, Maria. Patricia. *For We Are Sold, I and My People: Women and Industry in Mexico's Frontier*. Albany: State University of New York Press, 1983.
Freeman, Carla. *High Tech and High Heels in the Global Economy: Women, Work, and Pink-Collar Identities in the Caribbean*. Durham, NC: Duke University Press, 2000.
Istanbul Interviews, conducted by Esra Sarioglu. May 2010-June 2011. Recordings of these interviews are in Ankara, in the author's possession.
Kearney, A. T. "*Global Retail Expansion: Keeps on Moving*." 2012. Accessed January 1, 2015. http://www.atkearney.com.tr/documents/10192/302703/Global+Retail+Expansion+Keeps+On+Moving.pdf/4799f4e6-b20b-4605-9aa8-3ef451098f8a.
Lee, Ching Kwan. *Gender and the South China Miracle: Two Worlds of Factory Women*. Berkeley: University of California Press, 1998.
Ong, Aihwa. *Spirits of Resistance and Capitalist Discipline: Factory Women in Malaysia*. Albany: State University of New York Press, 1987.
Otis, Eileen. "Beyond the Industrial Paradigm: Market-Embedded Labor and the Gender Organization of Global Service Work in China," *American Sociological Review* 73, no. 1 (2008): 15–36.
Peiss, Kathy. *Cheap Amusements: Working Women and Leisure in Turn-of-the-Century New York*. Philadelphia: Temple University Press, 1986.
Pettinger, Lynne. "Friends, Relations and Colleagues: The Blurred Boundaries of the Workplace," *Sociological Review* 53, no. 2_suppl (2005): 37–55.
Salzinger, Leslie. *Genders in Production: Making Workers in Mexico's Global Factories*. Berkeley: University of California Press, 2003.

Sarioglu, Esra. "Gendering the Organization of Home-Based Work in Turkey: Classical versus Familial Patriarchy," *Gender, Work & Organization* 20, no. 5 (2013): 479–497.

Standing, Guy. "Global Feminization through Flexible Labor," *World Development* 17, no. 7 (1989): 1077–1095.

TEPAV (Policy Research Foundation of Turkey). "*Women Outpace Men in Job Gains.*" 2014. Accessed January 1, 2015. http://www.tepav.org.tr/en/haberler/s/3744.

TESK (Confederation of Turkish Trades men and Craftsmen). "*Zincir ve Süpermarket Sayısı 11bini Aştı.*" 2012. Accessed February 7, 2013. http://www.tesk.org.tr/tr/calisma/sicil/ist.html.

Tiano, Susan. *Patriarchy on the Line: Labor, Gender, and Ideology in the Mexican Maquila Industry.* Philadelphia: Temple University Press, 1994.

Toksöz, Gulay. "The State of Female Labor in the Impasse of the Neoliberal Market and Patriarchal Family." In *Gender and Society in Turkey: The Impact of Neoliberal Policies, Political Islam and EU Accession*, edited by Yavuz Elveren and Saniye Dedeoglu, 47–64. London: IB Tauris Academic Studies, 2012.

TUIK, Turkish Statistical Institute. "*Istanbul 2013: With Chosen Indicators.*" 2014. Accessed January 1, 2015. http://www.tuik.gov.tr/ilGostergeleri/iller/ISTANBUL.pdf.

Warhurst, Chris and Dennis Nickson. "Employee Experience of Aesthetic Labour in Retail and Hospitality," *Work, Employment and Society* 21, no. 1 (2007): 103–120.

White, Jenny. *Money Makes Us Relatives: Women's Labor in Urban Turkey.* Austin, Texas: University of Texas Press, 1994.

Williams, Christine L. and Catherine Connell. "Looking Good and Sounding Right" Aesthetic Labor and Social Inequality in the Retail Industry," *Work and Occupations* 37, no. 3 (2010): 349–377.

World Bank. "*Labor Force Participation Rate, Female (% of Female Population, Ages 15+).*" 2017. Accessed August 31, 2017. https://data.worldbank.org/indicator/SL.TLF.CACT.FE.ZS?end=2016&start=1990.

7

GENDER, WORK, AND RECESSION

Two views from the United States

Brigid O'Farrell

> We should educate public opinion not to profit by labor anywhere unless it was done under decent living conditions.
>
> Eleanor Roosevelt (1933)

Myrtle Witbooi entered the large hall from the back, surrounded by fellow domestic workers. In her lilting South African voice, finger raised, she sang, "My mother was a kitchen girl. My father was a garden boy. That's why I'm a unionist." Before over a thousand union delegates at the 2013 AFL-CIO convention in Los Angeles, a beaming President Richard Trumka presented her with the Meany-Kirkland Human Rights Award as chair of the International Domestic Workers Network and honoring their work bringing the voices of domestic workers to the international level.

Magan Smith of Bricklayers Local 8 in Florida gave the national keynote speech to over a thousand tradeswomen—electricians, plumbers, carpenters, iron workers, and laborers attending the national 2015 Women Build Nations Conference in Los Angeles. An Air Force veteran, she told her inspirational story of challenges and successes in apprenticeship. Terry O'Sullivan, president of the Laborers International Union, concluded his speech that day by pledging, "I am committed to standing shoulder to shoulder with you to bring full gender equity not only to our movement, but to our entire country."

These highly visible occasions indicate slow, but promising changes in the workplace. Emerging from the Great Recession, which officially lasted from 2007–2009, women have regained jobs lost, but they have not achieved greater equality in the labor market. This study explores two occupational categories to highlight ongoing job segregation within the global economic framework, the hardships and harassment many face, and the actions women and unions are taking to empower women in the post-recession recovery. While slow progress has been made, women's jobs remain concentrated in low-wage work, such as domestic caregiving, and women are rarely found in higher-wage jobs, such as those in the construction trades. The decent living conditions called for by First Lady Eleanor Roosevelt in 1933 remain elusive for many. Examples set by domestic workers and tradeswomen provide insights into strategies for achieving gender equality despite economic setbacks, increasing class inequality, and political resistance from conservative governments in the United States and around the world.[1]

Historical context

On October 11, 1963, President Kennedy's Commission on the Status of Women—chaired by Eleanor Roosevelt, international human rights leader, former first lady, and union member—issued its final report, *American Women*, under the direction of the Women's Bureau at the U.S. Department of Labor. The Commission, a long-time goal of union women, was led by Esther Peterson from the Amalgamated Clothing Workers of America, the highest-ranking woman in the Kennedy Administration and a union activist (Cobble 2004; O'Farrell 2015).

For the first time, the federal government evaluated the status of women as homemakers and workers and acknowledged discrimination against women in all walks of life, including education, employment, community, and the law. In 2013, the fiftieth anniversary of the report, these findings were used as a benchmark to assess changes in women's work lives and the policies developed to achieve equity, as captured in Figure 7.1, an employment graph expanded on in a series of papers commissioned by the Department of Labor (U.S. Department of Labor, Women's Bureau 2014).

As the graph and the related papers show, progress has been made. Today women are healthier, living longer, and have more opportunities in the paid workforce, where their numbers have dramatically increased. Not only are women able to serve on juries, they are now also serving as Supreme Court justices. They have a significant impact on elections and hold leadership positions in the major political parties. The personal stories of female Supreme Court justices, Olympic gold medal winners, scientists, and astronauts provide inspiration for millions of young women (O'Farrell 2015).

Women's progress in the area of education provides one example of such change (Carnevale and Smith 2014; Matz and Hedgepeth 2014). Women now outnumber men at all levels of education. They are more likely to complete high school, graduate from college, and go on to receive graduate degrees. Women constitute almost half of the students in medical school and law school and a third of those in business school. Title IX of the Education Act of 1972 played a critical role in advancing women in higher education as well as revolutionizing the role of women in sports, both amateur and professional (Hill and Prangley 2014).

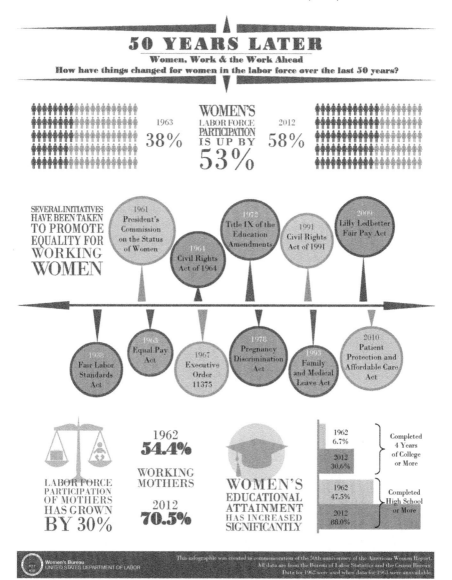

FIGURE 7.1 Labor force changes for women over the past fifty years
Source: U.S. Department of Labor, Women's Bureau (2015).

Changes in women's progress in employment status offers another example. Women now make up almost half of the workforce. The greatest difference has been for mothers. The number of mothers now in the workforce who have children under eighteen years of age has risen from 28 percent in 1960 to 70 percent in 2017. Almost two-thirds of mothers with a youngest child under the age of six (63.9 percent) are in the workforce (U.S. Department of Labor, Women's Bureau 2015). According to the Pew Research Center, mothers are now the sole or primary earners in 40 percent of households with children under eighteen (Wang et al. 2013).

Women now have access to many more occupations and leadership positions, which adds to their economic independence. According to the Bureau of Labor Statistics (U.S. Department of Labor, Bureau of Labor Statistics 2017a), 38 percent of physicians and surgeons and over 35 percent of lawyers are women, up from single digits in the 1960s. People working in the category of management, business, and financial operations are 51.5 percent women. Almost half of bus drivers in what was once a male-dominated field are now women. It is no longer unusual for a woman to hold a cabinet-level position in a presidential administration. Women serve as chief executives of major corporations and presidents of labor unions. The last barriers to women's full participation in the U.S. military forces have fallen. Women now compose almost 15 percent of the active-duty military and serve in combat on the ground, piloting planes, commanding units, and directing training (U.S. Department of Defense 2013). Growing faster than the national average, in 2016 the number of women-owned firms was almost 11.3 million. The percentage of women-owned businesses owned by women of color grew from 17 percent in 1997 to 44 percent in 2016 (American Express OPEN 2016).

Moreover, women now make up almost half of the members of the labor movement (Anderson et al. 2015). The AFL-CIO represents fifty-seven unions and over thirteen million members, almost half of whom are women. Liz Shuler, from the International Brotherhood of Electrical Workers, is the first woman and youngest person ever elected secretary-treasurer of this labor federation. The top three officers of the affiliated 1.5 million-member American Federation of Teachers are women. Unions not part of the AFL-CIO include the Service Employees International Union, more than half of whose 2.1 million members are female and whose president is Mary Kay Henry. Women represented by unions earn, on average, 13 percent more than similar women in non-union jobs (about $2.50 more per hour). There is a union wage advantage across all racial and ethnic groups. Union workers are also more likely to have health insurance and pensions, paid sick days, paid personal leave, short-term disability, dependent care reimbursement, and childcare (Jones et al. 2014).

These changes reflect many factors over the last fifty years, including legal, cultural, technological, and economic shifts. According to *New York Times* columnist Gail Collins (2009), this was *When Everything Changed* for American Women. As the women's movement began to grow, Title VII of the 1964 Civil Rights Act, for example, prohibited sex discrimination in employment. Class action complaints of sex discrimination were taken up by the Equal Employment Opportunity Commission in the 1970s, compelling the airline industry and corporate giants like AT&T and General Motors to reassess their recruitment, hiring, and promotion policies at all levels of their organizations. The 1978

Pregnancy Discrimination Act amended Title VII to stop discrimination based on pregnancy, childbirth, and related medical conditions. Through litigation, the courts defined sexual harassment and found it to be illegal. Superiors could no longer pressure subordinates for sex or sanction workplaces where women were demeaned, harassed, or sexually assaulted (Baker 2008; MacLean 2006). Public opinion changed as well. According to a Pew Research Center survey, only 18 percent of adults surveyed in 2012 believed that "women should return to their traditional role in society," and 58 percent "completely disagreed" with that view, up from 29 percent in 1987 (Milkman 2016, 287).

Problems persist

Despite progress toward gender equality in the workplace, problems have persisted and become the subject of much study. Research on occupational sex segregation, sexual harassment, and work/family balance has been conducted in sociology, economics, psychology, law, and the human relations departments of the nation's business schools. In the 1980s, the National Academy of Sciences, for example, established a Committee on Women's Employment and Related Social Issues. Leaders from academia, business, and labor came together and produced reports on the effects of technology on working women, the causes and consequences of occupational sex segregation in employment, the topic of equal pay, and the challenges of balancing work and family, (e.g., Reskin and Hartmann 1986). In the 1990s, Congress passed legislation creating the Glass Ceiling Commission at the U.S. Department of Labor brought together experts and policy makers to assess the barriers to women's full participation in the highest levels of the workforce (U.S. Department of Labor 1995). Since 1920, the Women's Bureau (U.S. Department of Labor, Women's Bureau 2012) has continued its long history of documenting women's employment problems and progress.

The pay gap between what women and men earn has narrowed from 60.7 percent in 1963 to 78.6 percent in 2013, but the gender gap persists, along with racial and ethnic disparities (U.S. Department of Labor, Women's Bureau 2015). Based on median annual earnings for full-time, year-round workers, white women earned just 75.4 percent of every dollar a white man earned. But while Asian women earned 83.5 percent, African American women earned less, at 60.5 percent, and Hispanic women only 54.6 percent. The wage gap also varied by state (Hess et al. 2015). Women in New York had the narrowest gap, earning 87.6 percent of what men earned, while those in Louisiana had the largest gap, earning 66.7 percent. This gap persists within all levels of education, but was smallest, 80 percent, for those with less than a high school degree or a doctoral degree (Hill and Prangley 2014, 225).

Significantly, the 78.6 percent average wage gap has been stagnant for the last ten years. Part of the earlier narrowing of the wage gap was, in fact, due to the stagnation in wages for men (Davis and Gould 2015). Occupational segregation continues and is seen as a major source of wage inequality today, just as it was in 1963 (Hegewisch and Hartmann 2014). Women continue to hold fewer than 3 percent of construction trade jobs and are underrepresented in the fast-growing and higher-paying jobs in STEM (science, technology, engineering, and math). As Sheryl Sandburg, chief operating officer of Facebook, pointed out in her bestselling book, *Lean In* (2013), fewer than 5 percent of CEOs of Fortune 500 companies are women. The United States remains the only developed nation without a paid maternity leave policy, and the availability of quality affordable childcare is no more a reality today than it was in 1963.

While women now make up almost half of the labor movement, overall union membership has declined from a high of 35 percent of workers fifty years ago to 10.7 percent of workers today. According to the Department of Labor (2017b), just 6.4 percent of workers in the private sector belong to a union. Corporate resistance to unions has grown dramatically. U.S. labor laws are weak and provide only minimal penalties for violations. Workers are fired in one out of four organizing drives that are conducted under the supervision of the National Labor Relations Board (Bronfenbrenner 2009). Far from securing the right to join a union at the state level as recommended by the president's 1963 Commission on the Status of Women, right-to-work laws that make it harder to maintain unions have passed even in such union strongholds as Michigan and Wisconsin (Anderson et al. 2015). A national right-to-work law was introduced in Congress in 2017.

Globalization, combined with other factors such as outsourcing and technological innovation, have strongly affected women's employment. Huwat and Verdier define the economic consequences of globalization as "the increased international trade in goods and services, of course, but also the evolution of MNE's [multinational enterprises], the organization of industrial production across borders, and the global crisscrossing of workers and students spurred by economic need" (2013, 13). While they find that some jobs have been lost, others have been gained. There are many reasons for these shifts and much debate about cause and effect, but one motivation for and result of these movements has been reduced costs to employers through lower wages for workers.

In 1989, for example, the United States had twice as many higher-paying manufacturing jobs as lower-paying service-sector jobs; now the numbers are nearly equal (Eidelson 2013). Many of these lower-paying service jobs are held by women, often by immigrant women and women of color. The devastating effects of outsourcing and plant closures on people and their communities have been captured most recently by Paul Theroux (2015) in his travels across the Deep South. Lazonick (Lazonick and the Academic-Industry Research Network 2015) argues that the basic structural changes that have occurred in the United States now affect white-collar and professional jobs as well as blue-collar manual and service jobs and have led to the widening income disparity and the decline in middle-class jobs. The most recent Great Recession threw these changes into stark relief.

The great recession

Women and men in all types of jobs were hard hit by the Great Recession. According to the National Bureau of Economic Research, the recession officially lasted from December 2007, the peak of the business cycle, through June 2009, the low point of the business cycle. An analysis by the Institute for Women's Policy Research found that American workers now hold more jobs than they did when the recession officially began, as seen in Figure 7.2. Women lost a smaller share of their jobs, 4 percent, than men, who lost 9 percent. Women, however, regained their job losses in 2013, while men did not until 2014. As shown in Figure 7.2, in January 2017, women held 72,086,000 payroll jobs while men held 73,217,000, both more than the peak number of jobs in 2007. These numbers are from the Bureau of Labor Statistics' Employer Survey. Based on the Current Population Survey, which surveys households and includes more job categories, such as the self-employed and unemployed, men's labor force participation rate remains at 69 percent, higher than women's rate of 57 percent.

According to the Bureau of Labor Statistics (IWPR 2017), the overall unemployment rate was 4.7 percent in December 2016, down from a high of 10 percent in 2009. Among workers aged twenty and older, however, the unemployment rate remained highest for black men, 7.6 percent, followed by black women, 6.8 percent; Hispanic women, 5.9 percent; and Hispanic men, 4.9 percent. The lowest unemployment rate was 3.8 percent for white women, 4.1 percent for white men, and 2.6 percent for the Asian population. While declining, the number of long-term unemployed—those out of work for twenty-seven weeks or more—was almost a quarter (24.2 percent) of the 7.5 million unemployed.

Wages, however, remained stagnant. Between 1948 and 1979, productivity and hourly compensation grew in tandem. Since 1979, however, the nation's productivity has risen 62.7 percent, but workers' median hourly compensation has increased by just 8.0 percent. Almost all the gains from growth have gone to the top earners, with no relief in sight for other workers. Global trade and investment are recovering, but full-time employment and wages are not (Davis and Gould 2015). Sociologist Ruth Milkman, who has documented the class inequalities among women that have "expanded to an historically unprecedented degree" (Milkman 2016, 292), finds that occupational sex segregation has been reduced more for college-educated women in professional and managerial jobs than for women in blue-collar and service jobs. If anything, class inequality has grown even larger because more affluent women tend to marry or partner with high earners and they are more likely to have stable unions.

In an analysis of the hundred largest cities in the United States, Milkman et al. (2016) conclude that income inequality is a significant predictor of the increase in the proportion of women employed in paid domestic labor. As real wages decline for much of the population, it becomes easier for affluent households to hire domestic services. At the same time, men working in jobs like construction face

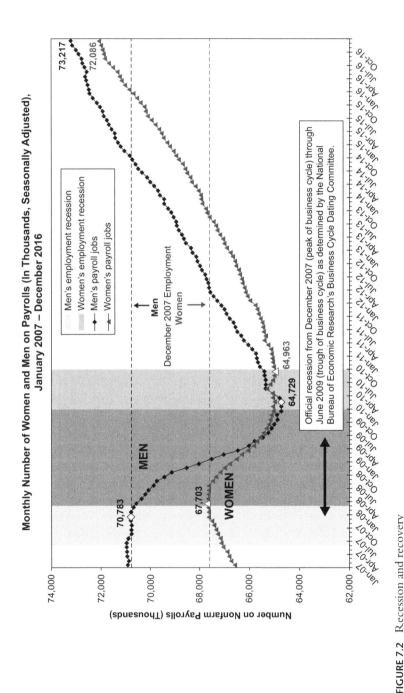

FIGURE 7.2 Recession and recovery

Source: IWPR analysis of U.S. Department of Labor, Bureau of Labor Statistics, Current Employment Statistics (January 6, 2017). Institute for Women's Policy Research, "Quick Figures," Washington, DC (January 2017).

stagnant wages, unemployment, and disdain from the affluent. Sean McGarvey (2015), president of North America's Building Trades Unions, recently decried the lawmakers and media elites who denigrate so-called "dirty jobs" and have little knowledge of, or appreciation for, the highly technical work required of workers in craft unions. Society at large has little collective understanding of why women or men would want to do this sort of "dirty manual work."

Two case studies

As the economy continues its slow recovery and income inequality continues to grow, domestic work and skilled trades provide two case studies to describe and analyze how female workers are challenging the continued segregation of women into low-wage jobs. Women in low-paid domestic work are organizing around the world, and women in high-paying construction jobs are looking for ways to increase their numbers. Table 7.1 compares available 2012 data regarding the numbers and earnings of in-home domestic workers and skilled trades workers.

There are almost two million people performing domestic work in homes. Some provide childcare in their own homes, while maids, housekeepers, and nannies offer services in their employers' homes. Those providing direct care for the elderly, convalescent, and disabled may be hired independently, but the majority work through agencies whose employees provide clients with assistance with daily living activities, offering services ranging from making beds and washing dishes to giving medications and monitoring health status. The majority

TABLE 7.1 Domestic work and skilled trades in the United States, 2012

Occupation	Total Number of Workers	Percent of Women	Worker Median Weekly Earnings**
Domestic/In-Home*	1,992,000	93.1%	$382
Maids, House Cleaners	328,000	96.8%	$337
Childcare Nannies	201,000	96.9%	$371
Childcare in Own Home	367,000	98.7%	$296
Direct Care, Not Agency	115,000	86.2%	$421
Direct Care, Agency	981,000	89.6%	$388
Construction*	5,102,000	1.9%	$740
Electricians	574,000	1.9%	$932
Sheet Metal Workers	103,000	2.9%	$885
Construction Laborers	937,000	2.6%	$607
Carpenters	750,000	0.9%	$675

* Based on data in Shierholz (2013), Tables 1, 5, 6, and 8.
** Based on data in Shierholz (2013, 10).
*** Based on data from U.S. Department of Labor, Bureau of Labor Statistics (2013), Table 39, Construction and Extraction.

of these domestic workers are women, and the jobs are low-paying, with median weekly earnings ranging from $296 to $421 (Table 7.1). Their numbers are also growing. Home healthcare, for example, is one of today's fastest growing industries. According to the *Occupational Outlook Handbook* (U.S. Department of Labor, Bureau of Labor Statistics 2016), the number of home health aides will increase by 38 percent, to 1.2 million, by 2024.

The data regarding the skilled trades for that same period offer several important contrasts. As seen in Table 7.1, the median weekly earnings for full-time wage and salary workers were considerably higher than for domestic workers and ranged from $607 to $932. Both men and women felt the severe effects of the recession in the construction industry. Employment in such trades as electricians, sheet metal workers, carpenters, and laborers declined by 25 percent between 2006 and 2013 (Hegewisch and O'Farrell 2015). Employment fell from over seven million workers to less than six million. For women in the industry, however, this loss was 37 percent, and the percentage of women in the skilled trades declined from 3.0 percent to 2.5 percent. The proportion of women ranged from less than 1 percent of brick masons and roofers to 5.7 percent of construction painters. Construction and extraction occupations, however, are predicted to grow 10 percent by 2024, faster than the average of all occupations, but this will only bring the total number of jobs in this sector to the pre-recession level (U.S. Department of Labor, Bureau of Labor Statistics 2016).

Domestic workers

Myrtle Witbooi, chair of the International Domestic Workers Network and secretary-treasurer of the South African Domestic Service and Allied Workers Union (SADSAWU), told a powerful story when she received the AFL-CIO's human rights award at the federation's quadrennial convention in 2013. Describing herself as a worker, she told the union delegates that when an employer said, "Oh, you know Myrtle, she is part of the family," she retorted, "I am not part of your family. I will never be part of your family. If I am part of your family you need to let me sit at your table and you get up and you wipe the dishes." She then challenged the delegates, asking if they were able to attend the convention because they were paying a woman at home to take care of their family. If yes, were they providing those workers, not family members, with good wages, working conditions, and benefits.

Witbooi told her story to AFL-CIO delegates who were reaching out beyond the declining union base in the United States to work with alternative labor organizations as well as women's rights, civil rights, and environmental groups. They were also reaching out internationally. While labor organizations have long talked about globalization and the importance of international organizations, there is evidence of that more such action has begun both by unions, such as the Steelworkers' partnership with Los Mineros in Mexico, and the AFL-CIO using the human rights framework and ILO structures employed to protect workers in the United States (Gross and Compa 2009). By honoring Witbooi with their human rights award, they were highlighting those workers who were organizing in less conventional ways internationally as well as domestically and seeking legal means to gain their rights.

The International Labor Office estimates that at least 53 million workers worldwide and approximately 11.5 million children under the age of eighteen work as domestics (Varia 2016). They work in their home countries and cross borders around the globe. The call to treat those who provide care services for the most vulnerable with dignity and respect has a long history. When domestic workers were excluded from a convention providing six days of paid leave for workers in many industries during an ILO conference in 1936, one delegate protested that domestic workers "are wage-earners, and therefore entitled to protection in the same way as other wage-earners" (ILO 2013).

In the United States during the 1930s, Eleanor Roosevelt called for domestic workers, especially women who worked in other people's homes, to form unions and demand decent pay and fair treatment (O'Farrell 2010, 91). When southern conservatives accused her of encouraging black women in the South to form "Eleanor Clubs" and to defy their employers by refusing to follow the rules they had established for "the help," the First Lady asked J. Edgar Hoover, director of the FBI, to investigate the allegation. No such clubs or movements existed, but she told women that instead of joining clubs, they "should join unions." She also argued that they should be covered by labor standards legislation. Under Roosevelt's leadership, the President's Commission on the Status of Women (1963) also called for including domestic workers under the labor standards legislation and encouraged unionization, as well as for public and private agencies to develop specialties, training, placement, and monitoring of household skills to meet modern labor standards.

Rooted in the need to secure southern Democratic votes, however, both the National Labor Relations Act (1935) and the Fair Labor Standard Act (1938) excluded domestic workers, thus leaving many African American women unprotected. The effects of these exclusions are still felt today. While domestic workers take pride and satisfaction in their work, they continue to be excluded from many employment laws and standards and are prohibited from forming unions to bargain collectively for improved wages and working conditions. Their low pay and their poor and often dangerous working conditions have been documented (Burnham and Theodore 2012; Varia 2016). Many women and girls who work or live full-time in their employers' homes face language barriers, isolation, and psychological, sexual, and physical abuse. Domestic workers struggle to gain the minimum wage, pay for overtime work, sick leave, vacation, and access to healthcare. Human Rights Watch documented the exploitation and abuse of domestic workers in many countries, including the United States (Varia and Becker 2012).

Until 2015, direct care workers for the elderly and disabled were categorized as "companions" and therefore exempt from minimum wage and overtime protections of the Fair Labor Standards Act. Home care workers who live in their employers' homes are not covered by overtime provisions. Those employed by an individual to perform housekeeping, cooking, and caring for children are not protected by the Occupational Health and Safety Act of 1970. Civil Rights Laws, such as Title VII of the 1964 Civil Rights Act, cover only employers with multiple employees, thus excluding any worker employed in a home with just one or two domestic employees. At the state level, domestic workers are excluded in almost half of the states with minimum wage and overtime laws and in almost all of the states with civil rights and labor laws (Mercado et al. 2013).

Who are these workers? While more likely to be foreign-born and have less education than the majority of workers, they constitute a diverse workforce doing different types of domestic work. In 2013, economist Heidi Shierholz reports, two-thirds of in-home domestic workers (66.9%) were U.S.-born, and almost half (47.6%) were white. Over half of all maids and housekeepers, however, were Hispanic (54.3%), while the largest concentration of black workers (27.6%) was found in agency-based direct care services. One in five domestic workers, or 20.9 percent, had not completed high school, compared to 8.3 percent of people who were not in-home workers. Over one-third, or 37.9 percent, of maids and housekeepers had not completed high school, while 30.3 percent of all in-home workers had some college and 11.6 percent had a bachelor's or advanced degree. One in five were immigrants who were not naturalized citizens, considerably higher than the 8.6 percent of workers in other occupations, and Shierholz estimates that 15 percent of in-home workers were unauthorized immigrants. While many in-home workers work part-time, others have or want full-time work.

According to this economic analysis, the median annual salaries for these in-home workers ranged from $9,000 for nannies to $13,689 for agency-based direct-caregivers. Most workers did not have benefits and, after controlling for demographic differences with other workers, the poverty rate was almost 12 percent higher for in-home workers than for similar workers in other occupations. Almost one in four lived below the poverty line. The *New York Times* reported that of nearly two million home care workers classified as companions, 92 percent were women, almost 30 percent were black, and 12 percent were Hispanic. Almost 40 percent received government benefits such as food stamps and Medicaid (Greenhouse 2013).

International progress

On the international front as we see in chapter 1, domestic workers around the world have made progress with a major effort to have the paid work that they do in the home, whether in their own homes or in the homes of others, acknowledged, respected, and protected. Through the International Labor Organization and Convention 189 Concerning Decent Work for Domestic Workers, 187 states that are members of the ILO now have standards by which to measure and improve the wages and working conditions of domestic workers in their own countries.

This international convention was agreed to by governments, corporations, and unions in the member states with the active involvement of community organizations in 2011. Workers were formally represented in the discussions by the International Trade Union Confederation, including the International Domestic Workers Network led by Myrtle Witbooi.

For the first time, global labor standards were established, including working hours, a minimum wage, overtime pay, rest periods, social security, and maternity leave. Protections have been established against child labor, violence, and abuse. The convention regulates recruitment agencies and fees and establishes monitoring and enforcement mechanisms. Now the convention must be ratified and the standards incorporated into the laws of individual counties and then enforced. The International Domestic Workers' Federation (IDWN) was founded as a global trade union in 2013, leading the way for national reforms in the ILO countries. According to Varia, under IDWN leadership, "National groups have employed creative strategies and tactics to challenge social attitudes, including viral videos, celebrity spokespersons, and alliances with employers" (2016, 225). Twenty-three countries have now ratified the convention–the United States has not.

In the United States, there is a long history of arguing for human rights internationally while accepting inequality at home (Thomas 2016). President Kennedy's 1963 Commission called for the United States to take a leadership role at the United Nations in developing and adopting international standards relating to women's employment, but the recommendation was not followed. Instead, the United States continued to question many international agreements, with conservative members of the Senate often arguing that such agreements would violate national sovereignty and give decision-making power over the United States to international bodies. In fact, the United States did not endorse the convention on the political and civil rights of the Universal Declaration of Human Rights until 1992 and has still not agreed to the convention on Social and Economic Rights. The Convention on the Elimination of All Forms of Discrimination Against Women (CEDAW) has been ratified by 189 countries, but not by the United States.

National initiatives

Despite the failure of the U.S. government to support many of these international initiatives, the documents provide a global framework within which advocates work for change. In the United States, a major effort has focused on the state level using a range of tactics to improve workers' lives through demonstrations, legislation, education, and training. Domestic Workers United (DWU 2017), for example, was founded in 2000 by several groups representing Caribbean, Latina, and African nannies, housekeepers, and elderly caregivers in New York City.

DWU organized to demand "power, respect, fair labor standards and to help build a movement to end exploitation and oppression for all." Under director Ai-Jen Poo, in 2007 they joined with other organizations to form the National Domestic Workers Alliance (NDWA 2017). NDWA works for "respect, recognition, and inclusion in labor protections for domestic workers" across the country. The national alliance has sixty affiliate organizations in addition to the first local chapter in Atlanta, with more than twenty thousand members in thirty-six cities and seventeen states. They have worked successfully at the state level.

In November 2010, New York State passed the first Domestic Workers Bill of Rights. Approximately 200,000 nannies, health aides, housecleaners, and cooks gained access to the New York State Department of Labor to file complaints and receive back pay awards, while employers were fined for violations of the law. Hawaii passed a similar bill in 2013, followed by the California Domestic Bill of Rights, signed by Governor Brown on September 12, 2013. While narrower than the New York law, under the California bill, an estimated two hundred thousand housekeepers, child-care workers, and caregivers would receive overtime pay for working more than nine hours a day or forty-five hours a week. Massachusetts, Oregon, Connecticut, and Illinois now have such laws. Enforcement is difficult, however, and a local community survey after the New York law was passed found that only 15 percent of employers were paying the legal overtime rate, and less than half were paying any overtime at all (Lerner 2012).

At the federal level, in 2013, the Department of Labor announced a new rule extending minimum wage and overtime protections to nearly two million home care workers. These are workers who care for the elderly and disabled and were previously classified as "companions," a category including babysitters. While some of these workers received the minimum wage, few received overtime pay. This change was to go into effect in January 2015 but was delayed by legal challenges from home care associations. The new rule was unanimously upheld by the U.S. Court of Appeals for the District of Columbia, on August 21, 2015, and went into effect in November (U.S. Department of Labor 2015).

The National Domestic Workers Alliance, the Restaurant Opportunities Center (ROC), the Fight for 15, and Organization United for Respect at Walmart (OUR Walmart) have become known as alternative or "alt-labor" groups (Eidelson 2013). They receive small amounts of financial support from member dues, but are much more dependent on foundation grants and, in some cases, direct support from unions. In 2011, the AFL-CIO signed a historic partnership agreement with the Domestic Workers Alliance and the National Guestworkers' Alliance (Parks 2011). According to Trumka, "We are signing these partnership agreements because we can't rely on the law alone if we want to fight for the inclusion of all workers." This was followed by a joint letter from the AFL-CIO and the Domestic Workers Alliance to trade unions and national centers around the world encouraging multiple strategies and collaboration in areas such as organizing and education at the local level, while issuing a call to action to support the ILO Convention on Decent Work for Domestic Workers. According to the federation, this was "a unique and critical opportunity for trade unions and domestic workers to build meaningful relationships that will hold up against the threats of corporate greed and a global weakening of workers' voices" (AFL-CIO 2011).

Home care workers have unionized and are building large coalitions and mobilizing politically, outside the traditional NLRB procedures. Over 100,000 home care workers—often considered invisible, working in homes rather than factories or offices, their situation complicated by government funding for caregiving and the consumer-client relationships—were organized by the late 1990s (Boris and Klein 2012). Today, twelve unions and non-profit organizations have formed the Caring Across Generations Campaign (2017), co-directed by Ai-Jen Poo, to change how the nation values caregiving services provided to everyone from infants to the elderly. They estimate that by 2025, one in five Americans will be over age sixty-five and many will need care. Domestic workers and the unions are crossing traditional lines to increase their strength. In 2015, for example, the California United Homecare Workers (CUHW) labor union announced that it was merging with the United Long Term Care Workers (ULTCW) of the Service Employees International Union (SEIU) and the United Domestic Workers (UDW) of AFSCME to better serve home care providers.

In 2017, the AFL-CIO held the second Global Women's Leadership Program, bringing fifty U.S. trade union women together with thousands of women from around the world at the United Nations (UN) Commission on the Status of Women meetings. The theme was economic empowerment in the changing world of work. Issues for domestic workers were placed in a global framework that analyzed macroeconomic policy and trade policy, global supply chains, the impact of technology, and the growth of informal work (Balakrishnan et al. 2016). Working with union women from around the world, these local leaders honed their understanding of global issues and their leadership skills as part of this increasing activism for working women, including domestic workers, within and outside the labor movement.

The future of domestic worker organizations is vulnerable because foundations could move on to other projects, dues seem unreliable, and union resources are declining. As suggested by Eidelson (2013), becoming sustainable or self-sufficient is a struggle, yet these organizations gained strength during the recession and built on that foundation. Important legislative victories were won after the recession ended and continue to grow. Women in some of the lowest-paying jobs and in the most vulnerable workplaces are taking action and successfully changing their workplaces, despite strong resistance from employers, conservative state legislatures, and new conservative national leaders. Despite resistance at home, they are part of a global movement.

Tradeswomen

As just discussed, domestic workers, mostly women, have been seeking legislation to help improve their wages and working conditions, forming broad-based coalitions with social justice and labor organizations, and joining existing unions, all within an international framework. Tradeswomen, on the other hand, have long been covered by labor legislation and anti-discrimination laws and have higher unionization rates than other workers, especially in the private sector. As shown in Table 7.1, these jobs pay well and do not require a college degree. Skills are learned on-the-job and in the classroom through apprenticeship training programs where people are paid while they are learning. Construction trades are also some of the most dangerous jobs, with high fatality rates, difficult hours, and seasonal unemployment. Skilled trades in the construction industry were among the hardest hit by the recession, and while a large number of openings in the trades are expected during the next decade, job totals are not predicted to reach their pre-recession levels until 2024 (U.S. Department of Labor BLS 2015).

Despite almost forty years of public policies designed to end gender discrimination, construction workers remain mostly men. Having lost ground during the recession, women in 2017 are back to representing just 3 percent of the trades, exactly where they were in 2006 and in 1963 (U.S. Department of Labor, BLS 2017a). A recent study showed that women hold only 2.2 percent of apprenticeships, the entryway into the building trades (National Women's Law Center 2014). Nationally, two-thirds of women working in construction occupations identify as white, 9 percent as black, 19 percent as Hispanic, and 6 percent as either multiracial, Asian, or American Indian (Hegewisch et al. 2013). Hispanic women and men are overrepresented in the construction workforce compared to their share of the workforce, while black and Asian women are underrepresented. White women's share of female construction jobs is equivalent to their share in the female workforce.

Government policies

The 1963 President's Commission on the Status of Women noted the lack of women in trades and the role of vocational education and job training in reinforcing this system, which limited women's options for access to good-paying skilled jobs. The commission, however, recommended relying on persuasion as a strategy for private employers to open these jobs and a presidential executive order prohibiting sex discrimination for those with government contracts, but an executive order separate from the one banning racial discrimination among government contractors.

Title VII of the 1964 Civil Rights Act radically changed this entire debate. Once discrimination based on sex was included in the law, complaints of sex discrimination were followed by court cases, consent decrees, and affirmative action programs involving employers, unions, and joint apprenticeship programs. In the first year of the Equal Employment Opportunity Commission's administration of the new law, 37 percent of the complaints were based on sex discrimination, far more than anticipated (Kessler-Harris 2001, 246). President

Lyndon Johnson soon added Executive Order 11375 prohibiting sex discrimination by federal contractors to be administered under the direction of what is now the Office of Federal Contract Compliance Programs (OFCCP) in the Department of Labor.

Affirmative action guidelines in construction, however, did not include sex discrimination. In 1976, tradeswomen and newly formed women's organizations, including Seattle Women in Trades and NOW Women's Legal Defense and Education Fund, filed a lawsuit. Advocates for Women v. Marshall, challenged the Department of Labor's failure to require affirmative action, including goals and timetables, for women in federally funded construction (Baker 2008, 68–72). The case led to a consent decree with the Department of Labor in 1978. President Jimmy Carter issued new regulations that set affirmative action standards for women in federal construction projects and goals and timetables (not quotas, which were illegal) for hiring women in the construction industry. The first goal was to bring women to 6.9 percent of the hours worked by 1981. A committee would then make recommendations for future goals and timetables. The guidelines called for workplaces free of sexual harassment, with two or more women assigned to each project where possible, appropriate toilet and changing facilities, and the hiring of women from racial minorities similar to their share of the population (Baker 2008).

Several months later, goals and timetables were established for apprenticeship programs (29 CFR-30). The goal was initially set at 20 to 25 percent of each new class, based on an analysis of the workforce, with detailed procedures for establishing equal opportunity on construction sites and in classrooms. The OFCCP and the Bureau of Apprenticeship and Training in the Labor Department, as well as independent state apprenticeship agencies, were responsible for the registered apprenticeship programs. A major effort for recruiting and training women for skilled trades and apprenticeships began. This effort slowed considerably in the 1980s under the Reagan Administration and never returned to earlier levels of support. Goals were not extended, enforcement budgets were cut, and momentum slowed. Although specific lawsuits resulted in new programs and measurable progress for some women, in 2017, women's portion of trade jobs remains at 3 percent and the modest goal of 6.9 percent women remains unachieved.

In the 1970s, vocational education and job training laws moved forward to address occupational segregation by sex. Studies have found, however, that in the twenty-first century, federally funded job training programs have reinforced rather than eliminated gender differences in occupations (Hegewisch and Luvri, 2010).

On a much smaller scale, Congress addressed women directly. In 1992, Congress passed the Women in Apprenticeship and Nontraditional Occupations Act (WANTO). The Department of Labor defines as nontraditional those occupations in which fewer than 25 percent of the jobs are held by women. The Women's Bureau and the Office of Apprenticeship have awarded approximately a million dollars a year in competitive grants to community-based organizations to provide technical assistance for employers and unions to recruit, train, and retain women in nontraditional occupations and to assist women in pre-apprenticeship programs. In 2014, three two-year grants totaling $1.9 million were awarded to provide technical assistance on a regional basis to recruit, train, and retain women in high-skill occupations in advanced manufacturing, transportation, energy, construction, information technology, and other industries (U.S. Department of Labor, ETA 2014). The program continues today.

One evaluation of the WANTO program found that it had largely positive results despite its limited funding. Serving as a catalyst, it began to open doors for women (WESTAT 2003). Mastracci (2004) found that women were 5 to 15 percent more likely to be employed in a nontraditional job if they lived in an area with a WANTO program. WANTO, according to the study, provided the greatest promise "for actually altering the patterns of occupational segregation by gender." During the recession, however, one study found no relationship between the presence of a tradeswomen's organization and programs such as WANTO and the percentage of women working in the trades, citing cultural as well as organizational barriers (Wagner 2014). Author and tradeswoman Susan Eisenberg (1998) used tradeswomen's voices to document the successes in the 1970s, the opposition after 1980, and the failure to enforce the policies. Building on this work others have concluded that government support was critical for increasing the number of tradeswomen and that the lack of support starting in the Reagan Administration was a major problem (MacLean 2006).

Although the percentage of women in the trades remains small, it still represents many women. In 2006, before the collapse of the construction industry, there were approximately equal numbers of women working as physicians (278,000), construction workers (292,000), and lawyers (314,000). The percentage of women in construction jobs has been stuck at less than 5 percent since the 1960s, while the percentage of female doctors grew from one in six to one in three and the percentage of female lawyers from fewer than 5 percent to over 30 percent of the profession during the same period (Hegewish and O'Farrell 2015), thus contributing to the class inequality among women identified by Milkman (2016).

Successes and challenges

The thousands of women who have entered the construction field have consistently shown that they enjoy the work and are capable of performing highly skilled jobs, but barriers remain. Molly Martin reported both "struggle and success" among the tradeswomen she interviewed in *Hard Hatted Women* (1988). An in-depth look at tradeswomen in New York City was provided by Jane LaTour (2008) and in one large electrical union local by Francine Moccio (2009). Susan Eisenberg (1998) provided historical and policy analysis using the voices of tradeswomen from across the country. In all these works, tradeswomen tell stories of accomplishment, of taking pride in their work, and of the people who helped them, including male coworkers. The hostility women have faced in the industry was also clearly documented in these books, which draw on individual interviews, multiple court cases, thousands of formal complaints, and public hearings. Despite facing fines and court ordered programs, contractors and apprenticeship programs have refused to hire women. Tradeswomen repeatedly described working in isolation and repeated incidents of intimidation and harassment on the job, sometimes life-threatening, by managers, supervisors, and coworkers. Inadequate training, biased evaluations, unsafe assignments, sexual assault, and rape have all been documented. Resistance from male coworkers has also been linked to economic conditions and jobs being deskilled, devalued, or eliminated (O'Farrell 1999).

Starting with the lawsuit against the Department of Labor in 1976, women's advocacy organizations such as Equal Rights Advocates in San Francisco and the National Women's Law Center in Washington, D.C., have provided legal guidance and support. Others groups, such as Chicago Women in Trades and Nontraditional Training for Women (NEW) in New York City, which have often been started by tradeswomen, have provided training and outreach programs for women and technical assistance for employers and unions to recruit and retain women. In the 1970s tradeswomen formed their own support groups like Tradeswomen, Inc in San Francisco, and they have been joined more recently, by tradeswomen in new organizations, such as MN Tradeswomen in Minnesota, primarily to provide support for tradeswomen across unions and to influence local and state policies wherever possible. Others have disbanded including Wider Opportunities for Women in Washington, DC, after celebrating its fiftieth anniversary. Over the years, these groups have received varying degrees of support from the Women's Bureau at the U.S. Department of Labor, other federal and state agencies, foundations, and labor unions.

In a recent survey of over 200 tradeswomen, mostly union members, the picture regarding women in the trades was mixed, reflecting both progress and barriers (Hegewisch and O'Farrell 2015). A large majority of these women (79%) were the main wage earners in their households. At least 50 percent had worked for at least thirty-seven weeks, in the previous year and of those with income from the trades, 40 percent made more than $50,000 that year, and 16 percent more than $75,000. More than one in five, however, were unemployed, and 28 percent earned $25,000 or less during the year. Only three respondents said they learned about their jobs through a high school counselor or the American Job Center.

Almost half of the respondents reported always being treated equally regarding such factors as access to tools, hours of work, and job assignments. The majority of the women said they had experienced some sexual harassment, and almost one in three said that they always or frequently experienced sexual harassment. One in four reported that there was never another woman with them on the job. While younger women felt that they were more likely to be treated equally with men than did older women, there was no age difference regarding sexual harassment. Most women said they had dealt with harassment on their own or had received help in doing so from male colleagues, yet only one in ten had taken claims to the U.S. Equal Employment Opportunity Commission. The majority felt their claims took too long and were not satisfactorily resolved. Examples of discrimination ranged from being the last to get work and first to be laid off to being hit with a crane, intimidated in isolated areas, and inappropriately touched. One woman reported fearing for her life on the job.

Lack of funding and enforcement of government regulations continues. Over the last twenty years, the Equal Employment Opportunity Commission saw a 38 percent increase in claims of discrimination, but between 2000 and 2008, funding and staff were cut by 30 percent (Frederickson 2015). Funding increased moderately during the Obama administration. The EEOC recently initiated a case against a construction company for firing female sheet metal workers. According to the regional director, "They don't seem to think the laws apply to them." At a New York summit on women in construction, Pat Shiu, director of the OFCCP, recommitted her agency to ending discrimination and in fact hired more investigators, improved training for compliance officers, increased the number of construction reviews per year, and worked on updating regulations.

Yet in the 2014 presidential budget, OFCCP reported that it had completed "385 construction evaluations resulting in almost $1.1 million in back pay to almost 2,000 victims of discrimination, and created 68 job opportunities." That averages out to sixty-eight jobs and about $550 per victim—men and women. While the Department of Labor issued new Equal Employment Opportunity regulations for registered apprenticeship, the 1978 affirmative action regulations for federal contractors have not been updated.

Union tradeswomen, however, are gaining visibility and strength. While there have been local and national conferences since the 1970s, in 2013, the same year that Myrtle Witbooi was at the AFL-CIO Convention, Walter Wise, president of the Iron Workers Union, encouraged over 800 tradeswomen in their work and promised the backing of the union to the 120 female ironworkers in the audience, women who build and maintain bridges and high-rise buildings, from the Golden Gate Bridge in San Francisco to the new Freedom Tower in New York City. On January 20, 2015, LeDaya Epps, an apprentice laborer and member of LiUNA Local 300 in California, was asked to join First Lady Michelle Obama at the U.S. Capitol to listen to the president's State of the Union Address.

In May of 2015, over 1,000 tradeswomen, from the Bricklayers and Tile Fitters union to the United Auto Workers, from Alaska to West Virginia, gathered in Los Angeles for the annual Women Build Nations Conference (Chaplan 2015). Eighteen unions were represented, the largest number, 175, coming from the electricians, followed by 119 ironworkers and 104 laborers. Magan Smith, from Bricklayers Local 8, gave the national keynote The following year, fifteen hundred women attended the Women Build Nations conference in Chicago, and even more are expected at the 2017 conference.

The majority of tradeswomen at the conferences were union members. Overall, union membership in the trades has declined, but with membership hovering around 20 percent, it is still considerably higher than the 6 percent in the private sector nationally. Union membership in the trades has also increased since the low point of the recession. According to North America's Building Trades Unions (2017), if residential construction was excluded, union membership among the commercial, heavy, and industrial sectors was close to 45 percent, an increase of 5 percent in the last several years. While all unions are under attack from employers in the private sector and conservative politicians in the public sector, the building trades see potential for growth in the future for both women and men.

Clearly, thousands of tradeswomen are now earning good wages doing skilled work. Women work as apprenticeship directors, head a city building trades council, and Theresa King, IBEW Local 915, was the first woman elected president of the Florida Building and Construction Trades Council. Some women are beginning to retire after full careers in the trades. Tradeswomen's issues, actions, and stories are posted on the web page tradeswomentaskforce.org, and there are related Facebook and web pages in the United States and Canada. Having a construction laborer apprentice appear with the first lady at the State of the Union address in 2015 marked a new visibility.

Since the end of the 2007–2009 recession, there have been ongoing changes in government. The Women's Bureau at the U.S. Department of Labor (2017) renewed its focus on increasing the number of women in traditionally male blue-collar jobs, including tradeswomen, by updating and making resources available on its web page, "Women Build, Protect, and Move America" and by awarding WANTO grants in coordination with the Office of Apprenticeship. As part of a $20.4 million initiative to expand apprenticeship opportunities nationwide, the Department of Labor funded a consortium of tradeswomen organizations across the country to "scale and promote adoption of strategies that increase access to and retention in apprenticeships among women, especially women of color (Chicago Women in Trades 2016)." Co-directed by Chicago Women in Trades and Oregon Tradeswomen Inc., they are working with the International Union of Bricklayers and Allied Craftworkers, the International Ironworkers Union, the International Union of Painters and Allied Trades, and the Sheet Metal and Air Condition Industry.

Other craft union initiatives include work by the North America's Building Trades Unions (NABTU) with its affiliates to offer a Multi-Craft Core Curriculum as part of a pre-apprenticeship program to help recruit women and people of color. On January 26, 2017, the Department of Labor met with the NABTU and advocacy organizations for a Construction Industry Diversity Summit to discuss finding solutions for the projected skilled workforce shortages while opening up full careers to women and people of color who have been underrepresented. Following this summit, the Ironworkers (2017) became the first construction union to join with contractors and announce a paid maternity leave policy offering up to six months of pay pre-delivery and six to eight weeks of pay post-delivery.

Contributing to this effort, the NABTU Tradeswomen Committee and Jobs With Justice released a new report detailing two case studies of large construction projects (University of Massachusetts in Boston and Viking Stadium in Minnesota) that exceeded their goals for hiring and training women and people of color and offering strategies for other employers, unions, and community groups (Johansson and Woods 2016). The Women Build Nations Conference will again be held in Chicago on October 13–17, 2017.

The Trump administration, however, has clearly shifted the focus of the federal government to less regulation of private employers and has reduced programs at the Department of Labor and other employment-related agencies. While the apprenticeship and WANTO programs continue this year, the proposed 2018 fiscal year budget, for example, will cut OFCCP funds by 16 percent and merge the program with the EEOC, reducing the number of employees by over a hundred positions. The WANTO grants program will be eliminated entirely (U.S. Office of Management and Budget 2017).

Moving forward

Domestic workers and tradeswomen face new challenges with the Republican Congress and the Trump administration, both of which are opposed to government regulation of private industry, labor laws, and labor unions. Both groups of women face this challenge in occupations that are growing in the aftermath of the recession. Two major lessons can be drawn from this review of occupational sex segregation among the large percentage of women in low-wage domestic work and the small percentage of women in high-wage construction trades. First, it shows that legislation and enforcement provide a critical framework for achieving gender equity in the global economy, but, second, that legal strategies are not enough and legislation must be part of a broader coalition of women and men working together to improve wages, working conditions, and respect for workers in an increasingly unequal world.

First is the importance of legislation. This means not only having laws but also enforcing existing laws and enforcing new laws being passed at the state and federal levels. Domestic workers are increasingly included under existing laws at the federal level, and a number of states have or are considering new legislation to help ensure equal rights, fair wages, and safe working conditions for home-based workers. The recent international ILO Convention 189 established these standards across countries through the International Labor Organization and provided an important framework for advocacy at the national and state levels.

Tradeswomen, on the other hand, have had strong laws for over thirty-five years to open the skilled jobs to women, but these regulations have never been adequately enforced, a situation that will worsen under deregulation policies.

There is also evidence that technical assistance programs for women, employers, and unions can make a positive difference in recruiting and retaining women in the trades. Enforcement and technical assistance will also be necessary in order for the domestic workers' bill of rights to become reality.

The labor movement is also reaching out to unorganized workers through the newly emerging alt-labor organizations such as the National Domestic Workers Alliance and the International Domestic Workers Network. The construction trades are beginning to see more women in their unions, some in leadership positions, and some unions are working with tradeswomen organizations to recruit women into the trades and highlight strategies that increase the recruitment and retention of tradeswomen as apprentices and journey-level skilled workers including negotiating policies such as paid maternity leave in their contracts. Women continue working together to improve their jobs and to gain access to the positions they traditionally have been denied. Changes are happening at the state and local level. Yet to achieve change on a larger scale, labor laws need to be strengthened and enforced along with employment and civil rights laws. Employers, unions, contractors, and government agencies must be held accountable. Working women, their advocacy organizations, and their unions are important parts of this process.

The second conclusion we can draw from this analysis is that legislation and legal strategies address only part of the larger cultural barriers. Domestic work and the skilled trades are part of a larger world and highlight the class conflicts that remain in the U.S. workforce. A lack of respect for manual and caring labor and a denigration of those who do this work are common in today's society and consciously and unconsciously encouraged by elites in positions of power in employment, policy, and education (Bronson 2015). Women in management and professional jobs depend on domestic workers, often immigrants and women of color, to be able to go out to work each day. Are professional women willing and able to pay fair wages and overtime and to offer breaks during the day, Social Security and unemployment benefits, and days off with pay, or are they part of the problem? As historian Dorothy Sue Cobble (2004, 227) concludes, if class is not incorporated into this analysis, "the problems of one group of women end up being solved at the expense of another."

Gender and class stereotypes die hard, and most Americans imagine men rather than women in construction jobs when they think about these positions at all. Schools and education programs do little to reduce these stereotypes. Many women and young girls are unaware that these jobs are options for them. In a time of stagnant wages, declining unionization, recent recession, technological changes, and growing inequality, many men are afraid they will lose their jobs, which increases their hostility to newcomers. The emerging global economy has added to the insecurity felt by those who work with their hands. Policies must enable women and men of all colors to access and succeed in jobs that are vital to the infrastructure of our daily lives.

The number of women domestic workers is growing around the world. Jobs in this sector are projected to increase in the United States, and many will be filled by first- or second-generation immigrant workers. Most Americans expect that women will do this work. While low-paid workers in employers' homes are particularly vulnerable to abuse, female domestic workers are organizing to improve their wages and working conditions and demanding respect and dignity through new coalitions, international conventions, and country-specific legislation. Tradeswomen who have entered the world of traditionally male construction work have overcome many challenges and enjoyed successes. While structural and cultural constraints remain, their numbers are growing after the recession, and they are gaining visibility and leadership roles with increasing support from their unions.

At the White House Summit on Worker Voice in 2015, then-President Barack Obama cautioned, "You can't just keep on doing the same things thinking you're going to get a different outcome." He challenged the gathering to develop innovative new strategies and models for making a difference that included unions as well as alternative organizing efforts and organizations. Since the recession new strategies and models are being tried. Magan Smith and Terry O'Sullivan reflect change on the national front in the building trades. Myrtle Witbooi and Richard Trumka reflect international progress being made by domestic workers. We know that progress is slow towards improving conditions for domestic workers and opening trades jobs to women. Much work remains to be done. In her last book, *Tomorrow is Now*, Eleanor Roosevelt (1963, 2012) challenged us all to "think and plan on a broader scale than ever before, on a scale that goes beyond our own borders, a scale that encompasses the world." As this analysis has shown, under the new administration and in this time of globalization, this type of thinking and planning is more important than ever.

Note

1 I would like to thank Mary Frederickson, Susan Eisenberg, and Ariane Hegewisch for comments on earlier drafts of this chapter. All errors of fact and interpretation are, of course, mine.

References

American Express OPEN. 2016. *The 2016 State of Women-Owned Businesses Report*. Last accessed August 21, 2017 at htpp://www.womenable.com/content/userfiles/2016_State_of_Women-Owned_Businesses_Executive_Report.pdf.

AFL-CIO. 2011. "Open Letter from the AFL-CIO and National Domestic Workers Alliance (USA) to Trade Unions and National Centers Around the World." Last accessed August 21, 2017 at: http://www.idwfed.org/en/updates/usa-afl-cio-partners-with-domestic-workers-alliance-call-for-domestic-worker-representatives-at-ilc/ndwa-aflcio-open-letter.pdf.

Anderson, Julie, Ariane Hegewisch, and Jeff Hayes. 2015. *The Union Advantage for Women*. Washington, DC: Institute for Women's Policy Research. Last accessed August 31, 2017 at https://iwpr.org/publications/the-union-advantage-for-women/.

Baker, Carrie N. 2008. *The Women's Movement Against Sexual Harassment*. Cambridge: Cambridge University Press.
Balakrishnan, Radhika, Lisa McGowan and Cassandra Waters. 2016. *Transforming Women's Work: Policies For An Inclusive Economic Agenda*. Rutgers University, AFL-CIO, Solidarity Center. Last accessed August 21, 2017 at htpp://www.cwgl.rutgers.edu/docman/economic-and-social-rights-publications/784-transforming-women-work-policies-for-an-inclusive-economic-agenda/file.
Boris, Eileen and Jennifer Klein. 2012. *Caring for America: Home Health Workers in the Shadow of the Welfare State*. New York: Oxford University Press.
Bronfenbrenner, Kate. 2009. *No Holds Barred: The Intensification of Employer Opposition to Organizing*. Washington, DC: Economic Policy Institute.
Bronson, Brittany. 2015. "Do We Value Low-Skilled Work?" *New York Times*, October 1. Last accessed August 21, 2017 at http://www.nytimes.com/2015/10/01/opinion/do-we-value-low-skilled-work.html?_r=0.
Burnham, Linda, and Nik Theodore. 2012. *Home Economics: The Invisible and Unregulated World of Domestic Work*. New York: National Domestic Workers Alliance. Last accessed August 21, 2017 at https://www.2016.domesticworkers.org/homeeconomics/.
Caring Across Generations. 2017. Accessed August 22, 2017 at http://www.caringacross.org.
Carvevale, Anthony P., and Nicole Smith. 2014. *Women, Jobs and Opportunity in the 21st Century*. Washington, DC: Women's Bureau, U.S. Department of Labor. Last accessed August 22, 2017 at http://www.dol.gov/asp/evaluation/reports/WBPaperSeries.pdf.
Chaplan, Debra. 2015. "Conference Rundown." State Building and Construction Trades Council of California. Last accessed August 22, 2017 at http://www.sbctc.org/docuser files/files/2015%20conference%20follow-up%20.pdf.
Chicago Women in Trades. 2016. "New Gender Equity in Apprenticeship Initiative to Increase Women's Participation." Last accessed August 21, 2017 at https://www.eldia newschicago.com/single-post/2016/11/18/New-Gender-Equity-in-Apprenticeship-Initiative-to-Increase-Women%E2%80%99s-Participation.
Cobble, Dorothy Sue. 2004. *The Other Women's Movement: Workplace Justice and Social Rights in Modern America*. Princeton: Princeton University Press.
Collins, Gail. 2009. *When Everything Changed: The Amazing Journey of American Women from 1960 to the Present*. New York: Back Bay Books, Little, Brown and Company.
Davis, Alyssa and Elise Gould. 2015. *Closing the Pay Gap and Beyond: A Comprehensive Strategy for Improving Economic Security for Women and Families*. Washington, DC: Economic Policy Institute. Last accessed August 22, 2017 at http://www.epi.org/publication/closing-the-pay-gap-and-beyond/.
Domestic Workers United. 2017.Last accessed August 22, 2017 at http://www.domestic workersunited.org/index.php/en/
Eidelson, Josh. 2013. "Alt-Labor." *American Prospect*, January. Last accessed August 22, 2017 at http://prospect.org/article/alt-labor.
Eisenberg, Susan 1998. *We'll Call You If We Need You: Experiences of Women Working Construction*. New York: Cornell University Press.
Frederickson, Caroline. 2015. *Under the Bus: How Working Women Are Being Run Over*. New York: The New Press.
Greenhouse, Steven. 2013. "U.S. to Include Home Care Aides in Wage and Overtime Law." *New York Times*, September 17.
Gross, James, and Lance Compa, Eds. 2009. *Human Rights in Labor and Employment Relations: International and Domestic Perspectives*. Champaign, IL: Labor and Employment Relations Association Series.

Hegewisch, Ariane and Helen Luvri. 2010. *The Workforce Investment Act and Women's Progress: Does WIA Funded Training Reinforce Sex Segregation in the Labor Market and the Gender Wage Gap?* Washington, DC: Institute for Women's Policy Research: https://iwpr.org/wp-content/uploads/wpallimport/files/iwpr-export/publications/C372.pdf

Hegewisch, Ariane and Heidi Hartmann. 2014. *Occupational Segregation and the Gender Wage Gap: A Job Half Done.* Washington, DC: Women's Bureau, U.S. Department of Labor. Last accessed August 22, 2017 at https://www.dol.gov/wb/resources/american_women_paper_series.pdf.

Hegewisch, Ariane, Jeffrey Hayes, Tonia Bui and Anlan Zhang. 2013. *Quality Employment for Women in the Green Economy: Industry, Occupation, and Sate-by-State Estimates.* IWPR Publication #C402. Washington, DC: Institute for Women's Policy Research. Last accessed August 31, 2017 at https://iwpr.org/publications/quality-employment-for-women-in-the-green-economy-industry-occupation-and-state-by-state-job-estimates/.

Hegewisch, Ariane and Brigid O'Farrell. 2015. *Women in the Construction Trades: Earnings, Workplace Discrimination, and the Promise of Green Jobs.* Washington, DC: Institute for Women's Policy Research. Last accessed August 22, 2017 at https://iwpr.org/publications/women-in-the-construction-trades-earnings-workplace-discrimination-and-the-promise-of-green-jobs/.

Hess, Cynthia, Jessica Milli, Ariane Hegewisch, Stephanie Roman, Julie Anderson, Justing Augeri. 2015. *The Status of Women in the States: 2015.* Washington, DC: Institute for Women's Policy Research. Last accessed August 22, 2017 at https://iwpr.org/publications/the-status-of-women-in-the-states-2015-full-report/.

Hill, Catherine, and Erin Prangley. 2014. *Policy, Education and Social Change: Fifty Years of Progress.* Washington, DC: Women's Bureau, U.S. Department of Labor. Last accessed August 22, 2017 at https://www.dol.gov/wb/resources/american_women_paper_series.pdf.

Huwart, J. Y. and L. Verdier. 2013. *Economic Globalisation: Origins and Consequences.* OECD Insights, OECD Publishing. Last accessed August 22, 2017 at http://dx.doi.org/10.1787/9789264111899-en.

Institute for Women's Policy Research. 2017. *Quick Figures, Job Growth Among Men Improves.* Washington, DC: Institute for Women's Policy Research.

International Labor Organization. 2013. *Domestic Workers Across the World: Global and Regional Statistics and the Extent of Legal Protection.* Geneva. Last accessed August 22, 2017 at http://www.ilo.org/wcmsp5/groups/public/—dgreports/—dcomm/—publ/documents/publication/wcms_173363.pdf.

Ironworkers. 2017. "Iron Workers and Contractors Announce Paid Maternity Leave Benefits." Last accessed August 22, 2017 at http://www.ironworkers.org/news-magazine/news/2017/04/24/iron-workers-and-contractors-announce-paid-maternity-leave-benefit.

Johansson, Erin and Benjamin Woods. 2016. *Building Career Opportunities for Women and People of Color: Breakthroughs in Construction.* Washington, DC: Jobs With Justice Education Fund and North America's Building Trades Unions Tradeswomen Committee. Last accessed August 22, 2017 at http://www.jwj.org/building-career-opportunities-for-women-and-people-of-color-breakthroughs-in-construction.

Jones, Janelle, John Schmitt, and Nicole Woo. 2014. *Women, Working Families, and Unions.* Washington, DC: Center for Economic and Policy Research. Last accessed August 31, 2017 at http://cepr.net/documents/women-union-2014-06.pdf.

Kessler-Harris, Alice. 2001. *In Pursuit of Equity: Women, Men, and the Quest for Economic Citizenship in 20th Century America.* Oxford: Oxford University Press.

LaTour, Jane. 2008. *Sisters in the Brotherhoods: Working Women Organizing for Equality in New York City*. New York: Palgrave MacMillan.
Lazonick, William, and the Academic-Industry Research Network. 2015. "Labor in the 21st Century: The Top 0.1% and the Disappearing Middle Class." In *Inequality, Uncertainty, and Opportunity: The Varied and Growing Role of Finance in Labor Relations*, Christian E. Weller (Ed.). Chicago: Labor and Employment Relations Association.
Lerner, Sharon. 2012. "Domestic Workers' Rights." *The Nation*, June 12. Last accessed August 22, 2017 at http://www.thenation.com/article/168353/uphill-battle-enforce-domestic-workers-right.
MacLean, Nancy. 2006. *Freedom Is Not Enough: The Opening of the American Workplace*. Cambridge: Harvard University Press and New York: Russell Sage Foundation.
Martin, Molly, Ed. 1988. *Hard Hatted Women: Life on the Job*. Seattle: The Seal Press.
Mastracci, Sharon. 2004. *Breaking Out of the Pink-Collar Ghetto: Policy Solutions for Non-College Women*. Armonk: M.E. Sharpe Inc.
Matz, Lisa and Anne Hedgepeth. 2014. *Women and Work: 50 Years of Change Since the American Women Report*. Washington, DC: Women's Bureau, U.S. Department of Labor. Last accessed August 22 2017 at https://www.dol.gov/wb/resources/american_women_paper_series.pdf.
McGarvey, Sean. 2015. "Why the Disdain for American Blue-Collar Workers?" *Huffington Post*, July 7. Last accessed August 22, 2017 at http://www.huffingtonpost.com/sean-mcgarvey/why-the-disdain-for-ameri_b_7746642.html.
Mercado, Andrea Christa, Sarah Liberstein, and Haeyong Yoon. 2013. *Winning Dignity and Respect: A Guide to the Domestic Workers' Bill of Rights*. Washington, DC: National Employment Law Project, National Domestic Workers Alliance. Last accessed August 22, 2017 at https://ctpcsw.files.wordpress.com/2010/07/from-marla-shiller-winning-dignity-respect-9-27-13.pdf.
Milkman, Ruth. 2016. "Women's Work and Economic Crisis Revisited: Comparing the Great Recession and the Great Depression." In *On Gender, Labor, and Inequality*, R. Milkman (Ed.), 275–300. Urbana: University of Illinois Press.
Milkman, Ruth and E. Reese and B. Roth. 2016. "The Macrosociology of Paid Domestic Labor." In *On Gender, Labor, and Inequality*, R. Milkman (Ed.), 225–252. Urbana: University of Illinois Press.
Moccio, Francie A. 2009. *Live Wire, Women and Brotherhood in the Electrical Industry*. Philadelphia: Temple University Press.
National Domestic Workers Alliance. 2017. https://www.domesticworkers.org/home.
National Women's Law Center. 2014. *Women in Construction, Still Breaking Ground*. Washington, DC: Last accessed August 22, 2017 at https://nwlc.org/resources/women-construction-still-breaking-ground/.
North America's Building Trades Unions. 2017. "Union Construction Continues to Expand." February 7. Last accessed August 22, 2017 at http://gppma.bctd.org/News room/Union-Construction-Continues-to-Expand-And-That-s.aspx.
Obama, Barack. 2015. *President's Remarks at the White House Summit on Worker Voice*. Washington, DC. Last accessed August 31, 2017 at https://obamawhitehouse.archives.gov/the-press-office/2015/10/07/remarks-president-white-house-summit-worker-voice.
O'Farrell, Brigid. 1999. "Women in Blue Collar and Related Occupations at the End of the Millennium." *The Quarterly Review of Economics and Finance* 39: 699–722.
O'Farrell, Brigid. 2010. *She Was One of Us: Eleanor Roosevelt and the American Worker*. Ithaca, NY: Cornell University Press.

O'Farrell, Brigid. 2015. *American Women: Looking Back, Moving Ahead, 50th Anniversary of the President's Commission on the Status of Women Report*. Women's Bureau, U.S. Department of Labor. http://www.dol.gov/wb/PCSW-03-30-2015.pdf.

Parks, James. 2011. *AFL-CIO Partners with Domestic Workers Alliance, National Guestworkers' Alliance*. AFL-CIO Blog. Washington, DC: AFL-CIO.

Reskin, Barbara F. and Heidi I. Hartmann, Ed. 1986. *Women's Work, Men's Work, Sex Segregation on the Job*. Washington, DC: National Academy Press.

Roosevelt, Eleanor. June 15,1933. In *The White House Press Conferences of Eleanor Roosevelt*, Maurine Beasley (Ed.), p. 10. New York: Garland Publishing, Inc

Roosevelt, Eleanor. 1963, 2012. *Tomorrow Is Now*. New York: Penguin Classics.

Sandberg, Sheryl. 2013. *Lean In, Women, Work, and the Will to Lead*. New York: Alfred A. Knopf.

Shierholz, Heidi. 2013. *Low Wages and Scant Benefits Leave Many in-Home Workers Unable to Make Ends Meet*. Washington, DC: Economic Policy Institute. Last accessed August 22, 2017 at http://www.epi.org/publication/in–home-workers/.

Theroux, Paul. 2015. *Deep South*. Chicago: Houghton Mifflin Harcourt.

Thomas, Dorothy Q. 2016. "Human Rights and Women's Status in the USA." In *Women and Girls Rising*, Ellen Chesler and Terry McGovern (Eds.). New York: Routledge.

U.S. Department of Defense. 2013. "2012 Demographics Profile of the Military Community." Last accessed August 22, 2017 at http://www.militaryonesource.mil/12038/MOS/Reports/2012_Demographics_Report.pdf.

U.S. Department of Labor. 1995. *A Solid Investment: Making Full Use of the National's Human Capital, Recommendations of the Federal Glass Ceiling Commission*. Washington, DC. November. Last accessed August 22, 2017 at https://www.dol.gov/dol/aboutdol/history/reich/reports/ceiling2.pdf.

U.S. Department Labor, Bureau of Labor Statistics. 2013. "Labor Force Statistics from the Currnet Population Survey. Table 39. In "Median weekly earnings of full-time wage salary workers by detailed occupation and sex

U.S. Department of Labor, Bureau of Labor Statistics. 2016. *Occupational Outlook Handbook*. Last accessed August 31, 2017 at Home Health Aides: http://www.bls.gov/ooh/healthcare/home-health-aides.htm; Construction and Extraction Occupations: https://www.bls.gov/ooh/construction-and-extraction/home.htm).

U.S. Department of Labor, Bureau of Labor Statistics. 2017a. "Labor Force Statistics from the Current Population Survey. Table 11. Employed Persons by Detailed Occupation, Sex, Race, and Hispanic or Latino Ethnicity." Last accessed August 31, 2017 at http://www.gov/cps/cpsaat11.htm.

U.S. Department of Labor, Bureau of Labor Statistics. 2017b. "Labor Force Statistics from the Current Population Survey. Table 39. Median Weekly Earnings of Full-Time Wage and Salary Workers by Detailed Occupation and Sex, 2016." Last accessed August 31, 2017 at http://www.bls.gov/cps/cpsaat39.htm.

U.S. Department of Labor, Bureau of Labor Statistics. 2015. "Union Members Summary." Last accessed August 31 at http://www.bls.gov/news.release/union2.nr0.htm.

U.S. Department of Labor, Employment and Training Administration. 2014. "$1.9M in Grants to Support Women in Nontraditional Occupations Announced by U.S. Labor Department." Last accessed August 31, 2017 at http://www.dol.gov/opa/media/press/eta/ETA20141177.htm

U.S. Department of Labor, Women's Bureau. 2012. "Our History: An Overview, 1920-1912." Last accessed August 31, 2017 at http://www.dol.gov/wb/info_about_wb/interwb.htm.

U.S. Department of Labor, Women's Bureau. 2014. "A Paper Series Celebrating the 50th Anniversary of American Women: Report of the President's Commission on the Status of Women." Last accessed August 31, 2017 at https://www.dol.gov/wb/resources/american_women_paper_series.pdf

U.S. Department of Labor, Women's Bureau. 2015. "Data and Statistics." Last accessed August 31, 2017 at https://www.dol.gov/wb/stats/stats_data.htm.

U.S. Department of Labor, Women's Bureau. 2017. "Women Build, Protect, and Move America." Last accessed at August 16, 2018: https://www.dol.gov/wb/NTO/.

U.S. Office of Management and Budget. 2017. "Budget of the U.S. Government, A New Foundation for American Greatness Fiscal Year 2018." Last accessed August 31, 2017 at https://www.whitehouse.gov/sites/whitehouse.gov/files/omb/budget/fy2018/budget.pdf.

U.S. President's Commission on the Status of Women. 1963. *American Women, Report of the president's commission on the Status of Women*. Last accessed August 31, 2017 at www.dol.gov/wb/American%20Women%20Report.pdf.

Varia, Nisha. 2016. "Revaluing Caregiving, Recent Victories for Domestic Workers Rights." In *Women and Girls Rising, Progress and resistance around the world*, Ellen Chesler and Terry McGovern (Eds.). New York: Routledge.

Varia, Nisha and Jo Becker. 2012. *World Report 2012: A Landmark Victory for Domestic Workers*. Human Rights Watch. Last accessed August 31, 2017 at https://www.hrw.org/world-report/2012/country-chapters/global-0.

Wagner, Heidi. 2014. "Building Construction Tradeswomen Advocacy Organizations and the Number of Women Working in the Building Trades." *Housing and Society* 41: 1, 89–104.

Wang, Wendy, Kim Parker and Paul Taylor. 2013. Breadwinner Moms. Pew Research Center, Social and Demographic Trends. Last accessed August 31, 2017 at http://www.pewsocialtrends.org/2013/05/29/breadwinner-moms/

Westat. 2003. *Women in Apprenticeships and Nontraditional Occupations Grant Program: Final Report*. Report prepared for the U.S. Department of Labor Women's Bureau on Contract No. GS-23F-8144H.

PART II
Exploitation vs. opportunity

The exploitation vs. opportunity binary reflects the calculus of a globalized economy in which the corporate race to the bottom of the wage scale largely determines the location of industrial production and the sites of industrial expansion. The economic lives of women workers across the globe expose the results of this high stakes competition. The chapters in Part II of *Global Women's Work* explore how the financial crisis of 2007–2008, and the global economic recession that followed, shaped and changed the parameters of women's lives within this binary. In the face of worldwide economic volatility, new forms of exploitation developed, opportunities contracted, and in some cases prospects for work expanded. The broad range of national experiences examined in this section—from Russia to Mexico, Kenya, Egypt, the Gulf Cooperation Council Countries, and Iran—illustrates the multiple templates for women's work that exist simultaneously in different parts of the world.

While each population of women analyzed here experienced some effects from the global Great Recession, the impact varied from substantial (Kenya) to minimal (Iran). "When the U.S. sneezed," writes Kelly Pike, "Kenya caught a cold." The tight economic connection between Mexico and the United States meant that the effects of the recession "hit hard." On the other hand, women in Iran and the Gulf Council Countries, living in an economic world not bound by the rubrics of neoliberal economics, found themselves affected in unexpected ways, both economically and politically. The political repercussions in the nations of northern Africa and the Middle East were enormous, from the Green Protests in Iran, to the Arab Spring protests in Egypt. The hope and chaos of widespread uprisings throughout the Arab world coincided with and were in multiple ways fed by the global economic crisis. In Russia, as Carol Nechemias argues, the global economic crisis "engulfed and shocked" the country, produced a sharp downturn in GDP, an upswing in unemployment and poverty, and almost a decade of lower economic growth rates. In ways both large and small, the aftermath of the global economic recession has proved consequential for women's economic wellbeing in each of the national contexts examined here.

Scholars frequently convey the history of global women's work in narratives of exploitation: stories of the tragic deaths of over 1,000 young women workers in the factory collapse at Rana Plaza in Bangladesh; accounts of the migration of over 40 million Chinese women from rural areas to work in factories thousands of miles from their hometowns; chronicles of the long hours and low pay of homeworkers in India and domestic workers in Mexico. And while each of these narrations documents circumstances marked by unjust compensation, mistreatment, abuse and corruption, these histories simultaneously illustrate that the line between opportunity and exploitation is a thin one. Millions of women workers in Bangladesh and China have flocked to fill factory jobs, despite average monthly wages of $65 or less. Homeworkers in India make far less than those in workshops or factories, but by working at home women can earn money and take care of their families at the same time. Because exploitation and opportunity coexist in the lives of women workers across the world, they are often viewed by women as part of a continuum. Individual workers calculate trade-offs, subjecting themselves to various forms of exploitation, in order to achieve other goals: saving money to send home; caring for a family; sending children to school; making specific purchases—a refrigerator, a TV, an apartment. Women make multiple intricate trade-offs throughout their work and home lives, weighing the exploitation they must endure for the opportunities they seek.

The chapters in Part II provide powerful examples of the exploitation of and opportunities for women workers, from the low-wage exploitation of domestic workers in Mexico, to the increased exploitation of the export-processing zones (EPZ's) in Kenya as the global economic crisis deepened, to increasingly limited opportunities for women in the workplace in Egypt and Russia as the recession took hold. Opportunity hoarding, a useful concept first described by Charles Tilly, occurs when one group controls access to a scarce resource through outright denial, or by exercising monopoly control. As the global recession spread, opportunity hoarding—which together with exploitation, generates and perpetuates inequality—increased dramatically. As Carol Nechemias explains, in the years following the economic downturn of 2008, Russia has experienced a drift toward authoritarianism "wrapped in the imagery and rhetoric of a tough patriarchal masculinity." Moreover, the Putin regime has gutted electoral democracy and civil society, erased the issues of women's equality and women's rights, forged a close alliance with a renascent Russian Orthodox Church, and limited political debates about women's role to a focus on women's reproductive rather than productive role in society. These objectives reflect the agendas of long established patriarchal regimes in Iran, Egypt, and in the Gulf Cooperation Council countries. As Valentine Moghadam argues about the politics of women and work in Iran, women's marginal position [in the labor force] is reinforced by the presence of a neopatriarchal state and highly discriminatory laws and the absence of women-friendly social policies, safeguards for women in the work force, and affirmative action policies to encourage more women to join the workforce.

Moghadam (Chapter 13)

Patterns of opportunity hoarding permeate each of these policies and programs. A complex series of regulations and ideologies exclude women from the workforce, even as they exploit women's position within civil society, educational institutions, and the family.

While opportunity hoarding is key to controlling women in nations as different as Mexico, Kenya and Iran, women's organizing efforts, whether through unions, feminist organizations, or international alliances, have been important forms of resistance that even in regimes as repressive as those in Russia, Egypt, and Iran have at certain points in time made important inroads. But as Nechemias contends, since the global economic recession, feminist resistance in Russia has been almost impossible to sustain in an environment where a close ally of Putin's denounced feminism as "very dangerous, because feminist organizations proclaim the pseudo-freedom of women, which … must appear outside of marriage and outside of the family." The Russian Orthodox Church, she writes, "equates anti-feminism with resistance to globalization and western culture … rejecting the 'idea actively imposed by countries of the Western world'" about "the equal role played in society by men and women." A similar pattern has emerged in Iran where Moghadam reports that "[t]here is no doubt that a large proportion of educated women … who aspire to more personal freedoms … [even in] the context of a political system opposed to feminism and favorable to traditional gender relations." However, she continues,

> [d]espite the revival of the feminist movement in 2005–2006 and massive participation of women in the Green Protests of June 2009, there has been a powerful tide of conservative gender attitudes reinforced by Iran's Muslim Family Law and the absence of women from the labor force and political power.
>
> *Moghadam (chapter 13)*

Political power follows economic power, and in each of the national frameworks analyzed in Part II, conservative backlash and a decisive shift away from globalization followed the economic crisis that began in 2007–2008. Economic nationalism frequently became the focus as nations dealt individually with the longer-term consequences of the crisis. In this context in Mexico, as Georgina Rojas-García and Mónica Toledo González write, "Given the difficulties faced by domestic workers in Mexico—low wages, precarious job stability, the stressful balancing of production and domestic reproduction—a logical solution might be to organize the PDW sector politically or to unionize." While Mexican workers have made some progress regarding independent political organizing, multiple factors operate against it. Nevertheless, despite the lack of a "progressive and democratic vision of unions in the social imaginary," in Mexico, organizations like the Latin America and Caribbean of Home Workers Confederation (CONLACTRAHO) and Support and Training Center for Home Workers (CACEH) not only exist, but work hard to promote equity, social justice, and labor and human rights for domestic workers. These groups have strengthened women's leadership while pushing women's demands onto the political agenda. CACEH, specifically, has been very active in facilitating the movement toward ratification of the ILO Domestic Work Convention 189.

Still, the multiple factors operating against women workers organizing in Mexico can also be seen thousands of miles across the globe in Egypt. In her essay on "Women and Trade Liberalization" in Egypt, Heba Nassar focuses largely on the final decade of Mubarak's reign, a time when, beginning in 2000, the Mubarak government promoted women's rights, largely to meet international legal obligations under the Convention on the Elimination of All Forms of Discrimination against Women (CEDAW). Women activists, supported by First Lady Suzanne Mubarak set up the National Council for Women (NCW). Nassar argues that in the years leading up to the economic crisis of 2008, "economic growth through free trade increase[d] the resources available for the realization of human rights."[1] She documents the correlation between women in the workforce and the achievement of women's rights in government and civil society in the years before, during, and after the revolution of 2011.

Like Mexico, Egypt experienced strong repercussions from the 2008 global recession. Simultaneously, political uncertainty at the end of Mubarak's 30-year regime ushered in a period of violent backlash against women who sought equal engagement in civic life. The first post-Mubarak elections brought conservative Islamist forces into the Egyptian government favoring traditional roles for Egyptian women and reversing decades of progress in women's rights in Egypt, and civil rights and freedoms in general. Women activists united and mobilized in opposition to these attacks, gaining back under the new 2014 Constitution explicit guarantees of equality between men and women and the right of women to assume high positions in the state, including the judiciary. Current President Abdel Fattah el-Sisi has taken a number of concrete steps to empower women and made 2017 the "year of the woman" in Egypt. That said, as in so many nations around the world, government promises do not necessarily become reality, and Egypt stands as a stark example of how the line between the exploitation and opportunity remains remarkably thin when it comes to women's rights. In 2015, the World Economic Forum's Gender Gap Report ranked Egypt in the bottom 10 countries in the world, 136 out of 145 states for this critical indicator of social progress.

In ways similar to the work of Heba Nassar, Alessandra González and Valentine Moghadam offer detailed analyses of the exploitation vs. opportunity continuum in the heart of the Middle East by looking at the issue of women and work in the Gulf

Cooperation Council countries and Iran. González analyzes the paradox of women's high university graduation rates and low labor force participation in the Gulf Cooperation Council countries of Bahrain, Kuwait, Oman, Qatar, Saudi Arabia, and the United Arab Emirates. Her work asks important questions about and underscores the fact that in countries rigidly segregated by economic inequalities, gender equality largely remains the purview of those with privilege. As she argues, resolving the exploitation vs. opportunity paradox in these nations is crucial for their economic future. It is well documented that investment in education compounds opportunities for women at all levels of society and results in positive returns in the labor force, business, government, and civil society. In what ways, she asks, "does women's work or lack of participation in the labor force challenge the sustainability of current GCC economies and mobilize women's rights movements in opposition to existing economic structures?" As in the case of Egypt, she questions the role of international organizations and local activists in prompting women's increased labor force participation in the post-economic crisis world.

Valentine Moghadam asks a comparable set of questions as she focuses on the persistently low levels of women's labor force participation in Iran. As in Egypt and the GCC economies, there exists a powerful paradox between women's high levels of educational attainment and women's low levels of paid employment. Shaped by political, institutional, and economic factors and especially the role of the neopatriarchal state, the gender-based policies of the government have been "highly disadvantageous" to women's equality, participation, and rights. Through law and social norms, women's roles have been inextricably tied to the family, while men have been privileged as "breadwinners, decision-makers, and political leaders." Moghadam's careful tracing of the work lives of Iranian women, with special attention to class and demographic location, opens our eyes to the complexities of life under Sharia law. Despite the overwhelming impact of Sharia law on women's lives, she argues that groups like the National Syndicate of Women Workers, established in 2003 to protect women workers and fight for equal conditions in the workplace, have made a real difference in staunching the exploitation of women and expanding their opportunities within this legal framework.

History tells us that while individuals cannot choose the circumstances into which they are born, in many cases they can create their own opportunities within the constraints imposed by the sociopolitical context in which they live. The chapters in this section of *Global Women's Work* illustrate this powerfully. From the National Syndicate of Women Workers and the Green Protests in Iran, to the efforts of women workers in Russia to stop the opportunity hoarding that increased when Putin established power, to groups like CONLACTRAHO and CACEH in Mexico, hundreds of organizations and women activists work across the globe to expand women's opportunities in the face of continued exploitation. In the years since the crisis, women have worked toward regaining much of the ground they lost, and it is within the boundaries of race, class, and gender that patriarchal regimes impose, the struggle continues.

8
WOMEN IN THE RUSSIAN WORKFORCE
A retreat from equality?

Carol Nechemias

In the Russian Federation, any mid-career working woman in her forties has witnessed a sweeping transformation of her country.[1] These extensive changes include the collapse of the USSR and the redrawing of international borders; the painful transition from a socialist economy to a new capitalist order; the jettisoning of the rule of the Communist Party and of communist ideology in favor of a new and still-evolving regime characterized by a growing authoritarianism replacing the fragile democratization of the 1990s; and the initial opening of the country to global contact and influence giving way to an increasingly vigorous effort under Vladimir Putin's leadership to purge the country of undesirable "foreign meddling," primarily aimed at western promotion of civil society and human rights. Especially acute was the degree of devastation suffered in the economic transition of the 1990s, arguably the most severe economic decline in world history, in which statistical real wages in 1998 fell to only half of their 1985 level (Ashwin 2006a, 1). These shock waves had far-reaching effects on women's lives and received ample attention from scholars, who focused on such topics as rising unemployment, downward mobility, the feminization of poverty, the gutting of welfare benefits from pensions for the elderly to preschools and nurseries for the young, and the emergence of new independent women's organizations and a nascent women's movement (Nechemias 1991; Posadskaya 1994; Bridger et al. 1996; Lipovskaya 1997; Sperling 1999). Unlike the economic crisis of the 1990s, however, the impact of the 2008 global economic recession on women has remained largely unexamined. Coming on the heels of ten years of impressive economic growth, that crisis, though short-lived and less ruinous, nonetheless engulfed and shocked the country, producing a sharp downturn in GDP along with an upswing in unemployment and poverty and then ushering in an era of lower economic growth rates. The 2008 economic crisis highlights key questions regarding the trajectory of Russian society and competing visions of the pathway to modernization, choices of immense importance to women. This chapter focuses on how the Russian state has responded to the quandaries posed by globalization and western challenges and on current trends that promise to reshape gender ideology and women's societal status in wide-ranging ways as new opportunities and roadblocks surface for women (Johnson and Saarinen 2013; Smyth and Soboleva 2014).

Although President Putin recognizes that the world has become more open, transparent, and interdependent and that Russia is not immune from pressures stemming from globalization, he nonetheless argues that Russia must forge "new strategies to preserve our identity" in response to moral challenges from Euro-Atlantic countries (Putin 2013). These challenges from the West involve cultural values, not just economic or military measures. Putin accuses western nations of "rejecting their roots, including the Christian values that constitute the basis of Western civilization," of denying moral principles and all traditional identities—national, cultural, religious, and even sexual—and thereby of standing for a "genderless and infertile" morality and leaving Russia as the defender of traditional family values. In this view, protecting Russian society from the pull of western neoliberal thinking includes expressing hostility not only to gay rights but to western-style feminism (Temkina 2012).

To fend off unwelcome western values, deeply conservative and nationalistic courses of action have intensified and now occupy center stage in Russia. These include a drift toward authoritarianism, the emergence of demographic policy as a national priority (Cook 2013; Rotkirch et al. 2007), and, since 2012, the forging of a close alliance between a resurgent Russian Orthodox Church and the Putin regime, a relationship that boosts patriarchal gender ideologies and was famously challenged by the feminist punk rock group Pussy Riot (Johnson 2014; Sharafutdinova 2014; Sperling 2014b; Yablokov 2014).

The turn toward authoritarian rule has come wrapped in the imagery and rhetoric of a tough patriarchal masculinity, replete with naked torso pictures of Putin, "male-only locker room talk" (Johnson and Saarinen 2013, 547), and thinly veiled homophobic and sexist rhetoric (see Sperling 2014a). Authoritarian rule has gutted electoral democracy and civil society; women's rights groups and gender critiques have suffered along with human rights NGOs in general. Independent voices in parliament, the media, and the third sector, especially organizations funded by outside sources, have been targeted, while several small feminist groups try to draw attention to sexism and discrimination (Sperling 2014a) and the issues of women's equality and women's rights have virtually disappeared from the landscape. Insofar as women figure in political debate, it has overwhelmingly been in connection with demographic policy, with a focus on women's reproductive rather than productive role in society.

Russia does face an extraordinary demographic crisis that threatens President Putin's ambitions to resurrect Russia as a great global power. The fall of communism ushered in acute national depopulation: the population shrank by roughly 750,000 people per year from the early 1990s until 2006, an event unprecedented among industrialized countries in peacetime. The cause was not primarily Russia's low and falling birthrates, which were hardly unique among European countries and Japan, but rather an aberration by international standards: soaring mortality rates —especially premature deaths among men in the most productive age group. Male life expectancy fell to fifty-eight years in 1994, compared to sixty-seven in 1985. Modest improvements have occurred, with male life expectancy recovering to sixty-four years by 2014, still below the standards of the 1980s; the total fertility rate—the average number of children born per woman—has also risen to 1.61 in 2013 from a low of 1.16 in 1999. Despite these positive developments, the country stands on the cusp of powerful negative demographic pressures as the cohort of young women born in the "baby bust" years following the breakup of the USSR move up the age ladder into the prime childbearing age group. In the words of prominent Russian demographer Anatoly Vishnevsky, "there will not be enough women for reproduction" (2010).

In his 2006 state of the nation address to the Federal Assembly, President Putin described the demographic situation as "the most acute problem facing our country" (2006). In terms of detail and specificity and the high economic cost of the proposed measures, Putin's speech was without parallel, far more ambitious than earlier efforts like then–Party Chairman Brezhnev's pronatalist efforts in 1981. Factors like alcoholism, smoking, an inadequate health-care system, high accident rates, cardiovascular disease, immigration policy, and poor environmental and workplace conditions represent some of the major causes of the population decline. Putin chose, however, to highlight childbirth rates—more specifically, to encourage families to have at least a second child. To achieve this goal, Putin focused on economic incentives like the major upgrading of existing policies whose value or availability had eroded in the post-communist era, like child-care benefits, paid maternity leave for eighteen months, and the availability of subsidized preschools, with higher subsidies for the second and third child. He also recommended a new, highly innovative element: maternal capital (*материнский капитал*), a one-time payment of 250,000 rubles (about US$12,000 in 2012) to mothers who have a second or subsequent children; this money becomes available when the child turns three years old and can be spent on housing, the child's education, or invested in the mother's pension plan (Rivkin-Fish 2010).

Putin (2006) believes that maternal capital will not only raise the birth rate but women's status as well. He notes that "the state has a duty to help women who have given birth to a second child and end up out of the workplace for a long time, losing their skills" and often "in a dependent and frankly even degraded position within the family." While state policy has focused on the economic barriers to having children, like low incomes and inadequate housing, the necessity of a shift in cultural norms—the revival of the spiritual and moral traditions of family relationships—also has drawn governmental attention (see Putin 2007).

The Russian Orthodox Church (ROC) has spearheaded the restoration of conservative family values. Russians have been returning to religion: the share of the population identifying as Orthodox Christian skyrocketed from 31 percent in

1991 to 72 percent by 2008 (Pew Research Center 2014), and the ROC and its leader, Patriarch Kirill, rank high in public esteem (Levada Center 2016b). Religious attendance nonetheless remains low, and the extent to which the public has assimilated Church positions remains unclear. Yet there is no doubt about the clout of the Russian Orthodox Church in the contemporary political scene, especially on issues related to women, the family, sexuality, and reproductive rights.

The ROC has hammered home a distinct message on women's place in society. Patriarch Kirill, a close ally and vocal supporter of President Putin, denounces feminism as "very dangerous, because feminist organizations proclaim the pseudo-freedom of women, which ... must appear outside of marriage and outside of the family" (as quoted in Elder 2013). As he explains,

> Man has his gaze turned outward—he must work, make money—and women must be focused inwards, where her home is. If this incredibly important function of women is destroyed then everything will be destroyed—the family and ... the motherland.
>
> *(as quoted in Elder 2013)*

Although the Church does not object to women working, even in predominantly male professions like politics or business, it does call on women to place a high priority on their home life.

The Russian Orthodox Church equates anti-feminism with resistance to globalization and western culture. As prominent ROC theologian and church official Metropolitan Hilarion of Volokolamsk (2012) notes, the Church rejects the "idea actively imposed by countries of the Western world" about "the equal role played in society by men and women." Instead, he argues, "the 'strong' and the 'weak' sexes should complement each other and play special, not identical, roles in the society, family, and Church"; in this equation, women's special role is as "guardian of the home, loving and careful wife and mother." This view that men and women have fundamentally different, God-given primordial destinies shares much in common with the communist legacy that embraced essentialist or biological beliefs about gender differences.

Minus the God-given argument, officials in the communist era had preached a similar essentialist view of sex differences that held that biology, not society, pegged women by nature for motherhood, nurturing, and managing a cozy household and generated natural differences in personality traits and inclinations. Communism strongly embraced work for all citizens as a moral duty, the worker-mother model; as a consequence, women's underrepresentation in high-level politics, among factory managers, in the Academy of Sciences, and so on were readily dismissed as stemming not from discrimination but rather from women's "natural" desire to favor devoting more time to family obligations than to the pursuit of high-powered careers (Ashwin 2006b, 34). Women's integration into the workforce thus did not challenge the traditional gender order when it came to domestic responsibilities. Current Russian policy incorporates much of the late-Soviet discourse about women, referring to women as the weaker sex or the fair sex and to men as the stronger sex and framing policies geared toward helping women reconcile their work and family lives as part of the state's responsibility to protect motherhood and children. In contrast to welfare states in many western countries, where family policies not only support parenting and work responsibilities but encourage changes in gender role attitudes and behavior, including domestic responsibilities, Russian policies emphasize traditional gender roles (Montiejunaite and Kravchenko 2008).

The end of communism did, however, end at least one aspect of the gender order. Communism often celebrated women's entering formerly male-dominated fields of study or occupations like engineering, technology, and metallurgy, although this position "sat uneasily with the idea of different biological destinies which was also endorsed by the state and had deeper roots" (Kozina and Zhidkova 2006, 58). In the late 1980s, under perestroika, the practice of publishing images of women wielding shovels on road construction sites and the like came under fire in parliament and in the mass media as violating women's femininity (Nechemias 1991, 82). In the post-communist transition, Irina Kozina and Elena Zhidkova contend, such earlier challenges to traditional "conceptions of gender-appropriate employment" have largely disappeared, and "deeply ingrained beliefs regarding biological difference have now acquired a new power and legitimacy" (2006, 58).

Nonetheless, the state can ill afford to pursue pronatalist policies and traditionalist ideologies that would reduce women's participation in the workforce. The present demographic policy and the economy's demand for labor involve agendas at loggerheads with one another: if women bear more children, they will leave the labor force at least temporarily, depriving the labor market of workers who play a vital role in economic modernization. In 2015, by the time workers reached the prime of their careers at age 40, women outnumbered men in the workforce (Goskomstat 2016, 31). And when it comes to human capital, the male population exhibits certain shortcomings: in 2005, Vladimir Yakovlev, then the Minister of Regional Development, noted that there are millions of working-age men of little use to the general economy because they sit in prisons, serve in the armed forces and the police, rescue, and secret services, or have succumbed to chronic alcoholism or drug addiction (as cited in Bigg 2005). In light of these demographic pressures and in a nod toward recognition that young women have interests beyond motherhood, new proposals are now emerging, such as the promotion of flexible work hours and the development of retraining programs for women reentering the workforce after years devoted to raising young children (Putin 2007). As Putin concedes, women are motivated by a number of factors, including a desire to not "lose their skills ... to retain their place on the labour market and to progress in their careers" (2014b).

Along with the impact of a still-emerging market economy, these trends in Russian society—authoritarian crackdowns, a priority on boosting birth rates, and a resurgent Russian Orthodox Church—impact women's workplace status and prospects for political empowerment.

Before exploring the influence of the 2008 global financial crisis on women's status, this essay will first examine specific labor force issues in Russia to provide a context for current trends.

Women in the labor force

To provide an overview of women's position in the Russian labor force, this section will explore a number of key aspects of women's working life: workforce participation, professional preparation, horizontal and vertical patterns of sex segregation, gender gaps in remuneration, unemployment, and discriminatory practices.

Labor force participation

In the Soviet era, women's participation in the labor force reached 90 percent, the highest in the world, with women forming 50 percent of the workforce by 1960 (Tsentral'noe statisticheskoe upravlenie RSFSR 1986, 233). Unlike during the communist era, it is no longer a duty for women to work, although economic conditions generally dictate a continuing presence in the workforce and a positive attitude toward women's employment persists. Labor force participation remains high: in 2013, 76 percent of women aged sixteen to fifty-four were economically active versus 83 percent of men aged sixteen to fifty-nine (Goskomstat 2014), rates that have exhibited a high degree of stability through the period preceding and subsequent to the 2008 economic crisis. Survey data show strong support for both women's right to work outside the home and the desirability of work-force activity. In 2010, the PEW Global Attitudes Project found that 95 percent of Russians agreed that women should be able to work outside the home and 74 percent considered marriages where both husband and wife have jobs more satisfying, up from only 47 percent in 1991 and 56 percent in 2002 (Pew Research Center 2010, 2, 6). This upward trend suggests that the "send the women home" rhetoric that accompanied the collapse of the Soviet Union, backlash against women's liberation communist style, and fears of mass unemployment that favored women stepping out of the workforce did influence public opinion for a time but has eroded and that longstanding norms have reasserted themselves (Nechemias 1991).

New wrinkles in women's labor force involvement have appeared, particularly with respect to older and younger women. Although Russian state statistics treat fifty-four as the cutoff year for women of working age—fifty-five is the legal age of retirement for women (sixty for men), current realities show a changing picture. Pensioners, predominantly older women, have endured one of the major negative impacts of the economic transition: their pensions, which were gutted by inflation in the 1990s, now barely exceed subsistence levels. The result for those in the age group fifty-five to fifty-nine has been soaring workforce participation rates, increasing from 39 percent in 2000 to 55 percent in 2013 (Goskomstat 2014). The bulk of that upward surge occurred in the early 2000s, reaching 51.3 percent in 2005 and dropping to 47.8 percent during the 2008 economic crisis before recovering and exceeding earlier rates. For some occupations, women of pension age now form a significant labor resource: for example, twenty percent of urban schoolteachers now fall in the age range of fifty-five to fifty-nine (Nikolaev and Chugunov 2012, 23). Workforce participation rates for women over age sixty also have risen but to the more modest level of 18 percent. The transition to a market economy and the collapse of communist-era social guarantees clearly wrought tremendous changes in the lives of senior citizens and their families, as grandmothers' social role has changed from retiring and helping raise grandchildren to working hard, leaving their grown children more dependent on finding preschools, nannies, and babysitters.

Another shift in workforce status involves the young—women and men under the age of twenty and in the twenty to twenty-four age bracket. Among women, labor force participation for the youngest group fell from 16 percent in 2000 to 8 percent in 2013; the comparable figures for those in their early twenties were 63 percent and 54 percent (Goskomstat 2014). The young do have a more difficult time securing work, but the larger story involves striking increases in access to higher education that brought Russia into the top ranks internationally with respect to the proportion of young people enrolling in tertiary education, all the more remarkable in that this occurred against the backdrop of the introduction of fee-based costs that affect about half the students attending public institutions. Recent data show that women especially enjoyed a marked upswing in attendance: the ratio of seventeen- to twenty-two-year-olds enrolled in higher education institutions rose from 28 percent in 1990–1991 to 84 percent in 2010–2011 (Nikolaev and Chugunov 2012, 48); for women, the ratio stood at 87 percent in 2013, compared to 65 percent for men (World Economic Forum 2013, 57). A large part of the expanded access came from a specifically post-Soviet phenomenon: the founding and growth of private higher education institutions plus the addition of new disciplines associated with the global private-sector economy, particularly the development of hundreds of new business programs.

Young women have good reason to seek as much education as they can get. According to S. Yaroshenko et al. (2006, 144), 72 percent of economically comfortable women possess a higher education, compared to 51 percent of their male counterparts. While men enjoy multiple pathways to pecuniary success, women rely more on getting as much education as they can get. We now turn to an examination of newly emerging patterns in the acquisition of educational credentials.

Human capital

Russian women bring substantial human capital to the table, building on legacies from the communist era. Women already had secured strong access to higher education under communism; for the past forty-plus years, women have formed a majority of higher education enrollees. In the post-communist era, women further expanded their advantage and constituted 54 percent of higher education enrollees in the 2013–2014 academic year (Goskomstat 2014). When it comes to skills, knowledge, and experience, women shine, representing 56 percent of professionals with higher education qualifications among economically active Russians (Goskomstat 2014). Toward the close of the communist era, women were enrolled in a wide array of academic specializations.

Yet disturbing signs of stagnation, if not retreat, are evident. Despite their longstanding status as the majority of higher education undergraduate students, women are underrepresented among graduate students. Their share has been stuck at the 43–47 percent mark since 1996, and they are concentrated in areas like pedagogy, psychology, medicine, philology, and culture and the arts (Goskomstat 1997, 2014). Moreover, although rules governing paid versus free education appear gender-neutral, 55 percent of women pay fees for their higher education, compared to 47 percent of their male counterparts (Baskarova et al. 2006, 43). Worse, a comparison of undergraduate enrollment patterns in 1996–1997 with those of 2013–2014 show a deterioration in women's access to educational specialties associated with well-paying, high-growth areas of the economy (Goskomstat 1997, 41–42, 2014). Natural resources, in particular oil and natural gas, loom huge in Russia's economy, but women's share of students in geology, prospecting, and the exploitation of natural resources fell from 29 percent to 16 percent during that period, while the respective figures for the information sciences and computer technology were 30 percent and 24 percent.[2] Women are losing ground in stereotypical male specializations like chemistry and its associated technologies, where during the same period women's share of students fell from 60 percent to 51 percent, and in metallurgy and mechanical engineering, where the figures were 29 percent and 17 percent, respectively. In stark contrast, a newly created discipline that leads to poor pay—social work—has been female-dominated.

Overall, basic gender patterns in higher education persist from the communist period. Women remain overrepresented in the humanities and social sciences, where they formed 57 percent and 78 percent of the student body, respectively, for the 2013–2014 academic year (Goskomstat 2014). They continue to dominate the fields of healthcare and education. But the restructuring of the economy has recast the relative prestige of various specializations, including improving the standing of some female-dominated fields. These include specializations connected with accounting, finance, and banking, which were poorly paid and regarded as monotonous, routine work during communism. As we shall see, female occupations whose pay scales have risen significantly have experienced an influx of men.

Remuneration and horizontal and vertical sex segregation

A major gender asymmetry in Russian life involves higher female educational attainment yet lower female wages. Toward the end of the Soviet era, women earned 70 percent of men's wages. The gender gap in earnings grew, dropping to 58 percent in 1994, reaching about 64 percent in the late 1990s, and remaining frozen in the 60 to 65 percent range through 2013, figures that suggest that a stable plateau has been reached at a level below that achieved by women in 1985 (Baskakova et al. 2006, 69; Mezentseva 2006; World Economic Forum 2013, 50).[3] The failure to close the pay gap, despite women's educational advantage, traces to several causes, including horizontal and vertical segregation in the workforce, employment discrimination, and inequality at home.

Horizontal sex segregation in the workforce

Experts point to occupational sex segregation as the primary factor underlying the gender gap in remuneration. The communist experience was mixed, encouraging women to enter many traditionally male fields of work while other areas became increasingly feminized. Beginning with the introduction of five-year plans in 1928 and Stalin's push for rapid industrialization, the Soviet state called on women to become skilled workers who could contribute to the building of socialism (Lapidus 1978). Women engaged in physical labor and ultimately formed a hefty 49 percent of the industrial manufacturing workforce (Buckley 1981, 87), although they were particularly concentrated in the lower-priority and lower-paid area of light industry (textiles, food processing) rather than in the state-favored branches of heavy industry. By the close of the communist era, women constituted an impressive 33 percent of the Soviet Union's engineers, 70 percent of physicians, 40 percent of academics, 65 percent of economists, and 38 percent of agronomists and veterinarians (Nechemias 2003, 547). At the same time, however, other job categories became heavily female, with women forming 80 percent of workers in trade and retail, 77 percent of educators, 85 percent in the field of health, 87 percent in credit and finance, and 69 percent of state bureaucrats (Nechemias 2003, 550).

A complementary pattern associated with occupational segregation involves the public–private sector gap, a post-Soviet labor force development. It is no longer the case that virtually all Russian citizens work for the state. The large-scale structural changes associated with the transition from communism to a market-oriented economy meant that between 1992 and 2007, employment in state-owned companies fell from 70 percent to 32 percent, while private domestic and foreign companies upped their share to 56 percent and 4 percent, respectively (Organization for Economic Co-operation and Development 2011b, 48). Men gravitated out of public-sector employment seeking higher wages, while women continued to work for lower wages but greater security in the state sector. As "public budget" employees, women working in healthcare, education, and the social services received salaries that placed them well below the minimum subsistence level by the turn of the new millennium, widening the gender gap in earnings and leading to the appearance of a new category, the working poor (Menzentseva 2006, 2).

Pay for these large numbers of professional women still lags behind average salaries in the economy as a whole. Female teachers earn less than the average female salary and roughly half the average male salary in the economy as a whole. The situation with medical doctors is especially interesting, as market pressures may nudge the government toward increased compensation in the future. Currently, doctors fall among those with the lowest salaries, along with nurses, shop assistants, secretaries, and street cleaners, earning on average about 18,300 rubles (US$650) per month in 2010 ("Moscow to Double City Doctors' Salaries by 2016." 2011), a figure below women's national average monthly earnings of 19,219 rubles and far below the comparable figure for men of 30,005 rubles (Goskomstat 2014). On the other hand, widespread corruption supplements doctors' salaries: it has been estimated that the greatest volume of bribes paid by the public—about $1.2 billion in small payments—goes to the health-care system (Lally 2012). Even with opportunities for under-the-table payments, more lucrative and more rewarding options with pharmaceutical companies or with opportunities abroad are proving attractive to doctors, resulting in a shortage of physicians that the state can address only by increasing remuneration (Spinella 2012).

The undervaluing of women's work thus persists from the socialist to a market economy. The patterns of horizontal sex segregation in the economy are familiar ones cross-nationally. Where women dominate, the pay is low; where women work in male-dominated occupations, they exceed the average pay for their gender; in either case, men earn more than their female counterparts. The influence of capitalism has recast some occupational categories. For example, banking and finance, which was a low-prestige, low-paid female field under socialism, has boomed and now represents one of the highest paid salary categories in Russia. In a pattern familiar in many societies, the rise in standing of this professional field drew an influx of men and a drop in the share of women from 89 percent to 67 percent from 1985 to 2013 (Kozina and Zhidkova 2006, 69; Goskomstat 2014).

Vertical sex segregation in the workforce

If horizontal sex segregation squeezes women into low-paying sectors of the economy, vertical sex segregation forms a powerful glass ceiling that prevents entry into higher-paying leadership positions. The communist past does not include a legacy of women in top positions in the economy: women accounted for only 6.5 percent of factory managers in the Russian Republic. Women rise to middle-level managerial positions but rarely to the top. The Organization for Economic Development and Cooperation (OECD), using a measure that targets chief executives, senior managers, and legislators, finds that Russia falls just below the OECD average and well behind the United States, New Zealand, and the United Kingdom (OECD 2011a). In contrast, Grant Thornton's 2014 International Business Report places Russia first in the world with respect to the proportion of women in senior management positions, a result the survey attributes at least in part to women's demographic advantage in key age groups (Grant Thorton 2014, 10). The Thornton report differs from the OECD study in that it covers only private-sector, mid-market businesses with 100–499 employees, which have a higher proportion of family-owned businesses, and throws the net widely to include positions like sales director, human resources director, chief information officer, chief marketing officer, and so on.[4] Thus, while the OECD report credits Russian women with holding just 5 percent of high-level positions, the Thornton survey concludes that 43 percent of managerial positions are held by women.

In either case, a glass ceiling clearly presents a barrier for women's upward mobility. Data for virtually any occupation reveal that the proportion of women declines in the higher and more responsible decision-making positions. The academic community offers a typical example: women make up 63 percent of the teaching corps in higher education but hold only 13 percent of the top position of rector. The propensity for women to fill positions as talented, reliable assistants to leading officials is commonplace; in this case, women fill 31 percent of the positions of vice rector and heads of branch campuses. Women also cluster toward the bottom of the teaching hierarchy, with only 32 percent reaching the level of professor (Goskomstat 2014).

Russian women have successfully pursued one path that avoids the issue of promotion within the workplace—being their own boss. The fall of communism opened the door to private entrepreneurship, an opportunity that many women seized to create small businesses. Despite the less-than-stellar record of gender equality in post-Soviet Russia (see UN 2005, 2010), small businesses present a bright spot with respect to women's achievements (McMahon 2001). According to the prominent sociologist Olga Kryshtanovskaia, "In business women play a rather significant role—you cannot say that about politics" (quoted in Kakoe mesto 2006, 5). Another leading scholar, Galina Sillaste (as cited in Shevchenko 2006) argues that no one predicted that Russian women would take up entrepreneurship so rapidly (see also Bridger et al. 1996, 117). Women now head up to 40 percent of small and medium-sized business ventures in Russia, a figure consistent with advanced market economies and among the highest internationally, leading the Russian president of Magram Market Research, Marina Malykhina, to assert that "Russia is the only country in the world where women strive to become entrepreneurs more than men" (quoted in Elkov 2008, 6).

Some scholars assign great promise to this phenomenon, although its potential is not yet fulfilled. According to R. A. Vardanian and E. V. Kochkina, Russian businesswomen form "a new female estate," a new social milieu that shows the "rudiments of a different way of life among women" but whose success in business has not yet translated into political and civic positions (2008, 59). Similarly, Edvard Radzinsky (2005, A-10), writing in the *Wall Street Journal*, suggests that traditional roles for women began to change when "the first Russian businesswomen came onto the scene." In his view, it is "in business, not politics, that the road to true gender equality in Russia began to be laid."

Women's prominent role in small businesses stems from several factors. A major impetus involved sheer economic survival—the need to feed a family—particularly in the initial years of economic transition in the 1990s, when large numbers of well-educated women lost their jobs and faced downward deployment, moving, for example, from a job as an engineer to one as a sales clerk. But the shift toward a market economy also meant a burgeoning demand for consumer goods and services, sectors of the economy that had suffered from severe deficits under communism but where women enjoyed considerable pre-eminence and where, for once, the stereotype of "women's work" held advantages. In contrast to industry and agriculture, employment opportunities in the service sector especially have grown. Women's high level of education and workforce experience contributed significantly to women's success, as these first waves of women entrepreneurs were self-taught rather than products of business or marketing programs.

A word of caution is warranted, however. The small and medium-sized business sector in Russia currently plays a much smaller role in the overall economy than in developed countries and in comparable developing ones as well (European Investment Bank 2013, 8). There is considerable growth potential, and in principle the Russian government supports the expansion of this sector of the economy as a key means of diversifying and modernizing a Russian economy that features state-led monopolies and dependence on natural resources, though in practice the Russian bureaucracy seems to distrust free individuals and free businesses. The International Finance Corporation (IFC) has directed attention toward the goal of increasing access to finance for women entrepreneurs in Russia, noting that "Russian banks have largely ignored this sizable, untapped market segment" (2014). Whether the small business sector secures a larger foothold in the Russian economy and whether women entrepreneurs play a transformative role in forging new gender relations in the future remains uncertain.

Unemployment

Unemployment as a major problem has shrunk in significance over the post-Soviet period. During the deep economic decline of the 1990s, unemployment reached a peak of 13 percent in 1998; rather than shed labor, many enterprises resorted to late payment of wages, enforced leave, and shortening work hours (Ashwin 2006a, 1). As the economy regained traction after 2000, unemployment rates dropped, from 8.2 percent in 2000 to 6.4 percent in 2008, kicking upward to 8.4 percent in 2009 as a result of the 2008 global financial crisis before falling to 4.9 percent by July 2014, the lowest rate in the past twenty-one years (Goskomstat 2014; Statista 2014). These figures, however, mask striking regional variations. Unemployment has dipped to a stunningly low 1.5 and 1.4 percent in the cities of Moscow and St. Petersburg, respectively, while reaching 34.7 percent in war-torn Ingushetia in the North Caucasus (ITAR-TASS 2014). Across Russia as a whole, tight labor market conditions have favored women's opportunities, a situation that has somewhat eroded in light of predictions of economic contraction after the introduction of the first round of western sanctions against Russia in 2014 due to Russia's military intervention in Ukraine.

Despite low rates of joblessness, unemployment not only exists but exhibits gender-related patterns. Two types of official unemployment statistics capture divergent and seemingly contradictory aspects of joblessness. Government survey data collected since 1992 suggest that men's jobless rates have consistently exceeded women's; the July 2014 figures, for example, show an unemployment rate of 5.2 percent for men but 4.5 percent for women (Goskomstat 2014, 221). Yet by a second measure, unemployed workers registered with the Federal Employment Service, women have steadily formed the majority over the years; currently they constitute 56 percent of those registered (Goskomstat 2012). It should be added that the Federal Employment Service has a reputation for providing its services–benefits, job placement, and retraining—in a rude and humiliating fashion (Ashwin 2006a, 10–12). Only a small percentage of the unemployed actually register with the Federal Employment Service, but on the surface, it seems odd that the two measures of unemployment consistently go in opposite directions with respect to who suffers more from unemployment, women or men.

Part of the explanation lies in women's longer periods of unemployment; 65 percent of citizens experiencing more than a year's break in their working life are female (UN 2000, 11). There is a serious mismatch between the jobs—overwhelmingly low-skilled and poorly paid—offered by government employment offices and the generally well-educated women who show up seeking assistance with finding work. In addition, women and men without work tend to utilize "gendered" approaches to landing a new position, differences that operate to men's advantage. When the unemployed are asked to identify their job search strategies, women's most popular choice is the Federal Employment Service; for men, it is networking—turning to friends, relatives, and acquaintances—a crucial resource for securing scarce and valued items in the Soviet period and a prime means of obtaining a good job in post-transition Russian society (Goskomstat 2012; see also Tartakovskaya and Ashwin 2006, 164–192). The gap in turning to personal networks is rather sizeable: 56 percent of men versus 44 percent of women. Men also reported greater enlistment of other avenues of action than women, such as turning to commercial employment services and directly approaching administrators or employers.

Aside from this greater dependence on state assistance, motherhood extracts a price in the job market. In 2013, the unemployment rate for women with children up to age eighteen stood at 4.9 percent, a rate that increased in a monotonic fashion from 4.3 percent for women with one child up to 15 percent for women with four or more children. For women with children up to six years of age, the unemployment rate was 6.4 percent (Goskomstat 2014). As we shall see, employers often have negative attitudes toward hiring young women.

Discrimination against women

There is evidence of discriminatory attitudes on the part of the mass public and employers, as well as state laws that bar women from a long list of occupations. Extensive cross-national surveys like the World Values surveys, Pew Global Attitudes surveys, the Gallup International Millennium Survey, and the World Public Opinion Project endorse the view that post-communist countries like Russia prove less egalitarian toward sex roles than post-industrial countries (with the exception of Japan) and Latin American nations. Russian mass public opinion shows little to no sign of swinging in a more egalitarian direction. World Values Survey data for 1995 and 2014 indicate that agreement that "men make better political leaders than do women" actually increased from 1995 to 2011, reaching 65 percent among men and 51 percent among women in 2011 (World Values Survey Waves 3; World Values Survey Wave 6). A large part of the Russian population does buy into the view that men and women have different societal responsibilities—58 percent of men and 54 percent of women support that position, which is consistent with an essentialist interpretation of sex differences (Levada Center 2012).

Looking more specifically at workplace issues, the Russian public recognizes that women encounter obstacles in pursuing a career. When asked in a public opinion survey whether women and men have equal opportunity to advance in the workplace, a 2012 survey that did not break down responses along gender lines found that 48 percent of those surveyed thought men held an advantage, while 32 percent believed that men and women enjoyed equal opportunity. Curiously, a whopping 20 percent considered the question too difficult to answer (Fond Obshchestvennoe Mnenie 2012). An earlier poll using different wording investigated whether the public believed that women faced greater difficulty in pursuing a career: in this case, 55 percent of men and 62 percent of women agreed that women encountered greater difficulties (Petrova 2004). A national poll that elicited the respondents' general opinion on which sex most often makes a good boss showed that 43 percent of men and 31 percent of women considered males better as workplace leaders, while 46 percent of men and 52 percent of women saw both genders as equally fit (Vserossiiskii Tsentr Izucheniia Obshchest-vennogo Meneniia 2004). A preference for women as workplace leaders drew only a small degree of support from both genders.

Widespread support for equal rights and even the acknowledgment of discrimination does not equate with regarding women's equality as a high-priority problem. A Pew Global Survey showed that Russians ranked low internationally with respect to believing that more change was needed to give women equal rights with men; in the same vein, a Program for Public Consultation project showed that Russians were less likely than western and Latin American nations, as well as China, Kenya, Nigeria, and Indonesia to support further government action to promote women's equality (Pew Research Center 2010; The Program for Public Consultation 2008). Women themselves do not necessarily regard instances of discrimination that they personally experience as unjust. Many women have absorbed societal attitudes that handicap them on the job market. Young women particularly encounter discrimination due to employers' reluctance to hire them because they are likely to become pregnant or already have young children; in the eyes of employers, this leads to absences from work, lower labor productivity due to the distractions of family life, and maternity leave and other social benefits that the employer will have to shoulder (Kozina and Zhidkova 2006, 72). Young women who experience unequal access to jobs often consider employers justified in rejecting females who will be looking after a sick child or pose a financial burden to employers while on maternity leave; moreover, women see themselves as lacking the flexibility a male offers to private employers in terms of physical strength to lift items, do repairs, work extra hours, or guard the workplace (Kozina and Zhidkova 2006, 73–75). Further, women tend not to question traditional gender roles that assign them the bulk of household work and treat men as the primary breadwinner (Ashwin 2006b, 32–56).

In contrast to the early period of the post-communist transition, when women were typically the first to be let go, discrimination by employers now takes place during recruitment or hiring. Employers exercise stronger preferences for hiring male or female job candidates for job categories stereotyped as appropriate for one or the other sex; for example, from 1997 to 2001, employers' desire to hire a male engineer rose from 37 percent to 53 percent; for a programmer, the comparable figures were 27 percent and 46 percent (United Nations 2005, 19). The widespread practice of issuing job advertisements that contain a specific gender requirement facilitated this process (Kozina and Zhidkova 2006, 68–69). In a step forward, new regulations passed by the State Duma in 2013 ban job advertisements that stipulate the desired race, sex, ethnicity, marital status, faith, age, or physical appearance of candidates. The penalties for violating the new regulations are, however, paltry: fines ranging from 500–1,000 rubles (US$15 to $30) for individuals, 3,000– 5,000 rubles (US$90–$150) for individual entrepreneurs, and 10,000–15,000 rubles (US$300–$450) for legal entities ("Ban on Discrimination 2013). Nonetheless, this new law draws Russia closer to a Western mentality with respect to employment discrimination and could serve as a basis for long-term improvement.

The state itself practices discrimination through its labor code, which bans women from working in 456 jobs. The tradition of barring women from work conditions considered unsafe and a threat to women's health originated in the early days of the Soviet Union. The current Russian labor code was relaxed in 2000 so that a woman can take a listed position if the employer proves that the work situation is safe. The jobs that are off-limits to women include firefighter, blacksmith, bus driver, train operator, and ship's captain; the vast majority of these jobs, however, are in construction, metallurgy, and mining (Marquardt 2010). A rare legal challenge to the list occurred following the rejection of a St. Petersburg woman's application to be an assistant operator in her city's metro system. Despite the Russian Constitution's guarantee of equal rights and opportunities for men and women, the Russian Supreme Court upheld the state's position that the possibility of risk to a woman herself, or to others, must be excluded. Ultimately, tight labor market conditions may chip away at these restrictions, given the difficulties some employers—like the Moscow subway system—face in landing sufficient numbers of healthy men.

In light of this broad overview of women's position in Russia's labor force, how did the 2008 global financial crisis affect women's status in the short term and provide an impetus for the emergence of important new trends?

The 2008 global financial crisis

In Russia, the impact of the 2008 global economic crisis became apparent during the fourth quarter of 2008, shattering the confidence built by a decade of economic growth rates averaging 6.9 percent annually. Real GDP contracted by 9.8 percent during the first quarter of 2009, the deepest recession among major world economies. For Russia, a key element of the international crisis involved collapsing oil prices, highlighting its economy's dependence on export earnings from oil, gas, and other natural resources as a source of budget revenue; as a result, a fiscal budget surplus turned into a deficit. A credit crunch, a bursting real-estate bubble, devaluation of the ruble, falling consumer demand, and accelerated capital flight added to the painful mix of economic woes. That the Russian population experienced hardships is borne out in the Levada Center's surveys, which ask Russians at the end of each year whether this year was harder, easier, or the same as the previous year. Those surveys show a soaring proportion of the population characterizing 2008 and 2009 as worse than the preceding year, with the 2007 figure of 20 percent surging to 46 percent in 2008 and to 62 percent in 2009 before declining to 28 percent in 2011 (Levada Center 2016a, 6).

The economic downturn held mixed results for women and men. Unemployment grew more rapidly for men than women, rising from 6.6 percent in 2008 to 9.0 percent in 2009, while the comparable figures for women were 6.1 percent and 7.8 percent (World Bank 2014). The recession especially impacted male-dominated sectors of the economy like oil and gas, construction, and metallurgy, with women's public-sector employment in education, healthcare, and social services providing a measure of protection. But unemployment did adversely affect women working in the service and retail sector, the clerical/secretarial field, and as skilled industrial workers; compared with 2007, female unemployment rose in those fields, from 5.0 to 8.8 percent, 4.0 to 7.6 percent, and 6.0 to 10.8 percent, respectively. The group that bore most of the brunt of the economic hard times, however, consisted of the significant numbers of women operating small, marginal businesses in the informal sector of the economy—unregistered businesses that operate in the shadows and leave their proprietors ineligible for government assistance programs for the unemployed (Trefilov et al. 2015). With falling consumer demand, many of these small businesses lost their precarious toehold in the economy.

Compared with pre-crisis data, the unemployed reported that their job loss was involuntary, stemming from cutbacks or the outright collapse of their workplace organization. For women, the upswing in unemployment went from 19.0 percent in 2007 to 27.9 percent in 2009; for men, from 16.4 percent to 29.7 percent (Goskomstat 2008, 2010). By 2013, that figure had fallen to 17.2 percent for both genders (Goskomstat 2014). During the economic crisis, unemployed women and men both turned in greater numbers to state employment agencies for assistance in finding employment; for women, that percentage jumped from 37.6 in 2007 to 46.1 in 2009; for men, the comparable figures were 28.9 and 37.4 (Goskomstat 2008, 2010). In harsh economic conditions, strategies like personal contacts or independent job searches proved less effective. During the post-crisis economic recovery, the utilization of government employment services compared with other avenues of job seeking declined to close to their pre-2008 levels—32.4 percent for women and 27.1 percent for men in 2013 (Goskomstat 2014).

Although the economic crisis particularly hit male-dominated sectors of the economy, the crisis set in motion or strengthened trends that undermined women's prospects in the labor force. The face of unemployed women registered with state employment services is changing. In 2007, only 14 percent of those women had completed a professional higher education; during the economic crisis, that figure climbed to 18.7 percent and has continued to rise, reaching 21.4 percent in 2013 (Goskomstat 2008, 2010, 2014). The growing presence of well-educated women among the registered unemployed suggests a tightening of opportunities for well-educated women, a negative sign for women who have relied on a strong base of social capital in the form of educational achievement. Linked to this problem is the opportunity that the economic crisis provided employers to shed themselves of young women of childbearing age. Among unemployed women in the age group twenty to twenty-nine, the jobless rate for those in a registered marriage—as opposed to categories like single women and women in unregistered relations—climbed from 20 percent in 2009 to 28 percent by 2013; for men, the comparable figures held steady at 16 and 15 percent (Goskomstat 2010, 2014). It is this group of young women who loom, in the eyes of employers, as unreliable workers likely to go on maternity leave or neglect their workplace duties in favor of domestic concerns.

The global economic crisis also highlighted the failure to put a further dent in childhood poverty despite significant reductions in the overall level of poverty since the year 2000, a situation closely connected to high poverty rates among households headed by women. Official Russian poverty statistics, considered by many scholars to severely underestimate the level of poverty, show that the overall level of poverty declined from 29 percent in 2000 to 10.8 percent in 2013, with the 2008 economic crisis temporarily reversing and halting progress around the 13.4 percent mark. The story for children, however, is quite different: for those under the age of sixteen, the poverty rate in 2000 was 24.4 percent, a figure that declined slowly to 21.4 percent in 2007, increased during the economic crisis to 23.8 percent in 2009, and has continued to grow, reaching a level of 28.4 percent in 2013 (Goskomstat 2014). The 2008 global economic crisis ushered in heightened hard times for families with children, particularly for female-headed households.

Dramatic changes have occurred in the structure of Russian family life that bear directly on the consequences of the 2008 global economic crisis. By 2008, family patterns in Russia looked more like those of other developed countries such as the United States, Canada, and most European countries: the proportion of births outside of marriage had increased from 11 percent in 1980 to roughly 20 percent in 1993 to 30 percent by 2005. A growth in the number of single teen girls giving birth, along with one of the highest divorce rates in the world, have left large numbers of women economically vulnerable if not marginalized. As Iu. P. Lezhnina (2011, 23–25) notes, the most critical situation in 2008 consisted of incomplete families, typically headed by women with minor children; these families were among those most likely to fall into poverty. She also argues that the burden posed by children was not as critical earlier, but that the 2008 crisis worsened the level of well-being of these families and set in motion an accelerated pace of deterioration. By 2010, demographic changes meant that 29 percent of Russian households with children were headed by women, a factor significantly contributing to the growing levels of poverty among children.

The primary legacy of the 2008 economic crisis lies, however, in political decision-making that bodes ill for women's status. That crisis gave added impetus to a trend already visible as early as 2005: a decoupling of Russia from the West.

The 2008 financial crisis: political ramifications

The financial crisis represents a watershed moment, confirming for President Putin the dangers of a unipolar world dominated by the United States—which he blamed for the global financial damage—and boosting a more conservative Russian nationalist outlook that rejects the Western model of secularism, democracy, and capitalism. A conservative gender ideology became dominant, reflecting concerns about demographic problems and the need for a "national idea" that would not only unite Russian society but provide a foundation for an identity separate from the rest of the West. The Russian Orthodox Church has stepped into that role. For women, the road to modernization Russian-style omits gender equality as it is understood and promoted by the West and by the UN. Putin has committed the nation to pursing its own path to modernity and to taking its place as a major world player. Macroeconomic policy increasingly favors sharp increases in defense spending and the oil and natural gas sectors, while placing less emphasis on the promotion of economic diversification and the social sectors of education and health. These priorities hurt women's prospects for gains in the labor force. In an environment of growing authoritarianism and patriarchal approaches to gender issues, women face great challenges in posing countervailing positions in Russian society and within the political system.

Under President Yeltsin, women's issues and women's influence in the political arena gained some prominence (Slater 1995; Buckley 1997; Sperling 1999; Nechemias 2000), and several fragile steps toward enhancing women's equality did take place. Within the executive branch, newly created commissions provided points of access for women's groups, inflating the influence of feminist scholars and activists who offered ammunition in the form of gender expertise to the development of analyses and recommendations. These included the Commission on Women, Family, and Demography, established in 1993 and located within the president's office, shortly followed by the Commission on Improving the Status of Women in 1995, also set up by executive order and charged with preparing recommendations for moving Russian society closer to the international standards set forth in the Beijing platform and UN Convention on the Elimination of All Forms of Discrimination against Women (CEDAW). These commissions were advisory bodies, lacking any decision-making authority.

The most heralded event, however, involved action in the legislature—the State Duma's passage in 1997 of the "Legal Framework on Equal Rights and Equal Opportunities," described by the feminist activist Elena Kotchkina (1997) as a "feminist revolution." This document reflected words rather than action, in the sense that it created a backdrop for action by posing goals and strategies based on an assessment of women's status in Russia. It incorporated many suggestions made by feminist non-governmental organizations. But deeds, in the form of concrete measures to carry out the recommendations, failed to materialize; the inability to secure passage in the State Duma of a core element geared toward advancing the goals outlined in the "Legal Framework" was a great disappointment to many advocates of women's equality. This follow-up measure involved a piece of legislation entitled "On State Guarantees of Equal Rights and Equal Opportunities for Women and Men in the Russian Federation" (hereafter "On State Guarantees") that would have established legal definitions and state mechanisms for tackling discrimination against women.

A turn in the direction of gender policy became evident in Putin's first term as president from 2000 to 2004, when government reorganizations resulted in the dismantlement of the two women's commissions and the downgrading of their status. Currently, buried within the Ministry of Labor and Social Protection, there is an office for questions of gender equality located within a department on demographic policies and social policies; the same ministry also contains a coordinating council on gender problems. This organizational setup links gender issues more closely to demographic issues and social protection than to a framework emphasizing equal opportunity.

With the taming of the State Duma and the replacement of competing programmatic parties with United Russia, the dominant party responsible to the executive, the government dropped its support for the legislation "On State Guarantees" in 2003, tabling the proposal that had reached its second reading in the State Duma. Curiously, after an eight-year hiatus, yet another version of the bill was put forward in 2011 by Elena Mizulina, Chair of the State Duma's Committee on Family, Women, and Children. This version went beyond a focus on labor force issues like discrepancies in pay to include the underrepresentation of women in political office. Interestingly, Deputy Mizulina believed that the forward-looking climate nurtured by then-President Dmitry Medvedev with his talk about the need to democratize and modernize Russian society had renewed the opportunity to move forward on fighting sex discrimination (Lobzina 2011). But the proposal drew fire from Russian Orthodox officials, who charged that it reflected radical feminism and would bring about same-sex marriage and the destruction of the family (NEWSru 2012). The bill continued to languish, and Putin's return to the presidency in 2012 led to what one journalist called the "clear" button regarding Medvedev's term in office (Barry 2012).

The dearth of women in President Putin's administration demonstrates a near total disregard for moving women into high-level politics and smacks of patterns set during the Soviet era (Buckley 1989; Nechemias 2000). As of September 2014, there is one woman among the eight deputy prime ministers, and among the twenty-four ministries, one is headed by a woman. Both of these women hold "feminine portfolios": the deputy prime minister oversees demographic policies, healthcare, education, and social insurance, while the lone minister heads the Ministry of Health. Russia, however, is one of the rare countries where the banking system is headed by a woman, Elvira Nabiullina. The highest-ranking female politician in Russia is Valentina Matvienko, the former governor of Saint Petersburg and currently chair of the Federation Council, the upper chamber of parliament. Matvienko often represents the Russian state when a woman is called for to support regime goals; for example, she has participated in sessions of the Interparliamentary Association of the Commonwealth of Independent States (CIS) to discuss the creation of a Eurasian Women's Forum to foster integration across the Eurasian region (Interparliamentary Assembly 2013, IPA CIS Council 2013).

The handful of high-ranking women in the executive branch resemble their parliamentary sisters in terms of avoiding outspoken advocacy for women's rights. Linda Cook and Carol Nechemias (2009, 54) found that there was a decline after the 1999 parliamentary election in the representation of women's interests as well as broader societal interests within the State Duma in comparison with earlier stages of the Russian transition. United Russia (UR) commanded large majorities in the legislature after 1999, and UR women deputies almost uniformly denied that there were problems specific to women; instead, they saw issues in terms of material conditions common to society as a whole. The proportion of women serving in the State Duma rose to 14 percent by 2013, but a good many of them serve a decorative function reminiscent of the USSR Supreme Soviet, with the UR recruiting women opera singers and Olympic stars. Moreover, the parliament has been reduced largely to an element of "managed democracy," with little independent power.

Below the national level, the picture is not improved, as the pipeline contains only a trickle of potential leading women political figures. Across the eighty-five federal units (including Crimea) that compose Russia, only four women serve as the top executive official in 2017. An additional indicator of women's low political status involves women's presence in the legislatures of Russia's federal units, where they made up 13 percent of the deputies in 2014. In the formal political system, women do not walk the hallways of power.

Women did find a niche in the third sector during the post-Soviet transition, founding many new organizations, including a budding feminist women's movement (Sperling 1999; Nechemias 2006). But women's rights and feminist organizations have since virtually disappeared in Russia, in part because they relied heavily on western funding that had largely dried up by 2006 and because they did not develop a base of support within Russian society (Wedel 2001; Henderson 2003; Hemment 2007) and in part because of a growing authoritarianism that systematically targeted independent voices in the third sector, particularly human rights NGOs funded by outside sources. Janet Elise Johnson and Aino Saarinen (2013; see also Johnson 2009) point to a partial exception to this trend: the domestic violence movement, which, while significantly reduced in size, largely stripped of a feminist critique, less involved with the transnational women's movement, and disengaged from overt political activities like lobbying for stronger laws, nonetheless survives in the form of government-operated regional and municipal crisis centers that now greatly outstrip the role played by NGOs.

On the whole, however, as the prominent Russian feminist Olga Zdravomyslova (Heinrich Boll Stiftung 2011) points out, a "patriarchal renaissance" now characterizes Russia, with "no counterweight to that: the critical reflection or social movements which might offer a response . . . are almost non-existent now." Among the latest Russian organizations to fall victim to the Justice Ministry's enforcement of the 2012 law that requires NGOs engaging in political activity and receiving funding from abroad to register as "foreign agents" are the Saratov Center for Social Policies and Gender Studies and the rights group Don Women (Moscow Times 2014). Labeling groups as foreign agents evokes an ugly form of stigmatization reminiscent of Soviet-era charges of espionage. In contrast, limited support from the state is directed toward "traditional" women's organizations that support families with many children, single mothers, and children with disabilities.

According to James Richter, Putin sees the need to encourage popular initiatives if Russia is to be a great power, but he "seeks to orchestrate and constrain this initiative within boundaries consistent with the interests of the state" (2008, 195). An interesting example of a budding movement that does fall within the palette of acceptable activity—protecting mothers—is "Young Mothers for Just Law." An issue that surfaced during the financial crisis of 2008 involved pregnant women and young mothers who were fired by employers who sought to avoid paying maternity benefits; in some cases, companies simply disappeared. Street demonstrations and picketing in 2010–2011, along with direct appeals by the St. Petersburg NGO Egida to the State Duma and high officials, led directly to a Russian government decision to start paying maternity benefits and other types of welfare directly from Russia's social insurance fund, replacing the system by which employers took responsibility for these payments (Kononova 2011; Chernova 2012).[5]

Largely marginalized, feminist activism now centers on the informal politics of web sites, direct actions in the form of small public demonstrations, and occasional round tables organized by organizations like the Gorbachev Foundation, the political party Yabloko's gender section, and the Association of Russian Women Journalists. An especially lively group, the Initiative Group for Feminism (www.zafeminizm.ru), operates a website with up-to-date information and opportunities for discussion and occasionally organizes small public protests.[6] Sadly, however, Valerie Sperling's research (2014a) suggests that the pervasive atmosphere of misogyny and gay-bashing infects virtually all political forces, including the youth wings of political groups across the political spectrum, with the one exception of Yabloko, a liberal party that has failed to exceed the minimum electoral threshold required to gain seats via the proportional representation system for the past three parliamentary elections.

Conclusion

President Putin (2013) contends that questions about "who we are and who we want to be are increasingly prominent in our society" but rejects as unrealistic the views of those who favor a return to communism, those who idealize pre-1917 Russia, and those who support "an extreme, western-style liberalism." The Russian state has opted to pursue a path to modernization and national identity that excludes feminist approaches to women's rights and to build fences against global influence in the area of gender equality and human rights. These trends, accentuated by the 2008 global economic crisis and further heightened by later developments like the Ukrainian crisis, do not bode well for women.

While it appears that the Putin regime shares many policy positions and values with the mass public, gender ideology reflects a variety of influences, including socioeconomic change, globalization, and government policies. Scholars point to a shifting, age-driven evolution of public opinion that is bringing young, educated Russians closer to their European counterparts (White 2005). As Elena Balashova of Moscow State University's Department of Psychology argues, "While, in the past, we used to observe career-driven motivation among men, now there's a spike in career motivation among women" (quoted in Obrazkova 2013). As she explains, many women are putting their career first as professional growth opportunities "have increased from what they were thirty or forty years ago. There are opportunities for very serious financial gain, working abroad, or travel." Sergei Smirnov, director of the Social Policy Institute at the Higher School of Economics, also acknowledges that many young people are postponing marriage and having children in favor of getting a high-paying job. He adds that this is due in part to expanded opportunities for higher education and those who pay for their education wanting "to get their money's worth when they graduate" (quoted in Obrazkova 2013). Sociological reality and political propaganda about traditional values therefore may conflict, with the public embrace of Putin's policy declarations not necessarily in harmony with younger Russians' actions or true inclinations.

Notes

1 Heba Nasssar, "Women and trade liberalization in Egypt," in this volume.
2 The figures for 1996–1997 were calculated by the author; it was necessary to combine some categories from 1996–1997 to match those used in 2013–2014.
3 There are varying reports concerning the gender wage gap. The World Economic Forum's calculations, reported in "The Global Gender Gap Report 2013," put women's earning as 63 percent of men's in 2013, while official Russian Federation figures, published in *Zhenshchiny i muzhchiny Rossii: statisticheskii sbornik* 2014, give figures of 68 percent for 2011 and 74 percent for 2013. The latter figure would place women's average earnings in comparison to men's above the mark reached under communism.
4 Details provided by Thorton employee Dominic King in a private email communication to me, 23 June 2014.
5 Egida, founded in 2002, focuses its work on defending the rights of the socially vulnerable, particularly employment rights protection for women. After the victory over how maternity benefits are paid, Rima Sharifullina, the president of Egida, spoke about forming a new coalition called "Women's Voice" and working toward goals like the abolition of the list of occupations off-limits for women and the establishment of a 40 percent quota for women in government institutions (Konova 2010). The year 2013 was difficult for Egida. In March, a district-level procurator in St. Petersburg initiated a review of whether Egida was in violation of not registering as a foreign agent under the 2012 law on NGOs receiving foreign funds. A district court suspended Egida's activities. The St. Petersburg city court later set aside the suspension, and the organization was basically cleared in December 2013. Egida was defended in court by Vladimir Lukin, one of the most prominent human rights figures in Russia.
6 The Russian government has been taking steps to tighten control over the Internet, which has remained one of the few media outlets where people can freely express their views. A new law in 2014, for example, requires bloggers with more than three thousand daily readers to register with authorities, and penalties for publishing unverified information can result in fines or being blacklisted. Another law allows the government to block websites deemed to contain "extremist" content.

References

Ashwin, Sarah. 2006a. "Dealing with devastation in Russia: Men and women compared." In *Adapting to Russia's New Labour Market: Gender and Employment Behavior*, 1–31. Edited by Sarah Ashwin, London: Routledge.

Ashwin, Sarah. 2006b. "The post-soviet gender order: Imperatives and implications." In *Adapting to Russia's New Labour Market: Gender and Employment Behavior*, 32–56. Edited by Sarah Ashwin, London: Routledge.

"Ban on discrimination in job ads comes into force." 2013. *Moscow Times*, July 14. http://www.themoscowtimes.com/business/article/ban-on-discrimination-in-job-ads-comes-into-force/483112.html.

Barry, Ellen. 2012. "Putin's Russia hits the 'clear' button on the Medvedev Era." *New York Times*, September 20.

Baskakova, Marina, Elena Mezentseva, and Elena Zotova. 2006. *Gender Issues in Modern Russia: Based on Formal Statistics*. Washington, DC: World Bank. http://documents.worldbank.org/curated/en/227901468143682653/Gender-issues-in-modern-Russia-based-on-formal-statistics Accessed August 18, 2017.

Bigg, Claire. 2005. "Russian officials warn of population crisis." *Radio Free Europe Radio Liberty*, April 28. https://www.rferl.org/a/1058670.html Accessed August 17, 2017.

Bridger, Sue, Rebecca Kay, and Kathryn Pinnick. 1996. *No More Heroines? Russia, Women and the Market*. London: Routledge.

Buckley, Mary. 1981. "Women in the Soviet Union." *Feminist Review*, 8: 79–106.

Buckley, Mary. 1989. *Women and Ideology in the Soviet Union*. Ann Arbor: University of Michigan Press.

Buckley, Mary. 1997. "Adaptation of the Soviet Women's committee: Deputies' Voices from 'Women of Russia'." In *Post-Soviet Women: From the Baltic to Central Asia*, 157–185. Edited by Mary Buckley, Cambridge: Cambridge University Press.

Chernova, Zhanna. 2012. "Parenthood in Russia: From the State Duty to Personal Responsibility and Mutual Cooperation." *Anthropology of East Europe Review*, 30(2): 1–19.

Cook, Linda J. 2013. "The political economy of Russia's demographic crisis." In *The Political Economy of Russia*, 97–119. Edited by Neil Robinson, Lanham, MD: Rowman & Littlefield.

Cook, Linda J., and Carol Nechemias. 2009. "Women in the Russian Duma." In *Women in Power in Post-Communist Parliaments*, 25–59. Edited by Marilyn Rueschemeyer and Sharon L. Wolchik, Bloomington: Indiana University Press.

Elder, Miriam. 2013 (April 9). "Feminism could destroy Russia, Russian orthodox patriarch claims." http://www.theguardian.com/world/2013/apr/09/feminism-destroy-russia-patriarch-kirill Accessed September 11, 2014.

Elkov, Igor'.r'. 2008. "Biznes-amazonki." *Rossii'skaia gazeta*, No. 49 (March 6): 6.

European Investment Bank. 2013 (November). "Small and medium entrepreneurship in Russia." http://www.eib.org/attachments/efs/econ_study_small_and_medium_entrepreneurship_in_russia_en.pdf Accessed August 15, 2014.

Fond Obshchestvennoe Mnenie. 2010 (March 11). "O Rossiiskoi zhenshchine." http://bd.fom.ru/pdf/d09zhen10.pdf Accessed September 18, 2014.

Fond Obshchestvennoe Menenie (FOM). 2012 (September 2). "'Zhenshchina—Tozhe Chelovek': Predstavleniia Rossiian o Feminizme." http://fom.ru/TSennosti/10611 Accessed August 29, 2017.

Goskomstat. 1997. *Zhenshchiny i muzhchiny Rossii*. Moscow: Goskomstat.

Goskomstat. 2008. *Zhenshchiny i muzhchiny Rossii*. Moscow: Goskomstat. http://www.gks.ru.

Goskomstat. 2010. *Zhenshchiny i muzhchiny Rossii*. Moscow: Goskomstat. http://www.gks.ru.
Goskomstat. 2012. *Zhenshchiny i muzhchiny Rossii*. Moscow: Goskomstat. http://www.gks.ru.
Goskomstat. 2014. *Zhenshchiny i muzhchiny Rossii*. Moscow: Goskomstat. http://www.gks.ru.
Goskomstat. 2016. *Rabochaia Sila, Zaniatnost' i Bezrabotnitsa v Rossii 2016*. Moscow: Goskomstat. http://www.gks.ru/.
Heinrich Boll Stiftung. Gunda Werner Institute. 2011 (February 14). "Patriarchal renaissance in Russia—Interview with Olga Zdravomyslova". http://www.gwi-boell.de/en/2011/02/14/patriarchal-renaissance-russia-interview-olga-zdravomyslova Accessed August 27, 2017.
Hemment, Julie. 2007. *Empowering Women in Russia: Activism, Aid, and NGOs*. Bloomington, IN: Indiana University Press.
Henderson, Sarah L. 2003. *Building Democracy in Contemporary Russia: Western Support for Grassroots Organizations*. Ithaca, NY: Cornell University Press.
Hilarion (Metropolitan Hilarion of Volokolamsk) 2012 (March 22). "Metropolitan Hilarion of Volokolamsk answers questions from visitors to the website of the synodal information department." https://mospat.ru.en/2012/03/22/news60400 Accessed August 18, 2013.
International Finance Corporation. 2014. "In Russia, more financing for women entrepreneurs." http://www.ifc.org/wps/wcm/connect/region__ext_content/regions/europe±middle±east±and±north±africa/ifc±in±europe±and±central±asia/news/in±russia%2C±more±financing±for±women±entrepreneurs Accessed August 23, 2014.
Interparliamentary Assembly of Member Nations of the Commonwealth of Independent States. 2013 (November 13). "Valentina Matvienko proposed to create the Eurasian women's forum." https://iacis.ru/eng/pressroom/news/sovet_mpa_sng/valeentina_matvienko_proposed_to_create_the_eurasian_women_s_forum/ Accessed August 27, 2017.
ITAR-TASS News Agency. 2014 (July 6). "Statistics: Lowest unemployment rates in Russia are in central regions." http://en.itar-tass.com/russia/739206 Accessed August 15, 2014.
Johnson, Janet Elise. 2009. *Gender Violence in Russia: The Politics of Feminist Intervention*. Bloomington: Indiana University Press.
Johnson, Janet Elise. 2014. "Pussy Riot as a feminist project: Russia's gendered informal politics." *Nationalities Papers*, 42(4): 583–590.
Johnson, Janet Elise, and Saarinen Aino. 2013. "Twenty-first-century feminisms under repression: gender regime change and the women's crisis center movement in Russia." *Signs: Journal of Women in Culture and Society*, 38(3): 543–567.
"Kakoe mesto Zanimaet segodnia Zhenshchina v politike i biznese Rossii?" 2006. *Izvestiia*, No. 38, March 3. http://dlib.eastview.com/sources/article.jsp?id=9118785 Penn State University Library.
Kochkina, Elena. 1997. *Informational Update. Email received from The Gender Expertise Project, November 20, 1997*. Edited by Kristen Hansen, Moscow: ABA CEELI.
Kononova, Svetlana. 2011 (May 10). "A gift to mothers: Women's rights NGOs have won a victory in changing how maternity benefits are paid out to Russian mothers." Special to Russian Profile. http://russiaprofile.org/culture_living/36157.html Accessed July 20, 2014.
Kozina, Irina and Zhidkova Elena. 2006. "Sex segregation and discrimination in the new Russian labour market." In *Adapting to Russia's New Labour Market: Gender and Employment Behavior*, 57–86. Edited by Sarah Ashwin, London: Routledge.
Lally, Kathy. 2012 (December 20). "Russians still forced to pay bribes, despite corruption fight." *The Washington Post*. http://www.washingtonpost.com/world/europe/russians-still-forced-to-pay-bribes-despite-corruption-fight/2012/12/20/f422ec8c-4384-11e2-9648-a2c323a991d6_story.html Accessed January 20, 2015.
Lapidus, Gail Warshovsky. 1978. *Women in Soviet Society: Equality, Development, and Social Change*. Berkeley, CA: University of California Press.

Levada Center. 2012. "Rossiiane ob otnoshenii k seksual'nym men'shinstvam." http://www.levada.ru/06-11-2012/rossiyane-ob-otnoshenii-k-seksualnym-menshinstvam Accessed May 7, 2014.

Levada Center. 2016a. "Russian public opinion 2013-2015." http://www.levada.ru/cp/wp-content/uploads/2016/01/2013-2015-Eng.pdf Accessed August 20, 2017.

Levada Center. 2016b. "Church." Press Release (April 5). https://www.levada.ru/en/2016/04/05/church/ Accessed August 28, 2017.

Lezhnina, Iu. P. 2011. "Sociodemographic factors determining the risk of poverty and low-income poverty." *Sociological Research*, 50(2): 13–31.

Lipovskaya, Olga. 1997. "Women's groups in Russia." In *Post-Soviet Women: From the Baltic to Central Asia*, pp. 186–199. Edited by Mary Buckley, Cambridge, UK: Cambridge University Press.

Lobzina, Alina. 2011 (March 18). "Tackling Russia's sex discrimination troubles." The Moscow News. http://themoscownews.com/society/20110318/188506302.html Accessed July 16, 2012.

Marquardt, Alexander 2010. "Why can't Russian women drive buses?" ABC News. http://abcnews.go.com/print?id=8220576 Accessed March 24, 2010.

McMahon, Colin. 2001. "Russia women embrace entrepreneurial spirit: Business group bucks status quo." Chicago Tribune (September 7). Johnson's Russia List, No. 5432, September 8, 2001. http://russialist.org/ Accessed September 10, 2001.

Mezentseva, Elena. 2006. "Gender inequality in today Russia: Who bear the social costs of reforms?" http://www.indiana.edu/~reeiweb/newsEvents/pre2006/mezentseva%20paper.pdf Accessed August 15, 2014.

Moscow Times. 2014 (June 9). "Justice ministry adds 5 more Russian NGOs to 'foreign agent' list." https://themoscowtimes.com/news/justice-ministry-adds-5-more-russian-ngos-to-foreign-agent-list-36315 Accessed August 27, 2017.

"Moscow to double city doctors' salaries by 2016." (June 1). RIA Novosti. http://en.ria.ru/russia/20110601/164360247.html Accessed July 30, 2014.

Motiejunaite, Akvile and Zhanna Kravchenko. 2008. "Family policy, employment and gender-role attitudes: A comparative analysis of Russia and Sweden." *Journal of European Social Policy*, 18(1): 38–49.

Nechemias, Carol. 1991. "The prospects for a Soviet Women's movement: Opportunities and obstacles." In *Perestroika from Below: Social Movements in the Soviet Union*, 56–72. Edited by Judith B. Sedaitis and Jim Butterfield, Boulder, CO: Westfield Press.

Nechemias, Carol. 2000. "Politics in post-Soviet Russia: Where are the women?" *Demokratizatsiya*, 8(2): 199–218.

Nechemias, Carol. 2003. "Russia." In *The Greenwood Encyclopedia of Women's Issues Worldwide: Europe*, 545–575. Edited by Lynn Walter, Westport, CT: Greenwood Press.

Nechemias, Carol. 2006. "Women organizing women in the Russian Federation." In *The U.S. Women's Movement in a Dynamic and Global Perspective*, pp. 151–176. Edited by Lee Ann Banaszak, Boulder, CO: Rowman & Littlefield Publishers.

NEWSru. 2012 (February 7). "Religiia i obshchestvo." http://newsru.com/religy/07feb2012/dimitriy_smirnov_print.html Accessed February 16, 2012.

Nikolaev, Denis and Dmitry Chugunov. 2012. "The education system in the Russian Federation: Education brief 2012." *World Bank Studies*. Washington, DC: The World Bank.

Obrazkova, Marina. 2013 (August 26). "Russians put career before having a family." Russia Beyond the Headlines. http://rbth.com/society/2013/08/26/russians_put_career_before_having_a_family_29201.html Accessed July 14, 2014.

Organization for Economic Co-operation and Development. 2011a. Better Policies for Better Lives. "Percentage of employed who are senior managers, by sex." http://www.oecd.org/gender/data/proportionofemployedwhoareseniormanagersbysex.htm Accessed January 8, 2014.

Organization for Economic Co-operation and Development. 2011b. *OECD Reviews of Labour Market and Social Policies: Russian Federation 2011*. Paris: OECD Publishing.

Petrova, A. 2004 (March 4). "Zhenshchiny dolzhny byt' ravny," Fond Obshchestvennoe Menenie (FOM). http://bd.fom.ru/report/cat/socium/soc_gr/lady_man/of040805 Accessed December 7, 2008.

Pew Research Center. 2010. "Gender equality universally embraced, but inequalities acknowledged." http://www.pewglobal.org/2010/07/01/gender-equality/ Accessed September 2, 2014.

Pew Research Center. 2014 (February 10). "Russians return to religion, but not to church." http://www.pewforum.org/2014/02/10/russians-return-to-religion-but-not-to-church/ Accessed August 28, 2017.

Posadskaya, Anastasia, Ed. 1994. *Women in Russia: A New Era in Russian Feminism*. Trans. Kate Clark. London: Verso.

Putin, Vladimir. 2006 (May 10). "Annual address to the federal assembly." http://eng.kremlin.ru/transcripts/8231 Accessed September 11, 2014.

Putin, Vladimir. 2007 (Oct.9). "Ukaz Prezidenta Rossiiskoi Federatsii." No. 1351. "Ob utverzhdenii Kontseptsii demograficheskoi politiki Rossiskoi Federatsii na period do 2025 goda." http://document.kremlin.ru.

Putin, Vladimir. 2013 (September19). "Meeting of the valdai international discussion club". http://eng.kremlin.ru/news/6007 Accessed September 5, 2014.

Putin, Vladimir. 2014 (14 February). "State council presidium meeting on family, motherhood and childhood policy." http://eng.news.kremlin.ru/transcripts/6687/print Accessed July 2, 2014.

Radzinsky, Edvard. 2005. "The other Russian revolution." *Wall Street Journal* (Eastern edition). August 30: A-10.

Richter, James. 2008. "Integration from below? The disappointing effort to promote civil society in Russia." In *Russia and Globalization: Identity, Security, and Society in an Era of Change*, 181–203. Edited by Douglas W. Blum. Baltimore, MD: Woodrow Wilson Center Press and the Johns Hopkins University Press.

Rivkin-Fish, Michele. 2010. "Pronatalism, gender politics, and the renewal of family support in Russia: Toward a feminist anthropology of 'Maternity Capital'." *Slavic Review*, 69(3): 701–724.

Rotkirch, Anna, Anna Temkina, and Zdravomyslova, Elena. 2007. "Who helps the degraded housewife?: Comments on Vladimir Putin's demographic speech." *European Journal of Women's Studies*, 14(4): 349–357.

Sharafutdinova, Gulnaz. 2014. "The Pussy Riot affair and Putin's démarche from sovereign democracy to sovereign morality." *Nationalities Papers*, 42(4): 615–621.

Shevchenko, Darina. 2006. "Nas strigut pod anglii'skii' gazon." *Vechernaiai Moskva*, No. 126, July 18: http://dlib.eastview.com/browse/doc/12848861 Accessed through Penn State University Library.

Slater, Wendy. 1995. "'Women of Russia' and women's representation in Russian politics." In *Russia in Transition: Politics, Privatization and Inequality*, 76–90. Edited by David Lane, London: Longman Group.

Smyth, Regina and Irina Soboleva. 2014. "Looking beyond the economy: Pussy Riot and the Kremlin's Voting Coalition." *Post-Soviet Affairs*, 30(4): 257–275.

Sperling, Valerie. 1999. *Organizing Women in Contemporary Russia: Engendering Transition.* Cambridge, UK: Cambridge University Press.

Sperling, Valerie. 2014a. *Sex, Politics, and Putin: Political Legitimacy in Russia.* Oxford, UK: Oxford University Press.

Sperling, Valerie. 2014b. "Russian Feminist Perspectives on Pussy Riot." *Nationalities Papers*, 42(4): 591–603.

Spinella, Peter. 2012 (May 11). "Low state salaries at heart of doctor deficit." *The Moscow Times.* http://www.themoscowtimes.com/business/article/tmt/458289.html Accessed August 1, 2014.

Statista: The Statistics Portal. 2014. "Russia: Unemployment Rate from 2004 to 2014." http://www.statista.com/statistics/263712/unemployment-in-russia/ Accessed August 25, 2014.

Tartakovskaya, Irina and Ashwin, Sarah. 2006. "Who benefits from networks?" In *Adapting to Russia's New Labour Market: Gender and employment behavior*, 164–192. Edited by Sarah Ashwin, London: Routledge.

Temkina, Anna. 2012. "The Gender Question in Contemporary Russia." *Global Dialogue: Newsletter for the International Sociological Association.* Volume 3 (1). www.isa-sociology.org/global-dialogue/category/v3-i1 Accessed January 9, 2013.

The Program for Public Consultation. 2008. (March 5). "International poll finds large majorities in all countries favor equal rights for women." http://www.worldpublicopinion.org/pipa/articles/btjusticehuman_rightsra/453.php?lb=bthr Accessed August 15, 2014.

Thornton, Grant. 2014. Women in business: From classroom to boardroom. Grant Thornton International Business Report 2014. http://www.grantthornton.com.au/files/ibr2014_wib_report.pdf Accessed January 20, 2015.

Trefilov, Ivan, Il'ia Kizirov, Melani Bachina, and Valeriia Ostroumova. 2015. "Rossiia za chertoi bednosti." *Radio Svoboda.* June 22, 2015. www.svoboda.org/content/article/27085040.html Accessed October 23, 2015.

Tsentral'noe statisticheskoe upravlenie RSFSR. 1986. *Narodnoe Khoziaistvo RSFSR v 1985 g.: Statisticheskii ezhegodnik.* Moscow: Financy i Statistika.

United Nations. 2000. "Russian federation: Replies to the questionnaire of the United Nations secretariat on the implementation of the Beijing platform." http://www.un.org/womenwatch/daw/Review/responses/RUSSIAN-FEDERATION-English.pdf Accessed August 26, 2014.

United Nations. 2005. "Gender equality and extension of women rights in Russia in the context of the UN millennium development goals." http://www.undp.ru/index.php?cmd=publications1&lid=1&id=46 Accessed August 15, 2014.

United Nations. 2010. *Committee on the Elimination of Discrimination Against Women, 46th Session, 12–30 July 2010. Concluding Observations of the Committee on the Elimination of Discrimination against Women. Russian Federation.* New York: New York City.

Vardanian, R.A. and E.V. Kochkina. 2008. "Elections: The gender gap." *Russian Social Science Review*, 49(3): 49–69.

Vishnevsky, Anatoly. 2010 (January 30). "On Russia's brief population increase." demography.matters.blog. http://demographymatters.blogspot.com/2010/01/on-russias-brief-population-increase.html Accessed August 5, 2014.

Vserossiiskii Tsentr Izucheniia Obshchestvennogo Meneniia. 2004. Press Release No. 63. "8 marta: O Roli Zhenshchiny v Rossiiskom Obshchestve." www.wciom.com/archives Accessed May 13, 2011.

Wedel, Janine R. 2001. *Collision & Collusion: The Strange Case of Western Aid to Eastern Europe.* NY, NY: Palgrave.

White, Anne. 2005. "Gender roles in contemporary Russia: Attitudes and expectations among women students." *Europe-Asia Studies*, 57(3): 429–455.

World Bank. 2014. *Russian Federation Gender Assessment.* Washington, DC: © World Bank. https://openknowledge.worldbank.org/handle/10986/21121 License: CC BY 3.0 IGO.

World Economic Forum. *The Global Gender Gap Report 2013.* 2013. http://reports.weforum.org/global-gender-gap-report-2013/#= Accessed June 15, 2014.

Yablokov, Ilya. 2014. "Pussy Riot as agent provocateur: Conspiracy theories and the media construction of nation in Putin's Russia." *Nationalities Papers*, 42(4): 622–636.

Yaroshenko, Svetlana, Elena Omel'chenko, Natal'ya Goncharova, and Olga Issoupova. 2006. "Gender differences in employment behavior in Russia's new labour market." In *Adapting to Russia's New Labour Market: Gender and Employment Behavior*, 134–163. Edited by Sarah Ashwin, London: Routledge.

Zhenshchiny i muzhchiny Rossii: Kratkii statisticheskii sbornik. 1997. Moscow: Goskomstat.

Zhenshchiny i muzhchiny Rossii: Kratkii statisticheskii sbornik. 1998. Moscow: Goskomstat.

Zhenshchiny i muzhchiny Rossii: Statisticheskii sbornik. 2012. Moscow: Goskomstat. http://www.gks.ru/.

9

WORKING POOR WOMEN IN MEXICO FACING ANOTHER CRISIS

Domestic workers, struggling with structural disadvantages, and the 2008 recession

Georgina Rojas-García and Mónica Patricia Toledo González

After Mexico, the United States, and Canada signed the North American Free Trade Agreement (NAFTA) in 1994, the Mexican economy became even more vulnerable than it had been to fluctuations in the U.S. economy. In 2008, although the United States had officially acknowledged the recession caused by the subprime mortgage crisis, Mexican officials seemed nonchalant about the recession's likely consequences for the national economy. But the recession hit Mexico hard. Not only was the main customer for Mexican exports in the middle of a deep recession, but other sources of income from the United States—especially tourism and remittances—declined substantially.

Mexico surmounted the effects of the recession quickly, according to official numbers anyway, and its gross domestic product (GDP) recovered by 2010. Officials claimed that the quick recovery was owed to the stability that the Mexican economy had achieved after the mid-1990s peso crisis. Many ordinary citizens, on the other hand, have yet to see their standard of living rise—notwithstanding improved macroeconomic indicators.

This chapter examines the repercussions of the 2008 recession on labor and, in particular, on domestic workers in Mexico. Paid domestic work (PDW) is a key example of labor segregation by gender. It has also been characterized as having some of the most precarious working conditions among all jobs: instability, low pay, and no social security or benefits. Domestic workers are at the bottom of the occupation hierarchy, together with such other low-paying occupations as street vendors. The economic crisis exacerbated an already grim situation for these domestic workers.

This study addresses the following questions: how did the 2008 recession affect Mexican labor, in general? How did domestic workers, in particular, fare within the Mexican labor structure? What impact did the 2008 recession have on domestic workers' daily lives? How did they respond to it? How do they manage to fulfill their responsibilities both at work and at home today?

To answer these questions, the study employed a methodological strategy that combined both quantitative and qualitative information. The statistical data were provided by the National Survey on Occupation and Employment (ENOE, in Spanish) and depict a panorama of macro changes in the Mexican labor structure. The qualitative information was collected by firsthand observation and thirty-four in-depth interviews conducted between 2010 and 2011. The fieldwork was carried out in Mexico City and the state of Tlaxcala, both in central Mexico, between 2010 and 2011. To be included in this study, an interviewee must either have been working as a domestic at the time of the interview (thirty-two participants) or have left domestic work no longer than a year before the interview (two participants). The interviews included both live-in and live-out domestic workers.

The chapter is structured as follows. First, it describes the effects of the 2008 recession on Mexico's economy and labor structure. Second, it considers domestics' working conditions and their place within Mexico's labor structure. Next, it examines how domestic workers struggle daily to overcome the economic constraints imposed by the market, especially in the aftermath of the 2008 recession. It concludes with final remarks.

The 2008 recession and the Mexican labor market

The influence of the 2008 American recession in Mexico was preceded by two important periods of economic shock: the debt crisis of the 1980s and the peso crisis of the mid-1990s. Though the Mexican economy officially recovered from the last recession by 2012 (Salas 2013), its performance has been sluggish for decades. GDP grew at an average of 3.4 percent during the 1990s but slowed to less than half that, 1.6 percent annually, between 2000 and 2010—one of the lowest growth rates in Latin America (Salas 2013; Zepeda et al. 2009).

Mexico's structural shift to greater economic openness also heightened its vulnerability to economic downturns abroad, especially in the United States. About 90 percent of Mexican exports go to its northern neighbor. After NAFTA was signed, Mexico became the third largest exporter to the United States, although after 2002, it lost ground to other countries, especially China, which jumped from fourth place to second (Gallagher et al. 2008). Additionally, although exports have become diversified, encompassing the automotive, electronic, and textile sectors (among others), oil still accounts for about a third of Mexico's total foreign revenue (Zepeda et al. 2009). According to Zepeda and colleagues, the attraction of foreign direct investment may have tripled since the mid-1990s but has not raised total investment levels. The decline in public investment has not been compensated for by rises in private ones.

Since the signature of NAFTA, Mexico has become more dependent on external stability. According to Blecker, the Mexican economy "has become chronically dependent on external forces as the motor of its expansion and remains highly vulnerable to adverse external shocks" (2009, 1281). And the

American economy is the external factor upon which Mexico most depends. As Salas (2013) has demonstrated, the main external determinants of Mexico's economic growth are net financial flows, the real international price of petroleum, and the rate of growth of the American economy.

Because the 2008 recession decreased demand for Mexican exports, the price of raw materials dropped, capital costs increased, and credit contracted. Two important sources of revenue from the United States, remittances and tourism, declined sharply. Internally, the swine flu and the war on drugs both siphoned government resources and scared tourists away during the first half of 2009 (Ochoa 2013).

The Mexican government was slow in reacting, announcing specific policies only in 2009. These measures included increasing public spending and investment in infrastructure, supporting businesses to stanch layoffs, and implementing job programs such as the Temporary Employment Program. These measures did not suffice to counteract the crisis: the Mexican GDP registered the highest contraction in Latin America, falling by 6 percent in 2009 (Ochoa 2013); unemployment increased from 3.3 percent at the onset of the crisis to 6.4 percent at its height in September 2009;[1] average wages fell by 4 percent; and most new jobs were created by small firms rather than by large ones (Salas 2013).

Following Salas' argument, while these policies were approved by Congress and may have had the potential to be effective, their impact was severely curtailed by mid-2009 reductions in federal expenditures, a result of the government's underestimating the effect of the crisis on its own revenues. Subsequent recovery has been gradual, and while unemployment has fallen, it remains above the pre-crisis level, wages have increased only marginally, and small businesses continue to be the main locus of job creation (Salas 2013, 206). In the long run, consolidating macrostructural economic change has led to social costs that are reflected in the labor sphere.

Some characteristics of the labor structure in Mexico

The Mexican labor structure is polarized. Only a small segment of the workforce has access to decent jobs, while the bulk of the working poor have low-quality jobs. There are two salient structural characteristics of the labor market in Mexico: a low unemployment rate coupled with a stagnant economy and a large share of the workforce employed in informal, unprotected economic activities (Rojas and Salas 2008).

In the absence of proper unemployment insurance and real saving capacity, the bulk of workforce resorts to any activities that bring home a little more income. These underemployed workers artificially inflate employment registries (Salas and Zepeda 2003). For instance, during the mid-1990s crisis, the overall unemployment rate was 7.4 percent, the highest in Mexican history (Ochoa 2013). More recently, in 2009, when the recession hit hardest in Mexico, the unemployment rate barely exceeded 6 percent (Salas 2013). Mexico has one of the lowest unemployment rates among members of the Organization for Economic Cooperation and Development (OECD), even though it is one of the poorest OCDE members and is the country where job quality could be the worst.[2] That is, not only the salaries are the lowest among OCDE members, but also it characterizes by its lack of social security and very low rate of unionizing.

Informal employment—non-professional, self-employed, and paid labor in small firms of five employees or less that are not registered by Hacienda, Mexico's taxing authority—has grown since the 1980s (Roberts 1991a; Salas and Zepeda 2003). In 1976, informal workers constituted 39.4 percent of the total workforce (Roberts 1991a). During 2007–2008, however, informal employment had reached 58 percent, and in mid-2013 it was 59.1 percent (FORLAC 2014). With three-fifths of the labor force in informal jobs, informal employment has been a prominent, enduring feature of the Mexican labor market. Two factors closely associated with informal employment are the growth of the tertiary sector and dependence on small firms to create jobs (Salas 2013).

Such a reliance of the labor market on small firms is not a negative feature per se. In the Mexican case, however, it has meant that large firms, which are more prone to creating jobs registered with Hacienda, cannot stimulate the internal economy. Thus, small firms with five workers or fewer tend to provide low-paying and low-productivity jobs that are not covered by the social security system, meaning that workers neither have access to health services nor are able to participate in retirement funding plans. Although small firms provide inexpensive goods for the low-income population, they have masked what would otherwise appear in the statistics as unemployment among the Mexican workforce (Salas and Zepeda 2003).

In addition to these characteristics of the Mexican labor market, data from ENOE help identifying some repercussions of the 2008 recession on working conditions among some selected occupations. Among these occupational groups, "professionals"—including workers that hold a college or advanced degree—is the only group selected from the top rungs of the occupational ladder; Tables 9.1 to 9.3 contrast professionals working conditions with those of the other occupational groups.

Social security coverage is the first element of these examined conditions. In Mexico, social security refers to public health system access and retirement savings. Table 9.1 shows that while 42.5 percent of professionals were without social security in 2007, by 2012 that figure had dropped to 38.8 percent. Although this suggests that conditions for professionals were improving, it also reveals that the proportion without social protection was still high given their privileged position on the labor ladder. The other occupational groups in the table are semiskilled or unskilled manual workers, and except for those on the police force and in private security, who are mostly covered, large proportions of workers in all occupational groups have no social security. Street venders are left entirely on their own—practically none are covered. Interestingly, despite

TABLE 9.1 Lack of Social Security among Mexican Workforce, 2007–2012

Selected Occupations	No Social Security (%)		
	2007	2009	2012
Professionals	42.5	41.5	38.8
Merchants, Retail Sales, and Clerks	76.3	76.2	77.4
Street Venders	99.7	99.7	99.7
Service Workers	64.0	66.8	68.4
Domestic Workers	95.1	95.1	96.2
Transportation Operators	60.7	63.3	63.8
Police and Private Security	15.9	17.2	17.5
Skilled Blue-collar	64.1	67.2	64.2
Unskilled Blue-collar	75.6	76.3	77.3
All Occupations	64.0	64.6	65.1

Source: National Survey of Occupation and Employment (ENOE).

engaging in wage labor, few domestics have social security, a situation that seems to have worsened after the crisis.

Regarding the length of the workweek, Table 9.2 shows that while most groups saw an increase in their average workweek between 2007 and 2012, the number of hours worked per week decreased for some groups. Overall, the information suggests that most Mexican workers were employed full time and that average weekly hours worked increased after the 2008 recession. The 2009 figures are close to 2007 levels, but in most cases, 2012 showed moderate to sharp increases since 2009.

During this period, the workweek got longer for most occupational groups, whether professional or manual workers, supporting Cortés and Rubalcava's (1991) "self-exploitation" hypothesis, which posits that the Mexican workforce exploits itself to make ends meet. Yet for other groups, including domestic workers and street venders, working hours went down after the crisis. Why did these groups work less instead of more in the face of an economic downturn? The reason may lie in what the Mexican Census Bureau pithily calls "market reasons." Since potential employers had less disposable income, domestic workers had trouble finding work or had their hours reduced, lowering the average workweek for the group as whole. The chapter will return to this point in its later analysis of qualitative data.

Income deserves special attention in this analysis of Mexican labor. Since the structural adjustments of the 1980s, the containment of labor costs has been crucial in attracting foreign investment (Salas and Zepeda 2003). In general, Mexican labor is comparatively cheaper than labor in its northern neighbors. Within this general panorama of low-paying work, though, the Mexican labor structure exhibits great

TABLE 9.2 Weekly working hours among Mexican Workforce, 2007–2012

Selected Occupations	Avg. Weekly Work Hours		
	2007	2009	2012
Professionals	38.06	38.8	42.4
Merchants, Retail Sales, and Clerks	37.0	37.6	47.0
Street Venders	41.1	41.8	30.3
Service Workers	36.0	36.9	40.5
Domestic Workers	38.7	39.6	32.5
Transportation Operators	38.7	38.7	55.2
Police and Private Security	39.6	40.0	63.0
Skilled Blue-collar	38.2	38.9	43.0
Unskilled Blue-collar	29.7	30.5	42.6
All Occupations	37.6	38.1	41.9

Source: National Survey of Occupation and Employment (ENOE) data.

heterogeneity in the precariousness of working conditions. Nowhere is this reflected more acutely than in income (Rojas García and Salas 2008).

Data suggest that labor income in Mexico has deteriorated since the 2008 recession. Comparing income across occupational groups (Table 9.3), professionals' monthly income far outstrips the rest. The next highest-earning groups, transportation operators and security personnel, earn less than half of what professionals do. Domestic workers make roughly a fourth of professionals' income; they constitute the occupational group located at the very bottom of the earnings scale. Such disparity in labor income helps explain the socioeconomic inequality workers face in daily life in Mexico.

Segregation and domestic workers within the Mexican labor structure

Not only must women work in a labor market polarized by inequitably distributed income and social benefits, but they must also face an occupational structure highly segregated by gender. In Mexico, 98 percent of female workers cluster in ten occupational groups: professionals, managers, technicians, workers in education, manual and blue-collar workers, administrative workers, merchants, street venders, personal service workers, and domestic workers (Pedrero 2003, 409).

As in other parts of the world, a deeper gender-based critique would show that many of these occupational categories are considered socially appropriate female skills, such as manual dexterity, and (in keeping with the patriarchal stereotype) a "natural proclivity" toward caretaking. Such presumably female occupations include secretarial work; professional health and educational services; blue-collar

TABLE 9.3 Monthly income among Mexican Workforce, 2007–2012

Selected Occupations	USD Montly Income*		
	2007	2009	2012
Professionals	993.6	881.1	818.7
Merchants, Retail Sales, and Clerks	405.8	326.6	314.5
Street Venders	243.5	205.8	198.4
Service Workers	319.1	272.0	270.9
Domestic Workers	211.7	185.3	188.9
Transportation Operators	500.6	405.4	406.9
Police and Private Security	437.7	408.9	396.3
Skilled Blue-collar	390.1	327.0	323.2
Unskilled Blue-collar	298.5	263.3	264.5
All Occupations	433.1	365.4	348.6

* Nominal income was deflated by the Mexican Price Consumer Index and then translated into American dollars of every period
Source: National Survey of Occupation and Employment (ENOE) data.

maquiladora industrial work, a sector in which nimble fingers are needed to assemble small, fragile pieces; a wide range of personal services from beauty to childcare; and, last but not least, cleaning and cooking.

PDW in Mexico exemplifies both the wage polarization and gender segregation of the workforce. On the one hand, nine out of ten domestic workers are women. Gender segregation into different occupations and economic sectors also implies an income gap. Table 9.4 shows the share of women's income relative to men's in diverse economic sectors and compares the income of wage and non-wage workers.

As shown in Table 9.4, women's income is generally lower than men's in most sectors. Non-wage women earn even less than men and women enrolled in dependent activities, that is, salary relationships. The pattern repeats in almost every sector. Among wage workers, women's income represents 86 percent of men's average income; comparatively, among all non-wage workers, women's income reaches, on average, only 57 percent of that of their male counterparts.

It is important to note, as ample feminist literature has demonstrated, that the preference for female workers is based on two factors. First, a large share of the Mexican workforce is involved in jobs characterized by low wages, short-term contracts, low rates of unionization, few or no benefits, job insecurity, and a precarious labour environment. Second, a socioeconomically vulnerable female labor force, paid significantly lower wages than men, is readily available. In other words, women are a cheaper labor force (Tiano 1994; Vosko 2010; Ward 1990).

In Mexico, as in other parts of the world, the female workforce is concentrated on the lowest rungs of the occupational ladder. Based on the ENOE, in

TABLE 9.4 Percentage of women's average monthly wage relative to men's in Mexico, 2014

Sector	Wage and Salary workers	Non-wage workers
Agriculture, Forestry, Fishing and Hunting	0.96	0.84
Mining, Quarrying, and Oil and Gas Extraction	1.12	0.4
Utilities	1.04	0
Manufacturing	0.77	0.36
Construction	1.36	2.1
Wholesale Trade	0.9	0.56
Retail Trade	0.8	0.51
Accommodation and Food Services	0.75	0.52
Transportation and Warehousing	1.02	1.16
Information	0.85	0.28
Finance and Insurance	0.81	0.62
Real Estate and Rental and Leasing	1.02	0.79
Professional, Scientific, and Technical Services	0.72	0.86
Management of Companies and Enterprises	0.81	–
Administrative and Support and Waste Management and Remediation Services	0.82	0.79
Educational Services	0.85	0.83
Healthcare and Social Assistance	0.76	0.72
Accommodation and Food Services	0.91	0.65
Other Services (except Public Administration)	0.61	0.56
Public Administration	0.97	–
Total	0.86	0.57

Source: National Survey of Occupation and Employment (ENOE) data (Second quarter).

2015, eight out of ten workers enrolled in personal services were women—personal services include a wide spectrum of services that ranges from beauty parlors to sex service sold on the streets. In other activities, such as restaurant and hotel work, the figure was similar (7.6 women out of 10 workers), and six out of ten workers participating in retail commerce were women. A common thread in those activities, as for paid domestic work, is the lack of protection—fringe benefits, access to health services—which, added to the low pay, creates unfavorable working conditions for two-thirds of all Mexicans who participate in the labor market.

This segment of the workforce in Mexico corresponds to what was called the "informal proletariat" by Portes and Hoffman (2003) in their study of social stratification in Latin America. This category, the lowest in their rankings, includes non-contractual wage workers, casual vendors, and family unpaid workers. Although paid domestic workers share the precariousness of their working conditions with, for instance, street vendors and sex workers, there are some nuances among these groups of workers that are worth emphasizing.[3]

Comparatively, paid domestic workers are less vulnerable than the other two groups. Most of the domestic workers in Mexico are employed directly by a person with whom they establish a minimum agreement about tasks, salary, and schedule; whereas street vendors and sex workers must find casual customers. Although paid domestic workers enter an asymmetrical relationship, the fact that the two parties celebrate a verbal, face-to-face agreement gives the workers certain bargaining power with their employers. A third feature that makes a difference is the location of the work. Whereas casual vendors and sex workers use the street to find their customers, domestic workers are employed within a house. While this does not guarantee a violence-free working environment for domestics, working on the street makes casual vendors and sex workers prone to social stigmatization and vulnerable to violence.

Despite the relative advantage that paid domestic workers have in their working conditions, the applicable labor law is contradictory and allows for rights violations. On the one hand, Article 123 of the Mexican Constitution fully recognizes domestic work, stating,

> Every person is entitled to a dignifying and socially useful job; to this effect, creation of jobs and social organization for working shall be promoted, according to the law. Congress will pass labor law that will govern over industrial workers, day workers, domestic workers, handcrafters and, in general, every labor contract
>
> *(Mexican Political Constitution)*[4]

On the other hand, the Federal Labor Law classifies domestic work under "special jobs," which devalues it and exempts employers from required provisions regarding the length of the working day, minimum wage, social security, maternity leave, Christmas bonus, and paid vacation, among others. In practice, placing domestic workers in this "special job" status excludes them from their right to housing and social security (health services and a future retirement) or reinstallment in their jobs; deprives them of collective association and unionizing; and, in general, neglects their labor stability. This contradiction, compounded by virtually no enforcement of the protections that do exist, substitutes employers' good will for legal obligations present in other occupations.

In practice, too, Mexican labor law is discriminatory against paid domestic workers because social security registration is not compulsory and they do not benefit from housing programs. Contrary to what is stated under the Federal Labor Law for any other job, the law states that domestic workers should display "consideration and respect" toward their employer, the employers' family, and their guests. This statement leaves an aftertaste of medieval language and reveals expectations of servitude from the domestic worker instead of a contractual labor relationship.

Domestic workers in Mexico have also suffered from systematic discrimination, based on three interconnected dimensions: gender, class, and ethnicity. Such discrimination does not solely occur in face-to-face interactions but is also evident in the regulatory framework, the rights and obligations that arise in this working relationship (Goldsmith 2007). For example, Mexico has not yet achieved ratification of the International Labor Organization (ILO)'s Domestic Work Covention 189. This Convention promotes the labor rights of paid domestic workers. It establishes the legal principles and basic rights to which workers have access, as well as the role of States in ensuring them.

This analysis next considers the sociodemographic profile of Mexican paid domestic workers. Based on the ENOE, there were 1,347,885 paid domestic workers in 1995, representing 4.1 percent of the total economically active population (EAP). By 2012, those figures had reached 2,266,422, a slight increase to 4.6 percent of the EAP.[5] Macrostructural economic changes have resulted in different occupational distributions of women in the EAP over time (Rendón 1990). Among working women, a fifth were domestic workers in 1970, but in 1995, that percentage was 11.5 percent, where it appears to have plateaued. In 2012, 11.1 percent of working women were paid domestic workers.

Table 9.5 shows some demographic characteristics of domestic workers in Mexico in 2007 and 2014. Almost half were married (46 percent in 2007 and 49.9 percent in 2014), and their average age was 40.3 years old (INEGI 2014). In 2014, the bulk of domestic workers (59.6 percent) were of prime working age (twenty-nine to forty-nine years old), and 25.7 percent were fifty years old or above. Despite general education gains in Mexico's workforce, most domestic workers have attained very low levels of education: in 2014, 55.6 percent had completed only primary school (six years or less), and another 35.6 percent had achieved up to nine years of schooling (secondary school or junior high).

As Table 9.3 shows, domestic workers make the least money of all occupational groups. Table 9.4 provides a shaper picture of wages among such workers: 31.9 of domestic workers earned up to the minimum wage a day (US$4.94 dollars)—barely above a poverty wage, given that, according to ECLAC and ILO, the minimum wage in Mexico is below the poverty line (Moreno-Brid, Garry, and Monroy-Gómez-Franco 2014). An additional 39 percent made twice the minimum wage (9.88 dollars) or less, which means that 70 percent of domestics and their families had to live on less than US$10 a day.

INEGI (2014) also reports that only 7.4 percent of domestic workers are currently hired as live-in workers, and, as Goldsmith notes, "the articulation between the demand from middle-class and the supply of older and married (domestic) workers has implied that [the living-out modality] is growing" (2007, 286). This shift reflects a restructuring of PDW in response to converging factors. From the demand side, the middle-class has neither the space—a spare room— nor the money to house and feed an extra person. Culturally, most families appreciate their privacy and intimacy is in such a way that they prefer hiring a live-out domestic worker (Toledo Gonzalez 2014). This modality also responds to the needs of the supply side. Because most domestic workers are married and have children, their own domestic responsibilities are incompatible with a live-in commitment. The living-out modality gives them some flexibility in using their time and, as discussed below, helps them reconcile their needs in both the social reproductive and productive arenas.

This increase in live-out PDW has meant greater autonomy for the domestic workers themselves, such as more freedom to set schedules, define the types of work they wish to do, and so on. But that increased autonomy still carries a heavy price: PDW remains a precarious occupation. Domestics, either living-in or living-out, may be "fired" at any time because they do not have a written contract, which makes PDW highly unstable. Domestic workers generally do not have social security and their incomes are low, often barely poverty-level. Greater freedom often means greater freedom to be poor. And while in theory the increasing prevalence of living-out work could mean greater autonomy, in practice, domestic workers' margin for negotiating with employers is fairly limited. The overabundance of unskilled labor in the Mexican labor force means that paid domestic workers often work on terms defined mostly by employers.

Domestic workers facing the 2008 recession

This section turns to domestics' daily life experiences and examines their strategies for handling the impact of the 2008 recession. Next, it considers how these workers reconcile their economic needs with their responsibilities at home, that is to say, how they match their needs in the productive and reproductive spheres. Finally, it explores collective organization efforts made by domestic workers.

As stated earlier, we gathered qualitative data through thirty-four in-depth-interviews. The ages of the participating domestic workers ranged from nineteen to sixty years old—with an average of 37.1, similar to that of female EAPs nationwide. Their average schooling was 9.6 years. Most (twenty-five out of thirty-four) worked under the live-out modality. Although it cannot be claimed that this sample is broadly representative, their characteristics do generally reflect the national domestic worker's profile provided in Table 9.5.

We classified the interviewed domestic workers into three groups based on two criteria: their family structure and their vulnerability to poverty. Group I comprised single women whose incomes helped provide for their family of origin (five workers, or 14.7 percent of the total group). Group II contained married women with dependent children who shared household expenses with their husbands (seventeen women, or 50 percent). Group III was composed of women with dependent children who headed their households and were thus solo providers for their families (twelve women, or 35.3 percent).

Repercussions of the 2008 recession and the strategies for facing it

Wage stagnation has been endemic since economic restructuring took place in Mexico in the 1980s. Income fell after the 2008 recession (see Table 9.3). How did the participating domestic workers experience and deal with these declines?

TABLE 9.5 Sociodemographic characteristics and working conditions of domestic workers' Mexico by percentages, 2007 and 2014

Feature	2007	2014
Gender		
Male	9.3	10.3
Female	90.7	89.7
Total	100	100
Marital Status		
Single	34.6	31.5
Married	46.0	49.9
Once Married (Divorced, Widower, separated)	19.2	18.6
Not specified	0.1	0.0
Total	100	100
Age		
From 14 to 24 years old	18.9	14.7
From 25 to 49 years old	58.0	59.6
From 50 and above	23.0	25.7
Not specified	0.1	0.1
Total	100	100
Schooling		
Elementary or less (6 years or less)	68.6	55.6
Junior High (up to 9 years)	27.0	35.6
High School (up to 12 years)	3.4	7.0
College	0.6	1.6
Not specified	0.3	0.2
Total	100	100
Income Level		
Up to 1 Minimum Wage	30.4	31.9
More than 1 and up to 2 MW	38.4	39.0
More than 2 and up to 3 times the MW	19.6	18.1
More than 3 and up to 5 times the MW	5.8	3.5
More than 5 times the MW	0.7	0.4
Without pay	0.3	0.3
Not specified	4.8	7.0
Total	100	100
N	2,022,518	2,339,940

Source: National Survey of Occupation and Employment (ENOE) data.

Income is an important point of departure for understanding the recession's consequences on the daily lives of domestics and their families. In 2010–2011, the income of workers in our sample ranged from US$6.02 to US$17.33 per day.[6] Because they did not necessarily work a full week, their individual incomes fluctuated from US$45.21 to US$105.5 per week. Making ends meet was difficult for domestics and their families even in the best of times, even without being shaken by a recession.

The 2008 recession affected the participants' incomes in several ways. One was their employers' diminished capacity to pay them. Goldsmith (1990) reported that cutting some expenses, including domestic service, was a common response among the middle class to the effects of economic crises during the 1980s. Among the women in our sample, Lucía (Group III) remembered, "Back then [2009], the *señora* [employer] did not hire me for the whole week anymore. She said she was not able to pay me."[7] There were other cases in which the domestic's husband was laid off and the family had to find a coping strategy. Patricia (Group II) recalled that her husband, Pepe, used to be a blue-collar worker but was laid off. Pepe was told by the factory where he used to work that they had to cut the payroll, starting with those workers like him, who did not have at least a junior high education. For three months, he looked fruitlessly for a job. A *compadre* of Pepe's later helped him get a job as a public transportation driver. During Pepe's unemployment, Patricia was the only person in the home who was bringing in income for the family.

Since the 1980s, studies on the crises in Mexico and in Latin America have used the notion of "household strategy," which, according to Roberts, is "a set of activities consciously undertaken by one or more members of a household over a period of time, directed toward ensuring the longer term survival of the household unit" that provide a way of "organizing the household to get by in the short and medium term" (Roberts 1991b, 139). Using Roberts' framework to understand the actions of domestic workers and their families taken in response to economic pressures in everyday life, our evidence supports the earlier finding that Mexican working-class households try to better stretch their resources despite having little maneuvering room (Selby et al. 1990). Like other previous studies (Cortés and Rubalcava 1991; González De La Rocha 1988; Roberts 1991b), we found that the most recurrent coping strategies among the participants in our study were increasing the variety of economic activities to earn an income, deploying a larger workforce, and adjusting or reducing consumption.

The first response to the difficult economic situation that we found in the domestic workers' narratives was that household members who were already employed added more hours to their workweek or developed a multiactivity strategy. Some of our informants, still relying on paid domestic work, the activity they knew the best, tried to add more workdays or more houses to clean in a single day, or they performed specific domestic activities such as laundry, washing dishes, or ironing and were paid by the job. Raquel (Group III) cleaned a house from Monday to Saturday and on Sundays looked to neighbors for extra laundry work, washing eighty to a hundred garments on her "day off." Lorena (Group II) had an ex-employer who had previously hired her for the whole week and now called her from time to time to do cooking, which gave Lorena a "few *pesitos* more."

This multiactivity strategy basically consisted of carrying out other informal income-generating activities parallel to domestic work. One such activity was making food to sell at one's own home. For example, Rosa (Group III) worked as a domestic from Monday through Saturday and on Thursday and Friday also sold *antojitos* (Mexican snacks). She would set up her food stand outside her door during the evening and hawk different corn-based foodstuffs to her neighbors. Another activity that domestics performed during their "spare" time was doing others' household chores in exchange for payment, such as laundry and sewing. Aurora (Group III), for example, would "go to a workshop where I ask for work. I get a load of garments that I take home to sew. When I finish, I take it back and get some money." Similarly, Claudia (Group II) reported that she eventually works in a small textile workshop, "I do not sew very well, but I get some tasks that I can do. I fray. I work on removing the extra shreds of finished garments and folding them."[8] A third kind of activity reported by some participants was selling goods from a catalogue—shoes, clothing, makeup items, and kitchen utensils. Isabel (Group I) borrowed 500 pesos (US$37) from her father to invest in her "business" of selling shoes and makeup. She also knitted some items. Her target clients were her employers and neighbors.

Rosario offers another example of developing several activities simultaneously to make ends meet (Group III). When not doing PDW, she worked as a waitress or washed dishes at big events in her hometown. She occasionally prepared food to sell. She also constantly gathered aluminum cans and recyclable plastic bottles and sold them at recycling centers. In short, she did anything that helped to improve her income: "I say, you gotta look. Sometimes there's not enough [money], and what can you do? You gotta look."

The second survival or coping strategy we observed in our sample was sending household members who had not previously been working into the labor market. In the households studied, this was most frequently the case with children because the woman and her husband were already working. It is important to note that households often combine some of these survival strategies, meaning that households may mix them to become more efficient (Selby et al. 1990). In Viridiana's household (Group II), her daughter, Linda, not only took care of the household duties while Viridiana is at work but also worked several hours nearby to earn some extra income. These two strategies, sending other household members into the labor market and diversifying activities, are forms of self-exploitation (Cortés and Rubalcava 1991).

As a third strategy, families tighten their belts, postponing or eliminating what they consider non-critical expenses, such as healthcare and schooling for the kids. In our interviews, many informants reported putting off seeking healthcare. Lucía

(Group III) had not visited the doctor to seek care for one of her knees, which she assumed would require "a lot of medicine" that she could not afford. As ample feminist scholarship has pointed out, female members of the household often add caregiving for the ill and elderly relatives to their daily unpaid shifts. Lucía from Group III and Viridiana (Group II) decided to remove their daughters from secondary (junior high) school due to daunting immediate expenses despite the long-term effects it would have on their daughters' qualifications for work, thereby reproducing an unskilled labor force whose future might consist of precarious labor.

Although all of the women interviewed needed to work outside the home to contribute in household reproduction, there were sharp differences among the three groups of women, specifically regarding their labor relations (more or less stable and whether they have education or networks that eventually will help them find a more rewarding job), and family structure (either they are single mothers or have a partner that also provides income to the household, and whether they have economically dependent children or rather their offspring can also help).

Women in Group I had relatively greater autonomy in deciding whether to keep working in the same house and activities or to move on. Since they were childless single women, they helped provide financial assistance to their maternal homes, but nobody else depended directly on their earnings. Women in the other two groups, however, were more constrained. Although the women in Group II were not sole providers—they shared expenses with their husbands—the money they brought home did make a difference in their living standards, and they were co-responsible for their dependent children. Women in Group III had far fewer choices about where and when to work and about what work they could do. Their income was crucial for their households' survival.

These various coping strategies used to weather the 2008 recession not only had their limits, but might also have put the families' future resources at risk—for instance, when healthcare was postponed or children were taken out of school. Even so, not all domestic workers in our study were able to implement these strategies. Some faced external market restraints, such as lowered middle-class demand for their services. Some lacked access to money for investing in microbusinesses that might have allowed them to bring a little more income home. In the end, all these strategies helped participating domestics' households to survive, but none significantly changed their living standards.

Double-work shift versus negotiating unpaid social reproduction

Domestic work (paid or unpaid) has a basic role in social reproduction, because, as Laslett and Brenner write: "Feminists use social reproduction to refer to the activities and attitudes, behaviors and emotions, responsibilities and relationships directly involved in the maintenance of life on a daily basis, and intergenerationally" (1989, 383).

Thus, the abovementioned process has several components, such as:

> how food, clothing, and shelter are made available for immediate consumption, the ways in which the care and socialization of children are provided, the care of the infirm and elderly, and the social organization of sexuality. Social reproduction can thus be seen to include various kinds of work-mental, manual, and emotional-aimed at providing the historically and socially, as well as biologically, defined care necessary to maintain existing life and to reproduce the next generation. And the organization of social reproduction refers to the varying institutions within which this work is performed, the varying strategies for accomplishing these tasks, and the varying ideologies that both shape and are shaped by them.
>
> *(Laslett y Brenner, 1989, 383)*

The social organization of reproductive labor is shaped by multiple factors, such as gender roles, the sexual division of labor, class position, and resources available to a household. Patriarchal values continue to permeate both male and female ideologies in general in Mexico, cutting across social classes and gender. The traditional sexual division of labor is therefore generally not in question, and Mexican women tend to assume responsibilities in the domestic arena as their own (Rojas and Toledo 2013). As Rojas and Toledo argued, to accomplish all the activities involved in reproductive labor, Mexican women either do these activities themselves within the household or resort to the market. It is basically middle-class women who can pay for the necessary activities or services, such as cleaning, childcare and preparing food, for instance, resulting in the "stratified social reproduction" (Colen 1995). Thus the commodification of these daily reproductive activities helps, in turn, to reproduce structural gender and class inequalities. How do women in this study reconcile both their paid and unpaid household responsibilities?

Some patterns emerged from our interviews. Before looking for work outside the home to give husbands what women initially perceived as "some help" in making ends meet, many of the women in our sample had to "negotiate" with their husbands for permission to work outside the home. These "negotiations" sometimes turned into verbal confrontations. According to most husbands, the state, and society in general, a wife's priority must be keeping her own home, including cleaning, cooking for the family, and looking after the children. The husbands of the women we interviewed often conditioned "granting permission" to work outside the home on wives' guaranteeing fulfillment of these primary obligations.

The women in this study struggled daily to stretch the income provided by their husbands, who were socially expected to meet the responsibilities of the household's breadwinner. As Toña (Group II) described this struggle,

> Truly, his [the husband's] earnings are not enough, and I, as a housewife, am the one who suffers. For instance, he gives me 500 pesos [US$37.31] per week. From that I have to get food for all of us and even pay the kids' daily transportation to go to school. Sometimes I notice their shoes are not good anymore, or they are asked at school to bring a book. What he gives to me is not enough. I prefer to work, so when my kids need something [I can tell them], "Here my son, here you have [some money]."
>
> (Toña)

Toña reported that her husband would constantly remind her that she should not go outside the home to work but stay home "to take care of the kids and the house," but that she nonetheless felt squeezed by the need for additional income. Like Toña, other women in our study had learned to live with the internal conflict caused by violating a norm they had been socialized to embrace since a tender age, and as a result, many tried to figure out a way to survive on what their husbands provided. That was the case of Patricia (Group II), who, although she worked outside the home, stated, "I was taught that one stands by the husband, that one sticks to whatever he can give. And so it has to be; I must devote myself to my children."

The women who participated in our study generally resolved the dilemma posed by the conflict between the reproduction of their domestic units and working outside the home in two key ways: 1) intensifying their *doble jornada*, or double shifts, that is working outside the home and taking care of the households chores; and, 2) delegating their chores to someone else who lived in the house or nearby. At home, women often charged the older children (especially daughters), other female relatives, or even neighbors with specific domestic duties. Viridiana's (Group II) household organization typifies this arrangement. Viridiana had five children, three of which (two sons aged seventeen and four, and a fifteen-year-old daughter) still lived with her and her husband, who was a blue-collar worker. They lived in a rented house, for which they paid 500 pesos (US$37.31) a month. Linda, Viridiana's daughter, was not accepted at the high school she wanted to attend and decided that she would wait a year and apply to the same school rather than go elsewhere.[9] In the meantime, Linda stayed home to take care of her two brothers and worked part-time in a tortilla factory in the same neighborhood.

Viridiana would get up at six in the morning to fix breakfast and leave a previously prepared lunch (usually pasta soup or beans). Once she had made some progress in the kitchen, she woke her husband and children. She would serve breakfast, sweep their small apartment, and pick up the dirty clothes. If they happened to have running water, Viridiana would do some laundry by hand. On the way to work, she would take her youngest son to preschool and head to work in Naucalpan, northern Mexico City. Depending on traffic, it might take an hour or longer for her to get there.

Viridiana also relied on Linda to do some of the unpaid household chores. Linda would pick up her youngest brother from school and make lunch for her two brothers and father. Linda and her mother had an agreement: if Viridiana was able to finish preparing lunch before going to work, Linda would clean up the house, and if not, Linda would be in charge of cooking for everybody. Viridiana would get off work at 6:00 p.m. and, depending on traffic, might take two hours to get back home. In Viridiana's household, the distribution of daily tasks fell squarely on Viridiana's and Linda's shoulders; neither the father nor the oldest son, a seventeen-year-old, participated in these tasks, yet both women accepted this division of labor, and Viridiana acknowledged Linda's support: "She's the one who helps me a lot at home."

This tension between responsibilities in their own household and at the workplace was sharpest among the women in Groups II and Group III, as the women in Group I were not married, and thus, their domestic responsibilities were different. Eva (Group II) tried to augment the money her husband gives her by occasionally calling some *señoras* (likely employers) that she knows, hoping they might hire her for odd jobs. Eva would offer to clean their houses, even if not on a regular basis, and if they accepted, she was happy "to make a few extra pesos." At the time, Eva worked in different houses for three days out of the week. She would leave home once her children left for school at 8:00 a.m. and work from 10:00 a.m. to 3:00 p.m. Eva got some help from her mother with cooking and taking care of her five-year-old son.

Eva felt pressured to maintain her expected role in the family despite working: "The days before I work, I plan what my mother is going to cook and go get the ingredients for her. My mother will take care of my son." She would also clean her house and do the laundry before going to work so the chores "won't pile up." Eva also had some arguments with her husband, who thought she did not take proper care of him or their son. She tried to take care of everything before leaving home for work. Her main goals for working outside the house were to afford some items her son might need, to buy more food, and to avoid feeling too constricted by the amount of money provided by her husband. Said Eva, "There's nothing like having a little of your own money."

A common thread throughout these women's stories was that they did not challenge the socially sanctioned gender division of labor. If they must work outside the home, they believed, it was their responsibility to find somebody else—another woman—to take over their assigned tasks. Even when they found help, they still resorted to the *doble jornada*, prolonging their workday considerably, as they were responsible for domestic reproduction as well as production outside the home.

Toward the political organization of domestic workers in Mexico

Given the difficulties faced by domestic workers in Mexico—low wages, precarious job stability, the stressful balancing of production and domestic reproduction—a logical solution might be to organize the PDW sector politically or to unionize. Compared to achievements in Uruguay, another country in the region, Mexico has made some progress regarding political organizing, but a winding road lies ahead due to some converging factors that operate against it.

The first of these is the lack of recognition of PDW as "real" work. Legally, PDW is included in the labor law broadly but in such a way that, in practice, the rights and obligations acquired by the two parties—employer and employee—are neither explicitly established nor clear. Usually the "contract" is a verbal agreement under which such issues as job duties, schedule, and salary are set but social benefits for the worker are not considered. By law, not even a minimum wage is established for PDW; instead, it offers employers a series of convenient loopholes.

This legal negligence is reinforced by negative social perceptions toward domestic workers' rights. Interviewing domestic workers and their employers separately, Toledo Gonzalez (2014) found that both groups were hesitant to recognize domestics as rights holders. Similar responses were expressed by the participants in this study, such as Lucía (Group III): "We are domestics. What rights can we have?" Employers often reinforce this devalued vision of domestic workers as unentitled to labor rights. According to Cleo's (Group III) employer, "Only workers like office workers are entitled to paid vacation, not those who work in houses. She says we don't have the right to get vacation."

Second, domestic workers, in general, lack a collective identity as an occupational group. This factor is rooted in the gendered division of labor that associates only women with social reproduction (Rendón 1990). Social devaluation of domestic work and isolation hinder domestics from creating a collective identity. Paid domestic work is characterized by the isolated nature of each unique employer-employee relationship. Each worker separately negotiates working conditions such as hours, salary, and job duties with her employer. Domestics are also physically isolated from one another, working in the solitude of a house belonging to others, making it difficult to build a collective PDW consciousness.

Third, another particularity of this relationship is that intimacy can lead to affection. The affective bonds that domestic workers and employers often develop toward one another also inhibit unionizing by domestics. Domestic workers and their employers are socially located in asymmetrical positions marked by sharp economic differences and power imbalances within the work relationship. The latent conflict implicit in this asymmetrical work relationship often conflicts with the very real mutual affection that often arises in the course of the relationship, especially in cases where the domestic has been with the same family for a long time (Toledo Gonzalez 2014). Sharing the same time, space, and objects for several days a week over a long time gives domestics and their employers familiarity with one another, allowing for an uneasy intimacy framed by social distance and hierarchy.

The particular fondness between worker and employer, coupled with the state's detachment from and indifference toward PDW, leads to employers' goodwill replacing any notion of rights enjoyed by domestic workers. From this perspective, domestic workers feel lucky to find work with an employer who is simply "a good person." Here, goodness refers to employers who treat workers well and who help them out or do them "favors" such as lending money. Lupe (Group III) explained that her former employer

> was very good to me, never shouted at me, never hit me. Whenever I was sick, she took me to the doctor. She asked her children to treat me well. If she had some leftover food, she gave it to me to bring it to my kids. Toys, clothes, or other things that she was no longer going to use, she gave them to me.
>
> (Lupe)

In such relationships, rights and obligations become blurred in a subjective (and intersubjective) vision that obstructs domestic workers from the possibility of creating political organizations that would allow them to demand rights for themselves.

A fourth factor that works against political organization is the permanent tension between the demands that organizing makes on one's time and those necessitated by family survival. The former is subordinated to the latter because making ends meet is a pressing daily need. Furthermore, a job as physically demanding as PDW leaves domestics with little energy to devote to activism. Live-in domestic workers frequently use Sundays, their day off, for recreation, while live-outs are often overwhelmed by various strategies they are using to beat the recession, including diversification and intensification of PDW tasks, working double shifts, and so on.

Furthermore, common perceptions of unions and their leaders within Mexico also work against political activism. This perception is rooted in the Mexican history of the corporatist relationship between unions and the Mexican state. The Mexican Revolution—the civil war that took place between 1910 and 1917—ended with the signature of a deeply reformed constitution. Among several social claims, the right to a dignified job was pursued and finally reflected in the progressive Article 123. In the onset of the import substituting industrialization period (1940s), in which the state was a direct and prominent economic actor, the ruling Revolutionary Institutional Party (PRI, in Spanish) was able to politically control unions through a corporatist relationship. An exchange of "favors" among leaders helped the government avoid strikes and demands from workers, and corruption turned into a very common and well-known practice among union leaders. Authoritarianism, compulsory affiliation, and a patrimonial use of the system have been some characteristics of large and pro-governmental unions.

Given the lack of a more progressive and democratic vision of unions in the social imaginary, it is not surprising that the ordinary Mexican citizen has had a negative image of unionism. This generally bad reputation emerged in our interviews with domestic workers. Toña (Group II), imagining she would have to pay a fee to be a union member, declared, "No, unions only help leaders to become rich people." Regarding union dues, Eva (Group II) also worried that "our salary is so low that if dues are taken out of our pay, it'd be even worse." Union organization has been a prerogative of only those workers formally registered in the social security system, and primarily of industrial workers. The share of workers belonging to a union has been very low and has decreased in recent years: between 2005 and 2010, it dropped from 16.7 percent to 14.5 percent (De la Garza 2012, 467).

Given such an adverse panorama for politically organizing domestic workers, it seems a considerable achievement that organizations like CONLACTRAHO for Latin America and CACEH for Mexico even exist. The Support and Training Center for Home Workers (CACEH) is affiliated with the Latin America and Caribbean of Home Workers Confederation (CONLACTRAHO). From a gender perspective, both promote equity, social justice, and labor human rights for domestic workers (Goldsmith 2013). They seek to strengthen women's leadership while encouraging participation among their peers.[10] Their strategies have allowed them to make their demands more visible and get them included in the political agenda. For instance, in Mexico, CACEH has been very actively pushing toward ratification of the ILO Domestic Work Convention 189. Although much work remains to be done in the political organization arena, these organizations have undertaken important forays into it.

Conclusion

By relying on a methodological strategy that combined qualitative and quantitative data, this chapter has analyzed the interaction between the macro sphere and the responses at the micro level among domestic workers in Mexico. Unlike in some other Latin American countries (notably Brazil), the consequences of the 2008 U.S. recession in Mexico were deep owing to Mexico's institutionalized, structural dependence on the American economy that was further accentuated by NAFTA. Mexico's sluggish economic performance before the crisis, together with the Mexican government's lethargic reaction afterward, meant the recession made itself felt in ordinary citizens' pocketbooks long after macroeconomic indicators had declared an official end to the recession.

The Mexican labor structure has historically been characterized by its heterogeneity, meaning that only a relatively small segment of the workforce had access to non-precarious employment—or what the literature calls "standard" employment, stable, well-paid, with benefits and social protections (Rojas García and Salas 2008). Within this generally polarized labor structure, women—and particularly domestic workers—face the additional challenge of a labor market segregated by gender and discrimination in labor standards, such as the wage gap and the glass ceiling.

In Mexico, women workers are concentrated in some activities that Portes and Hoffman (2003) called "informal proletariat," which includes personal services, retail commerce, and domestic work and constitutes the lowest steps of the occupational ladder. Under NAFTA, a trend to pay substandard wages to the Mexican workforce was consolidated. Nowhere is the labor structure polarization better captured than in income. Quantitative information provided in this chapter showed that by 2012, labor income had not reached the level it was at before the economic shock of 2008.

The bottom line of this examination of the repercussions of the 2008 recession in Mexican domestic workers' daily lives, we argue, is that that domestics are working poor women who struggle to make ends meet, devising coping strategies to help them juggle the demands of domestic reproduction with the need to bring additional money home. Our interviews show that these women have mostly internalized social expectations regarding caregiving for children and relatives and doing domestic chores as exclusively their responsibility.

The recession increased the tension between the two fronts of domestic responsibility and work outside the home. In the labor arena, finding work became harder. Our research reveals that domestic workers essentially followed two main strategies to overcome hardships born of the recession. First, they moonlighted, taking on additional jobs or income-producing activities, attempting to diversity their sources of income. Second, they sought to increase their incomes by working longer hours in jobs they already had, even when forced to resort to self-exploitation (Cortés and Rubalcava 1991). Even as they worked harder, their responsibility for social production remained unabated: domestic workers scrambled to ensure that their household's own domestic responsibilities were met, either working more themselves or relying on other women—relatives or neighbors—in their close-knit networks. Domestics dealt with internal conflicts caused by "neglecting" their own homes in order to work in someone else's to earn income.

Unionizing might be a way to not only demand recognition and rights but also overcome subsistence-level living conditions. Although a challenging road lies ahead, some organizations in Mexico and Latin America have advanced the defense of domestic workers' labor human rights, equity, and justice. One of their immediate goals is to get the Convention 189 ratified.

Acknowledgements

The authors deeply appreciate Carlos Salas' and David Crow's comments on previous versions. They also thank the editors' observations. All of them undoubtedly helped improve the text.

Notes

1 http://www.inegi.org.mx/sistemas/bie/?idserPadre=10100070#D10100070 (consulted 21 May 2015).

2 http://www.oecd.org/mexico/EMO-MEX-EN.pdf
3 We distinguish prostitution from people trafficking, and here we refer to the former.
4 Own translation from:

> Toda persona tiene derecho al trabajo digno y socialmente útil; al efecto, se promoverán la creación de empleos y la organización social para el trabajo, conforme a la ley. El Congreso de la Unión deberá expedir leyes sobre el trabajo, las cuales regirán: Entre los obreros, jornaleros, empleados domésticos, artesanos y de una manera general, todo contrato de trabajo.

5 It is worth noting that although these figures could seem confusing, in 1995, domestic workers were 4.1 percent of 15,139,747 workers (the total size of the labor force in Mexico), whereas by 2012, even though the number of domestic workers had almost doubled, it represented 4.6 percent of 24,926,111 workers. In this period, the economically active population in Mexico increased considerably.
6 US$1 = 13.27 MXN. To make the change from pesos to dollars, we take an average of the time series of the exchange rate in 2014, which is published by the Bank of Mexico. http://www.banxico.org.mx/
7 All names are pseudonyms.
8 The Spanish word for this activity is *deshebrar*. At textile workshops, it is one of the lowest-paid activities.
9 In Mexico, public junior high and high schools have competitive admissions processes.
10 http://idwfed.org/es/relatos/caceh-15-anos-de-lucha-a-favor-de-las-trabajadoras-del-hogar

References

Blecker, Robert A. 2009. "External Shocks, Structural Change, and Economic Growth in Mexico, 1979–2007." *World Development*, 37(7): 1274–1284.

Colen, Shellee. 1995. "'Like a Mother to Them': Stratified Reproduction and West Indian Childcare Workers and Employers in New York." In *Conceiving the New World Order: The Global Politics of Reproduction*, edited by Faye Ginsburg and Rayna Rapp, 78–102, Berkeley, Los Angeles, London: University California Press.

Cortés, Fernando and Rosa María Rubalcava. 1991. *Autoexplotación forzada y equidad por empobrecimiento: La distribución del ingreso familiar en México*. Mexico City: El Colegio de México.

De La Garza, Enrique. 2012. "La polémica acerca de la tasa de afiliación sindical revisada al 2010." In *La situación del trabajo en México, 2012: El trabajo en la crisis*, edited by Enrique De La Garza, 453–472, Mexico City: Plaza y Valdés.

FORLAC – Programa de Promoción de la Formalización en América Latina y El Caribe. 2014. *Notas sobre formalización. El empleo informal en México: Situación actual, políticas y desafíos*. Organización Internacional del Trabajo. https://www.ilo.org/wcmsp5/groups/public/—americas/—ro-lima/documents/publication/wcms_245613.pdf

Gallagher, Kevin, Juan Carlos Moreno-Brid and Roberto Porsekansky. 2008. "The Dynamics of Mexican Exports: Lost in (Chinese) Translation." *World Development*, 36(8): 1365–1380.

Goldsmith, Mary. 1990. "El servicio doméstico y la migración femenina." In *Trabajo femenino y Crisis en México, tendencias y transformaciones actuales*, edited by Elia Ramírez Bautista, and Hilda R. Dávila Ibáñez, 257–272, Mexico City: Universidad autónoma Metropolitana- Xochimilco.

Goldsmith, Mary. 2007. "De sirvientas a empleadas del hogar. La cara cambiante del servicio doméstico en México." In *Miradas feministas sobre los mexicanos del siglo XX*, edited by Marta Lamas, 279–311, Mexico City: Fondo de Cultura Económica.

Goldsmith, Mary. 2013. "Los espacios internacionales de la participación política de las trabajadoras remuneradas del hogar." *Revista de Estudios Sociales*, 45: 233–246.

González De La Rocha, Mercedes. 1988. "Economic Crisis, Domestic Reorganization and Women's Work in Guadalajara, Mexico." *Bulletin of Latin American Research*, 7(2): 207–223.

Instituto Nacional de Estadística y Geografía. 2014. *Estadísticas a propósito del Día Internacional del Trabajador Doméstico*. Aguascalientes: INEGI.

JuanCarlos, Moreno-Brid, Sthefanie Garry and Luis Ángel Monroy-Gómez-Franco. 2014. "'El salario mínimo en México', l Salario Mínimo en México." *Economía*, 11(33): 78–93.

Laslett, Barbara y Johanna Brenner. 1989. "Gender and Social Reproduction: Historical Perspectives." *Annual Review of Sociology*, 15: 381–404.

Pedrero, Mercedes. 2003. "Las condiciones de trabajo en los años noventa en México. Las mujeres y los hombres: ¿ganaron o perdieron?" *Revista Mexicana de Sociología*, Año XLV(4): 733–761.

Portes, Alejandro y Kelly Hoffman. 2003. "Latin American Class Structures: Their Composition and Change During the Neoliberal Era." *Latin American Research Review*, 38(1): 41–82.

Rendón, Teresa. 1990. "Trabajo femenino remunerado en el siglo XX. Cambios, tendencias y perspectivas." In *Trabajo femenino y Crisis en México, tendencias y transformaciones actuales*, edited by Elia Ramírez Bautista and Hilda R. Dávila Ibáñez, 29–51, Mexico City: Universidad autónoma Metropolitana- Xochimilco.

Roberts, Bryan. 1991a. "The Changing Nature of Informal Employment: the Case of Mexico." In *Towards Social Adjustment*, edited by Guy Standing and Víctor Tokman, 115–140, Geneva: International Labour Office.

Roberts, Bryan. 1991b. "Household Coping Strategies and Urban Poverty in a Comparative Perspective." In *Urban Life in Transition*, edited by M. Gottdiener and Chris G. Pickvance, 135–168, London: Sage Publications.

Rojas García, Georgina and Carlos Salas. 2008. "La precarización del empleo en México, 1995–2004." *Revista Latinoamericana de Estudios del Trabajo* Segunda Época, Año 13(19): 39–78.

Rojas García, Georgina and Mónica Patricia Toledo González. 2013. "Reproducción social estratificada: El trabajo doméstico remunerado en México y la interacción entre mujeres de estratos medios y populares." In *Población y trabajo en América Latina: Abordajes teórico-metodológicos y tendencias empíricas recientes*, edited by Luciana Gandini and Mauricio Padrón Innamorato, 403–441, Rio de Janeiro: Asociación Latinoamericana de Población – Fondo de Población de las Naciones Unidas.

Salas, Carlos. 2013. "Labour, Income and Social Programmes in Contemporary México." In *Social Protection, Growth and Employment. Evidence from India, Kenya, Malawi, México, Tajikistan*, 201–234, New York: United Nations Development Programme.

Salas, Carlos and Eduardo Zepeda. 2003. "Employment and Wages: Enduring the Costs of Liberalization and Economic Reform." In *Confronting Development. Assessing Mexico's Economic and Social Policy Challenges*, edited by Kevin J. Middlebrook and Eduardo Zepeda, 522–558, Stanford: Stanford University Press.

Ochoa León, Sara María. 2013. *Riesgo y vulnerabilidad laboral durante la crisis financiera y económica del 2008-2009 en México*. PhD Dissertation. Mexico City: El Colegio de México.

Selby, Henry A., Arthur D. Murphy y Stephen A. Lorenzen. 1990. *The Mexican Urban Household. Organizing for Self-Defense*. Austin: The University of Texas Press.

Tiano, Susan. 1994. *Patriarchy on the Line: Labor, Gender, and Ideology in the Mexican Maquila Industry*. Philadelphia: Temple University Press.
Toledo González, Mónica Patricia. 2014. *Entre muchachas y señoras*. Arreglos particulares en el trabajo doméstico remunerado en México, PhD Dissertation. Mexico City: CIESAS.
Ward, Kathryn. 1990. *Women Workers and Global Restructuring*. Ithaca, NY: ILR Press.
Zepeda, Eduardo, Timothy A. Wise and Kevin P. Gallagher. 2009. *Rethinking Trade Policy for Development: Lessons from Mexico under NAFTA*. Washington: Carnegie Endowment for International Peace Policy Outlook.

10
WOMEN'S WORK IN KENYA'S ATHI RIVER EXPORT PROCESSING ZONE

Opportunity or exploitation?

Kelly Pike

In 1990, the World Bank funded the establishment of the Athi River Export Processing Zone (EPZ) just outside of Nairobi with the purposes of developing Kenya's garment industry, exporting business, and creating employment for thousands of Kenyans.[1] Similar to other African countries, where women traditionally maintain the home while their husbands go to work, a job in a clothing factory represented first-time employment for most women. With this came promises of independence, stability, skill development, mobility, and an improved quality of life.

In July 2013, I facilitated thirteen focus group discussions with factory workers in the Athi River EPZ to gain a deeper understanding of their working conditions and the subsequent impact that their working there had on household and gender dynamics.[2] Additionally, five hundred and fifty workers completed questionnaires[3] with questions related to their working conditions.[4] Though an opportunity to provide basic necessities for themselves and their families, work in the EPZ is highly exploitative in terms of the physical and emotional toll it is taking on women, in their lives both at work and at home. This is particularly evident in their descriptions of increasing economic hardship in the wake of the global financial crisis, the intensifying interplay between working conditions and household dynamics, and the evolving perceptions that these particular Kenyan women have of their ability to effect change.

Global women's work: what does it mean and to whom?

Before we can begin to explore the question of whether paid work truly represents an opportunity for these women, we must first examine some of our underlying assumptions about what work is and consider whether they are appropriate for a discussion of global women's work in transition. To begin with a more philosophical perspective, David Beatty (1980) once conceptualized the personal meaning of employment as the following:

> A vehicle which admits a person to the status of a contributing, productive, member of society, employment is seen as providing recognition of the individual's being engaged in something worthwhile. It gives the individual a sense of significance. By realizing our capabilities and contributing in ways society determines to be useful, employment comes to represent the means by which most members of our community can lay claim to an equal right of respect and of concern from others. It is this institution through which most of us secure much of our self-respect and self-esteem.
> *(Beatty 1980, 324)*

This, to most workers occupying jobs at the bottom of the global supply chain, might sound like a naïve definition of privileged work. Does the machine operator in a clothing factory in Nairobi feel connected to her work and derive her sense of self-respect and self-esteem from it?

There is a group of scholars who argue that, yes, women are not exploited or subjugated but rather earn self-respect through their work, and that this work can in fact be their route to freedom. Working makes a woman less dependent on her husband, according to this argument, and this financial independence not only increases her economic power (Trappe and Sørensen 2006) but also her household bargaining power, self-respect, and agency (Friedemann-Sanchez 2006). In addition to paid work, legal changes in married women's property rights have also contributed to women's household bargaining power and agency, though these changes have arguably been developing over a longer time period in advanced industrialized countries (Combs 2006; Rutterford and Maltby 2006) than in other, industrializing countries (Datta 2006). Even in countries where women conform to their "normalization as housewives" as "the preferred social ideal," Soni-Sinha (2006, 340) argues that they are investing in the discourse constituting their work as "help to their husbands" but that they can break that discourse, in particular as they work in supervisory roles at work, challenging the discourse of the seclusion of women and certain types of work belonging to men.

From a feminist political economy perspective, the underlying assumption of the "dual-earner female career model" that has emerged with neoliberalism is that women are primarily responsible for social reproduction – that is, provisioning all processes that sustain life on a daily and generational basis – and therefore not in need of support for this unpaid work in the family, household, and community (Bezanson 2006). Though women participate in the labor market just as men do, the expectation is that they will also take responsibility for the household. This puts women in a position of constantly negotiating their work and home lives, with some struggling more than others due to differences in cultural norms, promotion of women's rights, the presence of social assistance, etc. Women's work in social reproduction plays an important role in contributing to the economy, in large part because their unpaid work ("non-tradables") subsidizes paid work ("tradables") in the economy (Elson 1995). As Elson (1995) argues, however, women should not be seen as a "resource for the achievement of development" but rather as "people whose control over resources should be strengthened."

Control over resources is a theme that recurs in the literature on gender and labor. Whether these resources include money from paid work or other assets resulting from changes in property rights or divorce laws, etc., the argument is that control over these resources empowers women. However, in exploring the question of opportunity vs. exploitation, there are two underlying issues to consider. First, what is the nature of the work that enables accumulation of these resources and, second, what happens when control over these resources equates not to financial independence but rather to a basic survival strategy?

Some scholars argue that employment for vulnerable workers in the Global South is an opportunity for them to pull themselves out of poverty. A job is an opportunity to earn an income, to become more independent, and to develop agency, thereby allowing someone to become a better and stronger contributing member of one's family and society at large. As the old adage would have it, any job is better than no job.

The problem with this view is that it is intellectually rooted in something far from the realities of capitalism, industrialization, and the impact of the downward pressure on workers generated by a global competitive marketplace. In reverting to this interpretation, we falsely label their work as an opportunity and an opportunity alone (e.g., to grow out of poverty, to achieve independence, to become a contributing member of society and the economy, etc.). In reality, however, most workers might describe their work as a curse or a commodity, a burden necessary for human survival, where boundaries between opportunity and exploitation blur.

John Budd (2011) further elaborates on these different conceptualizations of work, arguing that work can be any one or more of many things. Budd creates a typology of work in ten forms, each of which represents a different way in which one might experience work depending on his or her particular context. According to Budd, work can be labelled as a curse, freedom, commodity, occupational citizenship, disutility, personal fulfillment, a social relation, caring for others, identity, or service (Budd 2011, 14). Broadly, these can be categorized as either negative or positive interpretations of work. On one hand, work is a necessary evil in which workers are treated like animals or machines, yet survival would be impossible without it. On the other, work is a source of pride, bringing with it financial and personal independence and bolstering a sense of identity and belonging.

When we think about global women's work and how it has changed over time, we need to be aware of what work means—particularly to the women whose personal and intellectual narratives are at the focal point of this investigation. If all they want is a bit of money, regardless of any negative outcomes that come with that work, then it may be partially true that there is value in having "any" job. If, however, abuses are so harsh that they not only make one's work unbearable but also begin to erode one's home life, then perhaps it is worth asking where along the way the value of a half loaf of bread surpassed the wholeness of humanity.

Among the women I interviewed in the Athi River EPZ, there was a great deal of discussion about exploitative conditions at work and how these spiralled into conflicts at home. On the other hand, they also spoke about the benefits of being able to afford basic necessities for their families. The notion of work that most closely resonated with them was that of "caring for others," which Budd defines as "the physical, cognitive, and emotional effort required to attend to and maintain others" (Budd 2011, 14). The fact that they were able to provide for their families by putting food on the table—and, for some, being able to send their children to school —was the foremost driver of their seeking work and enduring whatever conditions accompanied it.

Opportunity and exploitation

Transition to a modern industrial economy has been slow in Kenya, as it has been in other sub-Saharan African countries (Muasya 2014). According to the Kenya National Bureau of Statistics 2009 (cited in Muasya 2014, 149), 67.7 percent of Kenya's 38.6 million people live in rural areas. There has been, however, quite a bit of rural-urban migration in recent decades—mostly among women—in part because of declining land productivity and shrinking incomes from agriculture, as well as increasing levels of education among females in Kenya (Muasya 2014). However, because of unemployment in Kenya, these women end up taking jobs in the informal sector—the majority of them (70 percent) winding up in low-income jobs (Atieno 2010) with poor economic security, high levels of poverty, and poor access to social security (Mokomane 2009). They often end up as casual laborers, with flexible hours that allow them to continue tending to their household and child-care responsibilities.[5]

The emergence of the Athi River EPZ in Kenya signalled an opportunity for women to participate in full-time employment and contribute more to their families financially. In the early 2000s, there was a boom in foreign direct investment (FDI) in the sub-Saharan African apparel industry, in large part due to both the African Growth and Opportunity Act (AGOA) and Multi-Fibre Arrangement (MFA). AGOA allowed duty-free access to markets in the United States, and the MFA imposed quotas on imports from major Asian apparel-producing countries, the latter of which resulted in the spread of apparel production in industrializing countries. However, when manufacturers in other countries (e.g., Japan, Korea, China, and Taiwan) reached their quotas in their home economies, they began to move production into the least-developed countries where quotas were still unfilled, which resulted primarily in foreign-owned apparel firms in sub-Saharan African countries. Low-value added activities (e.g., basic cut-make-trim), external control of sourcing, and reliance on expatriates for management have resulted in little spillover effect and virtually no locally owned operations (Staritz and Frederick 2014).[6]

The majority of the 25,900 workers employed (Staritz and Frederick 2014) in Kenya's apparel EPZs are women. For the 550 questionnaires completed during my fieldwork in 2013, the gender breakdown is roughly 75 percent women to 25 percent men, with an average age of 30.5 years (29.37 for women and 31.76 for men). As discussed in more detail below, roughly 60 percent of these women were single, divorced, or widowed, and the remaining 40 percent were married or living with a boyfriend. Some young women in Kenya were unable to attend school and left with little choice but to work in the Athi River EPZ because their parents had been laid off or were unable to find work. For others, it was an opportunity to increase total household income and cost-share with their husbands. Now, ten years later, did the workers in the EPZ feel that the potential benefits of these opportunities had been actualized? The vignette in Figure 10.1 is telling.

With a long day at the factory ahead of her, she wakes up at 5:00 a.m., stumbling in the darkness to grab clothes and light a few candles. She manages to boil some water for tea and washing; wake, dress, and feed her children; and pack lunches and make breakfast for her husband before finally setting out to work. She walks an hour to the factory and works from 7:00 a.m. to 12:00 p.m. without a break. Her back is aching, her eyes are dry, her stomach rumbles – she didn't have time to eat breakfast. After a short lunch, she returns to work. It's hot inside, and someone is yelling because there have been too many mistakes with the stitching, so they're behind on their orders. It's 5:00 p.m. and she's being told she must work until 7:00 p.m. to meet her target, but there will be no overtime pay. She walks home in the dark, wondering whether she will be the next victim of those who wait to rob or rape, but luckily arrives safely at home – where her husband has been angrily waiting for her to make his dinner. She's tired. The children haven't eaten, the house is dirty, her husband questions whether she was truly at work this late and is frustrated that she's no longer taking care of him and the home the way she used to. Fatigued, she makes it through the evening, and when her husband desires more from her, she begs some time to rest, only to be blamed for finding excuses to avoid her "wifely duties." After three days of this, her husband has had enough and leaves her for someone else. It's 5:00 a.m. again.

FIGURE 10.1 A Woman's Work in the Athi River EPZ

Though some might argue that paid work should represent opportunities for greater financial security, independence, and quality of life, it appears to be creating an exploitative situation for female workers in Kenya's clothing industry, both at work and at home. To begin with, wages in the industry were and remain very low. As inflation has increased exponentially in Kenya, workers' wages have nudged up only slightly. As one woman remarked,

> The basic salary is low according to the standard of life today.... It can't manage for your housekeeping. You have a child who is in school, you have to pay the school fees, you have to provide for her clothes, food, so the money you are getting are very less.
>
> *(Martha, Focus Group #9, 28 July 2013)*

Table 10.1 shows these nominal changes in workers' wages between the years 2003–2013, including a decrease in 2005. In US dollar value, the value of wages decreases in 2005, 2009, 2011 and 2013.

Between 2005–2007, appreciation in the Kenyan shilling caused a disruption in the economy and contributed to declines in the EPZ after 2004. A dip in workers' wages in 2005 was caused by the expiration of the MFA, which had provided Kenya and other developing countries preferential access to the United States. Omolo (2006, 155) describes conditions in Kenyan EPZs at this time as characterized by unfair and restrictive labor practices including low wages, inadequately compensated overtime, sexual harassment and the violation of the organizational rights of workers. Another dip in 2009 can be explained by the economic impact of the global financial crisis. In 2009, exports from the EPZ clothing sector decreased by nearly US$64 million (from $228.5M to $164.6M), in large part due to the slump in demand in the context of the financial crisis (Staritz and Frederick 2014, 222). Between 2000 and 2010, the United States was Kenya's top apparel export market and accounted for between 94–97 percent of Kenya's apparel exports to the world in any given year. It is not surprising, then, that when the United States sneezed, Kenya caught a cold.

When considering all U.S. apparel imports from Kenya (both EPZ and non-EPZ sectors), the figures are slightly higher but follow a similar pattern.

TABLE 10.1 Average wages of Kenyans in EPZ employment

	2003	2004	2005	2006	2007	2008	2009	2010	2011	2012	2013*
Average wage per month	5,233 ($69)	7,198 ($91)	6,608 ($87)	7,279 ($101)	7,734 ($115)	8,404 ($122)	9,059 ($117)	9,624 ($122)	9,803 ($111)	10,585 ($125)	10,290 ($118)

Sources: EPZA Annual Performance report 2009; EPZA (2005–2012); *Author's questionnaire 2013 (Athi River EPZ only).

Table 10.2 shows U.S. apparel imports from Kenya for the period 1997–2011. Note a surge in new investment between 2000 and 2004 enabled by the passage of AGOA (McCormick et al. 2006, 84). There is a subsequent drop in 2005 after the expiration of the MFA, which continued to decline in the years 2006–2008, with a sharp drop in 2009 (due to the impact of the global financial crisis) before starting to improve again in 2010 and 2011.

How does all of this affect workers? First of all, as indicated in Table 10.3, the Export Processing Zones Authority (EPZA) reported a decline in employment of 1,407 workers in 2009 (from 25,766 in 2008 to 24,359 in 2009). In the years leading up to this, workers in the EPZ had already been experiencing similar if not worse losses – employment in the EPZs peaked in 2003 but then decreased every year through 2010. Athi River is the largest zone, one of two public zones controlled by the EPZA. The other of these two is Kipevu EPZ, located close to Mombasa. Existing zones in Kenya are situated in Nairobi, Voi, Athi River, Kerio Valley, Mombasa, and Kilifi. The country had 45 zones in 2012 but about half are single firms (Vastveit 2013). Between 2005–2009, almost 10,000 workers in the EPZs lost their jobs.

On one hand, it seems that the dip in 2009 is simply representative of an inexorable pattern of decline in the sector. One could argue that this downward trend would have continued regardless of whether there had been a global financial crisis. Therefore, it is not truly astonishing to witness a loss in exports, employment, or wages. On the other hand, making this argument is like throwing salt in the wounds of workers, who ostensibly do not experience diminishing returns of pain when it comes to poverty and instability. Workers are aware that vulnerability exists beyond the workplace level. They know that, despite the conditions of their work, the jobs themselves can disappear for larger reasons related to trade and other global business and financial activity. This in turn affects the degree to which someone might be willing to rock the boat when it comes to trying to improve working conditions. Next, we examine the interconnectedness of working conditions such as wages and working hours on workers' well-being.

Though employment in the sector has decreased, there are still some families in which both partners are working in the EPZ. Although some of these families now have two incomes to support their households, many are still unable to meet their expenses with their combined incomes. Of the 347 women who responded to the question "Is your income enough to sustain your household?" 97 percent answered "No." Similarly, 96 percent of the 204 men who responded said "No" to this question.

In addition to receiving inadequate salaries, several workers who participated in the focus groups complained about not being paid on time. This can have severe consequences, both in terms of being unable to replenish food and household supplies, and in terms of being unable to make payments on time, which means they can be kicked out of their homes. According to one woman:

TABLE 10.2 U.S. apparel imports from Kenya

	1997	2000	2001	2002	2003	2004	2005	2006	2007	2008	2009	2010	2011
SSA Total ($US Mil)	429	748	935*	1,098	1,610*	1,757	1,464	1,292	1,293	1,151	922	790	904
Kenya Total ($US Mil)	31	44		125	188**	277	271	263	248	247	195	202	261
Growth Rate (%)	14.1	11.8		94.6		47.6	-2.4	-2.8	-5.6	-0.6	-20.9	3.4	29.2
Share of SSA (%)	7.3	5.9		11.4	11.7	15.8	18.5	20.4	19.2	21.4	21.2	25.5	28.8

Source: United States International Trade Commission; *AGOA Info; **McCormick et al. 2006.

TABLE 10.3 Key indicators of Kenya's apparel export sector

	'00	'01	'02	'03	'04	'05	'06	'07	'08	'09	'10	'11
Number of firms	6	17	30	34	30	25	25	22	18	19	16	18
Share of EPZ firms	-	-	56%	53%	41%	37%	35%	31%	23%	23%	21%	23%
Employment ('000)	6.5	12.0	25.3	32.1	34.6	34.2	31.8	28.5	25.8	24.4	24.1	25.9
Share of EPZ empl.	-	-	93%	93%	90%	88%	85%	82%	84%	80%	77%	79%
Investment (Kshs mio)	1,200	3,740	6,908	9,710	8,595	9,977	10,317	8,314	7,578	5,490	-	-

Sources: EPZA (2005–2012); Staritz and Frederick fieldwork March 2012.

> They don't care which day they pay you, they just pay whenever they [feel] like paying. Now if they pay on the tenth, my house closes on the fifth, it's the [rent] deadline. So from the fifth to tenth, where will I sleep? Outside. I have kids. ... I have to get money on loan and if I can't get money on loan, I have to look for an alternative place to sleep.... [On the day they finally pay you] they can even start paying from 6:00 p.m. because they don't want to interrupt their target. They start paying from 6:00 p.m., they finish paying at 9:00 p.m. Now, at 9:00 p.m., you are leaving the company, you don't have any means of transport; you have money in your pocket, what if you are killed out there? Thieves know we are being paid on that day. They wait for us there and kill us and take the money.[7]
>
> *(Evalyne, Focus Group #9, 28 July 2013)*

In addition to low salaries and late payments, working conditions are poor, particularly employer abuses of overtime hours, which lends itself to a shift in household dynamics, sometimes with negative consequences. Husbands may reprimand their wives who return home late due to long overtime hours, which many women reported is leading to an increasingly higher rate of divorce. Though women are taking on greater responsibilities away from the home, they are still expected to maintain their traditional responsibilities in the home. This was a common theme that workers raised throughout the focus group discussions. In response to a question about whether the fact that women are working is changing their relationships at home, one woman said:

> For the advantages, you're cost-sharing. ... At least you can build up yourselves together. But most [relationships] are breaking, especially because of the working conditions. Sometimes you're supposed to work late and, if your husband is not working there, he will not understand that you're [returning] from job. So you find that there are a good percentage of break-ups in marriages ... because of the working conditions. Sometimes you're told to work up to 9:00 p.m. You have a child who has come from school. The husband is there waiting. He'll wait for two, three days ... he'll feel this is too much. So either you leave the job and become a housewife, or you break up and you go for the job.
>
> *(Janet, Focus Group #3, 20 July 2013)*

In this case, the flip side of the benefit of having a job is the requirement to work late hours, which poses a risk to both women's safety and the well-being of their home lives. In addition to these problems at work and home, there is the overarching issue of the precariousness of the sector itself. There is very little security in the future of the sector at the macro level: trade agreements are expiring, and stakeholders are unwilling to invest in infrastructure upgrades that would improve local capacity and add value (Staritz and Frederick 2014, 219). The jobs themselves are insecure at the micro or workplace level. As one worker explains:

> If we had job security, we could prosper. You could go to a bank, take a loan. But with the nature of our jobs, you cannot approach any financial institution for any loan. They tell you these institutions of ours (the factories), you can be easily fired, you can be easily hired, so we cannot give you any loan... If we could be assured our job security...at least you could do something, go to a bank, take a loan, buy land, get a mortgage. But for us, you can work for twenty years and you have nothing to show.
> *(Janet, Focus Group #3, 20 July 2013)*

Although paid work in the Athi River EPZ has fallen short of offering grand opportunities, some evidence suggests that women are not being entirely exploited in the workplace. Work offers some training related to health and safety, for example. Of the women who completed the questionnaire, 72 percent said that they have a health and safety policy at work, and another 42 percent said they had received training on health and safety issues. Forty-nine percent said they have an HIV/AIDS policy, and 55 percent had received training on it. However, knowing one's rights is certainly different from having the power to exercise them, and the women in this study alluded to the fact that they do not always have bargaining power to negotiate when and whether they have sex. So the extent to which this training can be applied in the home is unclear, although it is more likely that training on health and safety could result in improved practices both at work and at home. Furthermore, some women believe that there is a degree of gender equality at work. Fifty-three percent thought that men and women had an equal chance of being promoted, and 92 percent said that men and women receive the same pay for doing the same work. Though these numbers are not staggering, they represent a glimmer of hope for a foundation upon which better standards can be built.

Despite this glimmer of hope, however, women encounter an enormous amount of adversity at work, including sexual harassment. Several women reported that sexual harassment is a problem in their factories and that refusing unwanted advances can result in further harassment or expulsion from the factory. For example, as one woman reported, "We are not supposed to have sexual harassment in the factory, but it happens ... When they abuse us sexually, when you do not give them [what they want], they throw you out of the company."

In the few cases where workers mentioned that sexual harassment had "ceased," they pinned that success on the efforts of the trade union—namely, of one organizer in their factory. One woman spoke at length about the challenges of the sexual harassment they faced when her factory was first set up ten years ago. She explained,

> The superiors used to lure the female employees for work. You have to have sexual relations before he employs you. But down the line, some five years, we got a strong union, under the leadership of [our union organizer]. Now things have changed for good. Now the sexual harassment ceased.
>
> *(Anonymous, Focus Group, July/Aug 2013)*

The union that represents clothing and textile workers in Kenya, the Tailors and Textiles Workers Union (TTWU), was founded in 1948. Unfortunately, membership in the union is low (roughly 17.5 percent, according to a TTWU report collected during fieldwork), and there are divisions within the TTWU. This issue of internal divisions—according to workers, shop stewards, and some union organizers—is that the top union leaders are old, set in their ways, and trying to retain their places in the hierarchy by appealing to employers instead of their members.[8] There are two local organizers in the Athi River EPZ—one is a Kenyan of Somali descent, the other is a Kenyan from the same tribe as the union president. The issue of tribalism (that is, favoritism) exists at the different levels of the hierarchy—within the union (e.g., the president favoring one local organizer over the other), between supervisors and workers, and between the workers themselves. This creates barriers for workers of different tribes when filing complaints because which tribe they belong to influences when or whether their complaints will be heard. When a worker has a complaint, she brings it to her shop steward, who brings it to the local organizer. That organizer then chooses whether or not to take the issue to the union leadership, and this is where workers feel that their voices are being silenced.

In addition to this, I discovered a lack of transparency in the union. During my month of fieldwork, the union president delayed meeting me until the last few days, and shop stewards were told (by the local organizer from the same tribe as the president) not to attend any research meetings. Some were indeed intimidated by this, while others wanted to meet me in a neighboring town where they could have privacy, eager to tell their stories. None of the organizers or the shop stewards I met with had ever seen a copy of their union's constitution. A copy was not available online, and they were not given one upon joining the union (neither as an organizer nor as a regular member). Communication channels were blocked or cut off near the end, which appeared to be based on leaders' fear of losing power.

On top of this, there was not a lot of worker uprising in the Athi River EPZ. Increases in inflation, combined with stagnant wages, left many workers concerned about unemployment and therefore reluctant to rock the boat. Second, there was not a lot of pressure from the union leadership on employers to make any changes. There was only one factory that appeared to be taking workers' well-being into account. Onsite, they had a day-care center—the majority of factory workers are single mothers—as well as a cafeteria that provided lunch for the workers. The employer was connected with the Aga Khan foundation and was a believer in promoting the social welfare of workers in addition to the economic benefits of production. From what I was able to observe, this was not happening at any other factory. Very few workers even knew who they were supplying their products to, and the employers were highly secretive about whom their buyers were.

Unfortunately, dictatorial top-down leadership in the union had resulted in a system that placed union–employer relationships ahead of workers' interests, corrupting the process of union organizing and suffocating workers' voices. The end result was that workers were unable to follow the traditional channels for filing and resolving grievances and most of the time workplace issues were kept under a lid, rendering the union ineffective as an organization through which women could effect change. During fieldwork, workers did not talk about having any other organizations or networks to fill this vacuum, although one of the local organizers spoke about trying to reach out directly to buyers and international labor rights groups.

Is paid work, then, truly an opportunity in this context? At the least, paid work should offer a modicum of security. To some, having security may mean simply the ability to put food on the table. To others, security may mean having the ability to send their children to school, or to afford some of the finer things in life—new clothes, nice food, travel, and the opportunity to socialize with friends. To others, it might mean the freedom to work without being harassed. Regardless of how one defines security, the fact remains that paid work should represent an opportunity to attain it. But as is the case for many women in the global world of work, opportunity and exploitation are two sides of the same coin, and it is difficult in this case to understand how one can exist without the other.

Impact on women beyond the workplace

One day during fieldwork in the Athi River EPZ, a group of female factory workers was discussing "men these days." One woman began,

> The Child Act, chapter 45, says that the father or the mother, they should take care of the child no matter what, if they are living together or not. So the father has to provide the necessities for the child.[9]
>
> *(Ann, Focus Group #6, 27 July 2013)*

Laughter and murmurs rippled throughout the room. Another woman continued:

> I'm a single mother—a mother of two. In the EPZ, men there say the money is little. When the children are there we need school fees, food, we need house rent. When they see the responsibility is too high, they'll definitely run away and go to the girls who have no children. So I'll be left with the whole burden of the children. I have to work hard, so even if I'm abused in the factory, I'll always stay for my children. The men there

> are not responsible. Even some young men, they go to old ladies—sugar mummies who have money. They go there, they are taken care of. There, they are not asked for anything. They just eat and drink and dress.
>
> (Teresa, Focus Group #6, 27 July 2013)

In another meeting with a different group of women, one of the women continued with this theme, saying,

> You can get some men, they stay in the town center...and the mother is there in the *shamba*[10] [plot or land] picking tea, coffee, digging *shamba*, looking [after] kids alone. And the man is coming drinking, drinking, drinking, fighting. That's the problem.
>
> (Rosemary, Focus Group #10, 3 August 2013)

It is not the uniqueness of these narratives that gives us pause, for indeed they might be cast as common parlance among women working in patriarchal societies. Rather, they show how Kenyan women are handling their evolving responsibilities and how work has influenced those. When asked if the situation for women is the same today as it was for their mothers' generation, one woman responded,

> Before, men were supposed to take more responsibilities than woman, but it was vice versa then. Because they say they are the head, so whatever they say is what the ladies will follow. Nowadays ladies are becoming the head...even some are the breadwinners. Many ladies are single so they take care of their children alone, and they take them far.
>
> (Nancy, Focus Group #10, 3 August 2013)

Just one generation ago in Kenya, women did not go to work. They did unpaid work at home—tended to the children, did the cleaning, and were there for their husbands in whatever way they needed them to be. They did not argue or disagree with their husbands but rather obeyed them. Men went to work and were responsible for providing financially for their families—a roof over their heads, money for food, school fees, and clothes. They were there for their families and were (or tried harder to be) faithful to their wives. "*Mpango wa kando*" (Swahili for having "a side dish") is cited in the Kenyan news as a growing problem among couples in the country (see, for example, Kenya Forum 2015; Muiruri 2014). Some believe this is linked to the fact that women who work are becoming more empowered and therefore less submissive to their husbands. One male factory worker remarked,

> In cases where the husband is working, the marriages are usually very good. But the minute she acquires a job with the EPZ... She has her own money... From there, it will be difficult for the husband and the wife to live in harmony

> because the minute the husband asks the wife to assist him in doing something, she will excuse herself that she is tired and leave for the bed.
>
> *(Juma, Focus Group #1, 13 July 2013)*

According to the workers involved in this research, issues related to financial insecurity are also contributing to a higher divorce rate—in part because the threat of poverty is pushing people into marriage too early. A 2011 report entitled *Status of the Institution of Marriage in Kenya* found that "financial instability, social insecurity and the desire to share responsibilities are driving Kenyans to marry early" (cited in Kenya Forum 2015; also see Daily Nation 2010). According to the Kenya Forum, an online news and opinion forum for Kenyans, one of the leading causes of divorce today in Kenya is that people are marrying for "the wrong reasons," that is, for financial stability (Kenya Forum 2015).

In the Athi River EPZ, one of the main concerns among female workers is the difficulty they have in meeting their financial obligations, with the added challenge of doing this on their own. They report that the majority of workers are either single mothers or in a relationship with a male partner who does not "take his responsibility." As an illustration, roughly 60 percent of the 343 females who completed the work-related questionnaire for this study said they were divorced, separated, widowed, or single. The remaining 40 percent were either married or living with a boyfriend.

There is some sentiment among men that women's work in the EPZ is a double-edged sword. On one hand, they need women to earn an income so they can make ends meet, something they did not traditionally rely on when the cost of living was lower.[11] On the other hand, they feel that women who work are becoming too confident, too arrogant, and have unrealistic expectations about the degree to which a man should help at home. As one male worker said, "In those days, men never used to let women get jobs at the factories. But nowadays we don't live like they did because life itself has become too hard for us."

When a group of male workers was asked whether women's working in the EPZ has changed the dynamics between men and women at home, one man responded:

> For some, it has changed for better because most are not financially well off. Now when the wife is working, they are just about making ends meet. But…after their wife has got work, she is arrogant, like they're the same. When she comes [home] after job, whatever she does in the kitchen or whatever, she wants the husband to do the same because they have been working together, they are getting the same salary. Now let's say Janet is my wife and we go there, she's getting 10K, I'm getting 10K, when we go to the house there's nothing I can say to her because whatever I'm getting she's also getting. So most families, if they don't have that patience, they end up breaking because of that… Those simple-minded people will think that when she's working she can be able to control her man. And mostly in

the African culture, men don't want to be controlled by women much. So it ends up creating problems in the family.

(Muli, Focus Group #3, 20 July 2013)

Female workers also voiced a concern that relationships are suffering because of work in the EPZ, though most of them brought this up in the context of their working hours and expectations at home. As mentioned earlier, some women felt like they were being forced to choose between being a housewife or seeking a paying job because it was too difficult to do both due to the responsibilities they are expected to take on in both places. Feedback from workers indicates that, with the economy the way it is in Kenya, more women are opting for a job and more men are relinquishing their responsibility when costs at home become too burdensome. When asked if there was anything they would like to see change for women in the future, in addition to reiterating the need for men to take their responsibilities, several women talked about a desire for more empowerment, saying things such as "I think also women should be empowered more since they take more responsibility, so you should be the head of the family" and "I think women are supposed to be empowered. At least they can be given opportunities because they are the ones who seem to be more responsible than men. So if they are empowered, I think they can go far."

Conclusion

In the case of women workers in Kenya's Athi River EPZ—and, to be sure, for many other women in the global world of work—opportunity and exploitation cannot exist without one another. The possibilities that came with the arrival of paid work in Athi River were exciting and endless, but so have been the physical and mental side effects. For most, a job in the EPZ was their first form of paid work. Simply earning a salary has been empowering for many women. Beginning to break from the norm of women staying at home, these women have become more confident, and some are willing to stand up for themselves—both at work and at home. Understanding the challenges arising from these shifting dynamics, including the resulting impact on women workers, has been a key focus of this chapter.

As Chief Justice Dickson of the Supreme Court of Canada once said,

> Work is one of the most fundamental aspects of a person's life, providing the individual with a means of financial support and, as importantly, a contributory role in society. A person's employment is an essential component of his or her sense of identity, self-worth and well-being. Accordingly, the conditions in which a person works are highly significant in shaping the whole compendium of psychological, emotional and physical elements of a person's dignity and self-respect.
>
> *(Dickson 1987)*

The interconnectedness of working conditions and household dynamics is important to consider when talking about how women's work is changing in Kenya. Women's casual (non-permanent) work status leaves them vulnerable to being fired at any moment and disqualifies them from taking paid maternity leave. Receiving late wages means they are unable to pay their bills on time, leading to problems with lenders—they can be locked out of their homes or threatened with violence when it is time for their money to be collected. Long working hours, including unpaid overtime, result in poor health due to fatigue (and skipping meals) and added pressure on relationships at home. Many women, however, report being happy to have a job because it enables them to care for their children. Notably, they also report that they do not perceive they have opportunities for work outside the EPZ and that inflation makes it impossible not to work.

A first step to reducing the worst forms of exploitation of these women is to give them access to information about their rights. Workers accept certain abuses at work because they are unaware of what they are entitled to receive through their own labor and employment laws. Poor working conditions, as this study has considered, are a starting point in thinking about the interconnectedness of work and home life. Workers' ability to utilize law-enforcing machinery and the willingness of business or government to respond to their concerns may be a different story and the subject of additional research, but without this basic knowledge, workers will remain lost. Access to information has other benefits as well and raises the issue of a need for accountability among the stakeholders in the clothing industry. When this research was conducted, union organizers had never seen a copy of their union constitution, nor did they know which major U.S. companies were being supplied by their factories. Workers felt that they could not approach their union leader and that their government did not care about them, prioritizing business well above the fair treatment of workers.

By some definitions, women's work in the Athi River EPZ is purely exploitative. By others, having any job is an opportunity. For the women in the EPZ, work does not appear like a golden road to the pearly gates, but their toil puts something on their children's plates—and this, for now, seems to be satisfactory to many of them. There are those, however, who are frustrated and willing to fight for change, whether through involvement in their union, voicing concerns at work, or simply talking and sharing information with each other. When asked what they believed it meant to be empowered, one woman assertively but eloquently remarked, "I can say, if you help a lady, you have helped the whole world."

Notes

1 Although the Athi River EPZ was funded in 1990, the infrastructure was not completed until 1995, industrial growth was slow, and occupancy rates were low (Madani 1999, 88). It wasn't until the early 2000s that the clothing firms started to establish themselves.
2 To recruit participants, I was assisted by a union organizer from the Tailors and Textile Workers Union (TTWU), as well as two shop stewards from the union. All

focus groups were held off-site, away from the EPZ. The first three were held at a hotel in Kitengela (a village just outside Athi River where many of the workers live), and the remaining ten were held in the back patio area of a small restaurant in Kitengela, for added privacy. Ten of the focus groups were held with females, two with males, and one with a mixed gender group. The focus group guidelines consisted of four modules: module 1 dealt with working conditions and labor standards compliance, module 2 with available remedies and tools for addressing issues, module 3 with employment relations, and module 4 with gender relations. Focus groups lasted approximately 1–1.5 hours and were both audio and video recorded. Most participants spoke in English and, for those who needed assistance, a translator was present at all times.

3 The questionnaire was based on a questionnaire I developed for research with workers in Lesotho's clothing industry in 2011. The questionnaire included 110 items related to work background, employment conditions, occupational health and safety, education, training, dispute resolution, gender, HIV/AIDS, and household income. This was revised slightly for the research in Kenya to reflect: (1) differences in Kenyan labor law and (2) the emphasis that the commissioning research group placed on learning more about gender gaps in economic opportunities, women's voice and agency, living standards, and labor market outcomes. The questionnaire was pre-tested with a group of five shop stewards from the Athi River EPZ. A group of approximately ten shop stewards was then trained on how to administer the questionnaire, which they distributed as the workers went into work, during lunch, as they left work, and in their villages. In total, over 550 fully completed questionnaires were collected. (More than 300 were completed by women.)

4 The focus groups and questionnaire administration took place over a one-month period in July and August, 2013. This fieldwork was commissioned by the World Bank as part of a larger comparative project on the quality of employment for the poor in Kenya, Lesotho, Vietnam, and Cambodia. It also served as a baseline assessment of working conditions in Kenya and in considering the scalability of a program similar to the ILO-IFC's Better Work in other parts of sub-Saharan Africa. (The program is currently in place in Lesotho, Cambodia, Jordan, Vietnam, Nicaragua, Indonesia, Haiti, and Bangladesh.)

5 For examples of this in other African countries, see Ceita 1999 (Angola) cited by Gonzàlez and Grinspun (2001), JUDAI and Associates (2005) (Zambia), and Marcucci (2001) (Zimbabwe).

6 In Kenya, there are eighteen apparel firms operating in EPZs. Six firms are Indian-owned, with two having head offices in Dubai; four are from Taiwan; four are from China; one is from Hong Kong Special Administrative Region (SAR); two have joint ownership structures; and one is locally owned (Staritz and Frederick 2014).

7 When asked why the employers wait so long to pay them, the workers said it is because their employers are waiting for them to reach their production targets. Although employers have the money, they withhold it until the targets are met.

8 The TTWU is headed by the general secretary (GS), also called the president, who is elected by all union-eligible workers through delegates from all fourteen branches (covering forty-seven counties in Kenya). Other elected officers under the GS are the deputy GS, assistant GS, national chairman, first vice national chairman, second vice national chairman, national treasurer, deputy national treasurer, assistant national treasurer, national organizing secretary, three trustees, and six committee members.

9 The Children Act 2001 of Kenya defines parental responsibility as: "All the duties, rights, powers, responsibilities and authority which by law a parent of a child has in relation to the child and the child's property in a manner consistent with the evolving capacities of the child. This includes the duty to maintain the child and in particular to provide him with: (i) adequate diet; (ii) shelter; (iii) clothing; (iv) medical care including immunization; and (v) education and guidance."

10 *Shamba* is a Swahili word for a small plot used for growing subsistence crops and fruit-bearing trees, often including the farmer's dwelling.
11 This is not unique to the EPZ but rather a symptom of Kenyan society's adjustment to a growing awareness around gender equality and women's empowerment.

References

AGOA Info. "United States and EU Sourcing of Clothing from Sub-Saharan Africa". https://agoa.info/data/apparel-trade.html

Atieno, Rosemary. "Explaining Female Labor Force Participation: The Case of Kenya Informal Sector and the Effects of the Economic Crisis". Paper presentation, Annual IAFFE Conference, Buenos Aires, Argentina, July 22–24, 2010.

Beatty, David. "Labour Is Not a Commodity." In *Studies in Contract Law*, edited by Barry Reiter and John Swan, 314. Toronto: Butterworths, 1980.

Bezanson, Kate. *Gender, the State, and Social Reproduction: Household Insecurity in Neo-Liberal Times*. Toronto: University of Toronto Press, 2006.

Combs, Mary Beth. "Cui Bono? The 1870 British Married Women's Property Act, Bargaining Power, and the Distribution of Resources within Marriage." *Feminist Economics* 12, no. 1–2 (2006): 51–83.

Daily Nation. "Kenya: Survey Reveals Kenyan Marriages in Crisis Amid Pressures of Modern Life," 2010. Accessed January 8, 2015. http://www.nation.co.ke/news/New-survey-reveals-Kenyan-marriages-in-crisis/1056-942080-vtxrr8/index.html

Datta, Namita. "Joint Titling – A Win-Win Policy? Gender and Property Rights in Urban Informal Settlements in Chandigarh, India." *Feminist Economics* 12, no. 1–2 (2006): 271–298.

Dickson, Chief Justice and Robert George Brian. *In Reference Re Public Service Employee Relations Act (Alta.)*. 1987. Alberta Union of Provincial Employees, et al. v. Her Majesty the Queen in Right of Alberta as represented by the Attorney General of Canada, [1987] 1 SCR 313 at 368.

Elson, Diane. "Gender Awareness in Modeling Structural Adjustment." *World Development* 23, no. 11 (1995): 1851–1868.

Export Processing Zones Program Annual Performance Reports, 2005–2012. Available at http://www.epzakenya.com/index.php/annual-performance-report.html

Kenya Forum. "Marriage in Kenya – Breaking Up Doesn't Seem so Hard to Do These Days." Accessed January 8, 2015. http://www.kenyaforum.net/2012/12/19/marriage-in-kenya--breaking-up-doesn't-seem-so-hard-to-do-these-days/

Friedemann-Sanchez, Greta. "Assets in Intrahousehold Bargaining Among Women Workers in Colombia's Cut-Flower Industry." *Feminist Economics* 12, no. 1–2 (2006): 247–269.

González De La Rocha, Mercedes and Alejandro Grinspun. "Private Adjustments: Households, Crisis and Work." In *Choices for the Poor: Lessons from National Poverty Strategies*, edited by Alejandro Grinspun, 55–87. New York: United Nations Development Programme, 2001.

John Budd. *The Thought of Work*. Ithaca: Cornell University Press, 2011.

JUDAI and Associates. *Work and Family Conflict in Zambia*. Unpublished Working Paper. Geneva: Conditions of Work and Employment Programme, International Labour Organisation, 2005.

Madani, Dorsati. *A Review of the Role and Impact of Export Processing Zones*. Policy Research Working Paper 2238. The World Bank, Development Research Group, Trade, 1999.

Marcucci, Pamela Nichols. *Jobs, Gender and Small Enterprises in Africa and Asia: Lessons Drawn from Bangladesh, the Philippines, Tunisia and Zimbabwe In Focus Programme on Boosting Employment*. WEDGE, no. 58. Geneva: International Labour Organisation, 2001.

McCormick, Dorothy, Paul Kamau and Peter Ligulu "Post-Multifibre Arrangement Analysis of the Textile and Garment Sectors in Kenya." *Institute of Development Studies Bulletin* 37(1): 80-88.

Mokomane, Zitha. *Work Family Conflict and Gender Equality in South Africa*. Paper presentation, 26th International Population Conference, Marrakech, Morocco, September 27–October 2, 2009.

Muasya, Gladys. "The Role of House Helps in Work-Family Balance of Women Employed in the Formal Sector in Kenya." In *Work-Family Interface in Sub-Saharan Africa*, edited by Zitha Mokomane, 149–159. Switzerland: International Perspectives on Social Policy, Administration, and Practice, 2014.

Muiruri, Anne. "Rules of Engagement for 'Mpango Wa Kando." Accessed January 8, 2015. https://www.sde.co.ke/article/2000143135/rules-of-engagement-for-mpango-wa-kando

Omolo, Jacob O. 2006. "The Textiles and Clothing Industry in Kenya." In *The Future of the Textile and Clothing Industry in Sub-Saharan Africa*, edited by Herbert Jauch and Rudolf Traub-Merz, 133-164. Bonn: Friedrich-Ebert-Stiftung.

Rutterford, Janette and Josephine Maltby. "'The Widow, The Clergyman and The Reckless': Women Investors in England, 1830–1914." *Feminist Economics* 12, no. 1–2 (2006): 111–138.

Soni-Sinha, Uurvashi. "Where Are the Women? Gender, Labor, and Discourse in the Noida Export Processing Zone and Delhi." *Feminist Economics* 12, no. 1–2 (2006): 335–365.

Staritz, Cornelia and Stacey Frederick. 2014. "Sector Case Study: Apparel." In *Making Foreign Direct Investment Work for Sub-Saharan Africa: Local Spillovers and Competitiveness in Global Value Chains*, edited by Thomas Farole and Deborah Winkler, 209–244. Washington, DC: The World Bank, 2014.

Trappe, Heike and Annemette Sørensen. "Economic Relations between Women and their Partners: An East and West German Comparison after Reunification." *Feminist Economics* 12, no. 1–2 (2006): 643–665.

United States International Trade Commission. "Sub-Saharan Africa: US General Imports, Textiles and Apparel." https://www.usitc.gov/research_and_analysis/trade_shifts.htm

Vastveit, Lene Kristin. "Export Processing Zones in Sub-Saharan Africa – Kenya and Lesotho." Thesis submitted to Department of Economics, Univresity of Bergen. 2013.

11
WOMEN AND TRADE LIBERALIZATION IN EGYPT

Heba Nassar

While Egypt experienced relatively positive economic performance prior to the global economic and financial crisis that began in 2007–2008, important employment and labor market challenges persisted both before and after the worldwide economic downturn. Prior to 2007, and in the decade that followed, the Egyptian unemployment rate remained among the highest in the world. Moreover, the nation's labor markets have had a remarkably high incidence of underemployment, with jobs that do not provide enough paid work, or work that does not make full use of a worker's skills and abilities. Egyptians also rely on an enormous informal economy that is not included in the gross national product (GNP) or gross domestic product (GDP). This informal sector is not monitored by any form of government and is not taxed. In addition, poor working conditions persist across most occupational categories and the nation's workers, paid and unpaid, are rigidly segregated by gender. As Azita Berar Awad, Directoer of the Employment Policy Department of the International Labor Organization (ILO), wrote in 2011, "Gender inequalities and particularly the low labour force participation of women are issues of major concern." While the Egyptian economy has improved since 2007–2008, the aftermath of the global economic and financial crisis had a major impact that resulted in a significant economic downturn with prolonged increases in unemployment, poverty, and inequality that exacerbated public discontent, leading to the 2011 revolution. The revolution, in turn, caused an even greater economic slowdown as political and institutional uncertainty and rising insecurity hurt tourism, manufacturing, and construction (Nassar and Biltagy 2017).

In the years preceding the global financial crisis, Egypt carried out a series of economic reforms intended to facilitate economic growth and attract foreign investment (Abdel-Baki 2011). During these years there was a strong connection drawn between the establishment of international trade and the increased enjoyment of human rights. In Egypt, as elsewhere, economic growth through free trade increased the resources available for the realization of human rights. Parallels can also be drawn between the principles of fair competition and non-discrimination under trade law and World Trade Organization (WTO) agreements and between equality and non-discrimination under human rights law. Furthermore, the special and differential treatment offered to Egypt and other developing countries under WTO rules reinforced the concepts of affirmative action under human rights law.

This does not mean, however, that free trade and economic growth automatically led to greater promotion and protection of human rights. While the goals and principles of WTO agreements and international human rights law converge to some extent, the implementation of those goals does not always produce results that are consistent with human rights principles. Hence the relationship between free trade and economic growth raises two important questions from a human rights perspective. One is whether free trade entails more equitable distribution of income, more and better jobs, better wages, more gender equality, and greater inclusiveness. The other, even more important question, is how to channel economic growth through free trade equitably to ensure the implementation of the right to development and fair and equal distribution of wealth and promotion of human well-being (United Nations General Assembly 2000).

Trade, gender, and human rights

Analyzing the relationship between trade and gender within the framework of human rights raises two main questions: first, how can the relationship between trade and gender be explained within the framework of human rights? That is, in what way do trade outcomes affect women's rights? Second, how can the human rights approach to trade be constructed to ensure that the benefits of trade liberalization will be equally distributed among men and women? In this context, analysts differ about the potential positive or negative effects of trade.

Potential positive effects

Trade liberalization policies can offer women opportunities in terms of better jobs and an increased share of paid employment, which can help empower women and raise their status in the society. The growth of export-oriented manufacturing has benefited women, creating many jobs for them (both absolutely and relative to men) and often drawing them into paid work (Fontana et al. 1998).

The expansion of the horticultural products sector (fresh and processed fruits, vegetables, flowers, and nuts) has become particularly important for women, with female workers now comprising a significant proportion of the labor force. Export-oriented production has also helped increase off-farm employment opportunities for women in the short term. Examples from Ghana and Uganda show that although women's wages in off-farm employment are low, they nevertheless seem to contribute to rural poverty alleviation (UNCTAD 2004).

The impact of trade expansion on women's economic activity includes wider human resource development benefits as well as gender benefits. It gives women greater control of income. Child nutritional status and other human resource development indicators may rise, and the livelihood basis of households with women wage workers will be more secure, in particular girls' education (Fontana et al. 1998). The opening of borders in wealthier countries allowing the temporary movement of persons such as nurses and teachers can also help women in poorer countries improve the standard of living of their families with the increase in remittances (United Nations Office of the High Commissioner for Human Rights 2003).

Potential negative effects

Expanding trade liberalization can expose women to discrimination in terms of wages, work status, and working conditions. Trade liberalization has also led to informal employment arrangements and subcontracting in female-dominated industries (such as food and garment production) that threaten the security, status, and rights of workers (Association for Women's Rights in Development 2002a).

In addition, gender-based inequalities (especially in education, health, and training) hinder women's ability to take advantage of new opportunities created by trade liberalization, such as skilled employment and entrepreneurial opportunities. Gender inequalities in access to productive assets such as land and credit or to storage and transport facilities tend to constrain women's benefits from such policies. Moreover, women also tend to lack access to technology and training (Randriamaro 2006). Women are usually concentrated in unskilled and semi-skilled occupations (Association for Women's Rights in Development 2002a).

Impact of trade liberalization on gender: the Egyptian case

The Egyptian case illustrates that trade liberalization can have both positive or negative impacts on women. This depends mainly on the status of women and the pattern of gender segmentation in jobs and wages in the labor market. In Egypt several research studies show that there is a both a horizontal and vertical gender segmentation in the labor market, meaning that workers are distributed both across and within occupations, based on gender. As a result of gender segregation in the occupational structure in Egypt, women are squeezed into a limited number of occupations in the lower and the highest levels of the occupational ladder, correlating with education level. In 2005, almost a third of employed females were working as agricultural workers, about 22.4 percent as professionals or managers, and 16.7 percent in technical occupations, while only 1.3 percent were employed as production workers and 7.8 percent as sales workers. Although almost half of the working females in the informal sector at that time were illiterate (43.9 percent), most educated working females had secondary or university education (48 percent). In contrast, men from all educational levels were more evenly distributed among the various occupations. A fourth of the male labor force worked in agricultural occupations, about 11.3 percent in legislative and managerial jobs, 12.7 percent as professionals, 7.6 percent in technical occupations, 4.6 percent as craft workers, and 10.5 percent as sales workers and as plant and machine operators (CAPMAS 2005).

The relatively high percentage of women clericals, professionals, and farmers reflected the vulnerability of females with respect to privatization policies that were first launched in 1991, and then accelerated beginning in 2003 when the government pushed for liberalization of the Egyptian economy (CAPMAS 2005). Policies aimed at moving Egypt from a centrally planned to a free market economy included floating the rate of exchange of the Egyptian pound and fully or partially privatizing 382 State Owned Enterprises (SOEs) between 2003 until after the 2011 revolution when President Mohamed Morsi suspended the largely unpopular privatization program. This, as financial economist Karim Badr El-Din has argued, "sparked numerous labor stsrikes and fueled public rage against economic liberalization policies" (Badr El-Din 2014). Following the economic crisis, from 2008–2013, informal employment in Egypt fluctuated between 10.8 million in 2008, representing 48.1% of total employment, to 11.3 million in 2013, representing 47% of total employment. Jobs in this informal sector, while a major source of job creation, paid low wages and were marked by poor working conditions (Nassar and Biltagy 2017).

While many Egyptians saw trade liberalization and a free market economy as threatening to their economic well-being, others noted the correlation between these aspects of globalization and a significant improvement in the status of women (CAWTAR 2001). For women entrepreneurs, studies indicate that as of 2004, as the move toward trade liberalization accelerated, the percentage of micro, middle, and small enterprises (M/SME) owned by women was estimated to be 12.4 percent, compared to the 87.6 percent owned by males (El Meehy 2003; El Mahdi 2004). The World Bank/Social Research Center at the American University Investment Climate Assessment Survey in 2004, which included 1,053 industrial establishments, found that 24 percent of the industrial enterprises surveyed were owned by women, but only 13 percent as single owners, while the rest were only shareholders (Nassar 2005). Coke, petroleum, and chemicals represent the main sector for women entrepreneurs in the private industrial sector (36.9 percent of female-owned enterprises), followed by ready-made garments (11.8 percent). In 2004, among female-owned firms employing more than ten employees, about half were in the textiles sector, followed by metals, chemicals, and mining enterprises, which averaged around 28.5 percent. About a third (35.5 percent) of the female-owned firms employing more than ten employees were located in Cairo, followed by Giza (12.7 percent) (National Council for Women 2004). During these years of trade liberalization, many women started their own enterprises or worked with relatives in small businesses so that they could manage their responsibilities between their household and their work. As of 2004, female entrepreneurs, whether working formally or informally, seemed to be mainly active in two major areas: the trade and services sectors (El Mahdy 2004; Khattab and Sakr 2009).

Across all sectors, however, unemployment has been a problem affecting every individual member of Egyptian society who needs and is able to work. The unemployment rate in Egypt averaged 10.63 percent from 1993 until 2014, reaching the highest value of 13.4 percent in 2013 and the lowest value of 8.1 percent in 1999 (Nassar and Biltagy 2017). The majority of the unemployed is made up of young people, 15 to 29 years of age, who are seeking a job for the first time. In 2014, almost one-third of unemployed individuals in Egypt were university graduates (CAPMAS 2014). Overall, however, while unemployment affects both men and women, the impact of unemployment on women has been consistantly more intense. Women are more vulnerable when they enter the labor market, largely, although not exclusively, because of the large number of women working in the informal economy. Even among university graduates, however, the unemployment rate in 2014 was 40.1 percent among female university graduates and 24.4 percent among males (Nassar and Biltagy 2017). According to the Central Agency for Public Mobilization, the duration of unemployment is longer for females than for males. It reaches three years and above for 43.1 percent of unemployed females and 36.4 percent for unemployed males, while it is less than 12 months for 20.9 percent of females and 28.1 percent of unemployed males (Nassar 2017). The continuity of women's work can be interrupted for years by maternal responsibilities and the impact of the dual roles that women occupy, as unpaid household workers and as compensated workers in both the formal and informal economy. Women may be forced to leave their jobs for their responsibilities at home, which is usually not the case for men (Nassar 2006; Hassanien 2010).

Women in Egypt also suffer from wage discrimination. Wage discrimination for women in manufacturing, as well as in the agricultural sector, takes place because women work in low-skilled jobs and rarely become supervisors. Their lack of education and inferior status in the labor market are a result of limited access to technical, vocational, and entrepreneurial training that reduces their chances to be engaged in more capital-intensive industries with higher salaries. For these reasons, women's wages on average are far below men's in the same industrial branch. It is important to mention that this does not reflect inequities in the setting of wages, as the manufacturing sector is still dominated by public enterprises that set wages uniformly for both sexes. The explanation for these inequities lies in the different entry jobs for both sexes, different chances for promotion, limited chances for vocational training, and females' resistance to working overtime, as they are restricted by their parenting or household responsibilities (Khattab and Sakr 2009).

Egyptian labor laws have been equitable and favorable to women, but despite this fact, they frequently lead to employers' holding unfavorable perceptions of women's work. This is particularly true in the private sector, as opposed to state-run industries. Laws that provide for maternity leaves, child-care centers, and nursing breaks in the government and public sector make women expensive workers for employers. According to the Labor Law (2003) in Egypt, "Women workers are entitled to three months paid maternity leave and up to two years unpaid maternity leave available up to three times." Although this law was written to benefit women, it has also lead to discrimination against women in the labor market by employers opposed to lengthy maternity leaves (Nassar 2005). An analysis of job advertisements found that 69 percent of the private sector advertisements in September 2005 were for males. The New Labor Law (2011) also requires employers with a hundred or more female employees to set up a nursery close to the workshops far from noise, pollution and waste, and to allow for breastfeeding for not less than one-half hour twice a day. This law also protects women from hazardous work as well as night work. Even when night work is allowed, as in the tourist sector, the law requires employers to provide transportation for women after 8 p.m. However, evidence shows that implementation is lagging behind regulations (Nassar 2017).

Significantly, the new post-2011 employment law also gave workers the right to collective negotiation. Women workers had played a crucial role in the wave of strikes that swept across the public and private sectors, beginning in 2004. More than 1,900 strikes took place between 2004–2008, with an estimated 1.7 million workers involved. In 2006, for example, led by 3,000 women workers, the employees at the Ghazl Al-Mahala textile plant walked out demanding that the government fulfill its promise to pay a yearly bonus. Despite this activism, however, women's representation in official trade unions is still limited to lower-level positions. All twenty-three unions of the Trade Union Federation have some female officers, however, they constitute only 3.4 percent of all officers. In only four of the 23 trade unions, have women reached high-level leadership positions. Moreover, trade union representation is not even available for most women who work as domestic servants, for women traders, or generally for women operating in the informal sector (National Council of Women 2004; Sika and Khodary 2012).

Finally, women in the labor market face other forms of discrimination as well. The Labor Force Information Project indicated that as of 2004, females reported facing such kinds of discrimination as ill-treatment by male colleagues, directors, supervisors, and employees (41.7 percent); harassment by the public (32.8 percent); sexual harassment (65 percent); discrimination against women (5.4 percent); absence of transportation facilities (4.7 percent); problems with young children left alone and housework (4.7 percent); being requiring to perform favors that are not part of their formal job duties (2 percent); and gossip (1.3 percent) (Nassar 2004). Moreover, the aforementioned study also indicated job discrimination against working women with respect to promotions, appointments, wages, bonuses, types of work, attaining high-ranking posts, chances to travel abroad, and favors asked on the job. In rural areas, discrimination in wages is significant, followed by the type of work given to females. In the government, women considered disparities in travelling abroad the most important form of discrimination, followed by attaining high-ranking posts, and then the type of work given to women. In the public sector, women face discrimination in the process of appointment, followed by the type of work given to them and in the number of the work trips they take. In the private sector, the most important form of discrimination was the type of work given to women, followed by wages and then by favors asked of women (Nassar 2004).

A sectoral view

As of 2014, women's representation in the manufacturing sector was still limited and had stood at 13 percent since 2002. Women working in manufacturing were concentrated in such labor-intensive industries as textiles and garments, food processing, and pharmaceutical products. The textile and garments industry is of significant importance for the Egyptian economy, as it exceeds 30 percent of all value-added manufacturing. In 2006 the Egyptian textile industry represented 27 percent of the country's total manufacturing production, 3 percent of its GNP, and contributes about 23 percent of wages in the industrial sector. It is hence the largest provider of wages in the industrial sector, accounting for around 30 percent of total employment in the manufacturing sector (1.3 million workers) (Fawzy and Massoud 2003; Sakr 2006; Central Bank of Egypt 2013–2014).

An indication of the lower status of female workers in manufacturing in general is in the division of skills required by gender in this sector. The results of the survey of World Bank Investment Climate Assessment (ICA) in 2005 and 2016 showed that women are hired to cut, sew, sort, inspect, and packagage clothing; to work as production supervisors; and as accountants and secretaries. The skills most in demand for females in the chemical, food, and textile sectors (and other sectors with a high concentration of females) were in finishing, packaging and secretarial work (World Bank, ICA 2005a, 2014).[1]

On the other hand, looking at the difficulties facing textiles exporters in Egypt from a gender perspective, the ICA surveys show a relative similarity in the severity of obstacles faced by male- and female-owned textile-exporting firms. Both male- and female-owned firms ranked macroeconomic uncertainty as the most severe obstacle they tend to face (92.3 percent for females, 90.3 percent for males). In the second place, females ranked regulatory policy uncertainty (77 percent) as a constraint, while males ranked tax rates (87.1 percent) as the second most severe obstacle. Tax rates constituted the third most severe obstacle for business women (69.2 percent), while regulatory policy uncertainty came third for males (71 percent). Customs and trade regulation seemed to constitute a problematic obstacle for female-owned exporting firms, as it came in fourth place (61.5 percent); however, it seemed to be a much less problematic obstacle for males, as only 38.7 percent of the male-owned exporting firms mentioned that customs and trade regulation constitute a severe obstacle. On the other hand, both male- and female-owned exporting firms agreed that telecommunication and transportation constituted a non-problematic or minor obstacle (100 and 92.3 percent, respectively, for females, and 93.5 and 90.3 percent, respectively, for males) (World Bank (ICA) 2005a).

More than half of women workers are absorbed in the service sector in its broader definition, however women are more concentrated in some occupations rather than others. Females are concentrated in social services, with very low representation in transportation and communication services. They are better represented in commerce, hotels and restaurants services. No significant differences exist in the occupation rates of both sexes in the real estate, banking and insurance services (Nassar 2017).

Gender sectoral bias is apparent in Egyptian society, where most job opportunities for females in the formal sector have been concentrated in the government and to some extent in the public sector in comparison to the male labor market (Asaad 2002; Nassar and Biltagy 2017). Feminization of the government sector in Egypt is a result of the relatively better working conditions in this sector in comparison to the private sector for females. The percentage of females working in this sector to total working females, exceeds the similar percentage for males. The equal opportunity environment prevailing in the government sector has resulted in some progress for women in access to senior positions. Women have made significant advances in the government sector compared to the private sector, such as secure wage setting, equal regulations, and comfortable working hours. However, currently females in the public sector face several problems, including deterioration in the status of government employees as real wages decline. Secondly, privatization may have negative effects on females working in the public sector. Among public sector redundancies, the percentage of females is high. Women tend to work in clerical, secretarial, and administrative work, areas that are already saturated. During the privatization process, women are the first to leave, as working conditions in the private sector are unsuitable for most married females due to long working hours and serious competition. Meanwhile, the division of labor continues to render the vocational training process that accompanies the process of labor dismissal more suitable for men than for women. Moreover, women's household and child-care responsibilities tend to affect their productivity and result in persistent barriers against the engagement of females in the private sector (Moghadam 1995). In addition, women like to work in permanent jobs like the jobs in the government with a fixed contract rather than transitory jobs with period contracts.

The agricultural sector comes second after the service sector in absorbing female workers in Egypt. In general, Egyptian women are a major resource in agriculture and agribusiness. Given women's predominant role in agriculture, food production, and home-based income-generating activities, this is hardly surprising. Women work particularly long hours during planting, weeding, and harvesting times. The situation of women in rural areas (productive and reproductive) is critical. Women in rural areas work all day in domestic and productive activities that were not calculated in official statistics for a long time.[2]

According to the Central Agency for Public Mobilization and Statistics (CAPMAS) Statistical database for Egypt in the 2000s, the horticultural subsector is a major employer of women. Women participate actively at all levels of the subsector, from production to processing and marketing. The proportion of female participation, however, varies by commodity and task. For example, commodities such as grapes, strawberries, apricots, green beans, artichokes, and valley-grown potatoes employ more women than other crops since they require more manual labor during production and harvesting. In grape production, women provide as much as 56 percent of the total labor required for both pre- and post-harvest activities. In the food processing industry, particularly those using vegetables and fruits, women are the main source of labor. Women provide approximately 85 to 90 percent of the cleaning, sorting, grading and packing labor, which requires patience. Even in modern plants where the cleaning, sorting, and grading are done by machines, women provide the bulk of packing labor. For example, in frozen vegetable processing, women make up the bulk of unskilled labor required to perform basic routine tasks. As in horticultural production, women are generally hired on a seasonal basis. Men, on the other hand, tend to be mostly permanent workers—machinists, engineers, technicians, and supervisors—and are also hired to perform the heavier and harsher tasks often required in processing plants, such as stacking, hauling and lifting. These tasks are usually perceived by both employers and female employees as unsuitable for women (and El-Said 2000; CAPMAS 2014).

The agribusiness sector has long been one of the more dynamic sectors in the economy. Egyptian agribusiness enterprises are mainly focused on specific subsectors like cotton, wheat, rice, horticulture, and food processing. In many of these agribusiness enterprises, women provide a sizeable share of the total labor (El Sanabary et al. 1999).

Women also have represented as much as 50 percent of the employees in factory plant laboratories, tissue-culture labs, and quality control and quality assurance departments in the private sector. The percentage of women employees is also steadily increasing in accounting and bookkeeping departments as agribusinesses become more formal and sophisticated. As these export-oriented, labor-intensive agribusinesses expand, the demand for both skilled and less-skilled female labor will expand as well (Chaherli and Moataz 2000).

Livestock and dairy production is an integral aspect of the country's farming system. In Egypt in 2000, more than 90 percent of the five million cattle (buffaloes and cows) are owned by smallholder dairy farmers, with an average of one to three head of cattle per household. Smallholder dairy farmers hold about 80 to 85 percent of the country's productive capacity in milk. Although most of the milk is consumed and processed at home (for example, into cheese, butter, and cream), a sizeable amount gets sold in the local market. Milk marketing at the smallholder level is largely done individually, particularly during market days, although some sales are conducted through village milk collectors who collect milk twice a day from individual farms. Marketing of home-processed dairy products such as cheese, cream, ghee, and butter are done directly in the market by women.[3] (www.capmas.gov.eg)

The gendering of agriculture appears to be a function of strength and male dominance. Female engagement in agriculture has always been regarded as part of their role as housewives and for long periods was not counted as economic activity. In this sector, the basic problem facing women is not lack of work opportunities but that they are working all the time without adequate financial evaluation of their participation in this sector (Nassar 2004). Moreover, the system of land ownership for women is determined by religion, which entitles women to inheritance. However by tradition, women might not be allowed to have control over their land as long their relatives are alive under the notion that females are not breadwinners and should be supported by the men in their families.

Policy recommendations

To improve the situation for women under trade liberalization, two policy approaches can be applied in general: a bottom-up approach and a top-down approach.

The bottom-up approach

The bottom-up approach includes the participation of organizations such as women's organizations, NGOs, and trade unions. Women's organizations can establish meso- or microlevel links between human rights, gender equality, and trade unions through partnerships, networking, and coordinated efforts with women's groups, civil society organizations, and gender experts. Trade unions can play a role in raising awareness of private firms regarding the importance of providing their employees with continuous training to upgrade their skills. The International Men and Gender Equality Survey (IMAGES), the largest multi-country study of its kind in the Middle East and North Africa, conducted a survey in Egypt showing that only 20 percent of the surveyed firms offered training to their employees. The percentage was higher—59.1 percent—in the public sector than in the private sector—11.1 percent. Ensuring equal representation of men and women among trade decision-makers is important to promote gender equality (El Feki et al. 2017).

More support by governmental and civil society entities could be given to workingwomen's organizations, covering both formal and informal sector workers, to improve their access to information on labor rights and standards, and their ability to take collective action to uphold their rights and negotiate with management over voluntary codes of conduct. On the other hand, traditional forms of organization by trade unions have not achieved women's objectives, as they have little bargaining power, very often are not allowed to organize, and are not very amenable to listening to women-specific demands and including them in their negotiating strategies.

NGOs can play an increasing role in addressing such imbalances in the labor market through enhancing women's access to market information, credit, and extension services, as there is a need to create awareness among women of trade regulations (labor, quality, and environmental standards) that they need to fulfill when exporting to the world market. Increasing awareness is also necessary among agricultural workingwomen.

The top-down approach

There is a need for the formulation of specific measures to reduce discrimination against women in labor markets so as to bring about sustained improvements in women's labor market status. This could be done via two means: effective implementation of labor standards and of gender-sensitive rules for employment and social protection. Provision of protection for women in the informal sector is an important mechanism for protecting the most vulnerable workers. Concerning labor standards, it is important to note that without complementary measures, international adoption of labor standards may lead to further dualism in working conditions, with greater segmentation in the labor market between protected and unprotected workers than presently exists. Other actions supportive of workingwomen's rights (such as codes of conduct) should provide a means of protecting women workers from employment abuse. This is especially true in terms of wages and working conditions, around which abuses are likely to increase as competition for international markets intensifies (Fontana et al. 1998). Voluntary Codes of Conduct (VCC) could be one of the complementary measures to the adoption of the formal labor standards, as they require the main contractor to take responsibility for the pay and conditions of all workers at every stage of production. VCCs have brought into the public domain women's priorities that have often been overlooked by male labor representatives. They impose rights to appropriate pay for the job and to collective organizing and bargaining.

Further, education and training programs should prepare women for the requirements of new technologies (Moghadem 1995) so that women will not be stuck in low-paid employment, and the provision of education and training programs should be gender-sensitive. The reservation of some places in technical education and vocational training centers for girls is a crucial measure for increasing the enrollment of girls into vocational-technical programs in some regions in Egypt, especially Upper Egypt. The provision of informal vocational training in formal evening schools with closer ties with the community is an effective means for enhancing girls' enrollment in this kind of education due to societal concerns about the safety of females, girls in particular. Distance education through radios, televisions and correspondence techniques is an important measure to promote technical education in secondary and post-secondary education. Independent classes or classes connected with mother-child care centers or "productive families workshops" might be suitable for married women. Such diversification should allow for meeting the needs of those who wish to continue their education at a higher level, as well as the needs of those who need to be educated in order to perform their work in a more efficient manner (Nassar 2002).

Gender policies and human resource development

Development of gender-aware, strategic macroeconomic policies needs human resource training programs to enhance gender-sensitive macroeconomic and trade policymaking.

It is important as well to strengthen the capacity of women's organizations and communities to understand the impact of trade and finance liberalization on women. This also will require the increase in the number of seats held by women in the parliament to protect their rights.

Enhanced research to understand the various channels through which macroeconomic policies affect women and men, both directly and indirectly (via the public, formal market, informal, and care reproductive sectors) is also crucial. There is a need for comprehensive gender analysis of current trade policies, specific WTO agreements, different sectors, and the full range of trade-related issues. Such research will help parse when women stand to win and when they stand to lose from new trading relations and also how different trade-related policies impact women's empowerment. Researchers and women's rights advocacy groups need to work together to articulate appropriate alternative policies that guarantee women's rights (AWID 2002b).

There is a clear need for conducting quantitative analyses and field surveys of the relationship between changes in the export share of manufacturing output and agricultural exports and female participation in the labor force in the region. Given the role of the informal sector as a major employer for females in the region, there is in an important need to understand the characteristics of the informal sector in the context of trade reform. Comparative assessments of the array of informal sector employment opportunities open to women and men, respectively, are few and far between, and none has been done in the context of changes in trade policy. The subject could be studied at the country level or for different industrial branches across countries in the region (for example, textiles and ready-made garments are important industrial export sectors that employ a considerable portion of females). An evaluation of the working conditions and different forms of social protection offered for women workers is needed (e.g., health plans, collective bargaining, savings plans), as well as of forms of reproductive care provision that have been made in the informal sector (UNCTAD 2004). Special attention also needs to be devoted to women entrepreneurs and exporters in the region. Statistics about women's employment in the export industries, QIZ areas, and of women exporters also need to be developed.

Moreover, the impact of women's employment on their status within the family and household, and on their decision-making, self-esteem, and aspirations needs to be studied. Although some research has been done on the benefits of education and employment among middle-class and professional females, there is a need for more research concerning working-class women. Enhancing IT and language skills is also a crucial step toward enhancing women's status in different sectors. IT can be a major venue for increasing women's economic participation through providing women with access to inexpensive market information, e-commerce, and distance work. Working from home could be a very suitable option for many married women, as it would give them the opportunity to satisfy their career ambitious as well as carry out their reproductive and household responsibilities.

Using human rights impact assessments and consultations with individuals and communities to guide trade rule and policymaking is an important step towards the progressive realization of human rights. In this regard, it is worth mentioning that studying the gender impact of trade liberalization agenda has received very little attention in the Arab Region both on the governmental as well as the academic level and should be improved. Proposed steps include consulting with women's groups in the formulation of trade policies. For example, the United Nations Fund for Women (UNIFEM) was invited to be a rapporteur in the follow-up meeting of the Barcelona+10 Euromed Conference on Women held in Barcelona in November 2005 and in preparation for the Euromed Ministerial Conference in Istanbul in November 2006, which was attended by government and civil society representatives, researchers, bi- and multilateral organizations, and EU delegates to debate challenges and strategies to support women's participation in social, economic, and political spheres. UNIFEM participation as a rapporteur at this session was an important opportunity to put forward a series of recommendations and strategies on gender equality to be included into the Euro-Mediterranean agreement (UNIFEM 2006). This same opportunity arose for the Union of Arab NGOs organized on December 12–14, 2006, to raise awareness about the free trade agreements and their sectoral impacts.

Encouraging international cooperation and assistance

International cooperation must give developing countries adequate transitional periods to be able to undertake trade reform without having negative impacts on their population. Trade liberalization in agriculture could have a serious impact on women's food security. A human rights approach suggests additional mechanisms to deal with these sorts of situations, such as a mechanism setting different rates of liberalization for crops fundamental to rural employment or national food security or establishing social safety nets to deal with the shocks that can have a negative effect on the enjoyment of the right to food. Developed countries can contribute to the establishment of such social safety through providing financial aid, food aid, and transfer of know-how.

Finally, there is also a need integrate gender issues into international, regional, and bilateral trade negotiations. A good example is the gender policy of the COMESA, which aims at enhancing women's chances to benefit from trade liberalization. Similar gender policies need to be developed with the EU and the Arab countries. Arab women, for example, could benefit from access to technical and financial assistance opportunities offered by the EU within the context of the Euro-Mediterranean agreement. Special quotas can be granted to women in programs targeting enhancing the skills of workers and exporters, such as Egypt's technical and vocational education reform program and Industrial Modernization programs, which are one of the EU assistance components. Women workers as well as entrepreneurs should be ensured fair access to the services offered by these programs.

Free trade and economic growth do not automatically lead to the greater promotion and protection of human rights, including the rights of women in the workplace. However, based on the Egyptian case, periods of increased free trade and economic growth correlate with the creation of more and better jobs, better wages, more equitable distribution of income, and more gender equality. The challenge remains how to channel economic growth through free trade in an equitable way that insures the implementation of the right to development and the fair and equal distribution of wealth. The promotion of human well-being continues to challenge nations across the Middle East and North Africa region, including Egypt. While progress has been made, gender-based inequalities in education, health, and job training keep women from embracing the new opportunities created by trade liberalization and from full participation in the Egyptian economy. Going forward, women's roles in the economic, social, cultural, and political life of the nation will shape and be shaped by the cultural and economic decisions that have been made in the wake of the 2008 global economic crisis.

Acknowledgements

Thanks goes to Dr. Rania ElSebaie for assistance in data collection anddocumentation.

Notes

1 This part depends on analyzing data from the Investment Climate Assessment (ICA) which is a collaborative study, funded by the World Bank and conducted by SRC since September 2004 until now under the auspices of the Ministry of Investment. The objective of this survey is to inform public policymakers of the current performance, costs and constraints facing the private sector to help guide the future agenda of reforms set by the Ministry of Investment. The series of ICA surveys covers the manufacturing, trade and services companies in both the formal and informal sector. Nearly 1500 companies were sampled and interviewed in the 2014

ICA survey (used in this study), where the companies interviewed in the 2004, 2008 and 2011 surveys were re-interviewed and new companies were added to the survey.
2 www1.aucegypt.edu/srd/wsite1, research on women in agriculture.
3 Central Agency for Public Mobiliation and Statistics Database, www.capmas.gov.eg

References

Abdel-Baki, M. 2011. "The Efficacy of the Egyptian Bank Reform Plan in Mitigating the Impact of The Global Financial Crisis." *Econ Change Restruct* 44: 221–241. https://doi.org/10.1007/s10644-011-9100-5

Association for Women's Rights in Development. 2002a. "Women's Rights and Economic Change." *AWRID Newsletter*, no. 4, August.

Association for Women's Rights in Development. 2002b. *Women's Rights, The World Trade Organization and International Trade Policy*. Facts & Issues, no. 4. August. (United States) New York.

Badr El-Din, Karim. 2014. "Privatization: A Key to Solving Egypt's Economic Woes." *Voices and Views: Middle East and North Africa*. The World Bank. Tuesday, 03/11/2014.

Center for Arab Women Training and Research (CAWTAR). 2001. *Globalization and Gender: Economic Participation of Arab Women*. Tunisia: CAWTAR.

Central Agency for Public Mobilization and Statistics (CAPMAS). 2005. *Labor Force Sample Survey 2004*. Cairo: CAPMAS. (www.capmas.gov.eg)

Central Agency for Public Mobilization and Statistics (CAPMAS). 2014. *Labour Force Sample Survey 2014*. Cairo: CAPMAS. (www.capmas.gov.eg)

Central Bank of Egypt. 2013/2014. "Economic Research Sector." *Economic Review* 54: 1–165.

Chaherli, Nabil and Moataz El-Said. 2000. *Impact of the WTO Agreement on MENA Agriculture*. Cairo: Economic Research Forum.

El Feki, S., Heilman, B., and Barker,G. eds. 2017. *Understanding Masculinities: Results from the International Men and Gender Equality Survey (IMAGES)*. Washington, DC: UN Women and Promundo-US.

El Mahdy, Alia. 2004. "Women Entrepreneurs in Egypt: Realities and Hopes." Egypt Network for Integrated Development Policy Brief 019. http://www.enid.org.eg/uploads/pdf/PB19_women_entrepreneurs.pdf

El Meehy, Tamer. 2003. "A Proposed General Policy Framework for SME Development In Egypt," Presented to The Ministry of Foreign Trade & Micro, Small & Medium Policy Development Project (SMEPOL).

Fawzy, Samiha and Nada Massoud. 2003. *The Future of Egypt's Textiles and Clothing Exports in Light of New International Trading Rules*. ECES Working Paper, no. 86. Cairo, Egypt: Egyptian Center for Economic Studies.

Fontana, Marzia, Susan Joekes and Rachel Masika. 1998. *Global Trade Expansion and Liberalization: Gender Issues and Impacts*. BRIDGE Report No. 42. Brighton: Institute of Development Studies (IDS).

Hassanien, Dahlia. 2010. "Gendering Decent Work: Obstacles to Performativity in the Egyptian Workplace." *Surfacing* 3(1), 1–15.

Khattab, Abdullah S. and Hala Sakr. 2009. *Women's Economic Empowerment in Egypt: Challenges and Opportunities*. SRC/CIDA Research Program on "Gender and Work." Paper no. (1). Cairo: Social Research Center. The American University in Cairo.

Moghadem, Valentine. 1995. *Women Industrial Employment in the Middle East and North Africa.* ERF newsletter no. 2, Vol. 2, Cairo: ERF.

Nassar, Heba and Marwa Biltagy. 2017. "Poverty, Employment, Investment, and Education Relationships: The Case of Egypt." *SAGE Open* 7(2), 1–10.

Nassar, Heba. 2006. *"Skills Requirements of the Egyptian Labor Market: Gender perspective (Manufacturing Sector) Report of a field Survey.* Social Research Center (SRC) Working Paper no. 7. Cairo: Social Research Center – The American University in Cairo.

Nassar, Heba. 2005. *Impact of Globalization on Women.* Paper submitted to the National Council for Women, Cairo (Egypt).

Nassar, Heba. 2004. *Policies to enhance the economic participation of women in Egypt* Paper submitted to National Council for Women and UNIFEM, Cairo (Egypt).

Nassar, Heba. 2002. *Market Potential Capacity for Female Graduates of Technical Education* Report submitted to Ministry of Education, Mubarak Kohl Initiative and Social Research Center, American University in Cairo. Cairo (Egypt).

The National Council of Women. 2004. *The Status of Egyptian Woman.* Cairo: NCW.

Randriamaro, Zo. 2006. *GENDER and TRADE: Overview Report.* BRIDGE Report. Brighton: Institute of Development Studies, Sussex University.

El Sanabary, Nagat, Kamla Mansour, Lamia El Fattal, Bagie Sherchand, Amani El Fiki and Nihad Hassan. 1999. *Gender Issues in Privatization and Liberalization of the Agriculture Economy in Egypt: Implications for Policy Reform.* Cairo: Ministry of Agriculture and Land Reclamation.

Sika, Nadine and Yasmin Khodary. 2012. "One Step Forward, Two Steps Back? Egyptian women within the Confines of Authoritarianism." *Journal of International Women's Studies* 13(5), 91–100. Available at: http://vc.bridgew.edu/jiws/vol13/iss5/9.

UNIFEM. 2006. Report on UNIFEM participation to the Euro med Ministerial Conference: "An Action Plan to strengthen women's role in society" held in Rabat, Morocco (14–16 June 2006).

United Nations Conference on Trade and Development (UNCTAD). 2004. *Trade and Gender: Opportunities and Challenges for Developing Countries Prepared by Anh-Nga Tran-Nguyen and Americo Bevigilla Zampetti.* Geneva and New York: UNCTAD.

United Nations General Assembly. 2000. *Globalization and Its Impact on the Full Enjoyment of All Human Rights: Preliminary Report of the Secretary-General.* New York: United Nations.

United Nations Office of the High Commissioner For Human Rights. 2003. "Human rights and trade," Submitted to the 5th WTO Ministerial Conference, Cancun, Mexico, 10–14 September 2003.

World Bank. 2005a. *Investment Climate Assessment Survey (ICA) for Egypt.* Washington, DC: World Bank.

World Bank. 2005b. *The Economic Advancement of Women in Jordan: A country Gender Assessment.* Washington, DC: World Bank.

12
WOMEN'S UNIVERSITY ATTAINMENT AND LABOR FORCE PARTICIPATION IN GULF COOPERATION COUNCIL COUNTRIES

Alessandra L. González

While women's university graduation rates currently exceed those of men in Gulf Cooperation Council (GCC) countries, women's labor force participation has remained stagnant. To understand the causes of this increase in women's higher education and what keeps the resulting masses of university-educated women from exploding into the work force in the GCC, this study explores possible explanations for this graduation-to-work discrepancy, including economic, sociological, and political factors. Among economic factors considered are the historical legacy of colonial economic partnerships, the rentier state status of various GCC countries, the importation of foreign labor, and recent efforts to nationalize the workforce and diversify the economy. Among the sociological factors considered are traditional gender roles and demographic trends in the region. Lastly, political factors considered are relevant legislation and government policies related to women's work and larger geo-political issues that GCC countries face, such as pressures to modernize and security challenges in the region.

In light of these economic, sociological, and political considerations, this chapter addresses possible paths forward for addressing the challenges highlighted by the gender gap in GCC labor force participation. Among economic pathways, it considers the success of diversification attempts and changes in hiring practices to promote GCC women's labor force participation. This analysis provides a descriptive foundation from which future analyses of women's higher education and labor force participation in the GCC can be conducted.

Understanding the causes of gender inequality and inefficiencies in the labor markets of the GCC is of tremendous significance for the economic future of those nations and the countries that interact with them. As energy-producing countries, their success is extremely important to the global economy. As leading economies, these nations also provide jobs for expatriate laborers and remittances back to home countries, particularly to other Middle Eastern and South East Asian economies (Weyl 2018). In addition, studies of GCC labor markets have broader theoretical implications for the field because of the history of political Islam in the region and women's varied access to local institutions of higher education. If the insights of the vast amount of research on the positive returns to investment in education can be applied to questions of gender and development in the Middle East, the GCC experience should provide a case with interesting implications for the field.

This study uses secondary statistical data from the World Bank, the CIA World Factbook, and GCC country statistical abstracts and census data and publicly available data collected by independent private consulting companies. Methods of analysis include descriptive statistics of variables of interest (i.e., women's university attainment and labor force participation in GCC countries). While few studies have been done on this topic (Coleman and Abdelgadir 2016; Young 2016), this analysis provides a descriptive foundation for future analyses. That some data are missing within the World Bank data estimates (for example, for female and male tertiary enrollment) reflects the difficulty of obtaining relevant data from GCC countries at the aggregate level. That some GCC member countries do not make certain data publicly available demonstrates the importance of conducting in-country mixed method research to get a fuller picture of the conditions regarding female tertiary enrollment and participation in the labor force. Discrepancies in available World Bank aggregate data and self-reported GCC census figures do not allow this analysis to combine both estimates into one dataset.

History of women's access to higher education in the GCC

Table 12.1 provides a brief history of women's education in GCC countries from year of independence to date of first university inauguration to women's current rates of university graduation and labor force participation. Although few academic studies have investigated the link between women's access to local university education in the Gulf and its long-term effects on gender equality, González and Al-Kazi (2011) have found that Kuwaiti youth whose mothers had at least some college education were much more likely to believe in gender equality than their peers. Once GCC countries established their own governments and political forms of governance, most of which are characterized by strong executive ruling families consulting in various degrees with legislative and judicial branches, they soon took up the project of setting up educational institutions. The universities they founded took various forms, such as men's-only technical colleges (as in Bahrain) and co-ed liberal arts universities (as in Kuwait). Figure 12.1 shows the ratio of female to male tertiary enrollment in these countries.

What is not visible from these data is the self-selection among local populations as to who would be among the first to attend these local institutions of

TABLE 12.1 GCC women's education and labor force statistics

Country	Independence	University Inauguration	Women University Graduates (%, 2013)	Women Employed in Labor Force (%, 2013)
Bahrain	1971	1968	48	30
Kuwait	1961	1966	67	51
Oman	1970	1986	71*	25
Qatar	1971	1973	72*	36
Saudi Arabia	1932	1957	57	17
UAE	1971	1975	70	28

Sources: CIA World Factbook (2016); Paschyn (2013); Oxford Business Group (2015); UAE Embassy (2017).
* 1999 data.

higher education. It may be that the first locals to attend the newly established universities came from already educated, upper-class, secular elites, as these institutions were nationalist government projects and not schools exclusively for religious education. Pictures of graduating classes from Kuwait University in the 1960s, for example, depict mixed-gender classes, including women not wearing hijabs and women wearing mini-skirts (González 2013, 85). In photographs of more recent graduating classes, however, Kuwaiti youth wear more traditional dress and are segregated by gender, with more women wearing veils. Does this mean that Kuwaitis are more religious than they were in the 1960s? Not necessarily. A more plausible explanation is that the democratization of higher education in the last half century, during which families from rural bedouin backgrounds migrated to cities to enroll their children in the Kuwaiti education system, has expanded university access to a more representative segment of the population. This trend of rural migration into urban centers for educational and economic opportunities can be seen throughout the Gulf.

But what explains the meteoric rise in women's university enrollment, graduation rates, and performance? Perhaps social norms have changed to encourage women to attend university, whereas social conservatives had previously discouraged women from even learning to read. It may be that the increasing presence of private universities alongside the initial public universities has given local families even more choices about where to send their daughters to school and enabled more to attend. Or the increasing economic demands of the developing GCC economies may have encouraged families to give their daughters options aside from the marriage market to support themselves and future children. In addition, perhaps the rising divorce rate in the GCC (varying around

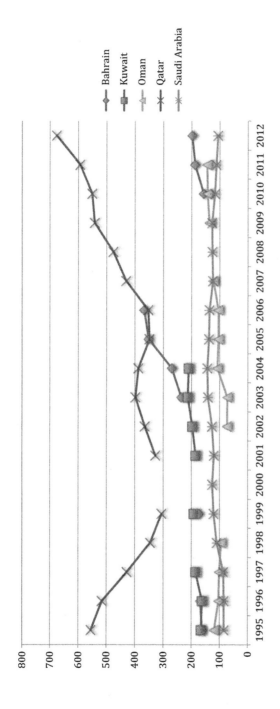

FIGURE 12.1 GCC ratio of percentage of female to male tertiary enrollment, 1995–2013, based on World Bank data. No data was available for the UAE. Missing data points mean no data was available for those years. These figures include non-national population.

30–40%) has made parents more aware of the security that a university education can provide their daughters in the event of a divorce. These hypotheses need further testing, but they could explain why women currently are vastly outnumbering and outperforming their male peers in university.

So what about the men? What does the rise in women's university graduation rates say about the incentives for men to succeed in school and their place in the labor market? Again, few academic studies have explored these questions, but some financial consulting companies have started to produce some data and evidence showing inefficiencies in GCC labor markets that do not reward returns on investments in education but rather maintain traditional cultural norms at the expense of economic progress (Paschyn 2013). In other words, there is some evidence that GCC employers still prefer to hire men rather than women, despite their academic performance.

Gender inequality in GCC labor force participation rates

Labor economists (see for example, Goldin 1995, 1990; Goldin and Olivetti 2013; Bertrand 2013; Bertrand, Chugh, and Mullainathan 2005) have suggested a few reasons for gender inequality in the labor market and its relationship to university education. Among these are discrimination by employers, women opting out of the labor market for the marriage market, and a mismatch between fields of study and fields ripe for employment. However, the regional particularities of GCC economies and their inextricability from social and political factors must be considered, as I do in this study.

The data in Figure 12.2 regarding recent trends in women's labor force participation reflect a discrepancy in the available aggregate and individual country-level data. The private company and self-reported figures provided in Paschyn (2013), for instance, report higher participation of Kuwaiti women than the World Bank data, perhaps because data regarding non-nationals is aggregated into the national data collected by the World Bank. But in general, we can see that women's labor force participation falls well below expectations based on their university graduation rates. In fact, some estimates show that unemployed women in the GCC report higher levels of education than employed men (Paschyn 2013; Solovieva 2013). This high level of female unemployment seems puzzling in light of the number of available opportunities for employment due to increased production in the energy sector (illustrated in Figure 12.3), although previous work (such as Ross 2008) has argued that oil-based economies restrain women's political participation through limited opportunities for economic participation.

Economic factors that constrain GCC women's labor force participation

Despite immense economic growth due to energy production over the last century, GCC women's labor force participation has been constrained by several

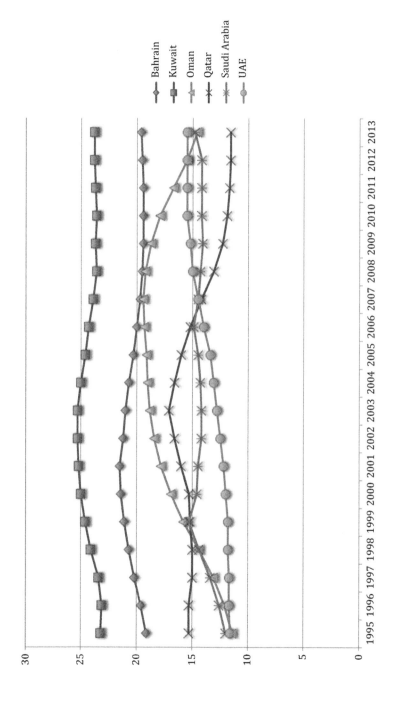

FIGURE 12.2 GCC Women Labor Force Participation Rates (%, Total Labor Force), based on World Bank data. These numbers include non-national labor force.

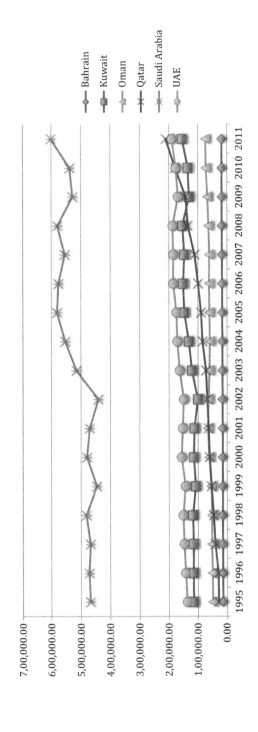

FIGURE 12.3 GCC Energy Production (kt of oil equivalent) (1995–2011), based on World Bank data. These numbers include non-national labor force.

economic factors. One is the historical legacy of colonial partnerships that has led many GCC countries, like other Arab countries in the Middle East North Africa (MENA) region, to set up favored trading and other economic partnerships with former colonial powers turned investors, such as the United Kingdom, the United States, and other Western powers. While new investors such as China and Russia have begun competing with some of these historical partnerships, GCC countries are nevertheless left with a heritage of governing and economic policies and institutional frameworks that, after being adapted to local cultural norms, have remained resilient despite economic pressures for change. For example, the Kuwaiti parliamentary system, which gives the executive branch veto power over their decisions and to dissolve the parliament, mirrors the British system. Facing greater political strains than their UK counterpart, Kuwaiti emirs have exercised their power to dissolve parliament more frequently, often disrupting legislative progress and economic management for political reasons (González 2013, 155). Other examples of colonial policies that have exerted economic strains on GCC labor markets include citizenship policies (e.g., citizenship is passed down by paternal lineage and women married to non-locals cannot pass their citizenship to their children) and the temporary status of third-country nationals who form a large part of the GCC labor force. Unless many economic, political, and social policies traced to their colonial heritage are reconsidered in light of modern economic needs, many GCC economies will arguably remain inefficient and underproductive, straining the entire labor force, not only women.

To a large degree, the constraints emanating from the rentier state status of various GCC countries have spurred many recent domestic and international efforts to nationalize the workforce and diversify the economy (Herb 2014, 23–24). These efforts include national plans labeled "Qatarization," "Kuwaitization," and the like to train locals to compete for jobs needed by the economy, including job training and skills development. These efforts, however, have ineffectively targeted women or been counteracted by national legislation constraining GCC women's ability to work unless they meet societal norms of propriety (Solovieva 2013). An additional area of possible economic growth and inclusion of women is entrepreneurship among young adults. Increasing numbers of GCC college graduates with business and leadership aspirations have expressed a desire to reform stagnant economic laws that stifle new businesses. Although some governments have publicly declared their openness to this desire for inclusion, more work needs to be done to to open space for youth to stake their claims in the modern economy.

Cultural constraints on GCC women's labor force participation

In addition to economic incentives and legislative policies that discourage women from participating in the labor force upon university graduation, several cultural constraints also impact GCC women's labor force participation, including pressure to maintain their traditional gender roles of managing household chores, providing childcare, and providing for the needs of extended family. It is still customary, and perhaps largely expected, that retired parents will go to live with their eldest sons, which transfers additional caregiving responsibilities to their daughters-in-law. Through their breadwinning husbands, these wives may be able to hire help for some of these duties, such as cleaning and childcare; but whether or not they have their own careers, they are expected to assume care not only for their immediate households but for their extended families. As has been shown in other settings, women's employment opportunities may trail or mirror men's shifting roles in the economy and be reinforced by popular media portrayals of normative female roles (Glazer 1993).

Government policies that discourage GCC women's labor force participation

The accompanying rise in gross domestic product (GDP) per capita rates (see Figure 12.4) also offers possible explanations for women's comparatively lower participation in the labor force. As GCC countries rise in wealth at the national level, for instance, they can support welfare-based maternity leave policies and subsidize women's work schedules to reduce their hours at work, as various GCC countries have done. Political liberals argue that generous state-welfare policies aimed at subsidizing women's traditional gender roles discourage them from working extra hours to gain promotion, staying in the workforce after having children, or joining the workforce in the first place (González 2013, 34–35, 64–65, 115–116).

Political and security challenges to GCC women's labor force participation

In addition to economc and legislative constraints, political and security challenges have also limited GCC women's participation in the labor force. On one hand, times of war can be important and transformative shocks to women's labor force participation by drawing women into traditionally male occupations out of economic or political necessity. Much has been written about the impact of World War II on women's entry into the labor force, including mass education in the technical skills of engineering and manufacturing to help the war effort (Goldin 1991; Goldin and Olivetti 2013; Greenwald 1980; Gregory 1974). Women's entry into political life and the labor market after the 1990 Iraqi invasion of Kuwait shows the effect of war on women's economic participation. During wartime, however, governments may also view the inclusion of women as a low-priority issue among the many others they face.

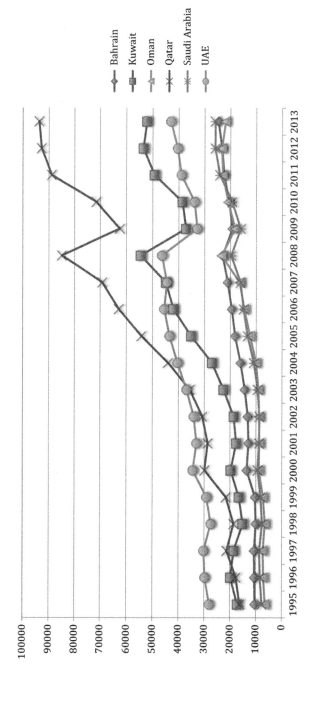

FIGURE 12.4 GCC GDP/Capita (1995–2013), based on World Bank data. These numbers include non-national labor force.

Conclusion

The inefficiencies of GCC economies, as evidenced by data regarding gender inequality in labor force participation and the various economic, political, and cultural constraints that contribute to them, suggest several avenues for future exploration by scholars studying GCC countries. First, an investment in more empirical research in this area is vital for more in-depth analysis as to the mechanisms and determinants of persistent female unemployment. Not only are current analyses of women's labor force participation inconsistent and difficult to find, but they fail to assess which legislative policies effectively meet the intended goal of encouraging women's participation in the workforce. Second, scholars should focus on the topic of youth engagement and youth entrepreneurship as one aspect of economic revitalization in which young female college graduates are participating. For policymakers, promoting incentives for entrepreneurship among talented youth is consistent with national strategies of economic diversification and efficient employment of the local labor force. If, in fact, additional research shows that GCC women graduates are not specializing in fields for which there is currently an economic demand, perhaps targeted partnerships with multinational corporations could sponsor female graduates in STEM fields or provide internships for university students to develop work experience and skills that would address some of those needs upon graduation. Lastly, because the retention of women in the labor market requires social as well as economic and political support, perhaps women's advocacy groups could be enlisted to focus their efforts on creating social support for women currently in the workplace through formal and informal mentorship and sponsorship programs. Such mentors and sponsors need not be senior women in the workplace, but, as previous research has shown (González 2013), can include male supporters, such as employed male family members, male university professors, or male employers.

This preliminary analysis of economic trends and gender inequality in GCC economies shows that many questions still remain about persistent gender inequality in the labor force despite women's university attainment. With additional scholarship investigating the link between women's university education and pathways toward economic labor force participation, researchers can begin to further unpeel the complex layers of economic legacy, legal structure, and societal conventions that keep women from equal participation in high-income, energy-producing GCC countries. Among the questions raised in this analysis are why GCC economies appear to be resistant to the labor force participation of increasingly qualified females. Does the return on investment in education not apply to GCC female university graduates? Or are political and sociological factors more likely to explain this persistent gender inequality and labor market inefficiency? What kinds of data and analytical methods are necessary to answer these research questions? Of particular research interest is isolating the cultural mechanisms that enable gender discrimination once economic and political explanatory factors are accounted for.

Natural extensions of this work include several other important potential research questions. In what ways does women's work or their lack of participation in the labor force challenge the sustainability of current GCC economies and mobilize women's groups in opposition to existing economic structures? In other words, how do women's increasing university graduation rates and stagnant labor force participation relate to women's future in the region? What is the effect of female politicians and government ministers on women's work legislation and policies? And what is the role of international actors in spurring women's greater labor force participation? In what ways does the gender gap in achievement at institutions of higher education challenge traditional gender roles? In what ways is the low achievement of male GCC students problematic for the labor force? Other potential research areas include investigations into the demand for women's work in GCC energy-producing countries, in particular among firms that are involved in energy extraction, production, and commercialization.

References

Bertrand, Marianne. 2013. "Career, Family, and the Well-Being of College Educated Women."*American Economic Review*, 103 (3): 244–250.

Bertrand, Marianne, Dolly Chugh, and Sendhil Mullainathan. 2005. "Implicit Discrimination." *American Economic Review*, 95 (2): 94–98.

CIA World Factbook. 2016. Accessed at https://www.cia.gov/library/publications/the-world-factbook/

Goldin, Claudia. 1990. *Understanding the Gender Gap: An Economic History of American Women*. New York: Oxford University Press.

Goldin, Claudia. 1991. "The Role of World War II in the Rise of Women's Employment." *American Economic Review*, 81 (4): 741–756.

Goldin, Claudia. 1995. "The U-Shaped Female Labor Force Function in Economic Development and Economic History." In *Investment in Women's Human Capital and Economic Development*, edited by T. Paul Schultz, 61–90. Chicago: University of Chicago Press.

Goldin, Claudia, and Claudia Olivetti. 2013. "Shocking Labor Supply: A Reassessment of the Role of World War II on Women's Labor Supply." *American Economic Review*, 103 (3): 257–262.

Coleman, Isobel, and Aala Abdelgadir. 2016. "The MENA's Woman Problem: Progress and Challenges in Women's Economic Participation." In *Women and Girls Rising: Progress and Resistance Around the World*, edited by Ellen Chesler and Terry McGovern, 243–257. New York: Routledge.

Glazer, Nona Y. 1993. *Women's Paid and Unpaid Labor: The Work Transfer in Health Care and Retailing*. Philadelphia: Temple University Press.

González, Alessandra L. 2013. *Islamic Feminism in Kuwait: The Politics and Paradoxes*. New York: Palgrave Macmillan.

González, Alessandra L., and Lubna Al-Kazi. 2011. "Complicating the 'Clash of Civilizations': Gender and Politics in Contemporary Kuwait." In *Annual Review of the Sociology of Religion*, Vol. 2, edited by Patrick Michel and Enzo Pace, 64–84. Boston: Brill.

Greenwald, Maurine Weiner. 1980. *Women, War, and Work: The Impact of World War I on Women Workers in the United Sates*. Westport, CT: Greenwood Press.

Gregory, Chester W. 1974. *Women in Defense Work During World War II: An Analysis of the Labor Problem and Women's Rights*. New York: Exposition Press.

Herb, Michael. 2014. *The Wages of Oil: Parliaments and Economic Development in Kuwait and the UAE*. Ithaca, NY: Cornell University Press.

Oxford Business Group. 2015. "Bahrain Works to Maintain its Regional Lead in Education." Accessed June 30, 2015 at http://www.oxfordbusinessgroup.com/overview/head-start-kingdom-striving-maintain-its-regional-lead-sector

Paschyn, Christina Maria. 2013. "Women in the Gulf: Better Educated But Less Employed." *Al-Fanar Media*, October 16. Accessed at http://www.al-fanarmedia.org/2013/10/women-in-the-gulf-better-educated-but-less-employed/

Ross, Michael L. 2008. "Oil, Islam, and Women." *American Political Science Review*, 102: 107–123.

UAE Embassy. 2017. "Women in the UAE." Accessed at http://www.uae-embassy.org/about-uae/women-uae.

Solovieva, Daria. 2013. "After University, Arab Women Struggle to Find Work." *Al-Fanar Media*, April 1. Accessed at http://www.al-fanarmedia.org/2013/04/after-university-arab-women-struggle-to-find-work/

Weyl, E. Glen. 2018. "The Openness-Equality Trade-Off in Global Redistribution." *Economic Journal*.

Young, Karen E. 2016. *Women's Labor Force Participation Across the GCC*. Issue Paper 10. Washington, DC: Arab Gulf Studies Institute in Washington.

13

THE POLITICS OF WOMEN AND WORK IN IRAN

Valentine M. Moghadam

A growing body of studies has noted the persistence of low levels of women's paid employment in Iran.[1] According to the 2006 Iranian population census (1385 by the Iranian lunar Islamic calendar), only 3.6 million women were employed, compared with 23.5 million men; women constituted just 16 percent of the non-agricultural paid labor force, and the highest urban female labor force participation rate was 23 percent for women aged twenty-five to twenty-nine. World Bank data for 2010 set the labor force participation rate of Iranian women at just 32 percent—up from 20 percent in 1980 and 29 percent in 2000 but still quite low by international standards. In 2015, the figures for female labor force participation and waged employment had not changed.[2] In contrast, women's educational attainment has rapidly increased since the 1990s, with high enrollments and graduation rates at the secondary levels (over 80 percent by 2011); women's enrollment rates at the tertiary level doubled between 1999 and 2011 to about 45 percent, and in most years exceeded men's enrollments (Islamic Republic of Iran, 2013).

Given women's educational attainment, one could reasonably expect growing levels of participation in senior decision-making positions and in university teaching. Yet according to census and international data, and despite a respectable share of civil service jobs (over one-third female) and professional jobs (35–45 percent), the proportion of women in administrative and management positions is surprisingly low. In 2013, decision-making positions at universities and other institutions were held overwhelmingly by men, and just 13 percent of the category "legislators, senior officials, and managers" were women (World Economic Forum 2013, 226). In the new century, women constituted between 20 and 24 percent of university teaching staff, proportions that are lower than in several other Middle East/North Africa (MENA) countries.

This chapter draws on data from official Iranian and international sources to show how patterns of women and work across social classes in the Islamic Republic of Iran have been shaped by political, institutional, and economic factors—notably the role of the neopatriarchal Islamic state, its legal and policy frameworks, and the continuing significance of the oil sector. It also focuses on education to show the disconnect between women's educational attainment and their employment. Comparisons with other MENA countries will highlight similarities as well as the specificities of the Iranian case. Finally, the study poses the question of whether, and when, the combination of household economic need and continued educational attainment of women could result in a shift to new labor and gender regimes. We begin with an overview of the gender policies of the Islamic Republic.

Background: gender policies in the Islamic Republic

In some ways, women's work in Iran has been in transition since the early years of modernization and industrialization. Elsewhere I have shown how patterns of women's work since the nineteenth century were aligned with shifts in political economy, especially during the transition from a rural and agrarian-based economy to a predominantly urban economy in which the oil sector and services played an increasingly central role in capital accumulation (Moghadam 2000). More transitions ensued following the Iranian revolution of 1979 and the establishment of an Islamic Republic with a highly ideological orientation rooted in the codification of a patriarchal version of Shia Islam. Policies and laws were not only gendered, but highly disadvantageous to women's equality, participation, and rights, given that the official ideology tied women's roles to the family and privileged men as breadwinners, decision-makers, and political leaders. The Iran-Iraq War (1980–1988) saw the military mobilization of a vast section of the male population, and while this eventually opened up some jobs for women in health, schooling, and—to a lesser degree—public administration, employment opportunities remained limited, and factory jobs for working-class women in particular became increasingly unavailable. A very conservative set of family law provisions inscribed in the Civil Code, along with discriminatory educational and employment policies, limited the fields of study and jobs available for women, such as in some engineering fields and the veterinary sciences.[3] In summary, the new gender policy was one that placed women under the control of husbands or male kin; restricted fields of study and jobs; and tied women to marriage, childbearing, and the family. By the end of the decade, both the total fertility rate and population growth had risen dramatically.[4] The unemployment rate among women was very high: 29 percent in the urban areas, compared to a 9 percent male unemployment rate.[5]

The presidencies of Ali Akbar Hashemi Rafsanjani and Mohammad Khatami from 1992 to 2005 brought about some relief. Some of the most egregious aspects of the regime's gender policies were overturned, and women began to gain admission to university programs in large numbers. Under Rafsanjani, the Women's Social and Cultural Council was formed to study and report on the legal, social, and economic problems of women and eventually lifted all academic restrictions on women in Iran's universities. The emergence and growth of the *Daneshgah-e Azad-e Islami* (Islamic Free University), which was not part of the country's system of public universities, reflected the Rafsanjani presidency's emphasis on privatization and liberalization but also had the effect of increasing educational opportunities for women. During the 1990s, women's enrollments grew and fertility rates declined, coinciding with a new family planning policy that encouraged small families through an active advocacy campaign. Health workers across the country were trained to teach married couples about the use and benefits of contraceptives and to deliver them free of charge (Islamic Republic of Iran 1999). The government organized mandatory seminars on family planning for couples planning to marry.

The picture of women in the labor force that was revealed by the Islamic Republic's second decennial census, which was completed in November 1996, was not as bright as the trends in women's educational attainment and fertility. In summary, women's share of the total economically active population was just 12.7 percent, and their share of the urban employed population was just 11.2 percent. (It should be said that the census has had a long practice of overlooking women's productive or domestic labor in rural settings. Moreover, continued rural-urban migration could have contributed to the shift to "housewife" status in the urban areas, while a larger proportion of young women who might otherwise have looked for work were in fact enrolled in university.) Of all public-sector wage earners, women constituted just 16.4 percent, a slight increase over 1986. Thus women's share of the labor force was very low by international standards. Women's total unemployment rate was 12.5 percent—considerably lower than in 1986, but still higher than men's (8.3 percent).[6] In fact, the female unemployment rate would increase noticeably in subsequent years.

In other domains, women made notable advances. The beginning of the Rafsanjani era saw the emergence of what feminist scholars in the Iranian diaspora termed "Islamic feminism," exemplified by the magazines *Zanan* (Women) and *Zan* and the women's studies journal *Farzaneh*. This period was defined by the flourishing and increasing international visibility of the Iranian film industry, which included outstanding films by woman directors, such as Marzieh Meshkini's "The Day I Became a Woman," Tahmineh Milani's "Two Women," and Rakhshan Bani Etemad's "Nargess," "The May Lady," and "Our Times." The presidency of Mohammad Khatami (1997–2005) coincided with the emergence of a political reform movement, a visible and vocal student movement, and the advent of women-led NGOs, some of which advocated for women's rights. In terms of formal political representation, fifteen women took seats in the fifth Majles, or parliament (1996–2000), including the feisty Faezeh Hashemi, a daughter of former president Rafsanjani and advocate for women's involvement in sports, including public bike-riding. The sixth Majles (2001–2005) had two fewer women, but most were women's rights advocates who influenced some reforms despite overwhelming challenges (Moghadam and Haghighatjoo 2016).

Educational advances

Admissions of women to universities increased steadily and dramatically during the period of liberalization and reform, with women eventually surpassing male enrollments. By 2001, women held 57 percent of total enrollments at the tertiary level. In 2002–2003, more women than ever before entered all fields of studies except engineering. The proportion of women doubled in most fields, and there was, indeed, a feminization in some fields; most dramatic was the increase of women in agriculture and veterinary sciences (from 2.5 percent to 51.1 percent) and in technical and engineering subjects (from 6.6 percent to 20.9 percent). In general, women were dominating not only the traditionally female-intensive humanities and the arts but also the sciences and medicine, with gynecology in particular becoming a female domain. According to an official report, the ratio of female to male students in tertiary education increased from 37.4 percent in 1990 to 110.5 percent in 2002 (Islamic Republic of Iran 2004, 19).

More women also completed degrees, and their share of degrees at various levels increased: of the bachelor's degrees conferred in 2003–2004, women's share was nearly 50 percent; their share of master's degrees was 27 percent; and their share of doctorate degrees was 24 percent.[7] By 2005, over 60 percent of urban women aged 18–30 had an upper secondary degree or above, compared with just over 50 percent of urban men. However, more men than women were enrolled in masters and doctorate degree programs (Rezai-Rashti and Moghadam 2011, Table 3). Surveys conducted in Iran within the framework of the World Values Survey found increasing societal support for women's education and disagreement with the statement, "University education is more important for a boy than for a girl" (Moaddel 2007, Table 9.3). Clearly, higher education was widely regarded as important to women's social status.

Progress in women's academic promotion within universities was nonetheless limited. This has been the case around the world, often as the result of implicit or explicit gender bias and the absence of support structures or policies that enable women to combine work and family. In Iran's case, a large proportion of female academics were employed as assistant professors, and although women's academic publications and research increased, they lagged behind men's. The female share of senior administrative positions remained low. Higher education attainment seemed to serve men better than women. In the academic market, for example, women in 2010 represented 63 percent of primary school teachers but only 19 percent of tertiary level instructors (see World Economic Forum 2010, 164).

Although unemployment became a problem for both women and men, in the rate of unemployment for university-educated men in 2002 was 8.8 percent, and for women it had increased to 19.6 percent.[8] Unemployment among educated youth increased significantly in the new century—and rates were twice as high for women as for men. This matched a trend in high unemployment rates, especially for educated youth in Arab countries (CAWTAR 2001). Unemployment in Iran was a consequence of structural and demographic factors, including sluggish economic growth, continued investments in capital-intensive rather than labor-intensive sectors, and rural-urban migration. High levels of female unemployment reflected the fact that a growing pool of women was available for work, but women's employment opportunities were blocked by gender bias as well as the aforementioned structural and sociodemographic factors.

The Khatami era brought with it not so much radical change as a gradualist approach to reform within the parameters of the existing Islamic and constitutional system. It allowed for the growth of civil society, including a burgeoning women's movement. Conservative forces led by Supreme Leader Ayatollah Khamenei remained opposed to change, and in this they were backed by the judiciary, the Guardian Council, and the armed forces. The authorities shut down over thirty newspapers and magazines, including *Zan,* arresting and prosecuting prominent journalists and reformists. More arrests were to follow during the presidency of Mahmoud Ahmadinejad. But first, the women's movement erupted in 2005, with the first large demonstrations since 1979, to protest Ahmadinejad's stated plan to close down NGOs; activists demanded an end to women's second-class citizenship inscribed in the country's discriminatory laws.

Backlash and setbacks under Ahmadinejad

The Ahmadinejad presidency (2005–2013) viewed women's issues through a neofundamentalist lens, resulting in the introduction of even more discriminatory legislation. Government concerns over late marriage, declining fertility, and women's higher enrollments in university—along with a harsh response to the liberal Green Protests of June 2009—were key features of this period. When he first took office, Ahmadinejad announced his intention to purge liberal and feminist professors; he accomplished that and later threatened those in the social sciences and humanities who were affiliated with the reform movement or had supported the Green Protests, and he accomplished that goal. By 2011, dozens of professors had been fired, forced to retire, or compelled to leave Iran and seek employment in other countries. A new decree would restrict women from entering the study of seventy-seven specific academic fields—mostly in engineering and related fields—in thirty-six government-run universities throughout the country. And in 2012, the government announced that it was reversing the family planning policy in an effort to raise the fertility rate (Roudi 2012).

What was behind the new measure against family planning? To be sure, sociodemographic changes in the Islamic Republic of Iran (and several other countries in the region) included ever-decreasing fertility, which by 2010 hovered at replacement level, a development that was tied to the prevalence of contraception, women's increased educational attainment, and the rising age at first marriage. The reversal of the family planning policy was no doubt motivated, at least in part, by the changed demographic reality and expected future "greying" of the population. Government policies, moreover, had not mitigated high unemployment among university graduates, which might have prompted the new restrictions on women. But the main explanation was arguably the neofundamentalist orientation of the Ahmadinejad presidency. The call for earlier marriage and larger families and the restrictions on fields of study for women at universities were likely intended to reverse social trends such as young women leaving their towns to study at a university in another city or province, young women living apart from their families and residing in a dormitory or even renting a flat with a group of other female students, postponement of marriage in order to meet the rigors of scientific study, increasing interaction between the sexes, and women overtaking men in entrance exams and in enrollments at the tertiary level. The return of a conservative gender ideology was driving the new education and family planning policies.

In many ways, Iran's political system operates in a manner not dissimilar to that of the United States, with its pendulum swings between liberals and conservatives. After Ahmadinejad's two terms as president, a cleric widely regarded as a moderate was elected president, and Hassan Rouhani went on to appoint more liberals to his government, including the articulate U.S.-educated Foreign Minister Mohammad Javad Zarif. This chapter will return to the Rouhani presidency in due course, but first it will review patterns of women's work in Iran.

Women, work, and social class

As noted at the start of this chapter, the 2006 (1385) census reported that just 3.6 million women were employed, compared with 23.5 million men; women constituted a mere 16 percent of the nonagricultural paid labor force, although they were well-represented in urban professional jobs. Key findings of the 2006 census for women's economic participation included the following:

- About 33 percent of Iran's female labor force was employed in professional jobs, concentrated in sex-segregated occupations within education, healthcare, and social services. Relatively few women held administrative and clerical or services and sales jobs.
- Some 20 percent of the female work force was employed in industrial employment, but mostly as unpaid family workers. Nearly half of rural women were found in industrial employment, involved mainly in craft work such as rug-weaving, but most were listed as unpaid family workers or contributing family workers.
- In terms of age-specific labor force participation, there was a sharp decline among women after the age of thirty.

What of subsequent years? By spring 2017 (1396), Iran's labor force survey reported a female labor force of about 5.4 million, compared with 21.3 million men; this came to a female labor force participation rate of just 16.4 percent. The majority of working women were found in the services sector (51.3 percent), followed by industry (where 25.4 percent of the female labor force was found), and then agriculture (with 23.2 percent). Despite the low rates of employment, women's unemployment rates have been consistently high, and about double those of men. The unemployment rates of young women are astonishing—on the order of 30 percent in 1997, 36 percent in 2000, 42.5 percent in 2004, for the age group twenty to twenty-four (Egel and Salehi-Isfahani 2010, Figure 1), and 44.6 percent in 2017 for women aged fifteen to twenty-nine, according to the government's labor force survey. These figures are perplexing and unsettling, but the implications for working-class women are even more so.

Middle class and working class women in the work force

Studies by the United Nations Educational, Scientific, and Cultural Organization (UNESCO) (2011) and the World Bank (2012) confirmed that by 2010, gender parity in Iran had been achieved at the secondary level; the majority of students in higher education were female; and fully 68 percent of science students were women. This was part of a regional trend in that female tertiary enrollments surpassed those of men in Jordan, Lebanon, Tunisia, and the West Bank.[9] However, educational attainment did not translate into employment increases across all occupations. The proportion of the female tertiary teaching staff in Iran did increase each academic year between 2001 and 2007, but only from 17 percent to 20 percent. In 2010, just over half of all teachers in Iran were women, but the female share of university teaching staff at different levels was reported to be about 24 percent (according to official Iranian sources). There is some discrepancy in the data, as the *Global Gender Gap Report 2011* reported a 19 percent share of women at the tertiary teaching level, compared with a 57 percent share of primary school teachers. (Data were not available for the proportion of female secondary school teachers.) A comparison of Iranian women's participation as teachers in the tertiary sector with that in other MENA countries in 2011 shows that women did better in Algeria (38 percent female), Tunisia (42 percent female), and Turkey (40 percent female). Iranian women's share of teaching jobs at the tertiary level was larger only than women's shares in Jordan, Morocco, and Yemen.

The data also show that women from working-class families, or those with less than a secondary school education, do not fare well in the labor force. University graduates have higher participation rates (but also higher unemployment rates) and more stable jobs than do women with less education, and they are more likely to work in the public sector. In 2009 (1388), of the women employed in the public sector—comprising 35.8 percent of the total 2.16 million Iranians in the public sector—some 741,610 women were employed under the civil service code (middle class), while just 10,000 were employed under the labor law (working class).[10] In general, the female labor force with secondary schooling or less was found in the private sector or in family employment, which was typically non-salaried. Over the period 1994–2007, women's average share of paid manufacturing employment was just 10 percent, largely concentrated in textiles and garments, food processing, and the production of office and medical supplies, predominantly in the private sector rather than in state-owned enterprises.

When examining Iranian women's employment patterns over several decades, it becomes evident that their access to employment has been very non-linear, unlike their access to education, which had continued an upward trend. The picture seems especially dire for working-class women. According to the Iran Statistical Yearbook 1391 (2012), out of a total economically active female population of about 3.5 million, some 2.7 million were employed. Nearly half of the employed women had higher-education credentials, while 36 percent had primary, "lower secondary," or "upper secondary" schooling. Women involved in production activities—craft and related trades workers, plant and machinery operators, elementary occupation workers—only added up to 437,000, or just 5 percent of the total workers in these categories. Working-class occupations, therefore, appeared closed to women. In contrast, the professions were far more open to (educated, middle-class) women; the roughly 760,000 women constituted fully 45 percent of all 1.7 million professionals in Iran.

According to Haleh Safarzadeh, an activist for women workers' rights cited in a recent report (Samimi 2014), "The minimum wage [that] women workers accept is so low that it has angered their male co-workers, who tell them these kinds of agreements may backfire on them and result in lower wages for the male workers as well." She also notes that "in certain instances, single women are employed in factories on condition that they commit to remaining single and/or refrain from becoming pregnant." The National Syndicate of Women Workers (NSWW) was established in 2003 to protect women workers and make serious efforts to create equal conditions in the workplace. According to an NSWW staffer cited in the same report, the number of women workers declined during the Ahmadinejad era; the adoption of a bill approving fewer working hours and telework for women was another blow to women's employment outside the home and in the manufacturing sector (Samimi 2014). Meanwhile, the government began to promote the ideal of larger families with more children and suspended its state-led family planning program. Paid maternity leave was extended from 90 days in 2010 to 270 days in 2015 (see World Economic Forum 2010, 2015). Such government measures seem to suggest that women do not belong in factory work—even though in some cases women workers are the family breadwinners—and that women really belong at home looking after the children. As if anticipating such attitudes and policies, an essay in the women's studies journal *Farzaneh* by Elaheh Koulaee, a female MP of the sixth parliament during the reformist era, criticized the conservatives in the Ahmadinejad government for their "traditionalist thinking" and outlook whereby women belong in the private sphere of the home while men should be out working to maintain the family (Koulaee 2008, 24).

The available data and studies indicate that whereas professional jobs are available in the health and education sectors for women with higher education attainment, and rural women engage in craft work (albeit largely as "unpaid family labor"), urban working-class or low-income women seem to be absent from the labor force. Decent jobs are more available for women with university degrees than for those with high school or vocational or less—even though women with higher education also suffer high rates of unemployment. Indeed, in Isfahan, some 75 percent of women university graduates remain without a job, a heavy price for a country aiming to grow its economy (Khajehpour 2014). Still, the vast majority of women from urban working-class families in cities such as Tehran, Isfahan, Tabriz, and Mashad either are discouraged workers and labor force dropouts, economically inactive or housewives, or engaged in informal, home-based, or voluntary activities.

During fieldwork in Iran in 1994, I noticed an array of home-based economic activities, including hairdressing and tailoring operations, run by women from lower-middle class and working-class families (Moghadam 1998, ch. 7). More recently, Roksana Bahramitash and Shahla Kazemipour (2008) and Fatemeh Etemad-Moghadam (2009) uncovered catering, counseling, childcare, and transportation services by such women, who supplement the incomes of their spouses and otherwise contribute to the household budget and have the flexibility needed to attend to domestic duties. In addition, many upper-middle-class women, they argued, engage in high-end home-based activities such as making and selling jewelry or special jams, providing catering services, tutoring or counseling, desktop publishing, and leading pilates or yoga classes. Such women may prefer to undertake work at home rather than acquiesce to the strictures of the dress code, untoward attitudes, and other irritants associated with formal sector employment. But they work individually rather than as part of a collective enterprise, and thus lack the conditions for collective action.

The preceding discussion raises a number of questions. Why are so few working-class women in paid occupations in the formal sector? Why were the graduates of secondary and tertiary education in the 1990s and the early years of the new century not eased into more employment? Why have women's unemployment rates remained so high? Why has the proportion of women in university teaching remained lower than in several Arab countries, and why has the category "legislators, senior officials and managers" not moved above a 17 percent female share? Is it because more men than women had graduate-level degrees? Has male bias impeded women's promotion to decision-making positions? Or could it be that women's own preference keeps them from gaining higher-level positions? After all, lack of confidence in the labor market generated by the high unemployment rate, the absence of social support for working mothers, and the male-dominated workplace environment could be reasons why many Iranian women prefer to remain outside of the labor force.[11]

Research has explained female labor supply and demand in terms of factors at the household, legal, and sectoral levels (see, e.g., Blau, Ferber, and Winkler

2016; Karshenas, Moghadam, and Chamlou 2016). Women's availability and willingness to work is usually shaped by a combination of educational attainment, marital status, fertility, and household economic need, and the present study has shown that those conditions are present in the Islamic Republic of Iran. The demand for labor is tied to the structure of the economy, development policy, and investment strategies, and in some cases, it can also be shaped by a country's institutional framework. In previous work, I have drawn attention to the role of the regional oil economy in shaping female labor supply and demand in MENA, and certainly the importance of the oil sector in Iran's economy has served to limit demand for female labor (see below). I also have posited that Muslim Family Law reproduces the patriarchal gender contract, or the male breadwinner/female homemaker ideal. In Iran's case, too, laws, policies, and norms can affect not only the demand for female labor but also the supply of women available for work. In turn, a small proportion of women in the workforce correlates with under-representation in the domain of formal politics.

Explaining women and work in Iran: structural and institutional factors

In the 1990s, although Iran's economy grew and the government developed new institutions that boosted opportunities for the expansion of modern services—education, medicine, finance, law, engineering, and the like—the demand for female labor remained limited. This calls attention to the economic development strategy that Iran has pursued, which favors the oil and gas sectors and, most recently, advances in nuclear power, fields that are capital-intensive and male-intensive. The presence of state-owned or parastate monopolies, combined with a strategy in the first two decades after the Revolution that favored self-employment and the expansion of the informal sector—as demonstrated by Farhad Nomani and Sohrab Behdad (2006)—created an economic and labor market environment that was not conducive to female labor incorporation. Looking through a gender-analytic lens, it would appear that the Iranian state favors the employment of some women in education and healthcare, if only to teach and administer healthcare to women and girls, but prefers that women generally remain at home and care for their families.

In 2011, Iran was the second-largest economy in the MENA region, after Saudi Arabia, with a gross domestic product (GDP) of US$400 billion; it had the second-largest population, after Egypt, with seventy-six million people.[12] Iran's economy was characterized by a large hydrocarbon sector, small-scale private agriculture and services, and a noticeable state presence in manufacturing and finance. In 2007, the service sector (including government) contributed 56 percent of GDP, followed by the hydrocarbon sector with 25 percent and agriculture with 10 percent. Iran ranked second in the world in natural gas reserves and third in oil reserves. It was the second-largest OPEC oil producer, with output averaging about four million barrels per day. Iran's chief source of foreign exchange came from oil and gas exports. Although Iran's economy had shifted toward a market-based economy, the financial sector was largely dominated by public banks, and the state still played a key role in the economy, owning large public and quasi-public enterprises in the manufacturing and commercial sectors. Over 60 percent of the manufacturing sector's output was produced by state-owned enterprises. The government envisioned a large privatization program in its 2010–2015 five-year plan, aiming to privatize some 20 percent of state-owned firms (SOEs) each year, although it appears that the assets of these SOEs were purchased largely by the Iranian Revolutionary Guards Corps or other semi-governmental enterprises. At the same time, macroeconomic policies had not counteracted boom–bust cycles in economic performance. The result was uncertainty faced by the private sector, which impeded investment and job creation. Meanwhile, the state sector continued to invest in the capital-intensive sectors of oil, gas, and nuclear energy.

What are the gender implications of the above trends? One is that the state-owned hydrocarbon sector and state presence in manufacturing and finance was more receptive to male than female labor. In principle, female labor should be found in large numbers in small-scale private agriculture and services, but according to the 2006 census, women made up just 17 percent of technical and related workers, less than 2 percent of plant and machinery workers, less than 7 percent of elementary workers, and a very small proportion of workers in the commercial and financial fields. If the rather conservative Iranian Revolutionary Guard had purchased "privatized" assets, that development, too, would be unlikely to favor the hiring of women. Iran does have free trade zones (FTZs), but they have not become the "back doors to the international economy" or foreign direct investment (FDI) that the authorities hoped for. Hassan Hakimian shows that while the free trade zones had a modest workforce to begin with, at some forty-five thousand, "female employment creation ... is very weak." He concludes that "Iran's experience of free zones in the past one and a half decades has failed to achieve its principal objectives of attracting FDI, diversifying non-oil exports and generating new jobs" (Hakimian 2011, 865, 871).

One reason why the Iranian state has been unable to attract FDI, especially of the type that might be labor-intensive and employment-generating, is the sanctions regime that has been in place and taken varied forms since 1979. That year, the United States first imposed sanctions against Iran and then expanded them in 1995; since then, it has filed legal suits against international firms or individuals that do business with Iran. In 2006, the U.N. Security Council imposed sanctions after Iran refused to suspend its nuclear enrichment program. On the positive side, sanctions, the absence of foreign banks in Iran, Iran's relatively closed economy, and its limited integration in the global economy insulated the country from the adverse effects of the global 2008 Great Recession. Although oil prices everywhere, including in Iran, plummeted after 2008, the government used funds from its reserve (the Oil Stabilization Fund) to offset the shortfall in the government budget. During this period, negotiations were held to end Iran's nuclear enrichment program and end the sanctions regime. The 2015 international nuclear deal was meant to accomplish this, and Iran agreed to tough inspections of its nuclear sector, but the Trump administration withdrew from the agreement and imposed new and punitive sanctions on Iran. In 2018 protests erupted against high prices, the declining value of the Iranian currency, high unemployment, and what many citizens see as government mismanagement of the economy.

Structural factors, therefore, have had adverse effects on women's employment opportunities. The state's strategy for development and growth, the tough sanctions, and the absence of investments in labor-intensive, female-intensive sectors all serve to limit women's gainful employment.

Institutional obstacles: the masculine state, its laws and norms

The Islamic Republic of Iran's very ambitious constitution of 1979 requires the government to provide its citizens with full employment, presumably including female citizens. But this constitutional guarantee has been undermined by a clause extolling the virtues of motherhood and emphasizing the ubiquitous Islamic criteria. Thus under the Islamic Republic's Sharia-based civil code, women cannot seek jobs or remain in their occupation of choice without the approval of their fathers or husbands, and major surgical operations require male kin approval (Tohidi 2010, 148). These are aspects of the patriarchal nature of the Iranian state and the male bias of its legal and policy frameworks.

The massive ideological campaign launched after the Islamic Revolution tied women to their family roles, and the new Islamic family law restored men's rights to polygamy, unilateral divorce, and automatic custody of children after divorce. Later amendments to the family law provisions allowed women to sue for divorce, but only under certain conditions, whereas no conditions existed for men. The 1998 documentary film by Kim Longinotto and Ziba Mir-Hosseini, *Divorce Iranian Style,* depicted women negotiating a divorce settlement or custody of a child. Although the film showed strong women determined to assert their rights under the law, it also drew attention to the arbitrariness or lack of sympathy of judges. In matters of inheritance, women became severely disadvantaged; for example, legally a man inherits all of his deceased wife's wealth, but the widow is entitled only to one-fourth (if her deceased spouse has no child) or one-eighth (if he had children) of his movable property and of the value of his estate. This pertains only to cases of spousal death in permanent marriages; partners in religiously sanctioned temporary marriages receive no inheritance.[13] In polygamous marriages (which are extremely rare in Iran), wives must divide among themselves the allotted inheritance, which, according to Article 942 of the Civil Code, can never exceed their designated one-fourth or one-eighth.

Article 1117 of the Civil Code stipulates that a man has the right to prevent his wife from becoming employed "if he deems such employment would be at variance with their family interests and values." As Ayatollah Khomeini's successor as Supreme Leader, Ali Khamenei, said in 1995,

> Islam authorizes women to work outside the household. Their work might even be necessary but it should not interfere with their main responsibility that is childrearing, childbearing, and housework. No country can do without women's workforce but this should not contradict women's moral and human values. It should not weaken women, nor compel them to bend or to stoop low.
>
> *(quoted in Kian-Thiébaut 2005, 55)*

Does "stooping low" refer to factory jobs and occupations requiring interaction with men? Iranian attitudes toward women working outside the home are ambivalent and reinforced by the absence of a network of subsidized and high-quality child-care centers. Iran's modernization trends of urbanization and nuclear families means that help from the extended family is not always available for women who might desire or need to work outside the home.

The condition of being outside the formal labor force, without an income and without political power, reinforces women's dependence on male kin for social insurance and retirement benefits and upon the *mahr*, or *mehrieh* in Persian parlance. A nuptial gift or "bride price," the *mehrieh* is normally specified in the Islamic marriage contract and is a promissory note to the bride by the groom after the marriage is consummated. It is usually divided into two parts: an amount that is paid after the marriage takes place and a deferred amount that is paid upon the dissolution of the marriage or after the husband's death. Prior to the 1979 revolution, the practice of negotiating *mehrieh* was declining among the elite stratum, as it was considered outmoded and incompatible with modernity. While supporters of the practice have always defended it as a form of social insurance or a means of asset building for the wife, opponents have argued that it presents the bride as an object for sale and encourages women's economic dependence. Anecdotal evidence indicates that in the new century, the practice of negotiating *mehrieh* has been growing rather than declining in Iran (Rezai-Rashti and Moghadam 2011). Could this be explained at least partly by the fact that women's employment opportunities were limited and women could not rely on a steady income? Could it also be explained by the ease with which men could divorce their wives under the post-revolutionary family law provisions?

Because Iran's Islamic family law makes it far easier for the husband to obtain a divorce than for the wife to do so, *mehrieh* can provide some leverage. Indeed, interviews in Iran conducted by Goli Rezai-Rashti in 2006 confirmed that women were employing *mehrieh* as a strategy to counter the legal discrimination and risk of divorce that women face under Iran's Muslim Family Law provisions. Still, it is not unreasonable to also suggest that the widespread practice of *mehrieh* and its monetary inflation have been associated with the denial of women's economic citizenship through limited employment opportunities and the absence of policies and mechanisms to enable work-family balance.

One can also identify class biases of both the employment policies and the family law, including the practice of *mehrieh*. Women with higher levels of education or from wealthy or well-connected families can negotiate higher *mehrieh*, but other women are left in a vulnerable situation after divorce, especially if they have married badly, cannot or will not remarry, or have dependents. The precarious situation of a lower-middle class woman after divorce is poignantly depicted in a 2002 documentary film by Rakhshan Bani-Etemad, *Our Times*. In the second half of the film, the protagonist Arezoo is divorced from a drug-addicted husband and works at an office job to support a small daughter and sightless mother but is bullied by her boss. She tries desperately to find a place to live after her landlady tells her she must leave to make way for the landlady's son and new daughter-in-law. Arezoo cannot afford to buy a home and cannot find a decent place to live because landlords prefer not to rent to single or divorced women.

Government policies not only ignore women like Arezoo but can also serve as a blunt instrument of patriarchal control. In 2007, the Ahmadinejad government introduced a controversial "Family Protection Bill" that would have consolidated the various family law provisions in the Civil Code and created a unified Family Law for the first time in forty years. Among other things, it would have imposed taxation of the *mehrieh*, removed the requirement to register temporary marriages, and eliminated the need for a husband to prove financial solvency or ask his wife's permission before marrying another woman. The bill caused a huge outcry and was eventually withdrawn.[14] Still, the overall climate for women within Iran's version of Muslim Family Law, along with the limited opportunities for salaried employment, have arguably compelled women to turn to *mehrieh* as a strategy for economic independence and as a patriarchal bargaining chip. The growing practice and value of *mehrieh* among the highly educated therefore provides women with some protection against the structural inequalities in marriage, in family law, and in employment that have not been mitigated by women's advances in higher education.

From Friedrich Engels to sociologists Rae Lesser Blumberg (1984) and Janet Chafetz (1984), the argument has been made that women's economic independence is a prerequisite for involvement in political society (see also Moghadam 1998, ch. 1). Given their low involvement in paid employment, it is no surprise that Iranian women have been severely underrepresented in formal politics, with a parliamentary share of a mere 2–6 percent of seats since the start of the Islamic Republic. These two measures—the female share of paid employment and the female share of formal politics—reveal the severity of gender inequality in Iran, a situation that has remained relatively stable over four decades of the Islamic Republic.

Women and political power and participation

The Islamic Republic of Iran has many discriminatory laws, but women have been a growing presence in public spaces since the 1990s. This presence takes the form not only of women walking, driving, shopping, and working but also taking part in public protests where possible, and their involvement in the public sphere includes the growth of women's websites, blogs, and petition campaigns as well as national debates and discussions about women's rights and legal reform. Women's paid and voluntary involvement in non-governmental organizations, activism in women's rights organizations, and visibility as writers, journalists, and artists also signal their growing social participation. Iranian women turn out in large numbers as voters and at times as candidates in the parliamentary and municipal elections. Still, they are excluded from the realm of political power. The situation persists despite women's impressive educational advances.

During the sixth parliament, the pro-women's rights members of parliament (MPs) managed to pass a bill that would commit the government to the UN Convention on the Elimination of All Forms of Discrimination against Women, but the Guardian Council refused to approve it. The female MPs of the sixth parliament also tried, mostly in vain, to place more women in decision-making positions across the ministries and as governors (Moghadam and Haghighatjoo 2016). International datasets show that over the past decade, just 13–18 percent of Iran's legislators, senior officials, and managers have been women (see Islamic Republic of Iran 1391/2012, Table 3.13; World Economic Forum 2011, 2015). The profession of judge became off-limits to women in Iran after the Islamic Revolution; in contrast, women constitute between 20 and 30 percent of all judges in Algeria and Tunisia, and indeed in a number of other Muslim-majority countries, such as Indonesia (see Sonneveld and Lindbekk 2017). Those women judges may be concentrated in juvenile courts or family courts and may not serve on Sharia courts, but their presence in such a traditionally male-dominated field enhances their social status and enables their entry into other domains.

The reality of Iranian women's leadership and decision-making exclusion makes the Iranian political system among the most masculinist in the world. Unlike many other countries, Iran has not instituted gender quotas for women's political participation, even though it has instituted quotas for fields of study, though in that case to limit rather than increase women's enrollments. And it has yet to become a signatory to the UN Convention on the Elimination of All Forms of Discrimination against Women. In Iran, women's underrepresentation in formal politics is a function of the masculine nature of the Iranian state, the male bias of its legal frameworks, and women's economic powerlessness.

What of public attitudes toward women, work, and power? Survey research conducted in Iran sheds some light on attitudinal changes with respect to women, work, family, and politics, although results across various surveys (especially those conducted in the early part of the century) show ambiguities and inconsistencies. A 2002 survey carried out by French-Iranian sociologist Azadeh Kian-Thiébaut found very positive attitudes. There was widespread agreement among the women respondents that women should have equal access to political activity, with rates as high as 59 percent among Persian-speaking respondents, 51 percent among Azeri-speaking, and a full 62.5 percent among Kurdish-speaking respondents; the average across the sample was 53 percent. Roughly the same proportions were found on the question regarding equal access to decision-making (Kian-Thiébaut 2005, Tables 10 and 11).

A 2003 survey conducted by Charles Kurzman and Kian Tajbakhsh, "The Iranian Family Attitudes Survey," confirmed the presence of conservative values and norms, though Kurzman (2008) sought to make a case for "a new feminist generation in Iran," especially among the educated population of young people. Some survey questions or statement prompted pro-feminist responses, others conservative views, and others inconsistencies. In response to the statement, "in general, men make better political leaders than women," just 38 percent of educated young women (and just 28.7 percent of "other Iranians") disagreed or strongly disagreed (Kurzman, Table 2), whereas another set of questions seemed to elicit high support for women's "equal privilege and rights" in political activity, high-ranking government posts, and local and national decision-making (Table 3b). Nearly 72 percent of educated young women agreed or strongly agreed that both wife and husband should earn income for the family (Table 2), but only 22 percent disagreed with the statement that "in general, family life suffers when a woman works full-time," and just under 24 percent disagreed or strongly disagreed that "the man's duty is to earn money; the woman's duty is to look after the family" (Table 1, 306–307). These results were thus largely consistent with the results of the Iran survey conducted during the fourth wave (1999–2002) of the World Values Survey, which showed some enlightened attitudes with respect to education and wife abuse but traditional views on single motherhood and on women's employment and leadership (Moaddel and Azadarmaki 2002).

There is no doubt that a large proportion of educated women in Iran aspire to more personal freedoms, which is a remarkable development in the context of a political system opposed to feminism and favorable to traditional gender relations. Despite the revival of the feminist movement in 2005–2006 and the massive participation of women in the Green Protests of June 2009, there has been a powerful tide of conservative gender attitudes reinforced by Iran's Muslim Family Law and the absence of women from the labor force and political power. What is needed is a stronger societal push for women's equal participation in politics, pressure on government for the adoption of a gender quota and other mechanisms, and decent job opportunities and institutional supports for working-class and lower-middle class women.

Conclusions

Women's work in Iran, as elsewhere, is shaped by political economy, gender ideology, and international influences and thus is always in transition, even as it reveals persistent patterns. This chapter has shown that although many Iranian women are available for work (as indicated by their high unemployment rate), a combination of structural and institutional factors preclude their incorporation into the labor force and affect attitudes toward women's employment. In addition to the nature of the economy, women's marginal position is reinforced by the presence of a neopatriarchal state and highly discriminatory laws, along with the absence of women-friendly social policies, safeguards for women in the work force, and affirmative action policies to encourage more women to join the work force. The state's legal and policy frameworks, and especially its family laws, reinforce conservative social norms regarding male and female roles. Such norms are internalized by many women themselves as well as by employers, thus affecting female labor supply and demand.

One may very well conjecture that in future years, and given the impressive expansion of higher education, more women will rebel against their marginal and subordinate place in the paid labor force and in political decision-making. If and when they do, the transition from patriarchal authoritarianism to a women-friendly democracy will finally be possible. This is a transition well worth anticipating, even though there are no indications at present that the current government is interested in transforming the labor and gender regimes in Iran. There was hope that the removal of sanctions with the successful conclusion of the 2015 the nuclear agreement (involving Iran, the five permanent members of the UN's Security Council, and Germany) would encourage more foreign investments in Iran and thus enhance women's economic participation through increased job opportunities. That hope dissipated with the U.S. withdrawal from the agreement. But even with more job opportunities, Iranian women would still have to face what so many of their sisters across the globe do: flexible labor markets, precarious employment, and the absence of support structures for working mothers. In that case, Iranian women would have to shift the focus of their grievances from the Islamist gender ideology to the neoliberal capitalist doctrine.

Notes

1. On women's employment in Iran, see V. M. Moghadam (1991, 1995, 1998, ch. 7, 2006); F. E. Moghadam (2009); Salehi-Isfahani (2005); Nomani and Behdad (2006); Farasatkhah (2008); Rezai-Rashti and Moghadam (2011); Majbouri (2015).
2. As we will see presently, women's labor force participation rates as reported by official Iranian surveys tend to disagree with international figures and in fact tend to be lower. Thus for 2017, the official labor force survey actually set the female labor force participation rate at a mere 16.4 percent. The female unemployment rate, by contrast, was reported as 20.9 percent. See Islamic Republic of Iran 2017 [1396], p. 4.
3. I have discussed this at greater length, and with full references, in Moghadam (2013), ch. 6.
4. Population growth was the result both of high fertility and of the wave of Afghan refugees fleeing the internationalized conflict in their country.

5 For details, see Moghadam (1998, 166–168), which draws on data from the 1370/1991 *Statistical Yearbook*.
6 Data from *Iran Statistical Yearbook 1375/1996* (Islamic Republic of Iran 1997), able 1–3, p. 70.
7 Data from a 2008 report by the Ministry of Science, Research, and Technology, cited in Rezai-Rashti and Moghadam (2011), table 7.
8 Data from Shahla Kazemipour (2007) cited in Rezai-Rashti and Moghadam (2011), table 3.
9 For details, see tables 4.2 and 4.3 in Moghadam (2013).
10 See *Iran Statistical Yearbook 1388*, table 3–24. http://salnameh.sci.org.ir.
11 On "preference theory," see Hakim (2003).
12 The discussion in this section draws on a paper by Massoud Karshenas titled "The Iranian Economy and the Contradictions of the Islamic Republic in Historical Perspective," prepared for a conference at Harvard University, August 2014; and on the World Bank's country analysis, Iran, available at: http://www.worldbank.org/en/country/iran.
13 Temporary marriage (*sigheh* or *muta'a*) is a fixed-term/temporary marriage contract between a man and woman in Iranian Shi'a practice that lasts only for a contractually specified period of time, after which neither party has responsibility for the other. It is practiced by some Shi'as but frowned upon by others. Sunni Muslims have a similar practice known as *urfi* marriage.
14 For an excellent discussion of the Family Protection Bill and the varied responses to it, see Bøe (2015).

References

Bahramitash, Roksana, and Shahla Kazemipour. 2008. "Economy, Informal Sector." In *Iran Today: An Encyclopedia of Life in the Islamic Republic*, Vol. 1, edited by Mehran Kamrava and Manochehr Dorraj, 156–159. Westport, CT: Greenwood Press.
Blau, Francine, Marianne Ferber, and Anne Winkler. 2016. *The Economics of Women, Men, and Work* (7th ed.). New York: Oxford University Press.
Blumberg, Rae Lesser. 1984. "A General Theory of Gender Stratification." *Sociological Theory* 2: 23–101.
Bøe, Marianne. 2015. *Family Law in Contemporary Iran: Women's Rights Activism and Sharia*. London: I. B. Tauris.
CAWTAR. 2001. *Globalization and Gender: Economic Participation of Arab Women*. Tunis: Center for Arab Women's Training and Research (CAWTAR) and the United Nations Development Programme (UNDP).
Chafetz, Janet Saltzman. 1984. *Sex and Advantage: A Comparative Macro-Structural Theory of Sexual Stratification*. Totowa, NJ: Rowman and Allanheld.
Egel, Daniel, and Djavad Salehi-Isfahani. 2010. *Youth Transition to Employment and Marriage in Iran*. Dubai: Dubai School of Government, Wolfensohn Center for Development, Middle East Initiative. Working Paper #11 (June). Available at https://www.brookings.edu/wp-content/uploads/2016/06/06_iran_youth_salehi_isfahani.pdf.
Farasatkhah, Maghsood. 2008. "Women, Higher Education, and the Job Market." *Pajoheshe Zanan* 2 (1): 147–163.
Hakim, Catherine. 2003. "A New Approach to Approaching Fertility Patterns: Preference Theory." *Population and Development Review* 29 (September): 339–345.
Hakimian, Hassan. 2011. "Iran's Free Trade Zones: Back Doors to the International Economy?" *Iranian Studies* 44 (6): 851–874.
Islamic Republic of Iran. 1997. *Iran Statistical Yearbook 1375 [1996]*. Tehran: Statistical Center of Iran.

Islamic Republic of Iran. 1999. *Human Development Report of the Islamic Republic of Iran, 1999.* Tehran: Plan and Budget Organization and the United Nations.
Islamic Republic of Iran. 2004. *Human Development Report of the Islamic Republic of Iran, 2004.* Tehran: Plan and Budget Organization and the United Nations.
Islamic Republic of Iran. 2012. *Iran Statistical Yearbook 1391 [2012].* Tehran: Statistical Center of Iran. Available at http://www.amar.org.ir/Portals/1/yearbook/1391/3.pdf.
Islamic Republic of Iran. 2013. *Iran Statistical Yearbook 1385 [2006].* Available at https://www.amar.org.ir/english/
Islamic Republic of Iran. 2016 [1395]. *Natayej-e Amar-geeri neerooye kar, tabestan 1395 [Results of the Labor Force Survey, Summer 1395].* Tehran: National Planning and Budget Organization, Statistical Center of Iran.
Karshenas, Massoud, Valentine M. Moghadam, and Nadereh Chamlou. 2016. "Women, Work and Welfare in the Middle East and North Africa: Introduction and Overview." In *Women, Work and Welfare in the Middle East and North Africa: The Role of Socio-Demographics, Entrepreneurship, and Public Policies*, edited by Nadereh Chamlou and Massoud Karshenas, 1–30. London: Imperial College Press.
Khajehpour, Bijan. 2014. "Women Can Play Larger Role in Iranian Economy." *al-Monitor* (26 March).
Kian-Thiébaut, Azadeh. 2005. "From Motherhood to Equal Rights Advocates: The Weakening of the Patriarchal Order." *Iranian Studies* 38 (1): 45–66.
Koulaee, Elaheh. 2008. "Iranian Women after the Reform Era." *Farzaneh: Journal of Women's Studies and Research* 7 (13): 21–34.
Kurzman, Charles. 2008. "A Feminist Generation in Iran?" *Iranian Studies* 41 (3): 297–321.
Majbouri, Mahdi. 2015. "Female Labor Force Participation in Iran: A Structural Analysis." *Review of Middle East Economics* 11 (1): 1023.
Moaddel, Mansoor. 2007. "The Saudi Public Speaks: Religion, Gender, and Politics." In *Values and Perceptions of the Islamic and Middle Eastern Publics*, edited by Mansoor Moaddel, 209–247. New York: Palgrave Macmillan.
Moaddel, Mansoor, and Taqi Azadarmaki. 2002. "The Worldviews of Islamic Publics: The Cases of Egypt, Iran, and Jordan." *Comparative Sociology* 1: 299–319.
Moghadam, Fatemeh Etemad. 2009. "Undercounting Women's Work in Iran." *Iranian Studies* 42 (1): 81–95.
Moghadam, Valentine M. 1991. "The Reproduction of Gender Inequality in Muslim Societies: A Case Study of Iran in the 1980s." *World Development* 19 (10): 1335–1349.
Moghadam, Valentine M. 1995. "Women's Employment Issues in Contemporary Iran: Problems and Prospects in the 1990s." *Iranian Studies* 28 (3–4): 175–202.
Moghadam, Valentine M. 1998. *Women; Work, and Economic Reform in the Middle East and North Africa.* Boulder, CO: Lynne Rienner.
Moghadam, Valentine M. 2000. "Hidden from History? Women Workers in Modern Iran." *Iranian Studies* 33 (3–4): 377–401.
Moghadam, Valentine M. 2006. "Maternalist Policies vs Economic Citizenship? Gendered Social Policy in Iran." In *Gender and Social Policy in a Global Context: Uncovering the Gendered Structure of "the Social"*, edited by Shahra Razavi and Shireen Hassim, 87–108. Basingstoke: Palgrave.
Moghadam, Valentine M. 2013. *Modernizing Women: Gender and Social Change in the Middle East.* Boulder, CO: Lynne Rienner Publishers, 3rd ed.
Moghadam, Valentine M., and Fatemeh Haghighatjoo. 2016. "Women and Political Leadership in an Authoritarian Context: A Case Study of the Sixth Parliament in the Islamic Republic of Iran." *Politics & Gender* 12: 168–197.

Nomani, Farhad, and Sohrab Behdad. 2006. *Class and Labor in Iran: Did the Revolution Matter?* Syracuse, NY: Syracuse University Press.

Rezai-Rashti, Goli, and Valentine M. Moghadam. 2011. "Women and Higher Education in Iran: What Are the Implications for Employment and the 'Marriage Market'?" *International Review of Education* 57 (3): 419–441. Available at http://link.springer.com/article/10.1007/s11159-011-9217-9/fulltext.html.

Roudi, Farzaneh. 2012. *Iran Is Reversing Its Population Policy*. Washington, DC: Woodrow Wilson Center. *Viewpoints* 7 (August).

Salehi-Isfahani, Djavad. 2005. "Human Resources in Iran: Potentials and Challenges." *Iranian Studies* 38 (1): 117–147.

Samimi, Mehnaz. 2014. "Women in Iran's Factories Face Hardship, Discrimination." *al-Monitor* (26 May).

Sonneveld, Nadia, and Monica Lindbekk (eds.). 2017. *Women Judges in the Muslim World: A Comparative Study of Discourse and Practice*. Leiden: Brill.

Tohidi, Nayereh. 2010. "Iran." In *Women's Rights in the Middle East and North Africa: Progress amid Resistance*, edited by Sanja Kelly and Julia Breslin, 121–156. Washington DC and Lanham: Freedom House and Rowman and Littlefield.

United Nations Educational, Scientific, and Cultural Organization (UNESCO). 2011. *Education for All Global Monitoring Report 2011: Regional Overview—South and West Asia*. Paris: UNESCO.

World Bank. 2012. Education Statistics. Available at http://data.worldbank.org/data-catalog/ed-stats.

World Economic Forum. 2010, 2011, 2013, 2015. *Global Gender Gap Report*. Geneva: World Economic Forum.

PART III
Negotiations of social and reproductive labor

The chapters in Part III of *Global Women's Work* explore women's renegotiations of social and reproductive labor under the expansion of women's employment that accompanied globalization. Much of the analysis in this section focuses on negotiations of women's agency: figuring out how to manage exploitation and maximizing opportunities in paid work, while continuing to perform gendered, socially ascribed, and unpaid social and reproductive work. This social and reproductive work encompasses unpaid work related to mothering, caring for the sick and elderly, providing emotional support for family members, and undertaking household labor including cooking, shopping, laundry, cleaning, among others. In the traditional gendered division of labor in households, mothers regularly hold the responsibility of fulfilling most of this unpaid social and reproductive work. The processes of pregnancy, birthing, and socializing children, primarily done on an unremunerated basis by mothers, includes the mental, manual, and emotional work central to the workings of the paid economy. It is within this unpaid sphere that the next generation of workers is created, and the current one sustained. While each of the essays included in *Global Women's Work* engage in a variety of ways with the negotiations of social and reproductive labor, the chapters in Part III narrow the focus to micro- and macronegotiations in households and communities in the context of paid employment and state policies related to caregiving and gender equity.

Unpaid social and reproductive work includes not only biological reproduction and family- and home-centered labor, but also the unpaid work community building through organizations ranging from religious groups to unions to political associations. In formal and informal institutions from one nation to another, women's agency often operates within informal sectors of the economy, in unpaid realms that exist within the larger and more formalized marketplace. In this context, women take on multilayered roles within homes, workplaces, and communities. As Eileen Boris argues in "Recognizing the Home Workplace" in Part I, the "outworker, household worker, working mother, employer of other women and consumer of their goods" is sometimes the same person. Historically and more recently in the context of the globalized feminization of the paid economy, an increase in women's waged employment rarely corresponds with a decline in their unpaid social and reproductive work. However, earning a wage and working outside the home can, and does, provide women with bargaining power, transforming—sometimes in contradictory ways—familial social relations, intimacy, and social and reproductive work undertaken within families.

Negotiations of social and reproductive labor takes on many forms. In India, for example, Meena Gopal pinpoints women's agency in the choice of young workers to migrate away from their hometowns for work, in response to changes in the labor market resulting from regional, national, and global dynamics, and documents this process in the work lives of women in the home-based beedi industry where women juggle their labor market opportunities with household work and child rearing. In a similar way, Ivis Garcia and Maura Toro-Morn carefully analyze these negotiations in their comparative study of Mexican and Puerto Rican women in Chicago during the early years of the Great Recession when lost jobs and the hypercompetitive conditions of the market unwound many families on Chicago's largely Latino West Side. Here, women turned to a combination of part-time work, reliance on extended family, and a retrenchment of personal economic and social goals that often included the acceptance of lower wages, foregoing homeownership, and letting go of the dream of living in a neighborhood with better schools. The impacts of these negotiations rippled out to families across local, national, and international economies—from children and spouses of India's beedi workers to diaspora relatives of the women on Chicago's West Side who were economically dependent on receiving regular remittances from abroad.

State responses to the 2007–2008 economic crisis further shaped women's choices related to combining paid work and childcare, often circumscribing their choices by defunding governmental programs, services, and agencies that provided a social safety and care net. In response, in Hungary as Erika Kispeter shows, part-time employment surged among mothers of young children seeking to balance state family leave policies with their desire to return to work. In Ireland, as Ursula Barry found, austerity measures put into place by the European Commission, the European Central Bank, and the International Monetary Fund, and slashing the budgets of key social and gender welfare departments and programs had the greatest negative effect on women—especially on young women, mothers in low-income households with three or more children, and female migrants. Specific gendered austerity policies related to the public sector and welfare recipients further exacerbated inequalities among these particularly vulnerable sectors of society. In Ireland and throughout the EU as Barry observes,

> [t]he entire infrastructure of public and statutory bodies that had been established to promote and advocate equality, monitor progress, enhance awareness, and develop new practices has been restructured, closed, subjected to drastic budget cuts, or absorbed into departments of government.
>
> *(Barry, Chapter 17, in this volume)*

The case study of social and reproductive labor in Sweden, analyzed here by Anita Nyberg, reveals a related pattern in which the global economic crisis exacerbated women's economic vulnerability. Nyberg's work helps us understand the complexity of how the "kick-start" public policies for promoting gender equality put in place in the 1960's led to a "u-turn" in gender equality in post-recession Sweden through a careful examination of the effects of income tax, childcare, and parental leave policies on gender equality, especially for women and men who are parents. In the course of this analysis, she emphasizes the high cost of social and reproductive labor for parents who take advantage of parental leave and publicly financed childcare—initially for women, and by the 2000s, for an increasing number of men. Sweden represents a particularly intriguing case because of its high rankings in gender equality and gender pay equity. The gender employment gap is small in Sweden, women enter traditionally male-dominated high-status jobs, the gender wage gap seems finally to be closing, women's paid working hours are increasing while men's are decreasing and fathers take on greater care responsibilities. However, as Nyberg argues, this does not mean that Sweden has reach gender equality because of the intransigence of the gendered division of unpaid household and care work.

The collective work in this section of *Global Women's Work* highlights a reality that cuts across time and place: in order to have gender equality in the labor market, gender equality in the family is needed. You cannot have one without the other.

14
CHANGE AND THE STATUS QUO IN HOME-BASED INDUSTRY IN SOUTH TAMIL NADU, INDIA

Women beedi workers confront shifts in the organization of labor and capital

Meena Gopal

This chapter looks at how the organization of labor within the home-based beedi industry in the Tirunelveli district of South Tamil Nadu has continued to perpetuate itself even as it deals with changes in the labor market for women workers (Gopal 2011).[1] Beedis are cheroots made of *tendu* leaves rolled with tobacco dust, which women produce by hand within their homes through a putting-out system. The women who collect the raw materials and deliver the finished beedis to subcontractors who set up units in the villages form about 90 percent of the workforce in the industry in Tamil Nadu. It takes a woman about eight hours to roll a thousand beedis, but since they combine this work with domestic and reproductive tasks within their homes, this beedi work spills into their other work within the household and draws upon the contributions of other members of the household, including children. Beedis account for about 50 percent of the tobacco consumption in India and are popular with the working classes in both rural and urban areas. In south Tamil Nadu, the beedi industry is about a century old and co-exists with agricultural labor and other non-farm activities.

Over the last three decades, subtle changes in the labor market for women in south Tamil Nadu, reflecting a pattern across India, include erratic work opportunities for women in agricultural labor and the recent emergence of a state-sponsored rural poverty-alleviation program that guarantees employment.[2] Even as these changes have emerged, women's labor within home-based beedi work persists as rural non-farm work even though many young women have been migrating to work in the spinning mills and garment factories in nearby districts that have emerged in the post-90s phase of economic restructuring (Ghosh 2009; Mazumdar 2007; Mazumdar and Neetha 2011).

The beedi industry consists of numerous small manufacturers operating in rural and urban areas across India under nearly three hundred brand names, none of which commands more than 5 percent of the national market share. Nearly twenty million workers are employed in the production of beedis across the country, with women in home-based production forming 90 percent of this workforce (Nandi et al. 2014; Tobacco Institute of India 2010). Compared to manufacturers in North India, South Indian entrepreneurs claim to provide better wages and work conditions. A comparison of wages for beedi work across India indicates that those offered in the southern states of Kerala and Tamil Nadu are Rupees (Rs.) 100 or above, while those in Madhya Pradesh or West Bengal hover around Rs. 60 or even less (Labor Bureau 2010).

With the small changes in the labor market for women's labor in Tamil Nadu, beedi workers of different ages and social locations have attempted to access these opportunities, juggling them with their own household work and other types of labor and confronting conflicting ideologies related to these labors. In the process, home-based work continues to remain entrenched, raising the question of whether there is something about the organization of labor in the beedi industry and the overall labor market that is leading women to attempt to access labor opportunities outside their homes while keeping a foothold within beedi work.

The organization of home-based beedi work

Beedi workers in south Tamil Nadu are not pauperized rural workers. In the Tirunelveli district in South Tamil Nadu, women beedi workers are home-based workers, unlike those in other parts of the state. Here women work through a putting-out or subcontracting system in which they obtain raw material from shops dispersed within their villages and are managed by subcontractors, who collect the beedis they produce and pay them weekly wages and other benefits. Some women beedi workers rely on beedi work as their only source of income, while others combine it with other livelihood options within the household (Gopal 1999), and thus the role played by beedi work and the income derived from it varies considerably within a village.

In south Tamil Nadu, the household relations and conditions of women are based largely on patriarchal notions of women as dependents whose primary roles are as homemakers and caregivers, despite also being wage earners engaged in non-farm work. This normative existence shapes their relationship to work and manifests in a lack of consciousness as workers that tends to make them unquestioningly accept self-limiting attitudes about their work as "women's work." The home-based nature of their work, the lack of a shared workplace, and the competitive and divisive relations of work with other women workers in the community combine to create the particular labor organization of beedi work. Among themselves, women lend and borrow beedis within a cooperative framework that often becomes competitive and in which some women are able to produce more beedis and thereby accumulate more earnings. Thus women's beedi work extracts the most out of them while simultaneously keeping them entrenched within a traditional social structure. Although employers claim that beedi work done by women within their households is done in their free or spare time, these women's tension-filled routines demonstrate that this claim is baseless. Furthermore, the manner in which women manage their food requirements and adjust their time, work, and leisure undercuts this "myth of convenience." Beedi work is devalued as "women's work" that men will not do, and the women beedi workers' atomized conditions of work, in which they lack a common place of work where they come together and share aspects of their work, means that they cannot easily achieve the unity required for collective efforts to resist these perceptions and practices. Given this background, these concepts of gender relations and work ideology reflect the various spheres of a woman's work and life, beginning with the household, and progressing to their work relations with one another, as well as with the beedi industry, their perception of their work and of themselves as workers, their capacity to bargain for their labor rights, and finally, their participation in the public sphere, in politics or in organizing themselves.

As this analysis shows, the organization of beedi work remains as entrenched in the second decade of the twenty-first century as it was in the mid-1990s, despite changes in the political economy and in the labor market for women. Although the state is welcoming investors who in turn are inviting rural unskilled workers to enter the labor market in new industrial enclaves such as special economic zones and export processing centers, this older form of labor organization persists even as entrepreneurs expand and diversify and women clamor for jobs in factories where they can work regular hours rather than drudge at home. The next section deals with the positive way entrepreneurs in the beedi industry represent themselves, not as capitalists who exploit labor as a matter of course. We also look at the entrepreneurs' view of the workforce, followed by an examination of how women perceive their home-based beedi work, especially in comparison with other work accessible in the local labor market.

Beedi entrepreneurship in the shadow of liberalization

Through the 1980s, the employment scenario in India was marked by a decrease in the importance of agriculture as the main source of livelihood coupled with an increase in employment opportunities in the non-farm sector. These opportunities included work in transport, communication, construction, and services and industrial employment related to agriculture and trade in farm products (Breman 1999b). The newly emerging entrepreneurs of the beedi industry in south India have followed this same path of creating opportunities.

There is a very clear distinction between the initial entrepreneurs in beedi capital and the later entrants. Today, the later entrants rule the roost, controlling the majority of the market for beedi sales. The beedi manufacturer credited with having brought beedi manufacture into Tirunelveli in the early part of the twentieth century is Sokkalal Ram Sait,[3] an entrepreneur from the Nadar caste who went to Bombay to learn the craft and taught it to men and women who were languishing in the drought then affecting agricultural regions of Ambasamudram in the Tirunelveli district of Tamil Nadu. Selling beedis under the brand Sokkalal Beedi, his headquarters still exist in the town of Mukkudal, although it is now a mere shadow of its earlier splendor. Sokkalal, whose name was Chokkalinga Nadar, took the appellation of "Sait," a generic North Indian name for a businessman or a moneyed man, to signify his pioneering role in the beedi business. Several of his relatives also became involved in the beedi industry. A significant number of the later entrants to the industry, however, were outsiders. Tamil Muslim merchants and traders who live in Tirunelveli or merchants and traders who migrated from the neighboring states of Kerala, Karnataka, and even Gujarat, to set up business in the southern districts of Tamil Nadu.

The early beedi entrepreneurs thus represented themselves in interviews as traders investing in their hometown and their people. In a similar vein, the later entrepreneurs claim to provide women with work they can do in their spare time in combination with their household chores, perpetuating a myth of convenience that absolves them of responsibility for providing work infrastructure, proper working conditions, or stipulated hours of work that have been gained elsewhere through the struggles of generations of workers.

A telling example of this self-representation observed by the author is a set of two photographs gracing the wall of the lobby of the Seyadu Beedi headquarters, named the House of Seyad (see Figure 14.1). One of these showed a man entering a corridor of a large warehouse carrying a tray stacked with beedis on his shoulders. The other

FIGURE 14.1 The headquarters of the Seyadu Beedi Company, referred to as the House of Seyad

Source: Photograph by the author, 2010.

showed the area outside that warehouse filled with beedi-stacked trays laid out in the courtyard to cure under the sun, a man on a bicycle riding along one side and two other men moving through the space carrying beedi trays. Both stylishly framed black-and-white photographs depicted the role of men in the curing and packaging of the beedis, completely obscuring the efforts of the women who produced these thousands of beedis before they reached the warehouse.

The beedi industry in south Tamil Nadu is thus largely controlled by the trading communities of the Nadars and Muslims. A few others, such as Mangalore Ganesh Beedi and Bharat Beedi, who are national players in the beedi industry, also have a presence in the district. The Nadars and Muslims began as petty commodity producers but, through the dint of their enterprise and the backing of their families, are today the barons of the beedi market. Today their commercial enterprises have substantially diversified into other consumer products such as oils; agro-products such as tea; health-care services such as ayurvedic care; and even running educational establishments such as residential schools. For instance, the Rajah Group, which manufactures beedis under the trademark Kajah Beedi, has ventured into the field of healthcare and the production of automobiles, software, and other consumer products.[4]

Beedis today account for 53 percent of domestic consumption of tobacco, compared to cigarettes at 19 percent. But in terms of revenue to the state between 2006 and 2009, they brought in much less than cigarettes, only about Rs. 400–500 crores (Rs.4–5 billion) compared to an increase from around Rs. 7,000 crores (Rs. 70 billion) to more than Rs. 9,000 crores (Rs. 90 billion) for cigarettes. Following the revision of the excise duty in 2007–2008, the revenue from other tobacco products, including gutkha and chewing tobacco, has also risen dramatically, while beedi's revenues have increased only marginally. In 2008–2009, beedi contributed the lowest amount in tax revenue among all tobacco products (Tobacco Institute of India 2010, 9). The beedi industry, spread in pockets across the country, obviously enjoys political protection that keeps it from not being heavily taxed, although the nicotine content of beedis is higher than cigarettes.

The movement of industries from their niche areas to diversify into newer areas with greater market potential received a boost in the late 1980s, when trade, investment, and exports were given a boost to improve the growth potential of their home countries. In the last three decades, the world has been further globalized in terms of certain markets, such as the market for the exchange of consumer goods, including media; the market for capital goods; and the financial market (Banerjee and Goldfield 2007). That this globalization has not affected the market for the labor of women has been far less discussed. The rise of the service sector and growth in global production chains has brought growing numbers of women into less skilled and more hazardous jobs that do not challenge the gendered division of labor. Many of these workers are migrants within their own countries. Another aspect of these changes that is less discussed is working conditions as large industrial concerns outsource work into home-based sweatshop conditions that leave women socially isolated from their co-workers, unable to come together to seek improvement in their conditions and wages. This is the shadow side of a globalizing India, where what shines is the beedi entrepreneurship displayed in in the glitzy building of the House of Seyad shown in Figure 14.1.

The owner-entrepreneurs of this shining India are praised by the state for their readiness to compete in the international market. Although beedi is not much of an export commodity, the incentive to diversify has encouraged entrepreneurs to enter into areas that make them claimants to this new entrepreneurial class. The globalization of capital has brought with it a mixture of both predatory and emancipatory possibilities. Despite the exploitative consequences of the situation of laborers within these industries, the success stories of local capitalists presents a different face of the globalization story. The garment businesses of western Tamil Nadu, for instance, are able to envision and enact a local form of capitalist enterprise that does not dispossess local communities from their lands,like the huge national and international corporate establishments that now are predators in the coal, bauxite, and other mines in the country. These businesses, like the labor they employ, are subalterns who present their lives as capital and labor as an aspect of the contested lived experience of modernity. They are able to rely on caste and kin affiliations to bind together pliable labor arrangements in their efforts to seek global markets (Chari 2004).

Historically, Western capitalist opportunities, when women and children entered industrial production in large numbers, initially provided an escape to women from familial exploitation. Like male workers, women workers aspired to break out of traditional systems of entrapment and work for wages, even if under deplorable conditions. I observed glimmers of such a desire among the beedi workers in south Tamil Nadu, some of whom expressed eagerness to leave their beedi trays behind for work in a factory. The jute and textile industries that had emerged in colonial India had provided such opportunities for men but for few women, foreshadowing women's limited participation in modern industry (Sen 1999).

The manufacturing factories today have molded themselves to suit women's needs but within limits. Women who envision a job for themselves in these factories are not free workers but are tied to familial obligations, social expectations, and actual material deprivation. I could see evidence of this scenario of young people seeking work, in the experience of young women and men who went to work in the factories and mills in faraway Coimbatore and Tiruppur in the northwestern region of the state. N, a beedi worker and mother of a young woman who was sent to work in a spinning mill near Coimbatore through kin networks in the village, noted that the conditions in the mills was no better than those of beedi work in the households, although it provided the young woman an opportunity to go out and work rather than sit at home and roll beedis, which she had hated. The young women in the mill followed exacting routines in which they had to stand throughout punishing shifts, although the attraction was the lump sum of Rs. 30,000 that would be paid to them at the end of their three-year contract. Young women were enticed to "earn" their dowry (an arrangement that employers in the garment industry termed *sumangali thittam*, "bridal scheme"), with some home visits, gifts, and even cash advances thrown in as incentives, but they also underwent constant sexual surveillance, rebukes, and moral control by the wardens and supervisors alongside their punishing work schedules. Many young women, unable to adjust, returned before their scheduled departure and thereby lost a lot of money. N's daughter did her three-year stint, loved the work in the mills, and earned her lump sum, which made a significant contribution to her household.

State officials and scholars have done a disservice to such women by misrepresenting the choices they make or castigating them as being trafficked or in need of protection. What we need to better understand is this urgency on the part of many women to get away, break out, and make changes in their lives and working conditions. Our ideological tendency to focus on the exploitative aspects of the work available to such women often misses the meaning that they make out of their own situations. The women I interviewed were articulating something by moving away from work at home and by their dream of factory work rather than white-collar jobs, which some of them equated with beedi work.

Women negotiating patriarchies: emerging identities through labor

Most of the middle-aged female beedi workers I interviewed recalled that the previous generation of women in their families had been Palmyra climbers who had also worked as poor agricultural workers once the palm season was over. Tapping toddy (liquor prepared from fermented palm juice) was the caste-based occupation of the Palmyra climbers, mostly poorer Nadars, which was considered lowly and carried a stigma. It was a family occupation in which men climbed palm trees and tapped the juice while women prepared palm sugar, toddy, and other byproducts for consumption and sale.

Since Palmyra climbing was seen as degrading and defiling, beedi work helped these women enact a generational shift from the stigmatized occupation for which Christianity and colonialism were also catalysts. Non-farm work such as beedi work provided income-producing opportunities for women outside of agriculture or caste-based occupations. Thus, for these women beedi work represents a *munnetram* (in Tamil, progress or improvement) away from caste-based occupations such as Palmyra climbing. Beedi work, like agriculture and trade, was responsible for lifting families out of starvation and social stigma. Women achieved new freedom and status, however marginal, in the uniform treatment they received as workers in the beedi shops. In a sense, the shift from the affiliations of caste disrupted the cultural meanings associated with these labors (Robb 1993).

But beedi work also enabled the next generation of women to utilize educational opportunities to move out of beedi work. In that way, it served as a steppingstone into another class domain: from being a beedi worker to admission into an educated class, assisted by the state and the institutional opportunities of education. Nonetheless, it was still considered "women's work" that men would not do, due its informal and home-based character. In this, it paralleled the sexual division of labor prevalent within the rural milieu of Tamil Nadu, including agricultural work, construction work, and other non-farm work in which men and women both participate but have specific tasks allotted to them by gender. Beedi work, women told me, offers somewhat similar wages as other work that would require them to do hard manual labor in the sun, while rolling beedis consists of hard work within homes.

T's history illustrates this social progress. The forty-two-year-old woman's parents were Palmyra workers. Her father used to climb the Palmyra trees to tap toddy and pluck nuts while her mother would make *karippatti* (palm sugar). Her in-laws were agricultural workers. Her husband still climbs palm trees and does casual labor. All five of their children, however, are educated, the first generation of their family to join the educated class. T described this movement, which she credited to beedi work, as *munnetram*, claiming that beedi work had done her family good and brought progress into their lives. Her daughter, M, is a first-generation college graduate. The eldest child in the family, she completed a bachelor's degree in mathematics at the Government College in Alwarkurichi, where her younger brother was also studying at the time.

Another widespread perception of beedi work among the women I interviewed was that it had brought them *nagareekam,* or a sort of civility or sophistication, especially in comparison to agricultural labor. They compared themselves as being equal to white-collar workers in their deportment, reporting to the subcontractors' shops well dressed and with their hair neatly done, just like young women going to work in offices and unlike unkempt field workers in agriculture. This fragile self-perception overlooks that beedi work done within the home, where women must compromise their food, rest, and leisure and work with tobacco dust and tendu leaves strewn all over, has left many women unfit for manual labor. In fact, some women beedi workers told me they envied agricultural laborers, who get to work set hours and return home to rest and prepare themselves for the next day's work, although some agricultural workers also combined agricultural labor with some amount of beedi work, sacrificing leisure and recuperation for the additional income. Nonetheless, these women viewed beedi work as sophisticated in comparison to the traditional occupations of women in the region and to agricultural labor, thereby privileging an urbanity that glossed over labor struggles within these new modes of production.

The pervasiveness of beedi work over the past couple of generations has prevented several middle-aged and almost all younger women from doing agricultural labor. While this may have bred contempt for work in the fields, it also instilled a fear of hard bodily labor among the beedi workers. While those critical of beedi work complained about how it spilled over in to all their other work in the home and compromised their health, they lacked the confidence to give it up and step out to work in the fields. Although participating in the public works projects of the Employment Guarantee Scheme gave some of the women a sense of confidence that they could manage hard bodily labor after years of beedi work, those women were from a class who could negotiate the division of labor with their families and had the wherewithal to take sufficient care of their bodily needs.

Of particular note for the purposes of this analysis is that these new meanings or ideologies associated with labor provided a veneer that did not reflect or have an impact on the structures and divergences within the labor processes from which they emanated. Instead, they helped mask the devaluation of that labor due to its continued location within the domestic sphere, camouflaging it from social commentary. These notions of glamour, sophistication, urbanity, and modernity are hallmarks not just of this rural home-based work but the mushrooming centers of labor-intensive, female-dominated manufacturing centers of numerous export processing zones and special economic zones. These new hubs of industrial production extract from labor much more than they give, especially from working-class women, as the state allies with capital to deprive labor of their legitimate rights. The movement of beedi workers from social disability to capitalist exploitation of the dependent poor should sound a warning note to those who propose this form of labor as a solution to the problems of the labor market or the entrenchment of a gender-based division of labor.

A further dimension of beedi work is observed in conjunction with the historical situation of caste and religious identities of the communities in this region, especially in terms of the relationship of beedi work with the caste-based occupations of these groups as we noted above. Both men and women of disadvantaged caste groups benefited from the efforts of Protestant missionaries in the nineteenth century to counter the historical degradation of those groups by the dominant castes and elites as the disadvantaged groups adopted norms of "respectability" that distanced them from their degraded pasts. These negotiations affected women from the Nadar community in interesting ways (Kent 2004). Both C and P are former beedi rollers who, through hard work and the congruence of family, caste, and religious factors, were able to move out of beedi rolling work. After being widowed in the mid-90s, C became the child nutrition worker (CNW) in the anganwadi (child-care center) run by Integrated Child Development Services (ICDS), a state program where preschoolers stay for a large part of the day when their parents are at work or busy with chores. Later she became the teacher in charge of another anganwadi in a hamlet of K panchayat. P, who was deserted by her husband in the mid-90s, took to beedi rolling and cooking food articles that she packed for children as part of their lunch or sold to children during their recess from school. She also did little odd jobs for the local schoolteacher to earn money to educate and take care of her two young children. Today her son runs a little furniture shop while her daughter has trained to be a nurse. Enterprise is deeply writ into the life trajectories of these women.

This enterprise reflects an unobtrusive grit and perseverance that women cultivate within the bounds of patriarchy, caste, and religious dictum while also constantly negotiating with them. This grit and courage was evident to an NGO worker that I interviewed who spoke of a woman beedi roller she encountered participating in a protest against a beedi entrepreneur who, after hurling a slogan at him outside his shop, promptly fainted and collapsed. At that moment, her strength crumbled in the collision between her "culture" as a woman and as a laborer. Just as her role as a woman required deference to patriarchal authority within her household, caste, and community, her role as a worker required a docility and submission to the arbitrary practices of employers. Women who are unable to think of themselves as workers because they work within the home contribute to a labor climate that makes them conducive to being taken advantage of by beedi entrepreneurs. This culture also neatly dovetailed with the entrenched social and the sexual division of labor and post-90s attempts to liberalize the economy, which in turn were aided by the development of such infrastructure as highways and communication networks. As it was, Tamil Nadu in the early 1990s boasted of a high level of urbanization and fertility reduction (Swaminathan 1996), both signifiers of a modern state that invited entrepreneurs to expand the beedi industry, although this did not even out the social conflicts emanating from the contradictions of caste riots and religious conversions. But the areas around K panchayat essentially comprised of docile workers conducive and suited to petty manufacturing.

Another change seen in the labor market is the migration of women from all districts of Tamil Nadu to the mills and garment factories of the northwestern part of the state. This migratory movement of young women is a recent phenomenon resulting from larger national, regional, and global dynamics in which family and other networks have widened to allow women to escape local work and move to other places for to earn a livelihood. While these offer some space for negotiation with family for young women, it includes a greater surveillance of their sexuality by not just the family but persons and systems that offer these opportunities. This collusion between capital and patriarchy in search of profits offers a veneer of growth and modernity, but the conditions of work are designed in such a way that the maximum is extracted from workers even as the cultural codes of family, community, and nation are maintained. Beneath this surface lie exploitative practices endured by young women kept under strict surveillance, resembling the numerous export-processing zones that emerged all along Latin America in the mid-90s employing young pliable female laborers who produced consumer goods for an international market.

Upon return to their families most of these young women returned to beedi rolling. What they craved when they set out for the mills was the shift in the location of paid work from the home to the factory, which they compared to the exploitative terms of the labor process by which home-based beedi work is organized. S had gone to work in the mill for two years but returned within a year, noting that although the conditions of work seemed better in the mills, she could earn more by rolling beedi and could work from home. According to S,

> at the mill that I worked, five hundred people were employed. I had gone there through an agent; and there were about forty odd young women from our Tenkasi area. One shift was from 5:30 a.m. to 2:30 p.m. And the other shift was from 9:00 p.m. to 6:00 a.m. We got a daily wage of Rs. 90, and so monthly it worked to Rs. 1,500–2,000, while the rest of the money was given at the end of three years as a lump sum amount. The daily routine began with a prayer and a *uruthi mozhi* [a vow], which we sang from a book of songs. Then there were exercises. On Saturdays, we go to the Ayyappa temple. We are taken on fun tours; the last time it was to Pollachi. During Deepavali festival, they give dresses as gifts to the girls. The girls then perform dance, drama, etc. The management even gives you a cash advance if you wanted. I did not stay long, though, but left in one year, after I intervened to help my friend who got into a relationship with a boy. The managers of the hostel beat up the boy. I was scolded for questioning this. But I created further trouble and then got out.
>
> Gopal (2011, p. 69)

Thus even though these young women had moved out of their own homes as adults, the continued surveillance of their sexuality was exercised strictly in this home away from home.

Ultimately, therefore, beedi work remains entrenched within a status quo that dictates gender inequality for women even as women access other forms of work, indicating the powerful role that ideologies play despite small shifts and changes in the labor market. As labor persists in their struggles with this status quo, beedi capital seems to have advanced in its expansion in diversifying the capital it has accumulated through the labor of women workers.

Notes

1 Most of the fieldwork for this paper was conducted as part of the Fellowship Program at the Nehru Memorial Museum and Library, New Delhi, in 2009–2011.
2 The rural employment guarantee scheme is a state program designed to provide livelihood security in the form of at least a hundred days of unskilled manual labor for wages in rural areas in such public works as land development, renovation of traditional water bodies, desilting tanks, and minor irrigation works (Ministry of Law and Justice 2005).
3 *Mudal Aandu Ninaivu Malar*, an undated publication commemorating the first anniversary of the death of Managing Director T. P. S Hariram Sait, who died in 1964, refers to his father, T.P Sokkalal Ram Sait, as the founder (moolakartar) of the southern Indian beedi industry. According to the legend of a photograph at the factory office, the factory was established by Beedi Chakravarti Ta Pi Sokkalal Ram Sait in 1898.
4 The Rajah Group website can be accessed at http://www.rg8.biz

References

Banerjee, Debdas and Michael Goldfield, eds. 2007. *Labor, Globalization and the State: Workers, Women and Migrants Confront Neoliberalism.* London: Routledge.

Breman, Jan. 1999a. "The Study of Industrial Labor in Post-colonial India—The Formal Sector: An Introductory Review." In *The Worlds of Indian Industrial Labor.* New Delhi: Sage, edited by Jonathan P. Parry, Jan Breman and Karin Kapadia, 1–41.

Breman, Jan. 1999b. "The Study of Industrial Labor in Post-colonial India—The Informal Sector: A Concluding Review." In *The Worlds of Indian Industrial Labor.* New Delhi: Sage, edited by Jonathan P. Parry, Jan Breman and Karin Kapadia, 407–431.

Chari, Sharad. 2004. *Fraternal Capital: Peasant Workers, Self-Made Men and Globalization in Provincial India.* Delhi: Permanent Black.

Ghosh, Jayati. 2009. *Never Done and Poorly Paid: Women's Work in Globalising India.* New Delhi: Women Unlimited.

Gopal, Meena. 1999. "Disempowered Despite Wage Work: Women Workers in Beedi Industry." *Economic and Political Weekly.* 34: WS12–WS20.

Gopal, Meena. 2011. *Shifts in Women's Work and Ideology in South Tamil Nadu: Labor Process and Gender Relations.* Unpublished report. New Delhi: Nehru Memorial Museum and Library.

Kent, Eliza. 2004. *Converting Women: Gender and Protestant Christianity in Colonial South India.* Oxford: Oxford University Press.

Labor Bureau. 2010. *Wage Rates in Rural India 2008–09.* Ministry of Labor and Employment. Chandigarh: Government of India.

Mazumdar, Indrani. 2007. *Women Workers and Globalization: Emergent Contradictions in India.* Kolkata: Stree.

Mazumdar, Indrani and Neetha N. 2011. "Gender Dimensions: Employment Trends in India, 1993–94 to 2009–10." *Economic and Political Weekly.* 46: 118–126.

Ministry of Law and Justice. 2005. *National Rural Employment Guarantee Act, 2005.* Ministry of Law and Justice, Legislative Department, Gazette of India. Accessed 15 July 2015. http://nrega.nic.in/rajaswa.pdf

Nandi Arindam, Ashvin Ashok, G. Emmanuel Guindon, Frank J. Chaloupka and Prabhat Jha. 2014. "Estimates of the Economic Contributions of the Bidi Manufacturing Industry in India." *Tobacco Control.* 1–8. 10.1136/tobaccocontrol-2013-051404

Robb, Peter. 1993. "Introduction: Meanings of Labor in Indian Social Context." *Dalit Movements and the Meanings of Labor in India.* Delhi: Oxford University Press, edited by Peter Robb, 1–67.

Sen, Samita. 1999. "At the Margins: Women Workers in the Bengal Jute Industry." *The Worlds of Indian Industrial Labor.* New Delhi: Sage, edited by Jonathan P. Parry, Jan Breman and Karin Kapadia, 239–269.

Swaminathan, Padmini. 1996. *The Failures of Success: An Analysis of Tamil Nadu's Recent Demographic Experience.* Chennai: Madras Institute of Development Studies. Working Paper no. 141.

Tobacco Institute of India. 2010. *The Golden Leaf in Parliament: A summary of questions and answers in Parliament.* New Delhi: Tobacco Institute of India. 9.

15
MEXICAN AND PUERTO RICAN WOMEN IN CHICAGO

A gendered analysis of the 2008 recession

Ivis García and Maura I. Toro-Morn

Rita, a Puerto Rican woman in Chicago, recognizes the effects of the 2008 economic recession and called for both individual and collective action:

> What about all these people that are going to lose their jobs? Are they going to get unemployment, and for how long? How do we keep up the community? Like Rosario said. There's no unity and no voice. Maybe we need stronger voices? I don't go out there and say, "Hey let's rally!" I'm one of the ones that learned how to survive; I don't go out there and rally. But you know what? Maybe there's got to be that one voice, where I can say this is a person that I can listen to, this is a meeting that I want to go to, here is going to be some kind of improvement for me and for my neighbor and for Rosario, this is going to help somebody. Maybe we need to hear that one voice out of so many that is going to make the difference.
>
> *(Focus Group)*

Rita's comments reveal her own awareness of the hypercompetitive conditions of the market forces during the recession and how these market forces destroyed families in her community. In other interviews conducted in Chicago's West Side—a community that is 41 percent Latino—it was also evident that unemployment, layoffs, and declines in wages meant significant social and economic vulnerability for women across nationalities. The 2008 economic recession created havoc in poor and working class communities around this nation, yet the general public knows little about how the economy disrupted Latino families and communities. This chapter seeks to address this problem by offering a case study of the impact of the 2008 economic recession on Latino women in Chicago.

Chicago has been home to a significant number of Mexican and Puerto Rican families arriving in the city in response to globalizing processes in both Mexico and Puerto Rico. This chapter explores how the development of export-processing zones in Puerto Rico and Mexico led to changes in women's employment patterns and reconstituted migration as a survival strategy for families across social classes. The historical perspective in the first part of this chapter offers readers an overview of these women's commitment to work, their families, and migration as a way to support their families. This historical background also offers readers an understanding of the role that Puerto Rican and Mexican women have played in the global assembly line that constitutes an important marker of globalization processes. In Chicago, Puerto Rican and Mexican women encountered a share of problems as well as opportunities. As a global city, Chicago has undergone the economic stages evident in most U.S. cities today—deindustrialization, globalization, and financialization—making it an important place to document the labor market experiences of Puerto Rican and Mexican women. This economic downturn, the most severe since the Great Depression, resulted in higher poverty rates and decreases in wages for people of color, but felt most pronouncedly by Latino/as. For example, Latinas could not afford to opt out of the labor force, thus their employment rates did not suffer as might have been expected. The neoliberal policies underlying the 2008 economic recession disrupted labor patterns thereby making women's labor conditions more precarious.

Using socioeconomic data from the American Community Survey (ACS) such as, labor participation rates, unemployment rates, poverty rates, and earnings from 2005–2012, this study examines the impact of the Great Recession on Puerto Rican and Mexican women in Chicago. Preliminary accounts suggest that the 2008 economic recession did not affect everyone equally, and thus it is necessary to deconstruct the gender and racial/ethnic differences that the aggregated data tend to mask. This chapter offers a comparative analysis of four ethnic and racial groups of women within the city of Chicago: Mexicans, Puerto Ricans, non-Hispanic whites, and non-Hispanic blacks. Although non-Hispanic whites and blacks are examined as a point of comparison, the emphasis here is on women of Puerto Rican and Mexican origin.

According to the 2010 decennial census, there were 778,862 Latinos living in Chicago, 74 percent of whom were Mexican (578,100). The number of Puerto Ricans in that group was 102,703, or 13 percent, making them the second largest Latino group in the city (U.S. Census Bureau). Given the size of the Mexican population, researchers studying the recession worry that the statistical analysis of Latinos is skewed toward representing Mexicans (Birson et al. 2013). Driven by the concern that Latinos are often examined without accounting for the substantial variation that exists between subgroups, this work seeks to disaggregate the socioeconomic effects of the economic downturn upon the two major Latino groups in Chicago: Mexicans and Puerto Ricans. A comparative perspective that sheds light on the differences and similarities between Puerto Rican and Mexican women can provide the initial tools for building solidarity between these groups.

Further, this chapter adds a layer of complexity to existing discussions of the recession by focusing on women. The recession affected individuals differently based on their gender (Pissarides 2013). In fact, popular culture has called it the "mancession" to express how the recession disproportionately affected males (Thompson 2009). According to the Bureau of Labor Force Statistics, the national unemployment rate peaked in October of 2009 at 9.9 percent; the unemployment rate for males peaked that same month at 11.0 percent, and women's unemployment rate peaked an entire year later at 8.8 percent. Analysts theorized that men were more susceptible to layoffs because they worked in the manufacturing and construction sectors as blue-collar workers or in finance and real estate as white-collar workers—the industries most greatly affected by the downturn (Perry 2010). Women, on the other hand, worked in education, healthcare, social services, retail, and other service-sector jobs (Perry 2010). In addition, more women worked for government agencies, which experienced fewer layoffs than the private sector at the peak of the financial meltdown (Kochhar 2011). Nonetheless, jobs in the public sector did contract after the recession due to general cutbacks in government expenditures, which meant that women started to lose these jobs after the height of the recession, but before it was declared officially over (Kochhar 2011). While the argument holds that the recent 2008 economic crisis initially affected more males, the experiences of women deserve to be analyzed, too. Women's experiences warrant analysis since the employment recovery for males has been much faster than for women, and, as this study will show, women in Chicago have higher unemployment rates now than during the recession. In addition, this study demonstrates that the effects of the recession on women differ across social classes and racial/ethnic groups. By noting the heterogeneous impacts across demographic groups, this chapter examines the recession's effects at the intersection of multiple identity categories.

The bulk of the analysis is offered in the third section, which focuses on recent socioeconomic data from the ACS to compare the different groups of women and understand their commonalities and differences after the Great Recession. Finally, the conclusion outlines existing and potential responses from policy makers and community members to counteract the negative outcomes that the crisis has had on women of color. In addition, this final section returns to the relevance of using a comparative ethnic-racial lens to understand women's work-life experiences.

The intellectual contributions of this work are many and at different levels. First, more comparative work is needed across Latino nationalities to be able to break homogenizing tendencies of pan-ethnic categories. Scholarly work that is attentive to deepening understanding of the intersections of gender, race, and social class across Latino groups also fills an important theoretical and empirical gap. Even more significantly, this research will ultimately help stakeholders—community activists, public officials, and others—take the steps needed to address the inequities and problems that Puerto Rican and Mexican women face as workers, mothers, and members of transnational communities.

Puerto Rican and Mexican women's labor histories: gender, globalization, and migration

Several decades of feminist research on neoliberal globalization processes has yielded some impressive and irrefutable findings. We know that neoliberal globalization processes have accelerated the entrance of women into the labor market, a process known as the "feminization of labor" (Acker 2004; Salzinger 2003). As Joan Acker describes it, "in country after country, women and often children have been drawn into production for the world market and into wage labor in transnational organizations" (2004, 33). Women's incorporation into wage processes has taken place in various arrangements, including work done in the home, export-processing zones, the informal economy, and on the street. We also know that the feminization of labor has been a rather bittersweet process for women across the world. As feminist scholar Alison Jaggar states,

> [N]eoliberal globalization is making the lives of many women better, [but] it is making the lives of even more women worse. The lives of many of the world's poorest and most marginalized women in the both the global South and the global North are deteriorating relative to the lives of better-off women and of men.
>
> *(Jaggar 2001, 301)*

Neoliberal globalization processes have also led to what social scientists have called the feminization of migration (Toro-Morn and Alicea 2004). Feminist scholars in a range of fields have documented the many ways that migration has affected women around the world. Today, women represent a significant percentage of the world's migrant population. The feminization of migration and labor have altered gender relations, families, and communities. This section offers a brief historical analysis of the ubiquitous global assembly line and how its development cuts through the lives and work experiences of Puerto Rican and Mexican women. It is no coincidence that in the aftermath of Operation Bootstrap, Puerto Rico's export-processing model, and Mexico's Border Industrialization Plan (BIP), massive out-migrations from these nations took place, bringing Mexican and Puerto Rican families to the U.S., including, most prominently, Chicago.

Both Operation Bootstrap and the BIP show how gender is embedded in the neoliberal globalization projects (Gottfried 2004). The following sections will discuss these two programs in more depth, as well as how they fueled out-migration.

Gender and Puerto Rico's operation bootstrap

Feminist scholar Palmira Rios argues that industrialization in Puerto Rico did not mean the exclusion or marginalization of women from the labor force (1990, 322). Instead, Operation Bootstrap, as the country's industrialization model is known, employed women in large assembly-line factories and in low-paid industries. Over a period of 30 years, fluctuations in the types of industries attracted to Puerto Rico caused women's employment patterns to suffer. For example, Rios shows that in 1952, the two leading manufacturing sectors were the apparel and food industries, but only the apparel industry tended to employ women (1990, 324). Similarly, in the 1970s, when the development program attracted heavy industries that privileged male workers, women's employment rates slowed. In the mid-1970s, however, four capital-intensive industries—electronic, chemical, machinery, and professional and scientific instruments—arrived on the island, improving women's employment rates. According to Rios, "the electronic industry alone added over 8,000 jobs from 1975–1980" (1990, 326). The foreign-owned subsidiaries that employed mostly women also paid those workers below-average wages.

A question that needs to be raised here is whether women's employment has benefitted them as individuals or their families. Even more importantly, have women been able to redefine or shift their gendered responsibilities? In the 1990s, research with working women in Puerto Rico reveals that although there have been some gains, for the most part, Puerto Rican women have not redefined their gendered responsibilities (Colón-Warren and Alegría-Ortega, 1998; Safa 1995). In her groundbreaking ethnography, *The Myth of the Male Breadwinner* (1995), anthropologist Helen Safa offers compelling evidence of the impact of women's employment patterns on gendered notions. In keeping with previous research findings, Safa found that working women in Puerto Rico made significant contributions to their family's income. In fact, women in her sample claimed that their family's survival depended on their salaries. She found that these women were aware of the problems they faced as women but powerless to address them. At the time, there was, however, little evidence of gender or class consciousness among working women. Although the state recognized their importance as wage earners, it continued to regard and treat them as supplementary workers with little legitimacy. Colon-Warren and Alegría-Ortega conclude that Puerto Rico's export-processing model facilitated women's integration in the formal economy and the public sphere but did not allow for a redefinition of gender roles and gender attitudes (1998, 102).

Puerto Rican feminist scholars have taken care to expose the deeply gendered and contradictory policies of Puerto Rico's development model that led to the massive movement of Puerto Ricans to New York City, a destination they had known since the turn of the twentieth century, and to new destinations, like Chicago. In Chicago, women were recruited to fill labor needs in the domestic labor sector (Toro-Morn 2001). Once there, many Puerto Ricans were deceived and exploited by employers and left domestic work in search of better employment prospects (Toro-Morn 2001; Rúa 2011). In the 1960s and 1970s, working-class families followed these early immigrants to Chicago. Puerto Rican women's work experiences in Chicago varied by social class. Working-class women found themselves employed in industrial, clerical, and service sector work (Toro-Morn 2001). In the 1960s and 1970s, there was a slight increase in the number of Puerto Rican women employed in white collar jobs, which can be attributed to the number of professional and educated women migrating from the island at the time. Working-class women found themselves balancing work and family responsibilities (Toro-Morn 2001) and the added transnational emotional labor of maintaining their families. There is no doubt that Puerto Rico "paved the way for the new international division of labor and that its basic components were tested in Puerto Rico before being exported to other developing nations" (Rios 1990, 332), just as in Mexico, the topic addressed next.

Gender and Mexico's maquila industry

In Mexico, the development of an export-processing model took place in the 1960s in the context of the Border Industrialization Plan (BIP), which created a 12.5 mile strip along the U.S.-Mexico border to attract transnational corporations. At the time, Mexico was a cheap alternative to the Asian export-processing zones. The BIP program resulted in the maquiladora factory system within the border cities along the U.S.-Mexico border. With the disappearance of agricultural production in rural areas and the Mexican government's interest in industrialization programs, Mexican men and women were driven from the countryside to perform low-wage labor for foreign manufacturing companies in urban areas. The program grew quickly, and by the end of the 1960s, 147 foreign companies participated in the BIP, hiring an average of 115 workers each (Taylor-Hansen 2003). The vast majority of the work in the maquilas was (and continues to be) performed by women. For example, in a 1975 study conducted in Cuidad Juárez, about 85 percent of those working on the assembly lines were women (Nash and Fernandez-Kelly 1983). In the 1970s, the maquila program was extended to the rest of Mexico with the hopes of encouraging economic investment in the country's interior. The first years of the maquila industry's job creation efforts produced only modest results, but with its expansion to the rest of Mexico, the number of factories grew, and women's employment with it. Susan Tiano (1994) reports that during the early years, women represented nearly 80 percent of the work force, but the privileging of some industries that employed mostly males led to fluctuations in women's employment.

In 1994, under the auspices of the North American Free Trade Agreement (NAFTA), the exploitation of women as a source of cheap labor became an institutional marker of the global assembly line. As in Puerto Rico, the exploitation of Mexican women workers meant employment in low-wage industries. These jobs were typified by long working hours without overtime pay, the inability to unionize, and poor working conditions that included verbal and physical abuse but no health or safety training. As of 2014, there are about 3,000 maquiladoras in the U.S.-Mexico border region with about 333 workers each. On average, workers were paid U.S.$1.50 an hour (Rosenberg 2014).

Decades of research about the maquila industry have revealed a work world that is shaped by exploitation and vulnerability. But there has also been research that complicates the narratives of neoliberal globalization as a "whirlwind descending upon" women and local women constituted as "never acting, always acted upon" (Salzinger 2003). Such research has documented that the image of maquila women as temporary and docile workers is both stereotypical and deeply problematic. Tiano's (1994) groundbreaking ethnographic work suggests that Mexican women in the maquila industry did not perceive their own work as temporary, and that if they demonstrated any ambiguity toward work and home roles, it was because of the inherent contradictions of capitalism. Although Tiano found that women were socialized to live in the tension between the roles of mother and worker, gendered socialization also "instilled in them a fundamental ambivalence about their identities as workers" (1994, 118).

Though geographically distant, the work experiences of Puerto Rican and Mexican women are connected by the global assembly line of neoliberal globalization sponsored by U.S. policies and capital. Both Operation Bootstrap and NAFTA were envisioned as experiments or models for others to follow on how economies of underdeveloped countries could modernize through industrialization. It was believed that the North-South development gap could be narrowed and that in both Mexico and Puerto Rico, earnings would rise while unemployment and poverty would decrease substantially. These expectations would lead one to speculate that, with the incorporation of women in the labor force, dual-income families would become wealthier and that immigration would cease as exports—rather than people—crossed borders. Paradoxically, Operation Bootstrap and NAFTA failed to fulfill these lofty expectations; rather, work for most women in low-wage industries became a means of survival for themselves and their families and led to massive flows of workers and their families to the United States.

Immigration, Chicago, and the great recession

In the annals of U.S. history, Chicago stands as out as a "city of immigrants" extraordinaire. In fact, poets, writers, and artists have captured the city's immigrant past and present with much flare. Poet Carl Sandburg called Chicago the city of "broad shoulders," evoking the industrial era of meatpacking and steel industries that dominated its economy for a significant part of the twentieth century. Immigrants then, and now, have supplied a great deal of the cheap labor needed for the steel industries of yesterday and the post-industrial service sector of today. According to the American Community Survey (ACS), in 2012 about 21 percent of the population in Chicago was foreign-born, and about half of that,

12 percent, was born in Latin America. At least 16 ancestry groups represented in the city had a population of more than 15,000, with Irish (200,724), German (200,624), Polish (163,966), and Italian (110,430) topping the list. The history of immigration is evident today in that the city is organized by distinct communities that are home to diverse ethnic and racial groups. The history of immigration will be evident in the city for years to come.

As a city of immigrants, each immigrant wave has constructed the community in unique ways, yet scholarly accounts have tended to privilege some accounts and obscure others. European immigrants were studied by the Chicago School of Sociology with great interest. Their story became the basis for one of the most popular frameworks against which all subsequent immigrants have been measured, namely assimilation theory. Similarly, the arrival of African Americans from the rural South at two distinct points in the twentieth century cemented the city's racial demography. Yet, as historian Lilia Fernández (2012) reminds us, in cities like Chicago, "the encounters, conflicts, and migrations of African American and whites" tell only part of the story.

Today, Latinos have surpassed African Americans as the nation's largest minority group. The Latino presence in Chicago has been apparent since the early decades of the twentieth century, yet the city continues to be (re)constructed in decidedly black/white terms. As anthropologist Merida Rúa (2011) notes, Mexicans and Puerto Ricans disrupted that social order with their racial ambiguity. Fernández agrees with Samuel Betances's assertion that blacks see Latinos as honorary whites while whites see Latinos as honorary blacks, leaving most Latinos in a racial no man's land. In Fernández words, "this racial ambivalence has made Mexicans, Puerto Ricans and other Latinos/as invisible as historical actors who have had experiences distinct from those of African Americans or European Americans" (2012, 5).

The most significant migration of both of these groups took place in the middle decades of the twentieth century, when, as Fernandez notes, "Mexicans and Puerto Ricans became subjects of state-sponsored mass labor importation programs in the United States" (2012, 24). Puerto Rican and Mexican migration to Chicago was decidedly gendered. The first group of Puerto Rican women who were recruited to work in the city were domestic workers (Toro-Morn 2001). The gender bias of Operation Bootstrap were revealed when policy documents and labor contracts showed the widespread sexism inherent in the program, promoting labor migration of young women to do domestic work in Chicago. Political officials in both Puerto Rico and the U.S. worried that population growth in the island would distort the success of the development program and hence promoted the massive out-migration of women of childbearing age from Puerto Rico to the United States (Toro-Morn 2001).

Mexican migration to the city was similarly gendered. Mexican men, mostly *braceros* (laborer), were recruited to meet labor needs in the city throughout the middle decades of the twentieth century. Historically, the stereotypical image most Americans had of *braceros* was that they were destitute agricultural workers, but the reality is that the labor contracts of *braceros* extended into industrial employment. Both Mexican and Puerto Rican workers faced many problems and experienced many abuses. Many broke their contracts and stayed in the city. Subsequent waves of immigration included the wives, children, and other family members of *braceros*. In all these cases, Fernandez states, Mexican Americans—*braceros* and Tejanos—and Puerto Ricans became part of the same occupational stratum—unskilled or semiskilled labor in agriculture and industrial jobs. Across the board, they also were relegated to the lowest-paid, most dangerous, and undesirable work. (2012).

Puerto Ricans and Mexicans in Chicago worked and lived together for many years. In fact, they also married each other in great numbers. But eventually, specific neighborhoods became identified as Puerto Rican and Mexican. Both Puerto Rican and Mexican women played many roles in the formation of their respective communities. They worked and supported their families and helped shaped their communities through their activism in schools, cultural groups, churches, and political groups.

Like many cities in the U.S. in the 1970s and 1980s, however, Chicago experienced industrial job flight—these jobs went from 64.3 percent of total employment in the city in 1970 to 32.9 percent in 1980, while service and retail positions went from 17.9 to 47.2 percent during the same time period. Both Puerto Ricans and Mexicans experienced massive job losses in manufacturing and unionized jobs, which traditionally had been paths to upward mobility for white males (Fernández 2012). Poverty rates rose in the inner city—from 1970 to 1980. For example, the percentage of families in Chicago living below the poverty level increased from 10.6 in 1970 to 16.8 percent in 1980 (U.S. Census Bureau).

Over the last 20 years, Chicago, unlike such other industrial cities in the U.S. as Detroit, Cincinnati, and Pittsburgh, was able to reinvent itself by implementing neoliberal policies characterized by the growth of construction, finance, insurance, and real estate, all quintessential neoliberal boom industries. In keeping with neoliberal tenets, Mayor Richard M. Daley (1989–2011) formed alliances with developers to build more market-rate housing in order to increase the tax base of the city and combat "blight" in the Central Business District and adjacent areas where Latinos and African Americans lived before they were displaced by these gentrifying forces (Betancur 2002). Chicago consolidated its reputation as a "global city" by attracting global capital and skilled and unskilled workers, including a sizable immigrant workforce (Sassen 2001). Table 15.1 provides some key demographic characteristics of the city.

Much of the earlier and recent internal migration of Mexicans and Puerto Ricans to Chicago can be linked to the complex interdependencies of the global economic structure. In the 1950s and 1960s, the most significant growth among industrial workers was seen among Latinos. Once the industrialization effort moved from the U.S. to other countries, the national economic strategy started to focus on the so-called service sector, which

TABLE 15.1 Key demographics in Chicago (1970–2010)

City of Chicago

	1970	1980	1990	2000	2010
Population (in millions)	3.7	3.0	2.8	2.9	2.7
Puerto Rican Population	72,223	112,074	119,866	113,055	102,854
Mexican Population	82,097	255,802	348,040	534,045	578,100
% Foreign Born	37.4	14.5	10.5	21.7	21.0
% White	58.2	43.2	37.9	31.3	31.7
% Black or African American	32.7	39.8	38.6	36.8	32.9
% Latino	7.3	14.0	19.6	26.0	28.9
% College Education	8.1	13.8	19	25.5	32.2
Median Family Income (Inflation adjusted)	57,560	39,873	51,232	54,101	53,338
% Families Below Poverty	10.6	16.8	18.3	16.6	17.2
% Manager and Professional Occupations	17.8	19.9	24.9	33.5	36.3
% Service and Retail Occupations	17.9	47.2	48.1	43.3	43.6
% Industrial Occupations	64.3	32.9	27.0	23.2	20.1

Source: U.S. Census Bureau data from 1970–2000 and 2010 American Community Survey.

needed more low-wage service workers but also made the economy dependent on FIRE (finance, insurance, and real estate) industries. Thus, the question needs to be asked: what did the 2008 economic recession mean for Chicago's Mexican and Puerto Rican women? Maria, a Mexican woman describes in her own words how she was laid off.

> I still remember the day I got laid off. As I entered the shop, I noticed a different air. Everybody was staring at me. Avoiding all eyes, I tried to make myself comfortable. Just then I got a call from the boss. I entered his office. He looked kind of distant. He said slowly, "Yolanda, you lost your job. I am sorry to say that, but you know, dear, how recession is. It is all from head office; there is nothing I could do. Are you listening?," he said. I only heard one thing, "You lost your job!" Having nothing to say, I collected my things and just left without any idea of what I was going to do. At that time, I wanted to leave the United States and return to Mexico. I thought that no dream could be fulfilled in this country. I thought to myself, how am I going to survive here with my little girls without a salary?
>
> *(Focus Group)*

Instead, she decided to find a way to stay in the U.S. in the hopes that her children would do better in the future:

> I was lucky I had family nearby; I shifted to my aunt's house that lived in Cicero [an Illinois suburb near Chicago]. It was months before I could find a new job. But thanks to my skills as a hairdresser and a little bit of savings, I was able to support my girls. After the bad times passed, I started to think that maybe this city can provide dreams to my girls, if not mine. Maybe I am never going to do anything big here, but I shall wait for my girls to grow and do better. I believe they will make their future here. It's for them I had to stay and keep searching for more earnings by any means necessary.
>
> (Focus Group)

Similarly, Juana, a Puerto Rican women also reflected on the meaning of her meager employment in the following quote.

> I had never considered myself lucky that I had so much when others had so little. I suppose I took it for granted. A small house to my name and an ordinary job sorting papers and making calls didn't feel like that much, especially not as a single mother to two teens. But when I lost my job, I started to realize how fortunate I had been.
>
> (Focus Group)

When seen in the larger context of the global financial crisis, for these Latinas, when the jobs disappeared so did the stability and security in their lives. Instead, they found themselves facing a range of insecurities and vulnerabilities, such as losing their home, as evidenced by the following quote from Juana:

> The last drop in the bucket was when my house was foreclosed. We were forced to move. Our new home was a tiny two-bedroom flat in a run-down area, which was all I could afford to rent. My children were forced to attend an equally run-down school where they felt pressured and neglected, and consequently their studies suffered. Over the next couple of years, I worked here and there at temp jobs, but finding reliable work was hard. Eventually, one of my part-time employers hired me full-time.
>
> (Focus Group)

Juana lost her means of making a living and her dream of becoming a homeowner. She could only hope that the dream of having her own house would be fulfilled in Puerto Rico. She still believed that it was important to provide a better future for her kids, and thus, like Yolanda, she decided to stay until they could make it on their own. She continued:

My children finished their studies and managed to get into community college despite their disadvantaged start. I could afford to rent in my old neighborhood again, though I found it hard to settle back in after so long. I just don't feel I belong anymore, because a lot of the people I knew are gone. I won't deny that I am fortunate. It could have been so much worse. But once my children finish school, I just want to get away from here, buy a home in Puerto Rico if I can, and live somewhere nice and quiet under the sun and waves.

(Focus Group)

These two stories are full of ambiguities. While on one hand, these women do not see any value in the cherished notions of the American dream, they still dream and hope that economic opportunities will be there for their children.

Neo-Marxist and Neo-Keynesians saw the crisis of 2008 as one of the many inevitable crises created by capitalism (Harvey 2010). David Harvey argues that economic recessions are inherent components of global capitalism and that many of these crises relate to housing developments, a new area of investment in the current global moment. Harvey offers as a parallel moment the stagflation of the 1970s, which he argues was a neoliberal moment when the deindustrialization of the U.S. created a push toward the commodification (through layoffs and union busting) of labor. As a point of reference, unionized jobs in Illinois fell from 35.6 percent in 1964 to 22.6 percent in 1984 to 18.7 percent in 2000 (Hirsch et al. 2001). In this new environment during the decades following this economic restructuring, housing more than ever became an investment, a means with which to leverage oneself or one's family against unforeseen economic shocks like illness or unemployment. Hence, the collapse of the housing market in the recent global recession can be seen as a manifestation of the liberalization of global markets, not a strange accident.

In 1999, the Glass–Steagall Act was repealed, eroding the distinction between commercial lending and investment banks. The abolition of the Glass–Steagall Act allowed financiers to bundle mortgages into securities, and those mortgages were given to subprime lenders. This securitization made it difficult to tell which of these bundles contained viable investment opportunities and which were full of undue risks—it turns out many of them were the latter. Bundling mortgages into securities and issuing subprime mortgages was an ongoing process, however, and nobody (or at least very few commentators) disputed the irrational exuberance of investors because "we thought that we were all going to benefit" (Balakrishnan 2014). Although everyone knows that bubbles have a tendency to burst, this possibility was largely ignored in favor of blaming low-income workers, many of them Latinas, for wanting to buy homes or the government for providing them with that opportunity.

As a result, in the City of Chicago, 16 percent of all properties holding a mortgage were foreclosed on between 2008 and 2012. This was more than a hundred thousand foreclosures in only four years (Woodstock Institute 2008–2012).

A Mexican woman shared her experience of becoming a homeowner, just to then lose her home shortly thereafter:

> I opened the door of our new house. I saw a clean house with all the amenities —washer, dryer, refrigerator, and dishwasher. Few months back, it all looked like a distant dream. "Oh God, we have waited a long time to reach here," I said to my husband. Having a refrigerator or a washer-dryer at home was a luxury for our family in Mexico. Like many other of my neighborhoods, my husband and I lost the house to foreclosure. Now, when I enter this rental apartment we are living, I see a place that is not mine and has no luxuries here. I cannot help the tears rolling down my cheeks when I think of my old house. I just hope I may have the strength to provide a secure future to my kids that I could never have.
> *(Focus Group)*

The Woodstock Institute also reported that Latinos in Chicago were among those most affected by the financial crisis, as 24 percent of all Latinos were victims of predatory lending. Additionally, Latina women in the Chicago Metropolitan Statistical Area were almost twice as likely as their white counterparts to receive a high-cost loan (National Community Reinvestment Coalition 2009). In 2008, home prices declined sharply, falling to about half of their original value. In aggregate terms, based on data from the Consumer Financial Protection Bureau on the amount of loans taken by Latinos, Latinos in Illinois experienced a total decrease in home value and wealth of close to $21 billion. According to the Pew Hispanic Center, 28 percent of the homes belonging to the Illinois Latino population were under water, meaning that the homeowners owed more than their homes were worth (Taylor 2012). Using data from the Consumer Financial Protection Bureau, we calculate that the net worth lost by residents in Chicago's West Side, where there is a high concentration of Latinos, was 47 percent. A final point, although not directly related to housing finance, is that during the crisis, conditions were so worrisome that a new trend emerged: Mexicans were returning to Mexico. It is estimated that during the recession period, about 280,000 Mexicans a year went back home, where unemployment was about half of that in the United States (Passel et al. 2012; Cafferty 2011).

Methodology

According to the Business Cycle Dating Committee of the National Bureau of Economic Research, the Great Recession lasted from December of 2007 until June 2009. In order to learn about the experiences of Chicago's Mexican and Puerto Rican women during the 2008 economic recession we conducted a focus group with four Mexican and five Puerto Rican women who lived in Chicago. The focus group was conducted June of 2012. Participants were recruited by sending emails to Latino community organizations author's had connections with. Participants were offered $20 for their participation. The focus group took one and a half hours. The conversation was recorded and trancribed.

The following analysis also employs publicly available 2010 U.S. Census data and one-year estimates from the U.S. Census American Community Survey (ACS) between 2005 to 2012 to examine how Puerto Ricans and Mexicans were affected by the Great Recession. Non-Hispanic white and black populations are used as points of comparison. Population data come from the U.S. Census, while socioeconomic data come primarily from the ACS. Although longitudinal data collected over nine years were examined, this analysis focuses on two points in time: 2005, about three years before the recession, and 2012, about three years after the recession. Hereafter, these dates will be referred to as pre-recession (2005) and post-recession (2012).

The labor force participation rate (LFPR), unemployment rate, median earnings, poverty rates for single-woman-headed households with children, and educational attainment are used as measures of the long-term socioeconomic effects of the recession on the various groupings of women. The first three are key indicators of conditions in the labor market. The LFPR is the percentage of people who are available to work—defined as those of working age (sixteen and older) and not attending school. This number represents both employed and unemployed individuals. On the other hand, the unemployment rate is calculated by dividing the number of unemployed by the LFPR. People are included in the unemployment ranks when they are actively trying to find work but have been unable to do so over the past four weeks. This means that individuals who give up looking for work and become discouraged workers will not be reflected in the unemployment rate.

Median earnings are different from income. Earnings take into account only the payments gained from work, either from an employer or self-employment. Only workers 16 years or older who worked full-time year-round are included in this figure. Median earnings would be much lower if this measure also included informal and part-time workers, who tend to be overrepresented by immigrant groups. In addition to these measures that focus mostly on the labor force, this study considers the poverty rates of households headed by single women with children, which are much more vulnerable than other types of families. For all these socioeconomic measures, the ACS uses estimates that are representative of the entire population.

Due to limitations in the publicly available data from the census and the ACS, it was impossible to disaggregate the data to Puerto Ricans and Mexicans born outside of the United States. Nonetheless, it is important to note that emigrants/immigrants are represented in the sample. In 2000 (the last year when this data was reported), there were 45,465 Puerto Ricans in Chicago who were born in Puerto Rico, out of 113,055, that is, about 40 percent (U.S. Census Bureau). Of the total 534,045 Mexicans in the city the same year, 283,531 (53 percent) were foreign-born.

Findings: the effects of the 2008 great recession

Table 15.2 shows that from 2005 to 2012, earnings for full-time white female workers in Chicago increased slightly (by 2 percent) but declined for all women

TABLE 15.2 Socioeconomic changes for women workers from 2005 to 2012

	2005	2012	Net Change from 2005–2012	Percent Change from 2005–2012	White women-gap 2005	White women-gap 2012
2.1 Median Earnings for Female Full-time, Year-round Workers						
Mexican	$27,793	$26,151	-$1,642	-5.91%	0.53	0.49
Puerto Rican	$35,274	$33,105	-$2,169	-6.15%	0.68	0.62
White	$52,248	$53,292	$1,044	2.00%	N/A	N/A
African American	$39,025	$37,682	-$1,343	-3.44%	0.75	0.71
2.2 Women in the Labor Force (ages 16 and older)						
Mexican	51.3	69.4	18.1	35.28%	-13.3	-3.5
Puerto Rican	55.8	62.6	6.8	12.19%	-8.8	-10.3
White	64.6	72.9	8.3	12.85%	N/A	N/A
African American	56.1	57.6	1.5	2.67%	-8.5	15.3
2.3 Women's Unemployment Rate (ages 16 and older)						
Mexican	15.9	14.3	-1.6	-10.06%	10.5	7.7
Puerto Rican	11	19.1	8.1	73.64%	5.6	12.5
White	5.4	6.6	1.2	22.22%	N/A	N/A
African American	18.5	24.8	6.3	34.05%	13.1	18.2
2.4 Poverty Rate for Female-Headed Household, with Children						
Mexican	38.8	47.9	9.1	23.45%	10.1	41.3
Puerto Rican	50.7	43.8	-6.9	-13.61%	22	37.2
White	28.7	20.8	-7.9	-27.53%	N/A	N/A
African American	48.3	54.4	6.1	12.63%	19.6	47.8

of color, and even more so for Latina women. For example, Puerto Ricans' earnings decreased by 6.15 percent, Mexicans' by 5.91 percent, and African Americans' by 3.44 percent. In addition, inequality between Latinas and white women increased slightly between 2005 and 2012. As the "white-gap" column shows in Table 15.2, in 2005, the Mexican earning gap was 53 cents to the dollar of what whites made and 68 cents for Puerto Ricans. In 2012, the gap was wider, at 49 cents and 62 cents, respectively.

Although women of all ethnic and racial groups have increased their labor participation rates, they have done so at different paces. Mexican women joined the labor force at an extraordinary rate. Female labor force participation rate of Mexican women went from 51.3 percent in 2005 to 69.4 percent in 2012, increasing by 18.1 points. While, the female labor force participation rate increased about 12 percent for both Puerto Ricans and whites and 2.7 percent for African Americans. A caveat here is that before the recession, the percentage of Mexican women in the labor force was lower than for any other group, and the racial difference between whites and Mexicans was thus the largest at −13.3 points. By 2012, the white-Mexican difference in labor participation rates had almost closed, which is indicative of a growing attachment to the labor of Mexican workers after the recession years.

Unemployment rates were very high for all minorities both before and after the recession. In 2005, unemployment was 15.9 percent among Mexicans, 11 percent among Puerto Ricans, 18.9 percent among African Americans, and only 5.4 percent among whites. By 2012, after the recession, unemployment had increased among everyone, with the exception of Mexican women. Although in 2012 Mexican women's unemployment rate was still very high (14.3 percent), it was lower than for Puerto Ricans (19.1 percent) and African Americans (24.8 percent). Because the Mexican unemployment rate decreased by 1.6 percent from 2005 to 2012, one can assume that as Mexican women joined the labor force, a large percentage were able to find employment. In comparison, as more Puerto Rican and African American women entered the labor force, many of them encountered rejection in the form of unemployment as a consequence of the recession. For Puerto Rican women, the chances of finding employment became even slimmer, as their unemployment rates almost doubled, from 11 to 19.1 percent. Nonetheless, African Americans still had higher unemployment rates than Latinas, which is evidence of the perceived racial preferences of employers—where Mexicans are believed to be hard workers, Puerto Ricans are right in the middle (often times this would depend on their race), and African Americans are at the bottom of the labor hierarchy (Kirschenman and Neckerman 1991).

During the recession years, poverty among single female-headed households with children increased for both Mexicans and African Americans, while it decreased for Puerto Ricans and whites. At 50.7 percent, Puerto Rican women's pre-recession poverty rate was higher than for any other group in the city. By 2012, Puerto Rican single female-headed households with children experienced a 13.6 percent decrease in poverty. Yet because the poverty rates of white single female-headed households with children experienced a substantial decrease, dropping by 27.53 percent, the relative inequality or white–non-white gap almost doubled for every minority group. The poverty rate for Mexican women with children increased from 38.8 to 47.9 percent. For African American women with children, the poverty rates in 2012, at 54.4 percent, were higher than for any other group of women (see Table 15.2).

Conclusion

This chapter has offered evidence of how gendered and racialized hierarchies have been historically reproduced and how in times of crisis, those hierarchies are exacerbated. As shown above, the crisis had profound consequences for the families and livelihoods of Puerto Rican and Mexican women in the United States. Taken together, these statistics and stories show that Mexican women remained more attached to the wage-labor market than Puerto Rican and African American women and that, because of the demand for low-wage laborers, the percentage of those out of work has decreased. Nonetheless, although Mexican women are gaining more employment in general, they have not experienced any gains in earnings. Since the recession, poverty has increased substantially for Mexican female-headed households with children. The story of Puerto Rican women is slightly different. While more women entered the labor force after the recession, more women have experienced unemployment. In addition, Puerto Rican women's wages have declined at a faster rate than those of any other group. The most positive changes for Puerto Rican female-headed households with children is that they have experienced decreases in poverty levels.

This analysis demonstrates that the experiences of women are varied and continuously in motion. More than ever before, women are part of the labor force, and therefore they have become highly susceptible to such structural changes in the economy as financialization and the boom-bust cycle. Yet some issues remain constant. As shown in this chapter, race and ethnicity are intrinsically linked to socioeconomic status, but both of these hierarchies are also deeply gendered.

Returning to the quotation that opened this chapter, it appears that even though Rita was able develop a skill for "surviving" in her daily life, she worried about those who did not. Rita experience illustrates the important need for policies that would increase redistribution and the social safety net for all Latino women, including Mexican women who are not citizens, many of whom do not have access to federal programs or are not protected by labor laws. Such policies would include as Individual Development Accounts, Earned Income Tax Credits, Head Start, Self-Help Homeownership Opportunity Program, and Emergency Unemployment Compensation. That six in ten minimum-wage workers in Illinois are women shows that the Equal Pay Act and raising the minimum wage

(National Women's Law Center 2014) are fundamental to improving women's work conditions.

Throughout the city, Latinas have been taking part in rallies and campaigns showing their support for raising the minimum wage. As Rita pointed out, maybe it is up to Latina women, the Latino communities, and women of color to "make the difference." In Chicago, Puerto Rican and Mexican women often build alliances to become agents of their own destiny. Together they are taking steps to directly confront structural and gender-based inequities by leading important organizations, such as *Mujeres Latinas en Acción,* a non-profit that empowers women through a multiplicity of legal, educational, and social services. This is to say, gender is and should be an organizing force. Women at the community level have the capacity to solve their own problems and create change individually and as group members. It will take both governmental and community action to effectively respond to problems originating in a global economy that has historically pushed women of color primarily into low-wage and precarious positions of employment in the labor force. If anything, the economic crisis of 2008 made clear to everyone who witnessed its consequences that social reform was urgently needed. Now it is up to policy makers and women of color to actively engage in improving the work-life chances of women, especially women of color.

References

Acker, Joan. "Gender, Capitalism and Globalization." *Critical Sociology* 30, no. 1 (2004): 17–41.

Balakrishnan, Radhika. 2014. "The Financial Crisis, the Global Recession and Women." Rutgers: The International Alliance of Women's Conference.

Betancur, John J. "The Politics of Gentrification: The Case of West Town in Chicago." *Urban Affairs Review* 37, no. 6 (2002): 780–814.

Birson, Kurt, Ramon Borges, and Kofi Ampaabeng. 2013. "The Asset Profile of Puerto Ricans and Latinos after the Great Recession: 2008–2010." Edwin Meléndez and Carlos Vargas-Ramos (eds.). In *Puerto Ricans at the Dawn of the New Millenium.* New York: Centro Press: 164–181.

Cafferty, Jack. 2011. "Illegal Aliens Leaving U.S., Returning to Mexico for Better Life?" August 3, 2014. http://caffertyfile.blogs.cnn.com/2011/08/03/illegal-aliens-leaving-u-s-returning-to-mexico-for-better-life/.

Fernández, Lilia. *Brown in the Windy City: Mexicans and Puerto Ricans in Postwar Chicago.* Chicago: University Of Chicago Press, 2012.

Colón-Warren, A. E., & Alegría-Ortega, I. (1998). Shattering the Illusion of Development: The Changing Status of Women and Challenges for the Feminist Movement in Puerto Rico. *Feminist Review*, *59*(1), 101–117. https://doi.org/10.1080/014177898339488

Gottfried, Heidi. "Gendering Globalization Discourses." *Critical Sociology* 30, no. 1 (2004): 9–15.

Harvey, David. *"Crises of Capitalism." John Adam Street.* London: Royal Society for the encouragement of Arts, Manufactures and Commerce, 2010.

Hirsch, Barry T., David A. Macpherson, and Wayne G. Vroman. "Estimates of Union Density by State." *Monthly Labor Review.* 124 (7), July 2001, 51-55.

Jaggar, Alison M. "Is Globalization Good for Women?". *Comparative Literature* 53, no. 4 (October 1, 2001): 298–314. doi:10.2307/3593521.

Kirschenman, Joleen, and Kathryn N. Neckerman 1991. "'We'd Love to Hire Them But....': The Meaning of Race for Employers." In *The Urban Underclass*. Washington, DC: Brookings Institution Press.

Kochhar, Rachel. *In Two Years of Economic Recovery, Women Lost Jobs, Men Found Them*. Washington, DC: Pew Research Center, Social and Demographic Trends, July 6, 2011.

Nash, June, and Maria Patricia Fernandez-Kelly. *Women, Men, and the International Division of Labor*. Albany: State Univ of New York Press, 1983.

National Community Reinvestment Coalition. *Assessing the Double Burden: Examining Racial and Gender Disparities in Mortgage Lending*. Washington, D.C. Community-Wealth.org, 2009.

National Women's Law Center. "Fair Pay for Women and People of Color in Illinois Requires Increasing the Minimum Wage and Maintaining a Strong Tipped Minimum Wage." National Women's Law Center, April 7, 2014. http://www.nwlc.org/resource/fair-pay-women-and-people-color-illinois-requires-increasing-minimum-wage-and-maintaining-s.

Passel, Jeffrey S., D'Vera Cohn, and Ana Gonzalez-Barrera "Net Migration from Mexico Falls to Zero—And Perhaps Less." *Pew Research Center's Hispanic Trends Project*, 2012.

Perry, Mark J. (2010, July 17). "The Great Mancession of 2008–2009." Retrieved from www.aei.org/speech/100152.

Pissarides, Christopher A. "Unemployment in the Great Recession." *Economica* 80, no. 319 (July 12013): 385–403.

Ríos, Palmira N. "Export-Oriented Industrialization and the Demand for Female Labor: Puerto Rican Women in the Manufacturing Sector, 1952–1980." *Gender & Society* 4, no. 3 (September 1, 1990): 321–337.

Rosenberg, Matt. "It's Where Your Stuff Is Made—What Are the Conditions and Pay in Maquiladoras?" *About.com Geography*, August 23, 2014.

Rúa, Mérida. *Latino Urban Ethnography and the Work of Elena Padilla*. Chicago: University of Illinois Press, 2011.

Salzinger, Leslie. *Genders in Production: Making Workers in Mexico's Global Factories*. Berkeley: University of California Press, 2003.

Safa, Helen Icken. *The Myth of the Male Breadwinner: Women and Industrialization in the Caribbean*. Boulder, CO: Westview Press, 1995.

Sassen, Saskia. *The Global City: New York, London, Tokyo*. 2nd edition. Princeton, NJ: Princeton University Press, 2001.

Taylor, Paul. "III. Latinos and Homeownership." *Pew Research Center Hispanic Trends Project* January 26, 2012. http://www.pewhispanic.org/2012/01/26/iii-latinos-and-home ownership/.

Taylor-Hansen, Lawrence D. "The Origins of the Maquila Industry in Mexico." *Comercio Exterior* 53 (11 November 2003), 1–16.

"The Great Mancession of 2008–2009," July 17, 2010.

Thompson, Derek. "It's Not Just a Recession. It's a Mancession!" *The Atlantic*, July 9, 2009.

Tiano, Susan. *Patriarchy On The Line: Labor, Gender, and Ideology in the Mexican Maquila Industry*. Philadelphia: Temple University Press, 1994.

Toro-Morn, Maura I. "Yo Era Muy Arriesgada: A Historical Overview of the Work Experiences of Puerto Rican Women in Chicago." *Centro Journal* 13, no. 2 (Fall 2001): 24–43.

Toro-Morn, Maura I., and Marixsa Alicea. *Migration and Immigration: A Global View.* Westport, CT: Greenwood Press, 2004.

U.S. Census Bureau. "American Community Survey," http://factfinder2.census.gov/.

U.S. Census Bureau. *Decennial Census.* Summary File 3, 1970–2010. https://www.census.gov/census2000/sumfile3.html

Woodstock Institute. "Foreclosure Updates," 2008–2012. http://www.woodstockinst.org/research/foreclosure-updates.

16
THE ECONOMIC CRISIS AND WOMEN'S PART-TIME WORK IN HUNGARY

Erika Kispeter

Introduction

Women in Hungary, as elsewhere, often seek part-time work to reconcile work and family responsibilities. Unlike in many Western European countries, historically the rate of part-time work in Hungary has been very low. Some argue that low rates of part-time work contribute to the country's large maternal employment gap. During the economic and financial crises the share of part-time employment among women increased a great deal: from 5.8 percent in 2007 to 9.8 percent in 2012 (HCSO 2017). This chapter aims to explore the impact of the crisis on women's work in Hungary at the microlevel, based on qualitative data gathered from focus groups of mothers of young children.

The analysis presented in this chapter complements the existing macrolevel studies on the gendered labor market effects of the crisis in Hungary (European Commission 2013; Frey 2014). Focusing on women's experience of finding employment during the financial crisis and the way they make sense of their work-care decisions, I will discuss how employment opportunities were shaped by the crisis. I will also examine the ways in which the crisis shaped women's gender ideologies, in particular their beliefs about combining paid work and childcare.

The key finding of this study is that a group of mothers, who lived in the more developed areas of Hungary and had access to some formal or informal childcare, benefited from the financial crisis in an unexpected way and found it easier than before to find part-time jobs. These job opportunities were created in reaction to the crisis and national government policy. I argue that the sense of insecurity associated with the crisis shaped women's decisions about paid work and childcare and made it easier for mothers of young children to resist societal pressures and resume work before their children reached the age of three.

The analysis is based on qualitative data, collected in five focus groups, which were conducted in 2013 in a relatively prosperous city in the Western part of Hungary. The city was selected because its local economy was strongly affected by the crisis (HCSO 2010) due to close links between its local manufacturing industry and global companies.[1] Mothers of young children were invited to participate in five focus groups, to which they were assigned according to their current parental leave status and formal educational qualifications. The groups included a total of thirty-one women, with the youngest participant in her early twenties and the oldest in her forties. Of these, fourteen women worked part-time or flexible hours during or immediately after their parental leave; some of them were employed formally, while others worked informally and received cash-in-hand payments.

Participants were initially recruited via local civil society organizations that organize activities for children and families or support parents. The discussions were audio recorded and transcribed verbatim. I read, reread, and coded the Hungarian language texts until patterns emerged. All translations in this chapter are mine. Names and some personal details have been changed to protect participants' privacy.

Theoretical considerations: mothers' paid work

In this section I will draw on two closely linked bodies of scholarship: theories of mothers' inclusion in the labor market and debates about women's work-care decisions. I will include literature that is specific to Hungary or the wider post-state socialist context.

Feminist scholarship on gender and work has shown that mothers of young children may be excluded from or marginalized in paid work because they do not conform to the norm of the "ideal worker," one who is free of caregiving responsibilities (Acker 1990; Hochschild 1997, 2005). At the same time, in certain feminized segments of the labor market, mothers may be the preferred choice of employers: as Rubery and Wilkinson argue, "the domestic circumstances of married women" make this group a source of flexible, cheap, yet committed labor (1994, 31–32).

In all state-socialist societies, mothers' participation in paid work was the norm: it was, in fact, an important element of the Marxist-Leninist project of women's emancipation and the state's commitment to full employment (Fodor 2003; Molyneux 1981; Zimmermann 2010). To reconcile the demands that full-time paid work and caring for young children place on women, an extended maternity leave (until the child's third birthday) with a job guarantee was introduced in Hungary in the late 1960s. Although this later became a gender-neutral parental leave policy, it continues to be used almost exclusively by mothers. Paid child-care leave days are also available for parents to look after their children when they are sick. These "maternalist" policies (Haney 2002) supported women's inclusion in the workforce, but at the same time contributed to their segregated and inferior position in terms of pay, prestige, and access to managerial authority (Fodor 2003), constructing women as "worker-mothers" rather than "workers" (Einhorn 1993, 40; Haney 2002).

After the collapse of state socialism the existing maternalist work-family policies remained in effect in Hungary.[2] In addition, a new, even longer parental leave was introduced and central government support for day care for children under the age of three was withdrawn in an attempt to reduce unemployment by withdrawing mothers of young children from the labor market (Kampichler and Kispeter 2014).

Although parental leave regulations continue to include a job guarantee, employers in the private sector now have considerable freedom in hiring and firing decisions, and rampant discrimination against mothers of young children emerged in the post-socialist period (Blaskó 2011; Glass and Fodor 2011; Szalai 2006). This is exacerbated by the fact that hiring and dismissing employees in Hungary is relatively easy and inexpensive, according to an international comparison (Cazes and Nesporova 2007). The maternalist policies are often quoted by employers as justification for not hiring mothers of young children, who they claim are less reliable and more costly employees than men or childless women (Glass and Fodor 2011). Part-time work, a common method of work-family reconciliation, remains rare in Hungary although research has demonstrated that middle managers and more senior staff may be allowed to work part-time or to work from home when their children are young, as companies are keen to retain their trusted employees (Glass and Fodor 2011; Oborni 2009).

In countries where child-care services and other work-care supports are not available, part-time employment has played a key role in promoting mothers' paid work (Hegewisch and Gornick 2011). However, in countries where good quality childcare is available and affordable, there is no clear link between motherhood and part-time work (Lyonette 2015). Rates of part-time work among employed women vary widely, from over 70 percent in the Netherlands and almost 50 percent in Germany to around 10 percent in Hungary and Poland in 2015 (Eurostat Database 2017).

Part-time workers often have a segregated or even marginalized position in the workforce, characterized by poor work conditions and low pay (Grimshaw and Rubery 2007). Among those with higher educational qualifications, part-time work often involves "working under potential," as part-time jobs typically are not available at senior levels (Grant et al. 2005). However, many women say they like working part-time (e. g. Scott and Dex 2009). A study conducted in Hungary in the early 2000s found that a quarter of women outside the labor force and 18 percent of those on parental leave said they would resume work if they could take a part-time job (Frey 2002). A recent qualitative study found that lacking reliable, accessible and affordable childcare, Hungarian mothers of young children could not meet the demands of full-time, inflexible jobs on offer in the formal labor market and they turned to informal work (Fodor and Kispeter 2014).

The second body of scholarship relevant to the analysis in this chapter is about women's work-care decisions. After long debates about women's so-called "choices" between paid work and family responsibilities (e. g. Hakim 2002, 2003; Crompton and Lyonette 2007), there is consensus in the research community that work-care decisions are influenced by multiple structural and interactional factors as well as an individual's gender ideology. In other words, mothers' decisions are necessarily constrained. The concept of gender strategy, defined as an attempt to implement one's gender ideology in everyday life, given the opportunities and constraints (Hochschild 1989) is very useful when analyzing such decisions.

Hungarians hold rather conservative gender ideologies (Blaskó 2005; Takács 2008). Takács et al. (2011) have shown that among the seventeen European societies they examined, Hungary was the only one where traditional attitudes to the gender division of labor did not decline between 2005 and 2010. Furthermore, while employees in most countries started to attribute higher value to the security of employment over this time period, employed women in Hungary continued to value the work-family balance aspect of jobs above all else. Regarding the employment of mothers with small children, "maternalist" parental leave policies and the gender ideology embedded in them, which focuses only on children's assumed needs, have mutually strengthened each other over the decades, establishing the "magical" status of children's third birthday and naturalizing the belief that children are not ready for day care before this age (Szikra and Haskova 2012). Blaskó (2011) has shown that while individual mothers do not necessarily share this maternalist gender ideology, it provides the discursive framework in which most work-care decisions are made, and mothers who take shorter parental leaves also make sense of their decisions by referring to their children's needs.

The Hungarian labor market and policy context

Women's position in the labor market

In the transition from a centrally planned to a market economy in the early 1990s, over a million jobs were lost—more than 20 percent of the total employment of Hungary at the time. Men and women were affected by these losses relatively equally (Frey 2014), but women's position in the labor market was weakened further by the backlash against their state socialist emancipation (Frey 2014).

In 2007, just before the financial and economic crisis hit Hungary, women's employment rate[3] was 51 percent, lower than the OECD average (57 percent) (OECD 2013). However, the female full-time equivalent employment rate (50 percent) was almost equal to the OECD figure (51 percent) for the same year, which indicates that the relatively few employed women worked long hours (OECD Database 2017). In 2012, immediately after the crisis, women's employment rate was slightly higher at 52 percent but the full-time equivalent rate did not change, which also shows that the women who entered the labor force tended to work fewer hours.

The "maternal employment gap," defined as the difference between the employment rate of women aged 25–49 years with at least one child below the age of 12 and their counterparts without such children was 29.9 percentage points in Hungary in 2010—the largest in the European Union (Miani and Hoorens 2014). This sizable gap is likely to be caused by the lack of child-care services and jobs suitable for mothers of young children as well as the maternalist gender ideology.

Parental leaves and public childcare services

New mothers who were employed before the birth of their child are entitled to a twenty-four-week paid maternity leave and to receive 70 percent of their previous pay. After this period, either parent (provided they are employed) is entitled to the insurance-based parental leave until the child's second birthday and to receive 70 percent of their former pay (with a rather low cap of twice the minimum wage). After the child's second birthday, either parent can take the universal parental leave, with a flat-rate benefit that equals the amount of the minimum old age pension. Uninsured parents can claim the universal parental leave and benefit from the birth of the child. Parents who raise three or more children can extend the universal parental leave with the flat-rate benefit until the youngest child reaches the age of eight—many Hungarians refer to this type of parental leave as "full-time motherhood."

Parents are allowed to work part-time while on parental leave (after the child's first birthday), but very few of them do (HCSO 2011), arguably because there are few day-care places for children under the age of three, especially in rural areas, and part-time jobs are rare. Most mothers take long parental leaves: about 10 percent of working-age women are on parental leave and counted in official statistics as outside the labor market. At the same time, less than 1 percent of those on parental leave are fathers (Frey 2014).

Publicly funded nursery places for children under the age of three are concentrated in cities, especially in the capital. About 10 percent of children between the ages of one to three are in nurseries, but almost none under the age of one (HCSO 2012).

The crisis and the reorganization of work hours

Hungary was strongly affected by the crisis (Karamessini 2014), which reached the banking sector of the country in autumn 2008. Employment began to decline at the end of 2008: in the first phase, primarily skilled male workers in the automotive, manufacturing, and construction sectors lost their jobs. By the end of 2010, the female employment rate had already reached its pre-crisis level, while that of men's remained significantly below its pre-crisis level (Frey 2014). Female employment rates bounced back due to a decrease in the number of women outside the labor market. Labor economists argue that this suggests an added worker effect: the labor supply of married women increased because their husbands became unemployed.

To cut labor costs, companies tended to freeze wages and reduce working hours in addition to layoffs. The two governments in office during the crisis (2006–2010 and 2010–2014) introduced a number of policies to mitigate the employment effects of the crisis. Employers who committed to keeping their staff, reduce working hours and use the "idle" time for training were given financial support (Hijzen and Venn 2011). This policy affected employed men and women alike. The second set of policies were aimed at mothers of young children: employers who rehired parents (in practice, mothers) returning from parental leave were also given financial support (Szikra 2013) and since 2010 public sector employers have been under a legal obligation to offer part-time jobs for employees raising a child under three (Frey 2014). It is important to emphasize that these policies have not been motivated by the goal of promoting gender equality but rather by policy makers' desire to increase the birth rate by making it easier for mothers to combine paid work and raising a family.

The share of part-time work among all employees rose during the crisis: among female employees, from 5.8 percent in 2007 to 9.8 percent in 2012 (HCSO 2017).

Analysis

In this section, I analyze the focus group data, starting with the impact of the crisis on women's paid work and their work-care decisions and outlining some of their stories and reactions. Then I discuss how the women talked about their decisions: what arguments they used and what discourses they drew on. Finally, I outline how women talked about the influence of their partners on their work-care decisions. When analyzing how the women explained their decisions about combining paid work and childcare, it is important to bear in mind that the different arguments I have identified were closely intertwined, as it will be clear from the quotations.[4]

The impact of the crisis on women's work-care decisions

Some focus group participants reported work-care decisions that were directly linked to the financial crisis: women decided to go back to work because they had foreign currency bank loans, and as the Hungarian forint became very weak, their monthly mortgage payments skyrocketed.[5] Mariann, for instance, did not feel ready to go back to work, but her earnings were needed. She is working full-time, but from home:

> It is very difficult to work from home. In fact, I only chose to do it because the mortgage was about as much as my parental leave pay. We were living

on my partner's salary, and after a year it was quite hard. So really, it was a necessity... I went back to work, but I am working from home.
(Mariann, Focus Group 2 [9 March 2013])

When she started work, however, she realized that it was very important for her to regain her financial independence: "When the first month ended, it was like coming up from under water. I didn't go shopping immediately, but it was great to know that I could." (Mariann, Focus Group 2 [9 March 2013]).

Nelli said that they could have continued to live on her husband's salary despite the mortgage, but she decided to go back to work (part-time) because she needed her financial independence:

It drove me mad... The parental leave pay arrived in my bank account, and it went on immediately to pay the mortgage, and then my balance was almost zero... My husband kept telling me that I should tell him if I needed money, which really got to me... I felt so dependent... He is the more dominant person in our relationship anyway, and this made it worse.
(Nelli, Focus Group 2 [March 9 2013])

Timea was working from home to supplement the parental leave pay, but the work was drying up after the crisis hit local businesses. Luckily, she managed to find a part-time job and soon realized that she preferred going out to work. Her only complaint was that she was expected to work long hours: "I officially work six hours, but it's always more than six." She was conscious of the time she spent at work not only because she wanted to spend more time with her family, but also because she continued to do ad hoc jobs from home to supplement her part-time salary: "I also do some extra work, so that we are financially secure." (Timea, Focus Group 3, [11 March 2013]) This example shows that women may be reluctant to give up their informal "mini jobs" (Fodor and Kispeter 2014) even when formal employment is available.

The women quoted above decided to take up part-time or flexible work due to financial pressure, but discovered that they enjoyed their financial independence and the experience of leaving the home after years of parental leave.

The impact of the crisis through the employers

While many companies dismissed workers or at least did not hire new ones during the economic crisis, some employers decided that taking back women after the parental leave might benefit their business. The women whose stories are discussed below were already well known to their managers and had established a working relationship with them prior to the parental leave. In addition, as mentioned above, special policies were introduced during the crisis that provided financial incentives to companies if they hired parents returning from leaves.

Nora wanted to stay at home for three years with her children, but when she received a call from her employer asking her to resume work, she said yes, as long as she could work part-time. This way she could remain on parental leave but also keep her job:

> I got a call, and they told me that I can go back, but I was only two years into the parental leave. At first, I didn't know what to do. I could have stayed at home, but what if they won't take me back in a year's time?... So ... I told the HR manager that I can work four hours a day and we'll see how the children put up with it.
>
> *(Nora, Focus Group 1, [9 March 2013])*

She was satisfied with this decision and now wanted to work six-hours days. Nelli was the only mother in the focus groups who wanted to return before the parental leave ended and was very happy to hear that her manager wanted her back, especially as she was offered reduced working hours. She suspected that she got the job because her manager wanted to take advantage of a recently introduced government policy:

> This "workplace protection action plan"[6] ... was certainly beneficial for me... When we sat down with my boss to see whether I can return or not, he said he would consider it, and then a couple of months later he said there was a four-hour position. He said that ... there was a budget only for four hours, and I said, that's great!
>
> *(Nelli, Focus Group 2, [9 March 2013])*

Regardless of what motivated her manager to offer a part-time position, Nelli felt very lucky with the part-time offer.

Renata was convinced that she was offered a job because the company could save on the social insurance contributions, which reduced the costs of employing her. She was the only person on the shop floor of the local company to have a part-time job:

> A friend took my CV to the production manager and recommended me. Then I was called in to do a test, and I did okay, but I didn't hear from them for weeks. When they finally called me, they said I could have a job working twenty hours a week.
>
> *(Renata, Focus Group 4, [13 January 2014])*

While the women above felt happy about resuming work before they used all their parental leave, Dori felt coerced into work. She told us that her manager had unexpectedly asked her to return from parental leave, adding that if she did not take this opportunity, she would lose her job. Dori went back to work because she knew that finding another job, especially a part-time one, would be very challenging:

> My boss told me that either I go back to work now, or I don't have to go back at all. At the end of the day, it is fantastic that I can work six hours a day, but my daughter is passed from one grandparent to the other, because we didn't get a kindergarten place. She's really unhappy, but there is nothing I can do about it, unfortunately.
>
> *(Dori, Focus Group 3, [11 March 2013])*

Even though her manager's behavior was against the Labor Code, Dori blamed the state for her situation, arguing that she had to take her employer's offer because the low parental leave benefit did not allow her to stay at home longer: "And the state doesn't help much either, with the parental leave benefit. So it's really not great at the moment." (Dori, Focus Group 3, [11 March 2013]) In contrast, a few women said they were happy to be on parental leave and receive the benefit, as their jobs were lost due to the economic crisis: "The crisis did not help jewelry shops, a lot of them closed down. Now I'm on parental leave, but I don't know what job I will find and where." (Anna, Focus Group 3, [11 March 2013])

Others were affected by the crisis through their husbands' losing their jobs or having their working hours and earnings reduced, which put pressure on the women to become "breadwinners." Emma was employed in the third year of her parental leave, earning the minimum wage. Her partner, who had a well-paid job in a local factory, often made fun of her because she earned so little. Emma was planning to reduce her working hours at least for a few months when their daughter started kindergarten (after attending the nursery), to help the child adapt to the change:

> The kindergarten opens at 7:30, and I have to start work at 7:00. So I didn't know how to drop her off in the morning. I thought I would ask if I can work part-time for a few months, until she gets used to the new place.
>
> *(Emma, Focus Group 4, [13 January 2014])*

Then her husband suddenly lost his job, and Emma became the sole earner in the family. Although her husband soon found another though less well-paid job, Emma did not ask for a reduced hours contract but continued to work full-time and paid a babysitter (from her minimum wage) to help out in the mornings. She seemed to have learned that she could not count on her partner's income and became more committed to her own job.

Kinga learned a different lesson when she faced the insecurity of her husband's job, stating that the parental leave benefit was much more reliable than wages:

> I think the main advantage of social benefits is that they are reliable. Your husband's job is not secure, but you can rely on the parental leave benefit: it will arrive on your account for two years, every month. Nowadays, this is a major advantage.
>
> *(Kinga, Focus Group 3, [11 March 2013])*

Most of the women quoted in this section took up jobs during the economic crisis despite their preferences. In other words, they have responded to the changing circumstances by changing their gender strategy: they still believed that the extended parental leave is the best for children, but they adapted their behavior. Some of them felt coerced into work but their anger was not directed at their employers, rather at the state which did not offer a parental leave benefit that would be a good alternative to their wages.

In the next section, I will highlight a few examples where women talked about how their partners were involved in their decisions concerning combining paid work and childcare.

The influence of partners on work-care decisions

Nelli and her husband agreed that it was a good idea for Nelli to work for pay, but the husband insisted that self-employment was the best option, while she argued, based on her own negative experience, that it was not right for her:

> My husband is still pushing me to be self-employed, because he is convinced that it's good for a mother. [He says that] "You can go home whenever you want, you can work whenever you want and you can schedule your own time." I don't think it is like that at all. When you are working from home, can you tell your children to play quietly?... My son is hanging around my neck all the time. I can't even write a single letter.
>
> (Nelli, Focus Group 2, [9 March 2013])

Other women mentioned that their partner or husband was concerned about losing his job and "encouraged" the woman to start earning while on parental leave. Erika told us that her husband kept suggesting that she should go back to work. She agreed with him that they needed more money and that she might be happier if she worked. As she explained, "My husband would like me to work part-time, for financial reasons and because he thinks it would make me happier. It's been too long, three years at home." (Erika, Focus Group 3, [11 March 2013]) However, she was not yet ready to go back, partly because she felt that her children benefitted from having a stay-at-home mother and partly because she did not want to take any odd job that did not match her qualifications: "I have invested a lot in my studies; I am a dance therapist and I want to work as a dance therapist. This is what I like. I do not want to be a self-employed consultant." (Erika, Focus Group 3, [11 March 2013]) She felt it was better to invest in further training, hoping that she would find a job that she likes at the end of the parental leave.

Only one mother mentioned that her partner actively supported her return to paid work by sharing childcare. Adel's husband took the last year of parental leave with their son while she went back to a full-time job:

> When I went back to work, my husband was there, he was willing to take parental leave. Not all men are capable of this, and with the older children he wasn't, either. But he was there for our son from the age of two to three.... That's how I could become an employee again, working from 8:00 to 4:00.
>
> *(Adel, Focus Group 2, [9 March 2013])*

It is somewhat ironic that despite all the praise for flexible and part-time working options, Adel was happy to resume a regular full-time job when her husband was willing to share the child-care responsibilities.

So far the analysis has concentrated on how women responded to labor market changes during the crisis. Many of the quotes above include references to why and how they made decisions. I will now discuss how the women made sense of the developments.

Arguments used when talking about work-care decisions

Based on the discussion above, it is safe to argue that the hightened risk of unemployment and the anxiety related to the austerity measures made the employed women in our study feel insecure about their financial situation and their employment options. In response, some of them resumed work earlier than planned while others came to appreciate their existing jobs more. Nora, seemed grateful to her employer for giving her a job at all, despite her two young children: "I really like my job because they don't mind that I have two kids and I'm raising them alone.... The company is very understanding, or rather, my managers are, so I can't complain." (Nora, Focus Group 1, [9 March 2013])[7]

Yet women's ideas about good mothering did not change overnight, and despite the economic crisis, they considered paid work acceptable only as long as it didn't "harm" their children. Veronika stated clearly that money was important but that, for her, the children came first:

> When you have children, you need more money, but it is very important [to decide] how much you can work, how you can fit in work. I have three kids and they come first, so I can only work part-time. Motherhood is my full-time job, and work is part-time.
>
> *(Veronika, Focus Group 1, [9 March 2013])*

Timea, a professional woman who wanted to start work during the parental leave also emphasized that it should not "harm" the child: "It's best to start work gradually, [to get] some extra money and some experience. This would not be harmful to the child." (Timea, Focus Group 3, [11 March 2013])

Apart from financial pressure and employment insecurity, when talking about their decisions to resume paid work, many of them referred to the tenet of popular psychology that only a happy woman can be a good mother. Women with lower- and higher-level qualifications stated that paid work makes them happy and improves their mental health:

> I know that work is good for me, or doing things that I like is good for me, and if it's good for me, it's good for the child, too. Even if I spend less time with them, they get a mother who is in better mental health. I can be myself with them.
>
> *(Adel, Focus Group 2, [9 March 2013])*

In this framework, paid work is seen as something that mothers do for themselves and that makes them happier, which is also good for their children.

Another argument that many women in our study relied on when talking about their decision to resume paid work was that it provided them with "self-realization." When Mariann, a professional, explained what she missed when not working, she said, "What I was missing the most was a sense of success and a sense of cooperation." (Mariann, Focus Group 2, [9 March 2013])

Arguments about work being good for mothers and a form of self-realization, were interconnected and both were linked to the argument about children coming first, as the following quotation from Timea illustrates:

> If I could work legally ... in a way that does not take time from the children ... that would be great. It would keep my brain active, and I would ... meet other people and use my creativity, my adult creativity. And when it's the end of the [parental leave], I could say, yes, it's me who did all these things.
>
> *(Timea, Focus Group 3, [11 March 2013])*

All the arguments quoted were concerned with combining work and motherhood. Another important aspect of women's gender ideologies is their beliefs about the gender division of labor with their partner. While many women criticized their partners for not sharing housework, only one of them referred to the link between her unpaid work in the household and her partner's ability to devote himself fully to his career. Anita argued that women who were fully responsible for childcare and the household because their partners worked in demanding and well-paid positions should not depend on their husbands' earnings. Rather, she claimed, the state should acknowledge their work and compensate them, interestingly, not for their care work, but for the sacrifice they make by giving up their own careers for their families. When she argued against the patriarchal arrangement of the wife depending on her husband financially, Anita referred to a woman's right to self-realization through paid work:

> For those women who are at home to ensure the background for their husband who has a high-level position and high salary, it shouldn't be

the husband who gives them a monthly allowance for caregiving but the state. ... The state should honor it to some extent that the woman pushes herself into the background for a few years.

(Anita, Focus Group 2, [9 March 2013])

Conclusion

This chapter has explored the ways in which the economic crisis has impacted mothers' decisions about combining paid work and childcare in a Hungarian city, focusing on women's working arrangements and the way they talked about and made sense of their decisions. As it has shown, the economic crisis opened opportunities for some mothers of young children to engage in part-time or flexible forms of paid work, a development that was the outcome of several factors, including government policies and employers' interest in reducing labor capacity and costs.

The economic crisis motivated some mothers who were on parental leave to look for jobs and reconsider their beliefs about ideal mothering, and while some women in this study felt pressured to give up full-time childcare and work for pay, most of them found something positive about their jobs in addition to their earnings.

The majority of the women interviewed for this research were happy to work part-time or from home because it made work-care reconciliation, especially child-care arrangements, easier for them. Part-time work also fit with the motherhood ideologies of these women, most of whom believed that their children would suffer harm if they worked full-time when the children were still very young. Their gender ideology remained unchanged, but they adapted their gender strategy to the new circumstances.

When making decisions regarding paid work and childcare, the children's well-being was the most important factor. Arguments linking maternal well-being to work were also invoked, and paid work was often discussed as something that the mothers enjoy and chose to do for themselves. Professional mothers tended to emphasize the self-realization aspect of their paid work over their earnings.

Overall, I argue that this group of mothers, who lived in the more developed areas of Hungary and had access to some formal or informal childcare, benefitted from the financial crisis in an unexpected way and found it easier than before to find part-time, flexible employment. The analysis highlighted the "path dependency" of women's relationship to paid work (Pfau-Effinger 1998): the long parental leave policy which originates in state socialist policymaking had a very strong influence on women's practices and beliefs and many of them felt that it was ultimately the responsibility of the state and not that of employers to support women in combining work and childcare.

The analysis also revealed that women's relationship to paid work and their gender ideologies are shifting: they are shaped by the available employment opportunities and the wider labor market context.

Although motherhood ideologies change slowly, the general sense of insecurity associated with the financial and economic crisis made it easier for mothers to resist societal pressures and resume work before their children reach the age of three. In other words, the economic crisis shaped the ideological context in which their work-care decisions were made.

Notes

1 The city was included in the European Commission-funded project 'FLOWS: impact of local welfare systems on female labor force participation and social cohesion' as the Hungarian case study.
2 This was not the case with all post-socialist countries: the maternalist arm of the welfare state has been largely dismantled in Poland (Glass and Fodor, 2007).
3 Defined as a proportion of employed women of all women aged 15–64.
4 Several other types of arguments were made about paid work and childcare, but here I concentrate on those that were related to the economic crisis.
5 The devaluation of the Hungarian currency (forint) meant that those who had taken out foreign currency loans started to be charged very high monthly mortgage payments.
6 The government policy which offered financial support to employers who rehired parents returning from leave.
7 This comment illustrates how natural it seems to have become to mothers of young children that they are routinely discriminated against in the labor market; see Glass and Fodor (2011).

References

Acker, Joan. 1990. "Hierarchies, Jobs, Bodies: A Theory of Gendered Organizations." *Gender and Society* 4(2): 139–158.
Blaskó, Zsuzsa. 2005. "Dolgozzanak-e a nők? A magyar lakosság nemi szerepekkel kapcsolatos véleményének változásai, 1988, 1994, 2002" (Should Hungarian Women Work? Changes Concerning the Opinion of the Hungarian Population on Gender Roles, 1988, 1994, 2002). *Demográfia* 48(2–3): 259–287.
Blaskó, Zsuzsa. 2011. "Hároméves kor alatt mindenképpen megsínyli? Interjús kutatás kisgyermekes anyák körében" (Is it Always Harmful to the Child under the Age of Three? Interviews with Mothers of Young Children). In *Szerepváltozások. Jelentés a nők és férfiak helyzetéről 2011*, ed. Ildikó Nagy and Tiborné Pongrácz. Budapest: TÁRKI, 156–170.
Cazes, Sandrine and Alena Nesporova. 2007. *Flexicurity: A Relevant Approach in Central and Eastern Europe*. Geneva: International Labour Office.
Collection of Focus Group Discussions. Conducted by Erika Kispeter, Eva Fodor and Dorottya Redai. March–December 2013. *Transcripts of the Discussions Are in the Author's Possession*.
Crompton, Rosemary, and Clare Lyonette. 2007. "Reply to Hakim." *The British Journal of Sociology* 58: 133–134.

Einhorn, Barbara. 1993. *Cinderella Goes to Market: Citizenship, Gender, and Women's Movements in East Central Europe.* London: Verso.
European Commission. 2013. *The Impact of the Economic Crisis on the Situation of Women and Men and on Gender Equality Policies.* Luxembourg: Publications Office of the European Union.
Eurostat Database. 2017. "Part-time Employment as Percentage of the Total Employment by Sex and Age [lfsa_eppga]." Available online: http://ec.europa.eu/eurostat/data/database.
Fodor, Eva. 2003. *Working Difference: Women's Working Lives in Hungary and Austria 1945-1995.* Durham: Duke University Press.
Fodor, Eva, and Erika Kispeter. 2014. "Making the 'Reserve Army' Invisible: Lengthy Parental Leave and Women's Economic Marginalisation in Hungary." *European Journal of Women's Studies* 21(4): 382–398.
Frey, Maria. 2002. "A gyermeknevelési támogatásokat igénybe vevő inaktív személyek foglalkoztatásának lehetőségei és akadályai" (Opportunities and Obstacles to Employing Inactive Persons on Parental Leave). *Demográfia* 45(4): 406–438.
Frey, Maria. 2014. "The Labour Market Impact of the Economic Crisis in Hungary through the Lens of Gender Equality." In *Women and Austerity: The Economic Crisis and the Future for Gender Equality*, ed. Maria Karamessini and Jill Rubery. Oxon: Routledge, 144–164.
Glass, Christy and Eva, Fodor. 2007. "From public to private maternalism? Gender and Welfare in Poland and Hungary after 1989." *Social Politics* 14(3): 323–350.
Glass, Christy, and Eva Fodor. 2011. "Public Maternalism Goes to Market: Recruitment, Hiring and Promotion in Postsocialist Hungary." *Gender and Society* 25(5): 5–26.
Grant, Linda, Sue Yeandle, and Lisa Buckner. 2005. *Working below Potential: Women and Part-Time Work.* Manchester: Equal Opportunities Commission.
Grimshaw, David, and Jill Rubery. 2007. *Undervaluing Women's Work.* Manchester: Equal Opportunities Commission.
Hakim, Catherine. 2002. "Lifestyle Preferences as Determinants of Women's Differentiated Labour Market Careers." *Work and Occupations* 29: 428–459.
Hakim, Catherine. 2003. *Models of the Family in Modern Societies: Ideals and Realities.* Aldershot: Ashgate.
Haney, Lynne. 2002. *Inventing the Needy: Gender and the Politics of Welfare in Hungary.* Berkeley: University of California Press.
Hegewisch, Ariane and Janet Gornick. 2011. "The Impact of Work-family Policies on Women's Employment: A Review of Research from OECD Countries. Community." *Work & Family* 14(2): 119–138.
Hijzen, Alexander, and Danielle Venn. 2011. *The Role of Short-Time Work Schemes during the 2008–09 Recession.* OECD Social, Employment and Migration Working Papers, No. 115. Paris: OECD Publishing.
Hochschild, Arlie. 1989. *The Second Shift: Working Parents and the Revolution at Home.* New York, NY: Viking.
Hochschild, Arlie. 1997. *The Time Bind: When Work Becomes Home and Home Becomes Work.* New York, NY: Metropolitan/Holt.
Hochschild, Arlie. 2005. "On the Edge of the Time Bind: Time and Market Culture." *Social Research* 72(2): 339–354.
Hungarian Central Statistical Office (HCSO). 2010. *A válság hatása a munkaerőpiacra.* (The Labour Market Effects of the Global Economic Crisis). Budapest: HCSO. Available online: http://www.ksh.hu/docs/hun/xftp/idoszaki/pdf/valsagmunkaeropiacra.pdf.

Hungarian Central Statistical Office (HCSO). 2011. *Munkavégzés és családi kötöttségek* (Paid Work and Care Responsibilities). Budapest: HCSO. Available online: http://www.ksh.hu/docs/hun/xftp/idoszaki/pdf/munkavegzescsalad.pdf.

Hungarian Central Statistical Office (HCSO). 2012. *Kisgyermekek napközbeni ellátása (Daycare for young children)*. Budapest: HCSO. Available online: http://www.ksh.hu/docs/hun/xftp/stattukor/kisgyermnapkozbeni/kisgyermnapkozbeni.pdf.

Hungarian Central Statistical Office (HCSO). 2017. STADAT Database. Table 2.1.11."Foglalkoztatottak száma rész- vagy teljes munkaidős foglalkozásuk szerint, nemenként (The Number of Employed People by Part- and Full-Time Employment and Sex)." Available online: http://www.ksh.hu/docs/hun/xstadat/xstadat_eves/i_qlf008.html.

Kampichler, Martina, and Erika Kispeter. 2014. "Public Maternalism in the Czech Republic and Hungary: Work Family Policies in Two Post-socialist Welfare States", *Socio.hu: The sociological aspects of Central Europe*. Available online: http://www.socio.hu/en/visegrad-issue.

Karamessini, Maria. 2014. "Introduction – Women's Vulnerability to Recession and Austerity: A Different Crisis, a Different Context." In *Women and Austerity: The Economic Crisis and the Future for Gender Equality*, ed. Maria Karamessini and Jill Rubery. Oxon: Routledge, 144–164.

Lyonette, Clare. 2015. "Part-time Work, Work-life Balance and Gender Equality." *Journal of Social Welfare and Family Law* 37(3): 321–333.

Miani, Celine, and Stijn Hoorens. 2014. *Parents at Work: Men and Women Participating in the Labour Force. Short Statistical Report 2*. Luxembourg: The Publication Office of the European Union.

Molyneux, Maxine. 1981. "Women in Socialist Societies: Problems of Theory and Practice." In *Of Marriage and the Market: Women's Subordination in an International Perspective*, ed. Kate Young, Carol Wolkowitz, and Roslyn McCullagh. London: Routledge.

Oborni, Katalin. 2009. *Imaginary Advantage – Invisible Exploitation in Part-time Work Positions at a Corporate Company in Hungary*. MA Thesis. Budapest: Central European University, Department of Gender Studies.

OECD. 2013. "Employment Rate of Women", *Employment and Labour Markets: Key Tables from OECD*, No. 5. Available online: http://dx.doi.org/10.1787/emp-fe-table-2013-1-en.

OECD Database. 2017. "Full-time Equivalent Employment Rate, by Sex." Available online: http://stats.oecd.org/index.aspx?queryid=54749.

Pfau-Effinger, Birgit. 1998. "Culture or Structure as Explanations for Differences in Part-time Work in Germany, Finland and the Netherlands?" In *Part-Time Prospects; Part-Time Employment in Europe, North America and the Pacific Rim*, ed. Colette Fagan and Jacqueline O'Reilly. London: Routledge, 177–198.

Rubery, Jill and Frank Wilkinson. 1994. "Introduction." In *Employer Strategy and the Labour Market*, ed. Jill Rubery. Oxford: Oxford University Press.

Scott, Jacqueline and Shirley Dex. 2009. "Paid and Unpaid Work: Can olicy Improve Gender Inequalities?" In *Sharing Lives, Dividing Assets: An Interdisciplinary Study*, ed. Joanna Miles and Rebecca Probert. Oxford: Hart, 41–60.

Szalai, Erzsébet. 2006. "Tőke-munka viszony és hatalmi szerkezet a magyarországi újkapitalizmusban." (Labor-Capital Relations in Hungarian New Capitalism). In *Társadalmi metszetek: Hatalom, érdek, individualizáció és egyenlőtlentség a mai Magyarországon*, ed. Imre Kovách. Budapest: Napvilág, 349–374.

Szikra, Dorottya. 2013. *Austerity Politics and Gender Impacts in Hungary*. Budapest: Friedrich Ebert Stiftung.

Szikra, Dorottya and Hana Haskova. 2012. "How Did We get the 'Magic 3? The Timing of Parental Leaves and Child Care Services." Paper Presented at the Workshop 'The Impact of Day Care Services for Children in the Visegrad Countries', Budapest, March 30–31.

Takács, Judit 2008. "Ha a mosogatógép nem lenne, már elváltunk volna" (If it Was not for the Dishwasher, We Would be Divorced by Now: Gender Division of Domestic Labor in International Comparison). *Esély* 19(6): 51–73.

Takács, Judit, Ivett Szalma, and Bernadett Szél. 2011. "Gender Role Related Attitudes before and during the Crisis." Paper Presented at the Conference "Crisis and Renewal: Welfare States, Democracy and Equality in Hard Times." Reykjavik, June 2–3.

Zimmermann, Susan. 2010. "Gender Regime and Gender Struggle in Hungarian State Socialism." *Aspasia* 4(1): 1–24.

17
GENDERED AUSTERITY POLICIES
Inequality on the rise in the European Union including Ireland

Ursula Barry

Debate on the economic crisis in the European Union (EU) has focused on the financial and banking crisis, contraction of paid employment, rise in unemployment, and huge household and sovereign debt that has been imposed on a number of EU economies (Greece, Spain, Ireland, Cyprus, Portugal, and Italy). The consequences of austerity policies have included increased levels of poverty and deprivation, extremely high levels of youth unemployment, dramatic reductions in public expenditures (on welfare, in particular), shrinking pension entitlements, and barriers to accessing affordable childcare and housing. Bailout programs imposed on EU countries by the European Central Bank (ECB) together with the International Monetary Fund (IMF) and the European Commission (EC)—known in Ireland as the *troika*—have been harshly criticized for turning the enormous private corporate debt of the banking sector into public or "sovereign" debt, resulting in major cutbacks to key public expenditure programs in order to finance impossible levels of debt repayments.

Ireland was the first EU country to officially declare itself in recession in August 2008 and the second Eurozone country (after Greece) to have a structural adjustment program imposed by the IMF, ECB, and EU. Specific countries, such as Greece, have had a wholly unmanageable and unsustainable debt repayment system forced upon them and their people, and no amount of savage reductions in social spending has been sufficient to meet the demands of the troika (see above). Ireland, in contrast, has now been held up as a country that has successfully exited the bailout program and in which employment growth has resumed. This talk of recovery of the Irish economy, however, deliberately ignores the major increases in poverty (particularly child poverty) that have taken place, the unresolved debt burden that has trapped tens of thousands of households in homes with mounting arrears in mortgage repayment, and the cruel impact of the loss of support to lone parents, those with disabilities and their caregivers, and the Traveller community, together with the rising level of homelessness and unacceptable treatment of asylum seekers.

Ireland has been through a boom–bust cycle of economic activity and economic policies characterized by crisis management focused on saving the entire banking system no matter what the economic consequences. Economic policy throughout the "boom decade" from 1998–2008, when Ireland was known as the "Celtic Tiger," was based on a neoliberal low-tax strategy, the consequences of which have shaped the particular way in which the economic recession unfolded and imposed a level of debt that will have an enormously negative impact on Irish public finances for generations to come. Since 2008, the Irish government has guaranteed the funds (not just of depositors but of all bondholders, secured and unsecured) in Irish banks and credit institutions, even those of institutions that had already failed. Key characteristics of the Irish economic crisis were, first, an overreliance on declining taxation income from a completely overstimulated property and construction sector and, second, a high level of public subsidy poured into a crisis-ridden Irish banking sector combined with enormous debt repayments as a result of the supposed bailout.

Each EU country that entered the bailout program became subject to a detailed memorandum of agreement signed with the troika that covered all areas of economic policy, including public expenditures and taxation policies, subject to quarterly review, including a commitment to repay all banking debt. Over the crisis years, this has meant a severe drop in public expenditures, a huge increase in public debt, rising poverty, and deprivation levels, and a decline in income levels that has had a particularly negative impact on those with low- to mid-level earnings, consequences of a high level of household debt and cutbacks in a wide range of public services.

In the early part of this century, Ireland was recognized across the EU as a country with a strong and comprehensive equality legislative and policy framework covering a broad range of discrimination grounds in relation to both employment and services and backed up with independent statutory agencies and organizations. That was until the onset of the economic crisis in 2008, when this situation changed radically. The entire infrastructure of public and statutory bodies that had been established to promote and advocate equality, monitor progress, enhance awareness, and develop new practices has been restructured, closed, subjected to drastic budget cuts, or absorbed into departments of government. The budgets of the Equality Authority and the National Women's Council were cut, prompting the resignation of both directors and considerable disquiet. The independence of important statutory agencies has been undermined as government departments have absorbed the work of key bodies such as the Combat Poverty Agency, the National Consultative Committee on Racism and Interculturalism, the Women's Health Council, and the Crisis Pregnancy Agency (Barry and Conroy 2014).

This chapter explores the consequences of the economic crisis and austerity policies for gender equality and the gender dimensions of the austerity policies that have been imposed across the EU. As has been demonstrated, there are gender dimensions to the policy processes that have been implemented at the EU level and to the policies that have been implemented in Ireland throughout the different phases of the crisis (Barry and Conroy 2014). This analysis therefore looks at the Irish situation but also takes a comparative perspective, drawing on analyses of core policies at the EU level to explore the gender patterns evident in the way in which economic and social policies have been developed and implemented and some of the consequences for women's economic position (ENEGE 2012; Oxfam 2013; Rubery and Karamessini 2014; Villa and Smith 2014).

EU policies toward gender equality

At the EU level, the increased emphasis on gender equality, particularly in employment policy, in the decade up to 2005 was transformed with the onset of the crisis. Gender equality had been a central feature of the development of a European Employment Strategy (EES), which, according to Villa and Smith (2014), was implemented in four phases. Phase I of the EES, during 1998–2002, saw gender equality designated as a "core priority" of EU employment policy and one of the four pillars of the strategy's framework for employment policy (which contained twenty-two guidelines, five of which came under the gender equality pillar). During this period, a new concept was also introduced: gender mainstreaming, which was to become a stated aim of establishing gender equality and in 1999 was adopted as a horizontal principle across all policy areas, not just employment policy. Linked to this stronger emphasis on gender equality in economic policy was the decision by the EU Council of Ministers meeting in Lisbon in 2000 to set a target for women's paid employment rate of 60 percent and for men's paid employment rate of 70 percent to be reached by 2010. Throughout this period (known as the Lisbon Process), the clear focus was on increasing employment rates, and women were seen as central to achieving that objective.

New changes were introduced during Phase II in 2003–2005, which coincided with the enlargement of the EU from fifteen to twenty-five member states. This phase resulted in redefining the EES to incorporate three overarching objectives and ten guidelines, only one of which was a gender equality guideline but which continued to include what it termed the mainstreaming of gender equality across all policy areas. This shift to gender mainstreaming has been viewed as the start of a weakened commitment to gender equality reflected in a loss of specific targeted programs (Bargwani et al. 2017). Within just a few years, further changes to the EES significantly reduced its gender equality emphasis. Phase III, which took place in 2005–2009, was characterized by the introduction of broad economic policy guidelines, which included twenty-four integrated policy guidelines. This time the framework contained no gender equality guidelines, just a statement in the preamble of the importance of gender equality, combating discrimination, and gender mainstreaming. The guidelines for Phase IV, covering 2010–2020, were developed in the midst of the crisis and saw a continuation of this process, resulting in just ten integrated policy guidelines. Yet again, this phase included no gender equality guideline and only a very simple statement in the preamble to the EES stating that visible gender equality is important in all relevant policy areas. Villa and Smith (2014) argue:

> The fourth phase was marked by the end of the Lisbon process in 2010 and the beginning of the formulation of a new strategy intended to take the EU to 2020. The new Europe 2020 strategy further marginalizes gender equality with none of the ten integrated guidelines related specifically to equal opportunities and only four related to employment. Moreover, gender mainstreaming is not even mentioned. Furthermore, this reformulation occurred in the middle of the crisis, when policy makers' attention was focused on its immediate impacts on male unemployment and declining youth employment, a context in which the gains made in raising female employment during the Lisbon process were quickly overlooked.
>
> *(Villa and Smith 2014, 278)*

As Table 17.1 shows, employment rates changed dramatically across the EU during the crisis years. Although the gender gap in employment rates between women and men has narrowed, this does not reflect a positive change toward greater gender equality but rather the faster deteriorating employment situation of men across the EU, particularly during the first stage of the crisis.

The negative impact of these policy changes at the EU level resulted in a change in policy priorities from a position in which targeted gender equality initiatives were supported to an initial process of mainstreaming gender equality across the policymaking process followed by a crisis period when it lacked any definite support for gender equality. Pfister (2008) makes the point that gender equality became increasingly marginalized within the EES, at least partly because of the vagueness of the concept of gender mainstreaming that effectively displaced the concept of gender equality. According to Pfister (2008),

> the gender equality dimension of the EES suffered from two main problems. First, its relative weight was affected by repeated attempts to refocus the EES (and the Lisbon strategy) on flexibility and activation in terms of employment

TABLE 17.1 Contraction in EU employment rates

Employment Rates (15–64 years)	*Women*	*Men*	*Gender Gap*
2008–2010 First Stage	60% to 56%	76% to 64%	15 points
2010–2014 Second Stage	56% to 55%	64% to 62%	9 points

Sources: www.ENEGE.eu and www.SAAGE.eu

rates. Although its importance or inclusion in the process has never been questioned, gender equality had been narrowed down, subordinated to other concepts and finally lost most of its visibility. Secondly, this shift of relative weight was aggravated by a shift of meaning of the already vague key concepts gender equality and gender mainstreaming... The principle of gender equality became increasingly *conflated* with the strategy of gender mainstreaming.

(Pfister, 2008, 232)

In Ireland, employment policy mirrored the changes happening at the EU level. Ireland had, in fact, reached the Lisbon targets by 2007, as women's employment rates had increased dramatically over the decade before the deep recession engulfed the country in 2008. The Irish Development Plan 2000–2006 adopted gender mainstreaming as a horizontal principle, and almost all measures funded under that plan had to be assessed from a gender equality perspective. While the gender impact assessment was limited in practice, it did reflect a greater recognition of gender equality in the policymaking process (McGauran 2005; Barry 2015). Once the crisis hit, employment policy priorities shifted. Gender equality was no longer specified as a core aspect of Irish employment policy, and the crisis years saw a move away from a policy of increasing the supply of labor through policies of gender equality that had promoted women's access to the paid labor market. As male unemployment levels surged, policies for reducing unemployment took priority. Gender equality was marginalized and in effect treated as a luxury that, due to the crisis, was rendered unattainable.

A report on the economic crisis across the EU compiled by the EU Network of Experts on Gender Equality and Employment, the ENEGE Report 2013, argues that specific austerity measures that were widely applied in EU countries had particularly negative impacts on gender equality. These include:

- Public sector cuts, including wage freezes or wage cuts; bans on recruitment; pension cuts and changes in eligibility requirements (applied in ten countries)
- Staffing freezes or personnel cuts in the public sector (applied in nine countries)
- Pension reforms that postponed age of retirement (applied in eight countries)
- Reductions and restrictions in caregiver supports; reductions in family payments, related benefits/allowances/facilities (applied in eight countries)
- Reduction of housing or family benefits (applied in six countries)
- Restrictions on eligibility criteria for unemployment and assistance benefits or reductions in replacement rates (applied in five countries)
- Increased charges for publicly subsidized services (applied in eight countries)

Interesting patterns became evident in the midst of this crisis both in Ireland and across the EU. One of the arguments for which there is strong supporting evidence is that the labor market behavior of women during this particular crisis has taken on a different character. Women in Ireland and elsewhere who have lost paid jobs maintained a strong attachment to the labor force, holding onto a self definition of being "unemployed," refusing to retreat into a self-definition of being "engaged in home duties" (the terms used in employment surveys). The traditional view that women serve as a reserve labor force to be brought into paid employment at significant levels only when demand increases and subsequently moved back into unpaid work when demand levels contract is not supported by the evidence documenting the experience of this crisis (ENEGE 2012). The reserve labor force is no longer gender specific. As the ENEGE report on this crisis highlights, "the contemporary *reserve labour force* are young men and women on temporary, short-term employment contracts and migrant workers." This report also presents new evidence of a change in women's economic roles across the EU. For example, where double-income/dual-earner couples have been reduced as a proportion of the workforce, this reduction has been replaced almost exclusively by female breadwinner couples, who have increased their share of the paid workforce by almost 10 percent (ENEGE 2013).

Another gendered trend across the EU over the crisis years is a rise in cases of discrimination against pregnant women in paid employment, a consequence of the crisis that specifically affects women in employment. The rights of pregnant women to maternity leave and benefits have been curtailed, and increased levels of discrimination against pregnant women have been documented in case law in many countries (including Ireland). A recent report in the United Kingdom revealed that discrimination cases involving pregnancy and maternity leave have increased dramatically during the crisis years:

> In 2005, three years before the global financial crisis of late 2008 and subsequent economic recession, a landmark study by the Equal Opportunities Commission (since merged with other bodies to become the Equalities and Human Rights Commission) found that half of all pregnant women suffered a related disadvantage at work, and that each year 30,000 were forced out of their job. Eight years on, the available evidence suggests that figure has ballooned to some 60,000. Since 2008, as many as 250,000 women have been forced out of their job simply for being pregnant or taking maternity leave.
>
> *(Maternity Action 2014, 35)*

A further critical conclusion from the ENEGE Report (2013) related to gender is that "household expenditure went down in most European countries for the consumption of items for which *women's unpaid work* is acting as a substitute." What is evident from this research is that cutbacks in services, particularly around caregiving, are being filled at the household and community level mostly by women's unpaid labor. A report by the European Women's Lobby (European Women's Lobby 2012) draws attention to the gendered implications of cutbacks in public sector employment given that women constitute 69 percent of public sector workers in the EU. According to this report, the "first wave" of the crisis was a private-sector crisis that had more of an impact upon male-dominated sectors of the economy (mainly construction), while in the "second wave," the crisis extended into the public sector where negative consequences were felt more harshly by women. The EWL document shows that cuts have hit female-dominated sectors of health and education hardest, as in the example of Latvia, where a teacher's minimum salary was cut by 30 percent to €6,000 per year and the gender pay gap increased from 13.4 percent to 17.6 percent. Significant layoffs among public sector workers are also noted in Greece (–25 percent), the United Kingdom (–20 percent), Romania (–10 percent), and Latvia (–10 percent). Wage cuts or freezes were recorded in at least thirteen countries, and increases in poverty rates between 2009 and 2012 were revealed to be especially high in Iceland, Latvia, Lithuania, Malta, Spain, and Ireland (for both men and women) (Barry 2016).

A key feature of the gender consequences of the crisis is the rise in part-time and casual employment, much of it involuntary. The European Parliament (EP) report on the gendered impact of the crisis underlines that the gender equality measures which have been cancelled or delayed and potential future cuts in public budgets will have a negative effect on female employment and on the promotion of equality. This report also argues that the economic downturn should not be used as an excuse to slow progress on work/life policies and that to cut budgets allocated for caregiving services for dependents and for leave arrangements would particularly affect women's access to the labor market. As it points out, "cuts in education, childcare and care services have pushed women to work shorter hours or part-time, thereby reducing not only their income but their pensions as well." Furthermore, the report states that studies have also shown that violence against women intensifies when men experience displacement and dispossession as a result of economic crisis (European Parliament 2013).

The latest Joint Employment Report (2015) from the European Commission recognizes that some effects of the economic crisis, such as persistent high unemployment and rising long-term unemployment, have increased "poverty or social exclusion in many Member States" (including a rise in the working poor), particularly affecting children. Specific sectors have experienced extremely high levels of unemployment, with youth unemployment rates of 20 to 50 percent in most countries. Employment rates of migrants within the EU have also seen a severe decline, falling from 62.4 to 55.4 percent between 2008 and 2014. A feature of the crisis has been a reduction in full-time jobs and a rise in part-time employment, including a significant amount of involuntary part-time work. Across the EU, "full-time employment has decreased by roughly 8.1 million between the first quarters of 2008 and 2014. Conversely, there has been steady growth in part time jobs in recent years, with 4 million more since the first quarter of 2008" (European Commission 2015, 11).

Women are strongly overrepresented in part-time work in the EU, accounting for 32 percent of women's paid employment, compared to just 8.3 percent of men's paid employment in 2015. Part-time work accounts for over 40 percent of women's paid employment in a number of Western European countries, such as Austria, Belgium, the United Kingdom, Germany, and the Netherlands, while the rate in Ireland is 35 percent. What is classified as involuntary part-time employment increased from 25.3 percent of the total to 29.6 percent between 2008 and 2013. A growing proportion of those in paid employment are in casual employment, made up mostly of women, young people, and migrants (Standing 2009). Young people across the EU account for 42.4 percent of temporary workers and 31.9 percent of part-time workers. Economic crises create opportunities to undermine employment and other rights (Klein 2007), and this latest crisis is no different. What Standing (2009) has identified as *the precariat*—those in the casual, marginalized parts of the workforce—sharply increased as the crisis presented an opportunity to curtail employment rights and consolidate employer-led flexibility. Low- or zero-hour contracts have become widespread, mainly in the retail and hospitality sectors. Workers have been forced into unprotected on-call systems without the possibility to plan their time and caregiving responsibilities. There is no indication that the "recovery" will redress this change.

The services sector in which women's jobs are concentrated now accounts for nearly three-quarters of all employment within the EU. Persistent gender pay gaps have been evident during the crisis years, particularly in private services employment, while public sector employment that had generated more diverse and secure flexible jobs has been shrinking. Women are paid on average 16 percentage points less per hour of work and experience a significantly higher earnings gap: "The gender gaps in employment, in number of hours worked and in pay add up and lead to a wide gender total earnings gap (37 percent across the EU)" (European Commission 2015, 30).

Gender segregation has been shown to be highly significant across the EU labour market, but marked differences between countries are also evident, even within the same occupational group, such as banking officials. Burchell et al. show that in the EU, just 18 percent of women work in mixed-gender occupations (with a 60/40 percent ratio of men to women), 69 percent work in female-dominated sectors (over 60 percent female), and only 13 percent in male-dominated occupations (over 60 percent male). This contrasts with only 15 percent of men who work in mixed-gender occupations and 59 percent in male-dominated occupations. They also argue that segregation may have both positive and negative effects. Although women make up the majority of public sector workers, with a significant portion of those in mid-level jobs, gender segregation also has negative consequences that are partially linked to austerity: "Segregation also limits employment choices and access to higher-level jobs and may lead to higher risks of job loss under austerity policies to reduce public sector jobs where women predominate. It may also facilitate the undervaluing of female-dominated occupations" (Burchell et al. 2014, 8).

Another consequence of the crisis has been the growth in inequality both within and between EU countries. Not surprisingly, countries whose economic policies have been dictated by the "bailout" terms of structural adjustment programs, are those in which inequality is relatively high and has increased since 2008 (Greece, Cyprus, Spain, and Portugal). In countries in which inequality is at its very highest (Latvia, Lithuania, Romania, and Bulgaria), the share of income among those in the top 20 percent was at least six times higher than that of those in the bottom 20 percent in 2013 (European Commission 2015).

Rising poverty levels have been a feature of this crisis in almost every country, affecting one in five of the population. Children in particular are experiencing growing levels of poverty, especially those in large families and in lone parent and low-income households. Migrants are another sector that has experienced a significantly higher than average risk of poverty and social exclusion, at 40.6 percent of migrants (aged eighteen to sixty-four years old) at risk of poverty and deprivation across the EU in 2013 (European Commision 2015). Pre-EU crisis policies focusing on early childhood education and child-care services became another victim of the crisis. Women, as primary caregivers, are on the front line in defending households against poverty, managing very limited household budgets, but there are other aspects to the ways in which poverty is gendered. For example, as pensions reflect earnings throughout life, the gender gap in pensions is wide (39 percent on average), and this is directly linked to a higher risk of poverty or social exclusion among women over fifty-five years of age in all EU countries.

A global perspective

Jane Lethbridge's 2012 report, *Global Context: Specific Impacts of Austerity on Women,* conducted for the Public Services International Research Unite (PSIRU), comes to a number of key conclusions that confirm EU-based research but looks further into the impact in poorer countries. Women workers and their children, in both the public and private sectors, are bearing the brunt of cuts in vital public services. As women are the majority among public sector workers globally, they therefore have lost more jobs as wage freezes and cuts have reduced the incomes and mobility of women who were already among the lowest paid. Letheridge argues that more women are working in insecure jobs with long hours, low pay, and poor working conditions to support their families and that reductions in public services and women's income will have long-term effects on the health, well-being, and future opportunities of their children. The gender pay gap has widened at a global level. Shelters for victims of domestic violence have been closed. In her view, the long struggle for equality has been set back by closures or funding cuts for public institutions that promote equality for women at work and in society.

Letheridge's work argues that those who are most vulnerable are being hurt the most, including girls in poorer countries who are dropping out of school to care for other family members while their mothers seek work and households that have to sell assets and thereby fall into chronic poverty. One of her important conclusions is that the economic crisis has reduced demand for exports from developing countries in sectors where most workers are female. She also points out that reduced access to health and education for women and girls will have long-term effects on their position in gendered societies. The effects of an economic crisis continue to be felt for many years and will likely slow improvements in the position of women over a long period of time. The impact of reduced access to healthcare and education for women and girls also has long-term effects on women's health and the position of women in society. The crisis has also created changes in the position of women in the labor market by pushing more women into a deteriorating labor market to make up for falling household income as a result of the rising rates of male unemployment. In effect, women are having to work harder and too often take on degrading activities.

Irish experience

Ireland is one of the countries that had a structural adjustment program imposed upon it, and the mismanagement of the crisis reinforced by austerity measures has had a negative impact on those most vulnerable. Ireland's continuing but still fragile economic recovery continues to be marked by increasing levels of poverty and disadvantage despite the continued significant reduction in unemployment rates to 8.6 percent, the lowest rate since the peak of almost 15 percent in April 2009 (and just above the EU-28 level of 8.5 percent for 2016). While male unemployment in Ireland rose steeply from 2008 due to the collapse of the construction industry and completely overinflated property sector, since 2012 male unemployment has been falling faster than female unemployment. The fall in unemployment has begun to have a positive effect in lowering the still-high levels of youth unemployment, particularly for young men aged fifteen to twenty-four years, whose rate has fallen significantly, from 36.4 percent to 29.8 percent, and for some young women, whose rate has fallen marginally from 24.0 percent to 23.5 percent (Barry 2016).

This gendered nature of economic activity in Ireland is reflected in the significant gender gap in employment rates, the predominance of women among low-paid workers, the significant gender pay gap (estimated at 14–20 percent), and the even greater level of gender inequality in the pension system. The negative economic impact of parenthood is also very evident in the gender gap in employment rates, which were 75.1 percent for men and 62.6 percent for women aged sixteen to sixty-five in 2015. Within specific age groups, the employment rate reveals significant gender differences. For example, among those aged fifty-five to sixty-four, rates among men showed a significant rise, from 59.3 percent to 64.9 percent between 2013 and 2015, whereas women's rates have risen more slowly but from what has traditionally been a significantly lower base, from 43.4 percent in 2013 to 46.4 percent in 2015. The rate of part-time employment in Ireland is also highly gendered and continues at a high level, accounting for 32.9 percent of women's employment (higher than the EU-28 average rate of 31.5 percent) and 11.3 percent of men's in 2015 (higher than the

EU-28 average rate of 8.2 percent). This high level of part-time employment is largely attributable to women's continuing to be the primary caregivers in their families and to child-care infrastructure receiving little public support. Among men, part-time employment grew consistently during the recession years and has now stabilized.

Gender differences within the pension system in Ireland are also marked. Women are far less likely to be covered by occupational pensions than men, and a significant number of women are classified as qualified adult dependants under the household-based claimant system. There is a marked difference in pension levels in Ireland between women and men aged sixty-five to seventy-four, reflected in a gender gap of 38.2 percentage points, a wider gap than within the EU-28 at 30.2 percentage points. This highly significant gender gap is linked to women's traditionally low level of access to paid employment and a system that has penalized women who have non-continuous participation in the labor market, in most cases due to the gendered pattern of caregiving responsibilities. Many women are penalized within the system because they have carried most of the social responsibility for unpaid caregiving work in families, which means that it is significantly harder for women to build adequate contributions in both private and public pension systems.

Austerity measures enacted during the crisis years exacerbated these inequalities, and nothing indicates that they will be reversed. The qualifying pension age rose from sixty-five to sixty-six years of age in 2010, will rise to sixty-seven in 2021 and again to sixty-eight years in 2028. There has been no corresponding change in the date for eligibility for the state pension, however, which means that those without occupational pensions are forced to sign up for Jobseeker's Allowance in the years before their pension entitlement can be activated. Changes have also been introduced to the pension system affecting primarily public sector pensions and employment, an important employer of women workers. Changes to the pension system for new entrants that were introduced in 2009 mean reduced pension entitlements for new public servants. Additional measures have been introduced for specific groups of public sector workers. Significantly reduced pay structures have been imposed for teachers and nurses, for example, who are mainly women, introducing a new gendered intergenerational inequality in public employment.

The increasing spread of low-paid employment in Ireland is linked to poor working conditions, and there is growing evidence of the widespread use of low- and zero-hour contracts in the retail, hospitality, and caregiving sectors. There is growing concern across the EU that casualization of working conditions and low pay have become endemic for women working in caregiving, hospitality, and retail jobs, a consequence of austerity policies and employer-centered flexibility on the labor market. The Organization for Economic Cooperation and Development (OECD) reported in 2013 that the United States and Ireland had the highest percentage of low-paying jobs among OECD countries, with low-paying jobs defined as those that earn less than two-thirds of the median income. The ratio in the United States was 25 percent, 22 percent in Ireland, and 21 percent in the United Kingdom, in contrast to Switzerland and Finland with ratios of 10 percent (OECD 2013a). The level of the statutory National Minimum Wage (NMW) in Ireland was static between 2008 and 2015, which in combination with additional taxes and charges, loss of benefits, and low-hours contracts has resulted in rising numbers of low-paid and low-income households.

Poverty levels in Ireland continue to rise, untouched by the recovery. The most recent EU data show that poverty increased substantially in Ireland between 2011 and 2015. EU-SILC data show the at-risk-of-poverty rate in Ireland was at 16.9 percent in 2015. The continued consequences of austerity are clear from the data, which show an increased deprivation rate that rose from 11.8 percent in 2008 to 30.5 percent in 2013, followed by a fall to a still-high rate of 25.5 percent in 2015 and a consistent poverty rate that rose from 6.9 percent in 2011 to 8.7 percent in 2015. Poverty levels among children have doubled since 2008, and the highest rate of poverty and social exclusion is experienced by lone parent families, at 57.9 percent (CSO 2015a). Of even greater concern is the increase in the deprivation rate for those at risk of poverty, rising from 46.8 percent in 2012 to 53.9 percent in 2013, followed by a slight fall to 51.5 percent in 2015. Those experiencing the highest poverty levels are adults (mainly women) and children in lone-parent households, in households in which no adult is in paid employment, and in large families. Specific minorities already experiencing disadvantage and poverty, such as Travellers, were hit hard by economic cutbacks, few of which have been reversed (Harvey 2013).

The particular vulnerability of lone parents (around 90 percent of whom are women) is confirmed by data from the CSO Household Finance and Consumption Survey 2013 that highlight that households with one adult and children were burdened with more debt than all other types of households (CSO 2015b). The gendered nature of poverty is also evident from recent figures from the Economic and Social Research Institute (ESRI), which show that women in couples experienced a 14 percent drop in income compared with a 9 percent drop for men in couples during the recession (ESRI 2015). Two particularly critical changes have targeted lone parents receiving payment under the One-Parent Family Payment (OPFP), including those who have part-time employment. The first is the significant reduction in the earnings disregard that enabled many lone parents to resume paid employment without loss of benefits. Severe reduction in the level of the earnings disregard has created new and deeper poverty traps for lone parents. The second policy change means that eligibility for OPFP will cease when the youngest child reaches seven years of age, which will compel the majority to rely upon Jobseeker's Allowance (a welfare payment paid at a lower rate than the OPFP). This is a form of compulsory training or employment, despite the lack of child-care support for those parents and the high cost of childcare in the private marketplace. Based on the government's stated aim of motivating single parents to return to the labor market, this policy change has been challenged by lone parent organizations, which have estimated that, despite possible access to some back-to-work financial support, losses to the income of lone parents with one child on the minimum wage will amount to between €25 and €51 per week (depending on hours worked). These factors, combined with the high cost of childcare, discourage households from benefiting through accessing paid employment (Barry and Conroy 2014; SPARK 2012).

Child-care costs are extremely high in Ireland, and affordability is a big issue. In 2013 European Anti-Poverty Network Ireland (EAPN Ireland 2013) estimated that child-care costs accounted over 50 percent of the total costs or around 30 percent of the disposable income of double-income households with two young children. It also reported that although financing was available for capital programs for child-care service providers, resources were limited for staffing and operating costs, so this burden was being increasingly passed to users many of whom cannot afford child-care services under these conditions (EAPN Ireland 2013). A 2010 report by the OECD revealed that households with young children in Ireland spent, on average, 41 percent of their income on childcare (OECD 2010). Another OECD Report (2013b) shows that Ireland spent less than 0.2 percent of its gross domestic product (GDP) on the care and education of pre-school children. 2013 OECD figures underscore just how much of an Irish family's income after taxes is consumed by child-care costs: 29 percent of a dual-income family's net income and 51 percent of a lone parent's (OECD 2013b). A 2013 research report that provoked much debate explored the extent to which the high costs of childcare act as a barrier to accessing paid employment, particularly among low-income households in Ireland. It concluded that 25 percent of parents had been prevented from accessing paid employment by the high costs of childcare, including 56 percent of parents in low-income households (Indecon Report 2013). Indecon estimated the cost of full-time childcare to be €16,500 per annum in a two-child household, making the cost of childcare in Ireland as a percentage of average wages the second highest in the OECD. Unless the availability and the cost of childcare are addressed, the policy changes that have cut child benefits, thus reducing resources at the household level, will continue to have a negative impact on low-income households, particularly lone mothers, and will do nothing to increase their participation in paid employment (Indecon Report 2013).

Key policies that researchers argue have directly contributed to increased poverty levels include changes in support to lone parents, reduction in payments by Jobseeker's Allowance to those under twenty-five years of age, discontinuation of the Cost of Education Allowance, reductions in Child Benefits, reductions in support for Traveller education, reductions in number and levels of important allowances for disability, loss of double welfare payments at Christmastime, declines in real value of state pensions as a result of changing eligibility criteria for medical cards, reduced allowance for telephone costs, increased payments for medical prescriptions, lower levels of fuel entitlements, and reduction of the value and taxation of Maternity Benefits (MB) (Barry 2016; European Anti-Poverty Network 2013; Barry and Feeley 2016). A particularly harsh measure introduced in 2011 is the Universal Social Charge (USC), a new regressive income tax paid on gross incomes of those earning only marginally above the minimum wage (Barry and Conroy 2014).

Issues faced by migrant women from non-EU countries can create precarious work situations in Ireland. Many women who travel or who join partners do not have work permits or visas in their own right and are vulnerable to super-exploitation by the labor market (many in the caregiving sector) and by the sex industry. Asylum seekers are locked into deep poverty and deprivation as by law they are denied the right to work and welfare entitlements are extremely limited. Institutionalized private profitmaking centers, characterised by overcrowding, lack of autonomy and dignity, in which asylum seekers are not facilitated to cook their own food, contravene basic human rights. Research has shown high levels of mental illness among women, men, and children forced into long-term stays in these unacceptable conditions (Irish Refugee Council 2014).

Budgets 2016–2018, Ireland's first post-recession budgets, introduced some new policy measures, including some that have had positive implications for gender equality. Because women constitute the majority of low-paid workers in Ireland, the proposed increases in the National Minimum Wage from €8.65 to €9.25 per hour and in the Family Income Supplement (FIS) as well as the removal of some low-paid workers from the penalizing Universal Social Change (USC) plan are important changes. Some new measures of child support intended to help support households with young children including an increase in the Universal Child Benefit and a second year of subsidized early childhood education, were introduced in September 2016.

Following Ireland's exit from the bailout or Structural Adjustment Program, the negative impacts of austerity policies are clear. This makes it urgent to address poverty levels among low-income (including lone parent) households and the high risk to children. Woman-headed households and households with three or more children comprise the majority of low-income households in Ireland. The abrupt withdrawal or reduction of benefits under austerity policies has played a significant role in trapping women and children in poverty and unemployment, and have had negative effects on young people, lone parents, and low-income households.

Conclusion

As this analysis has shown, gender equality was systematically deprioritized in national policies of the EU during the crisis years. Young people, lone parents, women in low-income households, migrants, and specific minorities have borne the brunt of the crisis in Ireland, a pattern at least partially repeated across the EU. Contractions in public expenditures (both across the EU and globally) have negatively affected women in particular. On the one hand, public sector employment is critical for women, and on the other, reductions in public services create new demands on women's unpaid labour. Gender blindness, or at best "gender neutrality" rather than gender equality is evident in the core policies of the recession period in Ireland, which has only been partially addressed under post-austerity policies.

The scant attention that has been paid to gender and equality has been compounded over the crisis years by a shift in economic policy from an emphasis on increasing women's employment rate to a new focus on (mostly male) registered unemployment, long-term unemployment, and the loss of traditional job opportunities. Women, who accounted for the majority of the growth in paid employment between 1997 and 2007, became marginalized in the attempt to prevent growth in the long-term unemployment of men. In employment policy, the hard-fought-for attention to gender equality in the 1990s and 2000s has almost disappeared, leaving few policies to address low pay, the gender pay gap, occupational segregation, and gender-related themes of poverty and social inclusion. Consequences of the failure to include a gender-equality perspective are particularly evident in rising levels of poverty, social exclusion of specific minorities, and inequality.

References

Bargawni, Hannah, Giovanna Cozzi and Susan Himmelweit (eds) 2017. *Economics and Austerity in Europe—Gendered Impacts and Sustainable Alternatives*. London: Routledge.

Barry, Ursula. 2016. *Gender Equality Policy in Ireland*. Report for the European Parliament. http://www.europarl.europa.eu/studies. Accessed October 17 2017.

Barry, Ursula and Feeely, Maggie. 2016. "Gender and Economic Inequality in Ireland." In *Cherishing All Equally 2016—Economic Inequality in Ireland*. TASC, Dublin.

Barry, Ursula. 2015. *Ireland: Policy on Gender Equality*. European Parliament, FEMM Committee. IPOL_IDA(2015)536450_EN.

Barry, Ursula and Pauline Conroy. 2012. *Ireland: The Untold Story of the Crisis Women, Gender and New Inequalities*, TASC.

Barry, Ursula and Pauline Conroy. 2014. "Ireland in Crisis: Women, Austerity and Inequality." In *Women and Austerity: The Economic Crisis and the Future for Gender Equality*, edited by Jill Rubery and Maria Karamessini, 187–206. London: Routledge.

Burchell, Brendan, Vincent Hardy, Jill Rubery and Mark Smith 2014. *A New Method to Understanding Occupational Gender Segregation in European Labour Markets*. www.enege.eu. Accessed 18 October 2017.

Central Statistics Office. 2013. *Women and Men in Ireland*. Dublin: CSO.

Central Statistics Office. 2014. *Employment and Unemployment Data*. Dublin: CSO.

Central Statistics Office. 2015a. *Household Finance and Consumption Survey*. Dublin: CSO.

Central Statistics Office. 2015b. *SILC Survey of Income and Living Conditions*. Dublin: CSO.

Economic and Social Research Institute and Equalit Authority. 2015. *The Gender Impact of Tax and Benefit Changes: A Microsimulation Approach*. www.equality.ie. Accessed 18 October 2017.

ENEGE. 2013. *The Impact of the Economic Crisis on the Situation of Women and Men and on Gender Equality Policies*. Brussels. www.enege.eu

European Parliament. 2013. *On the Impact of the Economic Crisis on Gender Equality and Women's Rights*. http://www.europarl.europa.eu/sides/getDoc.do?pubRef=-//EP//TEXT+REPORT+A7-2013-0048+0+DOC+XML+V0//EN [accessed 16 December 2015].

European Anti-Poverty Network (EAPN) Ireland. 2013. *Pre-Budget Submission to Government*. Dublin. www.eapn.ie. Accessed 18 October 2017.

European Commission. 2012. *The Gender Pay Gap in EU*. http://ec.europa.eu/justice/gender-equality/gender-pay-gap/index_en.htm.

European Commission 2013. *Assessment of 2012 National Reform Programme and Stability Programme for Ireland*," European Commission (COM, 2012, 316).

European Commission. 2015. *Joint Employment Report*. 2015 6142/15 SOC 68 EMPL 29 ECOFIN 95 EDUC 26 JEUN 11.

European Network on Employment on Gender Equality. 2012. *The Impact of the Economic Crisis on the Situation of Women and Men and on Gender Equality Policies*. Brussels. www.enege.eu. Accessed 18 October 2017.

EUROSTAT. 2011. *Living Arrangements in EU 27*. News Release 156/2011 Eurostat. Accessed 17 October 2017.

Klein, Naomi. (2007). *The Shock Doctrine*. New York: St Martin's Press.

European Women's Lobby. 2012. "The Price of Austerity—the Impact on Women's Rights and Gender Equality Issues." http://www.womenlobby.org/The-Price-of-Austerity-The-Impact-on-Women-s-Rights-and-Gender-Equality-in [Accessed 16 December 2015].

Harvey, Brian. 2013. *Travelling with Austerity: Impacts of Cuts on Travellers, Traveller Projects and Services*. Dublin: Pavee Point. www.paveepoint.ie. Accessed 17 October 2017.

HSE Crisis Pregnancy Programme & Equality Authority. 2011. *Pregnancy at Work—A National Survey*. Dublin: HSE and EA. www.equality.ie. Accessed 17 October 2017.

Indecon Report. 2013. *Support for Childcare for Working Families and Implications for Employment*. www.indecon.ie. Accessed 18 October 2017.

International Leave Network. 2013. *International Review of Leave Policies and Related Research*. www.leavenetwork.org. Accessed 18 October 2017.

International Monetary Fund. 2013. *Ireland's Economy 2013*. www.imf.com. Accessed 17 October 2017.

Irish Refugee Council. 2014. *Report of Conditions of Asylum Seekers in Ireland*. www.irishrefugeecouncil.ie. Accessed October 18 2017.

Mandate. 2012. *Decent Work? The Impact of the Recession on Low Paid Workers*. Dublin: Mandate Trade Union. www.mandate.ie. Accessed October 18 2017.

Maternity Action. 2014. *Overdue: A Plan of Action to Tackle Pregnancy Discrimination Now*. Maternity Action UK.

McGauran, Anne-Marie. 2005. *Plus ca Change? Gender Mainstreaming of the Irish National Development Plan*. Blue Paper. Policy Institute. Trinity College Dublin. www.policy.institute@tcd.ie. Accessed 17 October 2017.

National Women's Council of Ireland. 2008. *An Accessible Affordable Model of Childcare*. Ireland: NWCI. www.nwci.ie. Accessed 17 October 2017.

Organisation for Economic Cooperation and Development. 2010. *Gender Brief*. OECD.

Organisation for Economic Cooperation and Development. 2012. *Close the Gender Pay Gap Now*. Organisation for Economic Co-operation and Development. OECD.

Organisation for Economic Cooperation and Development. 2013a. *OECD Employment Outlook 2013*. Morgan Stanley Research. Geneva: OECD.

Organisation for Economic Cooperation and Development. 2013b. *Doing Better for Families*. OECD.

Oxfam. 2013. *The True Cost of Austerity and Inequality Ireland Case Study*. Oxford: Oxfam G.B.

Oxfam International and the European Women's Lobby. 2010. *Women's Poverty and Social Inclusion in the European Union at a Time of Recession—An Invisible Crisis*. Brussels: Oxfam and EWL. www.ewl.eu. Accessed October 18 2018.

Pfister, Thomas 2008. "Mainstreaming Away—Assessing the Gender Equality Dimension to European Employment Strategy," *Policy and Politics*, volume36, no. (4), pp. 521–538. The Policy Press. London.

Rubery, J. and Karamessini, M. 2014. *Women and Austerity – The Economic Crisis and the Future of Gender Equality*. London: Routledge.

SPARK. 2012. *Single Parents Acting for the Rights of Our Kids – Seven Is Too Young*. Pre-budget submission. Dublin: SPARK.

Standing, G. 2009. *The Precariat—The New Dangerous Class*. London and New York: Bloomsbury.

Villa, Paola and Mark Smith 2014. "Policy in the Time of Crisis: Employment Policy and Gender Equality in Europe" In *Women and Austerity—The Economic Crisis and the Future for Gender Equality*, edited by Marian Karamessini and Jill Rubery. London: Routledge.

18
FROM KICK-START TO U-TURN? GENDER EQUALITY IN SWEDEN

Anita Nyberg

In the 1960s, a vigorous and intense discussion got under way in Sweden concerning gender equality. In the 1970s, this discussion resulted in numerous decisive political measures, such as the introduction of individual taxation, parental leave, and expansion of publicly financed childcare, in order to further gender equality in the labor market and caregiving in the family. The discussion and political measures meant a kick-start for promoting gender equality in Sweden, which also seemed effective. Sweden has been number one in several lists ranking countries according to gender equality, including the World Economic Forum's Global Gender Gap list in 2006 and 2007; the Gender Equity Index of Social Watch in 2007, 2008, and 2009; and the Gender Equality Index of the European Institute for Gender Equality (EIGE) in 2005, 2010, and 2012.[1]

However, according to the Global Gender Gap, Sweden's rank slipped to number three in 2008 and to number four in 2009 and remained at that rank as of 2016; in the Gender Equity Index, Sweden regressed to number four in 2012; and in EIGE rankings, Sweden was still number one of the European Union (EU) countries in 2012 but its score was somewhat lower than in 2010. Was there a U-turn in gender equality? If so, was this because gender equality policies did not have intended effects, i.e. furthering gender equality in the labor market and in the family, or was it a result of changes in gender equality policies?

This chapter focuses on shifts in the situation for women in relation to men and on gender equality in the labor market and in the family in Sweden. The labor market is one of the areas that is included in all the above-mentioned indices and is often the focus when women's position and gender equality are studied. The gender division of unpaid household and care work is also often in focus when discussing gender equality. In order to have gender equality in the labor market, gender equality in the family is needed; you can't have one without the other.

As the World Economic Forum's report states, "national policy frameworks play a key role in influencing the magnitude and scope of gender gaps" (2013, 62), and notes that in this context, parental leave, availability of childcare, and type of taxation are especially relevant variables. Similarly, a cross-country study of the countries in the Organisation for Economic Co-operation and Development (OECD) concludes that gender equality in the labor market is higher in countries where the individual is the fundamental income tax entity, highly subsidized childcare is available, and parental leave allowances are tied to previous earnings of the mother (Jaumotte 2003).

The objective of this chapter is to investigate gender equality policies especially in three policy areas—individual taxation, publicly financed childcare, and parental leave, including parents' right to shorter working hours—and their outcomes in terms of women's achieving greater parity with men in the labor market and caregiving in the family in Sweden from the 1960s and 1970s to the middle of the 2010s.

The first section of the article analyzes gender equality policies, including discussions of gender equality policy in the 1960s and 1970s in general and then in each of the three identified policy areas. Yet trends in women and men's employment and gender equality policies cannot be considered as separate from or independent of general changes in the economy, in the labor market, and in policies other than gender equality policies. The second section of the article therefore briefly describes broader economic and policy developments during this period, followed by an investigation of the development of gender equality in employment, but also of absences from work, and working time in the labor market, since data on employment do not give an accurate picture.

The study makes use of macrolevel child-care data from the Swedish National Agency for Education (*Skolverket*), parental allowance data from the Swedish Social Insurance Agency (*Försäkringskassan*), labor force survey data from Statistics Sweden (*Statistiska Centralbyrån, SCB*), and earlier research concerning family policy, publicly financed childcare, parental leave, employment, etc.

Gender equality policy

Gender equality policy in the 1960s and 1970s

In the 1950s, probably nobody could have imagined that Sweden could be at the top of lists measuring gender equality. Policies then were designed in accordance with the discourse, if not always the reality, that men should be breadwinners and women should tend to domestic and caregiving work. To the extent that gender issues were politicized, they were discussed as women's issues. Over a very short period in the 1960s, however, the notion of women's issues was exchanged for one of gender equality, and the male-earner/female-caregiver family model was questioned and replaced as an ideal by a dual-earner/dual-caregiver family model.

The new norm was that men and women should have equal rights to employment and equal responsibility for home and children.

A very important factor in this change was an article, *"Kvinnans villkorliga frigivning"* (Women's conditional liberation), written in 1961 by Eva Moberg, a feminist and journalist. Moberg argued that instead of emphasizing women's two roles—i.e., both employment and work in the family—men's responsibility for home and children must also be taken into account.[2] Only if both women and men had dual roles could any substantial change take place. The solution, Moberg argued, was a redistribution of responsibilities between women and men rather than support for and recognition of women's two roles.

That gender equality must mean a change for both women and men was at the time a novel position. It was not presented as a conflict but instead emphasized common interests (Klinth and Johansson 2010, 49). The point of departure was that both women and men needed to be liberated from stereotypes and destructive expectations, i.e., from their sex roles, in the terminology of the time.

A number of researchers have tried to explain why there was a breakthrough for gender equality policy in Sweden in the 1960s and 1970s (Hirdman 1994; Florin and Nilsson 1999; Fürst 1999; Lindvert 2004). The main reasons identified in this research are the perceived need for women's labor in the labor market, demands for gender equality from women and women's organizations, a political will to create a fair and democratic society, economic and democratic forces resulting in new needs and dissatisfactions with the existing gender contract, women's increasingly being seen as individuals, and competition between the Liberal Party and the Social Democrats. If policies were to be instituted when the Social Democrats were in power, however, they also needed to be reformulated as a worker's (class) issue. To these factors could be added a strong central state, which made it possible to carry through the policies.

The gender equality debate at the time also had a redistribution and consensus logic that was part of a greater historical context. Redistribution was something that characterized the Swedish welfare state model during most of the twentieth century (Klinth and Johansson 2010, 52). Until the 1960s, the focus had been on redistribution between classes, which was then extended to also concern redistribution between women and men. The consensus that developed also has a historical background. In the Swedish model, the exercise of power has been based on inclusion and positive rights rather than exclusion and confrontation. Although the gender equality revolution in the 1960s and 1970s represented something new, it was also based on established ways of thinking and organizing politics (Lindvert 2002). The debates surrounding the redistribution of social roles described it as revolutionary, but it was a revolution in which all were winners. Gender equality was seen as sensible, functional, and liberating for men as well as women (Klinth 2002).

Several of the central arguments in the gender equality debate had their basis in economics. The traditional family structure meant that women were economically dependent on their husbands because they did not have an income of their own, which they would need in order to be liberated. Proponents also emphasized that women were needed in the labor market for economic reasons. Calculations showed that using women's underutilized labor could increase GDP by 25 percent (Holmberg 1966).

The process of intense policy formulation taking place in the 1960s resulted in a period of state institutionalization in the 1970s (Florin and Nilsson 1999, 66): individual taxation of income for wife and husband (1971), liberalized divorce laws in a new family law (1973), parents entitled to share parental allowances upon childbirth and a decision to expand publicly financed childcare (1974), a new abortion law (1975), a parliamentary commission on equal status and ordinance for equal opportunities in civil service (1976), agreement between employers and unions regarding equal opportunities (1977), right to shorter working hours for parents with small children (1979), and finally a law against sex discrimination in employment (1980) that instituted an equal opportunities ombudsman, an equal opportunities agreement with municipal and county governments, the opening of all professions to women including the defense sector, and a new law on succession to the throne in which the monarch's first-born daughter or son succeeds to the throne. These reforms provided a kick-start for gender equality and set the path for future development.

Much of the gender equality policy since then has been about implementing and extending the measures introduced in the 1970s. Since 2006, the overall objective of Sweden's gender equality policy has been to ensure that women and men have the same power to shape society and their own lives. There have been four subgoals of that policy, of which two were the main focus in the 1970s: economic equality between the sexes and equal distribution of unpaid care and household work. Another subgoal was that men's violence against women must stop, which was not discussed in the 1960s and 1970s and therefore will not be examined here. Another subgoal was equal distribution of power and influence, which was discussed in the 1960s and 1970s but also will not be looked at in this article, although it could be pointed out that the share of women in parliament in 1973 was 21 percent compared to 44 percent in 2014. The share has twice decreased when new right-wing populist male-dominated parties entered the parliament. Women made up 11 percent of the government in 1973, but have constituted approximately half of the members since the end of the 1990s.

Individual taxation

The first major measure to further women's employment and gender equality was the introduction of individual taxation in 1971. Development of this policy was very quick. In 1960, an almost unanimous parliament decided that joint taxation should be maintained (Elvander 1972, Chapter 7). Although the idea of individual taxation seemed very distant at that time, a couple of years later the situation was totally different. The debate regarding individual taxation was initiated by women with higher education without the support of any major organization.

They argued that joint taxation benefitted the "not fully occupied housewife without children," especially in high-income families. The conservative side of the debate maintained that the tax system should be neutral in relation to married women's employment; women's right to be supported housewives should not be questioned. The radical side objected that no tax system is neutral and that joint taxation was built on the old-fashioned idea that women should be supported by men, which was incompatible with a modern society.

The discussion about individual taxation can be seen as an offshoot of the intensive debate on sex roles and gender equality in the 1960s (Florin 1999). Women's organizations, researchers, journalists, and some politicians were of the opinion that women's liberation could only be achieved by women working for wages and having an income of their own, which demanded that economic obstacles to married women's employment be removed. Tax reform was needed to eliminate the tax penalty on married women's employment and to further gender equality. In an individual taxation system, women and men were seen as individuals, and it did not make a connection between taxes and marital status.

The political parties initially were divided and indecisive about individual taxation, but during the 1960s, all but the Conservative Party made up their minds in favor of individual taxation.[3] The Liberal Party was the party that was most energetically and wholeheartedly engaged in the move toward individual taxation. Their motivation was gender equality and was not directly related to the demand for married women's labor in the market.

For the Social Democratic Party, in comparison, the question of individual taxation was sensitive, and maybe especially so for Social Democratic women. The idea that married women might also be employed was not unfamiliar to Social Democrats. Married working-class women often worked part-time and in other peoples' homes, and women in agriculture, who were largely responsible for milking cows and tending to smaller animals, had always been gainfully employed (even if not counted as such in the censuses), and their work was crucial in a poor country such as Sweden at the beginning of the twentieth century (Nyberg 1989, 1994). The transition from an agrarian to industrial society meant that a relatively large share of married women became "housewives," although this lasted only for a short period, culminating in the 1950s when Sweden became richer and some male workers for the first time "could afford to support a housewife." As a result, many Social Democratic women were elderly housewives who could lose out with individual taxation.

The main problem for the Social Democrats was to design individual taxation in a way that did not primarily benefit high-income families. Alva Myrdal, a well-known Swedish feminist and Social Democrat, pointed out that the marginal effects of joint taxation also affected wives of low-income men (Elvander 1972, 256). Through this turn in the debate, taxation became a question not only about women but about class. This idea fell onto fertile ground among leading Social Democrats (Florin 1999, 114, 124, 131). In a newspaper article, Prime Minister Olof Palme put forward the Social Democratic arguments for individual taxation, declaring that it was first and foremost a reform of distribution to benefit those with low incomes, although he emphasized that it also concerned independence and equality for women. The dimension of redistribution and class thus was pushed to the foreground, and the gender equality aspect viewed as part of that dimension (Elvander 1972, 290).

In 1971, the time was ripe for the mandatory individual taxation reform. It meant that the two previous tax scales were replaced by a single tax scale for all (Lindencrona 1985). Additionally, the general tax deduction became the same for all individuals and could no longer be transferred from one spouse to the other. It was, however, pointed out that many families had only one wage earner, and in these families, the introduction of individual taxation meant a tax increase. In order to compensate one-earner families for the prospective adverse effect, they could use an extra deduction popularly known as "the housewife deduction." In 1971, this deduction was substantial, but the amount was kept at its nominal value, which meant that its value decreased over time (Gunnarsson 1995, 125).

In the new individual tax system, husband and wife were seen as two autonomous individual economic subjects. Also the social insurance system was discussed, and important representatives for the Social Democrats and the blue-collar union put forward a motion in 1967 arguing that the social security system needed to be overhauled (Lundqvist 2007, 221) against the background of married women's changed labor-market behavior. The social security system (which include unemployment benefits, sickness allowances, pensions, etc.) has the individual as its base, not the family. Additionally, most social security allowances are in one way or the other conditional on a previous work history, which is an incentive to be employed. Family legislation was also changed to emphasize that the family as a unit consisted of two autonomous individuals (Klinth and Johansson 2010, 56).

In certain respects, however, joint taxation was retained, such as individual taxation on business and farm income where one of the spouses was employed by the other. In 1976, individual taxation was introduced also in this case (Lindencrona 1979, 33). Still, the most important factor was that individual taxation covered only earned income. Unearned income (income from property, capital, capital gain, periodical support, and in some cases of enterprise and farm property) was jointly taxed until 1988, when a number of other joint taxation elements were also eliminated. The last remains of joint taxation of income and the "housewife deduction" were abolished in connection with a tax reform in 1991 (Gunnarsson 1995). Joint taxation of wealth was in force until such taxation was eliminated on January 1, 2007 by the newly elected Alliance (Moderate-Liberal-Centre-Christian Democratic Parties) government. This had nothing to do with gender equality; the reason behind it was that tax on wealth was seen as counterproductive, since it resulted in less investment, which was needed for economic growth.

An evaluation of the introduction of the individual taxation of earned income in 1971 shows that it spurred the female employment rate at the time

(Selin 2008; see also Gustafsson 1992). It can also be pointed out that wage policy in the 1960s and 1970s led to a radical equalization of wages. The motivation behind this policy was not to encourage gender equality, but to raise the wages of low-wage workers and diminish the general wage gap (i.e., a class perspective). The policy nonetheless was important in the shrinking of the gender wage gap up until the very beginning of the 1980s (Löfström 1989). Afterwards, the equalization of wages more or less ceased (Edin and Richardson 1997), although when using a standard weighting procedure taking occupation, sector, education and working time into consideration, the gender pay gap has decreased some, from 8.0 percentage points in 1996 to 6.0 percentage points in 2016 (SCB 2016).[4]

The introduction of individual taxation, social security allowances tied largely to earlier work history, and higher wages for women meant strong incentives for women to enter the labor market. As we might expect, these led to rising employment rates for women and thereby to increased gender equality in the labor market.

Publicly financed childcare

When increasing numbers of mothers entered the labor market in the 1960s and 1970s, there was very little publicly financed childcare available. An investigation published in 1967 showed that only 10 percent of the demand was covered, and another in 1971 estimated that 16 percent of the children who needed a place in childcare had one (Antman 1996, 128, 130). Many employed mothers engaged private family day care in the informal market. In 1966, the number of children in private family day care was 47,500, while the number in public family day care was 7,000 (Nyberg 1995, Table 3). In 1970, about half of the mothers with pre-school children (zero to six years old) were employed, while only around 10 percent of the children were enrolled in public childcare centers. The lack of publicly financed childcare was one of the reasons why "child care for all children" was a main demand of the radical feminist organization Group 8 and among working mothers in general.

In the context of facilitating women and mother's employment and laying the foundation of the dual-earner/dual-caregiver model in Sweden in the 1970s, publicly financed full-time day care constituted an important part of the social infrastructure (Bergqvist and Nyberg 2002). Earlier focus was on part-time playschools (Nyberg 1995), which were seen as a complement to childcare in the home and as positive for both mothers and children. The at-home mothers would get some relief from their "twenty-four-hour constraint." Full-time daycare centers were not seen as a positive alternative for children, but as a substitute for the care of the mother and as a necessity for single or poor mothers who did not have any other alternative. Indicative of this is when the central state increased grants to municipalities in order to expand childcare in the 1960s, it resulted in new places in part-time playschools rather than places in day-care centers (Nyberg 1995, Table 1). The number of places in part-time playschools was more numerous than in day-care centers until the end of the 1970s.

In 1973, the National Commission on Child Care (*Barnstugeutredningen*) laid the foundation for today's Swedish pre-school model: day-care centers and playschools were to be combined in a pre-school system that would serve the interests of children as well as allowing parents to work or study (SOU 1972:26, 27). Care and education were to be merged in a new way. Its intention was to erase the old-fashioned view that full-time day care was something for the poor while educational activities in part-time playschools were for the stimulation of better-off children.

In 1974, the Social Democratic government decided on an extensive publicly financed childcare program (Nyberg 2007a). However, it is the municipalities that are responsible for the supply of childcare, and the expansion was slow. Since many mothers with pre-school children were already in the labor market, the demand for childcare was much bigger than the supply. The gap between supply and demand for childcare was one important reason why in 1985—when the Social Democratic Party was again in power—the parliament decided that all children 1.5–7 years old with working or studying parents and all children who for different reasons need special support for their development were to be entitled to a place in public childcare by 1991. Yet, the expansion of child-care places was still too slow, and far from all parents who wished to have a place for their children were able to get one. Legislation was therefore tightened in 1995, when local authorities became duty bound to provide childcare without undue delay (within three to four months) to all children one to twelve years old with working or studying parents and children in need of special support.

Since the beginning of the 2000s, the right to a place in publicly financed childcare was expanded to cover not only children with working or studying parents but also those with parents on parental leave with a smaller child and unemployed parents. The right concerns fifteen hours per week for a fee. At the same time, all four- and five-year-olds became entitled, free of charge, to 525 hours of pre-school yearly, and in 2010 all three-year olds. In 2016, virtually all six year olds (97 percent) were in pre-school classes (Skolverket 2016g).

In spite of an economic crisis at the beginning of the 1990s and falling employment for mothers (and fathers), the number of children in publicly financed childcare increased dramatically. As can be seen in Figure 18.1 the proportion of enrolled two-, three-, four- and five-year olds increased from 55–67 percent in 1990 to 91–97 percent in 2016. No children below the age of one are in publicly financed childcare, since they are at home with a parent on parental leave. This is also true for a large proportion of the one year olds, since parental leave is longer than one year and can be spread over a longer period of time. However, the share of one year olds in childcare has increased from 35 percent in 1990 to around 50 percent since the end of the 2000s.

After-school care is also offered in leisure-time centers. If this was not the case, mothers might have to adapt their working hours to children's school hours by

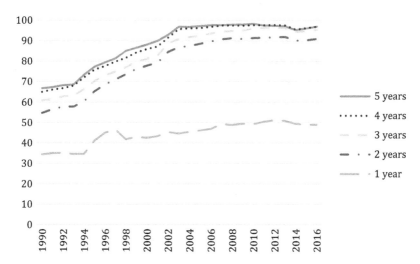

FIGURE 18.1 Percent of children aged 1–5 years in publicly financed childcare, Sweden, 1990–2016

Source: Figures for 1990–1993 are calculated from data on the number of children enrolled and the number of children in each age group in Statistisk årsbok 1992–1995; for 1994–1997 from Skolverket 1999 and Statistisk årsbok 2001, Table 433; for 1998–2010 from Skolverket 1998–2005, Table 1B and Skolverket 2006–2010, Table 1B; for 2011–2016 from Skolverket 2016a, Table 2B and Skolverket 2016b, Table 1B.

working part-time. The share of children in leisure-time centers has also increased considerably. The proportion of seven and eight year olds in leisure-time centers reached 86 and 87 percent in 2016 and 79 percent among nine year olds. Older children are more seldom found in publicly financed childcare. Among ten, eleven and twelve year olds, the share was 38, 18, and 8 percent, respectively, in 2016 (Skolverket 2016c, Table 2B).

While municipalities have the legal responsibility to ensure a sufficient supply of public childcare, child-care services can be provided by private companies, church organizations, parental and personnel cooperatives, etc. All these different forms of organizing childcare are financed by tax revenues as well as parental fees, which covered around 6 percent of the total costs in 2015 (Sjöquist 2017), on the same conditions as childcare run by the municipalities. In 2002, a low maximum fee was introduced in childcare (Nyberg 2007a).

In the 1970s and 1980s, publicly financed childcare expanded, but far from all children were able to find a place, and those who did were mainly upper-class families. The proportion of working-class children who went to publicly financed pre-school increased from 13 to 25 percent, while the proportion of children from the white-collar class increased from 16 to 54 percent in the cohorts born between 1966 and 1981 (Jonsson 2004, 105–108). One important exception to this was single mothers from all classes, whose children were prioritized in access to publicly financed childcare over children of married or cohabiting parents since they had to support themselves and their children. Today, the supply of childcare more or less meets demand; differences between children from different classes, marital status of parents, and ethnicities are small.

Political commitment to childcare has been motivated not only by wishing to enable mothers' employment but also to advance equality among children from different classes and a good social and pedagogical upbringing for all children (SOU 1972:26, 27; Bergqvist 1999). In other words, publicly financed childcare is seen as furthering not only gender equality but also class equality and equality between Swedish-born and foreign-born children. As an increasing number of children have been included in publicly financed childcare, it has also become a more important aspect of educational policy. The terminology has changed from *day-care centers* to *pre-schools,* and in 1996 the responsibility for publicly financed childcare was transferred from the Ministry of Social Affairs and Health to the Ministry of Education and Science and a special curriculum has been developed for children one to five years of age (Bergqvist and Nyberg 2002).

In Sweden, women entered the labor market long before there were enough places in publicly financed childcare. Instead, childcare was arranged in private family day care in the informal market, but informal care is not an alternative today. Informal day care is more expensive for parents than publicly financed childcare and parents believe that the quality is better in publicly financed childcare than in informal childcare.

Many studies find evidence of a strong positive effect of childcare on women's labor force participation. De Henau et al. (2010) conclude that when it comes to securing equal labor market access and conditions for mothers of young children and non-mothers, public child-care provision has the strongest impact.[5] Additionally, a Swedish study found that available childcare had a positive effect on the probability of mothers leaving unemployment, but did not have any effect on unemployed fathers (Vikman 2010).

In Sweden today, childcare is seen more in terms of education and children's rights than as furthering woman's employment. Still, with more than 90 percent of children aged two to five years in publicly financed childcare, it has without doubt had a positive influence on women's employment and gender equality in the labor market, in line with the research referred to earlier. But it does not automatically increase fathers' or men's contribution to unpaid care and household work and therefore to gender equality in that area. In fact, caregiving work might even be more feminized today than earlier, because paid childcare is more feminized than unpaid. Time-use studies show that 95 percent of co-habiting or married mothers of pre-school children spend on average two hours and twenty-eight minutes a day caring for children but also that 88 percent of the fathers spend on average one hour and forty-eight minutes. Compared to 1990–1991, this means a decrease among mothers of 2 percentage points or seventeen minutes and an increase among fathers of 7 percentage points or seventeen minutes (SCB 2012, Tables B:17a–b). Still, the expansion of publicly financed childcare has meant numerous job openings for women. Of the employees in publicly financed childcare, around 93 percent are women, who constituted at least 5–6 percent of all employed women in 2014.[6]

Parental leave and parents' right to shorter working hours

Parental leave

To further gender equality, maternity leave was transformed into parental leave in 1974. This change meant that paid leave following the birth of a child was no longer reserved for the mother, but could also be used by the father, although the father could transfer his right to the mother. This means that the parental allowance is an exception to other social security systems in Sweden, as it is based on the family rather than the individual. This makes parental leave optional for fathers in a way that is different from mothers, and whether fathers use it or not is their choice.

In 1974, the parental leave was six months, but in 1975 it was lengthened to seven months. Already at that time a governmental commission proposed a "father's month," i.e. a month reserved for the father, but it did not meet with approval. Instead, the parental leave was prolonged more or less in close connection to every election (Nyberg 2007a; Försäkringskassan 2011). By 1990, parental leave had reached fifteen months and today is sixteen months (Nyberg 2007b). When parental leave was introduced in 1974, the parental allowance was 90 percent of earnings. At the same time, the benefit became taxable and is considered when pension rights are calculated. In the wake of the economic crisis in Sweden in the 1990s, the parental allowance was lowered and today is about 78 percent of earnings and has a ceiling. Non-employed parents receive a basic amount. Additionally, since 1995, parents have a right to be absent from work to care for a child until the child is eighteen months, independent of whether the parent claims the parental allowance.

Since 2012, parents can take up to thirty days of leave at the same time until the child reaches one year of age. These days have been labeled "double days" (*dubbeldagar*). Parents can take 384 days before the child is four years old and save as many as 96 days of the total 480 parental allowance days until the child is twelve years old.[7] Parents of children born in 2014 or earlier must use all days before the child becomes eight years old.

Nearly all mothers use parental leave, but not all fathers. In 1974, only 3 percent of the recipients of the parental allowance were fathers and 97 percent were mothers, and fathers used only 0.5 percent of the total number of parental allowance days and mothers 99.5 percent (see Figure 18.2). By 1990, 26 percent of the recipients were fathers and fathers used 7 percent of the parental allowance days. Thus over time, the share of fathers taking parental leave grew, albeit very slowly. As a means of encouraging fathers to take more parental leave, the Liberal Party promoted a "father's month" (and corresponding "mother's month"), which was introduced in 1995: one month of the parental leave could no longer

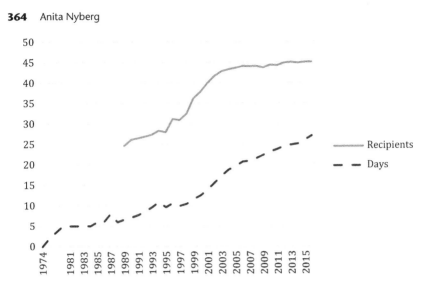

FIGURE 18.2 Percent of fathers among total number of recipients of parental allowance and of total number of parental allowance days, Sweden, 1974–2016

* Figures for recipients include only data from 1988–2016.

Source: For 1974–1988, SCB 1984,18 and 1993,28; for 1989–2016, Försäkringskassan 2016.

be transferred to the other parent, which in reality meant that the father could not transfer that month to the mother. In 2002, the Social Democrats prolonged parental leave with one month and at the same time introduced a second father's month, and neither of these sets of days can be transferred. The increase in the parental allowance days this time meant that fathers could use more leave without mothers having to use less.

A governmental commission appointed in 2004 proposed that a parental leave of fifteen months should be divided, with one third going to the mother, one third to the father, and one part divided as the parents choose (SOU 2005:73). This proposal was not endorsed despite the fact that the Social Democratic Party was in power in 2005 and that there were strong cross-gender alliances within and around the party supporting a more individualized parental leave (Bergqvist et al. 2013).[8] Opponents within the Social Democratic Party perceived that reform of the existing parental leave system was unpopular among the party's core voters in the working class and did not want to take any risks with an election coming the following year (which they lost nonetheless). Since 2014, however, the Social Democratic Party has again been in power, this time together with the Green Party, and has introduced a third father's month that has been in effect since January 1, 2016. This means that if parents want to use all sixteen months of parental leave, each parent must take at least three of those months, although the use of this right is not mandatory.

Of the total claimants of parental leave in 2016, fathers made up 45 percent and mothers 55 percent. While this seems to be a rather equal gender division of the parental leave, the proportion of all parental allowance days used by fathers is not equally impressive: just 27 percent, while mothers took 73 percent. However, the length of the leave differs considerably depending on how the leave is measured; if only the days with parental allowance is counted or if days without parental allowance also are included in the measurement makes a big difference. A 2014 study found that the average length of mothers' leave during the child's two first years was thirteen months, of which 9.5 months were taken with parental allowance (Duvander and Viklund 2014, 27, 45). For fathers, the average length was just 3.5 months, of which two months were taken with parental allowance. A common pattern was to use the parental allowance for five days a week and to take two days without pay.[9]

Besides introducing the first father's month, the same bourgeois government also launched cash-for-care in 1994. This could be seen as a contradiction, but resulted from a coalition government in which the Liberal Party favored a father's month and the Christian Democratic Party favored cash-for-care (Bergqvist and Nyberg 2002). After the election, when the Social Democratic Party again took office, they abolished the cash-for-care policy, which thus was in force only about six months. The argument especially put forth by Social Democratic women was that cash-for-care is a trap for women and supports a traditional family form.

In 2008, the Alliance government again introduced cash-for-care. This time municipalities could choose whether to introduce it or not. In 2013, around 100 of Sweden's 290 municipalities had introduced cash-for-care and half of all one to three year olds lived in municipalities that offered cash-for-care (SCB 2014). But only around 4 percent of the eligible children had parents who choose cash-for-care. Over 90 percent were mothers. Mothers who used cash-for-care had lower incomes and lower educational levels and were more likely to be foreign-born than other mothers. At the same time, a gender equality bonus was introduced in 2008 to encourage fathers to use more parental leave, but it did not have any effect (Inspektionen för socialförsäkringen 2012). Additionally, it was decided that the Swedish Social Insurance Agency (*Försäkringskassan*) should no longer work for an equal division of parental allowance days between mothers and fathers, but only inform parents on how they could use the days (Christenson and Rönngren 2011). However, the Social Democratic/Green Party government, back in power since the fall of 2014, again eliminated cash-for-care as of December 2015 and, as already mentioned, introduced a third father's month in January 2016 (Socialdepartementet 2015a, 2015b).

Parents' right to shorter working hours

Early on, shorter working hours were also seen as a gender equality measure. Six hours working time was proposed as a good idea by several well-known feminists (Myrdal and Klein 1956). In 1972, Social Democratic women demanded shorter working hours not only for parents but for everyone, which the party theoretically approved but resisted putting into practice (Karlsson 1996, 271ff).

In 1975, a commission proposed a part-time parental allowance (SOU 1975:62, 99) that would give each parent with a child younger than three years old the right to a six-hour working day for ten months. It was thought that this part-time parental leave would lead to a leveling of care and household work between parents. Social Democratic women opposed the proposal and were of the opinion that investments should be made in publicly financed childcare, longer parental leave, and an eventual six-hour work day for all (Karlsson 1996, 280ff). Many Social Democratic women believed (correctly, it would appear) that a solution in favor of parents would result in mothers' but not fathers' shortening their working day, which would strengthen gender differences in the labor market. However, the political decision makers decided to continue the status quo and define the unequal gender division of childcare as a problem of attitudes rather than as a structural matter in society. Since then, numerous campaigns have been waged to encourage fathers to use parental leave by ministries, governmental agencies, unions, and others.

In 1978, the government introduced a right to a special parental allowance for ninety days (SOU 2005:73, 109).[10] This special parental allowance could be used as in the form of a full, half, or fourth of a day of parental allowance. An obligatory division of the time between the parents was again discussed. But many argued that there were many situations when exceptions from an obligatory division and need for exceptions would create too much administrative trouble. The allowance was divided equally between the parents, but one parent (usually the father) could transfer the time to the other parent (usually the mother). In 1979, parents with children below the age of eight were also given the right to a partial leave of absence a fourth of full time without any economic compensation.

The parental allowance can today be used for whole days, but also for ¾, ½, ¼, and ⅛ of a day. But the use of paid parental leave for parts of days is very rare.[11] The right that parents have to shorten their working time without compensation is probably used to a much higher extent and almost exclusively by women.

The consequences of parental leave and shorter working hours are complex, but in general there seems to be a consensus that both part-time work and parental leave further women's employment. For example, when the possibility to work part-time increased in Sweden, the share of women who changed from working full-time to working part-time grew at the same time that the share of women changing from full-time to not employed decreased, and a large share of the women who entered the labor market did so on a part-time basis (Pettersson 1981, Chapter 3.4). In Sweden, a larger share of women work part-time after they have a child than before. Working part-time is especially common among women in blue-collar occupations, but since a larger share of them already work part-time before they have children, this change has been biggest among women in white-collar jobs (Westerlund et al. 2005).

Several studies have shown that parental leave policies that offer high replacement income strengthen women's attachment to the labor market by giving future mothers strong incentives to secure a stable position in the labor market prior to having a child in order to qualify for benefits and by raising the likelihood of their return to work when the parental leave expires (see, e.g., Ruhm 1998; Waldfogel et al. 1999). This is verified also by a study from Norway showing that entry into work is much faster among mothers on parental leave than among mothers not on leave and that entry into part-time work is much faster than entry into full-time work (Rønsen and Kitterød 2015).[12]

Fathers' greater use of parental leave seems to weaken the traditional gender division in the household. A Swedish study of time use indicates that while parenthood clearly strengthened the traditional gender division of labor in households in 1990–1991, this was much less the case in 2000–2001, when parenthood affected men and women in a more similar way (Dribe and Stanfors 2009). One reason for this was men's greater use of parental leave. This tendency is also showed in the time use study conducted in 2010 (Stanfors 2015).

Economic development and women and men in the labor market

Economic development

A 1962 long-range forecast for the Swedish economy predicted that in order for economic growth to reach 4 percent per year, the supply of labor had to increase. The shortage of labor was exacerbated by a process of shortening working hours from forty-seven hours per week in 1958 to forty-five hours in 1960 and to forty hours in 1973, in addition to the introduction of four weeks of vacation in 1963 (Nyberg 1996, Table 1). Since married women made up the biggest unused supply of labor, active labor market policy and family policy measures were needed to increase the employment rate of married women (SOU 1962:10, 96, 157).[13] The Swedish economy did develop very satisfactorily in the first half of the 1960s; most notably, the growth rate of production was higher than expected and much higher than it had been previously (SOU 1966:1, 14, 45). In the next long-range forecast, it was expected that growth in GDP could reach 4.2 percent in 1965–1970 if enough manpower (or rather women power) could be mobilized. The entire net increase in the supply of labor was expected to consist of women.

The positive state of the economy abruptly ended in the beginning of the 1970s with the international oil crisis (Eklund 2013; Ekonomifakta 2015). In Sweden, strong increases in wages and payroll taxes also led to high labor costs, leading inflation to rise and economic growth to stall. Production in manufacturing almost stopped altogether during the whole of the 1970s. But the public sector continued to expand, which led to fast-growing budget deficits and raises in national public debt. The Swedish krona (SEK) was devaluated in 1977, 1981, and 1982, which made the Swedish export industry competitive. The forest, steel, and engineering industries started to grow strongly. More people found employment, the state's revenues increased, and profits of Swedish companies rose, which led to a positive spiral for the whole economy. The second half of the 1980s witnessed a hectic economic boom.

This positive state of the economy again ended abruptly. At the beginning of the 1990s, Sweden experienced its worst economic crisis since the 1930s (SOU 2011:11; Nyberg 2014). This crisis consisted of three overlapping waves of employment losses: first, the "international phase," when employment losses hit the export sector and its subcontractors; second, the "real interest phase," which led to employment losses especially in goods-producing sectors selling to the domestic market; and, third, the "budget consolidation phase," with high employment losses in the public sector (Lundborg 2000). The recession in the early 1990s led to a number of retrenchment programs, and the following expansion did not really take off until after 1997. By 1998, the budget had achieved a balance of revenues and expenditures (Kautto 2000, 31).

In 2004, the dotcom bubble burst, economic growth slackened, and employment decreased somewhat (Nyberg 2014). But recovery was rapid and employment rose again, peaking in 2008. In 2009, however, there was a new recession, and GDP fell by 5 percent. The government allocated grants to local governments and introduced labor market measures. The floating exchange rate led to a fall in the Swedish krona (SEK), which boosted exports. These steps, combined with a relatively expansionary financial policy (against the background of a relatively low public debt) had a positive effect on the Swedish economy, and recovery was fast: In 2010, GDP had already increased by 6 percent (McKinsey Sverige 2012).

The situation during this recession was very different and handled differently than the recession in the early 1990s. Changes in the fiscal policy framework in response to the first recession led to a marked structural strengthening of public finances, which was helpful in the latter crisis. Despite the economic downturn in the late 2000s, the country faced only small budget deficits in 2009 and 2010 (Finanspolitiska rådet 2011; International Monetary Fund Sweden 2011). Thus deterioration in Swedish public finances was surprisingly small. One of the main reasons was the relatively small decline in employment compared to the substantial fall in GDP. Since local governments were affected by decreasing tax revenues due to the fall in employment and the rise in unemployment, the central government granted them temporary cyclical support in order to maintain employment and quality in welfare services (Sveriges Kommuner och Landsting 2011). The local government sector ended up with a large surplus in 2010, partly because local authorities were surprised by stronger than expected macroeconomic improvements and partly because of the temporary grants.

During 2008 and 2009, GDP fell as an effect of the financial crisis (Ekonomifakta 2015). 2010 was characterized by recovery and strong growth. This was also the case during parts of 2011, but the international debt crisis again slowed down the Swedish economy. During 2014, 2015, and 2016, Sweden started to move out of the recession and positive and stable growth was achieved, unemployment declined, and employment increased. However, uncertainties remain. Two such worries are how to increase the employment rate of foreign-born and the capacity of the public sector to recruit labor.

Employment

Women's situation in the labor market changed dramatically between 1963 and 1990 (see Figure 18.3). The employment rate for women between the ages of sixteen and sixty-four increased from 53 percent in 1963 to 81 percent in 1990. The increase in employment for mothers with children from zero to six years was even more dramatic: from 37 percent to 85 percent. In 1990, the employment rate of mothers in this group was as high as men's and higher than women's in general. During the same time period, men's employment also declined, from 89 percent in 1960 to 85 percent in 1990.

As can be seen in Figure 18.3, the year 1990 was a watershed year as far as women's employment is concerned. Before 1990, the rate increased continuously and drastically, while men's declined slightly; after 1990, men's—but also women's—employment rate decreased significantly, and thereafter the development was very similar for fathers, mothers, women, and men, with ups and downs in concord with the economic cycles. Today, mothers have a higher employment rate than non-mothers, which means that the presence of a child increases the employment rate for women as well as for men. Between 1990 and 2016, the decline in employment was about 6 percentage points for men and 5 percentage points for women. In 2016, the employment gap between fathers and

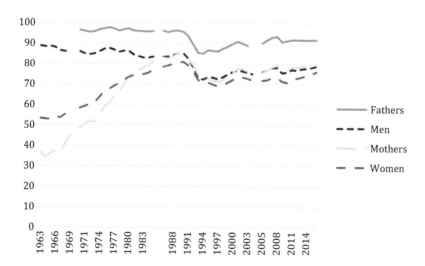

FIGURE 18.3 Percent of employed women and men 16–64 years and of mothers and fathers with children 0–6 years of age, Sweden, 1963–2016

* Figures for fathers include only data from 1970.

Source: SCB 1978, 1981, 1989, 2002, 2005a–2016.

mothers was 12 percentage points, down from 48 percentage points in 1970, and 3 percentage points between men and women, down from 35 percentage points in 1963. One important reason for the decline in employment in the early 1990s, besides the economic crisis, was that many more young people started to study at the university, especially women (Öhman 2011). The number of so-called "housewives" is extremely low in Sweden. In 1990, only 4.3 percent of women aged sixteen to sixty-four declared that they were working in the home, a rate that fell to 1.5 percent by 2016.[14]

Gender is today not the main factor that determines the employment rate. Of greater importance is whether a person is Swedish-born or foreign-born and their age (Nyberg 2015). Swedish-born women's employment rate is, for example, higher than foreign-born men's, and young women and men's (twenty to twenty-four years) employment rate is much lower than those in older age groups. Young persons' employment has decreased significantly especially after 1990; on the other hand, older persons' employment rate has increased.

Developments in employment in the public sector and especially at the municipality level have been extremely important for women's employment. As Figure 18.4 shows, the biggest change was the increase in the number of women (743,000) employed by municipalities between 1964 and 1990, but that growth was also large among men (128,000). The municipalities expanded in order to satisfy demand for services and reduce queues, which meant higher taxes. It also meant increased demand for women's labor, since employment in education, health, child and elderly care, and social welfare have traditionally been

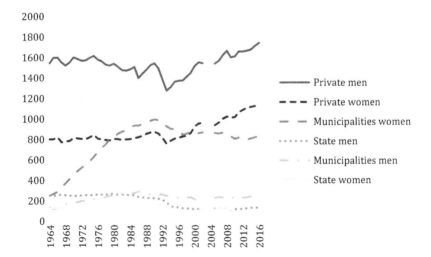

FIGURE 18.4 Number of employees, in thousands, women and men in different sectors, Sweden, 1964–2016

* Data for 1964–1975 include employees between 16–74 years old; for 1976–2016, 16–64 years old.

Source: SCB 1978, 1986, 2005b, 2005a–2016.

considered jobs suitable for women. Many of the new jobs could be filled with women with little education, which is unique for Sweden, compared to many other countries where highly educated women are employed but not women with little education. Many older women also found a job in elderly care, and younger women, often with children of their own, in childcare as day-care workers (Antman 1996). But between 1990 and 2016, the number of women employed in the municipalities decreased by 160,000 and the number of men by 8,000.

The number of employed men in the private sector fluctuated with the economic cycle before 1990 and then plummeted with the economic crisis at the beginning of the 1990s. The number of women in the private sector did not change much until toward the end of 1980s, when it increased some but then fell in the crisis, though less than among men. Between 1964 and 1993—the bottom of the crisis—men lost 269,000 jobs and women 43,000. Since the crisis, both men's and women's employment in the private sector has grown substantially. A comparison of 1993 and 2016 finds that men gained 465,000 jobs and women 392,000.

The decline in the number of public employees is not only a result of budget consolidation and austerity policies but also of other political decisions. Since the early 1990s, local government (municipalities and counties) increased the outsourcing of welfare services to private providers (Hartman 2011). During the following years in which the Social Democratic Party was in power, outsourcing slowed, but there were no serious attempts to reverse policy. When the Alliance government came into power in 2006, policies favoring more competition and private entrepreneurs again received new impetus, and local governments' procurement of services from private-sector providers increased substantially (Konjunkturinstitutet 2010, 2011). As a consequence, there has been an employment transfer in which local government employment has been transferred to the private sector but is still paid by taxes. As an example, the number of employed workers in private companies within health, school, and caregiving services increased from 90,000 in 2000 to 236,000 in 2013 (SOU 2016:78, 138). Given occupational gender segregation, we can assume that the transfer of care workers and teachers from the public to the private sector has been mainly a transfer of female employees, which to a certain extent explains the increasing number of employed women in the private sector.

The total number of employees in the state sector is small. It had increased until the middle of the 1980s and then started to fall: between 1964 and 2016, men lost 117,000 jobs and women gained 27,000 in this sector. There has also been movement of labor from the state sector to the private sector due to political decisions aimed at deregulating and converting public utilities into independent subsidiary companies, which explains a great deal of the shrinking number of men in the state sector.[15] The increasing number of women is almost certainly a result of women's higher educational level, since many highly educated persons work in the state sector.[16]

Gender equality in employment increased until 1990. After the economic crisis in the beginning of the 1990s, however, the gender employment gap has varied between 3 and 5 percentage points without seeming to close further, making it appear that gender equality in employment has come to a halt. Reasons for this can be found in the composition of the labor force. The gender employment gap is bigger among older women and men (between fifty-five and sixty-four years) than other age groups, and since this category constitutes a bigger share of the employed today than earlier, this sustains the total gender employment gap. The employment rate of older women and men is increasing, but faster for men than for women. Another reason is the growing share of foreign-born workers in Sweden, among whom the employment rate is lower. The difference in employment rate between Swedish-born and foreign-born women is much bigger than between Swedish-born and foreign-born men, which preserves the total gender employment gap. A majority of the newly arrived foreign-born are refugees or family members of refugees. To enter the labor market is especially difficult for foreign-born workers in their first years after arriving in Sweden, since the newly arrived have limited networks in Sweden and limited knowledge of the Swedish language.

Absence from work

As already discussed, women's employment increased significantly between the beginning of the 1960s until 1990, and by the beginning of the 1990s women and men's employment rates were almost the same. Since then the employment rate has been relatively gender-equal. Yet given the higher incidence of female absence from work and part-time employment, the employment rate overestimates women's labor market participation and gender equality. In fact, today the employment rate is not a very good indicator of gender equality in Sweden.

In 2012, the average time of absence among employees corresponded to 21.0 percent of the agreed working time (SCB 2013). Of these absences, 9.8 percent was for vacation, 3.2 percent for sickness, 3.2 percent for parental leave, 2.6 percent for holidays falling on workdays, and 2.3 percent for other reasons. A comparison between the sexes shows, as would be expected, that women's total absences were higher than men's, mainly because women use parental leave much more than men. Women's absence because of parental leave was three times higher than men's, and because of sickness was 50 percent higher than men's.

Figure 18.5 shows the share of employed women and men who were absent from work. In the 1960s, the difference in absences was smaller but increased as more and more married or cohabiting women and mothers entered the labor market and the length of parental leave became longer and longer. Toward the end of the period, the difference had decreased some. Absence was higher for both women and men when the employment rate was high in the 1980s and decreased in the economic crisis in the beginning of the 1990s.

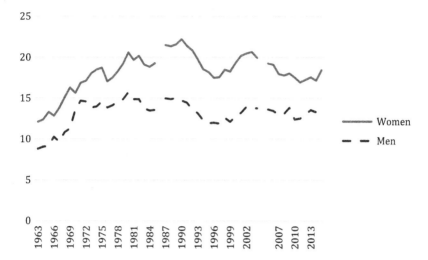

FIGURE 18.5 Percent absent of the employees, women and men, Sweden, 1963–2015
* Data for 1963-1975 include workers in the age group of 16–74 years old; for 1976, 16–64 years old.
Source: SCB 1978, 1986, 2005b, 2005a–2016.

Women's higher absence rates means that the gender gap is bigger between women and men if people "at work" is used as a measurement rather than employment rates. On the one hand, while parental leave gives women strong incentives to be employed before having children and to return to employment after parental leave, on the other, parental leave increases women's absence from employment, which negatively influences women's incomes and economic independence.

Working time

Even if absence is taken into account, women's labor market participation and gender equality is still overestimated because women's working hours are shorter than men's. It should be pointed out that a large majority of part-time employed women in Sweden work long part-time hours, ranging from twenty to thirty-four hours per week. The share of part-time employed women and mothers increased between the middle of the 1960s and the first half of the 1980s, at the same time their employment grew dramatically (see Figure 18.6).

Since the middle of the 1980s, the share of women and mothers working part-time has decreased, while the share of men and fathers working part-time has increased continuously but very slowly. In 2016, 30 percent of employed women and 12 percent of men worked part-time, as did 40 percent of mothers and 9 percent of fathers (SCB 2005a–2016).[17] Part-time work is also a matter of class among women, but not among men. In 2010, half of the women belonging to a union of blue-collar workers were employed part-time,

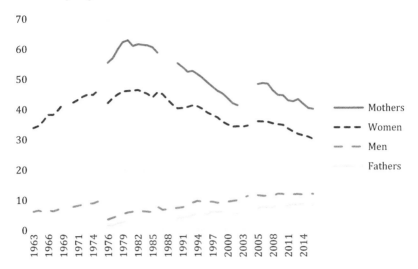

FIGURE 18.6 Percent part-time employed of the employed, mothers and fathers with children 0–6 years old and working age women and men, Sweden, 1965–2016

* Data for 1965–1975 include workers 16–74 years old; for 1976–2016, 16–64 years old. Data for fathers are available only for 1970. Observe that there are breaks in the series. Statistics Sweden (SCB) cannot explain the big difference in the share of part-time working mothers between 2002 and 2005. There is no change in the definition (Samuelsson, SCB).

Source: SCB 1978, 1981, 1986, 1988–2002, 1989, 2005b, 2005a–2016.

compared to a third of white-collar workers and only a fourth of professional women (Larsson 2010). Among men, the percentage was similar in all three categories. The decline in women's part-time work from the middle of the 1980s is most likely a result of a high demand for labor in the service sector and of women's higher educational levels and thereby stronger work orientation (Stanfors 2003, 123).

The gender gap in employment, therefore, is no longer the most important indicator of gender equality, replaced instead by the gender gap in working time (Nyberg 2015). Men's paid working time is on average longer than women's, irrespective of age and country of birth. For example, young men work longer hours than "prime age" women, and foreign-born men work longer hours than Swedish-born women. Women's working time has been prolonged, including among married or cohabiting women and single mothers since the middle of the 1980s. Men's working time, in comparison. has become shorter, including among married or cohabiting men and single fathers with children, but the big decline in men's working time took place when the norm for full-time work changed from forty-seven hours per week in 1958 to forty-five hours in 1960 and then to forty hours in 1973 (Nyberg 1996, Table 1).

It is well known that women tend to choose to be employed part-time in order to take care of children. In 2016, around 131,800 or 22 percent of part-time employed women and 22,000 or 8 percent of part-time employed men in Sweden stated that the reason they worked part-time was to care for children (SCB 2016). Much less known is that many more testified that they worked part-time because "suitable full-time work is unavailable/looking for full-time work": 193,700 or 27 percent of the part-time employed women and 84,900 or 32 percent of the part-time employed men.

The Labor Force Surveys classify a person as underemployed if she/he is employed but works less than she/he would like. Persons who are employed even one hour a week are classified as employed even if they are absent that hour or if they would like to work forty hours and thereby might be seen as unemployed thirty-nine hours per week. Furthermore, a person who works full-time but states that she/he would like to work more hours is also defined as underemployed.

Figure 18.7 presents the share of underemployed among the employed in Sweden between 1965 and 2016. As it shows, women's underemployment is much higher than men's during the whole period, except at the very end. That share increased drastically in the economic crisis in the beginning of the 1990, and much more for women than for men.[18] In the beginning of the 2000s, the share declined again. For women, it has not increased since then, but men's underemployment is approaching the level of women's. In 2009, 80 percent of the underemployed women worked part-time, while 40 percent of the underemployed men worked full-time (SCB 2009, 5, 13).

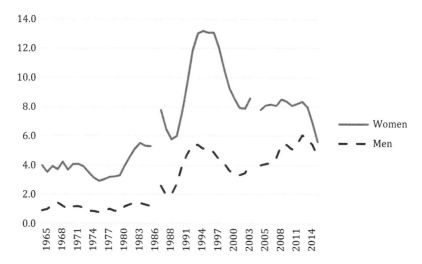

FIGURE 18.7 Percent underemployed of the employed, women and men, Sweden, 1965–2015

* For 1965–1985, the underemployed are persons 16–74 years old who are working part-time but would like to and are able to work more hours; for 1987–2016, they are persons 16–64 years old who are employed either part-time or full-time but would like to and are able to work more hours.

Source: SCB 1978, 1981, 1986, 2005b, 2005a–2016.

The share of underemployed has been highest among young women (between ages of fifteen and twenty-four), though young men come second and their share has been growing (Nyberg 2015). This is also the case somewhat among men twenty-five years and older, but not among women in the same age category. The share of underemployed has increased among foreign-born women and men and among Swedish-born men, while the share among Swedish-born women has changed very little.

A big majority of the underemployed—around 80 percent—wished to increase their working time in their present work. A 2009 study found that underemployment was highest among hotel and restaurant workers (16 percent)—among both women and men—and lowest among construction workers (3 percent) (SCB 2009). Care and social welfare workers dominate the underemployed, including many women in working-class occupations in the public sector.

Involuntary part-time work, especially in the public sector, has recently become a high-priority area in Sweden's gender equality policy (Prop 2013/14:1; Uo. 13, 59), although underemployment and part-time unemployment received very little attention in earlier budget bills (Nyberg 2015). But today much of the policy debate on gender equality revolves around "full-time employment as a right and part-time as a possibility." This is a demand put forward by the Social Democratic Party, the Social Democratic women, the Leftist Party, the Green Party, and the Women's Association of the Alliance, a coalition of Moderate, Center, Liberal, and Christian Democratic women. Today not only the government but also employers in the public sector see the need for more full-time employment as a result of the demographic situation among other factors. According to the Swedish Association of Local Authorities and Regions, the share of part-time work in municipalities decreased by 5 percentage points between 2008 and 2014, all of it among women (Prop 2016/17:1).

Although Swedish unemployment data show that the difference in women and men's unemployment is small, this analysis argues that such data underestimate women's unemployment because they measure only full-time unemployed and many women are part-time unemployed. If both unemployment and underemployment are counted as unemployment, then women's unemployment has been much higher than men's. The disparity between women and men's underemployment was highest between 1995 and 1998, when the difference reached 8 percentage points. In 2016, that difference had fallen 1 percentage point. A decrease among women and an increase among men have resulted in increased "gender equality" in underemployment. On the one hand, the right of parents to shorten their working hours makes it easier for some women to be employed; on the other hand, it also results in involuntary part-time unemployment and underemployment.

Conclusion

The title of this article raises a question: did the kick-start in gender equality policies in the 1960s and 1970s end in a U-turn? If so, was this because gender equality policies did not have the intended effects, i.e. promoting gender equality in the labor market and in the family, or was this a result of changes in gender equality policies? The answer to these questions are, I argue, that gender equality policies did go from a kick-start in the 1970s to a U-turn starting in the 2000s, which continued up until the last couple of years, when gender equality policies again appeared to be more determined. Throughout this whole period, however, women have strived for greater parity with men in the labor market and in the family, and gender equality has indeed increased in these areas.

A decisive year in the development was 1990, not because of gender equality policies but because of the economic situation and developments in the labor market before and after that year. In the 1960s, there was an intensive discussion in Sweden concerning women and men's roles and widespread agreement that they had to be changed so that both women and men could be employed and share unpaid household and caregiving work. To encourage this shift, during the 1970s individual taxation was introduced, publicly financed childcare was expanded, and maternity leave was transformed to parental leave, and gave parents the right to shorter working hours. But these decisions were only the beginning of a process. Although individual taxation was introduced in 1971, for instance, in 1990 the "housewife deduction" was still in place, as was joint taxation of wealth. A decision to expand publicly financed childcare was taken in 1974, but until the end of the 1970s more places were offered in part-time playschools than in full-day day-care centers, and for a long time the demand for publicly financed childcare was much larger than the supply. There were still queues in 1990 even though 55–67 percent of the two, three, four and five year olds were enrolled in publicly financed childcare at that time. When maternity leave was turned into parental leave in 1974, fathers were very hesitant to use it. Twenty years later in 1994, only 28 percent of the receivers of the parental allowance were fathers, and fathers took only 11 percent of the parental allowance days. Early attempts to individualize parental leave failed. Fathers' caregiving responsibilities for their children became voluntary and dependent on their choice to a much greater extent than for mothers. When the right of parents to shorten their working hours were also introduced, women's part-time work increased, but not fathers'. On the other hand, shortening ordinary working time from forty-seven hours to forty hours between the end of the 1950s to 1973 also meant that almost all men's working time was shortened significantly because almost all men worked full-time.

Nevertheless, the introduction of individual taxation, parental leave, expansion of publicly financed childcare, and parents' right to shorter working hours can be seen as providing a distinct kick-start for the dual-earner/dual-caregiver model and for greater gender equality in the Swedish labor market. Women and mothers' increasing employment took place in the fast-growing public sector and increased significantly from the beginning of the 1960s to its peak in 1990. During the same period, men's and fathers' employment rates decreased some and gender equality in employment was boosted. Simultaneously, the share of employed women who were absent from work also reached a peak in 1990, and the gender gap in absence from employment was the largest during the whole period. On the other hand, the share of women working part-time started to decline in the middle of the 1980s, which meant that gender equality in working time increased. Parental leave and parents' right to shorter working hours encouraged women's and mothers' employment but also their part-time work and absence from work.

The path started in the 1970s continued despite the severe economic crisis in Sweden at the beginning of the 1990s, in which employment for both women and men decreased dramatically and many jobs in the public sector were lost. The "housewife deduction" was abolished in 1991 and joint taxation of wealth in 2007. Expansion of publicly financed childcare continued, and by 2016, 91–97 percent of children aged two to five had a place and publicly financed childcare was viewed as an essential aspect of the country's educational policy.

In order to encourage fathers to take more parental leave, a "father's month" was introduced in 1995, which did encourage more fathers to use parental leave. However, when in 2002 a second fathers' month was introduced by the Social Democrats, the parental leave was prolonged at the same time, which meant that fathers could take longer leave while mothers still were away from the labor market long periods of time.[19] The Social Democrats choose not to individualize parental leave in 2005. The Alliance government introduced cash-for-care, which was almost exclusively used by mothers, and decided that the Social Insurance Agency should no longer promote an equal division of the parental allowance days between the parents. Together, these developments can be perceived as a U-turn in gender equality policies in the 2000s, though one that seems to have been reversed in the middle of the 2010s, when cash-for-care again was abolished and a third so-called father's month was introduced.

Still, even if the development in gender equality policies did take a U-turn, this does not mean that gender equality in the labor market and the family did the same. The gender employment gap was only around 1–2 percentage points in the beginning of the 1990s, mainly because men's employment decreased faster than women's. In the second half of 2000s, the gap increased to 4–5 percentage points, but had closed some in 2015 and 2016 to around 3 percentage points. Additionally, the gender absence gap has diminished recently and women work ever-longer hours, meaning that gender equality has increased in employment rates, at-work rates and working hours since 1990. Additionally, if women continue to educate themselves to a greater extent than men, enter traditionally male-dominated high-status jobs, and break up the gender-segregated labor market, the gender wage gap has finally begun closing. Changes are also taking place among men, including a decrease in working time among fathers. Parenthood affects men and women in a more similar way today than earlier. One reason given for this is men's greater use of parental leave. While the working mother is here to stay, it appears that the caring father is on his way.

Notes

1 The Global Gender Gap Report's index assesses four areas: economic participation and opportunities, educational attainment, health and survival, and political empowerment (World Economic Forum 2006–2016). The Gender Equity Index of Social Watch is based on three dimensions: education, economic participation, and empowerment (Social Watch 2007, 2009, 2012). The EIGE Gender Equality Index consists of six core domains and two satellite domains: work, money, knowledge, time, power, health, violence, and intersecting inequalities (European Institute for Gender Equality 2015).
2 Moberg referred to a book by Myrdal and Klein, *Women's Two Roles: Home and Work*, published in 1956.
3 The Conservative Party (*Högerpartiet*) changed its name in 1969 to the Moderate Party (*Moderaterna*).
4 According to the Discrimination Act (*Diskrimineringslagen*), employers are required to undertake pay surveys and to draw up a written action plan to accomplish equal pay.
5 See also, for example, Mandel and Semyonov (2003); Kalmijn et al. (2005); Kenjoh (2005); Pettit and Hook 2005); Lefebvre and Merrigan (2008); Steiber and Haas (2009).
6 Calculated from Skolverket (2016d), Table 2A; Skolverket (2016e), Table 1A; Skolverket (2016f), Table 2A; and SCB (2006a–2015), Table 1.
7 The father or other parent of the child is entitled to a temporary parental benefit for ten days in connection with the birth of a child or adoption. There is also a law that enables parents to take paid care leave for sick children (sixty days per year and per child) up to the child's twelfth birthday compensated at almost 80 percent of previous earnings.
8 The Social Democratic Women's Association, the Social Democratic Youth Organization, the blue collar union (LO), and the Minister for Gender Equality were in favor of a more individualized parental leave, while the prime minister, minister of finance, minister for social affairs, and the party secretary were against it.
9 The flexibility of the Swedish parental leave, where paid and unpaid days can be mixed, makes comparisons with other country's systems complicated.
10 Since January 1, 1980, this has been 180 days (Pettersson 1981, 53)
11 In 2014, the share of part-time (net) days amounted to around 10 percent of the total number of parental allowance days for both mothers and fathers (Försäkringskassan 2016)
12 Many studies also show that long parental leave negatively affects women's careers (Datta Gupta and Smith 2002; Rønsen and Sundström 2002; Aisenbrey et al. 2009; Evertsson and Duvander 2010; Evertsson and Grunow 2012), women's wages and earnings (Ruhm 1998; Albrecht et al. 1999, 2003; Pylkkänen and Smith 2003; Kennerberg 2007; Lindström 2010; Angelov et al. 2013), and men's wages and incomes (Stafford and Sundström 1996; Jansson et al. 2003; Thoursie 2005) and that fathers' use has a positive effect on mothers' income (Lindström 2010).
13 Another but much smaller source was immigrants.
14 Calculated from SCB, AKU, 1990, Tables 1 and 31, and SCB, AKU, 2016 Tables 1 and 16.
15 Privatization of state-run companies has involved such areas as steel production, telecommunications, banking, forestry, medicine, and the production of liquor (Calmfors 2012). Employees in air traffic control, electricity generation and distribution, postal services, and railway and other transport who were previously considered state employees are today included in the private sector.
16 It is worth pointing out that gender segregation in the labor market not only changes because women enter traditionally male-dominated sectors or men enter traditionally female-dominated sectors, but also because industries are reclassified from one sector to another.
17 There is a break in the data in 2004, and therefore data are not altogether comparable.

18 Unemployment, on the other hand, rose more for men than for women.
19 Additionally, twenty-six years after maternity leave was transformed into parental leave, two weeks of obligatory maternity leave was introduced in 2002 as a concession to the EU.

References

Aisenbrey, Silke, Evertsson, Marie, and Grunow, Daniela. 2009. "Is there a Career Penalty for Mothers' Time Out? A Comparison of Germany, Sweden and the United States." *Social Forces*, 88: 573–606.

Albrecht, James, Björklund, Anders, and Vroman, Susan B. 2003. "Is There a Glass Ceiling in Sweden?" *Journal of Labor Economics*, 21: 145–177.

Albrecht, James W., Edin, Per-Anders, Sundström, Marianne, and Vroman, Susan B. 1999. "Career Interruptions and Subsequent Earnings: A Reexamination Using Swedish Data." *Journal of Human Resources*, 34: 294–311.

Angelov, Nikolay, Johansson, Per, and Lindahl, Erica. 2013. *Is the Persistent Gender Gap in Income and Wages Due to Unequal Family Responsibilities?* IFAU Working paper 2013: 3. Uppsala: IFAU.

Antman, Peter. 1996. *Barn- och äldreomsorg i Tyskland och Sverige. Sverigedelen.* Skriftserien: Fakta/kunskaper Nr 5. Stockholm: Norstedts Tryckeri AB.

Bergqvist, Christina, (ed.). 1999. *Likestilte demokratier? Kjønn og politikk i Norden.* Oslo: Universitetsforlaget/Nordisk ministerråd.

Bergqvist, Christina, Bjarnegård, Elin, and Zetterberg, Pär. 2013. "Analysing Failure, Understanding Success: A Research Strategy for Explaining Gender Equality Policy Adoption." *NORA – Nordic Journal of Feminist and Gender Research*, 21, 4: 280–295.

Bergqvist, Christina, and Nyberg, Anita. 2002. "Welfare State Restructuring and Child Care in Sweden." In *Child Care Policy at the Crossroads: Gender and Welfare State Restructuring*, edited by Sonia Michel and Rianne Mahon, 287–307. New York: Routledge.

Calmfors, Lars. 2012. *Sweden – From Macroeconomic Failure to Macroeconomic Success.* CESifo Working Paper Series 3790, Munich: CESifo Group.

Christenson, Gerda, and Rönngren, Jenny. 2011. "Alliansen smygavskaffade mål om delad föräldraledighet." *Feministiskt perspektiv.* Available from: http://feministisktperspektiv.se/2011/10/14/alliansen-smygavskaffade-mal-om-delad-foraldraledighet/. Accessed 7 January 2017.

Datta Gupta, Nabanita, and Smith, Nina. 2002. "Children and Career Interruptions: The Family Gap in Denmark." *Economica*, 69: 609–629.

De Henau, Jérome, Meulders, Danièle, and O'Dorchai, Sile. 2010. "Maybe Baby: Comparing Partnered Women's Employment and Child Policies in the EU-15." *Feminist Economics*, 16, 1: 43–77.

Dribe, Martin, and Stanfors, Maria. 2009. "Does Parenthood Strengthen a Traditional Household Division of Labor? Evidence from Sweden." *Journal of Marriage and Family*, 71: 33–45.

Duvander, Ann-Zofie, and Viklund, Ida. 2014. "Kvinnors och mäns föräldraledighet." In *Lönsamt arbete – familjeansvarets fördelning och konsekvenser*, SOU 2014:28, 22–61. Stockholm: Fritzes.

Edin, Per-Anders, and Richardson, Katarina. 1997. "Lönepolitik, lönespridning och löneskillnader mellan män och kvinnor." In *Kvinnors och mäns löner – Varför så olika?* SOU 1997:136, edited by Inga Persson and Eskil Wadensjö, 87–103. Stockholm: Fritzes.

Eklund, Klas. 2013. *Vår ekonomi: en introduktion till samhällsekonomin.* Lund: Studentlitteratur.

Ekonomifakta. 2015. Available from: http://www.ekonomifakta.se/sv/Fakta/Ekonomi/Tillvaxt/BNP-per-capita/. Accessed 7 January 2017.

Elvander, Nils. 1972. *Svensk skattepolitik 1945–1970. En studie i partiers och organisationers funktioner.* Stockholm: Rabén & Sjögren.

European Institute for Gender Equality. 2015. *Gender Equality Index 2015. Measuring Gender Equality in the European Union 2005–2012.* Available from: http://eige.europa.eu/rdc/eige-publications/gender-equality-index-2015-measuring-gender-equality-european-union-2005-2012-report. Accessed 7 January 2017.

Evertsson, Marie, and Duvander, Ann-Zofie. 2010. "Parental Leave- Possibility or Trap? Does Family Leave Length Effect Swedish Women's Labour Market Opportunities?" *European Sociological Review,* 27: 1–16.

Evertsson, Marie, and Grunow, Daniela. 2012. "Women's Work Interruptions and Career Prospects in Germany and Sweden. Special issue on Welfare State Regulations and Mothers' Labour Market Participation in an Internationally Comparative Perspective." *International Journal of Sociology and Social Policy,* 32: 561–575.

Finanspolitiska rådet. 2011. *Svensk finanspolitik. Finanspolitiska rådets rapport 2011.* Stockholm: Finanspolitiska rådet.

Florin, Christina. 1999. "Skatten som befriar. Hemmafruar mot yrkeskvinnor i 1960-talets särbeskattningsdebatt." In *Kvinnor mot kvinnor,* edited by Christina Florin, Lena Sommestad and Ulla Wikander, 106–135. Stockholm: Norstedts förlag.

Florin, Christina, and Nilsson, Bengt. 1999. "Something in the Nature of a Bloodless Revolution …' How New Gender Relations Became Gender Equality Policy in Sweden in the Nineteen-Sixties and Seventies." In *State Policy and Gender System in the Two German States and Sweden 1945–1989,* edited by Rolf Torstendahl, 11–77. Uppsala: Department of History. St. Larsgatan 2, SE-753 10 Uppsala, Sweden.

Försäkringskassan. 2011. *Föräldrapenning. Båda föräldrarnas försäkring.* Socialförsäkringsrapport 2011: 13. Stockholm: Försäkringskassan.

Försäkringskassan. 2016. *Föräldrapenning. Antal mottagare, barn, nettodagar och belopp efter ålder.* Available from: https://www.forsakringskassan.se/statistik/statistik_och_analys2/barn_fa milj/foraldrapenning. Accessed 7 January 2017.

Fürst, Gunilla. 1999. *Jämställda på svenska.* Stockholm: Svenska institutet.

Gunnarsson, Åsa. 1995. *Skatterättvisa.* Uppsala: Iustus förlag.

Gustafsson, Siv. 1992. "Separate Taxation and Married Women's Labour Supply. A Comparison of West Germany and Sweden." *Journal of Population Economics,* 5, 1: 61–85.

Hartman, Laura. 2011. "Inledning and Slutsatser." In *Konkurrensens konsekvenser Vad händer med svensk välfärd?* edited by Laura Hartman, 9–31. Stockholm: SNS.

Hirdman, Yvonne. 1994. *Women – From Possibility to Problem? Gender Conflict in the Welfare State – The Swedish Model.* Research Report No. 3. Stockholm: Arbetslivscentrum.

Holmberg, Per. 1966. *Kynne eller kön?: om könsrollerna i det moderna samhället: en debattskrift.* Stockholm: Rabén & Sjögren.

Inspektionen för socialförsäkringen. 2012. *Ett jämställt uttag? Reformer inom föräldraförsäkringen.* Rapport 2012: 4. Stockholm: Inspektionen för socialförsäkringen.

International Monetary Fund Sweden. 2011. *Concluding Statement of the Article IV Consultation Mission.* Available from: http://www.imf.org/external/np/ms/2011/053011.htm. Accessed 10 July 2015.

Jansson, Fredrik, Pylkkänen, Elina, and Valck, Lizbeth. 2003. *En jämställd föräldraförsäkring?* SOU 2003:36. Bilaga 12 till Långtidsutredningen 2003. Stockholm: Fritzes.

Jaumotte, Florence. 2003. *Female Labour Force Participation: Past Trends and Main Determinants in OECD countries.* Working Paper 376. Paris: OECD Economics Department.

Jonsson, Jan O. 2004. "Förskola för förfördelad?" In *Familj och arbete – Vardagsliv i förändring*, edited by Magnus Bygren, Michael Gähler, and Magnus Nermo, 90–121. Stockholm: SNS förlag.

Kalmijn, Matthijs, Uunk, Wilfred, and Muffels, Ruud. 2005. "The Impact of Young Children on Women's Labour Supply A Reassessment of Institutional Effects in Europe." *Acta Sociologica*, 48, 1: 41–62.

Karlsson, Gunnel. 1996. *Från broderskap till systerskap*. Lund: Arkiv förlag.

Kautto Mikko. 2000. *Two of a Kind*. SOU 2000: 83. Stockholm: Socialdepartementet.

Kenjoh, Eiko. 2005. "New Mothers' Employment and Public Policy in the UK, Germany, the Netherlands, Sweden, and Japan." *Labour*, 19–51, Special Issue: 5–49.

Kennerberg, Louise. 2007. *Hur förändras kvinnors och mäns arbetssituation när de får barn?* Rapport 2007: 9. Uppsala: Institutet för Arbetsmarknadspolitisk utvärdering (IFAU).

Klinth, Roger. 2002. *Göra pappa med barn. Den svenska pappapolitiken 1960–1995*. Umeå: Boréa.

Klinth, Roger, and Johansson, Thomas. 2010. *Nya svenska fäder*. Umeå: Boréa.

Konjunkturinstitutet. 2010. *Kommunalt finansierad sysselsättning och arbetade timmar i privat sektor*. Fördjupnings-PM Nr. 6 2010. Stockholm: Konjunkturinstitutet.

Konjunkturinstitutet. 2011. *Konjunkturläget mars 2011*. Stockholm: Konjunkturinstitutet.

Larsson, Mats. 2010. *Arbetstider år 2009: heltids- och deltidsarbete, vanligen arbetad tid och arbetstidens förläggning efter klass och kön år 1990–2009*. Stockholm: LO.

Lefebvre, Pierre, and Merrigan, Philip. 2008. "Child-Care Policy and the Labor Supply of Mothers with Young Children: A Natural Experiment." *Journal of Labor Economics*, 26: 519–548.

Lindencrona, Gustaf. 1979. *Trends in Scandinavian Taxation*. Deventer, The Netherlands: Kluwer.

Lindencrona, Gustaf. 1985. "Juridiska nationalrapporter. Sverige." In *Familjebeskattningen i Norden. Rapporter och inlägg vid Nordiska skattevetenskapliga forskningsrådets seminarium i Moss i oktober 1984*, Nordiska skattevetenskapliga forskningsrådets skriftserie NSFS 15, Stockholm: Liber.

Lindström, Elly-Ann. 2010. *The Effect of Own and Spousal Parental Leave on Earnings*. IFAU Working Paper 2010: 4. Uppsala: IFAU.

Lindvert, Jessica. 2002. *Feminism som politik*. Umeå: Boréa.

Lindvert, Jessica. 2004. "Spelets regler. Att göra politik av genusfrågor." In *Framtiden i samtiden. Könsrelationer i förändring i Sverige och omvärlden*, edited by Christina Florin and Christina Bergqvist, Stockholm: Institutet för framtidsstudier.

Löfström, Åsa. 1989. *Diskriminering på svensk arbetsmarknad. En analys av löneskillnader mellan kvinnor och män*. Umeå Economic Studies No. 196. Umeå: Umeå University.

Lundborg, Per. 2000. "Vilka förlorade jobbet under 1990-talet?" In *Välfärdens förutsättningar*, SOU 2000: 37, edited by Johan Fritzell, Stockholm: Fritzes.

Lundqvist, Åsa. 2007. *Familjen i den svenska modellen*. Umeå: Boréa.

Mandel, Hadas, and Semyonov, Moshe. 2003. *Welfare Family Policies and Gender Earnings Inequality: A Cross-National Comparative Analysis*. Luxembourg Income Study Working Paper Series No. 364. Available from: http://citation.allacademic.com/meta/p_mla_a pa_research_citation/1/0/9/0/3/pages109039/p109039-1.php. Accessed 7 January 2017.

McKinsey Sverige. 2012. *Tillväxt och förnyelse i den svenska ekonomin. Utveckling, nuläge och prioriteringar inför framtiden*. Available from: http://news.cision.com/se/mckinsey-com pany-sverige/r/tillvaxt-och-fornyelse-i-den-svenska-ekonomin,c9265225. Accessed 7 January 2017.

Moberg, Eva. 1961. "Kvinnans villkorliga frigivning." In *Unga liberaler. Nio inlägg i idédebatten*, edited by Hans Hederberg, Stockholm: Bonniers.
Myrdal, Alva, and Klein, Viola. 1956. *Women's Two Roles: Home and Work*. London: Routledge & Kegan Paul.
Nyberg, Anita. 1989. *Tekniken – kvinnornas befriare? Hushållsteknik, köpevaror, gifta kvinnors hushållsarbetstid och förvärvsdeltagande 1930-talet – 1980-talet*. Linköping: Tema Teknik och social förändring, Linköping University.
Nyberg, Anita. 1994. "The Social Construction of Married Women's Labour-Force Participation: The Case of Sweden in the Twentieth Century." *Continuity and Change*, 9, 1: 145–156.
Nyberg, Anita. 1995. "Barnomsorgen. Ett kvinnligt nollsummespel eller?" In *Medmänsklighet att hyra? Åtta forskare om ideell verksamhet*, edited by Erik Amnå, 47–84. Örebro: Libris.
Nyberg, Anita. 1996. "Arbetstider ur jämställdhets- och familjesynpunkt." In *SOU 1996:145 Arbetstid längd, förläggning och inflytande. Bilagedel*, 223–296. Stockholm: Fritzes.
Nyberg, Anita. 2007a. "Lessons from the Swedish Experience." In *Kids Count. Better Early Childhood Education and Care in Australia*, edited by Elizabeth Hill, Barbara Pocock and Alison Elliott, 38–56. Sydney: Sydney University Press.
Nyberg, Anita. 2007b. "Desarrollo del modelo de dos sustentadores/dos cuidadores en Suecia: el papel del sistema de educación infantil y de los permisos parentales." In *Economía e igualdad de género: retos de la hacienda pública en el siglo XXI*, edited by Maria Pazos Morán, Madrid: Instituto de Estudios Fiscales.
Nyberg, Anita. 2014. "Women and Men's Employment in the Recessions of the 1990s and 2000s in Sweden." In *European Labour Markets in Times of Crisis. A Gender Perspective*, edited by Anne Eydoux, Antoine Math and Hélène Pérvier, 303–334. Revue de lÔfce Paris: SciencesPo.
Nyberg, Anita. 2015. *Ekonomisk självständighet och ekonomisk jämställdhet*. Underlag till Jämställdhetsutredningen U2014:06 Delmål 2: Ekonomisk jämställdhet (exklusive utbildning). Available from: http://www.sou.gov.se/wp-content/uploads/2015/03/Anita-Nyberg-Ekonomisk-j%C3%A4mst%C3%A4lldhet.pdf. Accessed 7 January 2017.
Öhman, Berndt. 2011. "Två kriser – en analys av den aktuella arbetsmarknaden." *Arbetskraftsundersökningarna (AKU) 50 år*. In *Fyra forskarperspektiv på arbetsmarknaden*, 33–62. Stockholm: SCB.
Pettersson, Marianne. 1981. *Deltidssökningens orsaker, deltidsanställdas levnadsförhållanden*. Stockholm: Arbetslivscentrum.
Pettit, Becky, and Hook, Jennifer. 2005. "The Structure of Women's Employment in Comparative Perspective." *Social Forces*, 84, 2: 779–801.
Prop. 2013/14:1 *Budgetpropositionen för 2014. Uo. 13*. Stockholm: Finansdepartementet. Available from: http://www.regeringen.se/49bb15/contentassets/f764ba87c27347588b4f4bb51c412688/utgiftsomrade-13-integration-och-jamstalldhet. Assessed 6 January 2017.
Prop. 2016/17:1 *Budgetpropositionen för 2017. Uo. 13*. Stockholm: Finansdepartementet. Available from: http://www.regeringen.se/4a6968/contentassets/e926a751d9eb4c978c4d892c659ebc8e/utgiftsomrade-13-jamstalldhet-och-nyanlanda-invandrares-etablering. Assessed 6 January 2017.
Pylkkänen, Elina, and Smith, Nina. 2003. *Career Interruptions Due to Parental Leave Matter in Europe. A Comparative Study of Denmark and Sweden*. OECD Social, Employment and Migration working Papers No. 1. Paris: OECD.
Rønsen, Marit, and Kitterød, Ragni Hege. 2015. "Gender-Equalizing Family Policies and Mothers' Entry into Paid Work: Recent Evidence From Norway." *Feminist Economics*, 21, 1: 58–89.

Rønsen, Marit, and Sundström, Marianne. 2002. "Family Policy and After-Birth Employment among New Mothers – A comparison of Finland, Norway and Sweden." *European Journal of Population*, 18: 121–152.

Ruhm, Christopher J. 1998. "The Economic Consequences of Parental Leave Mandates: Lessons from Europe." *The Quarterly Journal of Economics*, 113: 285–317.

Samuelsson, Daniel. 2012. SCB, email 8 August 2012.

SCB. 1978. *SM Am 1978: 32.Arbetskraftsundersökningarna 1963–1975*. Stockholm: SCB.

SCB. 1981. *SM Am 1981: 33.Arbetskraftsundersökningarna 1970–1980*. Stockholm: SCB.

SCB. 1984, 1993. *På tal om kvinnor och män* Stockholm: SCB.

SCB. 1986. *SM Am 12 SM 8602. Arbetskraftsundersökningarna 1976–1985*. Stockholm: SCB.

SCB. 1988–2002. *AKU. Arbetskraftsundersökningarna. Årsmedeltal*. Stockholm: SCB.

SCB. 1989. *Arbetsmarknaden i siffror. Sysselsättning, arbetslöshet mm 1970–1988*. Stockholm: SCB.

SCB. 2002. *Arbetskraftsundersökningarna. Sysselsättning och arbetslöshet 1975–2001. Information från Arbetskraftsundersökningarna 2002:1*. Stockholm: SCB.

SCB. 2005a–2016. *AKU. Grundtabeller. År*. Stockholm: SCB. Available from: http://www.scb.se/hitta-statistik/statistik-efter-amne/arbetsmarknad/arbetskraftsundersokningar/arbetskraftsundersokningarna-aku/pong/tabell-och-diagram/icke-sasongrensade-data/grundtabeller-aku-1574-ar-ar/. Accessed 7 January 2017.

SCB. 2005b. *Sysselsättning och arbetslöshet 1976–2004. Information från Arbetskraftsundersökningen 2005:1*. Stockholm: SCB.

SCB. 2009. *Arbetsmarknadssituationen för hela befolkningen 15–74 år, AKU 4: e kvartalet 2009. Tema – Undersysselsatta*. Statistiska meddelanden AM 11SM 1001. Stockholm: SCB.

SCB. 2012. *Nu för tiden. En undersökning om svenska folkets tidsanvändning*. Stockholm: SCB.

SCB. 2013. *Arbetad tid 2012 – Hur mycket arbetar vi och när?* SOS AM 110 SM 1301. Stockholm: SCB.

SCB. 2014. *Lägre inkomster bland föräldrar med vårdnadsbidrag*. Available from: http://www.scb.se/sv_/Hitta-statistik/Artiklar/Lagre-inkomster-bland-foraldrar-med-vardnadsbidrag/. Accessed 7 January 2017.

SCB. 2016. *Tema Jämställdhet*. Available from: http://www.scb.se/jamstalldhet/. Accessed 7 January 2017.

Selin, Håkan. 2008. *Four Empirical Essays on Responses to Income Taxation*. Uppsala: Department of Economics, Uppsala University.

Sjöquist, Peter. 2017. SKL, email 4 January 2017.

Skolverket. 1998–2010. *Inskrivna barn i procent av samtliga barn*. Available from: http://www.skolverket.se/statistik-och-utvardering/statistik-i-tabeller/forskola/barn-och-grupper. Accessed 7 January 2017.

Skolverket. 1999. *Barn och grupper. Inskrivna barn 1994–1999*. Available from: http://www.skolverket.se/statistik-och-utvardering/statistik-i-tabeller/forskola/barn-och-grupper/1999-1.29030. Accessed 7 January 2017.

Skolverket. 2016a. *Förskola – barn och grupper – Riksnivå. Inskrivna barn 2007–2015. Andel av alla barn i befolkningen*. Available from: http://www.skolverket.se/statistik-och-utvardering/statistik-i-tabeller/forskola/barn-och-grupper/barn-och-grupper-i-forskolan-15-oktober-2015-1.248719. Accessed 7 January 2017.

Skolverket. 2016b. *Pedagogisk omsorg – Barn och grupper – Riksnivå. Andel inskrivna barn av samtliga barn i befolkningen 2010–2015*. Available from: http://www.skolverket.se/statistik-och-utvardering/statistik-i-tabeller/annan-pedagogisk-verksamhet/pedagogisk-omsorg. Accessed 7 January 2017.

Skolverket. 2016c. *Elever och grupper i fritidshem 15 oktober 2015*. Available from: http://www.skolverket.se/statistik-och-utvardering/statistik-i-tabeller/fritidshem/elever-och-grupper. Accessed 7 January 2017.
Skolverket. 2016d. *Förskola – Personal – Riksnivå*. Available from: http://www.skolverket.se/statistik-och-utvardering/statistik-i-tabeller/forskola/personal. Accessed 7 January 2017.
Skolverket. 2016e. *Pedagogisk omsorg – Personal – Riksnivå*. Available from: http://www.skolverket.se/statistik-och-utvardering/statistik-i-tabeller/annan-pedagogisk-verksamhet/pedagogisk-omsorg. Accessed 7 January 2017.
Skolverket. 2016f. *Fritidshem – Personal – Riksnivå*. Available from: http://www.skolverket.se/statistik-och-utvardering/statistik-i-tabeller/fritidshem/personal. Accessed 7 January 2017.
Skolverket. 2016g. *Statistik om förskoleklass*. Available from: http://www.skolverket.se/statistik-och-utvardering/statistik-i-tabeller/forskoleklass. Accessed 6 January 2017.
Socialdepartementet. 2015a. *Ds 2015: 8 Ytterligare en månad inom föräldrapenningen reserveras för vardera föräldern*. Available from: http://www.regeringen.se/rattsdokument/departementsserien-och-promemorior/2015/01/ds-20158/. Accessed 7 January 2017.
Socialdepartementet. 2015b. *Ds 2015: 19.Det kommunala vårdnadsbidraget avskaffas*. Available from: http://www.regeringen.se/rattsdokument/departementsserien-och-promemorior/2015/03/ds-201519/. Accessed 7 January 2017.
Social Watch. 2007, 2009, 2012. *The Gender Equity Index*. Available from: http://www.socialwatch.org/publications. Accessed 7 January 2017.
SOU. 1962: 10 *Svensk ekonomi 1960–1965. Betänkande från 1959 års långtidsutredning*. Stockholm: Fritzes.
SOU. 1966: 1 *Svensk ekonomi 1966–70 med utblick mot 1980*. Stockholm: Fritzes.
SOU. 1972: 26 SOU 1972:27 *Förskolan, del I och del II*. Stockholm: Fritzes.
SOU. 1975: 62 *Förkortad arbetstid för småbarnsföräldrar: betänkande/av Familjestödsutredningen*. Stockholm: Fritzes.
SOU. 2005: 73 *Reformerad föräldraförsäkring: kärlek, omvårdnad, trygghet: betänkande/av Föräldraförsäkringsutredningen*. Stockholm: Fritzes.
SOU. 2011: 11 *Långtidsutredningen LU 2011 (2011). Huvudbetänkande*. Available from: http://www.regeringen.se/49bb35/contentassets/2969767dc25446d69a200f2d1b579744/sou-201111-langtidsutredningen-2011-huvudbetankande. Accessed 7 January 2017.
SOU. 2016:78 *Ordning och reda i välfärden. Betänkande till Välfärdsutredningen*. Available from: http://www.regeringen.se/4ab5e0/contentassets/da2ccefb5dc84389b79b48b06a5e000a/ordning-och-reda-i-valfarden-sou-201678. Accessed 5 January 2017.
Stafford, Frank P., and Sundström, Marianne. 1996. "Time Out for Childcare: Signalling and Earnings Rebound Effects for Men and Women." *Labour*, 10, 3: 669–629.
Stanfors, Maria. 2003. *Education, Labor Force Participation and Changing Fertility Patterns: A Study of Women and Socioeconomic Change in Twentieth Century Sweden*. Stockholm: Almqvist & Wiksell.
Stanfors, Maria. 2015. *Delmål 3: Det obetalda hem- och omsorgsarbetet. Underlag till Jämställdhetsutredningen U2014:06*. Available from: http://www.sou.gov.se/wp-content/uploads/2015/03/Maria-Stanfors-Det-obetalda-hem-och-omsorgsarbetet.pdf. Accessed 7 January 2017.
Statistisk årsbok. 1992–1995, 2001. Stockholm: SCB. Available from: http://www.scb.se/statistiskarsbok_sos_1914-/. Accessed 8 January 2017.
Steiber, Nadia, and Haas, Barbara. 2009. "Ideals or Compromises? The Attitude-Behaviour Relationship in Mothers' Employment." *Socio-Economic Review*, 7: 639–668.

Sveriges Kommuner och Landsting. 2011. *The Economy Report. On Swedish Municipal and County Council Finances – December 2010*. Available from: http://webbutik.skl.se/sv/artiklar/the-economy-report-may-2010.html. Accessed 7 January 2017.

Thoursie, Anna. 2005. "Föräldraförsäkringens effekter på sysselsättning och löner – olika för kvinnor och män?" In *SOU 2005:73 Reformerad föräldraförsäkring, bilagedel. Bilaga 7*, 193–288. Stockholm: Fritzes.

Vikman, Ulrika. 2010. *Does Providing Childcare to Unemployed Affect Unemployment Duration?* Working paper 2010: 5. Uppsala: IFAU.

Waldfogel, Jane, Higuchi, Yoshio, and Abe, Masahiro. 1999. "Family Leave Policies and Women's Retention after Childbirth: Evidence from United States, Britain, and Japan." *Journal of Population Economics*, 12, 4: 523–546.

Westerlund, Lena, Lindblad, Jenny, and Larsson, Mats. 2005. *Föräldraledighet och arbetstid– hur mycket jobbar föräldrar som varit hemma med barn*. Stockholm: LO.

World Economic Forum. 2006–2016. *Global Gender Gap Report*. Available from: http://www.weforum.org/issues/global-gender-gap. Accessed 7 January 2017.

INDEX

2008 great recession, effects (findings), 312–15
2008 recession: gendered analysis, 299; impact (Mexico), 200–10; labor market, relationship (Mexico), 191–5; repercussions/strategies (Mexico), 200–4

abortion, illegality, 7–8
Abrakasa, Ayebatonye, 1
activism, power, 2
Advocates for Women v. Marshall, 141
aesthetic labor, practice, 116–17
AFL-CIO: delegates, impact, 134–5; Global Women's Leadership Program, 139
AFL-CIO, union representation, 128
African Americans, unemployment rates, 314
African Growth and Opportunity Act (AGOA), 218
agarbatti (incense sticks), 17
agency: agency-based direct care services, 136; Bartolinas, 66–7; Bolivia global recession, peasant women's agency, 56; women, agency, 13
Agrarian Reform Law, 59–60
agriculture, trade liberalization, 246–7
Ahmadinejad, Mahmoud (presidency), backlash/setbacks, 267–8
All China Women's Federation (ACWF), 45–7; integration, 47–8; publications, discourse, 47
AMEJ, 64
American University Investment Climate Assessment Survey, 237

American Women report, 126
anti-crisis measures, 99–100
apparel: export sector (Kenya), 222t; imports (United States), 222t
apparel production (Bolivian women), 71, 80–3; questionnaire, usage, 85–9
Arab Springs, protests (Egypt), 155
Ardaya, Gloria, 63
Athi River Export Processing Zone (EPZ) (Kenya): "dual-earner female career model," 216–17; economy, disruption, 220; emergence, 218–19; Export Processing Zones Authority (EPZA), 221; female factory workers, discussion, 226–7; global women's work, 215–18; low-value added activities, 218–19; men/women dynamics, change, 228–9; opportunity/exploitation, 218–26; paid work, problem, 224; Tailors and Textiles Workers Union (TTWU), founding, 225; top-down leadership, 226; tradables, non-tradable subsidization, 217; women, work, 215
at-home mothers, twenty-four-hour constraint, 359–60
austerity measures (Ireland), 346
average wages, EPZ employment (Kenya), 220t
Awad, Azita Berar, 234

Bahramitash, Roksana, 271
Barry, Ursula, 336

Bartolinas, 56; effects, 60–1; goals, 65–6; identity/agency, 66–7; identity, maintenance, 67; illiteracy fight, 64–5; local context (Santa Cruz de la Sierra), 63–6; male chauvinism, 65; priority, expression, 66; self-perception, 64
Bartolinas, women (participation), 60–3
beedi workers, impact, 287
Behdad, Sohrab, 272
Berloffa, Gabriella, 13–14, 91
Bertrand, Marianne, 254
Bhatt, Ela R., 21, 23–4, 26
"Bill for the Protection of Home-Based Workers," Bhatt introduction, 23
Blackett, Adelle, 27
blue collar girls/boys (China), 43–4
Blumberg, Rae Lesser, 276
Bolivia: diaspora, 74; difference, social markers, 80; double lives, 58; economic crisis results, 57–8; entrepreneurial Bolivians, 72; family members, decisions, 62; feminine expertise, 83; gender equalities, reproduction, 81–2; global recession, peasant women's agency, 56; government initiatives, 59; gross domestic product (GDP), deceleration, 75; gross domestic product (GDP), growth rate, 57; low-income peasant women, crisis (impact), 58; macroeconomic/macro social data, 77; *mulieres advenus* migration, 15; oppression/agency, 73; poverty, concentration, 59; revolution (1952), organization, 61; self-employment, migrant refuge, 80; structural repulsion factors, 75
Bolivia, women: apparel production, 71, 80–3; entrepreneurs, 71; questionnaire, 85–9; work/poverty, 58–60
Bono Juana Azurduy (subsidy), 64
Bono Juancito Pinto (social support program), 64
Boris, Eileen, 17
Bourdieu, Pierre, 115
braceros (stereotypical image), 306–7
Brazil: apparel industry, outsourcing, 73–4; attraction factors, 75–6; census, migrants profile, 76–7; diaspora, 77–8; gross domestic product (GDP), 73; macroeconomic/macro social data, 77; private unilateral remittances, 75; sewing work, dynamics, 78; structural constraints, 79
"bride price," 275
Brown, Jerry, 138

Building Trades Unions, 133
Business Cycle Dating Committee (National Bureau of Economic Research) data, 311

CACEH. *See* Support and Training Center for Home Workers
California United Homecare Workers (CUHW), 139
Calla, Pamela, 66
capitalism, realities, 217
capitalist development (China), 36
capital organization, women beedi workers (impact), 287
CAPMAS. *See* Central Agency for Public Mobilization and Statistics
caregvier supports (EU), reductions/restrictions, 340
caretaking, natural proclivity, 195–6
cash-for-care (Sweden), 365
"Celtic Tiger" (Ireland), 337
Central Agency for Public Mobilization, 238
Central Agency for Public Mobilization and Statistics (CAPMAS), 242
Chicago: 2008 great recession, effects (findings), 312–15; 2008 recession, gendered analysis, 299; blight, combat, 307; city of immigrants/city of broad shoulders, 305–6; demographics, 308t; immigration, great recession (relationship), 305–11; Latinos, financial crisis (impact), 311; population, characteristics, 305–6; property foreclosures, 310–11; reinvention, 307; women workers, socioeconomic changes, 313t
Chicago, Mexican/Puerto Rican women, 299; great recession, examination methodology, 311–12; labor histories, gender/globalization/migration, 302
child-care costs (EAPN Ireland) estimates, 348
childcare, political commitment (Sweden), 362
child-care responsibilities, sharing (Hungary), 329
child-care services: public childcare services, 323; unavailability, 321
children, poverty levels (Ireland), 347
China: All China Women's Federation (ACWF), 45–6; blue collar girls/boys, 43–4; capitalist development/women worker, 36; class inequality, 47–8; Cultural Revolution, 40; economic

reform era, 43; gender equality, 37–41; "iron girl" model, 39, 45; labor, purpose, 43; migrant workers/retirees, ethnographic stories, 37; modernity, notion, 46; money economy, gender inequality, 41–4; paternalistic power, continuation, 44–8; rural migrant workers, gender discrimination, 48; rural-to-urban migration, 49; socialist construction, 40; socialist market economy, 41; socialist traditions, maintenance, 44–5; society, devotion, 40; state feminism, 39–40

China, migrant women workers: family devotion, 52; problems, 44; status, increase, 50

China, women: bodies, commodification, 42; exploitation, condemnation, 36–7; institutional/organizational arrangements, 45; roles, 42; social status, improvement, 41; state protection, limitation, 39–40

China, women workers: market, relationship, 41–4; role, 48–53; state, relationship, 44–8

Chinese Women, 47

Civil Code, Articles 942/1117, 274–5

Civil Rights Act, Title VII, 128–9, 137, 140–1

Civil Rights Laws, 136

civil society, western promotion, 161

class inequality (China), 47–8

Cobble, Dorothy Sue, 147

COMESA, gender policy, 247

Commission on the Status of Women, 126

Committee on Women's Employment and Related Social Issues (National Academy of Sciences), 129

communism, cessation, 165

community (construction), immigrant wave (impact), 306

companions, categorization/classification, 135–6, 138

comparative histories, 7–8

Confederación Nacional de Mujeres Campesinas Indígenas Originarias y Afrodescendentes de Bolivia-Bartolina Sisa, movement, 56

Confederacíon Sindical de Comunidades Interculturales de Bolivia (CSIB), 61

Confederation of Intercultural Communities of Bolivia, 61

CONLACTRAHO. *See* Latin American and Caribbean Confederation of Household Workers

Construction Industry Diversity Summit, 145–6

Construction trades, danger, 140

Consumer Financial Protection Bureau data, 311

Convention, 177, 23–7; ILO passage, 19; ratification, 27

Convention 189 (ILO), 146, 158; impact, 136–7

Convention on the Elimination of All Forms of Discrimination against Women (CEDAW), 158, 179

Cook, Linda, 180

Country Specific Recommendations (CSRs), 92, 96–7; analysis, 97; content, 96

crisis (2008), 74–5; financial crisis (2008), political ramifications, 178–82; global financial crisis, 176–8; international immigration, 73–80; neo-Marxist/neo-Keynesian perception, 310

cross-fertilization, 24

CSO Household Finance and Consumption Survey (2013), 347

CSUTCB, 60–2; male partners, 67; regulations, 66

Cultural Revolution, 40

customary discrimination, 25–6

Daley, Richard M., 307

Daneshgah-e Azad-e Islami (Islamic Free University), emergence/growth, 265

day-care centers, pre-schools (terminology change), 362

decent work, ILO focus, 28

del Campo, Esther, 67

Delors, Jacques, 92

de los Milagros Infante Ramirez, Marcolina, 29

de Pérez, Hilda Villalba, 63

developing country, 112

de Villegas, Gisela Schneider, 24

difference, social markers, 80

direct care workers, companion categorization, 135–6

"dirty jobs," denigration, 133

discrimination (Russian Federation), 174–6; state practice, 175–6

Divorce Iranian Style (Longinotto/Mir-Hosseini), 274

doble jornada (intensification), 206

domestic life, destabilization, 26

domestics, work, 27–30; United States, 133t

domestic violence, 83

domestic workers, 134–6; 2008 recession, impact (Mexico), 200–10; call, 135; political organization (Mexico), 207–10; segregation, Mexican labor structure, 195–200; sociodemographic characteristics/working conditions (Mexico), 201t
Domestic Workers United (DWU), founding, 137–8
dotcom bubble, bursting, 368
"double days" (Sweden), 363
double lives, 58
double-work shift, unpaid social reproduction (contrast), 204–7
dual-earner/dual-caregiver family model, 354–5, 359
dubbeldagar ("double days"), 363

economically active population (EAP), 199–200
Economic and Social Research Institute (ESRI) data, 347–8
Economic Commission for Latin American and the Caribbean (ECLAC), 57, 59, 199
Economic Commission for Latin American and the Caribbean (CEPAL) data, 77
economic crisis (EC), 342
economic crisis (Hungary), 319
economic crisis (2008), Bolivia (results), 57–8
economic crisis (Ireland), consequences, 337–8
economic development (Sweden), 367–9
economic growth, engine, 25
economic hegemony, 4
economic independence, 128
economic restructuring, 310
economies, focus, 5
Education Act (1972), Title IX, 126
Egypt: agricultural sector, 241–2; agriculture, gendering, 243; agriculture, trade liberalization, 246–7; Arab Spring, protests, 155; Central Agency for Public Mobilization, 238; COMESA, gender policy, 247; economic growth, facilitation, 234–5; economic reforms, 234–5; gender-based inequalities, 236; gender policies, human resource development (relationship), 245–6; gender sectoral bias, 241; gender, trade liberalization (impact), 236–43; global recession, impact, 158; government sector, feminization, 241; gross domestic product (GDP), 234; gross national product (GNP), 234; horticultural products sector, expansion, 235–6; human rights, impact, 246; Industrial Modernization programs, 247; international cooperation/assistance, encouragement, 246–7; International Men and Gender Equality Survey (IMAGES), 243; labor laws, equitability, 239; manufacturing, female workers status (lower level), 240; New Labor Law, 239; occupational structure, gender segregation, 236–7; QIZ areas, 246; State Owned Enterprises (SOEs), privatization, 237; technologies, women (preparation), 244–5; trade expansion, impact, 236; trade liberalization, policy recommendations, 243–245; unemployment, problem, 238; Voluntary Codes of Conduct (VCC), 244; women (economic activity), trade expansion (impact), 236; women/trade liberalization, relationship, 234; women, wage discrimination, 238
Eisenberg, Susan, 142
El-Din, Karim Badr, 237
"Eleanor Clubs," 135
El Salvador, minimum wage (increase), 79
el-Sisi, Abdel Fattah, 158
employees, absence time (Sweden), 372
employers: crisis, impact, 325–8; discrimination, 25–6
employment: gender equality, increase (Sweden), 372; gender gap (Sweden), 374; global gender gap, 6; insecurity (Hungary), 329–30; rate, increase (Sweden), 369; statuses, probabilities, 101t–103t
employment (Sweden), 369–72
empowerment, 36
Engels, Friedrich, 276
English, Beth, 1
ENOE. *See* National Survey on Occupation and Employment
entrepreneurship, understanding, 72–3
entrepreneurs, women (Bolivia), 71
Epps, LeDaya, 144
EPZ employment, Kenyan average wages, 220t
Equal Employment Opportunity, 144
Equal Employment Opportunity Commission (EEOC), impact, 140–1
Equality Authority budget, 337
Equal Rights Advocates, 143
Etemad-Moghadam, Fatemeh, 271

Eurasian Women's Forum, creation, 180
European Anti-Poverty Network Ireland (EAPN Ireland), child-care cost estimates, 348
European Central Bank (ECB), 336
European Commission (EC), 336; economic crisis, effects, 342
European economic integration, process (initiation), 92–3
European Economic Recovery Plan, 98–9
European Employment Strategy (EES): analysis, 91; country recommendations/viewpoint, 96–8; development, 338; emergence/governance mode, 92–3; evolution, 93–6; feminist approach, comparison, 97f; gender equality, 91–8; gender equality approach, 98; gender equality, visibility, 93–6; gender position, change, 94t; inception, 13; pillars, 95
European Expert Group on Gender and Employment (EGGE), 100
European Institute for Gender Equality (EIGE), 353
European Union (EU): anti-crisis measures; austerity measures, impact, 340; bailout program, 337; caregiver supports, reductions/restrictions, 340; crisis years, gendered trend, 341; employment policy coordination, 91; employment rates, contraction, 339t; fiscal consolidation, 99; gender effects, 104; gender equality guidelines, 339; gender equality policies, 14, 338–44; gender mainstreaming, 338–9; gender pay gap, 344; gender segregation, 343; global perspective, 344–5; housing/family benefits, reduction, 340; inequality, increase, 336; Network of Experts on Gender Equality and Employment (ENEG) Report (2013), 340–1; paid employment, access barrier, 348; pension reforms, 340; poverty levels, increase, 344; public sector cuts, 340; recovery, indication (absence), 343; reserve labour force, 341; soft law mechanisms, 93; staffing freezes/personnel cuts, 340; unemployment/assistance benefits/reductions, eligibility criteria (restrictions), 340; Universal Social Charge (USC), 349; women, part-time work (overrepresentation), 342–3; women, unpaid work, 341–2; working conditions, casualization, 346–7
European Women's Lobby (EWL) report, 341–2

Executive Order 11375, 141
exploitation, opportunity (contrast), 155–9
export-oriented manufacturing (Turkey), 110
export processing zones, 20
export-processing zones (EPZs), 156
Export Processing Zones Authority (EPZA), 221

failure, symbol, 11
fair globalization, ILO focus, 28
Family Income Supplement (FIS), 349
"Family Protection Bill" (Iran), 276
family, women workers (roles), 48–53
Farzaneh (journal), 265, 270
"father's month," proposal (Sweden), 363–4
Federal Employment Service (services benefits), 173
Federation of Peasant Women, founding, 61–2
female retail workers (Turkey), demographic characteristics, 114
female workers, leisurely pursuits, 120–1
female workforce, characteristics (Turkey), 112
feminimization labor patterns (Turkey), 109
feminine expertise (Bolivia), 83
feminine portfolios, 180
feminist approach, EES approach (comparison), 97f
Fernandez, Lilia, 306
finance, insurance, and real estate (FIRE) industries, economic dependence, 308
financial crisis (2008), political ramifications, 178–82
financial independence, example, 325
financial pressure (Hungary), 329–30
"foreign agents," registration, 181
foreign direct investment (FDI), 273
foreign meddling, 161
formal economics, focus, 5
Frederickson, Mary E., 1
free trade zones (FTZs), 273
free will, act, 43–4
Friedman, Thomas, 8

Galhera, Katiuscia Moreno, 14–15, 71
Gallup International Millennium Survey, 174
gender: importance, 30; inequality, GCC labor force participation rates, 254–8; mainstreaming, 95, 99–100, 338–9; maquila industry (Mexico), relationship, 304–5; marginal effects, probabilities,

101t–103t; negative effects, 236; pay gap (EU), 344; perspectives, 1; policies, human resource development (relationship), 245–6; position, change, 94t; positive effects, 235–6; Puerto Rican/Mexican women, labor histories (Chicago), 302; Puerto Rico, operation bootstrap (relationship), 303–4; segregation (EU), 343; themes, 4–5; trade/human rights, relationship, 235–6; trade liberalization, impact, 236–43; United States, 125

gender equality: change, 355; country recommendations/viewpoint, 96–8; EES approach, 98; empirical evidence, 100, 104; EU austerity measures, impact, 340; EU policies, 338–42; European Employment Strategy (EES), 91–8; great recession, 98–104; importance (EU), 339; labor market, 97f; Maoist approach/impacts, 37–41; Sweden, 353; visibility, 93–6

Gender Equality Index (European Institute for Gender Equality), 353

Gender Equality Strategy for 2010–2015, 95

Gender Gap Report (World Economic Forum), 158

Ghazl Al-Mahala textile plant, employee walkout, 239

Glass Ceiling Commission (U.S. Department of Labor), 129

Glass-Steagall Act, abolition, 310

global 2008 Great Recession, effects, 273–4

global capitalism, racist/patriarchal structures, 4

Global Context (Lethbridge), 344

global economic crises: Russian Federation, 178; side effects, 71

global economic recession, 3

global economic restructuring, 111–12

global financial crisis (2008), 176–8; jobs, disappearance, 309

Global Gender Gap Report (2011), 269

globalization: fair globalization, ILO focus, 28; impact, 9; passive agents, 72; Puerto Rican/Mexican women, labor histories, 302

global labor standards: establishment, 137; workers, creation, 17

global markets, liberalization (manifestation), 310

global recession, 5–6; peasant women's agency, 56

Global Women's Leadership Program (AFL-CIO), 139

global women, work (meaning), 215–18

Gonzaléz, Alessandra L., 158–9, 250

Gonzalez, Toledo, 208

Gopal, Meena, 287

Gorbachev Foundation, 182

Governing Body (GB), 19, 28

government regulations, funding/enforcement (absence), 144

great recession (Great Recession), 4, 7, 131–3, 155; effects, 15; emergence, 125–6; examination, methodology, 311–12; gender equality, 98–104; immigration (Chicago), relationship, 305–11

Green Protests (Iran), 155, 267

"Growth, Competitiveness and Employment" (Delors), 92

Gulf Cooperation Council (GCC) countries, 155; economic laws, expression, 257; economies, 159; economies, regional particularities, 254; energy production, 256f; female/male tertiary enrollment, percentage ratio, 253f; GDP/capita, 259f; gross domestic product (GDP), ris, 258; higher education, women access (history), 251–4; labor markets, economic strains, 257; labor markets, gender inequality/inefficiencies, 250–1; mixed-gender classes, depiction, 252; social norms, change, 252, 254; technical skills, mass education, 258; women, education, 251

Gulf Cooperation Council (GCC) countries, labor force: participation, 250; participation rates, gender inequality, 254–8; statistics, 252t

Gulf Cooperation Council (GCC) countries, women: education, 252t; labor force participation constraints, economic factors, 254, 257; labor force participation, cultural constraints, 257–8; labor force participation (discouragement), government policies (impact), 258; labor force participation, political/security challenges, 258; labor force participation rates, 255f; university attainment, 250

habitus, notion, 115
Hacienda, registration, 193
Hakimian, Hassan, 273
Hard Hatted Women (Martin), 142

Harvey, David, 310
Hashemi, Faezeh, 265
Henry, Mary Kay, 128
higher education, women (access), 251–4
home-based beedi work, organization, 288–9
home-based economic activities, 271
home-based industry (South Tamil Nadu), change/status quo, 287
home-based labor, action, 25
home-based workers, 29
home labor, 17–18
HomeNet Thailand, 17, 28
home workplace, recognition, 17
home work, spread, 21
Hoover, J. Edgar, 135
horizontal sex segregation (Russian Federation), 169–71; workforce, 169–70
household responsibilities, tension, 207
"household strategy," 202
housewife deduction (Sweden), 358
"housewives" (Sweden), 357
human capital (Russian Federation), 168–9
human resource development, gender policies (relationship), 245–6
human rights: impact, 246; negative effects, 236; positive effects, 235–6; trade/gender, relationship, 235–6
Hungary: child-care responsibilities, sharing, 329; economic crisis, 319; employers, crisis (impact), 325–8; employment security, 329–30; financial independence, example, 325; financial pressure, 329–30; job loss, 328; Labor Code, manager behavior (problem), 327; labor market, policy context, 322–4; labor market, women (position), 322–3; maternal employment gap, 323; maternalist parental leave policies, 322; maternalist policies, 320–1; mini jobs, relinquishment, 325; mothers, paid work (theoretical considerations), 320–2; parental leave, 323, 326–7; public childcare servies, 323; publicly funded nursery places, 323; self-realization, 330; state socialism, collapse, 321; training, idle time, 324; wages, freeze, 324; work-care decisions, discussion/argument, 329–31; work hours, crisis/reorganization, 323–4; working hours, reduction, 324; workplace protection action plan, 326

Hungary, women: choices, 322; emancipation (Marxist-Leninist project), 320–1; employment rate, increase, 322–3; part-time work, 319; part-time work, analysis, 324–31; work-care decision, crisis (impact), 324–5

Illinois, unionized jobs (decline), 310
illiteracy, Bartolina fight, 64–5
immigration (Chicago), great recession (relationship), 305–11
immoral western values, encroachment, 7
individual taxation (Sweden), 356–9
industrialization, realities, 217
Industrial Modernization programs, 247
informal economics, focus, 5
informal employment, 193
"informal proletariat" (Mexico), 197
in-home workers, median annual salaries, 136
Initiative Group for Feminism, 182
interactive service workers, work experiences, 113
International Business Report (2014), 171
International Confederation of Free Trade Unions (ICFTU), 22
International Domestic Worker Network (IDWN), 19, 147; founding, 137
International Finance Corporation (IFC), attention, 172
international immigration (2008 crisis), 73–80
International Labor Office, worker estimates, 135
International Labor Organization (ILO): Convention, 189, 146; Convention on Decent Work for Domestic Workers, 138–9; Domestic Work Convention, 189, 158; Domestic Work Convention 189, ratification, 199; impact, 136–7
International Labour Conference (ILC), 19
International Labour Organization (ILO): convention-making process, 19–20; labor categories, 13; organization, disjunction, 26
International Men and Gender Equality Survey (IMAGES), 243
International Monetary Fund (IMF), 336
International Textile, Garment, and Leather Workers' Federation (ITGLWF), 25
International Union of Food, Agricultural, Hotel, Restaurant, Cathering, Tobacco and Allied Workers' Associations (IUF), 24

International Women's Day, 9
Interparliamentary Association of the Commonwealth of Independent States (CIS), 180
intersectionality, 67
Investment Climate Assessment (ICA), World Bank, 240
involuntary part-time work, priority (Sweden), 376
Iran: agreement, Trump administration withdrawal, 274; "bride price," 275; class biases, identification, 276; "Family Protection Bill," 276; female labor supply/demand, 271–2; foreign direct investment (FDI), 273; free trade zones (FTZs), 273; Green Protests, 155, 267; gross domestic product (GDP), 272–3; home-based economic activities, 271; Muslim Family Law provisions, 275–6; National Syndicate of Women Workers (NSWW), establishment, 270; unpaid family labor, 271; work force, middle class/working class women (impact), 269–72
Iranian Revolutionary Guards Corps, SOE purchases, 273
Iran-Iraw War, military mobilization, 264
Iran, women: economic participation, 268; employment pattaerns, 270; ignoring, government policies (impact), 276; leadership, reality, 277; political power/participation, 277–8
Iran, women/work: institutional obstacles, 274–6; politics, 263; social class, relationship, 268–72; structural/institutional factors, 272–6
Ireland: at-risk-of-poverty rate (EU-SILC data), 347; austerity measures, 346; austerity policies, 337–8; bailout, 349; "Celtic Tiger," 337; children, poverty levels, 347; economic activity, gendered nature, 345–6; economic activity/policies, boom-bust cycle, 337; economic crisis, consequences, 337–8; experience, 345–9; gender equality, economic crisis/austerity policies, 337–8; inequality, rise, 336; Irish Development Plan (2000–2006), 340; National Minimum Wage (NMW), 347; pension system, gender differences, 346; poverty levels, 347; structural adjustment program, 345; Structural Adjustment Program, 349
"iron girl" model, 39, 45
Iron Workers Union, 144

Islamic Republic: Ahmadinejad presidency, backlash/setbacks, 267–8; educational advances, 266–7; feminization, 266; gender inequality, severity, 276; gender policies, 264–8; ideological campaign, launch, 274; neopatriarchal Islamic state, role, 264; population, greying, 268; Sharia-based civil code, 274; unemployment rates, 267; women/men, unemployment (problem), 266–7
Islamic Republic, women: academic promotion, progress, 266–7; economic participation, 268; labor force, 265; political power/participation, 277–8

Jeppesen, Anne Marie Ejdesgaard, 14, 56
Jhabvala, Renana, 24
job loss (Hungary), 328
Jobseeker's Allowance, 347–8
Johnson, Janet Elise, 181
Johnson, Lyndon B., 141
joint taxation, retention, 358
Jucumari, Quenta, 30

Kazemipour, Shahla, 271
Kelles-Viitanen, Anita, 24
Kennedy, Marie, 2
Kenya, apparel export sector, 222t
Kenya, Athi River EPZ (women, work), 215; employment, average wages, 220; global women, work (meaning), 215–18; opportunity/exploitation, 215, 218–26; text, 219f; workplace, women (impact), 226–9
Kenya, U.S. apparel imports, 222t
Khamenei, Ali, 275
Khatami, Mohammad, 264–5, 267
Kian-Thiébaut, Azadeh, 277
King, Theresa, 145
Kispeter, Erika, 319
Kochkina, E.V., 171
Koulaee, Elaheh, 270
Kozina, Irina, 165
Kryshtanovskaia, Olga, 171
Kurzman, Charles, 278
Kuwaiti women, participation (increase), 254
Kuwaitization, 257
Kvinnans villkorliga frigivning (Moberg), 355

labor: identity emergence, 293–7; ILO categories, 13; organization, women beedi workers (impact), 287; purpose (China), 43; reproductive labor,

Index 395

negotiation, 283–5; reserve army, Marxist paradigm, 112; social labor, negotiations, 283–5; structure (Mexico), domestic workers (segregation), 195–200; worth, dismissal, 30
Labor Code, manager behavior (problem), 327
labor, feminization: patterns (Turkey), 109; women workers (Turkey), 115–17
labor force: changes (women), 127f; Russian Federation, 166–76; statistics (GCC), 252t; women, GCC labor force participation rates, 255f
Labor Force Information Project, 239–40
labor force, participation, 166–7; constraints, economic factors, 254, 257; cultural constraints, 257–8; Gulf Cooperation Council (GCC) countries, 250; rates, Gulf Cooperation Council (GCC) countries, 254–8
labor force participation rate (LFPR), 312
labor market: gender equality, 97f; gender gaps, 6; Mexico, 2008 recession (relationship), 191–5; policy context (Hungary), 322–4; women, entry (Sweden), 362; women/men, involvement (Sweden), 367–76; women, position (Hungary), 322–3
Latin America, macroeconomic/macro social data, 77
Latin American and Caribbean Confederation of Household Workers (CONLACTRAHO), 28, 158–9, 210
Latinas (job disappearance), global financial crisis (impact), 309
Latinos: financial crisis, impact (Woodstock Institute report), 311; minority group, size, 306
LaTour, Jane, 142
Lazarte, Silvia, 56–7, 64
Lean In (Sandburg), 130
legal challenges (women), 78–80
"Legal Framework on Equal Rights and Equal Opportunities" (1997), 179
legal negligence, reinforcement, 208
leisure sociability, functions, 120
leisure spaces, women (involvement), 119–21
León, Marxa Chávez, 67
Lethbridge, Jane, 344
liberalization, beedi entrepreneurship (relationship), 289–93
Liberal Party, Social Democrats (competition), 355

Linera, Álvaro García, 67
live-out PDW, increase, 200
Longinotto, Kim, 274
Los Mineros, 134–5
Loutifi, Martha, 24
low-income peasant women, crisis (impact), 58
low-status kin position, denotation, 118

Magram Market Research, 171
MajorMarket, 115, 118–19
male chauvinism (Bartolinas), 65
male-earner/female-caregiver family model, 354–5
Malykhina, Marina, 171
maquiladora, 196
maquila industry (Mexico), gender (relationship), 304–5
market. *See* labor market: challenges (woman), 78–80; economy, impact, 165–6; women workers, relationship, 41–4
Martin, Molly, 142
maternal employment gap, 323
maternal homes, financial assistance, 204
maternalist policies, 320–1
Maternity Benefits (MB), value/taxation (reduction), 348–9
Matteazzi, Eleonora, 13–14, 91
median earnings, income (contrast), 312
Medvedev, Dmitry, 180
mehrieh (negotiation), 275–6
men, labor market involvement (Sweden), 36–76
MERCOSUL Agreement about Residence for National from the States Parties, Chile and Bolivia, 79
Mexican Constitution, Article, 123, 198
Mexican Revolution, 209
Mexicans: state-sponsored mass labor importation programs, 306; unemployment rate, decrease, 314
Mexican women (Chicago), 299; labor histories, gender/globalization/ migration, 302; work experiences, 305
Mexico: 2008 recession, repercussions/ strategies, 200–4; caretaking, natural proclivity, 195–6; double-work shift, unpaid social reproduction (contrast), 204–7; economically active population (EAP), 199; economic restructuring, 200, 202; external stability, dependence, 191–2; gross domestic product (GDP), recovery, 190; household responsibilities,

tension, 207; "household strategy," 202; informal employment, 193; "informal proletariat," 197; labor analysis, income (attention), 194–5; labor market, 2008 recession (relationship), 191–5; legal negligence, reinforcement, 208; maquila industry, gender (relationship), 304–5; maternal homes, financial assistance, 204; multiactivity strategy, 203; paid domestic work (PDW), 156, 190, 196–200; patriarchial values, 205; reproductive activities, commodification, 205; self-exploitation hypothesis, 194; social reproduction, feminist usage, 204–5; "special jobs," 198; structural shift, 191; unemployment insurance, absence, 192–3; women/men, average monthly wage comparison, 197t; working poor women, crisis, 190

Mexico, domestic workers: 2008 recession, impact, 200–10; political organization, 207–10; sociodemographic characteristics/working conditions, 201t; structural disadvantages/recession (2008), 190

Mexico, labor structure: characteristics, 192–5; domestic workers, segregation, 195–200

Mexico, workforce: monthly income, 196t; social security, absence, 194t; weekly working hours, 195t

micro, middle, and small enterprises (M/SME), ownership, 237

middle class women, work force presence (Iran), 269–72

Middle East North Africa (MENA), 263–4, 269; female labor supply/demand, shaping, 272; trading/economic partnerships, 257

migrant domestic work, transnational forces, 28

migrant women workers: family devotion, 52; problems, 44; status, increase, 50

migration, Puerto Rican/Mexican women (labor histories), 302

mini jobs, relinquishment, 325

Mir-Hosseini, Ziba, 274

mixed-gender classes, depiction, 252

Mizulina, Elena, 180

Moberg, Eva, 355

Moccio, Francine, 142

Modern Family, 47

modernity, notion, 46

Moghadam, Valentine M., 156–9, 263

money economy, gender inequality, 41–4

Money Makes Us Relatives (White), 117

Monje, Patricia Costas, 67

monthly income (Mexican workforce), 196t

monthly wage (average), women/men (comparison), 197t

Morales, Evo, 59; government, support/acceptance, 64, 66

Morsi, Mohamed, 237

mortgages, bundling, 310

"mother's month" (Sweden), 363–4

mothers, paid work (theoretical considerations), 320–2

Movement for Socialism-Political Instrument for the Sovereignty of the Peoples (MAS-IPSP), 60, 64, 67

Movimiento Revolucionario Nacional, El (MNR), 61

Mpango wa kando (Athi River Export Processing Zone), 227–8

Mubarak, Suzanne, 158

mulieres advenus migration, 15

multiactivity strategy, 203

Multi-Fibre Arrangement (MFA), 218

multinational enterprises (MNEs), evolution, 130

Municipal Women's Federation (Chongqing), 46

Myrdal, Alva, 357–8

Nairobi Conference on Women, 23–4

Nassar, Heba, 158, 234

National Bureau of Economic Research, Business Cycle Dating Committee data, 311

National Commission on Child Care, pre-school model, 360

National Confederation of Peasant Workers in Bolivia, 14, 56

National Council on Women (NCW), setup, 158

National Domestic Workers Alliance (NDWA), 147; organization/formation, 8, 138

National Labor Relations Act, 135

National Labor Relations Board (NLRB): procedures, 139; supervision, 130

National Minimum Wage (NMW), 347, 349

National Survey on Occupation and Employment (ENOE), 191, 193, 199

National Syndicate of Women Workers (NSWW), establishment, 270

National Women's Council budgets, 337
National Women's Law Center, legal guidance, 143
Nechemias, Carol, 7, 155, 161, 180
negative global GDP growth, 5
neoliberal globalization, narratives (complication), 305
Network of Experts on Gender Equality and Employment (ENEG) Report (2013), 340–1
New Labor Law, 239
New Political Constitution, 59–60, 64–6
Nomani, Farhad, 272
non-familial space (work), 117–19
nongovernmental organizations (NGOs), 22, 162; assistance, 28; consultation, 19; Egida, 182; role, increase, 244
non-mandatory employment guidelines (GLs), 93
Nontraditional Training for Women (NEW), 143
North American Free Trade Agreement (NAFTA), 190; failure, 305
North America's Building Trades Unions (NABTU), 145–6
NOW Women's Legal Defense and Education Fund, 141
Nyberg, Anita, 353

Obama, Barack, 9, 148
Obama, Michelle, 144
Occupational Health and Safety Act (1970), 136
occupational segregation, 6
occupational sex segregation, 169
O'Farrell, Brigid, 8, 15, 125
Office of Federal Contract Compliance Programs (OFCCP), 141; report, 144
offshore production, spread, 21
One-Parent Family Payment (OPFP) eligibility, 347
Open Method of Coordination (OMC), 91, 96
Operation Bootstrap, failure, 305
opportunity, exploitation (contrast), 155–9
Organization for Economic Development and Cooperation (OECD), 171, 193; gender equality report, 354; report, 346–8
Orleck, Annelise, 2
O'Sullivan, Terry, 125, 148
Otis, Eileen, 42–3
"Out of the Shadows," 28
outwork, 18–21
OXFAM, 22

Pact for Gender Equality, 95
paid domestic work (PDW), 156, 190, 196, 203; consciousness, building, 208; detachment/indifference, 208–9; live-out PDW, increase, 200; organization/recognition, 208; physical demands, 209; restructuring, 199–200; tasks, diversification/intensification, 209; vulnerability, reduction, 198
paid employment, access barrier, 348
Palme, Olof, 357–8
parental allowance (Sweden), 366
parental leave (Hungary), 323, 326–7; regulations, 321
parental leave (Sweden), 363–5
paternalistic power, continuation, 44–8
patriarchial renaissance, 181
patriarchial values, 205
patriarchies, women negotiation, 293–7
Patricia, Mónica, 190
Paulson, Susan, 66
pension system, gender differences (Ireland), 346
PEW Global Attaitudes Project, 166
Pew Hispanic Center, home data, 311
Pike, Kelly, 155, 215
Plurinational Legislative Assembly, women (percentage), 60
political power, women (participation), 277–8
post-communist transition, 175
poverty (Bolivia), 58–60; manifestation, 59; negative aspects, 83
poverty levels (Ireland), 347
poverty levels, increase (EU), 344
poverty rates, 312
Powe Global Survey, 175
President's Commission on the Status of Women, 140
private sector, male employment (Sweden), 371
private unilateral remittances, 75
(re)productive space (women), 77–8
Programme on Rural Women, 24
protests, spread, 2–3
Prügl, Elisabeth, 26
Pryce, Shirley, 29
public childcare: services (Hungary), 323; supply (Sweden), 361
publicly financed childcare (Sweden), 359–63

publicly funded nursery places, 323
public sector cuts (EU), 340
public sector, employment developments (Sweden), 370–1
Puerto Ricans, state-sponsored mass labor importation programs, 306
Puerto Rican women (Chicago), 299; employment, meaning, 309; labor histories, gender/globalization/migration, 302; work experiences, 305
Puerto Rico (operation bootstrap), gender (relationship), 303–4
Putin, Vladimir, 8, 156, 161–2, 180; administration, women (absence), 180; ambitions, 162–3
putting-out systems, 17–18

Qatarization, 257
QIZ areas, 246

Radzinsky, Edvard, 172
Rafsanjani, Ali Akbar Hashemi, 264–5
Rana Plaza, collapse, 9–11, 156
recession: great recession, 131–3; great recession, gender equality, 98–104; Mexico, labor market (relationship), 191–5; recovery, relationship, 132f; repercussions/strategies, 200–4; United States, 125
religiosity, problems, 110
replacement income, offering (Sweden), 366–7
reproductive activities, commodification, 205
reproductive labor, negotiations, 283–5
reproductive work distribution, 78f
reserve labour force (EU), 341
Revolutionary Institutional Party (PRI), 209
Richter, James, 182
Rojas-García, Georgina, 190
Roosevelt, Eleanor, 11, 126, 135, 148
Rouhani, Hassan, 268
Rousseau, Stéphanie, 67
Rúa, Merida, 306
rural migrant workers, gender discrimination, 48
rural-to-urban migration, 49
Russian Federation, women: discrimination, 174–6; economic downturn, 176–7; economy, restructuring, 168–9; equal rights, support, 175; family structure, changes, 178; feminine portfolios, 180; gender gaps, 166; gender policy, 179–80; global economic crisis, 178; horizontal/vertical sex segregation, 169–71; human capital, 168–9; joblessness rates, 173; labor force, 166–76; labor force participation, 166–7; maternal capital, 163; occupational segregation, complementary pattern, 169–70; patriarchial renaissance, 181; pre-crisis data, 177; remuneration, 169; sex differences, 164–5; stagnation, signs, 168; unemployment, 172–4; workforce, 161; workforce status, 167
Russian Orthodox Church (ROC), 178–9; family value restoration, 163–4

Saarinen, Aino, 181
Safarzadeh, Haleh, 270
sameness, 39
Sandburg, Carl, 305
Sandburg, Sheryl, 130
Sanmiguel-Valderrama, Olga, 1
Santa Cruz de la Sierra (Bartolinas context), 63–6
São Paulo, women (apparel production), 71, 80–3; emancipation, possibility, 82–3; formal education, 80; oppression, 82–3; origins/acculturation, 81–2; tasks, distribution, 82f
Sarioglu, Esra, 109
science, technology, engineering, and math (STEM) jobs, 130
Seattle Women in Trades, 141
sectoral segregation, 6
segregation, domestic workers (Mexican labor structure), 195–200
Self-Employed Women's Association (SEWA), 17–19; approach, 24; emergence, 22; Reception Centre, 23; self-employed inclusion recommendation, 25
self-employment, migrant refuge (Bolivia), 80
self-exploitation: forms, 203; hypothesis, 194
self-realization (Hungary), 330
Service Employees International Union (SEIU), 139
service industries, labor feminization (Turkey), 113
sex segregation (Russian Federation), 169–72
Seyadu Beedi Company (House of Seyad) headquarters, 290f
Sharia law, 159
Shierholz, Heidi, 136
Sillaste, Galina, 171

Sindicato Agrario, 62
sindicatos de base (community-based unions), 61
Singh, Andrea M., 24
single female-headed households, poverty (increase), 314–15
single-woman-headed households, data, 312
skilled trades (United States), 133t; data, 134
small businesses, women (role), 172
Smith, Magan, 125, 148
Sobhan, Zafar, 10
sociability, requirement, 118–19
sociable space (work), 117–19
social class, women/work relationship (Iran), 268–72
Social Democratic Party: childcare programs, 360; comparison, 355, 357; opponents, impact, 364; power, 371
social impediments, countering, 22
socialist construction, 40
socialist market economy, 41
socialist traditions, maintenance, 44–5
social justice, quest, 18
social labor, negotiations, 283–5
social norms, change, 252–3
social reproduction, feminist usage, 204–5
social safety net, impact, 6
social security, absence (Mexico workforce), 194t
Soft law mechanisms, 93
Soul Mate, 47
South African Domestic Service and Allied Workers Union (SADSAWU), 134
South Tamil Nadu (India): home-based beedi work, organization, 288–9; home-based industry, change/status quo, 287; labor/capital organization, women beedi workers (impact), 287; labor, identity emergence, 293–7; liberalization, beedi entrepreneurship (relationship), 289–93; patriarchies, women negotiation, 293–7
"special jobs" (Mexico), 198
"Special Rules on Labor Protection of Female Employees," 45
Sperling, Valerie, 182
stagnation, signs, 168
State Duma: regulations, 175; taming, 180
state feminism, 39–40
state-owned enterprises (SOEs), 52, 273
State Owned Enterprises (SOEs), privatization (Egypt), 237
state sector, employee numbers (Sweden), 371
state socialism, collapse, 321

Status of the Institution of Marriage in Kenya, 228
Stephens, Hester, 29
Structural Adjustment Program (Ireland), 349
structural repulsion factors, 75
suffering, relief, 30
Support and Training Center for Home Workers (CACEH), 158, 210
Sweden: absent employees, percent, 373f; at-home mothers, twenty-four-hour constraint, 359–60; cash-for-care, 365; change, 355; childcare, political commitment, 362; co-habiting, 362–3; *dubbeldagar* ("double days"), 363; economic crisis, 360; economic development, 367–9; economy (deceleration), international debt crisis (impact), 368–9; economy, positive state (cessation), 368; employed women/men, percent, 369f; employed women/men, percent unemployed, 375f; employees, absence time, 372; employees, number, 370f; employment, 369–72; employment, gender equality (increase), 372; employment, gender gap, 374; "father's month," proposal, 363–4; fiscal policy framework, changes, 368; gender equality, 353; Global Gender Gap data, 353; housewife deduction, 358; "housewives," 357; individual taxation, 356–9; involuntary part-time work, priority, 376; joint taxation, retention, 358; labor market, women/men (involvement), 367–76; Liberal Party, Social Democrats (competition), 355; "mother's month," 363–4; National Commission on Child Care, pre-school model, 360; parental allowance, 366; parental allowance days, fathers (percentage), 364f; parental leave, 363–5; part-time employed, percent, 374f; policy, 354–6; policy formulation, process, 356; private sector, male employment, 371; public childcare, supply, 361; publicly financed childcare, 359–63, 361f; public sector employment (developments), 370–1; replacement income, offering, 366–7; state sector, employee numbers, 371; tax penalty, elimination, 357; tax reform, necessity, 357; wages, equalization, 359; women, absence rates (increase), 373; work, absence, 372–3; working hours, reduction (parent rights), 363, 365–7; working time, 373–6

Swedish krona (SEK), devaluation, 367–8
Swedish Social Insurance Agency, 365

Tailors and Textiles Workers Union (TTWU), founding, 225
Tajbakhsh, Kian, 278
tasks, distribution, 82f
Tate, Jane, 24
tax penalty, elimination (Sweden), 357
Tazeen Fashions garment factory, fire, 10
Temporary Employment Program, 192
Theroux, Paul, 130
Thornton, Grant, 171
Tilly, Chris, 2
Tomei, Manuela, 29
Tomorrow Is Now (Roosevelt), 148
Toro-Morn, Maura I., 299
Trabajo de la Mujer Imigrante en São Paulo, El, 85–9
trade: gender/human rights, relationship, 235–6; negative effects, 235; positive effects, 235–6
trade liberalization: impact, 236–43; women, relationship, 234
tradeswomen (United States), 139–46; conference presence, 145; government policies, 140–2; successes/challenges, 142–6
training, idle time (Hungary), 324
transnational forces, impact, 28
treatment, equality, 26
troika, 336
Trumka, Richard, 148
Turkey: aesthetic labor, practice, 116–17; export-oriented manufacturing, 110; female retail workers, demographic characteristics, 114; female workers, leisurely pursuits, 120–1; female workforce, characteristics, 112; global economic restructuring, 111–12; global era, new workers, 110–1; interactive service workers, work experiences, 113; labor, feminization, 115–17; labor, feminization patterns, 109; leisure sociability, functions, 120; low-status kin position, denotation, 118; low-wage service occupations, types, 113–14; religiosity, problems, 110; research setting/method, 113–15; retail stores, organizational culture (non-familial aspects), 117–18; secular republic, 109; service industries, labor feminimization, 113; sociability requirement, 118–19

underemployed, Labor Force Surveys classification, 375
unemployment: benefits/reductions (EU), eligibility criteria (restrictions), 340; examination (Russian Federation), 172–4; gender gaps, 6; insurance, absence, 192–3
unemployment rates, 312–14; decrease, 131
unions, 22–3
United Auto Workers, 144–5
United Domestic Workers (UDW), 139
United Long Term Care Workers (ULTCW), 139
United Nations Convention on the Elimination of All Forms of Discrimination against Women, 277
United Nations Educational, Scientific, and Cultural Organization (UNESCO) studies, 269
United Nations Fund for Women (UNIFEM), 246
United Nations Women's Conference (1995), 24
United Russia (UR), legislature command, 180–1
United States: apparel (Kenya imports), 222t; unionization rates, 140
United States, domestic work/skilled trades, 133t; domestic workers, 134–6; international progress, 136–9; national initiatives, 137–9; tradeswomen, 139–46
United States, gender/work/recession, 125; case studies, 133–46; historical context, 126–9; problems, persistence, 129–30
Universal Child Benefit, increase, 349
Universal Social Charge (USC), 349; plan, penalization, 349
unpaid family labor, 271
unpaid social reproduction, negotiation, 204–7
U.S. Census American Community Survey (ACS) data/estimates, 312

Vardanian, R.A., 171
Veiga, João Paulo Candia, 14–15, 71
vertical sex segregation (Russian Federation), 169–71; workforce, 170–2
Villa, Paola, 13–14, 91
Vishnevsky, Anatoly, 163
Voluntary Codes of Conduct (VCC), 244

wages: equalization, 359; gap, narrowing, 129–30; stagnancy, 131
weekly working hours, Mexican workforce, 195t
When Everything Changed, 128
White House Summit on Worker Voice, 148
White, Jenny B., 117
Wildcat strikes, 2
Wise, Walter, 144
Witbooi, Myrtle, 137, 144, 148
women: absence rates, increase (Sweden), 372; agency, 13, 15; beedi workers, impact, 287; Bolivia, 58–60; contexts, 20–1; discrimination (Russian Federation), 174–6; education (GCC), 252t; educational attainment, 263; emancipation, Marxist-Leninist project, 320–1; emancipation, possibility, 82–3; employment rate, increase (Sweden), 369; labor force changes, 127f; labor market entry (Sweden), 362; labor market involvement (Sweden), 367–76; labor participation rates, increase, 314; labor, undervaluing, 8; legal/market challenges, 78–80; leisure spaces, 119–21; maternalist parental leave policies, 322; men, average monthly Mexican wage (comparison), 197t; middle class/working class women, work force participation (Iran), 269–72; oppression, 82–3; participation, Bartolinas (relationship), 60–3; part-time work (Hungary), 319; part-time work, overrepresentation (EU), 342–3; pay gap, 129; (re)productive space, 77–8; rights, endurance, 2; roles (China), 42; social status, improvement (China), 41; structural/institutional factors (Iran), 272–6; trade liberalization (Egypt), 234; tradeswomen (United States), 139–46; unemployment (Russian Federation), 172–4; university attainment, Gulf Cooperation Council (GCC), 250; unpaid work (EU), 341–2; work, Athi River EPZ (Kenya), 215; work-care decisions (Hungary), crisis (impact), 324–5; workforce (Russian Federation), 161; working poor women, crisis (Mexico), 190; workplace, impact (Kenya), 226–9; work/social class, relationship (Iran), 268–72; work, undervaluing, 170
"Women and Trade Liberalization" (Nassar), 158
women, apparel production (Bolivia), 71, 80–3; questionnaire, 85–9
Women Build Nations Conference, 144–5
Women in Apprenticeship and Nontraditional Occupations Act (WANTO), 141–2, 146
women, politics (Iran), 263
Women's Charter, 95
Women's Marches, characteristic, 1–2, 9
women workers: China, 36; market, relationship, 41–4; roles, 48–53; socioeconomic changes (Chicago), 313t; state, relationship, 44–8
Woodstock Institute report, 311
work: absence (Sweden), 372–3; Bolivia, 58–60; concerns, 5; decent work, ILO focus, 28; domestic work (United States), 133t; global women, work (meaning), 215–18; hours, crisis/reorganization (Hungary), 323–4; Kenya, Athi River EPZ, 215; non-familial/sociable space, 117–19; outwork, 18; permission, granting, 205; perspectives, 1; politics (Iran), 263; reproductive work distribution, 78f; Russian Federation, women (workforce), 161; structural/institutional factors (Iran), 272–6; themes, 4–5; United States, 125; women/social class relationship (Iran), 268–72; work-care supports, unavailability, 321
work-care decisions: crisis (Hungary), impact, 324–5; discussion, arguments, 329–31; partners, impact, 328–9
workers: domestic workers, 134–6; domestic workers, 2008 recession (impact), 200–10; female workers, leisurely pursuits, 120–1; women workers, 36, 41–53; women workers, socioeconomic changes (Chicago), 313t
workforce: experience, 172; female workforce, characteristics (Turkey), 112; horizontal sex segregation, 169–70; Mexico, social security (absence), 194t; Mexico, weekly working hours, 195t; vertical sex segregation, 170–2
working class women, work force presence (Iran), 269–72
working conditions: casualization (EU), 346–7; domestic workers (Mexico), 201t
working hours: reduction (Hungary), 324; Sweden, reduction (parent rights), 363, 365–7

working poor women, crisis (Mexico), 190
working time (Sweden), 373–6
workplace protection action plan (Hungary), 326
World Economic Forum: Gender Gap Report, 158; report, 354
World Public Opinion Project, 174
World Trade Organization (WTO) agreements, 235, 245

xenophobia, impact, 73

Yakovlev, Vladimir, 165
Yaroshenko, S., 167
Yeltsin, Boris, 179

young children (mothers), gender/work (feminist scholarship), 320
young Europeans: empirical evidence, 100, 104; employment statuses, probabilities, 101t–103t; gender marginal effects, probabilities, 101t–103t
Yunus, Muhammad, 9–10

Zambrana, Ivis Garcia, 299
Zarif, Mohammad Javad, 268
Zdravomyslova, Olga, 181
Zedong, Mao, 39–41
Zhang, Xiaodan, 7, 14, 36
Zheng, Tiantian, 42–3
Zhidkova, Elena, 165